Organizational
COMMUNICATION
Strategies for Success

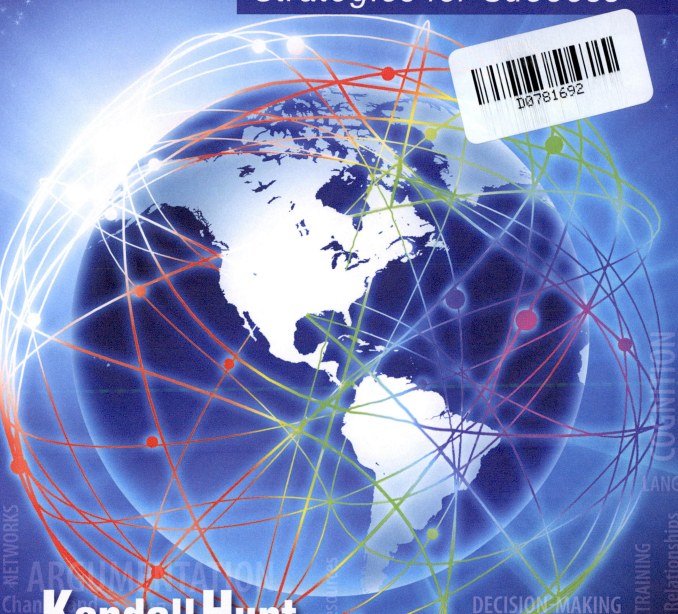

Kendall Hunt
p u b l i s h i n g c o m p a n y

Second Edition

Theodore A. Avtgis | **Andrew S. Rancer** | **Corey J. Liberman**

Ashland University   **University of Akron**   **Marymount Manhattan College**

Book Team

Chairman and Chief Executive Officer   Mark C. Falb
President and Chief Operating Officer   Chad M. Chandlee
Vice President, Higher Education   David L. Tart
Director of Business Partnerships   Paul B. Carty
Editorial Manager   Georgia Botsford
Senior Editor   Angela Willenbring
Vice President, Operations   Timothy J. Beitzel
Assistant Vice President, Production Services   Christine E. O'Brien
Senior Production Editor   Mary Melloy
Senior Permissions Coordinator   Renae Horstman
Cover Designer   Heather Richman
Web Project Manager   Jade Sprecher

Cover image © 2012 by Kendall Hunt Publishing Company

Kendall Hunt
publishing company

www.kendallhunt.com
Send all inquiries to:
4050 Westmark Drive
Dubuque, IA 52004-1840

Copyright © 2012 by Kendall Hunt Publishing Company

ISBN 978-1-4652-0390-8

Printed in the United States of America
10 9 8 7 6 5 4 3 2 1

Dedication

To our loving families
Mary, Aiden, Kathi, Aimee, Sara, and Hailey

Language and Interaction 79

Language Expectancy Theory 84

Language and Sexual Harassment 86

Summary 89

Questions for Discussion and Review 90

References 90

Chapter 5 Defining Relationships 95

Learning Objectives 95

Key Terms 95

Types of Organizational Relationships 97

Superior–Subordinate Organizational Relationships . 99

Advantages of Organizational Relationships . . . 100

Complications Associated with
Organizational Relationships 103

Organizational Social Networks 105

Strength of Organizational Ties 109

Relationships and Public Relations 110

Methods for Studying Organizational Relationships 110

Summary 112

Questions for Discussion and Review 112

References 113

Chapter 6 Personality and Organizational Life . . 117

Learning Objectives 117

Key Terms 117

Personality Traits 119

Japanese Blood Typing 121

The Chinese Zodiac 121

General Personality Traits 122

Communication Conflict–Related Traits 126

Verbal Aggressiveness 127

Argumentativeness 129

Brief Contents

Part 1 Foundations of Organizational Communication   1

  Chapter 1 Organizational Perspectives and Perceptions 3

  Chapter 2 Ways of Organizing Human Beings . . 23

  Chapter 3 Defining Organizational Culture 49

Part 2 Navigating Relational Rules of the Organization   69

  Chapter 4 Language in the Workplace 71

  Chapter 5 Defining Relationships 95

  Chapter 6 Personality and Organizational Life . . 117

  Chapter 7 Defining Small Groups 145

Part 3 Character and Leadership in the Organization   171

  Chapter 8 Strategic Leadership and Entrepreneurial Spirit 173

  Chapter 9 Ethics and Expression in the Workplace . 197

Chapter 10 Decision Making, Organizational
Information Processing, and
Organizational Change 217

Part 4 Applied Organizational Communication   245

Chapter 11 Communication and Training 247

Chapter 12 Communication and
Organizational Development 283

Chapter 13 Analyzing Organizational
Communication 309

Contents

Preface xvii
Acknowledgments xxiii
About the Authors xxvii

Part 1 Foundations of Organizational Communication — 1

Chapter 1 Organizational Perspectives and Perceptions 3

Learning Objectives 3
Key Terms 3
Evolutionary/Ecological Perspective 6
Systems Perspective 7
Critical Perspective 9
Organizational Perception 11
Attributing Meaning to Behavior 12
Rules for Attributing Meaning to Behavior 13
Biases in the Attribution Process 14
Employee Perspectives 15
Morgan's Multiple Perceptions 16
Summary 19
Questions for Discussion and Review 20
References 21

Chapter 2 Ways of Organizing Human Beings . . 23

Learning Objectives 23
Key Terms 23
Classical Management Approaches 26
    Taylor's Time-Motion Efficiency 26

Weber's Bureaucracy 28
Fayol's Lateral Communication 29
Human Relations Approach 31
Hawthorne Studies 31
Human Resource Approaches to Management . . . 33
Likert System 4 Management Approach 33
McGregor's Theory X and Theory Y 34
Ouchi's Theory Z 35
Argyris' Model I and Model II Approach 37
Blake and Mouton's Managerial Grid 39
The Theory of Independent Mindedness 41
Summary 44
Questions for Discussion and Review 45
References 46

Chapter 3 Defining Organizational Culture . . . 49

Learning Objectives 49
Key Terms 49
Defining Organizational Culture 50
Factors Associated with an Organization's Culture . 52
Organizational Socialization 56
Organizational Culture as Enabling and Constraining 60
Summary 64
Questions for Discussion and Review 64
References 65

Part 2 Navigating Relational Rules of the Organization   69

Chapter 4 Language in the Workplace 71

Learning Objectives 71
Key Terms 71
Language Styles 74
Language Perception 76
Language and Power 77

Taking Conflict Personally 130
Tolerance for Disagreement 131
Competence-Related Traits 133
Communicator Style 133
Cognitive Flexibility 134
Communicative Adaptability 135
Summary 137
Questions for Discussion and Review 138
References 139

Chapter 7 Defining Small Groups 145

Learning Objectives 145
Key Terms 145
Different Types of Small Groups 147
Stages of Group Formation 149
Advantages of Small Groups 151
Disadvantages of Small Groups 154
Roles in Small Groups 157
Types of Small Group Networks 160
The Role of Technology in Small Groups 163
Summary 164
Questions for Discussion and Review 165
References 166

Part 3 Character and Leadership in the Organization   171

Chapter 8 Strategic Leadership and
Entrepreneurial Spirit 173

Learning Objectives 173
Key Terms 173
Leadership 174
Leadership Perspectives 175
Organizations as Leaders 179
Applied Leadership 181

Motivation 183

    Maslow's Hierarchy of Needs 184

    Motivator Hygiene Theory 185

    Acquired Needs Theory 186

Entrepreneurial Spirit 187

    Background and Personality Factors 190

Summary 191

Questions for Discussion and Review 192

References 193

Chapter 9 Ethics and Expression in the Workplace . 197

Learning Objectives 197

Key Terms 197

Ethical Perspectives 198

    Foundational Ethical Perspective 199

    Situational Ethical Perspective 199

    Deontological Ethical Perspective 200

    Utilitarian Ethical Perspective 200

    Rights/Justice-Based Ethical Perspective 200

    Relationship-Based Ethical Perspective 201

    Stakeholder Theory 201

Ethical Considerations in Communication 202

    Nonverbal Behavior and Ethics 202

Practices of an Ethical Organization 205

The Ethical Wheel 205

    Personal Dimension of Ethics 206

    Primary Social Group Dimension of Ethics 206

    Secondary Social Group Dimension of Ethics . . . 206

    Professional Dimension of Ethics 206

Organizational Dissent 207

    Dimensions of Dissent 207

    Issues of Dissent 208

    Strategies of Dissent 209

Whistleblowing 209
Indirect Interpersonal Aggression 210
Real-World Misbehaviors in the Workplace 211
Practical Advice on When to Speak 212
Summary 213
Questions for Discussion and Review 214
References 215

Chapter 10 Decision Making, Organizational Information Processing, and Organizational Change 217

Learning Objectives 217
Key Terms 217
Decision Making 218
  Functional Approach 218
  Thompson's Uncertainty Model 219
  Vroom's Decision-Making Styles 220
  Simon's Activity Approach 222
  Decision Making as Art and Politics 223
  Idea Generation 226
  The Inventional System 226
Information Processing 228
  Information Systems Theory 229
  Informational Reception Apprehension 232
  Uncertainty Management Theory 233
Organizational Change 236
  Strategic Change 236
  Organizational Innovation 237
Summary 240
Questions for Discussion and Review 241
References 241

Part 4 Applied Organizational Communication   245

Chapter 11 Communication and Training 247

Learning Objectives 247

Key Terms 247

Defining Organizational Training 248

Organizational Training in the Structure of
the Organization 249

When Training Is Needed, and When It Is Not . . . 249

The Role of the Communication Trainer 251

   Skills and Abilities Critical for a Career in Training . . 253

The Need for Training 256

Levels of Competency 257

Creating an Interactive Training Program 258

   Conducting a Needs Assessment 258

   Selecting and Narrowing the Topic 260

   Conducting Research and Developing Content . . . 260

   Writing Instructional and Behavioral Objectives . . . 262

   Reasons for Objectives 263

Writing the Instructor's and Participants' Manuals . 264

   The Instructor's Manual 264

   The Participants' Manual 267

Delivering the Program 267

   Delivering a Lecture 268

Designing and Including Experiential Activities
in Training 269

   The Role-Play 269

   Case Studies 269

   Games 270

   Instruments 271

Using Instructional Aids 272

Essential Presentation Skills 273

Evaluating Training 274

The Efficacy of Communication Training 276

Summary 277

Questions for Discussion and Review 278
References 279
Appendix to Chapter 11 281

Chapter 12 Communication and
Organizational Development 283

Learning Objectives 283
Key Terms 283
What Is Organizational Development? 284
The Roots of Organizational Development 285
Action Research: The Foundational Method for
Organizational Change 286
Resistance to Change 287
Managing Organizational Change 288
Lewin's Three-Step Model of Organizational Change . 288
The Role of Communication in Managing
Organizational Change 289
A Blueprint for Communication During the
Implementation of Organizational Change 290
Case Studies in Managing Organizational Change . . 292
Two Approaches to Communication and
Organizational Development 295
Appreciative Inquiry 295
An Assessment of the AR and AI Models of
Organizational Development and Change 298
Team Building 300
An Appreciative Inquiry Approach to Team Building . 301
Summary 304
Questions for Discussion and Review 305
References 305

Chapter 13 Analyzing Organizational
Communication 309

Learning Objectives 309
Key Terms 309

communicate with one another. The chapter ends with a discussion about the role of technology in the small-group decision-making process.

Organization of the Text

Part 1: Foundations of Organizational Communication

Part 1 introduces the concept of "organization" and the study of organizations in both a historical as well as a contemporary treatment. It presents a thorough understanding of the ways organizations have developed over time and how perceptions of organizations influence organizational practice. This section also traces organizational development and practice and presents how the interaction between societal culture and organizational culture form unique environments from which people practice organizing.

Chapter 1, *Organizational Perspectives and Perceptions,* introduces the reader to the basic assumptions of organization and the perceptual process. Several management perspectives and philosophies are presented in ways that allow the student to understand many different ways of looking at and interpreting work.

Chapter 2, *Ways of Organizing Human Beings,* provides a comprehensive review of management evolution as well as a historical and contemporary view of management and organization. The review in this chapter spans centuries and highlights the most noteworthy breakthroughs in understanding how and why people work.

Chapter 3, *Defining Organizational Culture,* provides a detailed account of the role of culture in the social construction of an organization. This chapter highlights the elements part of an organization's culture, as well as ways that employees begin to "learn the ropes."

Part 2: Navigating Relational Rules of the Organization

This section exposes the reader to the interpersonal dynamics associated with organizational life. Aspects that influence relational dynamics include language use, personality characteristics, and our style of working with others. In today's organizations, people are engaged in relationships that are bound by power and status. This poses unique challenges to workers at all levels of the organization, as navigating such relational dynamics can mean the difference between success and failure. By accounting for such important interpersonal dynamics, the reader will gain a unique understanding of the research and problems that can exist as a result of a person's choice of words, predispositions toward behavior, and ability to coordinate with coworkers.

Chapter 4, *Language in the Workplace,* exposes the reader to the ways in which language has evolved and is practiced within organizations. Language

The Importance of Assessing Organizational
Communication 310

What Is a Communication Assessment? 311

Benefits of Conducting a Formal Organizational
Communication Assessment or Audit 313

Survey Research in the Organization 313

Advantages of Organizational Survey Research 314

The Seven Steps of Effective Organizational
Survey Research 316

The Issues of Reliability and Validity in
Organizational Survey Research 326

Benefits of Conducting a Communication Audit . . . 329

Established Communication Assessment
and Audit Tools 330

The International Communication
Association (ICA) Audit 330

The Downs-Hazen Communication
Satisfaction Questionnaire 340

Organizational Identification and
Organizational Commitment 342

Organizational Identification 342

Organizational Commitment 344

Communication Network Analysis 348

Summary 351

Questions for Discussion and Review 352

References 352

Conclusion 357

Glossary 359

Subject Index 389

Author Index 401

Preface

Background and Philosophy

The field of organizational communication refers to a complex and highly differentiated discipline comprising research and scholarship from several disciplines as well as the day-to-day workings of employees in organizations throughout the world. Approaching organizational communication in this way allows for a more inclusive, holistic, and relevant body of knowledge from which to draw.

The vision of this book came from years of searching for a student resource that would be of value for its theory as well as for relevant skills orientation. After years of listening to colleagues, students, corporate professionals, and researchers, we have developed what we believe is a unique organizational communication text that addresses the frustrations that instructors and students, alike, have been sharing with us for so many years.

The approach of this book has also been informed by our careers. The authors have served in the full range of the discipline as researchers of organizational and corporate communication, teachers of undergraduate, graduate, and professional students, as well as consultants and trainers for governmental and corporate organizations. It was our intention to produce a text that would not further divide the field of organizational communication, but serve as a resource for several diverse audiences. This includes the student who wants to study relevant organizational theory and the professional who is working toward the development of the necessary skillsets required for conducting communication training, assessment, and organizational development efforts.

This text is unique in that it:

- Is primarily social science–based, yet addresses important critical cultural elements.
- Presents a dynamic balance between theory and application.
- Utilizes communication research as well as research from other disciplines (e.g., Psychology, Business, Management, and Sociology).
- Is written in an accessible way for both undergraduate and graduate students.
- Offers an entire section (three chapters) dedicated to the practice of organizational communication.

- ◆ Offers a how-to approach for the organizational consultant interested in organizational development, organizational communication training, and organizational communication assessment.

- ◆ Bridges the gap between organizational communication as a course and organizational communication as a profession.

- ◆ Provides one of the most comprehensive glossaries on the market, which serves as an invaluable study guide and resource for students.

- ◆ Is written in a way that gives the extra background information for many concepts that traditionally are often superficially addressed (e.g., Hawthorne Studies and Motivator Hygiene Theory).

- ◆ Is written by communication scholars who have professional experience in all applied levels of organizational communication (organizational training, organizational assessment, and organizational development efforts).

- ◆ Utilizes the latest SMART technologies such as Quick Response (QR) Codes that can be scanned for quick reference to web materials.

Additions to the New Edition

Chapter 3

This chapter now focuses on the communicative construction of an organization's culture with a particular emphasis on the role of artifacts as informing employee behavior. The role of employee dress code, an organization's mission statement, an organization's symbol, and an organization's metaphor are discussed in relation to employee expectations and on-the-job decision making. In addition, there is a new focus on the advantages and disadvantages of an organization's culture.

Chapter 5

This chapter now focuses on types of relationships, with particular emphasis on the advantages of creating social ties with others who have limited resources. The advantages and potential disadvantages of relational construction are discussed as well as the role of organizational social networks in employee communication.

Chapter 7

This chapter now focuses on the types of small groups that exist within an organization as well as the stages through which groups pass during the formation process. The advantages and disadvantages of small groups are discussed, followed by a discussion of the types of group networks that are contrived and that emerge when employees begin to work and/or

is perhaps one of the most misunderstood communication concepts and is responsible for many costly mistakes and lawsuits. The chapter underscores that using language mindfully and powerfully has profound effects for organizational members.

Chapter 5, *Defining Relationships,* explores the many types of relationships that employees create within the organizational environment and the effects of them. This chapter highlights the role of social networks in employee behavior and employee decision making, with a particular emphasis on discussing the advantages and disadvantages of relationships within the workplace.

Chapter 6, *Personality and Organizational Life,* explores individual differences that make people behave differently within the organization. A historical perspective of personality is presented, followed by more contemporary methods of employee selection. Types of behavior typical of certain personality and communication traits are also presented.

Chapter 7, *Defining Small Groups,* presents a detailed account of the types of small groups within which employees find themselves embedded, highlighting the benefits and potential problems associated with group communication. Particular emphasis is placed on the types of small-group networks that emerge within organizations and the communicative and behavioral effects of them.

Part 3: Character and Leadership in the Organization

Part 3 presents the dynamics that pervade the practice of contemporary organizations and the choices people make to further the interests of the organization. As the contemporary work landscape allows for greater mobility and individual career focus, the ability to motivate people and innovate becomes more difficult and idiosyncratic. Information processing that leads to decision making is one of the most overlooked aspects of organizational communication. Readers are exposed to ways of becoming mindful to stimuli in the environment that may otherwise go unnoticed.

Chapter 8, *Strategic Leadership and Entrepreneurial Spirit,* traces the historical roots of leadership and provides a detailed explanation of contemporary ways of conceptualizing leadership and leadership qualities. Motivation and the different perspectives of employee drive are presented. The elements of innovation and entrepreneurship are also discussed in terms of their influence on the employee and the organization as a whole.

Chapter 9, *Ethics and Expression in the Workplace,* presents the reader with several ethical perspectives that both the worker and the organization possess and practice daily. Organizational dissent and expressions of displeasure are presented in terms of their efficacious and ethical implications.

In Chapter 10, *Decision Making, Organizational Informational Processing, and Organizational Change,* presents several models for decision making, along with techniques to generate solutions and clarify the approach that will be utilized when engaging in decision making. The use and implementation of information as well as information processing models are presented and discussed.

Part 4: Applied Organizational Communication

The final section exposes the reader to the practice and profession of organizational communication. To practice organizational communication or to be an organizational communication specialist requires a skillset consisting of the ability to diagnose problems, execute sound research design, and educate workers on communication skills that are necessary to improve performance. The information in this section can be considered a "tool box" from which a student wanting to become involved in communication careers such as organizational training or organizational development can draw from.

Chapter 11, *Communication and Training,* presents the contemporary approaches to the development and delivery of effective communication training within organizations. Specific skillsets and practices are presented and discussed in terms of their effect on both organizational and employee goals.

Chapter 12, *Communication and Organizational Development,* exposes the reader to the process of organizational development and the requisite skills and abilities needed to effectively engage in the development process. Historical and cutting-edge approaches to organizational development are presented, and strengths and weaknesses of all approaches are identified and discussed.

Chapter 13, *Analyzing Organizational Communication,* presents the most popular communication assessment tools available and step-by-step instructions on how to utilize such assessment instruments. The student is exposed to a variety of assessment instruments as well as the research methods necessary to administer such assessment tools.

Student-Oriented Pedagogy

Because we recognize the importance of assessing student learning, we have included features in each chapter that facilitate student learning and help instructors measure learning outcomes.

- **Learning Objectives** help students focus on the overall concepts, theories, and skills discussed.
- **Key Terms** list important concepts.
- **Running Glossary** provides a quick definition of key terms within the text.
- **Bolded Concept**s within the text indicate important information explained in the text and defined in the Glossary.
- **Figures and Tables** visually illustrate chapter concepts.

- **Summary** effectively reviews elements presented throughout the chapter.
- **Questions for Discussion and Review** encourage students to further explore the concepts they learned.
- **References** document the extensive research cited in the text.
- A comprehensive **Glossary** at the end of the text serves as a helpful reference tool.
- **Quick Response (QR) Codes** provide students with a way to electronically access some of the chapters' key concepts.

Instructional Online Enhancements

Both students and instructors have access to online content that is integrated chapter by chapter with the text to enrich student learning. The Web access code is included on the inside front cover of the textbook.

Look for the Web icon in the text margins to direct you to various interactive tools.

Student Web Content

- *Video interviews* showcase experts' explanations of concepts.
- *Case studies* allow students to explore concepts in real-life scenarios.
- *Flash cards* offer an interactive version of the key terms and their definitions.
- *Activities* provide extensive content review and application of concepts.
- *Movie clips* allow students to see the intersection of theory and practice.
- *Interactive games and projects* offer students the opportunity to engage in exercises dealing with "best practices."

Instructor Web Content

- *Chapter outlines* highlight central ideas for each chapter and can serve as lecture notes.
- *Comprehensive test bank* offers different question formats to better assess student knowledge.
- *PowerPoint*™ slides illustrate important chapter concepts and can be made accessible to students.
- *Recommendations* for movie and other media clips highlight key chapter concepts.
- *Recommendations* for class activities allow students to put theory into practice.

Acknowledgments

We would like to acknowledge the work of our most dependable team at Kendall Hunt publishing. Thanks to our editor Angela Willenbring and director of businesss partnerships Paul Carty for providing us with all the resources necessary to create a second edition that we believe captures the essential elements of organizational communication. Thanks to Megan Wise (Ashland University) for her work in developing the instructor materials. Last but certainly not least, we would like to also thank our families for their continued support and colleagues throughout the world who found the first edition to be of value and who provided valuable feedback for the second edition.

TAA
ASR
CJL

We gratefully acknowledge the constructive comments of the colleagues who provided content reviews for the first edition. They include:

Carey Adams
Missouri State University

Kathryn Archard
Bridgewater State College
Suffolk University

Kenneth Bagley
Portland State University

Michael Bannon
University of Pittsburgh

Beryl Bellman
California State University–
Los Angeles

Janet Bodenman
Bloomsburg University

Charlotte Brammer
Samford University

Michele Bresso
Bakersfield College

Pamela Brooks
ASU-Polytechnic

Amy Buxbaum
North Central College

Deborah Chasteen
William Jewell College

Carolyn Clark
Salt Lake Community
College

Stephanie Coopman
San Jose State University

Stephen Curtis
Eastern Connecticut State
University

Scott Dickmeyer
University of
Wisconsin–LaCrosse

Kristina Drumheller
West Texas A&M
University

Laura Eurich
University of Colorado–
Colorado Springs

Diane Ferrero-Paluzzi
Iona College

Ron Fetzer
Miami University–Ohio

Peggy Fisher
Ball State University

Kathryn Fonner
University of
Wisconsin–Milwaukee

Susan Fredricks
Penn State Brandywine

Joseph Ganakos
Lee College

Melissa Gibson Hancox
Edinboro University of
Pennsylvania

Bethany Goodier
College of Charleston

Robert Greenstreet
East Central University

John Gribas
Idaho State University

Philip Grise
Florida State University

Sandy Hanson
University of North
Carolina–Charlotte

Janie Harden Fritz
Duquesne University

Jessica Jameson
North Carolina State University

Mark Johnson
Pittsburg State University

Chris Kasch
Bradley University

Susan Klingel-Dowd
Ball State University

Geoff Leatham
University of Rhode Island

Canchu Lin
Bowling Green State University

Meina Liu
University of Maryland

Shawn Long
University of North Carolina–Charlotte

Joseph Martinez
El Paso Community College

Lee McGaan
Monmouth College

Janet McKenney
Oakland University/ Macomb Community College

Jeff McNeill
University of Hawaii–Manoa

Mary Meares
Washington State University

Kossuth Mitchell
Pikeville College

Megan Moe-Lunger
Lee University

Alfred Mueller II
Penn State Mont Alto

Gina Neff
University of Washington

Christine North
Ohio Northern University

Michael Pagano
Fairfield University

Terri Patkin
Eastern Connecticut State University

Kathleen Pederson
Hennepin Technical College

Richard S. Pressman
St. Mary's University

B. J. Reed
University of Wisconsin–Platteville

Larry Dale Richesin
University of Alaska–Fairbanks

Ken Robol
Beaudort Community College

Kay Rooff-Steffen
Muscatine Community College

Jeremy Rose
University of Minnesota

Noreen Schaefer-Faix
Defiance College

Tim Steffensmeier
Kansas State University

Robert Steinmiller
Henderson State University

Marlane Steinwart
Valparaiso University

Tim Thompson
Edinboro University

Jennifer Waldeck
Chapman University

Aimee Whiteside
University of Minnesota

Toni Whitfield
James Madison University

Bruce Wickelgren
Suffolk University

Edward Woods
Marshall University

Kathryn Sue Young
Mansfield University

About the Authors

Theodore A. Avtgis

(Ph.D.—Kent State University, 1999) is Professor of Communication Studies and Chair of the Department of Communication Studies at Ashland University. He is also an Adjunct Associate Professor in the Department of Surgery at West Virginia University School of Medicine. Dr. Avtgis has authored over 60 peer-reviewed articles and book chapters on organizational communication, communication personality, and their impact on the practice of healthcare. His work has appeared in journals such as *Management Communication Quarterly, Journal of Trauma: Injury, Infection, and Critical Care, Communication Education,* and *Communication Research Reports,* among others. He is co-author of six books and currently serves as Editor-in-Chief of *Communication Research Reports* as well as co-founder of the medical communication consulting firm *Medical Communication Specialists.* Among several awards, he was recognized as one of the Top Twelve Most Productive Scholars in the field Communication Studies (1996–2001), recognized as a member of the World Council on Hellenes Abroad (USA Region of American Academics), in 2009 named as a Centennial Scholar of Communication by the Eastern Communication Association, and the 2011 recipient of the ECA Past Presidents' Award.

Andrew S. Rancer

(Ph.D.—Kent State University, 1979) is Professor of Communication in the School of Communication, University of Akron. He has served as editor of *Communication Research Reports* (1999–2001) and the *Massachusetts Communication Journal* (1981). Among several honors, he is the recipient of the Eastern Communication Association's Past Presidents/Officers Award (1989) and the Distinguished Research Fellow Award (1997) and was a member of ECA's Committee of Scholars (1989–1990). In 2009 he received a Centennial Scholar of Communication Award from the Eastern Communication Association. He has published articles in *Communication Monographs, Human Communication Research, Communication Education, Communication Quarterly,* and *Communication Research Reports,* among others. He is the co-author of four books, including *Argumentative and Aggressive Communication* (2006) and *Arguments, Aggression, and Conflict* (2010).

Corey J. Liberman

(Ph.D.—Rutgers University, 2008) is Assistant Professor of Communication Arts at Marymount Manhattan College. His research in the area of organizational communication looks at the role of social networks on behavioral, psychological, and communicative phenomena, including such things as employee commitment, employee motivation, job satisfaction, and organizational identification, and how these variables are impacted by, and, in turn, come to impact an organization's culture. He routinely teaches courses in interpersonal communication, small group communication, organizational communication, and social network theory. He has authored or co-authored more than 15 papers that have been published as book reviews, proceedings, case studies, encyclopedia entries, and book chapters dealing with organizational communication, health communication, instructional communication, and social networks.

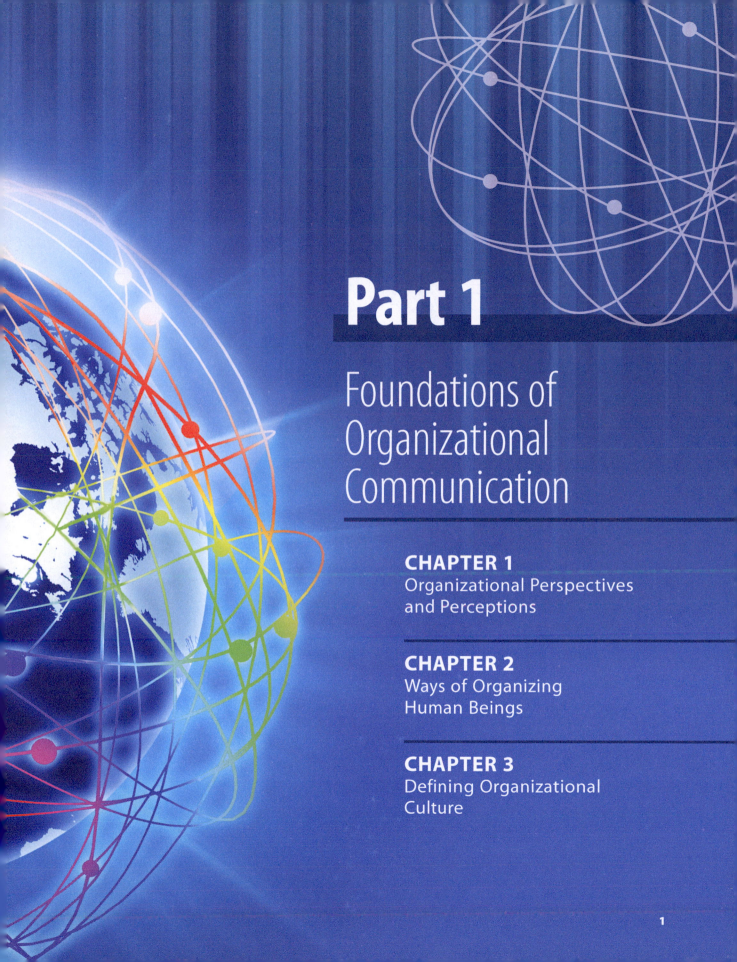

Part 1

Foundations of Organizational Communication

CHAPTER 1
Organizational Perspectives
and Perceptions

CHAPTER 2
Ways of Organizing
Human Beings

CHAPTER 3
Defining Organizational
Culture

Chapter 1

Organizational Perspectives and Perceptions

Learning Objectives

Upon completion of the chapter, the student should be able to:

- Compare and contrast the systems perspective with the critical perspective of organizations.

- Explain how the evolutionary perspective of organizations is effective in determining why some organizations succeed and some fail.

- Compare and contrast the three rules for attributing meaning to behavior.

- Compare and contrast the hedonic philosophy with the eudaimonic philosophy of organizational life.

- Compare and contrast Morgan's various perspectives.

Key Terms

Attribution	General Systems Theory	Organizational communication
Critical perspective	Hedonic view	Perception
Eudaimonic view	Imaginization	
Evolutionary perspective	Morgan's multiple perceptions	

The study of organizational communication as a scholarly discipline as well as a profession has revealed dramatic insights into how people choose to organize in efforts that bring about effective and ineffective outcomes. Now more than at any time in history, people are mobile and willing to relocate to further their professional development. Years ago, people would find employment, develop relationships with coworkers, and work at one organization until they retired. In an ever-evolving workplace, that level of stability may never be realized again. Change is the only constant in the contemporary workplace. The United States, and arguably the world, has experienced incredible financial instability, skyrocketing unemployment, and a general distrust of both governmental and financial institutions. Such institutions used to provide a degree of stability to our lives. When this distrust is coupled with technology that allows any person to instantaneously know about events occurring in the world, the concept of stability is measured in minutes or days as opposed to years and decades. In earlier times, we worked where we lived. In today's workplace, we live where we work.

With this decrease in stability comes a need for adaptation skills and ways of conceptualizing and reconceptualizing organizations. One of the most important adaptation skills is the practice of competent communication. That is, competent communication is the ability to be **effective** and **appropriate** when communicating. *Effectiveness* is the ability to achieve a desired outcome, whereas being *appropriate* reflects the ability to achieve desired goals in a socially appropriate way. The more we change jobs and organizations, the more we need to develop the communication skills required to form new relationships and maintain those relationships we have already formed.

Organizations are artificial environments when compared to the family environment or naturally occurring organizations where membership is based on free choice. That is, in organizations, we are forced to be in the presence of people whom we enjoy as well as people whom we do not enjoy. Navigating these organizational relationships has nothing to do with the specific tasks that we were hired to perform, yet has everything to do with the quality of the environment within which we perform our tasks. So, in effect, communication and the resulting work relationships we develop have major impacts on work enjoyment and overall psychological welfare. People who are not necessarily happy with their assigned tasks are more likely to stay in a job due to the relationships formed with the people they work with. On the other hand, people have a tendency to leave a job where they enjoy performing their assigned tasks but do not enjoy the relationships with coworkers. Communication in the organization, perhaps more than any other factor, influences how we feel about the organization and ourselves. Therefore, the study and understanding of organizational communication can dramatically increase our satisfaction with our work experience. **Organizational communication** is the process through which people, connected by and through a common mission, set of goals, and culture, create,

organizational communication The process through which people, connected by and through a common mission, set of goals, and culture, create, share, and distribute information to both internal and external constituents in an effort to achieve objectives and generate collective meaning.

share, and distribute information to both internal and external constituents in an effort to achieve objectives and generate collective meaning.

Understanding how communication affects people in the workplace is a fundamental competency for all organizational members regardless of their position. For example, as our society becomes increasingly service based, good interpersonal skills are no longer an added benefit but a necessity for organizational survival. This is evidenced by the number of college graduation requirements that involve some variety of communication skills. Through human relationships, we navigate our way through our work lives to create a career on which we can reflect with pride. The days of self-sustenance are long over. We depend on others for goods and services to ensure our existence. In the times when we grew our own food, made our own clothes, and so on, the need for managing relationships was not as important because people had no need of relationships beyond their immediate family and village. Although self-sustainability can be seen in communities such as the Amish, such people are seen as a novelty that exists within the larger culture of mass consumption. Mass production of goods and the development of urban centers, via the age of industrialization, traded our capacity to be self-sufficient for increased productivity and standardization. That is, we traded our ability to produce an entire product for an increase in the production of the number of products that others may consume. Perhaps one of the greatest examples of this concept is that of the interchangeable gun part. Before the interchangeable gun part, guns were produced as pieces of art in which the stock, barrel, and trigger assembly were unique to that one gun. Industrialization replaced the artisan or gunsmith who made the entire gun with standardized piecework. That is, one worker mass produces identical gun barrels, another worker mass produces identical stocks, and another employee mass-produces identical trigger assemblies. We make these standardized parts such that they are interchangeable with similar guns. What is gained is an increase in the number of guns produced. What is lost is any one person's ability to make an entire gun. Thus, we become dependent on others for our survival. Another example is the number and variety of undergraduate college majors students can choose from. Of the hundreds of possible majors leading to an undergraduate degree, most involve such specialized information and knowledge that, if one considers a career change, it can bring about anxiety because the skillset acquired for a particular major may be difficult to transfer to another discipline.

This chapter provides many perspectives concerning how we look at organizations and how we perceive work and work life. Understanding how we see work in relation to our life is an important and necessary component for professional development. Far too many people go through their work lives mindlessly. They tend to "fall" into their jobs as opposed to being proactive and "creating" their careers. Further, understanding our biases allows us to develop the skills needed to take multiple perspectives on any one event. For example, being able to hold our perceptual biases in check may allow us to develop other perspectives that can reveal new opportunities that would otherwise go unnoticed. The financial crisis currently affecting American business is considered a crisis for all Americans. However, consider the fact that when people cannot afford to purchase new automobiles, there is a dramatic increase in the use of and need for automotive mechanics to maintain older vehicles, and therefore there are new opportunities for existing and aspiring automotive mechanics. The assumption that a bad economy is bad for all is but one interpretation of the economy. Applying a variety of realities to a situation can dramatically improve our understanding of that situation and, subsequently, our decision making.

Evolutionary/Ecological Perspective

evolutionary perspective
A view of organizations that assumes that organizations are bound to other organizations of their kind and that some of these organizations will survive and some will become extinct. Only in stability can organizations survive.

The **evolutionary/ecological perspective** of organizations resembles that of any living species (Hannan & Freeman, 1989). That is, organizations of similar types are called **populations** that either prosper or decline in any given environment. The population ecology of organizations assumes that each organization is bound to others of its kind. For example, Walmart, Target, Kohl's, and so on are known as big box stores. Some of these organizations will survive and some will perish based on survival of the fittest.

Similar to the animal kingdom, organizations that do not adapt and change with the environment go extinct. The more variety within an organizational population, the more likely one or more forms will be optimal for adapting to change. The evolutionary/ecological view of organizations is Darwinian in nature. It is not that only strong organizations survive as much as only organizations that adapt best survive. An important concept of this view is **punctuated equilibria**, which occurs when there are long periods of stability interrupted by short periods of sudden change. Consider the electronics industry from post-World War II until the 1970s. The products available to consumers were relatively stable in terms of technological advancements. It is only in recent decades that rapid advances in technological products have been condensed into such a short time—so much so that by the time we purchase an electronic device, it is well on its way to being obsolete.

The concept of organizational change is generally seen as beneficial in organizational communication and business. However, the evolutionary/ecological perspective holds that only in stability (i.e., times of relatively little change and little innovation) can an organization thrive. This is due to the organization's dependence on scarce resources and production of output. In fact, change and innovation prompt the population (i.e., a group of similar organizations) to either adapt to change or die out. Once the organization adapts, it seeks stability so it can again thrive (Hannan & Carroll, 1992). Another assumption about organizational population concerns dealing with changes in the environment. That is, it is easier to survive by natural selection, or **replacement**, than it is to adapt an organization to a changing environment. For example, this occurs when a large corporation goes into bankruptcy (the death of the organization) to totally restructure and reemerge as a different organization better able to operate in the new environment (replacement). For example, companies such as K-Mart and General Motors declared bankruptcy in order to restructure and pursue a new business plan that better reflects changing consumer tastes.

The evolutionary/ecological view of individual organizations and their larger class of organizations is similar to that of an individual animal and its larger class of animal species. That is, this view seeks to describe why some survive and some do not. A final example is higher education. As consumers' (students') interests and desires change, educational organizations (colleges and universities) attempt to adapt to meet those changing consumer needs. These needs include offering more applied majors that result in an immediately relevant position upon graduation as well as an emphasis on internships, service learning, and real-world experience. There is also a pivotal change in higher education concerning online degrees and programs. The student dollar is a premium resource in higher education, and only those organizations that can adequately meet changes in the environment will survive (in this case, the changing demands of the education consumer).

Systems Perspective

The **systems perspective of organizations** is rooted in biology and uses the organism as a metaphor to explain organizations. Treating organizations as living organisms highlights the underlying assumptions of this perspective. Von Bertalanffy (1968), a biologist, is credited with the development of **general systems theory**. General systems theory applies the properties of living systems to a variety of phenomena, including organizations. Concepts such as **inputs** (elements flowing into the system), **throughputs** (elements flowing through the system), **outputs** (elements flowing out of the system), **permeable boundaries** (the limits of a system where elements are exchanged between the system and the larger environment), **homeostasis** (the dynamic balance of the system), and **equifinality** (multiple ways to reach the same goal) are relevant to organisms as well as organizations. In other words, a system is composed of a set of concepts and principles that are universal to all organizations.

general systems theory
Theory that applies the properties of living systems to a variety of phenomenon.

Systems theory is a macro view of organizations in that any given system is simultaneously a **subsystem** (a system that operates within a larger system) as well as a **suprasystem** (a larger system within which smaller systems operate). For example, the Walmart located in Little Rock, Arkansas is a subsystem of the Walmart Corporation but also a suprasystem to the electronics department that operates within the Little Rock Walmart. A communication studies department may be a subsystem of the university yet a suprasystem for the university chapter of the communication honor society, *Lambda Pi Eta*.

The systems perspective is highlighted by the idea that systems have permeable boundaries. For example, organizations constantly exchange information with the immediate environment. This is known as an **open system**. When a system does not exchange information with the immediate environment, the system becomes a **closed system** and eventually will die or move toward **entropy** (a system moving toward death). For example, consider a marketing department that is constantly soliciting feedback from customers to adjust to changing consumer needs. Further, the organization is composed of a set of interdependent systems. The marketing department would cease to function if the production department did not produce enough product. Each department within any given organization directly depends on the other for survival. From a systems perspective, organizations strive to maintain a level of homeostasis by balancing inputs, throughputs, and outputs (Farace, Monge, & Russell, 1977). For example, when production increases, the system provides feedback in the way of production reports to let the organization know if adjustments are needed. If the feedback indicates that production is decreasing, the system tries to maintain a homeostatic state by adjusting to increase production. This may take the form of hiring new employees to meet demand. Thus, bringing newcomers up to speed and integrating them into the system as quickly as possible is a response to feedback that prompted the system to take this course of action to reestablish the dynamic balance. **Feedback** is information obtained by the system that comes from the environment. Additionally, the systems perspective contains the idea of **nonsummativity**. The 2002 U.S. Men's National Basketball Team failed to medal in the World Championship Tournament. Although this may seem trivial, the team was composed of some of the best players in the National Basketball Association and thus the world. How could this team of stellar individual athletes lose? According to systems theory, having the best players does not mean you have the best team. The whole system is more than the sum of the system's parts (nonsummativity). A gelling of talent and personalities must occur for the system to run effectively. Sometimes ordinary organizations do extraordinary things.

The earlier example of increasing production levels illustrates the concept of a cybernetic system (Wiener, 1948). A **cybernetic system** is self-regulating based on feedback from the environment. Any self-regulating system uses feedback to either maintain (**system maintenance**) its current practices or adapt/change (**system adaptation**) current practices based on environmental changes. Let's look again at the example of production levels. If the organization were able to increase production to meet the increase in orders, the response to this feedback (increased orders from customers) would require the system to make no changes and maintain the status quo. However, if the feedback indicated that production was falling behind and the organization would be unable to meet the increased orders, the system would adapt to these changes by increasing current production practices to meet increased demand. This could take the form of increased hours for existing workers, additional equipment, or additional personnel.

In sum, it is important to recognize that organizations are complex and diverse just as organisms in nature. Like the human body, which is composed of systems (circulatory, musculoskeletal, nervous systems, etc.), the organization is composed of systems (the sales and marketing system, the manufacturing system, the engineering system, etc.). We are all a part of a greater whole in the notion of nonsummativity. The systems perspective of organizations offers a comprehensive and relatively simple understanding of how complex organizations function and are affected by subsystems and suprasystems that result in either organizational success or failure.

Critical Perspective

The **critical perspective** **of organizations** focuses on the concepts of **power** and **control** and seeks to uncover imbalances between those who have power and control over those who lack power and control. According to Marx (1964), there is an unequal distribution of power between management and workers, with the result being that organizations are viewed as battlegrounds due to the alienation of oppressed workers. Marx argued that in order for the **subjugated** (exploited) workers to free themselves from the **oppressors** (management), workers must take control of the means of production and, in doing so, will achieve **emancipation** (freedom and independence from oppression). However, often those in power tend to covertly control the oppressed, wherein the oppressed are unaware of their subjugated position.

The critical perspective gained popularity in the United States in the 1980s as social issues arose from the failure of trickle-down economics (Strine, 1991). Trickle-down economics was a response of political leaders who opposed the notion of progressive capitalism (paying workers enough so they can purchase the products they manufacture). The basic premise underlying trickle-down economics was to provide organizations with tax breaks and incentives, with the idea that these savings would flow to employees in the form of better wages and benefits. The result was a new category of workers called the **working poor**. The working poor could no longer meet typical household expenses. Thus, the expression "the rich get richer, and the poor get poorer" was coined. This development also resulted in the two-income household, which is now commonplace. In contemporary American society, two-income households are more the norm than single-income households.

According to the critical perspective, a fundamental goal is to uncover imbalances of power and control as well as make those who suffer from such oppression aware that this imbalance exists. Because newcomers are just entering the organization, the socialization process is an ideal mechanism for the hegemonic view of those in power to be instilled in the worker. According

critical perspective Focuses on the concepts of power and control and seeks to uncover imbalances between those who have power and control over those who lack power and control.

to Mumby (1987), the **hegemonic view** is based on the oppressed accepting the organization's ideology. In doing so, it reinforces the oppressed position. In simpler terms, hegemony involves subordinates accepting their role as the oppressed. This hegemony is created by the organizational elite as a set of rules and beliefs put forth to reinforce the interests of the organization over the individual. Thus, each time an employee follows these rules, he or she reinforces the hegemony (the requests of the elite) at all levels of the organization. Consider the college courses in which you are currently enrolled. Each course has a syllabus that puts forth control mechanisms, such as an attendance policy and homework assignments. Both mechanisms result in students behaving in ways that reinforce the policies of attending class regularly and completing homework assignments.

Similar to hegemony, manufactured consent and concertive control are additional tactics by which the organization maintains power and control over employees through their adherence to organizational rules. According to Habermas (1972), **manufactured consent** involves employees' willingness to adopt and enforce the organization's power and their subsequent oppression. For example, manufactured consent is at work when an employee says, "I was just doing my job," to justify a decision or action. According to Mumby (1987), if the actions of employees can be centered on a rule or a structure, employees are no longer responsible for actions or outcomes. Thus the organization maintains a level of covert control over employees through a series of rules and structures. This notion forwarded by Habermas led Barker and Tompkins (1993) to research self-managing teams and reveal the power of concertive control. According to Barker and Tompkins, **concertive control** is a consensus among employees to shape their behaviors in accordance with the organization's core set of values and vision. In other words, through hegemonic structures employees manage themselves in following the rules and values of the organization, and following these rules and values results in employee oppression. In this light, employees are willing, though unknowingly, participants in the creation of their own oppression.

In summary, it is important to remember that the critical perspective views organizations as a battlefield between management and employees as a result of management's desire to oppress employees. The employee's subjugated position is a result of the organization's control of and power over the employee. According to the critical perspective, the only way for an employee to be content is to escape from the oppressed state through emancipation.

Thus far we have discussed ways that organizations are conceptualized, and how various perspectives posit different assumptions about how organizations and workers function. In the next section we look at how employees observe, organize, and interpret information as well as how people develop "habits" of perception and attribute meaning to the behavior of other people in the workplace.

This QR code will take you to the home page of Noam Chomsky, where you can read more about manufactured consent and its impact on organizational communication practices.

http://www.chomsky.info/index.htm

Organizational Perception

Perception refers to things or data that people deem important and worthy of cognitive processing. For example, if you grew up in a small town and while visiting New York City you see a person dressed in a pink pig outfit, you may be surprised and puzzled; people dressing in costume is a more common occurrence in a big city than in a small town. However, if you grew up in New York City, a person dressed in a pink pig outfit may not attract your attention. **Perception** is a process that involves the selection, organization, and interpretation of stimuli in the environment. All of us are programmed to pay attention to certain types of information while ignoring others. For example, in a recent interview a highly successful manager was asked, "How do you determine who will make a good employee?" He answered, "I ask the applicant if he or she ever had a paper route as a child." To most people this type of question seems trivial at best and the data it reveals (through a yes or no answer) is seemingly meaningless. However, this manager interprets a job candidate who once delivered newspapers as one who internalized responsibility and accountability as a child and carries these behaviors into adult work behavior. Handshakes, style of dress, and the words we use are all types of information that may or may not catch our attention or be deemed important when making decisions within or outside the workplace.

perception A process that involves the selection, organization, and interpretation of stimuli in the environment.

The first step in the perception process is **selection** (which stimuli catch our attention). Generally, information that tends to gain our attention is *intense* (a coworker who is extremely short, wears too much cologne, is extremely hostile), *repetitious* (a boss who is chronically late for meetings), *contrasting or changing* (realizing how efficient your previous secretary was compared to your new, inefficient secretary), and influenced by your own *motivations* (you dislike a coworker so you focus on any possible negative behavior he or she engages in while simultaneously ignoring any positive behavior).

The next step in the perception process is **organization**, which occurs when we order incoming stimuli in an attempt to make sense of the world. Think about how many tens of thousands of pieces of information we are bombarded with during a typical workday. If all these different types of information catch our attention, we must put them into some order that enables us to interpret them. Each of us has a unique way to organize information. This way of organizing information, or stimuli, is called our **perceptual schema**. A perceptual schema is how we are "wired" to organize information. We develop set patterns in terms of how to organize stimuli. There are four types of categories, ranging from the physical to the psychological, that we use to organize information. When we organize data by *physical attributes,* we base our data organization on appearance (e.g., my boss is tall or my boss is a woman). When we organize data by *role attributes,* we rely on a person's role in society (coworker, boss, or CEO). We may also organize data based on a person's *interaction attributes* (this person is verbally aggressive, friendly, or argumentative). Lastly, we may organize data according to *psychological attributes* (this person is insecure, generous, or ambitious). We all use these categories to make sense of our world.

After we select and organize information, the next step in the perception process is the interpretation of information. **Interpretation** occurs when we make sense of organized data by giving meaning to it. Interpretation is based on many factors, including past experiences, expectations, personal moods, and assumptions about human behavior. For example, Becky has just started a new job. At her previous job, a coworker repeatedly sexually harassed her. Becky brought formal sexual harassment charges against her coworker, resulting in a lengthy investigation by human resources. The stress and frustration over the length of the investigation led Becky to resign her position. One day in her new position, a male coworker says, "Hey, Becky, that sweater looks so good on you." Given Becky's history, how do you think she would probably respond? If she never experienced sexual harassment, do you think she would react differently to this comment? This example illustrates how past experience shapes our perceptions of current events. The rule is that perception shapes reality. Another example of how past experiences can influence perception is the effect of the September 11, 2001 terrorist attacks on people's perception of firefighters as well as their perception of military reservists after the start of the war in Iraq. In these two examples, experience has dramatically altered most people's perceptions of these professions.

We now further discuss how people make sense of the behavior of others in and out of the workplace.

Attributing Meaning to Behavior

Given that human beings have an innate need to make sense of their world, making sense of situations related to the organization is no different. The way we attribute meaning to the behavior of other employees as well as our own behavior is called **attribution**. In other words, attribution is the process by which we give meaning to behavior (Heider, 1958).

attribution The process by which we give meaning to behavior.

Fundamentally, there are two types of attributions for behavior: **internal attributions** and **external attributions**. When we make an internal attribution, we attribute behavior to internal factors that are within a person, such as a personality trait, values, or attitudes. Internal factors are also known as **dispositional factors**. For example, when we see another employee with his feet on the desk and hands folded behind his head, we may conclude that this person is lazy. Laziness is an enduring characteristic and part of someone's personality. An external attribution reveals explanatory behavior based on factors outside the person, such as a situation, the environment, or the influence of other people. External factors are also known as **situational factors**. In the preceding example of the "lazy" employee, if we make an external attribution for his behavior, we may conclude that he probably did not sleep well last night or just finished an important report and is taking a quick break. External attributions tend to be shorter in duration and are more easily changed than dispositional factors or internal attributions.

Rules for Attributing Meaning to Behavior

People generally follow three rules when attempting to explain the behavior of others. First, we use the rule of **consensus**. The rule of consensus concerns whether the person is behaving in a way similar to others. Behaving like everyone else is also called following the norms of society. If there is high consensus, we make an external attribution. If there is low consensus, we attribute the behavior to internal factors. For example, if you see another employee cashing out the cash register at the close of the day, you would probably conclude that this behavior is what people normally engage in at the end of a business day (external attribution). However, if you see this same employee cashing out the cash register at 10 a.m. and knowing that closing time is not for another eight hours, you may conclude that is not what everyone normally does and therefore the person may be a thief or dishonest (internal attribution).

The next rule is **distinctiveness**. Distinctiveness is defined as whether a person acts differently to different people (e.g., is relaxed and at ease with most coworkers but is nervous and ill at ease with one or two specific coworkers). When a person exhibits low distinctiveness, we tend to make an internal attribution. On the other hand, when a person exhibits high distinctiveness, we tend to make an external attribution. For example, Tom is an employee who is friendly to everybody throughout the organization except for one employee named Janet. One day, you are having a friendly conversation with Tom. Janet walks into the room and Tom begins speaking in a hostile, verbally aggressive way. You would probably attribute Tom's behavior to Janet's presence (external attribution) and not to Tom being a hostile and angry person (internal attribution).

The final rule in determining the meaning of behavior is **consistency**, defined as whether a person behaves consistently with the same person over time. When a person exhibits high consistency, we tend to make an internal attribution, whereas when someone displays inconsistent behavior or low consistency, we tend to make an external attribution. For example, Mary is kind and always greets you with a smile and a warm greeting. After many occurrences of this behavior you would probably conclude that Mary is a warm and friendly person (internal attribution). However, one day, instead of a warm greeting you receive a sarcastic remark from Mary. Chances are you would not immediately conclude that Mary is a rude person but would conclude that something must have happened that led to her sarcasm (external attribution). Table 1.1 summarizes the concepts of consensus, distinctiveness, and consistency. Often we try to make sense of others' behavior only to come up with an interpretation of behaviors that serves to protect our own self-esteem ("I didn't do anything to Mary; she is just being a jerk!). This esteem protection can result in overly biased judgments about ourselves as well as other people, as we discuss next.

TABLE 1.1	Rules for Attributing Meaning to Behavior		
	Consensus	**Distinctiveness**	**Consistency**
High	External	External	Internal
Low	Internal	Internal	External

Biases in the Attribution Process

Sometimes when we try to make sense of our own behavior, as well as the behavior of others, we run the risk of making faulty judgments. **Basic attribution error** is defined as overemphasizing internal attributions (dispositional factors) in the behavior of others while underemphasizing external attributions (situational factors). In terms of our own behavior, we tend to underemphasize internal attributions (dispositional factors) and overestimate external attributions (situational factors) (Ross, 1977). If this type of interpretation is taken to an extreme, we end up with **ultimate attribution error,** which is the tendency to see the failures in others as internal (lack of intelligence or character flaws) and our own failures as due to the situation (the boss is a jerk or my coworkers just don't understand me).

There is also a difference in how we see negative behaviors. For example, what do you think when you see a coworker put a box of pens and a ream of paper in her briefcase just before going home for the weekend? Contrast that to how you feel when you put a box of pens or ream of paper in your briefcase just before leaving for the weekend. Odds are that you may interpret your coworker's behavior more negatively than your own behavior, even though the acts are exactly the same. This sort of bias is known as the **actor-observer bias**—that is, our actions are never interpreted as being as bad as the actions of others.

It has been said that "Perception is reality." Indeed, the way we perceive things influences outcomes. For example, one day your boss says to you in a serious tone, "I would like you to come to my office today at 4 o'clock. We need to discuss something." This request immediately has you thinking that you are in trouble, so you spend the next several hours thinking about what you could have done wrong and you expect to be yelled at or reprimanded for some failure. Upon entering your boss' office, you begin spouting justifications for any and all behavior that you think would have bothered him. By overjustifying your behavior, you anger your boss, which brings about the situation you thought would occur (the boss is mad at me). This is an example of the **self-fulfilling prophecy.** That is, false expectations about a situation often result in behavior that makes the false expectations come true. Yet another type of false perception is that of the **self-disconfirming prophecy,** which occurs when our original beliefs, perceptions, or expectations influence behavior in a way that prevents the original beliefs, perceptions, and expectations from being supported. In the previous example of the boss asking you to come into his office, you go into the boss' office and begin a friendly and kind exchange even though you think you are in trouble. Your boss responds in kind, and the meeting is filled with friendliness and respect as opposed to the anger and negativity you thought would transpire. Perceptions are a product of perspective, so our orientation toward events will inevitably influence how we perceive ourselves as well as those around us. In the next section, we discuss two main perspectives that influence perception.

Employee Perspectives

There is a great deal of variety in how people view an organization as well as how they view rewards and satisfaction in the workplace. Some people may see a satisfying workplace in an organization that is free of pressure and challenge. On the other hand, some people may see a satisfying organization as one that allows the worker to grow, maximize potential, and make a contribution to society. In American culture, there is a myth that everyone wants to have a rewarding career that is challenging and fosters personal growth. However, we all know someone who would love a job in which thinking is minimized, the work is unchallenging, the boss keeps a distance, and when the shift is over there is no thought about work until the next shift. These perspectives—the need to achieve as opposed to the need to do just enough to get a particular reward—have their roots in psychology as well as philosophy.

When people define a good work life as something that makes them happy, they are espousing a **hedonic view** of organizational life. That is, the hedonic view, dating back to the ancient Greeks, holds that the chief goal in life is the pursuit of happiness or pleasure (Kahneman, Diener, & Schwarz, 1999; Ryan & Deci, 2001; Waterman, 1993). The hedonic view of work is that we work because it provides us with a means to happiness. These means can include the pursuit of money, power, or prestige that allows us to "afford" happiness. Once the pleasure or happiness (in this case money, power, or prestige) is achieved, there is a continuing need to satisfy the desire for pleasure and happiness. In the workplace, this may take the form of someone switching jobs to increase earnings or move up in rank. Work life through the hedonic lens is a means to a desired end that brings about happiness for the person. This constant pursuit of pleasurable feelings keeps a person motivated. Therefore, an employee operating from the hedonic perspective is motivated by rewards that he or she perceives as pleasurable, such as an all-expense-paid trip, cash rewards, or an impressive title. Is the pursuit of happiness at work the only thing that makes for a successful work experience? Seligman (2002) argues that the pursuit of happiness for happiness' sake shortchanges the person of life experiences. He argues that reward and pleasure are realized only through the experience of adversity and challenges. Imagine being happy at work all the time. The experience of happiness would be lost because it is not in contrast with negative emotions or being challenged or being placed in an adverse situation. Many people would agree with

hedonic view A perspective that assumes the chief goal in life is the pursuit of happiness or pleasure.

the argument that their most significant professional growth came from an adverse situation or a challenge they had to overcome and conquer. It is only in professional struggle that significant accomplishment can be realized.

There is, however, another view, which assumes that we work to fulfill higher-level goals in which our talents are challenged and in which we function at an optimal level. More specifically, the **eudaimonic view** of organizational life concerns what Aristotle would call self-realization' or the pursuit of obtaining our inner potential. Self-realization or self-actualization is the process of allowing our value systems, personal needs, interpersonal needs, professional needs, and talents to drive our behavior in and out of the workplace. The eudaimonic perspective is derived from the ancient Greek word *daimon,* meaning "who you truly are." According to Baumgardner and Crothers (2008), "eudaimonia (or happiness) results from the realization of our potentials. We are happiest when we follow and achieve our goals and develop our unique potential" (p. 45).

A person who employs the eudaimonic view may gravitate toward a career that is not necessarily financially rewarding but involves serving others. For example, human services, social work, teaching, or employment with a nonprofit organization all reflect missions and philosophies that focus on making a change in the "bigger picture." These are but a few of the many occupations in which the greatest reward is obtained from making a difference in others' lives. Simply put, the need for contribution to the whole outweighs the need for material success and recognition.

The perspectives discussed in this section can influence how people view and, thus, communicate about their organization. The next section examines how the use of particular metaphors (i.e., a verbalized comparison of two unrelated things) can reveal much about a person's perspective.

eudaimonic view A perspective that assumes the chief goal in life is the pursuit of obtaining your inner potential.

Morgan's multiple perceptions The nine perceptions or images of organizations that are expressed through metaphors.

Morgan's Multiple Perceptions

How people view the organization sets the filter or perceptual system through which all events and occurrences are interpreted. Morgan (1986) believed that not only can people see the organization differently, but any one person can have multiple views of the organization. The argument here is that the more views or perspectives a person has of the organization, the more thorough the understanding of the organization. **Morgan's multiple perceptions** give rise to new ways of innovating and managing. There are nine perceptions or images of organizations that are expressed through metaphors and consist of perceiving organizations as (1) machines, (2) living organisms, (3) brains, (4) cultures, (5) political systems, (6) psychic prisons, (7) roles, (8) systems in flux or change, and (9) institutions of domination (Pugh & Hickson, 1997).

The **organizations as machines** metaphor assumes an orderly, logical arrangement of clear authority and structure. This includes a stable environment with explicit rules for discipline and equal treatment for all in the organization. This "reality" works well in the fast food industry because the clear structure and orderly functioning make it easy not only to train employees, but to replace them. However, the organization as machine metaphor tends to de-emphasize the growth of employees because it treats them like cogs in a machine.

The **organizations as living organisms** metaphor is based on biology and concerns the ability of the organization to adapt to the environment. The benefit of this metaphor is that the organization is flexible and open to the full range of human potential. However, that potential also has built-in biases (i.e., cancers) that can go undetected by the organization until the organization can no longer adapt. The systems and evolutionary perspectives discussed earlier fit with this metaphor in that adaptation and change are core assumptions.

The **organizations as brains** metaphor assumes that intelligence is found at all levels of the organization. In fact, this perception assumes the organization is in a constant state of learning and correcting faulty ways of operating. This view of the organization also includes the ability to accept criticism and use this criticism to optimize performance. In this metaphor we see characteristics of the systems and evolutionary perspectives, in that the organization as brains is a cybernetic system that changes based on feedback from the environment.

The **organizations as cultures** metaphor assumes the organization has an overall corporate culture comprised of many subcultures. When people share a common culture, this shared culture helps shape a common reality for all employees. This similarity in perception keeps all organizational members focused on their mission. One unique benefit of the cultural view is that an organization can shift its culture and, in doing so, reinvent itself. For example, when a company begins referring to its members as a family instead of employees, this forms a new reality. Once this perception is shared by the vast majority of members of the organization, reality is changed. This is characteristic of the structuration approach to culture (see Chapter 3), in that culture is created and recreated by the interactions of organizational members.

The **organizations as political systems** metaphor assumes that we see the organization as a place where politics are at work, and these politics range from *autocratic* to *democratic*. The political view holds that every part of the organization acts in its own best interest. That is, the organization as a whole, individual departments, and individual employees are all political agents acting on behalf of their own self-interest. Although this metaphor represents a cynical perspective with regard to human behavior, it allows people to question the motivations of those within the organization as well as the organization itself. The organizations as political systems metaphor reflects the hedonic view of work and the pursuit of happiness and pleasure.

The **organizations as roles** metaphor envisions a workplace that provides us with purpose and structure. Our role in the organization then becomes our reality. For example, consider an employee who is promoted to

This QR code will take you to an article appearing in *Executive Insights,* which highlights the use of power in organizations.

http://www.unc.edu/~wfarrell/ SOWO%20874/Readings/ maturepower.htm

management status. All the misbehaviors the employee previously engaged in and at one time interpreted as fun (e.g., surfing the Web on company time, taking long lunches, playing practical jokes on coworkers) now are reinterpreted as laziness and wasteful of company time and resources. This shift in perception is due to the employee's new role as manager. The role and the expectation of the new role mandate a change in member behavior.

The **organizations as psychic prisons** metaphor assumes that employees give the organization power over their thoughts and behaviors. This perception results in thinking patterns that are confined and controlled by the organization. This is not as far-fetched or bizarre as it may appear. Consider someone who, when speaking about her organization, says things such as "They simply won't let me" or "They would kill me if I spoke up." "They" in this case is the organization. This metaphor also reflects the critical perspective in which the employee willingly or unwillingly gives control to the organization and is subjugated as a result.

The **organizations as systems in flux** metaphor sees organizations in a state of constant transformation. That is, the organization is in a constant state of creating and recreating itself. By changing organizational practices, the organization brings about a transformed version of itself that is only as stable as the organizational practices that occur within it. This metaphor is reflective of the structuration approach to organizational culture (see Chapter 3).

The metaphor of **organizations as a place of domination** sees the organization as questing for power. The organization is also seen as a source of stress, sickness, pollution, and human exploitation. In other words, the many are exploited for the benefit of the few. The critical perspective is reflected in this metaphor in that the organization is seen as an overt and covert exploiter of people.

imaginization The reinterpretation of ourselves as well as the work we perform.

The overall benefits of Morgan's (1986, 1993) organizational perceptions are that they allow for a range of explanations for the same phenomenon. Morgan also advanced the concept of **imaginization**, which concerns the reinterpretation of ourselves as well as the work we perform. For example, a person who works at a McDonald's restaurant may see his role as important in that he is part of a team that makes sure thousands of customers are served breakfast so they can go to work nourished and thus provide for their families. This image is radically different from the more typical image of a fast food worker. The way in which we interpret our organization and our purpose is a free choice that each of us makes. However, effective managers and leaders use multiple perceptions to uncover problems and opportunities that may have been overlooked or hidden by using only one perceptual view. The nine metaphors discussed in this section provide various ways in which people express their perspectives of organizational life.

Summary

Throughout this chapter we presented various organizational perspectives as well as employees' perceptions of organizational life. The perspective that you and your organization adopt will exert great influence on how you see yourself in relation to your job, coworkers, and superiors as well as on how your organization views employees. Whether you see the organization as an evolutionary species, a living organism, or a place of oppression, you are guided by these assumptions when communicating with coworkers. Although people generally have a "default" perspective regarding work life, the ability to understand how others view the same organization is the mark of an effective and intelligent organizational member. This is not to argue that one perspective is superior or inferior to another. In fact, in any given situation, problems within the organization may be due to the perspective that members employ when encountering problems or making decisions in the workplace.

Perception is a dynamic and individualistically unique process that should be understood by all organizational members regardless of their position. As stated earlier in the chapter, perception is reality. People vary in terms of what stimuli they pay attention to and how those stimuli are organized. However, once the stimuli are ordered, our interpretation is based on our unique psychological experiences. This uniqueness of perception is inevitable in a pluralistic and democratic society in which people enjoy freedom of thought as well as freedom of speech. Earlier in this chapter we reviewed the hedonic and eudaimonic views of organizational life and how these views drive our perceptions and motivations for working. Whether it be working for the pursuit of pleasure or for self-actualization, everyone in the organization has a motive for being there.

The attribution of behavior is another perception-related process that can lead us to misinterpret behavior. Whether this misinterpretation stems from a need to protect our own self-esteem or is based on faulty information, we can make mistakes in concluding why people behave the way they do. Again, multiple perspectives can lead a person to a "better truth" than one obtained by only one perspective. As indicated in the example of the sexually harassed female worker, the intent behind any comment is less important than the meaning attributed to the comment. That is, many times charges of harassment of any type are a receiver-based construct and are not based on what we intended to say. This concept is discussed in Chapter 4.

Now that we have reviewed the perspectives of organizations and perceptual issues related to how people interpret work, we discuss how organizational communication differs based on the management style we employ. Chapter 2 traces the history of organizations and reveals how communication practices are valued or devalued based on how people are organized and on the relationship between workers and management.

Questions for Discussion and Review

1. Based on the evolutionary/ecological view of organizations, how do organizations resemble the animal kingdom? How does the concept of punctuated equilibria view organizational change? Provide examples to support your answer.

2. Explain how biology and the organizational system are related. Describe how the concept of nonsummativity is at the center of the systems perspective. Explain how the systems perspective can provide a unique lens for evaluating organizational structures such as in the example of Walmart. Provide a similar breakdown of an organization you have been affiliated with.

3. According to Marx, organizations are battlegrounds in which power and control are the primary areas of contention. Explain in detail how Marx believed that power and control differences in the workplace can be managed. Do you feel that these power and control differences still exist? Provide support for your answer. Do you agree with the expression "the rich get richer, and the poor get poorer"? Provide details to support your answer.

4. Define organizational perception. Explain how perception shapes our view of an organization. Provide examples to support your answer. Outline the steps in the process of perception formation. How does the idea of attributing meaning affect perceptions? Provide examples to support your answer.

5. Based on the information provided in this chapter, what are the three rules people generally follow when attributing meaning to a situation? Which of the three rules do you feel is most important or is one that you best relate to? Give an example to support your answer.

6. Explain what is meant by the idea of biases in the attribution process. How can these biases distort our perceptions? Give examples to support your answer. What is known as basic attribution error? What do you think of the notion that perception is reality?

7. Explain the differences between the hedonic and eudaimonic views of organizational life. Discuss the positives and negatives associated with each view and how these views impact the organization and employee motivation.

8. List and describe Morgan's nine perceptions or images of organizations (metaphors). Explain how these metaphors can describe an organization. Which of the nine perceptions do you feel most accurately matches your perceptions of your workplace or another organization you are associated with (e.g., social club, church group, fraternity/sorority)?

References

Barker, J., & Tompkins, P. (1993). Identification in the self-managing organization: Characteristics of target and tenure. *Human Communication Research, 21,* 223–240.

Baumgardner, S. R., & Crothers, M. K. (2008). *An introduction to the research and theory of positive psychology.* Boston: Pearson/Prentice Hall.

Farace, R. V., Monge, P. R., & Russell, H. M. (1977). *Communicating and organizing.* Reading, MA: Addison-Wesley.

Habermas, J. (1972). *Knowledge and human interests.* London: Heinemann Educational Books.

Hannan, M. T., & Carroll, G. R. (1992). *Dynamics of organizational populations.* New York: Oxford University Press.

Hannan, M. T., & Freeman, J. (1989). *Organizational ecology.* Cambridge, MA: Harvard University Press.

Heider, F. (1958). *The psychology of interpersonal relations.* New York: Wiley.

Kahneman, D., Diener, E., & Schwarz, N. (Eds.). (1999). *Well-being: The foundations of hedonic psychology.* New York: Russell Sage Foundation.

Marx, K. (1964). *Early writings.* (T. B. Bottomore, Trans. & Ed.). New York: McGraw-Hill.

Morgan, G. (1986). *Images of organizations.* Thousand Oaks, CA: SAGE Publications.

Morgan, G. (1993). *Imaginization: The art of creative management.* Thousand Oaks, CA: SAGE Publications.

Mumby, D. (1987). *Narrative and social control.* Newbury Park, CA: SAGE Publications.

Pugh, D. S., & Hickson, D. J. (1997). *Writers on organizations* (5th ed.). Thousand Oaks, CA: SAGE Publications.

Ross, L. (1977). The intuitive psychologist and his shortcomings: Distortions in the attribution process. In L. Berkowitz (Ed.), *Advances in experimental social psychology* (vol. 10, pp. 173–220). New York: Academic Press.

Ryan, R. M., & Deci, E. L. (2001). On happiness and human potentials: A review of research on hedonic and eudiamonic well-being. *Annual Review of Psychology, 52,* 141–166.

Seligman, M. E. P. (2002). *Authentic happiness: Using a new positive psychology to realize your potential for lasting fulfillment.* New York: Free Press.

Strine, M. (1991). Critical theory and "organic" intellectuals: Reframing the work of culture critical. *Communication Monographs, 58,* 195–201.

Von Bertalanffy, L. (1968). *General system theory: Foundations, development, applications.* New York: George Braziller.

Waterman, A. S. (1993). Two conceptions of happiness: Contrast of personal expressions (eudiamonia) and hedonic enjoyment. *Journal of Personality and Social Psychology, 64,* 678–691.

Wiener, N. (1948). *Cybernetics: On control and communication in animal and machine.* New York: Wiley.

Chapter 2

Ways of Organizing Human Beings

Learning Objectives

Upon completion of the chapter, the student should be able to:

- ◆ Compare and contrast the scientific management perspectives of Taylor, Weber, and Fayol.

- ◆ Explain the Hawthorne effect and how it impacted management thought.

- ◆ Compare and contrast the human relations approach to management with that of the human resource approach.

- ◆ Compare and contrast McGregor's Theory X and Y with Ouchi's Theory Z.

- ◆ Compare and contrast Agyris' Model I and Model II approach with Blake and Mouton's managerial grid.

- ◆ Explain the Theory of Independent Mindedness and why it is considered a true communication theory.

Key Terms

Bureaucratic management

Hawthorne studies

Human relations approach

Human resource approach

Managerial grid

Model I management

Model II management

Scientific management

System 4 management approach

Theory of independent mindedness

Theory X

Theory Y

Theory Z

The history of human productivity has centered on organizing human efforts to achieve a desired goal. Human organization has provided a means for survival and a better quality of life. In 1900, the average life expectancy in the United States was just under 50 years. Today, that life expectancy is over 78 years. Improvements in human organization that led to technological advancements and life-extending breakthroughs in medical science were a major factor in increasing life expectancy. On the other hand, human organization has also been used to exploit and oppress people and, in so doing, served to maximize human output for the benefit of a select few. In such cases, there is an exploiter and an exploited. Have these exploitative uses of organization changed over time? Will we continue to see human organization targeted at improving human existence as well as human organization used as a tool to exploit and oppress people?

For centuries, getting someone to be productive was as simple as a threat issued by the person in power. For example, "Do this or I'll make your life miserable!" From a productivity standpoint, this is an effective way to get people to perform a task, yet has no regard for human dignity or justice. Perhaps you've had a summer job at which your supervisor was constantly threatening to inflict some degree of retribution if his or her orders were not followed. Such a summer job experience is something that most teens can probably relate to. This type of situation occurs most often when those in power provide the powerless with shelter, food, and clothing. However, a civilized society is severely threatened if it accepts such harsh ways of treating people. We don't have to go back to ancient times or far-away civilizations for examples of worker mistreatment. America has its own well-documented history of worker exploitation. A large portion of this country was built on the backs of those who did not share in equal power. For example, the **robber barons** of the 19th century controlled entire industries, crushed competition, and amassed incredible personal wealth. These businessmen regularly used unfair business practices for their own maximum benefit and with little benefit for the workers or laborers. In fact, Thorstein Veblen's 1912 book, *The Theory of the Leisure Class: An Economic Study of Institutions,* equated robber barons with barbarians in that barbarians conquered weaker people with brute force, maximized opportunity, and lived off the materials and goods produced by those they conquered. Although robber barons seldom used brute force, they regularly used economic, psychological, and social force. Such force can be easily seen today in the way countries institute sanctions on each other, threatening to withhold commodities such as oil, electronics, food, medicine, etc. Other scholars argue that these robber barons used extortion, deception, and dishonesty as well as other felonious behaviors to acquire personal wealth. Individuals in American history associated with the term robber baron include John D. Rockefeller, Andrew Carnegie, and J. P. Morgan. Table 2.1 lists some of the most famous robber barons along with the industries they attempted to dominate.

TABLE 2.1	Well-Known Robber Barons and the Industries They Sought to Dominate	
Name	**Industry**	**Location**
Jay Cooke (1821–1905)	Finance	Pennsylvania
Daniel Drew (1797–1879)	Finance	New York
James Fisk (1834–1872)	Finance	New York
Jay Gould (1836–1892)	Finance/Railroads	New York
Andrew Mellon (1855–1913)	Finance	Pennsylvania
J. P. Morgan (1837–1937)	Finance	New York
Andrew Carnegie (1835–1919)	Railroads/Steel	Pennsylvania
Charles Crocker (1822–1888)	Railroads	California
Harry Flagler (1830–1913)	Railroads/Oil	New York
Edward Henry Harriman (1848–1909)	Railroads	New York
Collis P. Huntington (1821–1900)	Railroads	California
Mark Hopkins (1813–1878)	Railroads	California
Cornelius Vanderbilt (1794–1877)	Railroad/Shipping	New York
James J. Hill (1838–1916)	Railroads	Minnesota
George Mortimer Pullman (1831–1897)	Railroads	Chicago
Henry Clay Frick (1849–1919)	Steel	Pennsylvania
John Warne Gates (1855–1911)	Steel/Oil	Pennsylvania
John D. Rockefeller (1839–1937)	Oil	Cleveland

This maltreatment was not only reserved for adult workers. Children were also used as a means of production. Our own personal experience of childhood labor probably includes summer jobs such as being a ticket taker at an amusement park, babysitting, serving food, delivering newspapers, or laboring at a construction site. These types of jobs are common employment opportunities for American youth. However, contemporary news stories from Third World countries often report business practices that include the regular use of child labor in ways that bear no resemblance to our own child-hood work experiences. In the United States, exploitative types of child labor were common until the late 1930s, when child labor laws were enacted. These child labor laws restricted children under the age of 13 to relatively minor labor endeavors (e.g., babysitting, newspaper delivery). These types of jobs are enjoyed today by many children and are one way in which children are socialized to a work ethic that will serve them later in life.

With the advent of industrialization came a major shift in population from America's farms and agricultural centers to its urban manufacturing bases. This shift moved us away from the once common belief that we "work

where we live." In agricultural America, family and community relationships were of primary importance, and people generally found jobs in the immediate geographical location where they grew up. A shift in the American culture to consumerism and individual advancement resulted in a vastly different belief system, at the center of which is the idea that we "live where we work." This belief assumes that the pursuit of career goals and professional opportunity is of primary importance and can supersede more traditional concepts of service to the family, service to community, and citizenship in general. Modern technological advancements such as the Internet and SMART technology make it easy for people to stay in touch even though they may be separated by great distances. People are tethered to family and friends through technology that enables instantaneous communication despite great geographical distances.

With the massive influx of people into the industrial centers, it became necessary to organize labor in ways that promoted production and efficiency (e.g., shift scheduling, skill training, and other functions needed to achieve the company's goals). Concern for the well-being of workers is a relatively modern concept. As discussed in the next section, early management strategies used workers as any other organizational asset (e.g., lathe, screwdriver). Once the worker could no longer function to the expectations of the organization, the worker was discarded. In other words, in the early years of organizing workers, organizations viewed workers as commodities, and when that commodity ceased to be of value, it was discarded.

Classical Management Approaches

Taylor's Time-Motion Efficiency

scientific management
Assumes any worker can be productive if given a scientifically efficient task, will only perform if paid, and should be given simple and unambiguous tasks.

One of the first attempts to provide a comprehensive understanding of worker productivity was in the early 20th century. In 1911 Frederick Taylor developed a new perspective on worker productivity. At the Bethlehem Steel Mill in Cleveland, Taylor formulated his perspective, known as **scientific management**. In observing workers in the steel mill, Taylor concluded that the workers were purposely working well below their capacity. He termed this underachieving behavior **soldiering**. He believed that soldiering occurs because (1) workers believe that an increase in their productivity will result in the reduction of workers needed to perform that specific task; (2) a wage system that does not compensate more productive workers encourages lower productivity from all employees (e.g., if workers are paid for the number of pieces they produce [i.e., piece-work], they fear that reduced productivity will lead to a decrease in wages and thus they remain motivated to produce consistently at lower levels); and (3) when worker training is accomplished primarily through basic, unstandardized on-the-job training, the result is inefficiency and incorrect form and function. Only a task that has been scientifically analyzed and mastered for efficiency should be taught to every employee. A concept of soldiering similar to Taylor's that you may be more familiar with is herd mentality, which occurs when workers are not motivated to stand out from the crowd but are encouraged to revel in mediocrity. Perhaps you have heard phrases such as "Slow down! You're making me look bad," which is a phrase reflective of soldiering behavior.

There are three basic assumptions to the scientific management approach. First, any worker can be a top-producing employee if given a task that is **scientifically efficient**. In this view, every person has an equal chance at productivity as long as he or she is mastering a task in ways designed to make it optimally efficient. Second, workers are motivated by money and will only perform if paid. This principle cheapens human beings, because it assumes workers see no value in high levels of performance beyond that of achieving money or other goods. This view of working only to be externally rewarded is known as the **dangling carrot approach** to performance. Unfortunately, millions of people get up every morning and go to jobs only because the job pays well, not because they are proud of what they do or they feel a calling. Once the job stops paying well, the worker finds another well- paying job. Scientific management is not concerned with how you feel as much as how you perform. Finally, the scientific management approach holds that the tasks given to workers should be kept simple and unambiguous. This view degrades workers because it sees them as simple minded and easily overwhelmed.

Consider the act of shoveling coal into a furnace that's used for the production of steel. To make this task scientifically efficient, one would need to consider such aspects of the task as the distance of the coal pile from the furnace, the size and type of shovel, and the technique used to pick up, carry, and deposit the coal into the furnace. Once all the elements are analyzed, scrutinized, and made optimal, the result was the best technique for shoveling coal. This technique is then taught to all employees who are required to perform this task. As a result, this task has now become scientifically efficient. In a more recent example, consider the job of a contemporary athletic coach. In similar fashion, the coach breaks down particular sporting behaviors such as hitting a baseball, shooting a free-throw, or catching a football to its most basic movements and then has the athlete master each movement that comprises that entire sport behavior. Once each of the movements is mastered, they are put together with the hope that the entire movement is in the most efficient form possible.

The types of communication valued in a scientific management organization consist of messages that flow from workers to the supervisor (**upward communication**) and messages that flow from management to workers (**downward communication**). Messages that flow upward (these are sent with less frequency than downward messages) primarily concern alerting management to possible catastrophic consequences with regard to the tools or machines people are working with. It would be unheard of, especially during the age of industrialization, for employees to send messages upward regarding their feelings about company practices or employee benefits. Messages that flow downward from management to workers are generally task related and specific to that person's job. These messages focus on making the employee maximally productive and little more.

On the face of it, the principles of scientific management sound logical and simple to institute. But consider the underlying assumption about workers: Employees are viewed as cogs in a wheel or parts of a machine. They are not individuals, but rather are entities to be used at the discretion of the organization. This approach is similar to opening a kitchen drawer and retrieving a spoon to stir your coffee. If the spoon ceases to work, you discard it and retrieve another spoon.

Although this illustration may seem insensitive, the scientific management perspective was only concerned with productivity and output, which were the only marks of success in the early days of industrialization. One could argue that the pursuit of the almighty dollar still reigns supreme in today's corporate world. Can you think of organizations that use scientific management techniques in today's world? Perhaps you recently visited one for breakfast or lunch. The contemporary fast food industry is a great example. Consider the evolution of the modern-day drive-thru. From the early days of listening to an order taker through poor quality audio speakers to the modern-day two-lane, two-window, maximum-efficiency drive-thru, these fast food giants have a high employee turnover rate and exercise tight control over employee behavior. One would think that high employee turnover rates are costly, and generally they are. However, training new employees at fast food restaurants is so scientifically efficient that turnover does not adversely affect bottom-line profitability. These principles of scientific management best serve organizations in which employee innovativeness and creativity are devalued or not required.

Weber's Bureaucracy

bureaucratic management Perspective that advocates a tight structure with many levels in the hierarchy.

The need for tight structure and control over the employee was also put forward by Max Weber (1947). In his notion of **bureaucratic management**, he distinguished between the concepts of power and authority. **Power** is the ability to force people to do what you want, regardless of their willingness to do so. **Authority**, on the other hand, is getting people to obey orders voluntarily. Weber's most notable contribution was that of the **rational-legal authority system**. The term *rational* describes something that is designed specifically to achieve a certain goal. In this case, the organization is a fine-tuned machine that seeks maximum efficiency. The term *legal* refers to the use of authority through rules and regulations promulgated by the organization.

One main assumption of a bureaucratic structure is that it is believed to be the optimal means of organizing people. The bureaucratic structure has many levels set in a hierarchy, with each level regulating the level beneath it. There is also a strong emphasis on **depersonalization**; that is, there must be a clear separation between personal matters and business matters. Given a large organizational structure coupled with organizational rules and regulations, control and coordination of worker behavior can be achieved. However, depersonalization is believed to bring about little personal accountability for production. This lack of accountability is directly linked to worker depersonalization by the organization. There is a plethora of contemporary communication research linking worker depersonalization to lower levels of employee performance and employee commitment (see Jablin & Putnam, 2001). There is a common expression used by workers in what many consider to be one of the world's biggest bureaucracies, the U.S. government, that reflects this depersonalization: *Good enough for government work!*

Fayol's Lateral Communication

Another scientific management approach to organizations was put forward by Henri Fayol (1949). Fayol believed that management serves five functions: planning for the future, organizing, commanding, coordinating, and controlling. Given that his work was developed in the mid-1900s, it was far ahead of its time. Fayol is best known for his military-like principles of management. He believed there are 14 tenets of managerial effectiveness (see Table 2.2). Fayol's most significant contribution was the **scalar chain** concept of information transfer. The scalar chain is the clear hierarchical exchange of information. Fayol believed there should be clear lines of upward and downward communication, just as there are in the military. In addition, he believed managers who are at the same level of the organizational structure should be able to share information with each other as long as the organization is aware of the exchange. This lateral exchange of information, or **gangplank** (also known as **Fayol's bridge**), was a unique perspective for communication within any organization and can be easily seen in the communication structure of the U.S. military (see Figure 2.1).

As Table 2.2 indicates, Fayol was far ahead of his time in terms of management's function and concern for all aspects of the organization. In fact, several of his tenets are relationally and communication-based (e.g., authority, equity, esprit de corps). Although there is some concern for the worker in Fayol's approach, it is considered a scientific management approach because management's primary concern is organizational survival. Employee concern is a secondary goal to be pursued only after the primary goal of organizational efficiency is achieved. All the scientific management approaches to organizational productivity view the needs of the worker as, at best, secondary to and, at worst, unimportant to the goal of organizational profitability.

The classical management approach as a whole focuses primarily on processes and procedures, with people serving as an application of these processes and procedures. Ambiguity and uncertainty are seen as threats to efficiency and, as such, need to be reduced if not eliminated.

In the next section we show how the focus moves from people being an application of process and procedure to process and procedure being an application of people.

TABLE 2.2	Fayol's 14 Fundamental Tenets of Effective Management
Division of work	Workers who are trained in one task become experts and thus most productive.
Authority	The ability to issue orders as well as use power appropriately.
Discipline	Employees will only follow orders to the degree to which management provides effective leadership.
Unity of command	Employees should only have one manager; this keeps information clear and consistent.
Unity of direction	Employees who do similar tasks should all be given the same plan of action.
Subordination of individual interest to general interest	Management must put the needs of the organization above those of any single employee.
Remuneration	Compensation is an important motivating tool.
Centralization or decentralization	Which of the two theories management chooses should be based on current personnel as well as the current health of the organization.
Scalar chain	Clear hierarchy of information is necessary; lateral communication is encouraged.
Order	Order is needed at both the production and the personnel levels.
Equity	There must be a degree of respect for employees as well as equal justice throughout the organization.
Stability of tenure	Retaining quality management is crucial, given the cost and time involved in training new management.
Initiative	Employees at all levels of the organization should be allowed to be innovative.
Esprit de corps	Management is responsible for maintaining high morale levels for all employees.

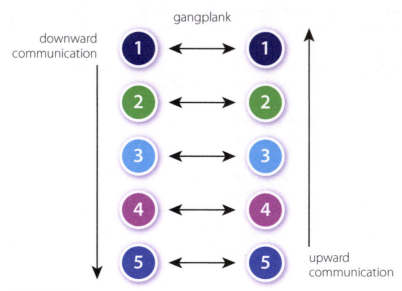

FIGURE 2.1
Fayol's Bridge.

Human Relations Approach to Management

As discussed previously, the eras of industrialization and scientific management were fraught with worker exploitation and human devaluation. During the late 19th and early 20th centuries, workers revolted against this maltreatment by banding together to form labor unions. In fact, one of the most famous workplace disasters served as a watershed moment in labor unionization in the United States. It occurred in 1911 at the Triangle Shirtwaist Company located on New York City's Lower East Side. A massive fire erupted that killed about 150 employees, most of whom were young women. Management had chained the emergency exits closed to reduce the loss of goods (i.e., employees were believed to be stealing items from the company) and, as a result, the victims were either burned to death or forced to jump to their death. This tragedy was more than the government and American people could tolerate. In the aftermath of the Triangle Shirtwaist Company disaster, many initiatives were passed to establish federal standards in industrial safety and methods of fire prevention. This watershed period of American labor history also served as a starting point for alternative conceptualizations of organization and management.

Hawthorne Studies

The **human relations approach** to management can be considered almost the diametric opposite of the scientific management approach. That is, this approach advocates that management should focus efforts on meeting the emotional needs of the worker and put less emphasis on production. The researchers most connected to this approach are Elton Mayo, Fritz Roethlisberger, and William Dickson. These researchers were consultants on what have become known as the **Hawthorne Studies**. Between 1927 and 1932, a series of experiments were conducted to determine the effect of lighting on productivity at the Western Electric Company's Hawthorne Plant in Chicago. Plant workers assembled induction coils for the telephone systems. Because assembling induction coils was considered a specialized job, a new management team was assembled to oversee this specialized production. Workers were assigned to either the experimental group, in which they assembled the coils in varied lighting situations, or the control group, in which they assembled the coils under normal lighting conditions. Other manipulations during the experiment included providing additional work breaks, changing wages based on performance, and altering lunch and work schedules. The initial findings indicated there was an increase in productivity as a result of these changes.

   Mayo and his team conducted several variations of this experiment to find out why workers in the experimental group were more productive than those in the control group. Mayo and his colleagues concluded that the

human relations approach
A management approach that advocates focusing on meeting the emotional needs of the worker with less focus on production.

Hawthorne studies A series of studies between 1927 and 1932 that gave rise to the human relations approach to management.

reason for this increased production was not due to the lighting conditions, but the attention given to the workers by the experimenter and supervisors. Further, the strong interpersonal relationships that developed among coworkers created a cohesive and supportive workgroup, which resulted in increased productivity. This increase in performance was thought to stem from strong relationships among the employees, who did not want to disappoint their fellow workgroup members by failing to perform at a high level.

Mayo believed that the employee's need for supportive and high-quality work relationships was a result of a breakdown in society (Roethlisberger & Dickson, 1949). In other words, as people lose the close attachments they share with family and friends, their unfulfilled relational needs must be fulfilled by the organization. Therefore, Mayo (1933) believed that one of the major management functions should be to provide **spontaneous cooperation**, or the fostering of relationships and teamwork. It was also a main tenet of the human relations management approach that conflict and competition should be avoided at all costs because they negatively influenced the goal of spontaneous cooperation. This perspective focused on relationships as opposed to production (recall that production was the main goal of the scientific management approach). Organizations that used the human relations approach to management often experienced lower productivity because the primary focus was the workers' psychological well-being, and the secondary focuses were organizational productivity and output.

Other research offers different interpretations of the findings from the Hawthorne Studies. Some scholars argue that the major findings of the study came about when one particular group, known as the Mica Splitting Test Group, was isolated from other groups in the experiment, and that this isolation resulted in a 15% increase in productivity. It was within this group that the **Hawthorne effect** was observed. The Hawthorne effect is defined as a threat to the internal validity of an experiment that occurs when a change in experimental conditions (moving the Mica Splitting Test Group into isolation) brings about a change in the behavior of the experiment's participants (Brannigan & Zwerman, 2001).

A recent re-analysis of the data from the original experiment found that managerial discipline, financial incentives, the economic hardship of the Great Depression, and increased rest periods significantly predicted worker productivity. In fact, although increased observation by management also led to increased worker productivity, it appears that the original researchers ignored the other factors that influenced performance and only focused on human relationships in an effort to forward the human relations ideology (Franke & Kaul, 1978). Simply put, the human relations approach to management met with little success because it was based on faulty information and interpretation of the Hawthorne Studies. However, the human relations approach did highlight the importance of management considering the psychological well-being of the worker and helped bring about positive changes in the way organizations treat employees.

This QR code will take you to documents produced by Harvard's Business School, highlighting the Hawthorne Effect and the Time Motion Studies.

http://www.library.hbs.edu/hc/hawthorne/09.html

Human Resource Approach to Management

Thus far, we have reviewed two perspectives with regard to productivity and quality of work life. As has been demonstrated, both scientific management and human relations management perspectives offer some interesting and effective insights into human organization as well as some negative consequences associated with each. That is, scientific management put productivity first with little concern for worker needs, whereas human relations management put worker needs first with less concern for productivity. However, there is an approach to management that considers both the needs of the organization and the needs of the worker in ways that are mutually beneficial. This perspective is known as the **human resource approach** to management. In this theory, the employee is seen as a valuable asset to the organization that must be developed and valued with regard to both the worker's needs and the organization's needs. This approach reflects a concern for both task and employee. Scholars interested in this management approach have provided several popular theories for both organizational effectiveness and enhanced worker well-being; many of these theories are practiced in contemporary organizations.

human resource approach Holds that employees are a valuable asset that should be developed for the benefit of both the organization and the worker.

Likert System 4 Management Approach

Several researchers have identified key differences between job-centered managers and employee-centered managers. One such effort was the **System 4 Management Approach** of Rensis Likert (1961, 1967). This system ranges from low concern for workers to high concern for workers. System 1 is the **exploitive-authoritative type** of management, which uses threats and fear to motivate employees. Decision making within this organization type is handled at the top levels and passed down. Downward communication is valued most within this system. Messages are primarily task centered and are handed down to employees from management. Upward communication is discouraged and kept to a minimum in an effort to keep supervisors and subordinates psychologically distant from one another.

system 4 management approach Ranges from depersonalization of employees to the full integration of employee input and potential.

System 2 is called the **benevolent-authoritative type** of management and is characterized by management's use of rewards for employee performance. However, management still devalues employee input and values management input. Communication is primarily downward but can flow upward in this type of organization. However, upward communication is limited to information that only management deems important.

System 3 is the **consultative type** of management and uses rewards and punishment but in a minor way involves subordinate input in the decision-making process. Although employee input is sought, major decisions are made at higher organizational levels. Only the smaller decisions or those decisions with less impact on the organization are left to lower-level employees. Communication associated with this management style involves both upward and downward communication. Unlike the previous two systems, System 3 contains some relational messages; however, the majority of messages are those that management prefers (i.e., messages that benefit the organization) as opposed to messages preferred by employees.

The most employee-centered system is System 4 and is known as the **participative type** of management. This system is most reflective of the human resource approach to management. In this system, management values and encourages input from subordinates. There is a strong psychological connection between superior and subordinate, and quality communication flows in both upward and downward directions. It is believed that the System 4 management style results in high productivity and quality interpersonal relationships at all levels of the organization. Further, employees in a participative organization tend to be committed to the organization. There is a premium on human needs and performance that emphasizes interpersonal relationships as a means to achieve maximum individual potential and promote organizational productivity.

Theory X Assumes workers are lazy, have little ambition, and are motivated by coercion and threats.

Theory Y Assumes workers are motivated by an internal need to excel and actively pursue responsibility.

This QR code will take you to a YouTube clip highlighting the differences between Theory X and Theory Y.

http://www.youtube.com/
watch?v=fd3-Esb-m3o

McGregor's Theory X and Theory Y

Douglas McGregor (1960, 1966) developed a way to explain managerial action based on the manager's assumption of employees' work ethic. In the early years of management research, scholars sought to explain how management controls and directs employees toward the organization's goals. McGregor's **Theory X** and **Theory Y** approaches to management are based on opposite assumptions about human behavior.

The Theory X management approach contains three basic assumptions (Pugh & Hickson, 1997). First, employees are basically lazy and have a tendency to do the minimum while actively seeking to avoid work. Management must constantly reward productivity and punish low production. Second, because of worker dislike for work, management must use motivating devices such as threats, coercion, control, and direction to achieve organizational goals. Third, employees want to be controlled and directed because they have little ambition and simply strive for a world free of uncertainty. Thus, by being controlled and directed, workers experience little uncertainty.

The Theory Y management approach contains six basic assumptions. First, productivity and the need to excel are internally motivating factors inherent in every worker. Second, managerial control of employees is only one of many devices that management can use to increase productivity. Third, the most valued reward for employees is the pursuit of satisfaction and the opportunity to become the best employee they can be. Fourth, employees can be taught not only to accept responsibility, but to actively seek opportunities for increased responsibility. Fifth, employees are capable of contributing more to creative solutions in the workplace than they actually do. Finally, as it currently stands, organizations do not maximize employees'

full potential as assets to the organization, thus missing out on untapped employee resources and talents.

As McGregor's theory indicates, Theory X exhibits more cynical and pessimistic assumptions about human beings when contrasted with Theory Y assumptions. Consider the example of a small business owner, such as a proprietor of a gas station or a sandwich shop. The Theory X manager will probably exhibit behaviors such as stopping by the store unannounced because he or she assumes the employees are lazy and will only work when supervised. Chances are that this sort of managerial behavior will result in high employee turnover as well as unsatisfied and suspicious employees. On the other hand, the Theory Y small business owner will behave in ways that empower employees to be creative and challenged. The Theory Y owner will instill a sense of pride and loyalty in employees, which will lead to better quality service and less employee turnover. Whether a person becomes a Theory Y or Theory X manager depends on their personality as well as on their assumptions about human beings in relation to work.

Ouchi's Theory Z

Traditionally it was common for management and organizational communication scholars to compare and contrast the management approaches of American organizations (**Type A organizations**) with those of Japanese organizations (**Type J organizations**); see Table 2.3. Type A organizations typically encourage individual decision making, short-term performance appraisals, and specialized career paths; whereas Type J organizations typically encourage collective decision making, long-term performance appraisals, and nonspecialized career paths. Comparing and contrasting Type A and Type J organizations were especially prevalent during the late 1970s and through the 1980s because of the incredible growth of Japanese organizations in the United States and international markets. There was an assumption that both management styles (Type A and Type J), which include both positive and negative aspects, could easily be imported and integrated into other countries and societies. However, most of these attempts to integrate management approaches specific to one culture were dismal failures.

William Ouchi (1981) believed the most effective management theory should be based on the society in which it is going to be applied. It is the ultimate goal of **Theory Z** to understand and coordinate the structure of society with organization management.

A key assumption of Theory Z is that workers actively involved in the processes and success of the organization represent the key to increased productivity. The theory is based on four components: (1) trust between superior and subordinate, in that all interactions and dealings between them are above board and conducted openly and honestly; (2) subtlety, which reflects the manager's implicit and personal knowledge of each employee and the use of this knowledge to match people who are compatible with one another to maximize efficiency (these similarities can be based on personalities,

Theory Z Advocates matching the organization's culture to that of the larger society and assumes that involved workers are the key to increased productivity.

| TABLE 2.3 | Ouchi's Comparison of Type A (American) vs. Type J (Japanese) Organizations |

Type A Organizations	Type J Organizations
Employment is short term.	Employment is long term and often for a lifetime.
Evaluation and promotion occur frequently and at a rapid rate.	Evaluation and promotion are slow and usually within the same organization.
Specialized career paths may lead workers to switch employment to competing organizations.	Nonspecialized career paths are malleable to the needs of the organization.
Explicit control mechanisms leave no ambiguity as to what rules and regulations the organization wants employees to follow.	Implicit control mechanisms reflect the more subtle organizational/societal expectations of worker performance and productivity.
Individual decision making is encouraged, and innovation and creativity are seen as individual pursuits that are the primary influence in decision making.	Collective decision making is encouraged, and individuality is discouraged; group rule and group harmony are primary influences in decision-making behavior.
Individual responsibility as a cultural assumption reflects accountability for themselves and not for coworkers. Employees are rewarded and punished based on individual performance.	Collective responsibility as a cultural assumption reflects that everyone has a stake in the whole organization, and a failure or success at any one level or by any one employee is a failure or success for the entire organization.
Segmented concern; cultural assumptions dictate localized problems and localized solutions without regard to implications for the greater good or the organization as a whole.	Holistic concern; cultural assumptions dictate the subordination of local concerns if those concerns are harmful to the whole. Individual sacrifices are expected if the organization as a whole will prosper.

Source: Adapted from Ouchi, 1981.

specialties, etc.); (3) productivity, which reflects a certain standard of performance is expected of all employees in the organization; and (4) intimacy, which reflects the practice of and belief in caring, support, and selflessness in social relationships.

Unlike the McGregor approaches, which focus on the manager's assumptions about employees' work ethic, Theory Z focuses on the attitude and individual responsibilities of employees. Ouchi (1981) believed that collective attitudes and beliefs of employees should be based on respect for one another as well as for the organization. Consider the concept of lifetime employment in Japan. Approximately 20% of the Japanese workforce is under lifetime employment in government and large corporations (Kato, 2001). Theory Z assumes that workers are loyal to their employer, are not looking to leave at the first sight of an advancement opportunity at another company, and will typically wait five, 10, or even 20 years for a promotion (which most often occurs from within their current organization). Contrast that to the typical American corporate culture, in which people are constantly looking to increase status, pay, and power. To understand how a person could wait so long for a promotion, we must understand the underlying societal values of loyalty, commitment, honor, and selflessness that are prevalent within Japanese organizations and the Japanese culture as a whole.

The Theory Z management approach requires that organizations spend a great deal of resources, such as time and money, in developing the interpersonal skills of every employee. Given the organization's stress on competent employee communication, processes such as decision making and information exchange are greatly improved. This results in a positive influence on employees' sense of pride in their organization as well as an improved organizational bottom line.

Argyris' Model I and Model II Approach

Another approach that uses the human resource perspective of management is the **Model I** and **Model II** approach to management developed by Chris Argyris (1965). Argyris believed that individuals' personal and professional growth is directly related to and affected by their work situation. Traditionally, management has been so focused on bottom-line productivity and profit goals that managers become communicatively incompetent or lack the social skills with regard to growing their employees and using employee creativity and potential.

This myopic focus on the bottom line, as characterized by the scientific management approach, results in employees developing a preventative or reactive posture as opposed to a proactive posture. These preventative or reactive postures are known as **defensive routines** (Argyris, 1985). In other words, people are so resistant to change, even when change can enhance their careers, that they develop a "work to not get fired" perspective as opposed to a "work toward excellence" perspective. When the "work to not get fired" perspective becomes internalized, the employee develops a **learned helplessness** (Seligman, 1992). For example, an employee who has shown initiative on the job and continually receives negative feedback for proactive behaviors eventually stops showing initiative. This condition is not self-induced but organizationally induced, in that organizations tell employees to focus on long-term personal and organizational goals but they evaluate employees in short-term cycles (e.g., quarterly job performance review) based solely on productivity. Moreover, organizations depersonalize the work through controls, such as time-motion studies and cost accounting that further stifle employee creativity and instill a fear of failure. This paradox of long-term performance expectations and short-term performance evaluation is but one of many paradoxes that workers face on a daily basis.

Chris Argyris and Donald Schon (1978) argued that workers are constantly caught in a paradoxical situation, or "a contradiction that follows correct deduction from consistent premises" (Watzlawick, Beavin-Bavelas, & Jackson, 1967, p. 188). For example, we are constantly encouraged by management to "think outside the box," but doing so requires us to break existing organizational rules. We all know that breaking organizational rules most

Model I Assumes unilateral goals, self-reliance, failure to disclose negative opinions, and reliance on objectivity and logic.

Model II Assumes proaction, consultative decision making, solution implementation, and the ability to adapt if the solution needs adjustment.

often results in reprimand, demotion, or termination. This type of paradox confounds employee growth and creates a constant state of uncertainty.

The models proposed by Argyris and Schon (1978) highlight differences between what a manager *says* are his or her behavior, ethics, philosophy, and the like (**espoused theory**) versus his or her *actual* behaviors, ethics, and philosophy (**theory in use**). For example, a manager may tell her employees that she has an open door policy and that no issue is too small to discuss. This constitutes the manager's espoused theory. However, when this manager is approached by an employee with an issue, she appears hurried, condescending, and uninterested. The manager's actual behavior constitutes the manager's theory in use, which in this case directly contradicts the manager's espoused theory. The communication style that managers espouse (e.g., being outgoing and collaborative) should correspond to their actual communication behavior.

Two types of theory in use approaches are Model I and Model II. Model I assumes four types of managerial behavior: (1) The manager sets unilateral goals that are then pursued. (2) The manager is so self-reliant that he or she maximizes success and minimizes failure. (3) The manager doesn't express negative behavior in public and keeps opinions and attitudes to him- or herself. (4) The manager treats all issues objectively and rationally to the point that emotional expression is minimized.

The type of learning the Model I approach generates is known as **single-loop learning**. Argyris (1985) believes this type of learning is self-oppressive. Single-loop learning is the understanding of *how* a process is conducted, not *why* the process is conducted the way it currently is. For example, there is a lot of single-loop learning in the fast food industry. Consider the process of making French fries. When the fryer light goes on and the beeping sound signals that the French fries have finished cooking, the employee immediately takes the fry basket out of the oil, puts the new fry basket containing uncooked potatoes into the fryer, then pushes the reset button to begin the next cooking process. This process takes place dozens of times a day at thousands of locations throughout the world. But how many of the employees who perform this French fry process actually know *why* they perform this task in the way they were trained? Managers shouldn't confuse the word *how* with the word *why*. In a sense, we cheapen human beings by simply telling them what to do without telling them why they are doing it.

In some of your college classes each semester, you are provided syllabi that state how many tests, quizzes, papers, and so on you are required to complete. Have you ever been told why the professor chose particular tests (the type of test), quizzes (the type of quizzes), and papers (the type of papers)? The answer will most likely be no. If you were told why the professor chose the format used to evaluate your course performance, you would probably respect the assignment and understand how the assessment of course material will benefit you in the future.

The Model II approach to management allows for organizational learning and growth. Model II managers regularly engage in the following three behaviors: (1) The manager acts on information he or she sees as valid. (2) The manager consults all people who are both relevant to the decision and competent to make the decision, and then acts on that decision. (3) The manager is committed to the decision and is active in its implementation yet willing to adjust if unsuccessful.

Managers using the Model II management approach are open to feedback and trust others, which results in **double-loop learning**. Double-loop learning is also known as **generative learning**. Generative learning entails learning the process, understanding the rationale for the process, and understanding how the process contributes to the functioning of the entire organization. Unlike Model I management, which only results in single-loop learning, Model II management results in a more complete understanding of the process. Revisit the example of the fryer in the fast food restaurant. A Model II manager instructs the employee in the proper process for operating the fryer and explains why the steps are performed as they are, thus tying the task into the overall success of the organization. In the case of the college course example, generative learning would be reflected in your professor telling you why your test is in an essay format and why your paper needs to be 20 pages long. This process allows for feedback, identifying possible misunderstanding, and possible changes to the process. Recall the systems perspective discussed in Chapter 1. The concept of **cybernetic learning** is based on feedback that allows the system to self-regulate and adjust to the environment. Double-loop learning is similar to a cybernetic system in that both rely on feedback for self-correction.

It is possible to change a Model I organization or manager into a Model II organization or manager. Argyris (1993) conducted a five-year study resulting in a seminar directed at training Model II communication and management skills to organizational members with a goal of overcoming the defensiveness and mistrust that signify a Model I management approach. The effectiveness of management training indicates that people can and do change their management practices. As the work of Chris Argyris indicates, effective management is a skill, and all skills can be learned.

Blake and Mouton's Managerial Grid

Another way to conceptualize different management styles is to use concern for workers and concern for task as two separate dimensions that combine to form a management style as opposed to treating concern for worker and concern for task as an either/or proposition (as demonstrated in McGregor's Theory X and Theory Y approach). Robert Blake and Jane Mouton (1964, 1978) developed the **managerial grid** for assessing the focus of managerial efforts. Managers are assessed on a scale from 1 (very low) to 9 (very high). This scale measures the degree to which managers have concern for their workers and/or concern for the task at hand.

managerial grid
A management approach that treats concern for workers and concern for task as two separate dimensions resulting in five management styles.

This QR code will take you to an article discussing Blake and Mouton's Managerial/Leadership Grid, produced by *Mind Tools*.

http://www.mindtools.com/pages/article/newLDR_73.htm

The manager who has low concern for people and low concern for task is labeled an **impoverished manager** (i.e., scoring at or near 1 on concern for workers and at or near 1 on concern for task). These managers are very ineffective, are costly to the organization, and generally have less tenure in management positions. People with this management style may also exhibit communication apprehension, verbal aggression, antisocial behavior, low self-esteem, or depression (see Figure 2.2).

A manager who reports high concern for workers and low concern for task is known as a **country club manager** (i.e., scoring at or near 9 on concern for workers and at or near 1 on concern for task). This type of manager is valued by subordinates because his or her high level of communication and relational competency foster positive affect (feelings) from subordinates. However, this person is not valued by the organization's upper-level management. The country club manager is more concerned with being liked than with being effective. This management style resembles the human relations approach (see Figure 2.3).

The manager who displays a high concern for task and low concern for workers is called a **task manager** (i.e., scoring at or near 1 on concern for workers and at or near 9 on concern for task). This type of manager is very productive and efficient and often generates an improved bottom line, which higher-level management appreciates. However, because of the exclusive focus on productivity, relationships with subordinates suffer. The task manager is not well liked by subordinates. The task manager may simply be an incompetent communicator. That is, task managers may lack the skills required to develop quality relationships with subordinates. This management style is reflective of the scientific management approach (see Figure 2.4).

The next type of management style consists of a person who is moderate in both concern for task and workers (i.e., scoring at or near 5 on concern for workers and at or near 5 on concern for task). Managers scoring moderate on both are known as **moderate managers**. This type of person will realize average success with regard to productivity and average levels of appreciation and liking from subordinates. Given that the scores for the moderate manager are in the middle for both task and workers, there are more moderate managers

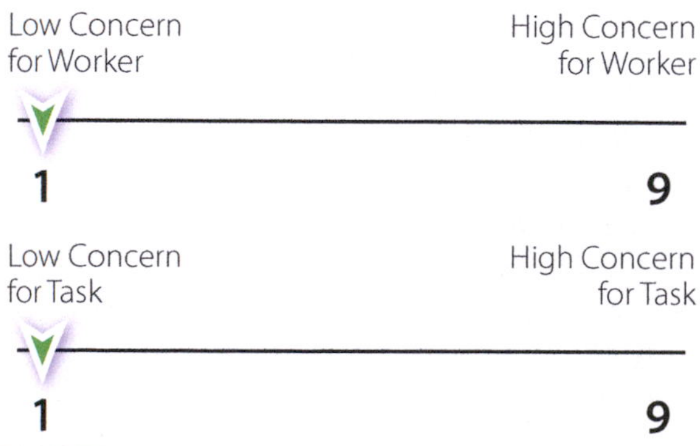

Low Concern for Worker	High Concern for Worker
⌄	
1	9

Low Concern for Task	High Concern for Task
⌄	
1	9

FIGURE 2.2
Impoverished Manager.

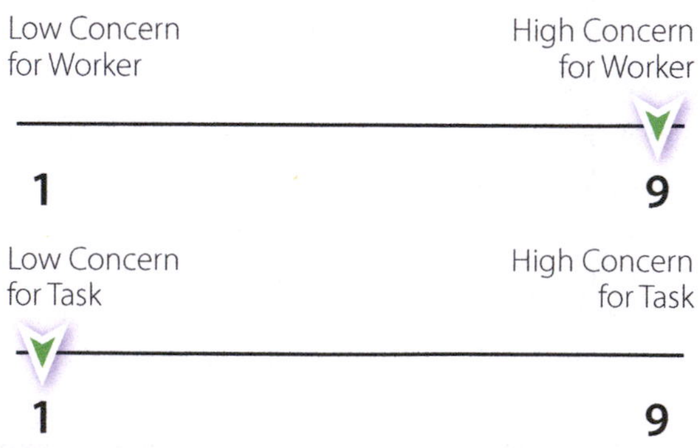

Low Concern for Worker	High Concern for Worker
	⌄
1	9

Low Concern for Task	High Concern for Task
⌄	
1	9

FIGURE 2.3
Country Club Manager.

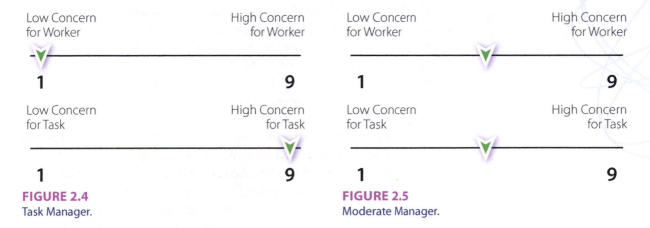

FIGURE 2.4
Task Manager.

FIGURE 2.5
Moderate Manager.

than any other type of manager because fewer people score on the extremes of these measures (e.g., country club and task manager) (see Figure 2.5).

The manager who displays high concern for both task and workers is known as a **team manager** (i.e., scoring at or near 9 on concern for workers and at or near 9 on concern for task). This person enjoys both high levels of productivity and quality interpersonal relationships with workers. The team manager is the optimal management style in that both domains of task and workers are fully addressed (Blake & Mouton, 1982). Dean Tjosvold (1984) found that people reported working their hardest when the manager was high in both concern for task and workers. In contrast, people reported working the least for a manager who was high in concern for workers and low in concern for task (i.e., country club manager). The team manager style is most reflective of the human resource approach. The value of the Blake and Mouton (1964, 1978) managerial grid is reflected in the many combinations of management styles that can be derived from treating concern for the task and concern for the workers as independent dimensions that range from low concern to high concern (see Figure 2.6).

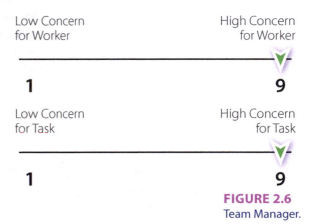

FIGURE 2.6
Team Manager.

The Theory of Independent Mindedness

The next theory is based on the communication skills of both the supervisor and the subordinate. This contemporary communication theory is in the human resource management tradition and is called the **theory of independent mindedness** (TIM) (Infante, 1987a, 1987b). This theory is uniquely communication based as opposed to economic-, business-, or psychology-based, which are representative of some of the other approaches discussed earlier. The TIM seeks congruity or similarity between the culture created within the specific organization (i.e., microculture) and the larger culture (macroculture) within which the organization operates (Infante,

theory of independent mindedness A management style that advocates cultural congruity between the organization and the larger culture within which it operates.

1987b). This cultural coordination is also the foundation of the Theory Z style of management discussed earlier. American culture values freedom of expression and individual rights. Both of these cherished values are made explicit in the United States Constitution and are fiercely protected by its citizens. According to the TIM, these values should not only be reflected, but fostered in the organization. Figure 2.7 highlights the need for congruity between the micro- and macrocultures.

This corporatist theory, which considers the bottom line (e.g., profit) as much as it does employee needs, is believed to bring about more motivated, satisfied, and productive employees. According to the TIM, employees should be active members in decision making, and there should be a robust exchange of ideas and perspectives between employees and managers. In contrast with most Eastern management approaches, power and status differences should not be diminished but acknowledged and emphasized, because they are part of American organizational life (Avtgis & Rancer, 2007a).

This theory is a radical departure from scientific management-based theories that emphasize the use of unilateral control and power (Ewing, 1982; Infante & Gorden, 1987). In fact, this perspective assumes that power and control are fluid ideas that move both downward from employer to employee as well as upward from employee to employer. In an effort to exert control and power appropriately, communication skills must be developed. More specifically, there are three communication traits that bring about a state of independent mindedness in the superior-subordinate relationship: **argumentativeness** (Infante & Rancer, 1982), **verbal aggressiveness** (Infante & Wigley, 1986), and **communicator style** (Norton, 1978).

Argumentativeness is a stable communication trait that can be defined as a person's predisposition to advocate positions on controversial issues while simultaneously attacking the positions others take on those issues (Rancer & Avtgis, 2006). Argumentativeness is considered a subset of assertiveness in that all argument is assertive communication but not all assertive

If a≠b then cultural mismatching is present and thus detrimental to organizational success and productivity

If a=b then cultural matching is present and thus optimal for organizational success

FIGURE 2.7
Theory of Independent Mindedness.

communication involves argument (Avtgis & Rancer, 2007b). Within the organization, high levels of argumentativeness have been linked to a host of positive outcomes, such as more appropriate use of dissent strategies (Kassing & Avtgis, 1999), subordinate relational and job satisfaction (Infante & Gorden, 1985), and the use of solution-oriented conflict strategies (Martin, Anderson, & Sirimangkala, 1997). Overwhelmingly, evidence supports the notion that the more one is argumentative, the more successful one is in the workplace. However, there is a slight gender bias to this generalization that is discussed in Chapter 6. There is a cultural assumption that arguing is the same as a verbal fight. Arguing, in the case of the TIM, is the ability to articulate ideas and think critically about the positions that others present. This concept of arguing is a positive and prosocial expression and should not be confused with fighting.

The second communication trait, verbal aggressiveness, is defined as the tendency to attack the self-concept of another person with the intent to inflict psychological harm (Infante & Wigley, 1986). Unlike argumentativeness, verbal aggressiveness is a subset of hostility and has been linked to a variety of negative organizational outcomes. For example, verbal aggressiveness has been linked to inattentiveness and unfriendliness, decreased organizational satisfaction (Infante & Gorden, 1989), and use of ineffective or inappropriate organizational dissent strategies (Kassing & Avtgis, 1999). It is in relation to verbal aggression that the term *arguing* is incorrectly substituted. As stated earlier, arguing is a positive and constructive type of communication.

The final communication trait in the TIM model is communicator style, which is defined as "the way one verbally and para-verbally interacts to signal how literal meaning should be taken, interpreted, filtered, or understood" (Norton, 1978, p. 99). This trait contains 10 communicator style dimensions: **dominant style** (communicating in a way that takes charge of a situation), **dramatic style** (communicating in a way that either understates or overstates information), **contentious style** (communicating in a combative or antagonistic way), **impression-leaving style** (interacting in a way that is memorable), **animated style** (frequent use of nonverbal behaviors), **relaxed style** (communicating in a way that lacks anxiety or tension), **open style** (communicating in an extroverted and spontaneous way), **attentive style** (communicating in a way that gives other people the impression that you are listening to them), **precise style** (communicating in a way that is exact and detailed), and **friendly style** (communicating in a more intimate way). There are particular combinations of these styles that validate the self-concept of others. For example, being relaxed, attentive, open, friendly, and impression-leaving validates the other person's self-concept. When we communicate in a way that validates another person's self-concept, we are displaying an **affirming communication style**. Other combinations of styles, such as dramatic, dominant, contentious, precise, and animated, negate or threaten the self-concept of other people. When we communicate in a way that negates or threatens another person's self-concept, we're displaying a **nonaffirming communication style**.

TABLE 2.4	Communication Trait Profiles of the Theory of Independent-Mindedness	
Profile	**Trait Level**	**Outcome**
One	High Argumentativeness	High Employee Commitment
	Low Verbal Aggressiveness	High Employee Satisfaction
	Affirming Communicator Style	High Employee Productivity
Two	High Argumentativeness	Moderate Employee Commitment
	Low Verbal Aggressiveness	Moderate Employee Satisfaction
	Nonaffirming Communicator Style	Moderate Employee Productivity
Three	Low Argumentativeness	Low Employee Commitment
	Low Verbal Aggressiveness	Low Employee Satisfaction
	Affirming Communicator Style	Low Employee Productivity
Four	Low Argumentativeness	Low Employee Commitment
	High Verbal Aggressiveness	Low Employee Satisfaction
	Nonaffirming Communicator Style	Low Employee Productivity

Infante and Gorden (1987) proposed four profiles of communication traits that comprise the range of styles, from complete independent mindedness (profile 1) to the absence of independent-mindedness (profile 4). Table 2.4 illustrates the four profiles.

The TIM requires that all members of an organization be trained in argumentation; that is, the ability to formulate and deliver effective arguments as well as skills to control verbal aggression. This type of training will move organizational members toward a state of independent-mindedness. It is assumed that liberty-loving people who value individual expression are well served in a workplace that values such foundational rights. We cannot ask people to suspend core cultural values at work and resume those values outside the organization. To date, the TIM remains the only communication-specific organizational theory available to social scientific researchers that's based on cultural congruity. Recall that Theory Z seeks coordination between the societal culture and the organizational culture but was developed in the field of business, not the field of communication.

Summary

This chapter provides a variety of perspectives that assume different ideas about human beings. Some of these perspectives place a premium on the value of human life, whereas others take a more mechanistic view. Are human beings to be the most valued asset of the organization? Or are human beings just another resource to be used and controlled by management?

The answer to these questions lies in the perspective of the specific person answering them. In today's society, we see all these management perspectives employed with a range of success and failure.

Evidence of effectiveness as well as ineffectiveness has amassed for all the management and communication approaches presented in this chapter. Regardless of the approach we take, they are all based on Western civilization and the notion that effectiveness and productivity can only be achieved through the efficient management of human beings. It has been less than a century since researchers began theorizing about organizing and controlling human output. Relatively speaking, our management and communication strategies are still in their infancy and will probably grow by leaps and bounds in future decades.

Managers should adopt the management and communication approaches that best represent their personality and life perspective. That is, trying to implement a management approach that does not match your personality will probably result in less-than-optimal productivity and a less-than-satisfying work experience. Similar to the cultural matching advocated in the Theory of Independent-Mindedness and Theory Z, managers should seek to match their attributes to an organization that will value and foster those attributes. By doing so, managers will implement their own management style rather than accept the organization's prescribed management style, which may be incongruent with their own self-concept.

Questions for Discussion and Review

1. Recall the discussion of scientific management. List and explain the major contributions made by Taylor, Weber, and Fayol.

2. How might the 14 tenets of effective management put forth by Fayol be used in organizations today? Which of the 14 tenets do you agree with and which do you disagree with? Explain your rationale.

3. Argue why human relations management was successful. What led the movement away from the human relations perspective?

4. For the three management perspectives listed in the chapter (i.e., scientific, human relations, and human resources), show how communication is at the center of these perspectives.

5. Define McGregor's Theory X and Y management styles. What role do you think the organization's management perspective plays in the use of either X or Y management styles? Explain your answer.

6. Based on Argyris' two types of theory in use, Model I and Model II, explain the basic idea behind both approaches and state whether you agree with one of the models more than the other. Explain your choice.

7. Recall the discussion of Blake and Mouton's managerial grid. Define each of the different management styles and explain why certain styles are preferred over others. Explain which style you prefer.

8. Recall from the chapter Type A and Type J organizational models and Ouchi's Theory Z management type. Define each organizational type. Explain how American culture would have difficulty adapting to a J type of organization and a Theory Z management style.

9. Define the theory of independent-mindedness (TIM). Explain the idea behind the micro- and macrocultural matching model. List and define the communication traits associated with TIM. Referring to Table 2.4, explain what's meant by complete independent-mindedness and absence of independent-mindedness.

References

Argyris, C. (1965). *Organization and innovation.* Scarborough, ON: Irwin.

Argyris, C. (1985). *Strategy, change, and defensive routines.* London: Pitman.

Argyris, C. (1993). *Knowledge for action: A guide to overcoming barriers to change.* Hoboken, NJ: Jossey-Bass.

Avtgis, T. A., & Rancer, A. S. (2007a). The theory of independent mindedness: An organizational theory for individualistic cultures. In M. Hinner (Ed.), *The role of communication in business transactions and relationships: Freiberger beitrage zur interkulturellen und wirtschaftskom—munikation: A forum for general and intercultural business communication* (pp. 183–201). Frankfurt: Peter Lang.

Avtgis, T. A., & Rancer, A. S. (2007b). A communication trait based approach to superior-subordinate relationships: The theory of independent mindedness. *Business Research Yearbook, 24,* 867–873.

Argyris, C., & Schon, D. (1978). *Organizational learning: A theory of action perspective.* Boston: Addison-Wesley.

Blake, R. R., & Mouton, J. S. (1964). *The managerial grid.* Houston, TX: Gulf Publishing.

Blake, R. R., & Mouton, J. S. (1978). *The new managerial grid.* Houston, TX: Gulf Publishing.

Blake, R. R., & Mouton, J. S. (1982). A comparative analysis of situationalism and 9, 9 management by principle. *Organizational Dynamics, 24,* 20–43.

Brannigan, A., & Zwerman, W. (2001). The real 'Hawthorne effect.' *Society, 38,* 55–61.

Ewing, D. (1982). *'Do it my way or you're fired': Employee rights and the changing role of management perspectives.* New York: John Wiley & Sons.

Fayol, H. (1949). *General and industrial management.* New York: Pitman.

Franke, R. H., & Kaul, J. D. (1978). The Hawthorne experiments: First statistical interpretation. *American Sociological Review, 43,* 623–639.

Infante, D. A. (1987a, July). Argumentativeness in superior-subordinate communication: An essential condition for organizational productivity. Paper presented at the *American Forensic Summer Conference of the Speech Communication Association,* Alta, UT.

Infante, D. A. (1987b, May). A*n independent-mindedness model of organizational productivity: The role of communication education.* Paper presented at the annual meeting of the *Eastern Communication Association,* Syracuse, NY.

Infante, D. A., & Gorden, W. I. (1985). Superior's argumentativeness and verbal aggressiveness as predictors of subordinates' satisfaction. *Human Communication Research, 12,* 117–125.

Infante, D. A., & Gorden, W. I. (1987). Superior and subordinate communication profiles: Implications for independent-mindedness and upward effectiveness. *Central Speech Journal, 38,* 73–80.

Infante, D. A., & Gorden, W. I. (1989). Argumentativeness and affirming communicator style as predictors of satisfaction/dissatisfaction with subordinates. *Communication Quarterly, 37,* 81–90.

Infante, D. A., & Rancer, A. S. (1982). A conceptualization and measure of argumentativeness. *Journal of Personality Assessment, 46,* 72–80.

Infante, D. A., & Wigley, C. J. (1986). Verbal aggressiveness: An interpersonal model and measure. *Communication Monographs, 53,* 61–69.

Jablin, F. M., & Putnam, L. L. (Eds.). (2001). *The new handbook of organizational communication: Advances in theory, research, and methods.* Thousand Oaks, CA: SAGE Publications.

Kassing, J. W., & Avtgis, T. A. (1999). Examining the relationship between organizational dissent and aggressive communication. *Management Communication Quarterly, 13,* 100–115.

Kato, T. (2001). The end of lifetime employment in Japan?: Evidence from the national surveys and field research. *Journal of the Japanese and International Economies, 15,* 489–514.

Likert, R. (1961). *New patterns of management.* New York: McGraw-Hill.

Likert, R. (1967). *The human organization: Its management and value.* New York: McGraw-Hill.

Martin, M. M., Anderson, C. M., & Sirimangkala, P. (1997, April). The relationship between use of organizational conflict strategies with socio-communicative style and aggressive communication traits. Paper presented at the annual meeting of the *Eastern Communication Association,* Baltimore, MD.

Mayo, E. (1933). *The human problems of an industrial civilization.* New York: Macmillan.

McGregor, D. (1960). *The human side of enterprise.* New York: McGraw-Hill.

McGregor, D. (1966). *Leadership and motivation.* Cambridge, MA: MIT Press.

Norton, R. (1978). Foundation of a communication style construct. *Human Communication Research, 4,* 99–112.

Ouchi, W. G. (1981). *Theory Z: How American business can meet the Japanese challenge.* Reading, MA: Addison-Wesley.

Pugh, D. S., & Hickson, D. J. (1997). *Writers on organizations* (5th ed.). Thousand Oaks, CA: SAGE Publications.

Rancer, A. S., & Avtgis, T. A. (2006). *Argumentative and aggressive communication: Theory, research, and application.* Thousand Oaks, CA: SAGE Publications.

Roethlisberger, F. J., & Dickson, W. J. (1949). *Management and the worker.* Cambridge, MA: Harvard University Press.

Seligman, M. E. P. (1992). *Helplessness: On development, depression, & death.* New York: Freeman.

Taylor, F. W. (1911). *Scientific management.* New York: Harper & Row.

Tjosvold, D. (1984). Effects of leader warmth and directiveness on subordinate performance on a subsequent task. *Journal of Applied Psychology, 69,* 222–232.

Veblen, T. (1912). *The leisure class: An economic study of institutions.* New York: Macmillan.

Watzlawick, P., Beavin-Bavelas, J., & Jackson, D. D. (1967). *Pragmatics of human communication: A study of interactional patterns, pathologies, and paradoxes.* New York: Norton.

Weber, M. (1947). *The theory of social and economic organization* (A M. Henderson & T. Parsons, Trans). New York: Oxford.

Chapter 3

Defining Organizational Culture

Learning Objectives

Upon completion of the chapter, the student should be able to:

- ◆ Define and explain the role of culture in the creation of an organization.

- ◆ Explain how Social Identity Theory comes to inform the creation and manifestation of an organization's culture.

- ◆ Describe the artifacts that are part and parcel of an organization and give an example of the role that each artifact plays in the organizing process.

- ◆ Differentiate among the three stages of organizational socialization and explain the role of communication in each.

- ◆ Explain how organizational cultures can be framed as both enabling and constraining.

Key Terms

Anticipatory stage

Artifact

Corporate we

Encounter stage

Ideology

Metamorphosis stage

Metaphor

Organizational culture

Organizational socialization

Social identity theory

Symbol

Defining Organizational Culture

As both personal history and historical fact attest, no two organizations are the same. In light of this statement, we have to pose the following question: What differentiates one organization from another? Anyone who has held several jobs can say, with certainty, that some organizations are better to work for than others. But what makes one organization better and another worse in terms of employment experience? Edgar Schein, a prominent management and leadership scholar, claims that it's an organization's culture that differentiates it from others (Schein, 1985). **Organizational culture** can be defined as a socially constructed way of thinking, feeling, and doing that provides a blueprint for employee action, and that has both psychological and behavioral effects. If an employee claims that she does not like working for a particular organization because of the leadership style, the way that feedback is offered, the way that rewards and incentives are distributed, the design of office spaces, or the level of mentorship, then she is speaking about the negative implications of an organization's culture, as all these factors are outcomes of the practices that are created, recreated, and maintained by the organization.

This chapter highlights the role of culture in an organization, including the elements that are part of an organization's culture, the effects of an organization's culture on the employee base, the processes by which employees are socialized into an organization's culture, the existence of potential subcultures, and reasons why a culture can be framed as both enabling and constraining.

To truly understand an organization, we must understand its culture (Schein, 1996). A culture can be considered a constellation of rules, regulations, mission, symbols, and the effect(s) that each has on employee well-being. Simply put, it is important to conduct studies *in* organizations, not studies *of* organizations. As Schein points out, an organization's culture is something that gives common meaning and common understanding to a group of interconnected beings, making an organization a collective unit. This closely aligns with Kenneth Burke's (1950) discussion of employee identification, whereby an organization's culture becomes one of the variables necessary for organizational unity and provides a sense of collective membership (see Chapter 13). Perhaps the greatest contribution provided by Burke (1950) to the study of organizations was his notion of the "**corporate we**," symbolizing a unified identity among employees. Much scholarship since has framed an organization's culture as the independent variable that predicts such unification (Denison & Mishra, 1995). That is, it's the organization that predicts the collective identity, not the collective identity that predicts the organization.

Think for a moment about the culture that has emerged among your closest group of friends. There are clearly certain cultural elements that define your group that promote as well as inhibit membership. For example,

Organizational culture
A socially constructed way of thinking, feeling, and doing that provides a blueprint for employee action and that has both psychological and behavioral effects.

corporate we A unified sense of identity among employees.

perhaps your group of friends likes sports, fast food restaurants, video games, carbonated soft drinks, comedy movies, and romance novels. Henri Tajfel and John Turner (1986) are prominent social psychologists who are perhaps best known for the development of **Social Identity Theory**. This theory argues that people construct a certain sense of self based on the groups in which they find themselves embedded. They claim that such small group characteristics play a large role in the creation and maintenance of group membership (Tajfel & Turner, 1986). Given the previous example, one would only be part of this group if, in fact, he or she enjoyed sports, fast food restaurants, video games, carbonated soft drinks, comedy movies, and romance novels. This provides a sense of in-group membership. At the same time, however, this also bars membership to those who dislike sports, dislike fast food restaurants, dislike video games, dislike carbonated soft drinks, prefer horror movies, and read historical autobiographies. This, according to Tajfel and Turner (1986), creates an out-group. This in-group/out-group partition is exactly what creates and inhibits group membership (Mael & Ashforth, 1992). In essence, we are in groups where people enjoy and dislike similar things. There exists a longstanding joke in the New York City area whereby fans of the New York Mets root for two teams: the Mets and whichever team is playing against the New York Yankees. In other words, Mets fans clearly want the Mets to win, but they also want the Yankees to lose, as this rivalry has come to define what part of the city you are from as well as a host of other characteristics that separate one New York sports fan from another. This idea of team allegiance illustrates and promotes the idea of group membership. Those who are part of the group like and dislike the same things, creating psychological and behavioral contagion. **Contagion** is the process through which attitudes and/or behaviors are either adopted or barred by people, based on the number of others who have created similar attitudes or engaged in similar behaviors, as they make both collective and individual decisions.

Organizations, too, foster a sense of in-group mentality through culture (Martin & Siehl, 1983). Imagine a world without rules or norms. At first glance, it might sound luxurious. There would be no such thing as a legal drinking age, no such thing as a speed limit, no such thing as cheating on an exam, no such thing as wearing too much cologne, etc. However, it is likely that, over time, the nonexistence of rules and norms would prove challenging, perhaps so much so that we would be faced with too much ambiguity about the difference between right and wrong to the point that we would be ill equipped to navigate our social worlds. We might not like a particular speed limit, but we feel comfort in the fact that we know what such a limit is and why it was put in place. We might not like that the drinking age is so high, but we feel comfort knowing what is legal and illegal. We might not like that cheating is banned, but we feel comfort knowing that it is a punishable offense. In other words, we live in a social world rife with rules, rites, regulations, and policies that dictate human behavior.

Social Identity Theory
The idea that individuals construct a certain sense of self based on the groups in which they find themselves embedded.

This QR code will take you to an article on the role of culture in an organization's social existence.

http://www. organizationalculture101.com/

Organizations are no exception. They, too, have rules, rites, regulations, and policies that drive employee action. That is, organizations have cultures. Consider perhaps the largest organization in the United States, the U.S. government. In the United States, home ownership is considered a positive practice for social, moral, and civic order. How can the government create or influence a culture to strongly believe that home ownership is something that is sought by its citizens? Some ways include offering tax breaks for first-time homebuyers, low-interest federal loans, tax savings for home improvement, etc. All of these "organizational practices" serve to influence the culture in terms of how people view home ownership and, as a result, have both attitudinal and behavioral implications.

Factors Associated with an Organization's Culture

ideology A set of ideas that inform employees about their organization's goals, practices, aspirations, needs, and expectations.

artifact A symbolic element that comes to shape and create employee knowledge and understanding.

An organization's culture provides an **ideology**, or set of ideas, that informs employees of its goals, practices, aspirations, needs, and expectations (Mumby, 1989). According to Schein (1985), the foremost ideological indicator is the collection of an organization's artifacts, which are those elements that shape and create employee knowledge and understanding. In fact, the term **artifact** comes from the anthropological world, wherein paleontologists attempt to discover information about ancient cultures by digging up remains and fossils to better understand a life that once was. For example, we know about dinosaurs because of the fossils that remain and we know about ancient man because of the bones that have been unearthed. These, in essence, are cultural artifacts that provide anthropologists with information about once-existing cultures. The same would be true if an anthropologist visited an organization.

One artifact this anthropologist would be interested in studying would be an organization's dress code, which, according to Schein (1985), is among the many organizational artifacts. Like fossils and bones, a dress code provides much information about an organization. Assume, for example, that an anthropologist enters an organization where the dress code is extremely formal. In a not-so-popular movie from the 1980s called *The Secret of My*

TABLE 3.1	Artifacts Associated with an Organization's Culture
Artifact	**Cultural Effect**
Dress Code	Formality/Informality
Office Space	Reliance on Hierarchy/Flattened Structure
Mission Statement	Organizational Purpose
Symbol	Organizational Representation
Metaphor	Organizational Analogy

Success, Michael J. Fox's character, Brantley Foster, is hired as a mailroom clerk, and he and his fellow mailroom employees refer to those in administrative positions as "the suits." The suits were those in the marketing, finance, and operations departments. In organizations, if those in such hierarchical positions, or the "suits," are dressed in formal garb, this speaks a lot about the organization's culture. Compare this with an organization that fosters less formal dress, or what is today termed business casual. It is likely that an organization with a formal dress code is more vertically structured and more formal in terms of communication and the construction of interpersonal relationships (see Chapter 7). On the other hand, it is likely that an organization with an informal dress code is more horizontally structured and more informal in terms of communication practices and relationship development (Pratt & Rafaeli, 1997). Just as bones and fossils serve as an indicator about a life that once was, dress code can serve as an indicator of an organizational life that currently is being lived (see Chapter 9 for a discussion of nonverbal aspects of organizational life).

In addition to dress code, another cultural artifact within an organization is the physical layout of the office spaces (Schein, 1985). An organization that has a lock-and-key office for every employee communicates something quite different when compared to the organization that has offices for only those in administrative positions, the organization that forces employees to share offices, or the organization that has employee cubicles. This is not to say that having an office for each employee is preferred. It is to say, however, that an organization's physical layout depends on the culture that it wants to create. A formal organizational culture would probably have a more formal dress code and individual offices (likely larger for those in more superior positions), whereas an informal organizational culture would likely have a more relaxed, informal dress code with perhaps a more open layout (such as cubicles) (Deal & Kennedy, 1982). In fact, architects and interior designers have become very important in terms of aesthetics that are consistent with the organization's mission. For example, consider the architectural layout of new hospitals geared toward children, cancer patients, or other specialized populations. The environment is carefully manipulated to communicate the organization's vision and purpose. Thus, both dress code and physical layout say a lot about the culture of an organization.

In addition to dress code and physical layout, another cultural artifact about which Schein (1990) speaks is an organization's **mission statement**. Mission statements provide both employees and consumers with information about what the organization in question deems most important (Fairhurst, Jordan, & Neuwirth, 1997). A prime example of a mission statement that is extremely informing of its organizational practices is that of *Johnson and Johnson,* one of the world's leading pharmaceutical companies. Their organizational mission statement, or Credo, includes the information about the employees being "respected" and "recognized," meaning that they truly are the ties that bind *Johnson and Johnson* together. What does this credo say

This QR code will take you to the website of *Johnson & Johnson*, where you will be able to locate their organizational credo.

http://www.jnj.com/connect/

about the organization and its culture? As is likely evident from even the quickest, cursory read of this mission statement, the organization is very attuned to the needs of its employees. Think about an organization that fosters dignity, recognition, mindfulness, opportunity, advancement, and competency, and does so in written form. Such a mission statement eliminates guesswork and provides direction and understanding (Pearce, 1982). Like bones and fossils, and dress code and physical layout, mission statements provide much information about organizations and how they function.

symbol A type of sign that is human made or an artificial phenomenon.

Another interesting cultural artifact that speaks volumes about an organization is its **symbol** (logo), or the socially constructed representation of its organizational image (Pettigrew, 1979). Organizations have long understood the importance of symbols to promote an organization and to inform its employees and consumers. For example, the Nike swoosh, the golden arches of McDonald's, Disney's Mickey Mouse ears, Mercedes Benz' three-pointed star, Audi's four interlocking circles, Geico's gecko, and Starbucks' long-haired female siren all inform both employees and consumers about the organization's culture and what the organization stands for.

As Linstead and Grafton-Small (1992) claim, however, it is exponentially more difficult to decipher and decode an organization's symbol than it is to create it. For example, what does the Nike swoosh truly mean? In other words, what is the symbolic meaning of this organization's logo? Is the symbol arbitrary and meaningless? Does it come to represent a check mark, indicating that no matter what, the Nike organization has what you want? Does it mean, similar to the check mark that appears when a text message is sent from one cellular device to another, that this company delivers? Those who are well-versed in the historical trajectory of Nike might know that Carolyn Davidson, the 1971 creator and designer of the company's logo, meant for it to represent the wing of Nike, the Greek goddess of victory. What is important, however, is not why or how the symbol is encoded, but rather how it is decoded (Feldman, 1986). In other words, how does the employee or consumer translate this symbol and create meaning from it. This, in essence, highlights the role of an organization's symbol in the creation of its culture and how it comes to represent its mission, goals, purpose, and values. To illustrate this point further, assume two people look at the same Nike swoosh logo and attempt to garner meaning from it. One person conjures a warm and happy thought of his time on the college basketball team, where Nike was one of the team's sponsors, while the other person conjures a vision of her pair of Air Jordan sneakers that were less than ideal for competitive tennis matches. Clearly, this presents problems in terms of decoding an organization's symbol.

metaphor A term that comes to symbolically and comparatively represent, by association, something else.

A fifth cultural indicator within an organization is its **metaphor**. A metaphor is defined as a term that comes to symbolically and comparatively represent, by association, something else. For example, if your dorm roommate tells you that your side of the room is a pigsty, he or she is implying that it is time to clean up. Within organizations, a metaphor comes to symbolically represent the way employees communicate and engage in their work practices (Morgan, 1980). An organization metaphorically analogous to a machine is strikingly different from the organization that is metaphorically analogous to a family, a circus, a prison, or a group. What, however, is different? The difference, according to Dose (1997) and Putnam (1998), is that metaphors are emblematic of an organization's set of work values or the norms by which an organization operates. Gareth Morgan, an organizational behaviorist best known for his research on metaphor analysis, concurs. He claims that metaphors give both organizations and employees direction, definition, and a sense of group membership (Morgan, 1983). Recall in Chapter 1 that we discussed Morgan's (1986) multiple perspectives, which consist of nine metaphors commonly used to characterize organizations.

Kendall and Kendall (1993) offer different categories of metaphors consisting of the following: organization as game, as machine, as journey, as jungle, as family, as zoo, as society, as war, and as organism. Each of the nine metaphors carries with it a different connotation about an organization and the practices and processes that accompany it.

The organization metaphorically analogous to a:

- ◆ *game* connotes the idea that an organization works as a collective group of people, all having a different role or position, attempting to win.

- ◆ *machine* connotes the idea that each part of an organization must work together as well as independently. If even one part of the organization fails to produce, the machine stops working and failure results.

- ◆ *journey* connotes both the possibilities and troubles associated with tackling the unknown, starting at one point and having a clearly defined goal.

- ◆ *jungle* is one where there is an "every man for himself" mentality, where chaos is not only omnipresent, but is also highly endorsed and valued.

- ◆ *zoo* connotes an organization that partitions employees based on departmental membership, where a leader is necessary to keep the livelihood of the collection of workers.

- ◆ *society* is one with its own set of rules and makes certain to adhere to the needs, desires, and wants of internal members, paying particular attention to politics and the communication and behavioral processes that accompany them.

- ◆ *war* is one that seems to always be in battle, where leaders must stand at the front line and have their employees ready, willing, and able to attack if and when necessary.

- ◆ *organism* is one that understands the importance of birth, development, and death, paying particular attention to the role of innovation, change, and adaptation in organizational success.

TABLE 3.2 Organizational Metaphors	
Metaphor	**Implication**
Game	Need to win at all costs
Machine	All parts work together
Journey	Must move from Point A to Point B
Jungle	Chaos and elements of individuality
Family	All in it together
Zoo	Partitioning based on departmental membership
Society	Politics are governed by leaders
War	Potential battle is always possible
Organism	Birth development and death are inevitable

In the end, an organization's metaphor, which is both produced and enacted by employees, explains how it runs and provides an organizational blueprint for employee action and communication (Morgan, 1980).

Collectively, the combination of an organization's artifacts, including its dress code, its office layout, its mission statement, its symbol, and its metaphor, is indicative of its character, and truly provides employees with a way of doing, a way of thinking, and most importantly, a way of communicating (Wilkins, 1983). All organizations have artifacts and, according to Schein (1990), these are instrumental in differentiating one from another. From an effects perspective, an organization's culture provides uniform expectations, uniform understanding, and a collective, uniform identity, all of which are linked to such things as employee productivity, employee well-being, employee motivation, job satisfaction, and organizational tenure.

Organizational Socialization

Up to this point we have discussed many aspects of an organization's culture and its importance. Now we discuss how employees learn about an organization's culture. If you have ever visited a different college or university, travelled to another country, attended a ceremony for a religion you are unfamiliar with, gone to see a sports event at an opposing team's stadium, or had dinner at a friend's house, you have encountered a cross-cultural situation. Such cross-cultural experiences are both exciting and anxiety producing. They are exciting because of the novelty, though they are anxiety producing because of the potential lack of information about behavioral norms and social rules needed to successfully behave in this new culture.

Organizations are no exception, as they, too, have embedded cultures that are both novel and exciting. Such practices must be taught to new employees as they begin their organizational experiences. Frederic Jablin, an influential and well-established researcher in the field of organizational communication, spent most of his academic career studying the many processes involved in **organizational socialization**, or the process by which newcomers learn the ropes of their organization's culture (Jablin, 1987). Even though artifacts, such as those mentioned in the previous section, exist, there is not much information about them in any form of written correspondence or house organ. Therefore, there is a need to teach new employees about the organization's culture and its way of doing things. This is primarily achieved through verbal dialogue with veteran employees. While a person can read about an organization, its mission statement, its earnings, etc., it is through communication that the learning of an organization's culture really takes place. According to Jablin (1987), the process of organizational socialization includes three stages, appropriately termed *anticipatory, encounter,* and *metamorphosis.*

As Jablin (1987) notes, there are times in one's childhood, adolescence, and young adulthood when he or she develops an interest in a particular area of work. This is not to say that children, adolescents, or young adults know, at an early age, that they want to work for Apple or Pfizer or Dannon or Starbucks. This is to say, however, that it is not uncommon to hear teachers, construction workers, police officers, doctors, or military personnel claim that they knew from an early age that this vocation/career was exactly what they wanted to do. With such knowledge comes expectation. Although every organizational culture is different, there are certain expectations that accompany professional membership. For example, teachers will not be surprised to learn that their workday begins at 7:45 a.m.; police officers will not be surprised to learn that they will have periodic weekend commitments; and construction workers will not be surprised to learn that certain holidays do not warrant time off. According to Jablin (1982), the reason there is little surprise is because such employees have been able to (knowingly or not) anticipate life in their organization.

Think for a moment about your choice to attend your college or university. Did you know for certain what was in store for you regarding the reality of attending your institution? Probably not. But merely by being provided information about the population of the school, the male/female ratio, the average SAT/ACT scores of students admitted, the percentage of students who graduate in four years, the percentage of students who are commuters, the

organizational socialization
The process by which newcomers learn the ropes of their organization's culture.

TABLE 3.3	Stages of Organizational Socialization
Stage	**Effects**
Anticipatory	Expectations are created
Encounter	Norms are taught
Metamorphosis	Employees become organizational insiders

anticipatory stage The first stage of the socialization process within which employees begin to anticipate life within the organization.

percentage of students who participate in extracurricular activities, and the number of students per major, you learned a great deal about the institution. In addition, you probably visited the school and were able to ask current students about their experiences and what they liked and disliked about being there. You may have even been fortunate enough to have a friend or family member attend the same school to give you useful, practical advice. These are examples of the types of information provided during the **anticipatory stage** of socialization, before you even entered the college or university.

The same things occur in organizations, where newcomers enter with a lot of information about such things as its practices, its culture, and its employee base. Gaining a lot of important and valid information about an organization prior to entry, according to Van Maanen and Schein (1979), is a strong predictor of job satisfaction. It is likely that if you know someone who transferred from your school before graduation, he or she said, in one form or another, that the reality of being there did not match their expectations. Valid expectations, according to Jablin (1982), are a key ingredient for organizational success.

The second stage of the organizational socialization process is known as the **encounter stage**, or what Jablin (1982) and Van Maanen (1975) call the **breaking-in period**. If one was able to appropriately and adequately gain enough information during the anticipatory stage, then much of the information provided from more experienced employees during the **encounter stage** would be repetitive. If, for one reason or another, one was not able to gain much valid, explanatory data prior to joining the organization, then much about the organization's goals, mission, culture, rules, behaviors, and norms would probably be a surprise. However, as mentioned previously, newcomers enter with much information about both the organization and the profession within which the organization is embedded. Most importantly, it is during this second stage of the socialization process that expectations are learned and sense making occurs (Jablin, 1987). A good example of the encounter stage is when a person experiences corporate training (see Chapter 11). The majority of organizations have training programs, either informal or formal, wherein new employees are taught norms about such things as formal correspondence with superiors, how to deal with negative feedback, the role of technology in organizational practices, how to deal with multiculturalism, how to effectively manage interpersonal conflict, how to delegate responsibilities, how to work and excel in small-group situations, and how to deal with troubled coworkers. Clearly, these are not things that will surface informally during the anticipatory stage, though they are important for on-the-job decisions and understanding an organization's cultural norms (Falcione & Wilson, 1988). Most of the research in this area has concluded that much of what an employee learns during the encounter stage occurs during communication with the newcomer's supervisor (Jablin, 1982). Research also points to the important role that coworkers play in the process of newcomer learning.

encounter stage The second stage of the socialization process within which employees begin to learn the ropes and experience the realities of the organization.

Assume that you have an exam forthcoming in one of your advanced communication courses, but have never before had the instructor and become worried about the nature of the exam (e.g. how much material is covered, how difficult the exam will be, how much of the exam will be devoted to the outside readings, etc.). From a communication perspective, it seems as though there are two ways to gain such necessary information. The first option, which is likely something that some undergraduate students take advantage of, is to speak to the instructor directly. This, clearly, would provide the most useful and valid information. However, there is oftentimes something inherent in such a situation that discourages students from approaching the information-gathering process this way. As a result, this student might choose a less direct strategy, such as speaking to friends about the instructor's exams. This information would come from students who have already taken the course with the same instructor, so that such academic testimony is based on a "been there, done that" mentality. The first example, where the student speaks directly to the instructor, would be similar to the employee who gains information from his or her supervisor (Jablin, 1994). Although this is very important, and probably optimal for accurate information, engaging in such a social situation is filled with feelings of inequality and nervousness on the part of the student. If such inequality and nervousness trump the need for direct, valid information, then students might speak to friends who have either taken the course, studied with the instructor, or, in a perfect world, both. This would be similar to an employee gaining salient organizational information from coworkers using evidence-based testimony (Jablin, 1987). Although such information is valuable, it is perhaps prejudiced because of differences in individual needs and individual perceptions. For example, the student who wants to take an "easy" class will likely claim that the instructor's exams are difficult merely because of the density and difficulty of the material. This friend will likely create nerves in the mind of the student and, in the end, this information could prove disadvantageous for exam preparation. Given this example, the student would be provided a biased perspective because of the cognitive perception of his/her friend. In the end, there are both opportunities and problems associated with gaining information from supervisors and coworkers during the encounter stage of socialization, though it is important to do both if one is to get a well-rounded, comprehensive view of an organization and its cultural artifacts.

The final stage of the organizational socialization process, according to Jablin (1982), is metamorphosis, which is analogous to the caterpillar that turns into a butterfly. From an organizational perspective, then, the employee turns, communicatively and behaviorally speaking, from an outsider to an insider by not only learning the values, norms, expectations, rules, regulations, and standards of the organization, but also by behaving in ways illustrative of them (Falcione & Wilson, 1988). For example, it is not only learning that an organization deals with conflict through cooperative, rather than competitive strategies. It is also enacting the cooperative strategy during the

This QR code will take you to a YouTube clip highlighting the benefits of successful and effective organizational cultures.

http://www.youtube.com/watch?v =wSZ3IPDmqCg&feature=related

metamorphosis stage
The third and final stage of the socialization process within which employees begin to accept and manifest organizational norms and become organizational insiders.

conflict resolution process. In essence, the anticipatory stage might best be defined as the "expectation stage," the encounter stage might best be defined as the "understanding stage," and the **metamorphosis stage** might best be defined as the "change stage." A good example of the metamorphosis stage is formal recognition of a new brother or sister into a collegiate fraternity or sorority. Students decide to pledge a particular Greek organization because of the inherent value of such membership. That is, one decides to pledge a fraternity or sorority because they anticipate that the rewards that come with membership will not only be great, but also will be greater than joining any other Greek organization. This is an example of *anticipation*. During the pledge process, potential organizational members learn about the organization, including its mission, its history, what its Greek letters stand for, its philanthropic duties, as well as the sisters or brothers who are members of the local chapter. This is an example of **encounter**. Finally comes the pin ceremony, a momentous event for most fraternities and sororities, during which time new members are officially "sworn in" by the existing sisterhood or brotherhood. This is emblematic of the formal acceptance of new members based on knowledge of and appreciation for the organization's mission and goals, and the cultural indicators that accompany them. This is an example of metamorphosis. By becoming an organizational insider, and being metamorphosized, employees accept the organization's culture and the practices and processes associated with it.

In the end, the process of organizational socialization is important for organizations and the employees who are part of them. In essence, it is during the anticipatory, encounter, and metamorphosis stages that employees expect, learn, and manifest certain organizational norms. Without such socialization, either formal, informal, or a combination of both, employees might not know or understand their organization's ways of doing things. This, unfortunately, could have serious negative ramifications at both the employee and organizational levels.

Organizational Cultures as Enabling and Constraining

Organizational cultures are necessary for employees to understand how to perform normal, daily, routine tasks. For example, it is an organization's culture that determines how one provides positive and negative feedback, how and when small groups are more conducive than individual efforts, if and how to ask a manager for time off, how one is commended for his or her accomplishments, and how to deal with troubled coworkers (Schein, 1992). As the information in this chapter illustrates, there seem to be two overarching benefits, or enabling factors, that are realized when one properly understands an organization's culture. First, cultures provide a blueprint (Hofsteade, 1998). Simply put, a **blueprint** is a prototype or design that documents the ways in

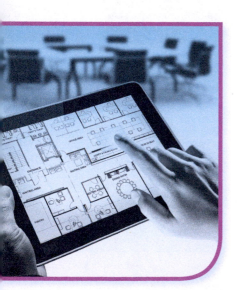

TABLE 3.4	Enabling and Constraining Factors Associated with an Organization's Culture
Enabling Factors	**Constraining Factors**
Provides an organizational blueprint	Becomes overly restrictive
Promotes a sense of collective identity	Difficult to change
	Potential for subcultures to emerge

which certain interdependent parts of the organization work together. Just as an architectural blueprint informs the architect about the construction plans for a building or home, a culture provides the employee with a blueprint for organizational operations. For example, an organization's symbol and mission statement provide a blueprint for action. That is, whether it is the golden arches of McDonald's, the bulls-eye of Target, the silver boomerang of Nike, American Express' "we value our people, encourage their development, and reward their performance," Family Dollar Stores' "a compelling place to work … by providing exceptional opportunities and rewards for achievement," or Amazon's "to build a place where people can come to find and discover anything they might want to buy online," these cultural artifacts are informative. Entering into an organization where the "suits" and the "nonsuits" are geographically dispersed based on office design, where lock-and-key offices are for those in managerial positions and cubicles are for those in nonmanagerial positions, can provide a lot of information about the communicative and behavioral practices of employees. Having an employee of the month program, where achievements are recognized, speaks a lot about an organization's method of reward and acknowledgment. Although these are not things that an employee can necessarily anticipate, such cultural artifacts are learned during the encounter stage, become part of employee life during the metamorphosis stage, and provide a behavioral blueprint for organizational action.

Second, an organization's culture shapes a sense of collective identity among employees (Ravasi & Schultz, 2006). That is, although organizations are composed of people with different backgrounds, genders, expertise, departments, experiences, morals, work ethics, and aspirations, the one attribute that all employees share is organizational membership. Much research on organizational identity concludes that an organization's culture is one of the strongest predictors of collective membership and identification (Tajfel & Turner, 1986). For example, if you have ever been to Johnny Rockets, a franchise best known for its hamburgers, you likely will not be surprised when the wait staff begins to dance at every 15-minute interval. If you have ever been to Cold Stone Creamery, offering what the organization calls "the ultimate ice cream experience," you probably will not be surprised when the staff begins to sing when patrons leave a tip. If you have ever been to TGI Fridays, a casual dining franchise, you likely will not be surprised when the wait staff begins to (perhaps embarrassingly) celebrate your birthday through song and cheer. It is these seemingly small, trivial cultural norms

FIGURE 3.1
Examples of
Organizational Symbols

that set organizations apart. Being part of a collective, or what Tajfel and Turner (1986) call the in-group, has been predictive of such things as organizational commitment, job satisfaction, a sense of community, increased involvement, organizational motivation, and feelings of self-worth. It is likely that if you asked the managers of Johnny Rockets, Cold Stone Creamery, and TFI Fridays why they do these communicative norms, they will say that it is just part of who they are. This sense of organizational self results in a collective sense of identity, created by cultural artifacts that are both understood and performed by all employees (Ashforth & Mael, 1989).

However, organizational cultures are not without problems, as they carry with them constraining factors that might ultimately inhibit certain employee practices. For example, cultures might be seen as constrictive, meaning that as much as they provide a blueprint for action, they also prohibit certain behaviors from occurring. Assume, for example, that Barry is in disagreement about an idea that Brian brought forth at a recent organizational meeting. Rather than speaking to Brian privately after the meeting or sending him an email or speaking to Brian's supervisor, Barry decides to publicly reject Brian's idea. After the meeting, Barry's boss, Sayre, brings him into her office to tell him of her disappointment. In so doing, Sayre tells Barry that "this is not the way that we do things around here." Given this example, as much as an organization's culture provides a blueprint for acceptable behavior and communication, it also implicitly provides a blueprint for behavior and communication that is deemed unacceptable. In a sense, then, culture can be enabling on one hand (e.g., providing necessary organizational information), though constraining on the other (e.g., norms become firm and steadfast).

In addition to organizational cultures being constrictive, they are also difficult to change (Schein, 1985). Much research over the past decade has focused on cultural change during organizational transition in the wake of a **merger** or **acquisition**. A merger is when two organizations combine to create a new entity, whereas an acquisition is when one organization takes control of another. Cartwright and Cooper (1993) argue that a successful cultural "marriage" must occur for successful mergers and acquisitions. For example, the merger of United Airlines and Continental Airlines required that a new organizational culture emerge. It's important to keep in mind that each organization operated as an individual entity prior to the merger in 2010. As such, each operated according to its own cultural norms. What is this new organizational entity to do? Should its administrative body determine which culture should become dominant? Should it combine the two once-existing cultures? Should it create a new culture from scratch? In addition, once such a decision is made, how are employees to be socialized into the new organizational culture? In other words, would employees merely be re-socialized, or will an entirely new training program need to surface? Such decisions, according to Giffords and Dina (2003), are extremely important, yet extremely difficult to make. In the end, cultural change becomes a potential constraining factor for organizations during times of transition.

Finally, and perhaps most problematic for employees, is the idea that certain subcultures are likely to emerge within organizations. That is, although an organization has one overarching culture, it's likely that departments have their own minicultures, teams have their own minicultures, and circles of friends have their own minicultures. This is the idea that there exist structures within structures within structures. It is likely that you have at least once said to yourself that you wished you had a different teacher for a course that you took. In fact, it is likely that certain sections of certain courses fill first during the registration process because of the instructor. What does this say about an organization's culture? It says that although courses, departments, instructors, and curricula are all housed within the college or university (the organization), departments and instructors might dance to their own tune. It is probable, therefore, that the history department differs from the communication department, which differs from the anthropology department, which differs from the political science department, which differs from the biology department. What becomes overly problematic about this is when cultures begin to compete. A friendly, democratic department housed within a bureaucratic college or university creates a dialectical tension for employees, meaning that it might be extremely difficult for a faculty member to design his/her own syllabus (democratic) within an organization where administrators make most of the salient decisions (bureaucratic) (see Chapter 5). If multiple cultures exist within a given entity, the likelihood of

This QR code will take you to an interactive website that allows you to gain practical knowledge of, and hands-on experience with, organizational mission statements.

http://www.missionstatements.com/

employee equivocality, or uncertainty, increases, which, according to Weick (1979), can be detrimental for organizations and the employees who are a part of them.

Summary

An organization's culture helps define what the organization is and ultimately provides a sense of shared community and collective identity for all members. Cultural artifacts, such as symbols, mission statements, dress codes, and physical office layouts provide direction and inform employees about behavioral norms. Given that organizational cultures exist before we even encounter them, employees must learn about them through formal training, informal discussions, and/or on-the-job encounters. For some employees, an organization's culture is inconsistent with their personal values and, as a result, they may decide to leave for another organization whose culture is more consistent with their values, desires, and motivations. For most employees, however, cultural understanding and acceptance occur and they become metamorphosized. It becomes clear that there are both enabling and constraining factors associated with an organization's culture, therefore making it important for organizations to harness the benefits and reduce the (potentially) harmful factors produced by culture. Merely by walking into an organization and seeing its cultural artifacts, an outsider can learn a great deal about its norms and practices. As fossils and bones provide the cultural anthropologist with information about a life that once was, an organization's culture provides information about a life and world that currently exists, and one that will likely exist well in the future.

Questions for Discussion and Review

1. Explain what is meant by *cultural artifact*. Give some examples of them within the organizational environment.

2. Create a new mission statement for your organization. Explain its role in informing employees about work practices and behaviors.

3. Choose two organizational symbols and compare and contrast them in terms of the meaning they represent for the organization and its employees.

4. Create a new organizational metaphor. Explain its utility for employees and the behavioral norms by which they operate.

5. Explain the role of the anticipatory, encounter, and metamorphosis stages of organizational socialization. Give examples of what occurs at each stage.

6. Explain what is meant by enabling and constraining factors. Give an example of each as they relate to an organization's culture.

References

Ashforth, B. E., & Mael, F. (1989). Social identity theory and the organization. *Academy of Management Review, 14,* 20–39.

Burke, K. (1950). *A rhetoric of motives.* Berkeley, CA: University of California Press.

Cartwright, S., & Cooper, C. L. (1993). The role of culture compatibility in successful organizational marriage. *Academy of Management Executive, 7,* 57–70.

Deal, T. E., & Kennedy, A. A. (1982). *Corporate cultures: The rites and rituals of corporate life.* Reading, MA: Addison-Wesley.

Denison, D. R., & Mishra, A. K. (1995). Toward a theory of organizational culture and effectiveness. *Organization Science, 6,* 204–223.

Dose, J. J. (1997). Work values: An integrative framework and illustrative application to organizational socialization. *Journal of Occupational and Organizational Psychology, 70,* 219–240.

Fairhurst, G. T., Jordan, J. M., & Neuwirth, K. (1997). Why are we here: Managing the meaning of an organizational mission statement. *Journal of Applied Communication Research, 25,* 243–263.

Falcione, R. L., & Wilson, C. E. (1988). Socialization processes in organizations. In G. M. Goldhaber & G. A. Barnett (Eds.), *Handbook of organizational communication* (pp. 151–169). Norwood, NJ: Ablex.

Feldman, S. P. (1986). Managing in context: An essay on the relevance of culture to understanding organizational change. *Journal of Management Studies, 23,* 587–607.

Giffords, E., & Dina, R. (2003). Changing organizational cultures: The challenge in forging successful mergers. *Administration in Social Work, 27,* 69–81.

Hofsteade, G. (1998). Attitudes, values, and organizational culture: Disentangling the concepts. *Organization Studies, 19,* 477–492.

Jablin, F. M. (1982). Organizational communication: An assimilation approach. In M. E. Roloff & C. R. Berger (Eds.), *Social cognition and communication* (pp. 255–286). Beverly Hills, CA: SAGE Publications.

Jablin, F. M. (1987). Organizational entry, assimilation, and exit. In F. M. Jablin, L. L. Putnam, K. Roberts, & L. Porter (Eds.), *Handbook of organizational communication: An interpretive approach* (pp. 679–740). Newbury Park, CA: SAGE Publications.

Jablin, F. M. (1994). Communication competence: An organizational assimilation perspective. In L. Van Waes, E. Woudstra, & P. Van Den Hoven (Eds.), *Functional communication quality* (pp. 28–41). Amsterdam: Rodpoi.

Linstead, S. A., & Grafton-Small, R. (1992). On reading organizational culture. *Organization Studies, 13,* 331–355.

Kendall, J., & Kendall, K. (1993). Metaphors and methodologies: Living beyond the systems machine. *MIS Quarterly, 17,* 149–171.

Mael, F. A., & Ashforth, B. E. (1992). Alumni and their alma mater: A partial test of the reformulated model of organizational identification. *Journal of Organizational Behavior, 13,* 103–123.

Martin, J., & Siehl, C. (1983). Organizational culture and counterculture: An uneasy symbiosis. *Organizational Dynamics, 122,* 52–65.

Morgan, G. (1980). Paradigms, metaphors, and puzzle-solving in organization theory. *Administrative Science Quarterly, 2,* 27–46.

Morgan, G. (1983). More on metaphor: Why we cannot control tropes in administrative science. *Administrative Science Quarterly, 28,* 601–607.

Morgan, G. (1986). *Images of organizations.* Thousand Oaks, CA: SAGE Publications.

Mumby, D. K. (1989). Ideology and the social construction of meaning: A communication perspective. *Communication Quarterly, 37,* 291–304.

Pearce, J. A. (1982). The company mission as a strategic tool. *Sloan Management Review, 23,* 15–24.

Pettigrew, A. M. (1979). On studying organizational cultures. *Administrative Science Quarterly, 24,* 570–581.

Pratt, M., & Rafaeli, A. (1997). Organizational dress as a symbol of multilayered social identities. *Academy of Management Journal, 40,* 862–898.

Putnam, L. L. (1998). Metaphors and images of organizational communication. In J. S. Trent (Ed.), *Communication: Views from the helm for the twenty first century* (pp. 145–161). Boston: Allyn and Bacon.

Ravasi, D., & Schultz, M. (2006). Responding to organizational identity threats: Exploring the role of organizational culture. *Academy of Management Journal, 49,* 433–458.

Schein, E. H. (1985). *Organizational culture and leadership.* San Francisco: Jossey-Bass.

Schein, E. H. (1990). Organizational culture. *American Psychologist, 45,* 109–119.

Schein, E. H. (1992). *Organizational culture and leadership* (2nd Ed.). San Francisco: Jossey-Bass.

Schein, E. H. (1996). Culture: The missing concept in organization studies. *Administrative Science Quarterly, 41,* 229–240.

Tajfel, H., & Turner, J. C. (1986). The social identity theory of intergroup behavior. In S. Worchel & W. G. Austin (Eds.), *The psychology of intergroup relations* (pp. 7–24). Chicago: Nelson-Hall.

Van Maanen, J. (1975). Breaking-in: Socialization to work. In R. Dubin (Ed.), *Handbook of work, organization and society* (pp. 32–103). Chicago: Rand-McNally.

Van Maanen, J., & Schein, E. H. (1979). Toward a theory of organizational socialization. In B. M. Staw (Ed.), *Research in organizational behavior* (pp. 209–264). Greenwich, CT: JAI Press.

Weick, K. E. (1979). *The social psychology of organizing.* Reading, MA: Addison-Wesley.

Wilkins, A. (1983). The culture audit: A tool for understanding organizations. *Organizational Dynamics, 12,* 24–38.

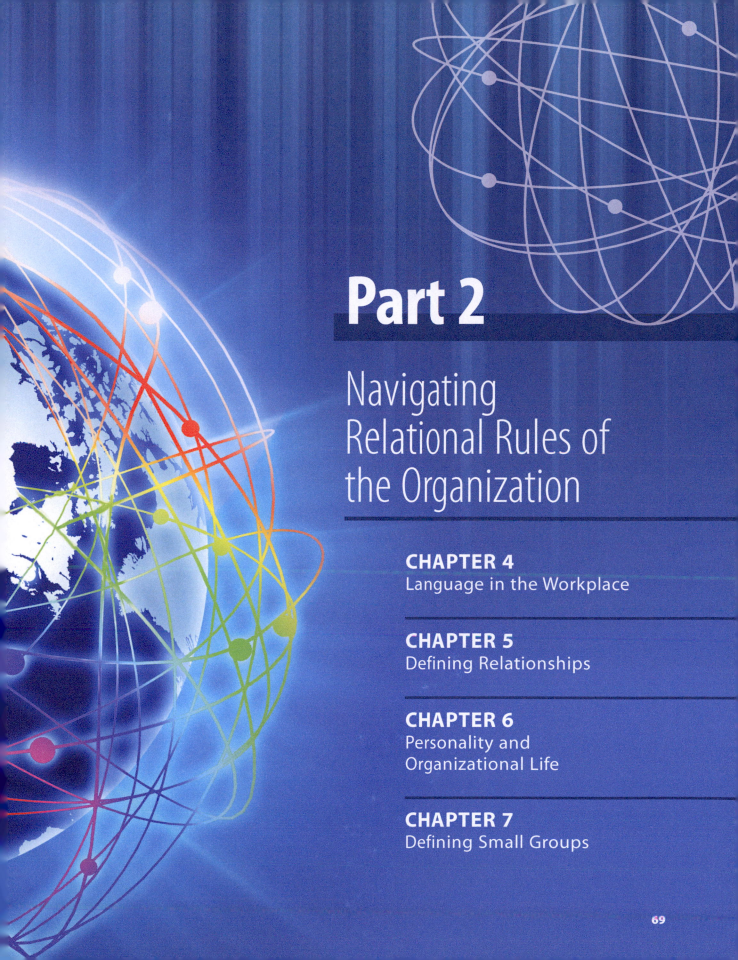

Part 2

Navigating Relational Rules of the Organization

CHAPTER 4
Language in the Workplace

CHAPTER 5
Defining Relationships

CHAPTER 6
Personality and
Organizational Life

CHAPTER 7
Defining Small Groups

Chapter 4

Language in the Workplace

Learning Objectives

Upon completion of the chapter, the student should be able to:

- Compare and contrast the three types of signs.

- Compare and contrast positive language use with negative language use.

- Explain the Sapir-Whorf hypothesis.

- Compare and contrast convergent communication strategies with divergent communication strategies.

- Compare and contrast reciprocating patterns with compensating patterns.

- Explain small bandwidth and wide bandwidth.

- Compare and contrast the different approaches to explaining sexual harassment.

Key Terms

Communication accommodation theory (CAT)

Convergence

Divergence

Interaction adaptation theory (IAT)

Language

Language expectancy theory (LET)

Mindfulness

Sapir-Whorf hypothesis

Self-handicapping

Sexual harassment

Theory of linguistic relativity

As we have alluded to earlier in this text, communication is the "glue" that keeps an organization together. One of the primary ways in which we communicate is through the exchange of verbal symbols, also known as language. Language use, especially within the workplace, has been studied in terms of appropriateness, effectiveness, constitutions of harassment, as well as many other aspects of symbolic exchange. This chapter discusses the basic elements of language and how language is created, learned, understood, and misunderstood within the organization.

language A collection of signs, symbols, codes, and rules used to construct and convey messages.

Language can be defined as "a collection of signs, symbols, codes, and rules used to construct and convey messages. These elements form the medium through which we communicate our ideas, desires, and feelings" (Infante, Rancer, & Avtgis, 2010, p. 185). The main function of language is to allow humans to stimulate meaning in the minds of other people (Steinfatt, 1977). According to many experts, humans have an innate ability to acquire a language. In other words, people are "hard wired" to acquire a language. The language people acquire depends on where they are born and raised. For example, people who are born in China are no different from people born in England in terms of the capacity to acquire language. Both people will acquire a language; in this example there is a high probability that one person will acquire the Chinese language, and the other will acquire the English language, respectively.

Just as society changes, so, too, do the means by which we make sense of those changes (i.e., language). Consider the English language. Every few years there are updated dictionaries printed with hundreds of new words that come about from the development of new ideas, technologies, common expressions, and so on. Words such as *byte, gigabyte, communibiology, positive psychology, hockey mom,* and *chill-out* have come about due to technological, academic, political, and societal change/evolution. Therefore, what was appropriate language in the workplace 25 years ago may now be interpreted as offensive and unacceptable.

Before we discuss the intricacies of language, it is important to distinguish between what is and what is not considered language. First, there are behaviors, called **signs**, that are not considered to be language. Signs are things that stand for or represent something else. The thing that the sign represents is called a **referent**. In other words, the sign indicates that something else is present. For example, in a bad national and local economy, employee downsizing is a common practice. Therefore, the sign of a bad economy can be an indicator of an organizational action, the referent is downsizing. The two types of signs are **signals** and **symbols**. Signals are direct one-to-one relationships with the things they represent. Gary Cronkhite (1986) defined a signal as "the type of sign that stands for its significate by virtue of a natural relationship, usually by some relationship of causality, contingency, or resemblance" (p. 232). One can also think of a signal as a **symptom** because it is a "sign that bears a natural relationship to that for which it stands" (Cronkhite, 1986, p. 232). For example, the symptoms of a runny nose, pounding head, and nausea all may indicate the onset of influenza, whereas coworkers who are happy, upbeat, and overall helpful may be indicating that it is Friday afternoon. The second type of sign is known as a symbol and reflects human-made or artificial phenomena. Symbols are considered arbitrary and ambiguous because people in a society simply agree that a particular word represents something and there is no direct referent with what the symbols represent. By *arbitrary* and *ambiguous* we refer to words such as *cool, nuts,* and *canned.* For example, if you think critically about the meaning of these words, *cool* can reflect a temperature or something that is desirable or correct, whereas the word *canned* can reflect something that has been sealed in a metal container, terminated from an organization, or a generic way of doing something. The fact that people have attributed these meanings to these symbols is something that just happened, not in science but because everyone has agreed to it.

The third type of sign is **ritual**. A ritual is a sign behavior that is neither totally arbitrary (like a symbol) nor symptomatic (like a signal). Consider sitting in a business meeting that started at 2 p.m. and is scheduled to conclude at 3:30 p.m. At about 3:20 p.m. people will begin to fidget and behave in ways that reflect slight discomfort. Some of these behaviors may be signs of being uncomfortable (a naturally occurring human response to discomfort) or signs that are intentionally displayed to send a message to the chairperson of the meeting (a carefully orchestrated behavior to send a message that time is running out). Students also display this behavior by rustling papers and gathering materials just as class is scheduled to end.

There is a truism in communication that *meanings are in people.* This suggests that language, although used by a sender to relay messages, is subject to the interpretation of the receiver. Consider the sentence "Report to the conference room immediately." This sentence can strike fear in one person (the recipient) and be intended as a harmless request by another (the sender). Therefore, there are two types of meaning that are given to language. **Denotative meaning** reflects the literal or dictionary meaning of a word. For example, according to the *Oxford Pocket Dictionary and Thesaurus* (1997), the word *boss* reflects being an employer; manager; overseer; being one who controls a political organization; treating domineeringly; being the master or manager of; or being a round knob, stud, or other protuberance (p. 82). Denotative meaning is also known as digital communication because it has a correct usage (i.e., the dictionary term). On the other hand, **connotative meaning** is the subjective association people attach to verbal messages. In connotative meaning, judgment and evaluation of language come into play. When a coworker asks you to go out for a couple drinks after work, what is he or she actually requesting? Have two drinks, 10 drinks, start an out-of-work friendship, start a romantic relationship, or something else entirely? Unlike the denotative meaning, which can be verified via dictionary, the connotative meaning is as varied and idiosyncratic as the person interpreting it. The simple words "You look nice today" can serve as both a compliment and an inappropriate sexual advance. Connotative meanings tend to be heavily influenced by the situation in which the language is used. If a supervisor during an open meeting says, "You look nice today," it becomes difficult to garner any other meanings than that a compliment is being served. However, if the supervisor and subordinate are alone after work hours, that phrase can easily take on a different meaning.

Language within the workplace takes on a unique significance in that language becomes particularly restricted and bound by not only societal rules, but by organization-specific rules as well. Something as simple as addressing people within the organization can become a difficult and complicated task. According to Michael Thomsett (1991), subordinates should follow some simple suggestions when addressing superiors in the organization. First, always use last names for managers and executives until told to do otherwise (i.e., Ms. Armstead instead of Barbara). If you witness most people in the organization using first names, then follow that pattern. Second, ask permission to address someone based on how he or she signs letters. If someone signs his letters "Bob," then ask if it's appropriate to address him as Bob. On the other hand, if someone signs his name as Mr. Kimble, then address him as such.

Language Styles

Whenever a person is exposed to new information, there is a reaction to the new information or perhaps a new way of thinking about old information. Much of our language choice and language use is done in a mindless fashion. Ellen Langer (1989) believed that people operate mindlessly when they interact in ways that are generic, without thought, and without regard to the specific context. For example, how many times a day does the average person say "Hi," "Hello," or "What's up" as if it is a generic script for acknowledging someone else? This **mindlessness** can become as second nature as shutting your eyes when you sneeze, so much so that we become almost unaware of it. Many times the categories we create for something can lead us to mindless thinking. For example, if someone believes that all union members are lazy or all managers are abusive, this person will interact in ways that relay this information even though the person may be unaware of it. On the other hand, **mindfulness** reflects being aware of your behavior and basing your behavior on the specific situation as opposed to simply enacting a generic script that you use for a variety of situations.

The same can be said for **positive language** and **negative language**. The use of negative language creates an impression of someone who is pessimistic, insecure, and threatened by situations, people, and places. The negative explanatory style is infectious and can turn a well-functioning work team into a dysfunctional group. For example, Jenny is new to an organization and projects a negative and sarcastic outlook on the workplace and people in general. Within her first month of employment, Jenny finds herself alone

mindfulness Being aware of your behavior and basing it on a specific situation as opposed to simply enacting a generic script used for a variety of situations.

and unappreciated by her boss and coworkers. She quickly concludes that they're all losers and do not appreciate her talents. On the other hand, use of positive language projects a confident, well-meaning, and team-oriented person. If Jenny adopts a positive, explanatory style, she will experience a more pleasurable work environment with supportive and encouraging colleagues. Table 4.1 reflects both negative and positive language styles.

Language use is influenced by our gender. Language has been studied from many perspectives, including language use differences employed by men and women as well as the male-based language that is often still found in today's organizations. Studies of this sort have been conducted for several decades (Bate & Bowker, 1997). In contemporary organizations, as well as in the culture at large, there has been a heightened sensitivity to language use and word choice. People tend to avoid using masculine pronouns and choose more gender-neutral terms for both males and females, as well as avoid language that stereotypes job titles based on sex. For example, *policeman, chairman, fireman,* and *stewardess* have been changed to *police officer, chairperson, firefighter,* and *flight attendant,* respectively. In the workplace, we generally address someone as Mr. or Ms., and this does not require us to know the marital status of the person we're addressing. Although there have been great advances with regard to using gender-neutral terms for describing occupations, some occupations still remain gendered by language. For example, when a male chooses the profession of nursing, he is commonly referred to as a *male nurse* as opposed to being referred to as a *nurse.*

In a study to provide evidence for gender and language use being culture specific (as opposed to biological), Anthony Mulac, James Bradac, and Pamela Gibbons (2001) found that although both men and women share the same language, they use that language in different ways because the culture at large dictates such language patterns. Much of this learning takes place in groups of same-sex peers between the ages of 5 and 15. Learning how to carry on friendly conversations in different social contexts can result in males and females having different language preferences. These learned differences

TABLE 4.1	Negative and Positive Language Styles
Negative Style	**Positive Style**
I would absolutely hate it if he …	Wouldn't it be better if he …
Why in God's name can't you …	How about if we …
This idea is doomed to failure …	Could we consider this option …
What absolute stupidity …	I don't think that this suggestion will be as fruitful as these others …
I can't stand him …	He certainly offers unique perspectives …
I hate that new policy …	The new policy certainly offers interesting challenges …
Don't you ever do that again …	Next time I would suggest considering another way to approach the situation …

often result in communication breakdowns when members of one sex try to use their language behaviors in speaking with members of the other sex. For example, men generally do not have as large a vocabulary when it comes to language about their emotional state. This may result in a variety of complex emotions being labeled as *anger* or *frustration.* If men and women disagree on the interpretation of a given communicative behavior due to their different language use, the interaction can be dramatically affected. For example, a man may interpret a woman's use of tag questions (adding questions to the end of statements) as a sign of uncertainty and low self-confidence whereas she may interpret the use of tag questions as a way to involve the other person in the conversation. These interpretive differences for the same act can result in organizational outcomes such as being passed over for a promotion, being viewed as wishy-washy, or being seen as a push-over.

Language Perception

theory of linguistic relativity Assumes that the structure of language we use influences the way we perceive the environment. Also known as the **Sapir-Whorf hypothesis**.

The language we use can tell a great deal about the way we view the world. There is a common phrase that reflects this: *Language shapes reality.* This phrase reflects the **theory of linguistic relativity**, also known as the **Sapir-Whorf hypothesis**, which assumes that all higher levels of thought depend on language and that the structure of language we use influences the way we perceive the environment (Chase, 1956). It is also a common assumption that the more words a given culture has for something, the more valuable it is to the culture and the more thoroughly the concept is understood. For example, a boss believes there are two types of people: people who are ambitious and people who are lazy. This categorization grossly oversimplifies the range of work performance that lies between being ambitious and lazy. Therefore, the boss' perception of employees is constrained by the language he uses to describe them. Throughout this book we stress the idea of communication competence being based on effectiveness and appropriateness. The language we choose when expressing our ideas directly impacts both our effectiveness and appropriateness. The greater the linguistic diversity, the more likely we will be able to be more effective critical thinkers.

The language we choose when posing questions to others also influences how people perceive and react to such questions. The language we use when developing questions can drastically change what is implied about the question as well as the relationship between the two people in the interaction. The following question is posed the same way with only the boldface word changing. Ask yourself the following question while stressing the boldface word:

1. **Could** you possibly work harder on this project?
2. Could **you** possibly work harder on this project?
3. Could you **possibly** work harder on this project?
4. Could you possibly **work** harder on this project?
5. Could you possibly work **harder** on this project?

6. Could you possibly work harder **on** this project?

7. Could you possibly work harder on **this** project?

8. Could you possibly work harder on this **project**?

As you can see from this example, each question takes on a unique meaning as the word emphasis changes. This variation is not due to the digital language (i.e., words that are said) but the **paralanguage**. Paralanguage is the use of all elements associated with the voice other than the actual words we use. Things such as inflection, tone, speech rate, and accent are all examples of paralanguage. Paralanguage can be mindful or mindless depending on the person using it. Competent communicators are aware of the paralinguistic messages they are sending, whereas less competent communicators may be unaware of the messages being sent and, in so doing, suffer negative relational and professional consequences.

This QR code will take you to a YouTube clip highlighting the role of language, and the Sapir Whorf hypothesis, as they relate to language within organizations.

http://www.youtube.com/watch?v=3pKB-xAx9wM

Language and Power

The pursuit of power, control, and status are believed to be at the core of many social relationships (Giles & Wiemann, 1987), especially those occurring within the organization. There are several types of language use that are especially revealing about power and status, but only if a person is trained to look for them.

Verbal intensifiers are words that increase the intensity of the emotion the speaker is experiencing, as opposed to the literal information contained in the message. For example, a coworker comes back from a meeting with her boss concerning her six-month performance review and, when asked about it, states, "It was such a wonderfully super-productive meeting!" The way the person feels (e.g., using verbal intensifiers such as *wonderful* and *super-productive*) about the meeting draws the listener's attention to the emotional state of the speaker and how the speaker feels about the meeting, and draws less attention to the content of the meeting. People should be careful when using verbal intensifiers because their chronic use communicates a powerless position. People who are lower in the organizational structure tend to use verbal intensifiers more than superiors and people at higher organizational levels, thus showing both respect as well as signaling acknowledgment and acceptance of their subordinated position.

Verbal qualifiers are words that reduce the strength and impact of the utterance. This type of language use is relevant in the speech patterns of the powerless person because it draws away from the speaker's certainty of the statement as well as the assertion made by the statement. For example, consider the following verbal qualifiers and it will become clear that their use can detract from a person's credibility.

1. I may be wrong but ...

2. This may sound dumb but ...

3. This isn't my area of expertise but …
4. We probably covered this earlier but …
5. I'm not as experienced as the rest of you but …

In a similar vein, **tag questions** are a form of powerless language use where questions are tagged onto the end of the statement (as opposed to verbal qualifiers, which are attached to the front of the statement) and greatly detract from the power and status of the speaker. By turning a statement into a question, speakers indicate to listeners that they are either unsure of their position on the issue or that the listener will not agree with the statement.

The **length of the requests** that people make also reveals interesting insights into both the sender and receiver of the message. Long requests are called **compound requests** and reflect a more powerless, less assertive, and lower status position. For example, the request "If you wouldn't mind, could you get me an application?" is a compound request because it asks the listener to (1) make a decision as to whether he or she minds completing the request, and (2) make a decision whether to comply with what is being asked of him or her. Generally speaking, more powerful people tend to make shorter requests than less powerful people. There is one caveat to this generalization: Powerlessness, as indicated by longer length of requests, should not be confused with politeness. Polite people, regardless of their organizational position, tend to have longer requests due to the addition of language that is affirming toward the person they are speaking to.

The perception of language can also be influenced by the gender of the person using it. Initial research indicates that women tend to use more verbal intensifiers, verbal qualifiers, tag questions, and longer requests than men (Lakoff, 1975). As shown in this and other research findings, female language styles are seen as less powerful than male patterns. There is a double standard when it comes to the use of powerful language and gender. Powerful language is perceived to be a male "type" of language. Therefore, when a male uses "male" language, people may describe him as confident, determined, and precise, whereas when a woman employs "male" language, she is viewed as difficult, hostile, and undesirable. This double standard has also been observed in argumentative training that targets female employees (Anderson, Schultz, & Courtney-Staley, 1987).

Language can also protect us from threats to our psychological well-being. What happens when we find ourselves in a situation in which our professional identity, which we have worked so hard to create, is threatened? Language can be used to protect ourselves from situations that can result in negative consequences. **Self-handicapping** is one such linguistic device and is defined as "the adoption or advocacy of impediments to success in a situation where the person anticipates failure. By assuming a self-handicap, the person has an excuse for the impending failure and thereby may maintain self-esteem and the illusion of competence" (Harris, Snyder, Higgins, & Schrag, 1986, p. 1191). For example, a manager expects you to provide a comprehensive report on a potential product that will be presented to the board

self-handicapping The adoption or advocacy of impediments to success in a situation where the person anticipates failure.

of directors on Friday afternoon. On Friday morning you show up and upon beginning the presentation, you mention how your 3-year-old child had the flu and this resulted in your missing several hours of sleep. By informing the people of such a situation, you have protected yourself to a certain degree from negative evaluation should your presentation fail. For example, someone may think, "If his child hadn't been sick, I'm sure that he would have been well rested and presented the report much more effectively."

As the previous example illustrates, a person can adopt a handicapping strategy with the hopes that it will deflect any esteem threat or negative competence attribution. Should the strategy be successful, the person will have a greater tendency to use the self-handicap in future situations that pose threats to his or her esteem. In our previous example, should the "lack of sleep" handicap prove successful, the person who successfully uses this strategy will have a greater tendency to use similar strategies in the future. **Verbal self-handicaps** reveal to the evaluator (via language) that the condition exists (telling you the child was sick resulting in my being tired, as opposed to actually acting tired) (Leary & Shepperd, 1986). The self-handicap serves as a controlling mechanism for a failed social performance by restoring the illusion of success if it were not for the presence of the self-handicap. For example, moodiness and premenstrual syndrome have been found to serve as effective strategies for failed social performances (Baumgardner, Lake, & Arkin, 1985; Mello-Goldner & Jackson, 1999). Aggressive communication has also been found to be a viable communication strategy in that people who have a high tendency to engage self-handicapping behavior reported significantly greater verbal aggressiveness than low self-handicappers (Avtgis, Rancer, & Amato, 1998). Self-handicapping is a clever linguistic device that people employ to protect against failure as well as accentuate success. For example, if you complain about being tired before an important presentation and then proceed to make an outstanding presentation, one such interpretation of the outcome is that you are so good at your job that even a lack of sleep can't keep you from a great presentation.

Language and Interaction

Language, its structure, and its use have served as the foundation for explaining human relationships in general and have also been applied to relationships within the organization. People generally equate language with a means of simply transmitting messages from one person to another. However, according to theories that are primarily based on language and verbal behavior, our language use and verbal behavior provide invaluable insight into many relational dynamics between communicators.

Communication accommodation theory (CAT) was developed to examine the underlying motivations and consequences of shifts in language patterns (Giles & Wiemann, 1987). The similarity-attraction principle influences CAT in that we use language to "fit in" with people we like and are

communication accommodation theory (CAT) A language theory developed to examine the underlying motivations and consequences of shifts in language patterns.

attracted to, much more than people whom we dislike. For example, consider an employee working for a company with a corporate culture that demands the use of formal titles when addressing other employees (i.e., Mr., Mrs., Dr., etc.) and a strict professional dress code. If this employee is offered a new position that's considered a "dream job" at another organization that embraces more informal verbal and dress codes, the employee will try, to the best of his or her ability, to adapt both verbal and nonverbal behavior to fit into the new culture. For example, matching the mode of dress, style of speaking, and word choice all represent ways of fitting in. Unless the new employee is a competent communicator, he or she may have a difficult time adjusting their behavior.

According to CAT, there are two central premises at work. First, when communicating with others, people try to accommodate or adjust their style of language to one another. Second, people perform this accommodation process to gain approval, increase communication efficiency, and create/maintain a positive self-image with the person with whom they are speaking (Infante, Rancer, & Avtgis, 2010). The degree to which we match or mismatch another person's language style is based on our perception of the other person and our motivation for engaging in a relationship with that person.

convergence How people use language to adapt to one another by slowing down or speeding up speech rates, lengthening or shortening utterances, and using pauses and specific forms of language.

divergence Reflects how people maximize vocal and linguistic differences to highlight differences between themselves and others.

People engage in two strategies when interacting with others: **convergence** and **divergence**. The choice of strategy is influenced by our interpretation of the other person's speech style (Giles, Mulac, Bradac, & Johnson, 1987). Convergence strategies reflect how people use language to adapt to one another by slowing down or speeding up speech rates; lengthening or shortening utterances; using pauses as well as specific forms of language, including tag questions, verbal intensifiers, and various forms of politeness, tone quality, vocal energy, phrasing, enunciation, and pronunciation. When we use convergence strategies we seek to increase liking, membership, and sociological status with the other person. When conveying language patterns, a person must be careful to not overly converge language patterns. **Overconvergence** occurs when a person adapts to the language patterns of another person to the point that the language use is perceived as condescending and ridiculing. For example, a 50-year-old manager attends lunch with a group of 20-year-old hourly laborers. The language use of the young laborers may be different from the language use of the middle-aged manager (e.g., frequent slang, profanity, and off-color humor). Therefore, the manager can converge patterns to a certain degree (e.g., snickering as opposed to laughing out loud at jokes that are not politically correct, not matching the extreme language as opposed to matching the degree of extreme language), but if the manager tries to converge to the point of actually having the communication patterns of a 20-year-old laborer, the manager's behavior comes across as suspect or inappropriate.

Divergence reflects how people maximize vocal and linguistic differences to highlight differences between themselves and others. People use divergence strategies when they want to maintain social distance, perhaps

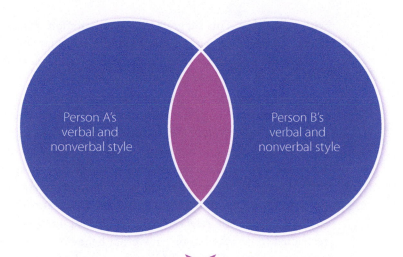

Convergence: Adapting to each other's style of communication

Divergence: Accentuating communication differences in order to point out social differences

FIGURE 4.1
Communication
Accommodation Process.

due to the belief that the other person belongs to an undesirable group, has distasteful attributes, or is in other ways undesirable to the speaker (Street & Giles, 1982). Divergence is also a strategy that people use to establish credibility. For example, if a CEO of an organization meets with assembly-line workers, the CEO will converge his or her language only to a degree. The difference in language patterns reinforces the CEO's higher-level position in the organization and the fact that he or she is not one of them. Figure 4.1 shows how communication accommodation takes place.

In a similar vein to CAT, **interaction adaptation theory (IAT)** was developed to explain conscious communicative behavior. That is, behavior that is "mindful, intentional, and symbolic" (Burgoon, LaPoire, & Rosenthal, 1995, p. 11). IAT assumes that our relationships with each other are based on both verbal and nonverbal messages adapted to the behavior of the interaction partner. **Adaptation** reflects the degree to which we alter our behavior in response to the behavior of another person. Further, adaptation during interaction serves as a signal to the interactants and observers of the interaction as to the nature or basis of the relationship between the two communicators (White, 2008). That is, the way people engage in adaptive behavior during an interaction relays important relational information that can include the type of relationship, degree of positive/negative affect between the interactants, as well as power and status differences. For example, how two coworkers interact, the type of language they use, and the topics discussed are all clues into the relationship dynamics between the two.

IAT assumes that adaptation is a systematic pattern of behavior that is in direct response to the interactive pattern of another communicator (Burgoon et al., 1995). Therefore, there are no random adaptations when people interact

interaction adaptation theory (IAT) A theory developed to explain conscious communicative behavior that is mindful, intentional, and symbolic.

with each other. This suggests that all adaptation is intentional. Simply put, if you are speaking with a coworker, all your adaptation is focused on and influenced by the other person, and vice versa. The major influence on your behavior is the behavior of the other person.

The two adaptation patterns that people use in an interaction reflect either **reciprocating patterns** or **compensating patterns**. Adaptation that uses reciprocating patterns reflects matching behavior, or reciprocating the behavior of the other person. This is similar to the Communication Accommodation Theory concept of converging our speech patterns to the other person to show liking and affiliation. Convergence means we adapt our interaction patterns to match those of the other person. Matching, within the IAT framework, refers to both verbal and nonverbal behavior and is not restricted to only verbal or paraverbal behavior, as it is in Communication Accommodation Theory. To illustrate how IAT patterns function, consider a scenario in which a close colleague is upset and discloses to you that she received an unfavorable performance evaluation. When communicating with this colleague, you will probably use matching adaptation reflecting behavior that is somber, empathetic, and caring.

Adaptation is a compensating pattern that reflects the balancing out of the other's behavior and seeks to represent the whole spectrum of the interaction. An example of this would be a subordinate who is incredibly excited and enters his supervisor's office to say that he is putting his entire life savings into the buying and selling of real estate based on an investment product he purchased from a TV infomercial. In this case, the supervisor's interaction pattern may be one of a cautious, reserved, and skeptical tone, thus not matching the euphoric, excited, and determined patterns of the subordinate. This concept of compensation is also reflective of the yin and yang in Chinese philosophy. The yin and yang concept reflects the intertwining of opposing forces. In the current example, the supervisor's cautious, reserved, and skeptical behavior is intended to balance out the subordinate's euphoric, excited, and determined behavior. The tone of one person's behavior is interdependent and gives rise to the other person's behavior in mutually reciprocating ways.

Although adaptation is considered nonrandom (i.e., intentional), IAT treats interaction adaptation as a primal survival need. That is, we choose our adaptation in a way that satisfies survival needs and seeks to establish important links to other people, thus ensuring or significantly increasing our probability of survival (i.e., strength in numbers). In organizations, we are constantly trying to "play the game" or navigate the politics and power of the organization. Thus, adaptation is vital for workplace survival. There is more to adaptation than the simple idea that we either engage in matching or compensating patterns or we do not. The theory also speaks to the amount to which we engage in adaptation. The degree of adaptation is influenced by both the role we play in society (i.e., societal norms) and idiosyncratic personal preferences. For example, a mortician will probably have a more restricted degree of adaptation than a professional football player because societal norms for a mortician's behavior are more conservative than they are for the professional football player. A mortician would not give coworkers high-five handshakes or do a victory dance after performing his or her job at a high level whereas a professional football player may very well engage in such behavior to the delight of fans.

IAT assumes there are several main factors (both socially and personally derived) that influence a person's needs, wants, and expectations of other people when engaged in interaction. More specifically, when we first encounter someone in conversation, we bring with us a host of **conversational requirements (R), conversational expectations (E),** and **conversational desires (D)** with regard to the person and the specific conversation. These three components are referred to as **RED** (Figure 4.2). It is assumed that our conversational requirements are a person's basic psychological/physiological needs related to approach-avoidance behavior (a.k.a. the fight-or-flight response experienced when interacting with others). These requirements are primarily unconscious and said to influence our conversational expectations. These expectations are formed by societal norms of appropriateness as well as the degree of knowledge that we have developed from past interactions with that specific person. These expectations, in turn, influence our desires, which are "highly personalized and reflect things such as one's personality and other individual differences" (White, 2008, p. 193). The three dimensions of RED are highly interdependent, and requirements, expectations, and desires can be weighted differently based on the specific interaction. In other words, in one interaction expectations may play more of a role than desires or conversational requirements, whereas in another interaction, a different factor may be weighted more heavily. For example, a person may have a great need to avoid a difficult coworker (i.e., conversational requirement). This need for avoidance can be so strong that it supersedes our desires (i.e., individual interests) and our expectations (i.e., what is socially appropriate behavior in that situation).

The three components of RED combine to form a unique collection of individualized communication information known as a person's **interaction position**. According to Burgoon et al. (1995), interaction profiles represent "a net assessment of what is needed, anticipated, and preferred as the dyadic interaction pattern in a situation" (p. 266). By understanding a person's interaction position, we can better predict how that person interprets a communication situation and the likely communicative behaviors he or she will enact.

Consider the example of a supervisor who is about to conduct a meeting with a subordinate concerning the subordinate's quarterly performance review. The supervisor has, throughout her career, engaged in many conversations with subordinates regarding both positive and negative aspects of their performance. According to IAT, any given conversation is influenced by the supervisor's psychological and/or physiological needs at any given time. These may take the form of the need to mentor, need for affiliation, need

Interaction Adaptation Theory

FIGURE 4.2
IAT Hierarchy of RED.

to control, and so on. This would constitute the supervisor's conversational requirements (R). Second, the supervisor has a general idea or expectation about how employees, in general, respond to negative evaluations and even more specific expectations about how a specific employee will respond to such information (e.g., anger, sorrow, remorse, embarrassment [E]). Finally, the supervisor has a desire for employees to be open, involved, and eager to make needed changes to improve performance (D). These RED factors constitute the supervisor's interaction position (IP).

A subordinate who has had a history of poor performance and a generally negative attitude was about to come into the office for a performance evaluation meeting. Based on the aforementioned description of the supervisor's IP, the supervisor was expecting a hostile and generally emotionally charged interaction. Therefore, the supervisor prepared herself to console the subordinate and to give some comforting words. However, when the subordinate arrived for the performance review, the subordinate was proactive in offering strategies to improve his performance and optimistic about his future contribution to the department and the organization as a whole (E). Interaction adaptation theory predicts the supervisor will have an interaction style of convergence, matching, and reciprocity because the subordinate's behavior was more positively valenced (more attractive) than the supervisor's interaction position. Therefore,

$$IP\ (\text{interaction position}) < E\ (\text{actual behavior}) = \text{Convergence, Matching, Reciprocity}$$

Understanding the basic components of how coworkers adapt allows us greater predictability of other people's behavior and, thus, can assist us in successfully navigating the workplace.

Language Expectancy Theory

language expectancy theory (LET) A theory that explains why some linguistic forms of persuasive messages are more effective than others.

Language expectancy theory (LET) was proposed by Michael Burgoon in 1995 and is based on an accumulation of research on how people are persuaded. LET focuses on language and how language affects both the change and reinforcement of attitudes and beliefs. This theory seeks to explain why some linguistic forms of persuasive messages are more effective than others (Burgoon, 1995; Burgoon, Denning, & Roberts, 2002). The concept of language expectation was originally adapted from the work of Brooks (1970), who believed our stereotypes (later called expectancies) about what a source has to say and how it will be said influence the attitudes and beliefs of the receiver. For example, consider a male coworker who has conservative views about financial investing and is about to hear a presentation from two speakers about the employer-sponsored retirement program. Both speakers share the same attitudes about investing (being fiscally conservative), yet one speaker is a male with a heavy Brooklyn, New York accent and an animated presentation style, whereas the other speaker is a Midwestern female with a more generic accent and reserved presentation style. Based on our expectations concerning how we "think they should speak" and their actual use of language, who will be more effective? Who will be less effective? LET is not concerned with each individual person's expectations (e.g., this woman looks like my ex-girlfriend, who was irresponsible with money, so therefore this female presenter has no credibility) as much as with the expectations set forth by society and our culture at large (e.g., what language expectations do we have about financial advisors? Male financial advisors? Female financial advisors? East Coast accents? Midwest accents?).

The idea that the strategic linguistic choices made by persuaders can significantly predict success was the impetus for the development of LET (Burgoon, Jones, & Stewart, 1975). LET assumes that language is a rule-governed system that people, through socialization by their home culture, come to expect; further, people prefer particular message and language strategies over others. That is, when people engage in persuasion, they need to consider how the audience was culturally programmed to determine what is considered competent and appropriate persuasive communication as well as what is considered inappropriate and ineffective language use (Burgoon et al., 1995). Further, these culturally/socially developed expectations impact persuasibility based on whether the language conforms (is consistent with) or does not conform (is inconsistent with) to our expectancies. When we violate linguistic norms (either positively or negatively), these violations affect the perceived appropriateness and effectiveness of the persuasive message. When we speak of cultures, we are also referring to organizational cultures and the cultures contained within particular sectors, such as the financial sector or education. For example, a subordinate who works for an organization with an organizational culture that values direct and truthful communication in the most concise way possible is about to ask for a salary increase. In this situation, speaking directly with the message "I deserve and want a salary increase" would be seen as more appropriate than asking in a way that is full of hedging, qualifiers, and other powerless language.

The formation of linguistic expectations can encompass entire social categories, such as sex, ethnicity, organizational position, tenure in the organization, and socioeconomic status. As such, these categories define what is considered appropriate communication behavior. For example, males have greater linguistic freedom than females. Having greater linguistic freedom is called having a **wide bandwidth**, and results in a greater variety of persuasive linguistic strategies that are seen as appropriate or within an expected range (Burgoon et al., 2002). Other social classes may be constrained to a **small bandwidth**, or not given a large degree of linguistic freedom regarding what is considered "appropriate linguistic strategies." These linguistic strategies can include variations in language intensity (e.g., fear appeals, opinionated language, and aggressive compliance-gaining strategies). Simply put, people with greater bandwidth are allowed to "get away with" using more linguistic variation than others. For example, a male supervisor addressing a work team about slumping sales would probably be afforded a greater bandwidth (e.g., using profanity, intimidation, sympathy, support) than would a female supervisor addressing the same group. Societal expectations concerning the female supervisor's linguistic strategies are more constricted when compared to those of the male supervisor, with the result that the perception of appropriateness is influenced by the sex of the supervisor.

As indicated in the previous example, bandwidth variations have been identified in the study of gender. According to Burgoon et al. (2002), rigid norms have developed concerning what is and what is not acceptable use of language by men and women, in that men are allowed more linguistic variability. For example, men are afforded the cultural expectation that use of intense language can still be persuasive. But women, when using intense language, were not seen as persuasive because intense language would be perceived as a violation of expectations regarding what constitutes appropriate and effective persuasive messages for use by females. **Source credibility** (i.e., the degree to which people are perceived as being trustworthy and having expertise) has also been interpreted using LET, in that people with high credibility are afforded greater bandwidth than people with low credibility (Hamilton, Hunter, & Burgoon, 1990). When we believe a person has a degree of expertise or is highly trustworthy, we tend to afford that person more latitude in the types of language he or she uses when trying to persuade us.

Language and Sexual Harassment

Although sexual harassment involves both verbal and nonverbal behavior, in this section we present the issues related to **sexual harassment** in the workplace as a function of language. According to the U.S. Equal Employment Opportunity Commission (EEOC) (2009),

> [U]nwelcome sexual advances, requests for sexual favors, and other verbal or physical conduct of a sexual nature constitute sexual harassment when this conduct explicitly or implicitly affects an individual's employment, unreasonably interferes with an individual's work performance, or creates an intimidating, hostile, or offensive work environment.

Further, EEOC states that the following circumstances/factors (among others) are commonplace for sexual harassment:

- The victim as well as the harasser may be a woman or a man. The victim does not have to be of the opposite sex.
- The harasser can be the victim's supervisor, an agent of the employer, a supervisor in another area, a coworker, or a non-employee.

sexual harassment
Unwelcomed sexual advances and other verbal or physical conduct of a sexual nature when this conduct explicitly or implicitly affects an individual's employment, interferes with an individual's work performance, or creates an intimidating, hostile, or offensive work environment.

- The victim does not have to be the person harassed but could be anyone affected by the offensive conduct.

- Unlawful sexual harassment may occur without economic injury to or discharge of the victim.

- The harasser's conduct must be unwelcome.

In 2005, of the 12,679 sexual harassment charges filed in the United States, 14.3% were filed by men (EEOC, 2006). In 2008, of 13,867 sexual harassment charges, 15.9% were filed by men. These suits resulted in $47.4 million in monetary benefits (not including money awarded through litigation) (EEOC, 2009). These statistics clearly show that sexual harassment is a major issue in today's organizations. The possibility of being charged with such an offense has had a chilling effect on how people interact in the workplace. Often people use the term **political correctness (PC)**, referring to language that is strategically used to replace other language so as not to be discriminatory, harassing, or offensive to others.

It is important for every member of an organization to realize that sexual harassment is primarily receiver based. That is, the intentions of the messages sent are of little importance when the receiver deems the message as harassing. There have been several ways of conceptualizing sexual harassment; all of them seek to explain this costly phenomenon. According to the EEOC (2009), sexual harassment can be based on two factors: (1) **quid pro quo**, defined as sexual behavior in exchange for something (e.g., promotions, pay raise, time off), and (2) the creation and maintenance of a **hostile work environment** that reflects a sexually charged work atmosphere. Although the quid pro quo standard is fairly easy to decipher (e.g., did he or didn't he offer you a promotion for sex?), the hostile environment criterion is based on more ambiguous judgment, such as the degree to which the person was victimized, if at all. Even though both factors are different in their definitions and level of provability, they both require that for behavior to be described as harassing, the behavior must be unwanted.

Many researchers have attempted to identify other factors that constitute sexual harassment and generate theories to explain/predict sexual harassment, including biological sex, sexual coercion, and unwanted sexual attention (Fitzgerald et al., 1988). The **sex-role spillover approach** assumes that when the sex ratio is disproportionate (i.e., more men than women or vice versa) there is a higher probability for sexual harassment (Gutek & Monarsh, 1982). By *disproportionate* we refer to sex ratio on the specific job (e.g., being a laborer for the local construction company), sex ratio based on the work role (e.g., female forklift operator), and sex ratio of the occupation (e.g., the ratio of women to men in the construction field).

The **power differential approach** assumes that the larger the power difference between people, the more probable that there will be sexual harassment (Fitzgerald & Shullman, 1993). As discussed in Chapter 2, organizations from individualistic cultures are based on great power differences as opposed to organizations in cultures with lower power differences. The

This QR code will take you to a very detailed assessment of sexual harassment policies and their relationship to organizational ethics.

http://www3.uakron.edu/lawrev/robert1.html

power differential approach goes beyond the organizational culture and to the culture at large (Gruber & Bjorn, 1986). As discussed in Chapter 9, people in positions of power frequently find themselves abusing the privileges granted to them by the organization. It seems that not a day goes by that we do not hear of an organization or head of an organization overstepping legitimate power and being caught in illegal activity. This power abuse phenomenon occurs when someone who holds considerable organizational power is named the perpetrator in a legal complaint by an employee at a lower level. In contrast, we rarely hear of complaints from people in powerful positions claiming to be harassed by subordinates. This is not to say that such incidences do not take place, but that the person in power usually has the ability to terminate the employee on the spot, thus effectively ending any further problems.

The **sociopsychological approach** assumes there are particular combinations of an individual's personality and specific situations that, when aligned, bring about sexual harassment (Pryor, Giedd, & Williams, 1995). That is, it is assumed that some people are predisposed to harass others, but having that predisposition does not mean a person will do so. Instead, sexually harassing behavior is most likely to emerge when a person with a predisposition for sexually harassing behavior is in a situation that fosters emergence of that behavior.

Elizabeth O'Hare and William O'Donohue (1998) proposed a **four-factor model** of sexually harassing behavior. These four factors consist of two internal factors and two external factors. The internal factors are **motives for harassment** and **overcoming internal inhibitors**. Motives for harassment can range from a need for power and dominance over someone else to a desire to exercise total control over someone. Regardless of whether the motivation is for power, dominance, or control, these motives can be channeled into harassing behavior. Overcoming internal inhibitors reflects the perpetrator's fears of victim retaliation and the perpetrator's personal sexual inhibitions. The external factors consist of **overcoming external inhibitors** and **overcoming victim resistance**. Overcoming external inhibitors consists of issues such as organizational reaction to the behavior and legal ramifications the harasser may encounter. Overcoming victim resistance concerns using power factors, such as job factors, which affords the more powerful person the privilege of being the initiator of most communication with subordinates; thus allowing an opportunity for the higher-status person to move beyond the victim's refutations. Whether the communicator is harassing or not, the higher status employee controls interaction time and topic and has the power to terminate the interaction. These factors, taken as a whole, reflect the internal and external barriers that a harasser must overcome/address when harassing the victim.

Up to this point, we have discussed sexual harassment as an interpersonal phenomenon. However, whenever a case is settled in a civil litigation, generally the accused harasser and the organization are identified as defendants.

It is therefore imperative for organizations to address problematic behavior before it starts. This is not only a moral argument; this is also a financial argument. Most, if not all, major corporations offer some form of training in identifying and addressing harassing behaviors.

Organizations suffer greatly from sexual harassment accusations. Organizations whose employees are convicted of sexual harassment are often seen by the public as being a "sponsor" of harassment (Keyton, 1996). This sponsorship effect influences the bottom line in terms of customer loyalty and interactions with other companies in the same industry. In 1999, the average cost of resolving a sexual harassment suit was $200,000, which is further exacerbated by increased absenteeism by the victim, increased turnover, therapy costs, and new employee training costs (Stanko & Schneider, 1999). In 2007, the EEOC reported that the average jury verdict for sexual harassment cases was $1 million. As evidenced in these figures, harassment has been and continues to be a costly operating expense for organizations and must be treated as any other liability that consumes organizational resources.

Of course, the most significantly impacted person in all this is the victim. Not only do victims suffer the immediate trauma that is induced by the harassing behavior, but victims also suffer the wrath of being labeled a troublemaker or whistleblower; many victims suffer from and receive treatment for posttraumatic stress disorder (Gutek & Koss, 1993). Victims are frequently blackballed from their respective industries and find themselves looking not only for a new organization, but a new career. Sexual harassment can be considered a crime of communication and language that brings with it a dramatic emotional, psychological, social, and financial cost to the victim and organization.

Summary

The study of language and how it influences workplace interaction will always be of value because both language and organizations are involved in constant evolution and change. Language is something that people possess as well as something that people express. This chapter introduced the practice of language and discussed how meaning is both literal and figurative. Looking at language as a style, we can see how the phrasing, attitude, and awareness of communicators all have a dramatic impact on organizational relationships. The use of power is conveyed through language. A person can use language to establish power dynamics as well as to protect possible threats to self-esteem.

This chapter presented several theories that use language as the foundation for explaining relationships. Whether we choose to adapt to or digress from the language patterns of other people provides clues to a host of communication and relational dynamics. Finally, this chapter presented the concept of language use as a vehicle for sexual harassment. Sexual harassment is one of the most destructive elements to organizational cohesion and team development. Awareness of how our messages affect others is crucial for a workplace free of bias based on sex, color, creed, or sexual orientation.

Questions for Discussion and Review

1. Explain what is meant by the adage "language is arbitrary." Provide some examples of this principle in your workplace.

2. Describe how people use language in mindless and mindful ways. How can mindless language be made mindful? Provide examples.

3. Explain the Sapir-Whorf hypothesis of language and culture. Do you agree with this hypothesis? Defend your answer using examples from your organization.

4. Describe the relationship between power and language use. Give examples of the types of language used by a powerful person.

5. Explain why someone would engage in self-handicapping behavior. Give an example of a self-handicapping strategy you have seen in the workplace.

6. According to communication accommodation theory, people either converge or diverge their speech patterns. Give two reasons why people would use convergent and divergent strategies.

7. According to interaction adaptation theory, people adapt their language behavior to other people. Explain the two types of adaptation patterns people use and provide examples of each.

8. Explain the concept of RED from interaction adaptation theory. Provide an example of the RED for a supervisor about to meet the star employee to discuss a well-deserved promotion.

9. Describe language expectancy theory and provide examples of a person with a wide bandwidth and a person with a small bandwidth.

10. Define sexual harassment and explain the influence of language on such behavior.

11. Describe the four-factor model of sexual harassment. Provide examples of each factor.

References

Abate, F. R. (Ed.). (1997). *Oxford Pocket Dictionary and Thesaurus* (American Edition). New York: Oxford University Press.

Anderson, J., Schultz, B., & Courtney-Staley, C. (1987). Training in argumentativeness: New hope for nonassertive women. *Women Studies in Communication, 10,* 58–66.

Avtgis, T. A., Rancer, A. S., & Amato, P. P. (1998). Self-handicapping orientation toward verbal aggressiveness. *Communication Research Reports, 15,* 226–234.

Bate, B., & Bowker, J. (1997). *Communication and the sexes* (2nd ed.). Prospect Heights, IL: Waveland Press.

Baumgardner, A. H., Lake, E. A., & Arkin, R. M. (1985). Claiming mood as a self-handicap: The influence of spoiled and unspoiled public identities. *Personality and Social Psychology Bulletin, 11,* 349–357.

Brooks, R. D. (1970). The generalizability of early reversals of attitudes toward communication sources. *Speech Monographs, 37,* 152–155.

Burgoon, M. (1995). Language expectancy theory: Elaboration, explication, and extension. In C. R. Berger & M. Burgoon (Eds.), *Communication and social influence process* (pp. 29–52). East Lansing, MI: Michigan State University Press.

Burgoon, M., Denning, V. P., & Roberts, L. (2002). Language expectancy theory. In J. P. Dillard & M. Pfau (Eds.), *The persuasion handbook* (pp. 117–136). Thousand Oaks, CA: SAGE Publications.

Burgoon, M., Jones, S. B., & Stewart, D. (1975). Toward a message-centered theory of persuasion: Three empirical investigations of language intensity. *Human Communication Research, 1,* 240–256.

Burgoon, J. K., LaPoire, B. A., & Rosenthal, R. (1995). Effects of preinteraction expectancies and target communication on perceiver reciprocity and compensation in dyadic interaction. *Journal of Experimental Social Psychology, 31,* 287–321.

Chase, S. (1956). Forward. In J. B. Carroll (Ed.), *Benjamin Lee Whorf: Language, thought and reality* (pp. v–x). Cambridge, MA: The MIT Press.

Cronkhite, G. (1986). On the focus, scope, and coherence of the study of human symbolic activity. *Quarterly Journal of Speech, 72,* 231–246.

Equal Opportunity Employment Commission (EEOC). (2006). *Sexual harassment.* Retrieved from http://www.eeoc.gov/types/ sexual_harassment.html

Equal Opportunity Employment Commission (EEOC). (2009). *Sexual harassment.* Retrieved from http://www.eeoc.gov/types/ sexual_harassment.html

Fitzgerald, L. F., & Shullman, S. L. (1993). Sexual harassment: A research analysis and agenda for the 1990s. *Journal of Vocational Behavior, 42,* 5–27.

Fitzgerald, L. F., Shullman, S. L., Bailey, N., Richards, M., Swecker, J., Gold et al. (1988). The incidence and dimensions of sexual harassment in academia and the workplace. *Journal of Vocational Behavior, 32,* 152–175.

Giles, H., Mulac, A., Bradac, J. J., & Johnson, P. (1987). Speech accommodation theory: The first decade and beyond. In M. L. McLaughlin (Ed.), *Communication Yearbook* (pp. 13–48). Beverly Hills, CA: SAGE Publications.

Giles, H., & Wiemann, J. M. (1987). Language, social comparison and power. In C. R. Berger & S. H. Chaffee (Eds.), *Handbook of communication science* (pp. 350–384). Newbury Park, CA: SAGE Publications.

Gruber, J. E., & Bjorn, L. (1986). Women's response to sexual harassment: A multivariate analysis. *Basic and Applied Social Psychology, 17,* 543–562.

Gutek, B. A., & Koss, M. P. (1993). Changed women and changed organizations: Consequences of and coping with sexual harassment. *Journal of Vocational Behavior, 42,* 28–48.

Gutek, B. A., & Monarsh, B. (1982). Sex-ratios, sex-role spillover, and sexual harassment of women at work. *Journal of Social Issues, 38,* 55–74.

Hamilton, M. A., Hunter, J. E., & Burgoon, M. (1990). An empirical test of an axiomatic model of the relationship between language intensity and persuasion. *Journal of Language and Social Psychology, 9,* 235–255.

Harris, R. N., Snyder, C. R., Higgins, R. L., & Schrag, J. L. (1986). Enhancing the prediction of self-handicapping. *Journal of Personality and Social Psychology, 51,* 1191–1199.

Infante, D. A., Rancer, A. S., & Avtgis, T. A. (2010). *Contemporary communication theory.* Dubuque, IA: Kendall Hunt.

Keyton, J. (1996). Sexual harassment: A multidisciplinary synthesis and critique. In B. R. Burleson (Ed.), *Communication Yearbook 19* (pp. 93–155). Thousand Oaks, CA: SAGE Publications.

Lakoff, R. (1975). *Language and woman's place.* New York: Harper & Row.

Langer, E. J. (1989). *Mindfulness.* Reading, MA: Addison-Wesley.

Leary, M. R., & Shepperd, J. A. (1986). Behavioral self-handicaps versus self-reported handicaps: A conceptual note. *Journal of Personality and Social Psychology, 51,* 1265–1268.

Mello-Goldner, D., & Jackson, J. (1999). Premenstrual syndrome (PMS) as a self-handicapping strategy among college women. *Journal of Social Behavior and Personality, 14,* 607–616.

Mulac, A., Bradac, J. J., & Gibbons, P. (2001). Empirical support for the gender-as-culture hypothesis: An intercultural analysis of male/female language differences. *Human Communication Research, 27,* 121–152.

O'Hare, E. A., & O'Donohue, W. (1998). Sexual harassment: Identifying risk factors. *Archives of Sexual Behavior, 6,* 561–580.

Pryor, J. B., Giedd, J. L., & Williams, K. B. (1995). A social psychology model for predicting sexual harassment. *Journal of Social Issues, 51,* 69–84.

Stanko, B. B., & Schneider, M. (1999). Sexual harassment in the public accounting profession. *Journal of Business Ethics, 18,* 185–200.

Steinfatt, T. M. (1977). *Human communication: An interpersonal introduction.* Indianapolis: Bobbs-Merrill.

Street, R. L., & Giles, H. (1982). Speech accommodation theory: A social cognitive approach to language and speech behavior. In M. Roloff & C. R. Berger (Eds.), *Social cognition and communication* (pp. 193–226). Beverly Hills, CA: SAGE Publications.

Thomsett, M. C. (1991). *The little black book of business etiquette.* New York: AMACOM.

White, C. H. (2008). Expectancy violations theory and interaction adaptation theory: From expectations to adaptation. In L. A. Baxter & D. O. Braithwaite (Eds.), *Engaging theories in interpersonal communication: Multiple perspectives* (pp. 189–202). Thousand Oaks, CA: SAGE Publications.

Chapter 5

Defining Relationships

Perhaps one of the most fundamental, underlying concepts of the term *organization* is that it is a function of the individuals part of it. That is, any definition of organizational communication explicitly or implicitly mentions the people who are unified around a common goal, common mission, and common work practices. To capture and appreciate the importance of communication in the organizational environment, it is necessary to understand the nature and function of the relationships in which employees find themselves embedded (Barry & Crant, 2000). This chapter focuses on the social construction of relationships and the role that these relationships play in everyday organizational practices, as well as the people who are affected by such practices.

A **relationship** can be defined as a symbiotic social connection between two people in which certain limited resources are shared, resulting in more effective and efficient productivity for both parties. Key to this definition is the term **limited resources**, which reflects that certain advantages exist in every organization, but not all employees have equal access to them (Boyd, 1990). One of the most important limited resources within an organization is access to information, which, if any employee finds himself or herself without it, can make performing a particular task very difficult. For example, assume that an employee is told to create a new RGK file using the company's software system, although he or she has no idea what such a file is or how the system works. This, unfortunately, becomes a resource whose lack of knowledge impairs productivity. Scholars and practitioners who study the relational dynamics of employees have concluded that creating and maintaining relationships with people who have access to organizationally relevant information is extremely profitable as such information tends to get shared (Monge & Contractor, 2001). There is an old saying that the most important people in any organization are administrative assistants, as an incredible amount of information flows through them on a daily basis. This access to information and the subsequent ability to share it with others is a form of social power and is emblematic of organizational significance.

The fact that information is not collectively shared among all employees can be problematic as this inhibits work practices of some and accentuates the work practices of others (Davenport & Prusak, 1998). On the other hand, from an individual employee perspective, this becomes a networking opportunity: to find those who have necessary and limited information and create a social relationship with them. For example, if Lee has access to information and Sara has a social relationship with Lee, then Sara also has access to this information. This relationship between Lee and Sara exemplifies the importance of not only having access to information, but also having a relationship with those who have access to the information. In the end, the only reason that Sara has access to information is because of her relationship with Lee.

In addition to forming relationships in order to have access to information, employees have a desire to create relationships with those in powerful positions. According to John French and Bertram Raven, two social

relationship A symbiotic social connection between two people in which certain limited resources are shared, resulting in more effective and efficient productivity for both parties.

limited resources A certain advantage that exists within an organization, but one that not all employees have equal access to.

TABLE 5.1	Types of Power
Type	**Source**
Reward power	Based on one's ability to provide incentives
Punishment power	Based on one's ability to administer negative consequences
Legitimate power	Based on one's hierarchical position
Expert power	Based on one's knowledge base
Referent power	Based on one's employee merit and social popularity

psychologists interested in the processes and effects of relational **power**, there are five primary reasons that people have power over others: reward power is based on a person's ability to provide incentives, punishment power is based on a person's ability to administer negative consequences, legitimate power is based on a person's official position within an organization, expert power is based on the knowledge that a person has about a particular topic, and referent power is based on a person's perceived worth and respect (French & Raven, 1959). Forming a relationship with a powerful other means, by definition, that the person in the less powerful position gains a more powerful status. For example, if Jodie has legitimate power and Mitchell shares a social relationship with Jodie, then Mitchell becomes more powerful. Just as employees seek to create relationships with those who have access to limited information, they also seek to create relationships with those who have power.

power An employee's ability to have certain control over others because of a limited resource that he or she possesses

A third reason that people form relationships is for access to the personal networks of the other person. That is, forming relationships with those who, themselves, have a lot of relationships or are popular translates into a desirable limited resource (Monge & Contractor, 2003). At a basic level, one who has relationships with others who are well connected within the organization's social structure increases the likelihood of access to more information as well as links to those who have at least one of the five sources of power. Therefore, by having access to information, employees become more relationally valuable; by having access to information, employees become more powerful; and by having access to and relationships with people who are well connected, employees find themselves embedded in social bonds that are rich in information, power, and opportunity. It should be apparent that constructing relationships with the *right* employees becomes advantageous and opportunistic and, some would argue, vital for success in the organization.

Types of Organizational Relationships

It was not until the early 1930s, when Elton Mayo and colleagues conducted experiments at the Western Electric Company's Hawthorne Plant in Chicago and concluded that worker productivity, motivation, satisfaction, and commitment are closely linked to interpersonal communication and quality organizational relationships, that scholars began to understand the importance of social connections (see Chapter 2). Among their findings was that workplace relationships were instrumental in fostering a sense of collective membership and a sense of psychological well-being (Mayo, 1933). Based on Mayo's (1933) findings, Gerald Goldhaber, an influential organizational communication scholar, claimed that organizations are an interdependent collection of the relationships in which employees find themselves embedded (Goldhaber, 1974). Simply put, relationships *are* the organization.

Since Mayo's studies of the 1930s, organizations have spent much time and energy not only determining which organizational relationships should and need to be developed, but also ways to facilitate such relational development. As research indicates, some organizational relationships are **contrived**, meaning that employees have no jurisdiction over them (McPhee, 1985). For example, departmental and team membership are often not under the volition of the individual employee, but rather those in administrative positions. The formation of departmental and team relationships are, in a sense, forced. For better or worse, it is rare that employees get to choose with whom they work. However, most organizational relationships are **emergent**, meaning that employees proactively determine with whom they network and construct relationships (Monge & Contractor, 2001). Ironically, these emergent relationships are often not task based, which are the primary means of organizational productivity, but socially based. The importance of emergent networks becomes evident when coupled with the fact that much of the social psychological research highlights the importance of relationships for the psychological and physical well-being of individuals.

To put the importance of quality social relationships in perspective, assume the average person works for 40 years (based on much data about the 65-year-old retirement plan) at 40 hours per week. Including vacations and days off, this means the average person works a total of 83,200 hours during his or her lifetime. Imagine you had to spend these 83,200 hours in social isolation. Is it possible you could remain productive and psychologically healthy? Probably, but not likely. Relationships, as interpersonal communication scholarship has dictated for the better part of the last 50 years, are essential to human functioning, with organizational relationships being no exception to this rule (Sias, Krone, & Jablin, 2002). Organizational downtime, or the time when employees interact about nonwork-related issues, has been found to be strongly correlated with organizational commitment, job satisfaction, morale, tenure, and productivity (Morrison, 2004). Although this discussion is not meant to imply that contrived (i.e., forced or assigned) relationships are never social and that emergent relationships are never task based, much scholarship has partitioned contrived and emergent relationships based primarily on the impetus for such connections (i.e., forced versus voluntary).

Superior/Subordinate Organizational Relationships

Regarding contrived relationships, the majority of research has focused on superior-subordinate communication (see, for example, Jablin, 1979). Research indicates that the nature of one's relationship with his or her boss has much to do with the organization's culture, centralization of authority and decision making, and the type of leadership (Krone, 1992). From a cultural perspective (see Chapter 2), an organization that is more horizontal, has informal lines of communication, and where information and influence are shared tends to contain relationships between superiors and subordinates that are more casual and relaxed in nature. By contrast, an organization that is more vertical or has many levels of hierarchy, tends to have more formal lines of communication, and where information and influence are in the hands of a few, likely fosters a relational situation that is task based, hierarchical, and formal in nature.

Assume, for example, that Jonathan works for a company that prides itself on cultural and communicative informality, wherein such things as title, hierarchy, status, and tenure are deemed insignificant. It is likely that Jonathan will create an informal relationship with his boss, creating a social situation rife with both task and social implications. In addition to speaking to Jonathan's boss about his job and the social processes that accompany it, he is also likely, based on the informal culture, to speak about "extra-organizational" topics, such as sports, food and drink, vacations, family, and recreational reading. Compare this situation to Bonnie, an employee of an organization that has a formal hierarchy and whose culture is more like a machine (see Chapter 2). It is unlikely that Bonnie, as compared to Jonathan, will cultivate a friendship with her boss, as her organization's culture is not conducive to such informal fraternizing. An organization's culture is clearly one of the predictors of informal superior-subordinate communication and the subsequent development of casual relationships (Kotter & Heskett, 1992). Simply put, there is a lot to be learned about organizational relationships based on the structure of the organization, the way people address one another, and the topics they speak about.

A second factor involved in the nature of superior-subordinate relationships is whether authority and decision making are centralized (Jablin, 1979). In other words, are power and influence in the hands of few or in the hands of many? If in the hands of a few, then this indicates an environment based on hierarchy and protocol. After all, it is power and influence that negate the introduction of a horizontal social structure and de-emphasize the creation of social relationships. With such a vertical structure in place, the relationship between a superior and his or her subordinate is likely to be task based only, representative of the time motion studies mentioned in Chapter 2. Among Frederick Taylor's (1911) results (see Chapter 2) was that formal, hierarchical figures are necessary in organizations to keep efficiency and effectiveness elevated. This, again, is not to say that an organization with a flattened hierarchy and informal superior-subordinate relationships is doomed to fail, while an organization with a vertical structure and formalized relationships is destined for success. It is to say, however, that much of the impetus for creating informal relationships is based on whether authority, status, position, tenure, and the power that accompany them are emphasized (Jablin, 1979). Taylor had a general distrust of the worker in that, unless supervised, the workers could easily adopt negative work habits, such as soldiering behavior.

A third factor involved in whether one creates a more social, informal relationship with his or her superior is based on the leadership practices of those in administrative positions. An example of this is Blake and Mouton's (1964) managerial grid, which highlights whether and to what extent leaders have a concern for employees, a concern for task, a concern for both, or a concern for neither (see Chapter 2). Using this managerial grid, it is more likely that employees will create informal relationships with their superiors if their leader is either a country club-style manager or a team manager, as opposed to an impoverished manager or a task manager, for the former two styles place more emphasis on employee well-being, whereas the latter two styles emphasize task. In the end, among the important independent variables that predict and explain informal superior-subordinate relationships include the culture of the organization, the centralization or sharing of authority and decision making, and the style of leadership practiced by management.

Advantages of Organizational Relationships

Fifty years of scholarship has indicated the overarching benefits of creating both formal and informal, as well as contrived and emergent, relationships within the organization (Jablin & Krone, 1994). First among these benefits is the basic need for social interaction. Abraham Maslow, an influential psychologist best known for his research on human needs, argued that social beings have an innate desire for belonging. That is, people would be emotionally and psychologically unfulfilled if not for the relationships they create over their entire lifespan (Maslow, 1943). In fact, many scholars believe that relationships serve a survival function. For the most part, it is one's informal organizational relationships that fulfill this need for belonging, wherein communication about nonwork-related topics transpires and people are able to meet interpersonal needs within the organization (Bridge & Baxter, 1992).

Using the example of the average person's working hours over a lifetime provided at the beginning of this chapter, imagine spending 83,200 hours without any informal relationships. Maslow found that such social isolation was likely predictive of such things as depression, lack of motivation, and feelings of ill-accomplishment (Maslow, 1943). If employees feel a sense of depression, lack of motivation, and feelings of ill-accomplishment, this can have serious negative ramifications for organizational productivity, job satisfaction, and organizational commitment (Morrison, 2004). Thus, the creation of informal relationships, or what Maslow would call a basic human need, is necessary within the organizational environment (see Chapter 8). Not surprisingly, results from a study conducted by Markiewicz, Devine, and Kausilas (2000) found a significant correlation between work friendships and job satisfaction, meaning that having informal relationships within the organizational environment is linked to being more satisfied with one's job.

Another advantage of creating interpersonal relationships within organizations is to cultivate a social support system that can provide advice, comfort, and solidarity (Kirmeyer & Lin, 1987). Think for a moment about a time when you were internally conflicted about something or someone. In all likelihood, you asked a close friend or family member for advice and confided in this person. In the end, even if your decision did not prove fruitful or successful, you likely felt comfort in the fact that another person in your personal network supported and encouraged a particular action or set of actions. This, in essence, is the idea of **social support** and **social solidarity**. Social support is defined as the support system created by in-group or network members. Social solidarity is defined as a network's or small group's willingness to agree that certain behaviors are deemed appropriate and others inappropriate. If others with whom we interact encourage behaviors, we are more likely to engage in these than if social network members disapprove or discourage them (Albrecht & Adelman, 1987). For example, assume that Jason is clearly upset about a decision made by his boss, Alexis. Rather than directly confronting Alexis, Jason first asks for the advice of his coworker Amber. Based on research that links decision making and interpersonal relationships, Jason is more likely to confront Alexis if Amber agrees that such a confrontation would be, in the end, rewarding. This is not to say that all decisions that gain the social support of others are successful. In fact, social support is exactly the prerequisite necessary for Groupthink (see Chapter 7), wherein those part of a collective social unit are fearful of not promoting a behavior or decision because of the inherent social dangers of nonconformity (Jablin, 1979). It is safe to say that employees often feel more comfortable and more willing to engage in certain behaviors if relational others substantiate them.

A third advantage of creating interpersonal relationships within organizations is the opportunity for minority influence or the influence of those whose position, opinion, or perspective is not shared by the majority or by people in power (Wood, Lundgren, Ouellette, Busceme, & Blackstone, 1994). For better or worse, the majority of organizational decisions are made because a collective body of employees agrees that a particular action is warranted or just. Much small-group communication research indicates that for a minority opinion to be adopted, there must be at least two individuals who advocate for it (Hirokawa & Poole, 1996). Assume, for example, that a group of nine employees from Abercrombie & Fitch was assigned the task of creating a new summer design and color for its men's collection. Assume further that only one member of the group brings forth the idea to initiate a new tight-fitting, pink, collared shirt (a decision that was made over a decade ago and subsequently proved to have been a pivotal, successful corporate move). Such an idea would likely be received with much hesitation and perhaps even ambivalence. Why? If only one person out of nine favors such a decision, it is difficult to convince others of the decision's merit.

Think, for example, about trying to convince your group of friends that *The Big Bang Theory* is the best TV sitcom presently aired, if you are the only one who believes this. You will likely realize that this is a difficult if not impossible feat. However, imagine that both you and another friend both endorse *The Big Bang Theory*. Merely because there are now two people in agreement, convincing others becomes more likely and, in a sense, easier. This, according to decision scientists, is known as **minority influence**, defined as a decision supported by few, but one that can be adopted if the "right" people use the "right" persuasive strategies. To have a decision result in adoption, often it is necessary to have at least two people favor it. These two people likely share a relationship and, as a result, minority influence becomes a possibility. Given the foregoing example, if two people favor the tight-fitting, pink, collared shirt from Abercrombie & Fitch, convincing the other group members likely becomes a more realistic task.

minority influence A decision supported by few, but that can be adopted if the "right" people use the "right" persuasive strategies.

A fourth advantage linked to organizational relationships refers to the necessary flow of information between and among employees. Much research in the early part of the 20th century indicated that information would flow throughout the organization based on hierarchical structuring (Glauser, 1984). That is, information would flow "down" the organization from top management, to middle management, then to nonmanagement employees. The problem with this is that information dissemination is time consuming and, as a result, inefficient. Assume that the president of a college or university needed to get an important piece of information communicated to all students concerning an incident on campus that requires rapid student feedback. Think about the time and energy needed to spread this message from the president to the vice president, from the vice president to the provost, from the provost to the deans, from the deans to the department chairs, from department chairs to faculty members, and from faculty members to students. This is a prime example of downward communication flow that becomes inefficient when there is a need for a message to be sent instantaneously. However, what if information flow and dissemination occurred based on friendship ties, rather than formal hierarchical positioning? Would such dissemination be more effective and efficient? In other words, if the president told the vice president, who told his friends, who told their friends, who told their friends, is it likely that the spread of such information would be eased? Based on much research of informal organizational relationships, the answer to this question is yes.

Complications Associated with Organizational Relationships

Although there are benefits associated with the creation of relationships within the organizational environment, such relationships are not without complications (Berman, West, & Richter, 2002). First among such complications reflects the negotiation of competing interpersonal needs (Baxter, 1988). A **relational dialectic**, defined as an inherent inconsistency between two salient variables, results when competing interpersonal needs surface at the same time. For example, in many interpersonal relationships that are intimate in nature, there is a need for both connection and separation. That is, people want to share their lives with others, but also want the autonomy to have social networks that extend beyond this specific, intimate relationship. In the movie *How to Lose a Guy in Ten Days,* Annie is romantically involved with Benjamin and she has trouble dealing with the fact that he routinely has a "guys night out." This is emblematic of a relational dialectic because there seem to be two competing needs for Benjamin. He seems to need both connection to and separation from Annie.

The same type of tension can occur within the organizational setting (Bridge & Baxter, 1992). As an example, assume that Joan and Kenneth share an interpersonal relationship with one another, though Joan is Kenneth's boss. This relationship is casual and informal, predicated on such things as humor, sarcasm, and jokes. This, according to much organizational communication research, is beneficial. However, assume that Joan calls Kenneth into her office to provide negative feedback about an organization-wide email that he had just sent complaining about certain organizational practices. What issues or needs could arise for either person? Relational dialectics would predict that Joan has two existing, yet competing, needs: the need to be "friend" and the need to be "supervisor." What might happen when Joan reprimands Kenneth for his email? Might he take such negative feedback sarcastically? Might he laugh about the issue rather than take it seriously? Might Joan have problems addressing such an issue because of the nature of their relationship? It is likely that the answer to all these questions is yes. In this case, the creation of such an informal, casual relationship between superior and subordinate becomes problematic because such competing dialectics might prove too difficult and because offering meaningful, constructive, effective feedback might become an arduous task. Recall that in Chapter 2, Max Weber's bureaucratic approach to organizing made a priority of separating work life from personal life. Although such a separation is difficult, if not impossible, it would negate such a dialectical tension as that being experienced by Joan and Kenneth.

A second complication associated with informal relationships within the organizational environment is the possibility for **upward distortion** and **downward distortion**. Upward distortion and downward distortion, in this context, are defined as one's decision to emphasize the positive

relational dialectic An inherent inconsistency between two salient variables, which results when competing interpersonal needs surface at the same time.

elements embedded in a message when communicating with superiors and subordinates. In short, we are likely to distort feedback to/from others when we share an interpersonal relationship with them for a variety of reasons (Athanassiades, 1973). For example, assume that Jaclyn and Greg work for the same organization, but are also friends. What happens if Jaclyn has to offer Greg negative feedback about how he handled an interpersonal conflict with his departmental coworker Michelle. Jaclyn might engage in downward distortion, where she tells Greg that "it's not the end of the world" or that "it wasn't such a big deal" or "not to worry because others aren't upset about it." However, what happens if it is "the end of the world" or if it was "a big deal" or it is "something others are upset about?" Although Jaclyn might have done this as a way to soften such negative feedback so as not to embarrass Greg, this downward distortion could have a negative effect on him.

As another example, assume that Amy needs to tell Thomas, her boss and friend, that other organizational employees are disappointed with his recent decision to eliminate the holiday reception. Could a similar thing happen regarding the information distortion? Amy may tell Thomas that "it's not a big deal, but certain people are a bit perplexed about your decision" or "don't worry about them, I don't agree." This also illustrates the potential issues with creating relationships with coworkers, insofar as providing feedback might become overly problematic, especially when providing feedback that is inherently negative (Jablin, 1979). Being mindful of such potential distortions can help one create messages about sensitive issues.

A third complication with forming relationships is interpersonal conflict. **Conflict**, defined as a disagreement that accrues within a relationship based on divergent viewpoints and perspectives, if constructive, task-based, and properly managed, provides a wealth of information and can be framed as something organizationally beneficial. However, conflict becomes problematic when it is unmanaged and character based (Putnam & Poole, 1987). For example, assume that Matthew and Pamela enter into a discussion-turned-argument about how to best market a new type of rechargeable battery. After Matthew explains to Pamela that she neglected to consider such things as market segmentation, price, placement, and media outlets, Pamela responds with a personal attack by telling Matthew that he does not belong in his administrative marketing position. This personal, socially based attack is likely to escalate and is likely to provide neither party with any benefit. Such interpersonal conflict is unwanted in any social situation, but is exponentially more difficult in organizations. Unfortunately, such interpersonal conflict might make the work environment bleak and unpleasant (Putnam, 1995).

Closely related to interpersonal conflict is **relational dissolution,** the fourth unwanted complication of friendships within organizations. Relational dissolution is defined as the process by which relationships come to an end, either through a gradual process (passing away) or an isolated incident or event (sudden death). I am sure that you can think of a time where interpersonal conflict resulted in the destruction of a relationship

conflict A disagreement that accrues within a relationship based on divergent viewpoints and perspectives.

TABLE 5.2	Advantages and Disadvantages of Relationships in Organizations
Advantages	**Disadvantages**
Fulfills basic need for interaction	Potential dialectics
Provides a system of social support	Upward distortion
Potential for minority influence	Downward distortion
Flow of information	Conflict
	Relational dissolution

and, for better or worse, you disentangled your life from your former friend's life. This was likely a difficult decision and the effects of such relational destruction were likely unfortunate. However, within the organizational environment, relational dissolution is overly problematic because the people whose relationship ends still must work together daily (Sias & Perry, 2004). Unfortunately, we rarely, if ever, are able to choose with whom we work and if such conflict results in relational dissolution, we are often told to "deal with it and manage." Clearly, as Frederic Jablin, a prominent organizational communication scholar, claimed, it is important to harness the benefits and eliminate the unwanted negative consequences of interpersonal relationships in the organizational setting (Jablin, 1979).

Although easier said than done, if employees can find ways to fulfill basic social needs, provide a social support system, become influential regarding a minority opinion, expedite the flow of information, alleviate potential relational dialectics, reduce the likelihood of upward and downward distortion, and reduce the likelihood of interpersonal conflict and relational dissolution, the benefits of organizational relationships will outweigh the potential difficulties associated with them (Sias & Cahill, 1998).

Organizational Social Networks

One area that has received a lot of attention, and whose practical implications are of great use to both management and workers, is the **organizational social network**. An organizational social network is a representation of how social actors within an organization are socially and structurally connected to others, providing an answer to the "who communicates with whom" question. By mapping an organization's social network, one can determine the presence (or absence) of relationships between and among organizational employees. Not only does such a social representation indicate where relationships do (and do not) exist within the organizational environment, but it also indicates who has potentially more influence and power (Monge & Contractor, 2001). For example, an employee who has connections to, or relationships with, nine others is potentially more important and more influential than the employee who has connections to only four.

organizational social network A representation of how employees are structurally and socially connected to each other.

TABLE 5.3	Types of Centrality
Type	**Effect**
Degree	More social ties as compared to others
Betweenness	Ability to connect previously disconnected people together
Closeness	Ability to reach all other in fewer steps as compared to all others
Eigenvector	Connected to others who are, themselves central

centrality The level of importance based on one's position within a given social network.

Linton Freeman, an influential sociologist best known for his research and theory of societal networks and how groups of people are socially connected to others, explained that social network positioning is extremely important for such things as social movements, community outreach, community leadership, and organizational practices. Among his important contributions to the study of social networks is his conceptualization of **centrality**, which is defined as the level of importance based on one's position within a given social network (Freeman, 1979). One's level of centrality (i.e., importance) in a network is based on the social relationships that he or she has with others. Therefore, the establishment and maintenance of organizational relationships is critical to network centrality.

One measure of centrality, according to Freeman (1979), is known as **degree centrality**, which is a quantitative measure of the number of relationships that a single employee has compared to all others. For example, assume that Lee has a social connection to 15 employees, whereas Lisa has a social connection to six. According to this example, Lee has more degree centrality when compared to Lisa. Having a high level of degree centrality has been linked to influence (Ibarra, 1993). In terms of Lee and Lisa, assume the organization for which they work is interested in creating a new organizational mission statement, and both Lee and Lisa have, independently, come up with ideas. Is it more likely that Lee's or Lisa's mission statement will be adopted by the collective body? Since Lee has more than twice as many connections, or relationships, as Lisa (15 vs. 6), it is likely that his statement will be seen as a better solution when compared with hers. This preference for Lee's decision

FIGURE 5.1
Degree Centrality

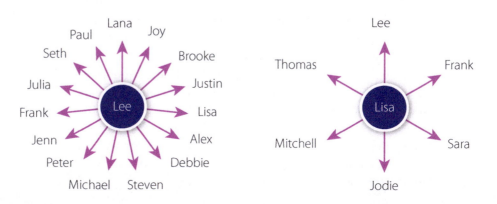

FIGURE 5.2
Betweenness Centrality

is largely based on the quantitative difference in relationships that each has created. Clearly, having many relationships becomes beneficial within the organizational environment (Higgins, 2000).

A second measure of centrality, known as **betweenness centrality**, is defined as one's level of importance based on his or her ability to socially connect previously disconnected people. According to Freeman (1979), if Timothy is friends with Jessica, and if Jessica is friends with Rachel, then it is likely that Timothy and Rachel, too, could be friends with one another. This thinking is much aligned with Fritz Heider's (1958) balance theory, which argues that the friends of your friends are friends themselves. Given the previous example, Timothy and Rachel would be friends because Jessica socially connected them. In other words, Jessica has a high level of betweenness centrality. What becomes advantageous about connecting previously disconnected people within the organizational environment? Research indicates that being such a connective agent promotes a sense of reciprocity or feelings of obligation (Brass, 1984). That is, since Jessica connected Timothy and Rachel, both Timothy and Rachel owe Jessica something in the future. It becomes evident that all three parties are now happy and satisfied. Jessica is happy because she is now connected to Timothy; Timothy is happy because he is now connected to Rachel; and Jessica is happy because both Timothy and Rachel owe her something in the future for having been the linchpin connecting the two of them.

These two measures of centrality indicate that the creation of organizational relationships has benefits, but for different reasons. It is beneficial to create the greatest number of relationships possible (degree) because of the amount of influence that surfaces as a result, though it is also beneficial to create relationships where one is able to become a bridge (betweenness), connecting others, because of the norm of reciprocity that emerges.

A third measure of centrality, according to Freeman (1979), is **closeness centrality**, defined as the number of steps necessary to reach all other parts of a given social network. Assume, for example, that an organization consists of 50 employees. If each employee had a direct social connection to all 49 others, this would mean three things. First, no individual employee has more degree centrality than anyone else, since all employees are socially connected to the same number of people. Second, no individual employee would have any betweenness centrality because there would be no employees disconnected from the organization's collective social network. Third, all employees would be able to reach all other employees in only one communicative step, meaning that each employee would have the same measure of closeness centrality.

This QR code will direct you to the International Network for Social Network Analysis, where you will be able to learn more about studying social networks in organizations.

http://www.insna.org/

FIGURE 5.3
Closeness Centrality

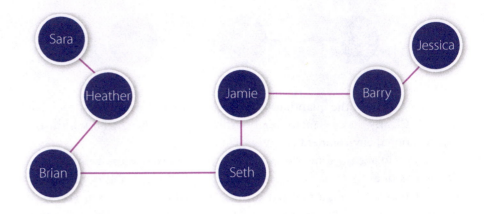

However, it is not realistic to assume an organization's social network is composed of employees who are connected to all others. Assume, therefore, that Sara is connected to Heather, who is connected to Brian, who is connected to Seth, who is connected to Jamie. Assume further that Jessica is connected to Barry who is connected to Jamie. Given these two examples, both Sara and Jessica have a social connection to Jamie, though Jessica, structurally speaking, can communicate with Jamie more easily than Sara, as the degree of separation between Jessica and Jamie is one, and the degree of separation between Sara and Jamie is four. As such, Jessica, compared to Sara, has a higher level of closeness centrality, as she can reach Jamie in fewer steps. From a relational perspective, closeness centrality is a salient measure of importance. It is easier to spread information to those with whom one creates a "close" network connection as compared to those with whom one shares a relationship with several degrees of separation embedded in it (Monge & Contractor, 2003).

A final measure of importance within a given network is **eigenvector centrality**. This is the idea that rather than being connected to the most people (degree), or being able to connect otherwise disconnected people (betweenness), or being able to reach all others in the social network in the fewest steps possible (closeness), a person's importance is based on whether he or she is connected to people with degree, betweenness, and/or closeness centrality (Bonacich, 1987). Thus, it becomes necessary to be socially connected to and share an interpersonal relationship with others who are important. For example, assume that Loryn has a social connection to 65 organizational employees. If Jason has a connection to Loryn, who, in this example, has high degree centrality, then he, by extension, has access to all the people connected to Loryn. As such, Jason, merely by having a connection to Loryn, becomes an important member of the organization's social network. Given this example, since Jason is connected to an employee with high degree centrality, he has a high measure of eigenvector centrality.

In the end, Freeman's scholarship has been extremely informing concerning relationships and social connections, and has pointed to the advantages of both the quantity (degree) and quality (betweenness, closeness, and eigenvector) of interpersonal communication within organizations.

Strength of Organizational Ties

An **organizational tie** is defined as any type of relationship that one employee shares with another. For example, employees have both formal organizational ties (supervisors, coworkers, team members) and informal organizational ties (friends). An important question surfaced in the early 1970s when Mark Granovetter, another important figure in the field of social psychology, asked whether it is more beneficial for organizational employees to cultivate strong or weak relationships with others. In other words, is it necessary to create strong friendships with others or is it equally beneficial to have merely organizational acquaintances? In Granovetter's (1973) strength of weak ties argument, he claimed that having weak ties, or relationships with others, characterized as being non-intimate, low on the time-consuming continuum, and emotionally non-intensive, can be beneficial. That is, having access to many people (degree centrality) becomes more important than cultivating strong, intimate relationships when it comes to such things as information dissemination and the accumulation of various resources.

Nearly 20 years later, David Krackhardt, a scholar of management and organizational behavior, argued the opposite: that the importance of creating relationships with others that are intimate, time-consuming, and emotionally intensive can be equally beneficial, but determining the benefit of any relational type must be based on the specific context and not applied as a general rule. For example, Krackhardt (1992) argued that strong ties are more effective than weak ties in situations that require social solidarity, such as organizational change and organizational development, whereas the opposite would be true in situations that do not require social solidarity or in times of organizational stability.

For example, what would happen if Alexander was in charge of disseminating information about a new organizational procedure? If he was asked to obtain input from others about a new organizational prototype? If he was asked to survey his fellow employees about perceptions of the organization's culture? Would Alexander likely be more effective if he had many weak ties or few strong ties? Since all three of these examples imply the dissemination or accumulation of information, weak ties would be acceptable (and even preferable), as access to more people would necessarily imply more feedback. However, what if Alexander was asked to create a new organizational procedure or create a new organizational prototype or change the organization's culture? Might Alexander benefit more by consulting his strong ties rather than his weak ties? Certainly. In fact, this is one of the major arguments made by Krackhardt (1992). Alexander would need his friends, those with whom he

organizational tie Any type of relationship that one employee shares with another.

shares a strong relationship, if such change is to occur. In the end, therefore, there is credibility and utility to both the strength of weak ties argument and the strength of strong ties argument. The difference depends on the role of such relationships. If the relationship is needed to spread information, then weak ties would be acceptable and suitable. If the relationship is needed to create organizational change, however, strong ties would be necessary. The key is to understand that both strong and weak relationships are important, just for different reasons and under different circumstances.

Relationships and Public Relations

public relations The communicative construction of an organization's public image, and the goodwill that results, for such external bodies as government officials, social activists, consumers or potential consumers, investors or potential investors, and media outlets.

Although intra-organizational communication is of great interest to scholars and practitioners, organizations need to cultivate relationships outside of the organization as well. Many students of organizational communication will find themselves in careers within the field of **public relations**. In short, public relations involves the communicative construction of an organization's public image and the goodwill that results for such external bodies as government officials, social activists, consumers or potential consumers, investors or potential investors, and media outlets. All these stakeholders are important for organizations, and public relations professionals are employed to create, strengthen, and/or solidify relationships with them. For example, in the wake of its 2010 oil spill, British Petroleum was forced to remedy its public image and regain the allegiance of its consumers, lobbyists, and investors. Although there is much debate about the effectiveness of BP's public relations behaviors after its 2010 oil spill, including its public apology, it is evident that the organization spent much energy rectifying its image through the recreation of important extra-organizational relationships, which Tony Hayward, the former Chief Executive Officer, knew were important for the organization's continued success.

This QR code will direct you to the homepage of the Public Relations Society of America, where you will be able to learn more about the role of public relations in organizational communication.

http://www.prsa.org/

Methods for Studying Organizational Relationships

There exist three important, yet very different, methodologies for studying relationships within the organizational setting. The first method for obtaining relational data is Nielsen, Jex, and Adams' (2000) *workplace friendship scale,* which assesses both opportunity for and prevalence of relationships. Although this questionnaire does not delve into who communicates with whom, it does assess the extent to which organizations endorse the formation of internal friendships. Some of the items include the following: "I have the opportunity to get to know my coworkers;" "In my organization, I have the chance to talk informally and visit with others;" "Communication among employees is encouraged by my organization;" "I have the opportunity to develop close friendships at my workplace;" "Informal talk is tolerated by my organization as long as the work is completed;" "I have formed strong friendships at work;" "Being able to see my coworkers is one reason why I look forward to my job." The workplace friendship scale has, according to Morrison (2004), become a reliable, valid, and useful tool for studying interpersonal relationships within organizations. Many scholars interested in workplace relationships use this scale in conjunction with other scales to determine the link between interpersonal relationships and such variables as job satisfaction, organizational commitment, intention to leave, organizational culture, organizational climate, and job involvement.

Although Nielsen et al's (2000) scale does not provide researchers with information about who, specifically, communicates with whom, many organizational scholars interested in workplace relationships have used Burt's (1984) **name generator technique** to gain such data. Through this technique, organizational participants are asked to name the five people with whom they communicate most often. From this, researchers will be able to extrapolate more about the nature of such relationships (e.g., level of trust, level of intimacy, level of reciprocity). Such a technique allows the organizational researcher to determine not only who has formed relationships with whom, but also allows the researcher to determine measures of centrality (i.e., degree, betweenness, closeness, eigenvector). Thus, whereas Nielsen, et al's (2000) scale provides data about nonspecific relationships and employees' rationale for their creation, Burt's (1984) name generator technique provides specific interpersonal data that provides the researcher the opportunity to track both individual relationships and overall organizational structures.

A final way to study organizational relationships is by using a conversation analytic approach (see Chapter 4), wherein the researcher gains access to verbal dialogue between employees to assess what the nature of talk says about the relationship among the interactants. As Watzlawick, Beavin, and Jackson (1967) noted, all communication has both a content element (what is said) and a relational element (how it is said and what such communication says about the interactants' relationship). By analyzing the communication that surfaces during interpersonal interaction, researchers are able to make conclusions about the nature of the employees' relationship (e.g., the levels of comfort, intimacy, respect, and openness).

Although each of these three methods is unique and advantageous in its own right, the combination of the three provides researchers with information about the rationale for the creation of organizational relationships, relationships themselves, and the nature of talk as informing of relationships.

Summary

Relationships are a necessary component of organizational communication. After all, the term *communication* implies that at least two social actors are involved in the dialogic process and being part of this process necessarily entails that a relationship has been created. Relationships serve basic human needs, are necessary for the creation of a social support system, help increase the likelihood of minority influence, and expedite the process of information flow within organizations. At the same time, however, relationships provide the opportunity for competing needs, increase the likelihood of upward and downward distortion, provide the potential for interpersonal conflict, and may create uncomfortable social situations if relationships dissolve. The key, therefore, is to magnify the benefits and minimize the potential disadvantages of interpersonal relationships within the organizational environment. Social network scholars have been able to identify the opportunities that accrue for social actors based on the relationships they have cultivated, whether it be influence, level of reciprocity, ease of information flow, or a combination thereof. Clearly, employees benefit from the relationships (both the quantity and quality) they create. Organizational communication scholars and practitioners are aware that relationships and communication are the ties that bind an organization together. Without relationships there is no such thing as communication and without communication there is no such thing as an organization. In the end, understanding relationships within the organizational setting is often the difference between success and failure for both the individual and the organization as a whole.

Questions for Discussion and Review

1. Explain the difference among the five sources of organizational power and give an example of an employee who has each source.

2. Explain the difference between an emergent relationship and a contrived relationship and give an example of each.

3. Explain the benefits and potential problems associated with informal relationships created between superiors and subordinates.

4. Differentiate between the advantages and disadvantages of creating organizational relationships. Make an argument either favoring or dispelling the idea that informal relationships within the organizational environment are good/beneficial or bad/disadvantageous.

5. Explain what is meant by a relational dialectic. Give an example of a dialectic related to organizational relationships, as well as a strategy for overcoming such a dialectic.

6. Differentiate among degree centrality, betweenness centrality, closeness centrality, and eigenvector centrality. Give an organizational example of an employee who has each.

7. It might seem as though having degree centrality is more beneficial for an employee than having any other type of centrality. However, betweenness centrality is also beneficial. Explain whether degree centrality or betweenness centrality is more beneficial and explain why.

8. Explain whether you think that weak ties or strong ties are more beneficial within the organizational environment. Provide examples to strengthen your arguments.

References

Albrecht, T. L., & Adelman, M. B. (1987). Communicating social support: A theoretical perspective. In T. L. Albrecht & M. B. Adelman (Eds.), *Communicating social support* (pp. 18–39). Newbury Park, CA: SAGE Publications.

Athanassiades, J. C. (1973). The distortion of upward communication in hierarchical organizations. *Academy of Management, 16*, 207–227.

Barry, B., & Crant, M. (2000). Dyadic communication relationships in organizations: An attribution/expectancy approach. *Organization Science, 11*, 648–664.

Baxter, L. A. (1988). A dialectical perspective on communication strategies in relationship development. In S. Duck (Ed.), *Handbook of personal relationships* (pp. 257–274). London: Wiley.

Berman, E. M., West, J. P., & Richter, M. N. (2002). Workplace relations: Friendship patterns and consequences (according to managers). *Public Administration Review, 62*, 217–230.

Blake, R. R., & Mouton, J. S. (1964). *The managerial grid*. Houston: Gulf Publishing.

Bonacich, P. (1987). Some unique properties of eigenvector centrality. *Social Networks, 29*, 555–564.

Boyd, B. (1990). Corporate linkages and organizational environment: A test of the resource dependence model. *Strategic Management Journal, 11*, 419–430.

Brass, D. J. (1984). Being in the right place: A structural analysis of individual influence in an organization. *Administrative Science Quarterly, 29*, 518–539.

Bridge, K., & Baxter, L. A. (1992). Blended relationships: Friends as work associates. *Western Journal of Communication, 56*, 200–225.

Burt, R. S. (1984). Network items in the general social survey. *Social Networks, 6*, 293–339.

Davenport, T. H., & Prusak, L. (1998). *Working knowledge: How organizations manage what they know.* Cambridge, MA: Harvard Business School Press.

Freeman, L. C. (1979). Centrality in social networks: Conceptual clarification. *Social Networks, 1,* 215–239.

French, J. R. P., & Raven, B. (1959). The bases of social power. In D. Cartwright (Ed.), *Studies in social power* (pp. 150–167). Ann Arbor, MI: Institute for Social Research.

Glauser, M. J. (1984). Upward information flow in organizations: Review and conceptual analysis. *Human Relations, 37,* 613–643.

Goldhaber, G. M. (1974). *Organizational communication.* Dubuque, IA: W. C. Brown.

Granovetter, M. S. (1973). The strength of weak ties. *The American Journal of Sociology, 78,* 1360–1380.

Heider, F. (1958). *The psychology of interpersonal relations.* New York: Wiley.

Higgins, M. C. (2000). The more the merrier: Multiple developmental relationships and work satisfaction. *Journal of Management Development, 19,* 277–296.

Hirokawa, R. Y., & Poole, M. S. (1996). *Communication and group decision making.* Beverly Hills, CA: SAGE Publications.

Ibarra, H. (1993). Network centrality, power, and innovation involvement: Determinants of technical and administrative roles. *Academy of Management Journal, 36,* 471–501.

Jablin, F. M. (1979). Superior-subordinate communication: The state of the art. *Psychological Bulletin, 86,* 1201–1222.

Jablin, F. M., & Krone, K. J. (1994). Task/work relationships: A life-span perspective. In M. L. Knapp & G. R. Miller (Eds.), *Handbook of interpersonal communication* (2nd ed.) (pp. 621–675). Newbury Park, CA: SAGE Publications.

Kirkmeyer, S. L., & Lin, T. (1987). Social support: Its relationship to observed communication with peers and superiors. *Academy of Management Journal, 30,* 138–151.

Kotter, J. P., & Heskett, J. L. (1992). *Corporate culture and performance.* New York: Free Press.

Krackhardt, D. (1992). The strength of strong ties: The importance of philos in organizations. In N. Nohria & R. Eccles (Eds.), *Networks and organizations: Structure, form, and action* (pp. 216–239). Boston: Harvard Business School Press.

Krone, K. J. (1992). A comparison of organizational, structural, and relationship effects on subordinates' upward influence choices. *Communication Quarterly, 40,* 1–15.

Markiewicz, D., Devine, I., & Kausilas, D. (2000). Friendships of women and men at work: Job satisfaction and resource implications. *Journal of Managerial Psychology, 15,* 161–184.

Maslow, A. (1943). A theory of human motivation. *Psychological Review, 50,* 370–396.

Mayo, E. (1933). *The human problems of an industrial civilization.* New York: Macmillan.

McPhee, R. D. (1985). Formal structure and organizational communication. In R. D. McPhee and P. K. Tompkins (Eds.), *Organizational communication: Traditional themes and new directions* (pp. 149–177). Beverly Hills, CA: SAGE Publications.

Monge, P. R., & Contractor, N. S. (2001). Emergence of communication networks. In F. M. Jablin & L.L. Putnam (Eds.), *New handbook of organizational communication* (pp. 440–502). Newbury Park, CA: SAGE Publications.

Monge, P. R., & Contractor, N. S. (2003). *Theories of communication networks.* New York: Oxford University Press.

Morrison, R. (2004). Informal relationships in the workplace: Associations with job satisfaction, organizational commitment, and turnover intentions. *New Zealand Journal of Psychology, 33,* 114–128.

Nielsen, I. K., Jex, S. M., & Adams, G. A. (2000). Development and validation of scores on a two-dimensional workplace friendship scale. *Educational and Psychological Measurement, 60,* 628–643.

Putnam, L. L. (1995). Formal negotiations: The productive side of organizational conflict. In A. M. Nicotera (Ed.), *Conflict and organizations: Communicative processes* (pp. 183–200). New York: State University of New York Press.

Putnam, L. L., & Poole, M. S. (1987). Conflict and negotiation. In F. M. Jablin, L. L. Putnam, K. H. Roberts, & L. W. Porter (Eds.), *Handbook of organizational communication: An interdisciplinary perspective* (pp. 549–599). Beverly Hills, CA: SAGE Publications.

Sias, P. M., & Cahill, D. J. (1998). From coworkers to friends: The development of peer friendships in the workplace. *Western Journal of Communication, 62,* 273–299.

Sias, P. M., Krone, K. J., & Jablin, F. M. (2002). An ecological systems perspective on workplace relationships. In M. L. Knapp and J. Daly (Eds.), *Handbook of interpersonal communication* (3rd ed.) (pp. 615–642). Newbury Park, CA: SAGE Publications.

Sias, P. M., & Perry, T. (2004). Disengaging from workplace relationships: A research note. *Human Communication Research, 30,* 589–602.

Taylor, F. W. (1911). *Scientific management.* New York: Harper and Row.

Watzlawick, P., Beavin, J., & Jackson, D. D. (1967). *Pragmatics of human communication: A study of interactional patterns, pathologies, and paradoxes.* New York: Norton.

Wood, W., Lundgren, S., Ouellette, J. A., Busceme, S., & Blackstone, T. (1994). Minority influence: A meta-analytic review of social influence processes. *Psychological Bulletin, 115,* 323–345.

Chapter 6

Personality and Organizational Life

Learning Objectives

Upon completion of the chapter, the student should be able to:

- Compare and contrast the neurobiological approach to personality and the social learning approach to personality.

- Compare and contrast constructive traits and destructive traits.

- Explain the difference between the clusters of communicator styles that form an affirming communication style with the clusters of communicator styles that form a non-affirming style.

- Compare and contrast communicator flexibility and communicator adaptability.

- Compare and contrast taking conflict personally and tolerance for disagreement.

Key Terms

Argumentativeness	Communicator style	Tolerance for disagreement (TFD)
Blood typing	Myers-Briggs Type Indicator	Verbal aggressiveness
Cognitive flexibility	Personality traits	
Communicative adaptability	Taking conflict personally (TCP)	

The study of personality pervades all contexts of communication and holds interesting insights on how people behave and what differentiates one person from another. The importance of accounting for individual differences is no less valuable in the organization. The study of personal and other individual differences has revealed important findings for researchers, scholars, CEOs, human resource directors, as well as any number of people involved in the study, management, and employment of people. This chapter presents some popular perspectives on personality and discusses some of the most important personality and communication traits that influence organizational behavior. The need to understand a person's predisposition toward communication and behavior is important because a person's predispositions are one of the best indicators of his or her actual behavior.

Have you ever known someone who moves from job to job because they never seem to be satisfied? This type of person will often say things such as "My coworkers are crazy!" "The company treats the employees like dirt!" or "They have no appreciation for how hard I work!" Sooner or later, the people who work with this person will probably conclude that it is not the jobs that are bad or unfulfilling, but the person's personality contributes to the negative work experience; therefore, no matter where they work the same types of problems arise.

The compelling question then becomes, Can this person change? The answer is, as is the answer to most questions, "perhaps." It is up to each of us to understand how our personalities are perceived by other people in the organization and how to use or manipulate our good qualities and de-emphasize the more negative aspects of ourselves in order to have satisfying work experiences. If we are unaware of a negative trait we possess, people's impressions of us may be negative. If we are unaware of how others perceive our behavior, then we are unable to change antisocial behaviors. The study of personality in the workplace has intrigued people in the organizational world for decades, if not centuries. Just as we seek regularities in our world, we simultaneously seek regularities within ourselves.

People argue that some personality traits are more beneficial or more appropriate than others. This assertion can be misleading. Our personality, regardless of what traits it is composed of, can be a benefit or a detriment, depending on the type of job or project being pursued. For example, if we are hiring a nurse, we would probably not offer the position to someone who appears overly task driven and aggressive. Instead, we may want to look for someone who displays high levels of compassion and empathy. However, if we are hiring a stockbroker, chances are we would be better off hiring the aggressive and task-driven person, who is more likely to perform at a higher level in this sales position when compared to our more compassionate and empathetic candidate. Although there are literally dozens of different personality traits, the traits presented in this chapter are some of the most well-researched traits in organizational communication. Table 6.1 lists some of the many traits that are used to distinguish one person from another in today's organizations.

TABLE 6.1	Personality and Communication Traits		
Achievement	**Affect Orientation**	**Argumentativeness**	**Assertiveness**
Attribution Style	Birth order	Charisma	Cognitive complexity
Communication apprehension	Communicator style	Dogmatism	Dominance
Empathy	Extraversion	Field dependence	Hostility
Interpersonal needs	Locus of control	Machiavellianism	Need for cognition
Perceived communication competence	Predisposition toward verbal behavior	Psychological gender	Repression-sensitization
Reticence	Self-awareness	Self-consciousness	Self-disclosure
Self-efficacy	Self-handicapping	Self-monitoring	Sensation seeking
Shyness	Singing apprehension	Sociocommunicator orientation	Sociocommunicator style
Taking conflict personally	Tolerance for ambiguity	Touch apprehension	Touch avoidance
Unwillingness to communicate	Verbal aggressiveness	Writing apprehension	

Personality Traits

What are personality traits? **Personality traits** are the idiosyncratic and individual factors that set one person apart from another. There is debate as to whether these personality differences are biologically rooted or socially learned. By biologically rooted we mean that our neurobiological composition (driven primarily by biology and heredity, not environment) is responsible for the way we behave. From this perspective, any behavioral training or skills learning will have little effect on our behavior. In Chapter 11 we present information on communication training. If we follow the assumptions of the biological explanation for personality development, we must recognize that little can be achieved through training designed to alter our personality, our behavior, or our perceptions (e.g., becoming more assertive or increasing our empathetic communication). The reason little change would be expected is that if biology truly controls behavior, then only biologically targeted treatments would be effective (e.g., administering medication for reducing the experience of communication anxiety). This is one effective way to temporarily alter biological influences on behavior so that a person can interact more effectively.

Some of you may have heard of the **Myers-Briggs Type Indicator**. This assessment is given to prospective employees to assess important personality characteristics and how these characteristics are tailored toward different careers.

personality traits Idiosyncratic and individual factors that set one person apart from another.

Myers-Briggs Type Indicator A test that assesses important personality characteristics pertinent to a person's preference for certain career paths.

The underlying assumption of this measure is that the most important aspects of an employee's personality determine what the person finds **energizing** (i.e., finding out what motivates him or her). For example, is the person motivated by outside factors such as people, places, and things (a.k.a. **extroverted**)? Or is the person internally motivated by emotions and internal perceptions of the world (a.k.a. **introverted**)? Another factor concerns the type of attending people do. Does the employee tend to see things at face value (**sensing**)? Or does the person tend to envision that which is not yet created (**intuition**)? A third category concerns how people make decisions (**deciding**). Does the employee use logic and structured information when faced with a decision (**thinking**)? Or does the employee make decisions with regard to how he or she feels or some other value-based judgment (**feeling**)? The final aspect of the Myers-Briggs assessment concerns people's preferred style of living. Does the person prefer an organized and structured life (**judgment**), or is the person more spontaneous and flexible (**perception**)? The Myers-Briggs employee assessment is the most widely used organizational behavioral/organizational psychology instrument in modern organizations. The success of the assessment in linking particular personality types to certain careers speaks to its popularity and relatively high cost. It is an invaluable tool for human resource managers interested in finding an ideal match between person and task.

A 2005 study conducted by the Society for Human Resource Management revealed that over one-third of employers give their job candidates some sort of personality test (Gunn, 2006). In fact, with our increasing ability to understand which areas of the brain are related to particular behaviors, there will be a day when prospective employees will not be given a paper and pencil test (e.g., Myers-Briggs Type Indicator) to determine whether they have the desired personality characteristics for the job. Rather, an appointment at a local health facility for a Functional Magnetic Resonance Image (MRI) of the prospective employee's brain might be required. This type of medical breakthrough will reduce the prospective employee's attempts to lie or embellish the truth and in so doing look like a more appealing candidate. For example, we know that under frustration-producing conditions, such as attempting to complete a difficult task, there are differences in the brain activation between proven leaders and those without leadership qualities. That is, our interpretation of the task (i.e., is this task perceived as a threat or an opportunity) and our predisposition to react in productive or unproductive ways are a function of the neurobiological connections that are activated in the brain. Researchers have recently identified a brain chemical that regulates how people cope with stressful events. The chemical is called brain-derived neurotrophic factor, or BDNF, and is located in the reward center of the brain (e.g., amygdala and ventral striatum). Thus, people with higher levels of BDNF do not cope with stressful events as effectively as those with lower levels of BDNF. This example of biological influences on our behavior is one of many efforts highlighting behavioral differences in people based on

This QR code will direct you to the homepage of the Meyers Briggs Foundation, where you will be able to learn more about issues of personality and its link to organizational communication.

http://www.myersbriggs.org/

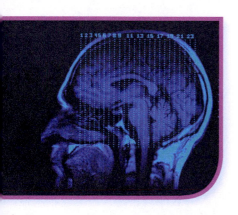

differences in brain activity. Let's move from this technologically advanced approach to assessing employee behavior and employee selection (e.g., fMRI assessment) to older and less technological approaches.

The need to predict and make sense of human behavior has long been an important aspect of civilization. Although rare in today's corporate world, there are still some old methods that separate prospective employees who are believed to possess the qualities of a productive worker from those of the unproductive.

Japanese Blood Typing

In Japan, **blood typing** is an assessment method that assigns particular personality characteristics based on a person's blood (Shintaku, 2006). For example, **blood type A** is associated with people who possess deep-rooted strength and are steady in times of crisis. They are also seen as responsible, they desire perfection, and they are the most artistic of the blood types. However, they are also seen as shy and tending to avoid conflict. **Blood type B** is the most practical of the blood types. These people direct all their attention to tasks and follow their goals until they are achieved. However, they also have a tendency to follow their own rules and ideas, they are individualists, and they follow logic rather than passion. They can also be unconventional in their ways of approaching tasks. The third blood type is **blood type O**. People with type O blood are social, outgoing, and energetic, and they value the opinions of others. However, they are known for giving up easily, being undependable, and speaking their mind without regard to appropriateness. In Japan, type O blood is considered the best blood type. This is culturally consistent in that type O blood is the most common of blood types, and Japanese culture values the idea of concern for the collective whole above concern for the individual. Therefore, the blood types of the "masses" tend to be more appealing to collectivist cultures. **Blood type AB** is considered the least desirable type of blood. Type AB people have both the characteristics of type A and type B blood, meaning that a person can be both outgoing and shy. AB people are trustworthy and responsible yet set their own rules and conditions for tasks. Few people want to work with type AB employees because of potential interpersonal problems stemming from a variable personality (ranging from the positives and negatives of possessing both types A and B blood) and little consistency. It is in this lack of consistency that makes the AB blood type so undesirable. Blood typing is a more primitive physiological assessment of personality than fMRI scanning.

blood typing An assessment method that assigns particular personality characteristics based on a person's blood type.

The Chinese Zodiac

If you have ever gone to a Chinese restaurant, you have probably encountered the **Chinese Zodiac** placemat. This is not simply a "prop" used to give you an authentic Chinese dining experience. Instead, this chronologically based personality assessment is grounded in ancient folklore. According to Chinese legend, Buddha summoned animals from throughout the land and honored them by naming a calendar year after them. The animals were so pleased with this honor that they in turn gave their personality characteristics to people born during their respective years (Chinese Animal Zodiac, 2006). Table 6.2 lists the animals, years of birth, and personality characteristics associated with each animal and birth year.

General Personality Traits

In more contemporary times, researchers are using social science principles to identify global as well as specific personality and communication traits that have become valuable to organizational researchers interested in explaining and predicting employee behavior. Recall from Chapter 2 that management's need to account for employee action as well as coordinate such action to maximize productivity is a fundamental goal of management. The

TABLE 6.2	Chinese Zodiac and Personality Attributes	
Animal	**Year Born**	**Personality characteristics**
Rat	1912, 1924, 1936, 1948, 1960, 1972, 1984, 1996	Charming, goal directed, successful, easily agitated, enjoys gossip
Ox	1913, 1925, 1937, 1949, 1961, 1973, 1985, 1997	Patient, soft spoken, mentally alert, stubborn, bad tempered, dislikes failure
Tiger	1914, 1926, 1938, 1950, 1962, 1974, 1986, 1998	Sensitive, sympathetic, deep thinker, suspicious, quick tempered
Rabbit	1915, 1927, 1939, 1951, 1963, 1975, 1987, 1999	Articulate, ambitious, trusted, enjoys gossip, conservative
Dragon	1916, 1928, 1940, 1952, 1964, 1976, 1988, 2000	Honest, brave, energetic, short tempered, stubborn
Snake	1917, 1929, 1941, 1953, 1965, 1977, 1989, 2001	Sympathetic, financially successful, self-reliant, hates failure, impatient
Horse	1918, 1930, 1942, 1954, 1966, 1978, 1990, 2002	Cheerful, financially skillful, wise, talks too much, impatient
Ram	1919, 1931, 1943, 1955, 1967, 1979, 1991, 2003	Highly accomplished, passionate, wise, pessimistic, shy
Monkey	1920, 1932, 1944, 1956, 1968, 1980, 1992, 2004	Clever, skillful, flexible, looks down on others, stubborn, impulsive
Rooster	1921, 1933, 1945, 1957, 1969, 1981, 1993, 2005	Talented, deep thinking, brave, moody, timid
Dog	1922, 1934, 1946, 1958, 1970, 1982, 1994, 2006	Loyal, honest, good leader, selfish, stubborn, sharp-tongued
Pig	1923, 1935, 1947, 1959, 1971, 1983, 1995, 2007	Honest, well liked, intellectually curious, quick tempered, impulsive

following traits represent some of the most significant personality characteristics that best predict and explain employee behavior. Knowledge of such personality and communication traits can allow management to tailor messages and alter working conditions in an effort to create the most satisfying environment for each worker, which, in turn, should result in higher levels of satisfaction and productivity. These personality traits include authoritarianism, dogmatism, Machiavellianism, and locus of control.

Authoritarianism

Authoritarianism is the predisposition to rely on structure and rules to determine what is right and wrong. High authoritarians respect the power and status given to them by the organization and demand that other people also respect that power and status (Adorno, Frenkel-Brunswik, Levinson, & Sanford, 1950). For example, if you work in an organization where people (especially those in superior positions) are called Dr., Mr., Ms., and so on, your organization values respect for power differences and formality. In addition, your organization probably has a high authoritarian type of organizational structure. Supervisors who prosper in this environment would probably be considered high in authoritarianism because they demand that status differences be recognized in most, if not all, interactions. Authoritarians tend to be suspicious by nature and do not view the organization as a place where people should "enjoy" themselves. In other words, work is a place for working, not playing. This sort of perspective is representative of the scientific management approach (see Chapter 2).

Research indicates that authoritarians, if not in a supervisory position, may have difficulty getting along with coworkers. Authoritarians need to follow the "rule of law." For example, consider people in subordinate positions that spend a good part of the workday engaged in non-organizationally sanctioned behaviors such as surfing the Internet, sending personal e-mails, developing personal friendships with coworkers, spending time trying to increase opportunities for individual growth to the neglect of job responsibilities, or simply attempting to get away with as much as they can without getting caught by management. Authoritarians would be angered by these behaviors because they see them as deviating from the employees' official job descriptions and detracting from the organization's mission.

Dogmatism

A trait similar to authoritarianism is **dogmatism**. A dogmatic person is often rigid in his or her belief system on what constitutes right and wrong. This is not the same as the rules that authoritarians use to determine right and wrong. In contrast to authoritarians, dogmatics are unwilling to consider the viewpoints of others (Rokeach, 1960). You have probably worked for a person who believed that she knew everything and you knew nothing. This person probably believed that the only correct and proper views are similar or identical to her own. The high dogmatic supervisor believes in the "my way or the highway" philosophy of management. If you are a high dogmatic subordinate, or if you someday manage a high dogmatic subordinate, you can expect an employee who may resist orders unless the orders are consistent with the subordinate's own worldview.

Research suggests that people who are high dogmatics are also high authoritarians, have a strong tendency to accept traditional ways of doing things, and resist changes in societal practices (Henkel, Sheehan, & Reichel, 1997; Kazlow, 1977; Levin & Spates, 1968). Further, in a study looking at the quality of message exchange between superior and subordinates, Fiechtner and Krayer (1986) found that high dogmatic group members focused their attention on the quality of the task-focused information (i.e., information targeted at completing the task) rather than the quantity of information. This finding illustrates that high dogmatics tend to scrutinize information to determine whether it fits their belief system and that they value efficient communication designed for optimal task accomplishment.

If you are a highly dogmatic person, developing skills to curb your rigid views of the world and developing the ability to consider alternative views will serve you well. If you are dealing with a highly dogmatic subordinate or supervisor, focus on the things you agree on and give less attention to areas of disagreement; focusing on disagreement only fosters a winless argument and animosity between you and the other person.

Machiavellianism

Have you ever worked for someone who would lie, cheat, and/or steal to get a desired reward? These people tend to do whatever it takes to obtain something they want. This personality trait is known as **Machiavellianism**, which is based on the ideas of Niccolo Machiavelli (1469–1527). Machiavelli wrote a book titled *The Prince* that focused on what royalty must know and do if it is to become successful. Although Machiavelli wrote this book centuries ago, the concepts are alive and well in contemporary society. Consider U.S. presidential candidates, who are surrounded by people who advise them on how to dress, what to say, how to say it, when to say it, and to whom to say it. These sorts of advisors are known as *king makers.* Our society almost demands that people, to succeed in corporate America and get elected public service, "bend" the truth. Consider advice given to graduating students by career service departments at every university and college campus throughout the United States. In preparing students for professional life, students are told how to dress, what to say, how to say it, when to say it, and to whom to say it.

Machiavellianism is the tendency to do whatever it takes to achieve a desired goal. Simply put, *the end justifies the means.* An employee high in Machiavellianism (also known as a *high mach*) will do whatever it takes to be successful. Success, in this case, can take the form of closing the sale, avoiding getting caught for some action, getting a promotion, making sure people donate money to a cause, etc. Some would argue that people who are higher Machiavellians are questionable in moral character, although this is not necessarily true. Higher machs are good in people professions such as sales, marketing, advertising, public relations, and journalism.

Research indicates that retail store managers who are high in Machiavellianism have greater job performance in a loosely structured work environment than in a highly structured work environment (Gable, Hollon, & Dangello, 1992). The loosely structured work environment allows more leeway for the high mach to strategize and manipulate toward success, whereas a highly structured environment minimizes opportunities to strategize and manipulate. In a study looking at the relationship between Machiavellianism, credibility, and motivation, Jason Teven, James McCroskey, and Virginia Richmond (2006) found that employees who reported working for a high mach supervisor saw the supervisor as less credible and less liked than non-high mach supervisors, and employees of high mach supervisors showed lower motivation and lower job satisfaction than those who worked for non-high mach supervisors. Investigating motivation, Becker and O'Hair (2007) found that workers who are high machs are concerned with impression management (i.e., making sure they create and maintain a desired impression in the eyes of others to achieve personal gain) significantly more than they are concerned for the values of their organization or society at large. Research specific to communication motives (i.e., communicating for pleasure, affection, inclusion, relaxation, control, and escape) revealed that high machs communicate to relax, escape, and control and are less concerned with the need for affectionate communication. As indicated throughout these research findings, high machs perceive, feel, and behave in ways that serve a desired, self-defined end.

Locus of Control

How employees interpret success or failure in their work lives directly relates to their degree of effectiveness and level of production. **Locus of control** is the way in which people interpret outcomes in their lives as being due to forces beyond their control or to their own actions (Rotter, 1966). The most basic distinction is between an **internal locus of control** and an **external locus of control**. People with an internal locus of control view outcomes in their life as due to their own purposeful actions, whereas people with an external locus of control believe that chance, luck, fate, or powerful other factors (e.g., their boss) are responsible for outcomes (Lefcourt, 1981).

These control expectancies are believed to be a learned behavior (Bandura, 1977). That is, we are conditioned by those around us (e.g., parents, mentors, supervisors) on how to interpret life events. The interpretation of these expectations for control becomes a self-perpetuating reinforcement cycle. For example, once you are trained to see things as beyond your control, all events will be interpreted as such.

Although locus of control concerns how people see things in their lives in general, people also develop control expectancies with regard to specific domains of their lives. For the purposes of this chapter, we are referring to

work-specific locus of control, which focuses on how people interpret events in the workplace (Spector, 1982, 1988). For example, consider two employees who receive the same promotion. The employee with an **internal work locus of control** will likely interpret the promotion as the result of hard work that has been recognized by management and duly rewarded. The employee who exhibits an **external work locus of control** will interpret the promotion as a matter of luck (e.g., "the boss likes me," "my prayers were answered"). As this example illustrates, people who see themselves as proactive agents in their success (i.e., internal control orientation) climb the corporate ladder faster than those who believe external forces are responsible for outcomes (Lefcourt, 1981).

In general, research indicates that people with an external locus of control are more persuaded and compliant than internals (Lefcourt, 1981), suffer more communication apprehension (i.e., fear of communicating) (McCroskey, Daly, & Sorensen, 1976), are more verbally aggressive and less argumentative (Avtgis & Rancer, 1997), and use more avoidant behavior and/or sarcasm during interpersonal conflict (Canary, Cunningham, & Cody, 1988). Within the organization, locus of control has also been found to significantly affect worker behavior. For example, Lilly and Virick (2006) found that workers with an internal locus of control report receiving increased levels of organizational support, procedural justice (i.e., belief that policies are enforced equally among all employees), and trust in their organization. Positive outcomes associated with an internal work locus of control also include job satisfaction (Luck, 2004) and a better quality work life (Rosen, 2000).

You may have already concluded that it is beneficial to develop an internal work locus of control orientation. However, internalizing all failure can be detrimental to a person's mental health. For example, think of a person who is passed over for a promotion. In this event, the employee with internal control expectancies may blame stable internal forces (e.g., "I am not smart enough," or "I am not management material"). The ideal locus of control profile would involve attributing success to **internal-stable factors** such as intelligence, drive, and character. Internal-stable factors do not change in a person. In contrast, an ideal locus of control profile attributes failures to **internal-unstable factors** such as motivation, hesitation, or lack of networking. Internal-unstable factors can be changed. By attributing failures to factors that can be changed (e.g., don't hesitate next time an opportunity arises, or start forming better networks), a person has the opportunity to achieve success in the future and maintain a sense of control over future outcomes.

Communication Conflict-Related Traits

There are clusters of specific communication traits that directly impact how we address workplace conflict. The experience of conflict in the organization, as evidenced by anyone who has been employed, affects every worker and pervades every workplace. Our ability to confront or avoid conflict can be directly influenced by our predisposition to communicate. More specifically, the communication traits of verbal aggressiveness, argumentativeness, taking conflict personally, and tolerance for disagreement are believed to strongly influence our behavior in the organization.

Verbal Aggressiveness

Not a day goes by that we don't read or hear about some sort of verbal abuse within the workplace. The workplace is increasingly becoming an uncivil environment in which people backstab each other in order to climb the corporate ladder. Consider TV shows such as *The Apprentice,* which pits talented executives against each other in an attempt to find out which one will "survive" the game. Survival in this case often involves abusive and destructive forms of communication. Are people doing this because it is required for success, or are they doing this because it is part of their personality? The answer is probably a mixture of both. A communication trait that encompasses terms such as *verbal bullying, intimidating communication, aggressive communication,* and *verbal abuse* is **verbal aggressiveness**.

Verbal aggressiveness is a predisposition to attack the self-concept of another person with the intent to inflict psychological harm or pain (Infante & Wigley, 1986). Verbal aggressiveness is a subset of hostility in that all verbal aggression is hostile but not all hostility involves verbal aggression. There are several reasons for verbal aggressiveness in the workplace. One explanation lies in the **temperament** of the person. This explanation holds that people are, or are not, verbally aggressive because they are biologically programmed to be that way. Our neurobiological circuitry influences the degree to which we are activated (angered) in different situations. Consider a supervisor who is always losing his temper no matter whom he is speaking with or what issue he is speaking about. This supervisor's aggressive behavior, according to the biological explanation, is rooted in his biology, not his psychology.

Another potential cause of verbal aggressiveness is **disdain**. This explanation holds that people use verbal aggression when they have a deep-seated dislike for a person. Generally speaking, however, if we have such a great dislike for someone, we would probably avoid him or her. In the case of disdain for a supervisor, we would probably ask for a transfer or quit. The **psychopathology** explanation of verbal aggressiveness contends that we carry repressed hostility from a past traumatic experience. When we are faced with a similar situation, we attack the person for the pain caused by the past experience as well as for the present situation. For example, if you had a terrible work experience with a supervisor years ago and encounter a supervisor who behaves similarly, you may verbally attack this person for perceived injustices done to you by a previous supervisor.

The final two explanations of verbal aggressiveness are **social learning** and **skills deficiency**. The social learning explanation assumes that we learn to use, or not use, verbal aggression in the workplace based on whether the

verbal aggressiveness A predisposition to attack the self-concept of another person with the intent to inflict psychological harm or pain.

behavior reaps a reward or a punishment. For example, if we see an employee use verbal aggression with a supervisor and reap some benefit from doing so (e.g., promotion, extra time off), we learn that aggressive behavior is rewarded. However, if we see an employee verbally attack a supervisor and the employee is reprimanded or terminated, we learn not to be verbally aggressive because such behavior has negative consequences.

The final explanation for verbal aggressiveness is skills deficiency. This explanation assumes that when an employee lacks the ability to make arguments, whether due to a lack of education or a general cognitive inability to generate arguments, this person can become frustrated and resort to personal attacks. Further, as part of the theory of independent mindedness (discussed in Chapter 2), teaching employees how to argue may reduce their tendency to use verbal aggression (Rancer & Avtgis, 2006).

What exactly constitutes a verbally aggressive attack? There are several forms of verbally aggressive communication, including **competence attacks** (attacking someone's inability to do something), **character attacks** (attacking someone for poor character, such as "You're a cheater!"), **profanity** (using obscene words and generally vulgar language), **teasing and ridicule** (making light of someone's shortcomings in an antagonistic fashion), **maledictions** (using phrases that wish someone harm), **threats** (insinuating physical or psychological harm to another person), **personality attacks** (attacking characteristics of the person's personality), and **nonverbal verbal aggression** (using nonverbal gestures to intimidate or humiliate another person). Any use of one or a combination of these message behaviors constitutes a verbally aggressive attack. People who are high in trait verbal aggressiveness use a greater variety and frequency of these messages than people who are low in verbal aggressiveness.

Research findings on verbal aggression in the workplace overwhelmingly endorse the notion that verbal aggression is destructive to the employee and the organization as a whole. Research indicates that employees who have a supervisor who is high in verbal aggressiveness report being less satisfied, less committed, and more frustrated on the job (see Infante & Rancer, 1996). Further, employees who are high in verbal aggressiveness report higher levels of burnout and use more displaced dissent (complaining to people outside the organization) and less articulated dissent (speaking directly to the boss about the problematic issue) than employees low in trait verbal aggressiveness (Avtgis, Thomas-Maddox, Taylor, & Patterson, 2007; Kassing & Avtgis, 1999). In short, if you tend to be high in verbal aggressiveness, work hard to curb your tendency to attack your coworkers' self-concept because doing so can cost you a promotion, a job, and/or friendships and may escalate a verbally aggressive encounter into a physically aggressive exchange. How verbally aggressive are you? Log on to the course website and complete the Verbal Aggressiveness Scale to determine your tendency to attack others' self-concept.

Argumentativeness

In contemporary American culture, people seem to be losing their ability to debate issues without resorting to personal attacks. In fact, if you ask any 10 people if they enjoy interpersonal conflict or arguing, it is likely that at least eight will respond "no." One of the primary reasons for this response is our inability to distinguish between discussing issues of difference and verbally attacking the person who disagrees with us. Conflict, by nature, should be a welcomed opportunity to work through areas of disagreement between two people. In contemporary society we are bombarded by media images reinforcing that conflict is painful and should be avoided, even if avoidance means psychological pain for all parties involved. Conflict and conflict resolution should be a growth opportunity for all parties and, as such, should be interpreted in a positive light. The next several communication traits concern the spectrum of conflict communication, from productive and constructive to unproductive and destructive.

The tendency to enjoy and appreciate an exchange of different ideas and debate is determined by biology as well as socially learned behavior. This concept is known as the **interactionist perspective of personality**. The tendency to approach or avoid arguing with others is termed **argumentativeness**. Argumentativeness is defined as a tendency to present and defend positions on controversial issues while simultaneously attacking the positions of others on those issues (Infante & Rancer, 1982). The focus of effective arguing is on *refuting the position* of the other person as opposed to *refuting the person*. Every person ranges from very low to very high in his or her **general tendency to argue** (ARGgt). This tendency to argue is composed of the degree to which we approach argumentative situations (**argument approach**, or ARGap) and the degree to which we avoid argumentative situations (**argument avoid**, or ARGav). This results in the following formula:

$$ARGgt = ARGap - ARGav$$

argumentativeness
The tendency to present and defend positions on controversial issues while simultaneously attacking the positions that others take on those issues.

People high in trait argumentativeness have a high approach tendency and a low avoidance tendency and, therefore, possess a high general tendency to argue. On the other hand, people low in trait argumentativeness have a low approach tendency and a high avoidance tendency and, therefore, possess a low general tendency to argue. Figure 6.1 shows both the approach and avoidance dimensions of argumentativeness.

Argumentativeness is a subset of **assertiveness** in that all argumentative behavior is assertive but not all assertiveness involves argument. Assertiveness is defined as a tendency to assert one's rights when a perceived wrong or injustice has occurred. Given that the ability to argue is a valued skill in the organization as well as the culture at large, argumentativeness is considered a constructive trait because it leads to many beneficial outcomes. Recall the theory of independent mindedness (discussed in Chapter 2). One of the basic assumptions of the theory is that training all organizational members (i.e., superiors and subordinates) in argumentation will have

FIGURE 6.1
Approach-avoidance motivations of the trait argumentativeness model.

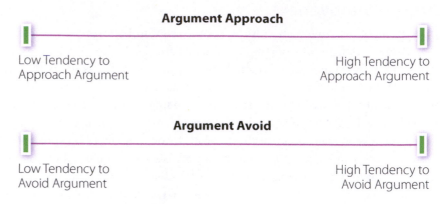

Argument Approach

Low Tendency to
Approach Argument

High Tendency to
Approach Argument

Argument Avoid

Low Tendency to
Avoid Argument

High Tendency to
Avoid Argument

bottom-line effects for the organization (Avtgis & Rancer, 2007). Other positive organizational outcomes associated with increased argumentativeness include greater feelings of employee voice and freedom of speech (Gorden, Infante, & Graham, 1988), greater use of articulated dissent strategies (i.e., going directly to your boss to discuss issues or difficulties you are experiencing) (Kassing & Avtgis, 1999), greater levels of subordinate work satisfaction (Gorden & Infante, 1987), and less tendency to suffer workplace burnout syndrome, which is characterized by feelings of failure, emotional exhaustion, and an interpersonal disconnect from others (Avtgis et al., 2007).

Although research shows that increased levels of argumentativeness are associated with positive organizational outcomes, there is also a gender effect. Shullery (1998) found that the optimal level of argumentativeness for women in the workplace is a moderate level of argumentativeness, whereas for men, high levels of argumentativeness appear to be most beneficial (Rancer & Avtgis, 2006; Shullery, 1998, 1999). Regardless of this gender effect, argumentativeness is a positive trait to possess and display because it results in numerous positive organizational outcomes. What is your level of argumentativeness? Log on to the course website and complete the Argumentativeness Scale to determine your tendency to attack others' positions on controversial issues.

Taking Conflict Personally

taking conflict personally (TCP) A communication trait that refers to the degree to which people view conflict as a punishing situation and something that should be avoided.

The communication conflict trait of **taking conflict personally (TCP)** refers to the degree to which people view conflict as a punishing situation and something that should be avoided. TCP is considered a trait in that people tend to experience negative consequences when engaged in conflict across a wide range of people and issues. In this light, TCP "refers to a general level of readiness to take conflict personally" (Hample & Dallinger, 1995, p. 306). The interpretation of conflict can range from an enjoyable experience to one of punishment. Therefore, people differ in their predisposition to being tolerant, trusting, self-interested, self-confident, generous in their attributions, and either more or less easily hurt when involved in a conflict situation.

Dale Hample and Judith Dallinger (1995) believe that TCP is recursive in nature. That is, negative feelings in the face of conflict can be manifest in avoidant or aggressive behavior that brings about a similar response from other people. The trait of TCP contains six dimensions related to conflict episodes: **Direct personalization** is the bad feelings people experience when in a conflict episode; **persecution feelings** are the feelings that one is being personally attacked when engaged in conflict; **stress reaction** is the psychological and physical discomfort a person experiences in a conflict episode; **positive relational effects** is the belief that conflict is positive and results in better quality relationships; **negative relational effects** is the belief that conflict is negative and only leads to damaged relationships; **like/dislike valence** is the degree to which people enjoy or do not enjoy engaging in interpersonal conflict.

Research shows that people who report feeling personally attacked, persecuted, and stressed and who perceive negative outcomes during conflict also report avoiding arguments with others as well as avoiding discussion of controversial issues. Within the organization, employees who report high levels of direct personalization, persecuted feelings, and stress reaction also report using nonconfrontational conflict styles. In other words, these employees use conflict styles that are more avoidant in nature than actually openly confronting the specific issue of conflict (Dallinger, 1991). Further, subordinates who report high levels of persecution feelings reported that their supervisor "forced the conflict issues" on them, which means they see themselves in an almost powerless or victimized position (Dallinger, 1991).

As these and other studies indicate, internalization of conflict leads to the belief that confronting any conflict episode, regardless of the issue or the people involved, is seen as inappropriate. Employees who are high in TCP also report lower levels of satisfaction with their supervisor and lower levels of communication competence (Barch & Dallinger, 1995; Hample & Dallinger, 1993). What is your level of taking conflict personally? Log on to the course website and complete the Taking Conflict Personally measure to determine the ways in which you personalize conflict.

Tolerance for Disagreement

Tolerance for disagreement (TFD) is defined as "the amount of disagreement an individual can tolerate before he or she perceives the existence of conflict in a relationship" (Richmond, McCroskey, & McCroskey, 2005, p. 178). TFD was originally developed by James McCroskey and Lawrence Wheeless (1976) and later expanded (Knutson, McCroskey, Knutson, & Hurt, 1979). Most conflict research relies on a unidimensional continuum that ranges from good conflict to bad conflict. McCroskey and Wheeless (1976) distinguished between **disagreement**, which is a difference of opinion on issues, and **conflict**, which involves competition, suspicion, distrust, hostility, and self-perpetuation.

tolerance for disagreement (TFD) A communication trait reflecting the amount of disagreement a person can tolerate before he or she perceives the existence of conflict in a relationship.

Although TFD was conceptualized as a product of the interaction and as relationship specific, Knutson et al. (1979) argued that because of each individual's unique interpretation of disagreement and conflict, these interpretations are cross-contextual and, thus, should be considered traitlike. More specifically, they argued that treating TFD as a trait allows us to account for why some people see conflict sooner than others. The distinction between disagreement and conflict is similar to the distinction between argument and verbal aggression, respectively (McCroskey, 2006). That is, argument (as well as trait argumentativeness) is considered constructive, whereas verbal aggression (as well as trait verbal aggressiveness) is considered destructive. All disagreement is considered constructive and all conflict is considered destructive to the relationship. The TFD trait is also influenced by situational factors, such as a low degree of affinity (liking) between the people involved in the disagreement. These situational triggers are similar to the situational triggers identified for verbally aggressive behavior (Wigley, 2006).

People who are high in TFD are reluctant to engage in conflict, whereas people low in TFD are more likely to engage in conflict across a wide range of relationships regardless of the specific subject of disagreement. These differences are based on a person's threshold at which disagreement transforms into conflict. This consistency in tendency to engage in either disagreement or conflict is rooted in the larger supertrait of assertiveness (which contains disagreement) and hostility (which involves conflict). Figure 6.2 illustrates the thresholds of disagreement and conflict.

Virginia Richmond and James McCroskey (1979) investigated the extent to which employee satisfaction related to both the employee's and supervisor's level of TFD. The findings indicated that employee satisfaction, which involves satisfaction with supervisor, work, and pay, was influenced more by the supervisor's TFD than by the employee's TFD. Therefore, the greater the supervisor's level of tolerance for disagreement, the more satisfied the employee. Further evidence reveals that TFD is also related to cognitive

This QR code will direct you to the Tolerance for Disagreement Scale, developed by Teven, Richmond, and McCroskey (1998), which helps highlight the role of disagreement during argumentation.

http://www.jamescmccroskey.com/measures/tfd.htm

FIGURE 6.2
Thresholds of Disagreement and Conflict.

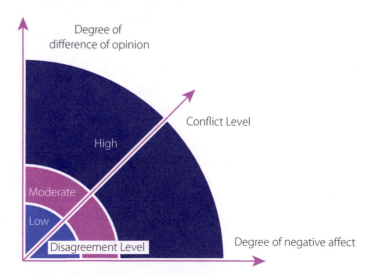

flexibility (Martin, Anderson, & Thweatt, 1998) in that "the flexible communicator appeared to be willing to argue and disagree with others. These individuals tend to approach arguments and do not avoid confrontations where there may be a difference of opinions" (Teven, McCroskey, & Richmond, 1998, p. 212). Log on to the course website and determine your tolerance for disagreement.

Competence-Related Traits

Just as some traits can have negative effects on behavior, other communication traits can have beneficial effects on behavior. The concept of communication competence refers to a person's ability to be both effective and appropriate in any given situation. Communication competence encompasses flexibility in thoughts, emotions, and behaviors to adapt successfully to a particular situation. For example, any competent supervisor will be able to adapt communication to the particular needs of the employee. The three most important communication traits that comprise a competent communicator are communicator style, cognitive flexibility, and communicative adaptability.

Communicator Style

The **communicator style** construct (CS) (Norton, 1978, 1983) is believed to be a significant factor in determining the quality of superior-subordinate relationships. The CS trait holds that people have stylistic differences and these differences between people are cross-contextual or carried across situations (i.e., our communication style is a trait). Communicator style is defined as "the way one verbally and paraverbally interacts to signal how literal meaning should be taken, interpreted, filtered, or understood" (Norton, 1978, p. 99). The construct contains 10 dimensions or substyles of interaction: **dominant** (communicating in a way to gain control of a situation), **dramatic** (communicating in a way that exaggerates information), **contentious** (communicating in an antagonistic and confrontational way), **impression leaving** (communicating in a unique fashion that leads others to remember you by your interaction style), **animated** (using physical and nonverbal behaviors extensively when interacting with others), **relaxed** (communicating in a way that reflects a lack of anxiety), **open** (interacting in a spontaneous and extroverted fashion), **attentive** (communicating in a way that suggests interest and involvement in a conversation), **precise** (interacting in a way that focuses on correctness and accuracy), and **friendly** (communicating in a way that shows increased intimacy). Collectively, these substyles combine to produce the **communicator image**, or the degree to which a person is seen as a competent and effective communicator. As discussed in Chapter 2, particular combinations of communicator style dimensions can be either prosocial or antisocial in nature. Particular combinations of styles either validate the self-concept of the other person (i.e., an affirming style)

communicator style A trait reflecting how a person verbally and paraverbally interacts with others.

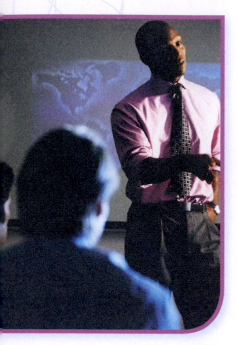

cognitive flexibility The degree to which a communicator considers options for behaving in different situations, as well as enacts the correct behavioral option in accordance with the situation at hand.

or threaten the other person's self-concept (i.e., nonaffirming style). The difference between these styles has been explored in general interpersonal relationships as well as within superior-subordinate dyads. An affirming style is reflected in communication that supports the face of both the supervisor and the subordinate (i.e., communication that shows that people are respected and valued by both interactants as well as the organization). The subcluster of relaxed, friendly, and attentive communication styles constitutes an affirming communicator style.

Earlier in this chapter, we presented research indicating the productive outcomes associated with trait argumentativeness. However, some research shows that, in certain cases, argumentativeness can be interpreted as a threatening form of communication (Rancer, 1995). Therefore, it is believed that displaying an affirming communicator style while engaging in argumentative communication allows people to engage in argumentative behavior while concomitantly benefiting from positive relational perceptions and outcomes as opposed to relationally damaging outcomes (Rancer & Avtgis, 2006). That is, when we argue with another person, the style in which we engage greatly influences the receiver (i.e., are we being prosocial and assertive or antisocial and aggressive?). Log on to the course website to see what type of communicator style you possess.

Cognitive Flexibility

The trait of **cognitive flexibility** was developed by Matthew Martin and Rebecca Rubin (1995), who defined cognitive flexibility as the degree to which communicators are "able to adapt their communication to meet the demands of the situations, and perhaps more importantly, to consider options and alternative ways of behaving in different situations" (Martin, Anderson, & Thweatt, 1998, p. 531). It is believed that people are aware of options and alternatives for behavior in any given situation, are motivated to be flexible in any given situation, and believe they have the ability to be successful in adapting to the situation at hand. Thus, someone who is high in cognitive flexibility can identify and enact a variety of behaviors as mandated by the situation. It is important to emphasize that not only must people be aware that they have behavioral options from which to choose, but they must also believe they can successfully enact those behaviors (i.e., self-efficacy). For example, consider someone who is well traveled and has a significant amount of intellectual training. This person probably has a wealth of behavioral options from which to choose in adapting to any given situation. However, if this person suffers from communication apprehension or the fear of communicating, he lacks the confidence to enact these behaviors and, thus, appears rigid or inflexible.

Flexibility in any given situation is an important factor in competent communication (Parks, 1994). In fact, cognitive flexibility has been positively associated with communication competence (Rubin & Martin, 1994). That is, as people's cognitive flexibility increases, so, too, does their level of communication competence.

In terms of relating cognitive flexibility to argumentative and aggressive communication traits, Martin, Anderson, and Thweatt (1998) found that the trait of argumentativeness was positively related to cognitive flexibility. That is, the greater tendency a person has to approach arguments, the more cognitively flexible that person is. Conversely, people who report greater trait verbal aggressiveness report having less cognitive flexibility. This study clearly indicates that cognitively flexible people are more adept at creating arguments that are appropriate to the particular issue or situation at hand and have decreased tendency toward verbal aggressiveness. Similarly, indirect interpersonal aggression (e.g., spreading rumors about another person, purposely not relaying important information to another person, intentionally jamming the copy machine to slow a coworker's production) appears to be related to cognitive flexibility. Chesbro and Martin (2003) found that people who are highly flexible use indirect interpersonal aggression more than people who are less flexible. That is, highly flexible people are more likely to spread rumors, withhold important information, betray confidences, and so on. Highly cognitively flexible people may not resort to overt verbal aggression because they know they can reach desired goals without resorting to a direct aggressive exchange and that direct aggressive exchanges are more face threatening than simply "working behind the scenes" to achieve their goals. However, indirect interpersonal aggression is within the realm of an aggressive personality (Rancer & Avtgis, 2006).

Cognitive flexibility is a critical factor in the larger construct of communication competence (Parks, 1994) and concerns higher level of thought (i.e., executive brain function) and greater ability to make appropriate and effective cognitive and behavioral alterations during a communication encounter. The cognitive flexibility trait will continue to aid researchers in understanding how people with higher order cognitive function and/or greater critical thinking skills adapt to a variety of organizational situations. Complete the Cognitive Flexibility Scale on the course website and determine your level of cognitive flexibility.

Communicative Adaptability

The **communicative adaptability** trait was originally developed as a way to integrate several dimensions of communication competence. Robert Duran (1992) defined communicative adaptability as "the ability to perceive socio-interpersonal relationships and adapt one's interaction goals and behaviors accordingly" (p. 320). The basic premise is that the greater a person's repertoire of social skills, the more he or she is able to display a successful communicative performance. Therefore, communicative adaptability is a conceptualization of social communication competence.

communicative adaptability The ability to perceive sociointerpersonal relationships and adapt interaction goals and interpersonal behaviors.

Communicative adaptability consists of six dimensions that are closely related to aspects of communication competence: **social composure, social confirmation, social experience, appropriate disclosure, articulation,** and **wit** (Duran, 1992). Social composure is the degree to which a person is calm, cool, and collected in social situations. Social confirmation is the degree to which a person can affirm or maintain the other person's face or self-image while interacting. Social experience is the degree to which a person actually experiences, or is willing to experience, novel situations. Appropriate disclosure is the degree to which a person reveals personal information in the appropriate amount as dictated by any given social situation. Articulation is the degree to which a person is proficient or skilled in the expression of ideas. Articulation includes the level of language mastery, such as appropriate syntax and semantic elements. The wit dimension reflects the degree to which a person uses humor in appropriate situations to diffuse escalating aggressive communication exchanges. As can be seen by the different dimensions of communicative adaptability, sociocommunication competence comprises psychological factors (social composure and social experience), sociological factors (appropriate disclosure and social confirmation), and communication factors (articulation and wit).

Results indicate that communicative adaptability is a causal factor in satisfaction with roommate relationships (Duran & Zakahi, 1988) and is related to interpersonal assertiveness (Zakahi, 1985). In a study of communicative adaptability and attractiveness, Robert Duran and Lynne Kelly (1985) found that the more adaptive people are, the more cognitively complex they are (they are able to develop multiple categories for describing abstract as well as concrete ideas). Further, adaptability is also linked to greater levels of interaction involvement (another communication competence-based construct that reflects the degree to which people are cognitively and behaviorally engaged in interpersonal interactions) (Duran & Kelly, 1988).

Focusing on the psychological trait of locus of control, Theodore Avtgis and Scott Myers (1996) found that people with an internal locus of control orientation (people who interpret outcomes in their lives as being a function of their own purposeful action) reported greater adaptability than people with an external locus of control (people who see outcomes in their lives as being due to chance, fate, or other people). More specifically, internally oriented people are more socially composed and have more social experience than externally oriented people. Recall that the cognitive flexibility trait requires that people believe they have control over their behavior and can successfully execute a given behavior. We can conclude from the Avtgis and Myers study that the belief in control over behavior (self-efficacy) is an important aspect of communicative adaptability.

Duran and Zakahi (1984) found communicative adaptability to be highly related to the communicator style construct. Their findings revealed that these two traits, when combined, form three "super traits." That is, all six dimensions of the communicative adaptability trait and the 10 dimensions from the communicator style trait, when combined, form three larger dimensions of *self-confidence, affect,* and *entertainment* (Duran & Zakahi, 1984).

In an effort to find a genetic basis for communicative adaptability, Michael Beatty, Lenora Marshall, and Jill Rudd (2001) administered the Communicative Adaptability Scale (CAS) to identical twins (monozygotic twin pairs) and fraternal twins (dizygotic twin pairs). The researchers hypothesized that monozygotic twin pairs are genetically identical whereas as dizygotic twins are about 50 percent genetically identical. The overall findings of this research indicate that the CAS dimension of social composure is 88 percent heritable, wit is 90 percent heritable, and social confirmation is 36 percent heritable. The other dimensions were found not to have a genetic basis.

The trait of communicative adaptability provides researchers in communication studies a trait that is considered a social competence and is generally stable over a variety of situations. Although there is overlap among communicative adaptability with other competence-related and adaptive traits, communicative adaptability is unique in that it encompasses cognitive, affective, and behavioral dimensions of competence. This is especially important in today's organizations because appropriate and effective behaviors are highly valued yet are ever-changing as the definition of appropriate organizational behavior changes. How adaptive are you? Log on to the course website and complete the Communicative Adaptability Survey to determine your type of adaptive behavior.

Summary

Throughout this chapter we have highlighted the importance of personality to an individual's organizational success. The conceptualizations of personality discussed in this chapter come to us from the Far East (China and Japan) as well as from more contemporary Western social science conceptions of personality and communication traits. Some of the personality characteristics in this chapter reflect differences in how people interpret events as well as how people behave in different ways to achieve the same goals. One theme that pervades all communication traits discussed in this chapter is that to be competent, one must engage in competent communication. Whether communication is conflict based or relationship building based, it must be done appropriately and effectively. The inability to develop these interpersonal skills (e.g., adaptability skills, argumentative skills) can affect employees negatively. An important point of this chapter is that we cannot be fully satisfied in the workplace if we cannot be ourselves. Therefore, we must strive to ensure that our chosen career matches our personality. If our chosen career is inconsistent with how we are programmed to behave, work is cumbersome and nothing more than a mandatory series of unpleasant tasks. Thus, the idea of worker/work congruity (i.e., who they are = what they do) is as important as worker skillset/job congruity (i.e., what they can do/what they actually do). This is known as **personality/task congruity**.

Imagine choosing a career that matches your personality. Chances are you will experience a wonderfully rewarding career and think, "I can't believe I am getting paid for doing something I enjoy!" You probably know several people who experience high levels of personality/task congruity. These people are probably happy with their position, their level of success, and their organization. On the other hand, most people "simply exist" in a career because they are too afraid of making a change that will correct the personality/task mismatch. It is important to understand your own personality and how it matches (or does not match) your present or future career opportunities. All people possess both positive and negative personality characteristics. Through embracing your traits, understanding the positive and negative impact of these traits on organizational life will help you establish personality/task congruity.

Questions for Discussion and Review

1. What is a personality trait? Explain how the Myers-Briggs Type Indicator assesses personality types. Do you think organizations should evaluate personality types as a process for screening job applicants? Explain your answer.

2. Based on the Chinese Zodiac, what animal are you? How well does this represent your personality? Argue your position on whether you believe this method of personality typing has merit.

3. Explain the characteristics of a dogmatic individual. How might this person be difficult to get along with in the workplace? Explain your answer.

4. Argue why it is believed that individuals who are high Machiavellians are often in management positions. Describe the behaviors of a person who is a high Machiavellian.

5. Explain the difference between internal and external locus of control. Which type of control is preferred in the workplace? Which do you believe fits your personality type? Explain your answer.

6. Define verbal aggressiveness. How might a person high in verbal aggressiveness be difficult to get along with in the workplace? Give three examples of verbally aggressive behaviors in the workplace.

7. List and explain why (as discussed in the chapter) individuals engage in verbally aggressive behaviors.

8. Define argumentativeness. Why is this considered a desirable communication trait?

9. Why is it important to display an affirming communicator style when being assertive? Can you be assertive without displaying an affirming communicator style?

10. Of the 10 communicator style characteristics, which of these best characterizes your communicator image? Discuss the benefits and negative aspects of your particular communicator image.

11. If we assume that traits can be influenced by both environment and biology, what advice would you give to a subordinate to make him or her more communicatively flexible?

12. Given that communicative adaptability concerns the ability to change one's interaction behavior to fit the situation, do you think a person can overcompensate for his or her behavior? Give an example.

13. Why do you think people internalize/personalize conflict? Do you think a person can be trained to interpret conflict differently? If so, how?

References

Adorno, T., Frenkel-Brunswick, E., Levinson, D., & Sanford, R. (1950). *The authoritarian personality.* New York: Harper & Row.

Avtgis, T. A., & Myers, S. A. (1996, November). Perceived control and communicative adaptability: How outlook on life influences ability to change. Paper presented at the annual meeting of the *Speech Communication Association,* San Diego.

Avtgis, T. A., & Rancer, A. S. (1997). Argumentativeness and verbal aggressiveness as a function of locus of control. *Communication Research Reports, 14,* 441–450.

Avtgis, T. A., & Rancer, A. S. (2007). The theory of independent mindedness: An organizational theory for individualistic cultures. In M. Hinner (Ed.), *Freiberger beitrage zur interkulturellen und wirtschaftskommunikation: A forum for general and intercultural business communication* (pp.183–201). Frankfurt: Peter Lang.

Avtgis, T. A., Thomas-Maddox, C., Taylor, E., & Patterson, B. P. (2007). The influence of organizational burnout syndrome on the expression of organizational dissent. *Communication Research Reports, 24,* 1–6.

Bandura, A. (1977). *Social learning theory.* Englewood Cliffs, NJ: Prentice Hall.

Barch, S. L., & Dallinger, J. M. (1995, May). Assessing HMO CEOs' communication competence and propensity to take conflict personally. Paper presented at the annual meeting of the *International Communication Association,* Albuquerque.

Beatty, M. J., Marshall, L. A., & Rudd, J. E. (2001). A twin study of communicative adaptability: Heritability of individual differences. *Quarterly Journal of Speech, 87,* 366–377.

Becker, J. H., & O'Hair, D. H. (2007). Machiavellians' motives in organizational citizenship behavior. *Journal of Applied Communication Research, 35,* 246–267.

Canary, D. J., Cunningham, E. M., & Cody, M. J. (1988). Goal types, gender, and locus of control in managing interpersonal conflict. *Communication Research, 15,* 426–446.

Chesbro, J. L., & Martin, M. M. (2003). The relationship between conversational sensitivity, cognitive flexibility, verbal aggressiveness, and indirect interpersonal aggressiveness. *Communication Research Reports, 20,* 143–150.

Chinese Animal Zodiac. (2006). *Chinese Culture Center of San Francisco.* Retrieved from http://www.c-c-c.org

Dallinger, J. M. (1991, November). Taking conflict personally, conflict resolution strategies and satisfaction in superior-subordinate conflict. Paper presented at the annual meeting of the *Speech Communication Association,* Atlanta.

Duran, R. L. (1992). Communicative adaptability: A review of conceptualization and measurement. *Communication Quarterly, 40,* 253–268.

Duran, R. L., & Kelly, L. (1985). An investigation into the cognitive domain of communicating competence. *Communication Research Reports, 2,* 112–119.

Duran, R. L., & Kelly, L. (1988). An investigation into the cognitive domain of communicative competence II. *Communication Research Reports, 5,* 91–96.

Duran, R. L., & Zakahi, W. R. (1984). Competence or style: What's in a name? *Communication Research Reports, 1,* 42–47.

Duran, R. L., & Zakahi, W. R. (1988). The influence of communicative competence upon roommate satisfaction. *Western Journal of Speech Communication, 52,* 135–146.

Fiechtner, S. B., & Krayer, K. J. (1986). Variations in dogmatism and leader-supplied information: Determinants of perceived behavior in task-oriented groups. *Group and Organization Studies, 11,* 403–418.

Gable, M., Hollon, C., & Dangello, F. (1992). Managerial structuring of work as a moderator of the Machiavellianism and job performance relationship. *Journal of Psychology: Interdisciplinary and Applied, 126,* 317–325.

Gorden, W. I., & Infante, D. A. (1987). Employee rights: Context argumentativeness, verbal aggressiveness, and career satisfaction: In C. A. B. Osigweh (Ed.), *Communicating employee responsibilities and rights* (pp. 149–163). Westport, CT: Quorum.

Gorden, W. I., Infante, D. A., & Graham, E. E. (1988). Corporate conditions conducive to employee voice: A subordinate perspective. *Employee Responsibility and Rights Journal, 1,* 101–111.

Gunn, E. P. (2006, October 16). It is in your head. *US News and World Report,* EE8–EE9.

Hample, D., & Dallinger, J. M. (1993). The effects of taking conflict personally on arguing behavior. In R. E. McKerrow (Ed.), *Argument and the postmodern challenge* (pp. 235–238). Annandale, VA: Speech Communication Association.

Hample, D., & Dallinger, J. M. (1995). A Lewinian perspective on taking conflict personally: Revision, refinement and validation of the instrument. *Communication Quarterly, 43,* 297–319.

Henkel, J., Sheehan, E. P., & Reichel, P. (1997). Relation of police misconduct to authoritarianism. *Journal of Social Behavior & Personality, 12,* 551–555.

Infante, D. A., & Rancer, A. S. (1982). A conceptualization and measure of argumentativeness. *Journal of Personality Assessment, 46,* 72–80.

Infante, D. A., & Rancer, A. S. (1996). Argumentativeness and verbal aggressiveness: A review of recent theory and research. *Communication Yearbook, 19,* 319–351.

Infante, D. A., & Wigley, C. J. (1986). Verbal aggressiveness: An interpersonal model and measure. *Communication Monographs, 53,* 61–69.

Kassing, J. W., & Avtgis, T. A. (1999). Examining the relationship between organizational dissent and aggressive communication. *Management Communication Quarterly, 13,* 100–115.

Kazlow, C. (1977). Faculty receptivity to organizational change: A test of two explanations of resistance to innovation in higher education. *Journal of Research & Development in Education, 10,* 87–98.

Knutson, P. K., McCroskey, J. C., Knutson, T., & Hurt, H. (1979, February). Tolerance for disagreement: Interpersonal conflict reconceptualized. Paper presented at the annual meeting of the *Western Speech Association,* Los Angeles.

Lefcourt, H. M. (1981). *Research with the locus of control construct: Vol. 1. Assessment methods.* New York: Academic Press.

Levin, J., & Spates, J. L. (1968). Closed systems of behavior and traditional family ideologies. *Psychological Reports, 23,* 978.

Lewin, K. (1951). *Field theory in social science; selected theoretical papers.* D. Cartwright (Ed.). New York: Harper & Row.

Lilly, J. D., & Virick, M. (2006). The effect of personality on perceptions of justice. *Journal of Managerial Psychology, 21,* 438–458.

Luck, G. (2004). The relationship of an innovative thinking style, locus of control, and perceived control on job satisfaction and workspace preferences among knowledge workers. *Dissertation Abstracts International, 65,* 2133.

Martin, M. M., Anderson, C. A., & Thweatt, K. S. (1998). Aggressive communication traits and their relationship with the Cognitive Flexibility Scale and the Communication Flexibility Scale. *Journal of Social Behavior and Personality, 13,* 531–540.

Martin, M. M., & Rubin, R. B. (1995). A new measure of cognitive flexibility. *Psychological Reports, 76,* 623–626.

McCroskey, J. C. (2006). Tolerance for disagreement. In A. S. Rancer & T. A. Avtgis (Eds.), *Argumentative and aggressive communication: Theory, research, and application* (pp. 244–245). Thousand Oaks, CA: SAGE Publications.

McCroskey, J. C., Daly, J. A., & Sorensen, G. (1976). Personality correlates of communication apprehension: A research note. *Human Communication Research, 2,* 376–380.

McCroskey, J. C., & Wheeless, L. (1976). *An introduction to human communication.* Boston: Allyn & Bacon.

Norton, R. (1983). *Communicator style: Theory, applications, and measures:* Beverly Hills, CA: SAGE Publications.

Norton, R. W. (1978). Foundation of the communicator construct. *Human Communication Research, 4,* 99–112.

Parks, M. R. (1994). Communication competence and interpersonal control. In M. L. Knapp & G. R. Miller (Eds.), *Handbook of interpersonal communication* (pp. 589–620). Beverly Hills, CA: SAGE Publications.

Rancer, A. S. (1995). Aggressive communication in organizational contexts: A synthesis and review. In A. M. Nicotera (Ed.), *Conflict and organizations: Communicative processes* (pp. 151–173). Albany, NY: State University of New York Press.

Rancer, A. S., & Avtgis, T. A. (2006). *Argumentative and aggressive communication: Theory, research, and application.* Thousand Oaks, CA: SAGE Publications.

Richmond, V. P., & McCroskey, J. C. (1979). Management communicator style, tolerance for disagreement, and innovativeness as predictors of employee satisfaction: A comparison of single-factor, two-factor, and multiple factor approaches. In D. Nimmo (Ed.), *Communication Yearbook, 3,* (pp. 359–373). New Brunswick, NJ: Transaction Books.

Richmond, V. P., McCroskey, J. C., & McCroskey, L. L. (2005). *Organizational communication: Making work, work.* Boston: Pearson

Rokeach, M. (1960). *The open and closed mind.* New York: Basic Books.

Rosen, I. C. (2000). Correlates of employee involvement: Quality of work life and locus of control orientation. *Dissertation Abstracts International, 61,* 1122.

Rotter, J. B. (1966). Generalized expectancies for internal versus external control of reinforcement. *Psychological Monographs, 80* (Whole No. 609).

Rubin, R. B., & Martin, M. M. (1994). The interpersonal communication competence scale. *Communication Research Reports, 11,* 33–44.

Shintaku, M. (2006). Personality traits by blood-type—A Japanese concept. *Bellonline: The Voice of Women.* Retrieved from http://www.bellaonline.com

Shullery, M. M. (1998). The optimum level of argumentativeness for employed women. *Journal of Business Communication, 35,* 346–367.

Shullery, M. M. (1999). Argumentative men: Expectations of success. *Journal of Business Communication, 36,* 362–381.

Spector, P. E. (1982). Behavior in organization as a function of employee's locus of control. *Psychological Bulletin, 91,* 482–497.

Spector, P. E. (1988). Development of the work locus of control scale. *Journal of Occupational Psychology, 61,* 335–340.

Teven, J. J., McCroskey, M. C., & Richmond, V. P. (1998). Measuring tolerance for disagreement. *Communication Research Reports, 15,* 209–217.

Teven, J. J., McCroskey, J. C., & Richmond, V. P. (2006). Communication correlates of perceived Machiavellianism and supervisors: Communication orientations and outcomes. *Communication Quarterly, 54,* 127–142.

Wigley, C. J. (2006). Verbal trigger events. In A. S. Rancer & T. A. Avtgis (Eds.), *Argumentative and aggressive communication: Theory, research, and application* (pp. 243–244). Thousand Oaks, CA: SAGE Publications.

Zakahi, W. R. (1985). The relationship of assertiveness to communicative competence and communication satisfaction: A dyadic assessment. *Communication Research Reports, 2,* 36–40.

Chapter 7

Defining Small Groups

Learning Objectives

Upon completion of the chapter, the student should be able to:

- Define a small group and explain the underlying logic behind the ceiling effect.

- Compare and contrast working groups, project groups, and quality improvement groups in terms of task and communication.

- Explain what occurs during each of the four stages of the group development process.

- Describe the advantages and disadvantages of working in small groups.

- Explain the role of a small group in the development of a risky shift mentality.

- Explain the potential problems that exist when a group experiences the unwanted consequences of the groupthink phenomenon.

Key Terms

Ceiling effect	Groupthink	Reinforcement
Conflict	Holism	Risky shift
Emergence	Maintenance role	Self-centered role
Group	Orientation	Task role

It is important for students, scholars, and practitioners of organizational communication to understand the difference between the terms *organization* and *organize*. The former is considered to be a product or effect, and the latter is considered to be the process involved in creating that product (Redding, 1966). Take, for example, Apple, Inc. From a product perspective, this organization exists because individuals (employees, consumers, investors) have a common interest in developing, producing, and distributing electronic goods. From a process perspective, this organization exists because these individuals organize themselves through such things as departmental membership, division of work and labor, work-oriented relationships, and even hierarchical structuring.

This chapter focuses on how people use groups as a means of achieving both personal and organizational goals. A **group** is defined as a collection of individuals, ranging in number from three to 11, all of whom are brought together because of a common interest and must work collaboratively and interdependently to achieve a collectively accepted goal. From a communication perspective, this quantitative range exists because fewer than three individuals would be considered either *interpersonal* (two individuals) or *intrapersonal* (one individual), whereas more than 11 oftentimes extends into the organizational or public realms (Bennis & Shephard, 1956). With an increase in the number of people as part of a given social entity, such things as decision making, argumentation, conflict resolution, task distribution, and individual and collective motivation become increasingly difficult and more diffused (Bonito & Hollingshead, 1997). To illustrate this point, consider trying to decide which movie to see this weekend. Chances are that such a decision would be easier when only three, four, or five individuals are part of the decision-making process as compared to nine, 10, or 11. Why? For one thing, it is easier to solicit and gather information from fewer as compared to more people (Wheelan & McKeage, 1993). For a second reason, the amount of conflict that arises during the decision-making process is likely to be greatly reduced when there are fewer as compared to more people involved (Farmer & Roth, 1998). For a third reason, it is more difficult to coordinate the collective activities of 11 individuals as compared to five (Mabry, 1999). The same underlying arguments hold true for group work in organizations, in that there tends to be a **ceiling effect**, which occurs when too many social actors part of the same group begin to counteract the benefits of being in such a group. Groups are difficult to create, manage, coordinate, motivate, and organize. And, despite the fact that many individuals are hesitant about working in groups, much organizational communication research points to the overarching benefits of this organizing strategy (Hirokawa, 1988). Simply put, groups work for organizations because they improve individual and organizational productivity.

group A collection of individuals, ranging in number from three to 11, who are brought together because of a common interest and who must work collaboratively and interdependently to achieve a collectively accepted goal.

ceiling effect The process by which too many parts of the same group begin to counteract the benefits of being in such a group.

Different Types of Small Groups

Given that organizational groups provide a way to organize individuals to meet both personal and organizational needs, we need to explore some basic distinctions. First, it is important to differentiate a contrived group from an emergent group. A **contrived group** is one that is deliberatively and artificially constructed (Monge & Contractor, 2001). For example, the product development team of McDonald's, whose responsibility is the creation of new menu items for the world's largest fast food chain, is a contrived group. The members of the group were chosen by those in upper administrative positions due to some talent or possible input. On the other hand, an **emergent group** is one that comes into being based on volunteerism, self-interest, and expertise (Rogers & Kincaid, 1981). An example of this can be seen in the wake of many natural disasters, when people who are part of disaster relief organizations, such as FEMA (U.S. Federal Emergency Management Agency), Habitat For Humanity, and the American Red Cross, have members come together to create groups to engage in such activities as providing medical assistance to disaster victims, promoting public safety postdisaster, and soliciting donations for those impacted by a natural disaster. To further illustrate this point, the National Communication Association held its annual 2011 conference in New Orleans, Louisiana, during which many scholars came together to provide a Day of Service, where volunteers went into some of the most devastated areas affected by 2005's Hurricane Katrina to assist in rebuilding efforts. Based on much research, there is often a pleasant mix of both contrived and emergent groups within organizations (Monge & Eisenberg, 1987).

Now that we have differentiated contrived and emergent groups, we examine how groups function. There are five major types of groups, although they are not necessarily mutually exclusive. The first group is known as a **work group**, which is a collection of individuals whose main purpose is to achieve an overarching task that ultimately benefits the organization and those who are part of it (Whitford & Moss, 2009). For example, even though many employees identify themselves by stating their departmental membership (e.g., "I'm part of the marketing department"), departments are, operationally speaking, work groups. Key to this definition is the term *overarching*, implying that a group's task or goal is broad and, as such, perhaps nonspecific. For example, the marketing team for Gap is responsible for creating the best products, selling these products at the best price, promoting these products through the most effective forms of media, and placing these products in the most effective distribution outlets. Through group communication, members of this marketing team must figure out the best possible strategies for achieving these four integrated goals.

Closely linked to a work group is a **project group**, whose ultimate objectives are more specific and more microdriven (Xia, Yuan, & Gay, 2009). Using the previous example of the Gap marketing team, whereas a work group would be responsible for the marketing strategies of all organizational products (jeans, sweatshirts, cologne, sunglasses, t-shirts), a project group might be responsible for only one (e.g., maternity pants, toddler pajamas). Given the previous differentiation between contrived and emergent groups, work groups are more likely to be contrived (e.g., assigned by management), whereas project groups are more likely to be emergent. It is important to note that individuals comprising project groups are often those from already-existing work groups. Assume, for a moment, that the head of the sales department for Nordstrom recently announced, at a corporate-wide meeting, that the company must determine why the sale of women's clothing in the Brass Plum department has recently dropped. It is likely that employees from the sales department (an example of a work group) would become part of this more specific, microlevel project group.

In addition to the work group and the project group is a **quality improvement group**, which is a collection of individuals whose main responsibility is to determine strategies for increasing an organization's effectiveness, efficiency, and productivity (Hoegl & Gemuenden, 2001). For example, assume that administrative members of the Campbell's corporation recently decided that they must determine why, based on consumer feedback, their Healthy Request split pea and ham soup has been very successful, but their Healthy Request minestrone soup has not received much public support. Might it be the taste of the soup? Might it be the price? Might it be the packaging? Might it be a combination of these three? A quality improvement group would form to figure out what it is about this product that has not led to the anticipated sales. Quality improvement groups, due to their nature, are no more likely to be contrived than emergent.

A fourth type of group within an organization is a **permanent group**, also known as a **standing group**, which is ever-present and rarely changes its members (Gersick, 1988). Those in administrative positions determine that certain groups must always be present. For example, most colleges and universities have an academic review board, whose responsibility is to determine the ramifications of academic dishonesty and plagiarism. However, this group only needs to meet when an issue of academic dishonesty or plagiarism surfaces. Perhaps the best example of a permanent group is a work group (e.g., department), again highlighting the fact that not all organizational groups are mutually exclusive and, in fact, often depend on each other for success.

TABLE 7.1	Types of Small Groups
Type	**Reason for its creation**
Work Group	Standing group responsible for a multitude of tasks
Project Group	Disbanding group responsible for a specific task
Quality Improvement Group	Group responsible for making necessary changes to products, ideas, promotions, and services

A fifth and final type of group within an organization is a **disbanding group**, also known as an **ad hoc group**, which organizes members for a particular reason and, either upon completion of the group's task or failure of the group to overcome internal conflict, these members part ways (Ancona, 1990). As an example, project groups are, by and large, disbanding. In other words, they are contrived or emergent entities whose members come together, make certain organization-related decisions, and then dissipate. Think, for a moment, about a legal jury. A group of people randomly selected from society come together to determine the verdict for a person accused of a crime or civil wrongdoing. The jury listens to the trial, deliberates together, delivers a verdict to the judge, and then goes its separate ways and disbands. Disbanding groups are those that are important for an organization at a particular time for a particular reason, but need not be permanent or omnipresent.

Communicatively speaking, there are many differences among work groups, project groups, quality improvement groups, permanent groups, and disbanding groups. For example, it is likely that communication is somewhat predictable and patterned in work groups (employees part of the same department come to create seemingly routine communication strategies). On the other hand, communication is somewhat novel and unpredictable in project groups due to the fact that they are likely to be emergent and disbanding and, as a result, communication occurs between and among employees not necessarily used to making decisions together. It is also likely, based on rational thinking, that communication in work groups is less informing and less effective because, after all, these groups are permanent, resulting in interactions that are both conventional and repetitive. Similarly, communication in project groups is likely to be more focused and task-centered because specific, microlevel decisions must be made between and among members whose organizational patronage is different and whose knowledge, expertise, and resources are diverse. In terms of communicative conflict, it is likely that those who are members of disbanding groups are more likely than those who are part of permanent groups to engage in intragroup conflict because membership is transient. Aren't we more likely to engage in conflict with others whom we do not need to work with all the time, as compared to those who are part of our department? In the end, it is not only important to understand the role of communication in the formation of small groups, and the communicative and behavioral effects of groups, but also how and why certain groups are more or less appropriate based on the organizational task at hand.

Stages of Group Formation

The group development process is perhaps the area in which communication has its most relevant and important role (Chang, Duck, & Bordia, 2006). That is, how does communication facilitate the small-group process, from the initial formation stage to the final stage in which the entire group makes a decision about something? B. Aubrey Fisher, one of the leading

orientation The first stage of the group development process wherein individuals begin to engage in informal dialogue in an effort to get to know one another and reduce the initial uncertainty that accompanies any novel social situation.

conflict The second stage of the group development process wherein group members oftentimes engage in constructive conflict, circulating a multitude of ideas, and bringing forth several decision alternatives.

emergence The third stage of the group development process wherein the development of a decision through communication by group members transpires.

reinforcement The fourth and final stage of the group development process wherein group members continue to rationalize their decision and reinforce its validity.

communication scholars interested in group decision making, created one of the prominent stage models explaining group processes (Fisher, 1970). In the first stage, known as **orientation**, individuals begin to engage in informal dialogue to get to know one another and to reduce the initial uncertainty that accompanies a novel social situation. According to Fisher (1970), it is during this first stage that psychological comfort is created, ultimately making communication less arduous. In fact, it is rare for group members to speak about task-related issues during this first stage, other than clarifying the group's task, as it is truly meant for individuals to get to know one another. During the second stage, known as **conflict**, communication concerning the task begins to occur. As the name of the stage implies, group members often engage in constructive conflict, circulating a multitude of ideas and bringing forth several decision alternatives (see Chapter 10 for effective ways of decision making and problem solving). For example, assume that a group of employees working for Verizon was charged with designing a case for its newest Droid phone. Everyone who is part of this group will likely have a different design idea, and must communicate the logic and rationale behind their ideas so the group can ultimately make an informed decision in the best interest of the customer and the organization. This type of constructive conflict is ultimately beneficial for a group, as the more debate and conversation there is, the more likely that the group will make the best decision possible (Alderton & Frey, 1986). It is also during the conflict stage that all task-related communication occurs.

The third stage, termed **emergence**, is characterized by the development of a decision through communication by group members. Regarding a final decision, some groups require a **consensus** (all group members are in agreement), while others find either **majority vote** (at least one more individual in favor of a decision than against it) or **compromise** (an agreement based on mutual concession) acceptable (Beatty, 1989). In the end, communication is likely to be most complex and problematic, and rife with conflict if a group's decision requires consensus as compared to a majority vote (Gouran, 1969). During the fourth and final stage, known as **reinforcement**, group members continue to rationalize their decision and reinforce its validity. Group unity and solidarity are created during this stage as members communicatively convince themselves that no other decision could have or should

TABLE 7.2	Stages of Group Formation
Stage	**Communication Process Involved**
Orientation	Group introductions and information about each other is shared
Conflict	Discussion about the merit and problems with vertain potential decisions
Emergence	Group conforms around one final decision
Reinforcement	Group reinforces the merit of its final decision

have been made. Those who were originally skeptical about the merit of the group's decision become accepting of it and nothing but pride, confidence, and agreement surface.

Advantages of Small Groups

Although it is difficult to work in groups, research indicates that the many benefits associated with collective thought outweigh the benefits of individual reflection. One of these benefits is the opportunity for a **diversity of ideas**, or the wide range of alternatives available to group members as they make a decision (Scheidel & Crowell, 1964). When working alone on a task, individuals become isolated from divergent perspectives and, as such, have no opportunity to hear a dissenting viewpoint. Although the mere addition of different ideas and perspectives in no way guarantees a better or more successful decision, it does guarantee more decision options. The key to harnessing the benefits associated with this increase in decision options is effective communication (Hirokawa, 1990). Realizing that all groups have interdependent goals and realizing that discussion about the merit of decision alternatives is a necessary byproduct of the group decision-making process, it is important that decision discussion be constructive and focused on the merit and limitations of ideas without prejudice about the people who proposed such ideas (Meyers & Brashers, 1998). Imagine for a moment that a group of marketers working in the corporate sector of Coca Cola was charged with redesigning the company's logo. Although such a group situation is rife with opportunity for a diversity of ideas, it is also rife with the opportunity for intragroup conflict. If managed properly, this diversity ultimately becomes the group's greatest strength, adding credibility to the "two heads are better than one" adage (Vinokur & Burnstein, 1974).

Another benefit of working in a group is **collective involvement** and **collective commitment**, indicating that group members will engage in work more productively when they know they are part of a communal body. When working alone, social beings know they are in charge of their own destiny (i.e., they get out what they put in). In other words, success or failure depends on individual action and productivity. Within groups, however, each social actor relies on and is relied on by others (Gustafson, Shukla, Delbecq, & Walster, 1973). Daniel Katz and Robert Kahn, two social psychologists interested in studying organizational structures and productivity, developed the concept of **holism**, which holds that individuals who are part of a group are only as strong as their weakest link (Katz & Kahn, 1966). Given the previous example of the Coca Cola marketing group, assume that four departments were consulted about the redesign of the corporate logo: the finance department (to determine how much this rebranding would cost the company), the training and development department (to determine how employees could use this new corporate logo to strengthen the company's image), the legal department (to make certain this logo earned copyright privileges), and

holism The idea that individuals who are part of a group are only as strong as their weakest link.

the sales department (to determine how the company can use this logo to increase profitability). However, after the decision was made, the person in charge of presenting these new ideas to those in upper administrative positions was ineffective in his persuasive attempt and, therefore, the group's pitch for a new logo was unsuccessful. Although only the presenter in this example seemed to pull the group down, the entire group suffered. This, according to Katz and Kahn (1966) is the holistic principle. Making certain that each individual member of any organizational group understands this principle of holism both increases the likelihood of success and increases the likelihood of collective involvement and commitment, thus adopting the idea of *we* instead of *I* (Burke, 1950).

A third advantage of working in groups deals with what is known as a risky shift. A **risky shift** is the idea that social beings are more likely to make a riskier, rather than safer, decision when working in a group with others (Cline & Cline, 1980). At the fundamental level, this increased motivation to make a riskier decision when part of a group stems from the need for individuals to deflect responsibility for a failed decision. When working in a group, such responsibility is shared (Wallach, Kogan, & Bem, 1964). In Chapter 4 we discussed the concept of self-handicapping as a means of protecting the self-esteem of a person from real or perceived failure. When discussing groups, this type of behavior can be considered a *group handicapping* behavior. From an organizational perspective, assume that you are the only individual responsible for creating a new menu item for Wendy's. This individual decision, for better or worse, is stress-inducing, as you know that if the new menu item fails, the responsibility falls squarely on your shoulders. After all, it was your idea and your decision. However, add another two, three, six, or nine others into the decision-making situation and suddenly there is a psychological and cognitive change. No longer does the responsibility of a failed, ineffective decision fall solely on one individual, but rather a collective group of people. This, based on group communication research, leads to decisions that are not so "safe" and are more "risky." Given the foregoing example, it is more likely that an isolated individual would propose a Cajun grilled chicken sandwich (a safe decision) than a stuffed flounder platter (a risky decision) for Wendy's. Although risky decisions are not guaranteed to be effective, they do carry with them increased creativity and, from a quasi-economic perspective, highlights the "no risk, no reward" paradigm. Such a paradigm is more likely to be enacted when working in groups as compared to working alone (Collins & Guetzkow, 1964).

The fourth advantage of working in groups, and is perhaps the most pragmatic advantage for an organization, is the idea of **task and role distribution**, which argues that group members have interconnected yet distinct duties and identities (Stasser & Titus, 1985). Although it is human nature to assume we can do anything and everything individually, manifesting the "Jack of all trades" ideology, it becomes obvious that certain organizational

risky shift The idea that social beings are more likely to make a riskier, rather than safer, decision when working in a group with others as opposed to when working alone.

employees are better at certain things than others. For example, some are "numbers people," some are "creative people," some are "people people," some are "social people," some are "logistical people," and some are "practical people." Anyone who has seen an episode of NBC's *The Apprentice* realizes that roles and duties are distributed among the group responsible for a given task. When working alone, one has to assume all these roles, and if one happens to be the "people person," but not the "creative person," then failure likely looms in the not-too-distant future. However, when working in a group, these roles can be distributed and individual members' strengths can be capitalized on (Bray & Brawley, 2002). Imagine, for example, that the executive chef of the Gramercy Tavern, an upscale eatery in Manhattan, had to design the restaurant, order the food, cook the food, plate the food, serve the food, wash the dishes, pay the employees, deal with the organizational finances, and market the establishment. In all likelihood, this executive chef would be charged only with cooking and plating the food, which is why an eatery often employs a hostess, a wait staff, and a kitchen staff.

Finally, the fifth advantage of engaging in organizational tasks as part of a group concerns **shared knowledge**, defined as the pooled information to which people have access that enables employees to engage in work practices (Shaw, 1981). Over the past two decades, scholars from the fields of organizational communication and information science have been interested in understanding where, in organizations, knowledge exists. Since knowledge resides in organizational employees, a more important question, especially from a communication perspective, is how knowledge is transferred between and among employees (Malone, 2002). Knowledge is often transferred during organizational entry and organizational change. Think, for example, about the employee who is hired to replace an existing organizational member. It is often the job of the existing employee to teach the incoming employee the ropes, or what is known as *knowledge transfer*. Unfortunately, however, there seems to exist a paradox or Catch 22. By having organizational knowledge that no one else has, an employee becomes powerful and is seen as an important organizational resource. It is this individual who becomes a crucial part of the organization's social network. From an individual perspective, employees like having power and like having resources that are considered to be both valuable and limited.

However, by sharing this knowledge, not only does this person lose (or have to share) power, this person also becomes more dispensable and, as a result, less important to the organization. This idea brings up an interesting organizational dialectic: Can the needs of the organization and the needs of the organizational employees be satisfied at once? From an organizational perspective, those in upper administrative positions want employees to have equal access to all organizational knowledge needed to perform work duties. From an employee perspective, however, individuals like having access to knowledge that others are barred from, as this translates, communicatively, into such things as power, prominence, authority, and centrality. The

"Knowledge is power" adage is seen most clearly within the organizational confines. In fact, Pelz (1952) found that knowledge is one of most important predictors of effective leadership within the organizational setting, further illustrating the link between knowledge and power. This idea has since become known as the *Pelz effect*. When organizational employees work as part of a group, knowledge and the social processes that accompany it become shared. There is an interdependent, holistic nature about working in groups that does not arise when working individually. That is, knowledge is not only increased and not only reflects diverse viewpoints, but is also shared (Hansen, Mors, & Lovas, 2005). In the end, although collective knowledge might seem, at first glance, to only benefit the organization, sharing knowledge between and among group members is among the most effective communicative strategies for increasing the likelihood of effective group discussion and effective group decision making.

Disadvantages of Small Groups

It is clear that working in groups is advantageous at both organizational and individual levels. However, anyone who has worked in groups knows that, due to the communication-intense nature of groups, they are prone to problems. First among these potential problems is the fact that an increase in the number of people who have to interact and coordinate makes the communication process more difficult (Gastil, 1993). Consider working on a project with just one additional person. Dividing up work, scheduling meetings, providing feedback, and preparing the final product is certainly no easy task. Now add two, three, six, or nine more individuals into the process and you will undoubtedly understand the communicative complexities involved in the group process. As a group moves through the four stages of the group decision-making process (orientation, conflict, emergence, reinforcement), it is communication that oftentimes is the difference between success and failure (Tuckman, 1965). Thus, it is important for members of groups to understand and appreciate that people engage in work processes differently and have different communication practices and patterns. Without such differences, a group would be unable to reap the benefits of diverse viewpoints. Anyone who has been part of and has witnessed firsthand the process of jury selection knows there is not much advantage of having a group of 11 homophilous (those who are demographically, attitudinally, and/or behaviorally similar) individuals determine the fate of the accused. Rather, the jury selection process entails getting voices from a divergent group of people, based on such things as age, education, gender, and socioeconomic status, among others. As advantageous as this heterophilous (those who are demographically, attitudinally, and/or behaviorally different) group might be, it remains a fact that an increase in the number of group members leads to an increase in communication difficulties (Saunders & Miranda, 1998).

The second potential problem lies in the idea that group members seem to easily fall prey to social influence and group cohesion. In one of the earliest studies of group cohesion, Muzafer Sherif, a prominent social psychologist, conducted a study dealing with what he called the autokinetic effect (Sherif, 1935). The researcher placed the subject (i.e., the person being experimented on) and a small group of confederates (people who are playing a specific role in the experiment and are told how to behave by the experimenter) in a dark room. He shone a steady, unmoving light beam on one of the walls in the room. He then told all participants that he was going to move the light beam and instructed the subject and confederates to determine how far the light beam moved from its original point of projection. Unbeknownst to the subject, the light beam never actually moved. However, after hearing obviously wrong answers from many of the confederates (ranging, on average, from 2 inches to 20 inches), the subject would choose a number somewhere in between the extremes. Once the experiment was over, Sherif told the subject that the light beam did not, in fact, move at all. This process was repeated dozens of times, with nearly universal results. In post-experiment interviews, many of the subjects claimed they knew the light beam had not moved from its original point of projection, but felt pressure from the confederates because of the small-group setting. In other words, the subjects knowingly gave wrong answers so as to not be the group's outcast. Simply put, it was better to be wrong than not belong.

This experiment, and many others since, points to the disturbing effects of group conformity during the decision-making process (Asch, 1951). That is, individuals who are part of a small group are likely to go along with the majority, even if they think the decision is rife with problems, merely out of fear of nonconformity. We have likely all been part of groups, in organizations or otherwise, where certain members, for one reason or another, merely say, "Good idea. Let's go with it." However, what becomes problematic is when this person truly does not believe that it is a "good idea" and is only on board to add psychological solidarity. This idea of social conformity is also known as the *groupthink phenomenon,* a term popularized by Irving Janis, a psychologist interested in studying small-group processes. **Groupthink** is the idea that members of a small group are likely to table their ideas if they are considered to be divergent from the majority view, so as to increase intragroup harmony, eliminate the potential for conflict, and become a cohesive body (Janis, 1972). It becomes important for groups to take advantage of their diversity and ultimately benefit from anticonformist discussions that have the potential to decrease the likelihood of groupthink emergence.

The third potential problem is that working and making decisions in groups, as compared to individually, takes more time (Bales & Borgatta, 1966). The "Time is money" axiom could not be more representative of group work, as the majority of group decisions have a static deadline. That is, groups are given both a task and a time by which this task must be completed. Although the four stages of the group decision-making process highlighted

This QR code will direct you to a *New York Times* article dealing with the role of Groupthink in organizational communication practices.

http://www.nytimes.com/2012/01/15/opinion/sunday/the-rise-of-the-new-groupthink.html?pagewanted=all

groupthink The process by which those who are part of a collective social unit are fearful of not supporting a behavior or decision because of the inherent social dangers of nonconformity.

TABLE 7.3	Advantages and Disadvantages of Working in Groups	
Advantages	**Disadvantages**	
Diversity of ideas	Difficult to coordinate	
Collective involvement	People and tasks	
Collective commitment	Potential for group cohesion	
Risky shift mentality	Takes more time to get work done	
Task/role distribution	Lack of individual accountability	
Shared knowledge		

earlier might lead one to assume that decisions are made quickly and without many problems, this is far from the truth. In fact, some groups find themselves in the conflict stage for so long without resolve that they never make the decision that necessitated the group formation process in the first place. What happens, for example, when an organizational group has one member who is ill, one member who cannot adequately balance time needed for home life and work life, and one member who is having trouble translating his ideas into a form accessible by others? This reality impinges on both productivity and timeliness, ultimately detracting from the small-group process. Group members must collectively engage in time management to avoid situations such as these, a practice much easier said than done.

Finally, the fourth potential problem with group work in organizations is the potential lack of individual accountability and recognition (Karau & Williams, 1993). When working in groups, the "win together, lose together" mentality is prominent, highlighting Katz and Kahn's principle of holism mentioned earlier in this chapter. The lack of individual accountability when working in groups has the potential to affect one's contributions to the task. Think, for a moment, about a group of market researchers attempting to determine what new coffee flavor Dunkin' Donuts consumers might want. If this group consists of six individuals, group research indicates that the likelihood of one or more of these members being either underproductive or unproductive increases (Ingham, Levinger, Graves, & Peckham, 1974). After all, if others exert all their energy to the task and if there is no such thing as individual recognition, what becomes the impetus to "give it one's all?" This individual becomes the group's **social loafer**, or the group member who exerts less energy and effort toward the group's task because they expect others to pick up the slack (Hoon & Tan, 2008). In other words, the social loafer adopts the "safety in numbers" mentality. This is one of the gravest negative and unintended consequences of working in groups. When we rely on others in small groups we oftentimes forget that others rely on us, too. Communicatively speaking, social loafing is a behavior that is likely to anger other group members, and the resulting conflict can do nothing but harm all individuals involved.

TABLE 7.4	Types of Small Group Roles
Type of Role	**Expectations of Role**
Task	Make certain that the project is achieving success
Maintenance	Make certain that the members of the group are working together harmoniously
Self-centered	Make certain that individual needs are being fulfilled

Roles in Small Groups

Whether an organizational group is contrived or emergent, disbanding or permanent, certain roles are needed for effective communication to transpire. Kenneth Benne and Paul Sheats developed three overarching social roles that group members adopt, each with its own focus: **task roles** (focus on productivity and making certain the group achieves its defined goals), **maintenance roles** (focus on interpersonal relationships and intragroup harmony), and **self-centered roles** (focus on disturbing intragroup harmony and detracting the group from its productivity) (Benne & Sheats, 1948). To illustrate the manifestation of task roles, maintenance roles, and self-centered roles, assume that a product development group working for Dolce & Gabbana is in charge of creating a new scent for the company's perfume line. Among the task roles for the group members is the **information seeker**, whose primary responsibility is to use communication to gauge member insight. At the basic level, the information seeker asks all members to propose certain ideas to help the group reach its goal. Given the present example, the information seeker attempts to determine what olfactory message those who purchase Dolce & Gabbana perfume want to communicate and how this could be translated into one's desire for a particular scent. Those group members who provide responses to the information seeker's query are known as the **initiators** or **contributors** (Benne & Sheats, 1948). Clearly, the role of initiator/contributor is relevant for groups, as without the generation of such new ideas, the group in question would have no fruitful avenue for success.

Given this example, the initiators/contributors might propose a floral scent that communicates elegance and tradition, an oceanic scent that communicates freshness and modernity, and a woody scent that communicates purity and richness. Once ideas surface, the **elaborator** is charged with explaining the ideas (not the merits of the ideas) to other group members to reduce any ambiguities. For example, the elaborator might explain that a floral scent can be created in one of two ways: a single floral scent is one that highlights the potent scent of one isolated flower, whereas a floral bouquet scent is one that highlights the complementary olfaction of several, related flowers. This elaborator might also give an example of each, claiming that the best known example of a single floral scent in the perfume market is Flower by Kenzo, whereas a popular example of a floral bouquet scent is Romance by Ralph Lauren. To determine the group's sentiments about the proposed

task role A small group role, the focus of which is on productivity and making certain the group achieves its defined goals.

maintenance role A small group role, the focus of which is on interpersonal relationships and intragroup harmony.

self-centered role A small-group role, the focus of which is on disturbing intragroup harmony and detracting the group from its productivity.

alternatives, the **opinion seeker's** role is to engage the members in discussion about the merits and drawbacks of all ideas presented (Benne & Sheats, 1948).

Given this example, the opinion seeker will ask group members what seems to be beneficial about having a floral scent that is elegant, what seems to be problematic about selling a perfume product that is perhaps too modern, and/or what is both opportunistic and limiting about marketing a perfume that creates an image of purity? Although all group members might not have the opportunity, for one reason or another, to emerge as information seeker or contributor, all group members can engage in discussion about the merits of proposed ideas, again solidifying the importance of communication within the decision-making process. To decrease the likelihood of group cohesion and groupthink, an additional small group role is the **evaluator/critic**, whose responsibility is to play devil's advocate. This individual group member oftentimes questions the validity of a proposed idea by bringing forth the "what would happen if" scenario. Given the current example, an evaluator/critic might ask the group about certain unintended consequences of marketing an oceanic scent or deciding not to adopt the woody scent. Although this role is often stigmatized for the ensuing conflict, it is a necessary component of the group decision-making process and provides the group with testimonial evidence about the rationale behind decision alternatives.

Finally, in addition to the information seeker, initiator/contributor, elaborator, opinion seeker, and evaluator/critic is the **recorder**, whose responsibility it is to keep track of everything communicated during small group deliberations. Revisiting the principle of holism, none of the aforementioned roles and the communication that accompanies them matter if there is no information on record. From a pragmatic perspective, the participants of the small group process, as well as those who will use the information provided, all need formal documentation of all proposed ideas and the strengths and weaknesses associated with them.

Although task roles are clearly most important for a group's productivity, one must not underestimate or devalue the importance of maintenance roles in the decision-making process. The maintenance roles in the group are predictive of group motivation, group commitment, group satisfaction, and overall group energy. Two of the maintenance roles that Benne and Sheats (1948) speak of are the **encourager** and the **harmonizer**. The encourager is the individual who provides praise and admiration for the ideas presented by group members. The effect of the encourager is an increase in group members' willingness to circulate ideas even if the merit of such ideas might be challenged. Using the current example of the Dolce & Gabbana marketing group, assume that a group member would rather hear a discussion about the merit of creating a citrus scent: one that is framed as natural and not overpowering. Even if it is clear group sentiments oppose this idea, the encourager highlights the positive contribution and, in the end, even if this individual's suggestion is not taken into consideration during the group

deliberation, he or she feels a sense of accomplishment and pride. Thus, the encourager plays an important role in fostering group harmony and feelings of praise and support (Benne & Sheats, 1948).

The harmonizer's role is to quickly and effectively diffuse the unwanted consequences of group conflict. It is important to remember that group conflict, if constructive and handled properly, is beneficial for groups. The problem, however, is when conflict becomes (a) aimed at personal rather than task issues, (b) omnipresent, and (c) overly difficult or impossible to reduce. If constructive conflict emerges, the harmonizer attempts to reduce unwanted tensions through communicative mediation. This individual reminds group members that the effort is collective and that, for purposes of the decision-making process, it is important to sideline conflict that extends beyond the discussion at hand. Given the Dolce & Gabbana example, the harmonizer could tell group members to "keep their eyes on the goal at hand" and to "extinguish any interpersonal tensions unrelated to the task." The group member adopting this role has an important responsibility and has the opportunity to mitigate unwanted and perhaps unintended consequences of intragroup conflict.

The final set of roles are those considered to be self-centered or those that satisfy the needs of the individual at the likely risk of hindering group effectiveness (Benne & Sheats, 1948). Among these roles is the **aggressor**, defined as the individual who makes personal attacks in the hope that such degradation will impede the small group process and lower the victim's assumed status. Although it is possible that such an individual will verbally attack one's input, it is likely the verbal attack will also be geared toward an individual, rather than the individual's idea. This, clearly, negatively impacts the entire group process and necessitates that the encourager and harmonizer work hard to remedy this and once again regain the accord that once existed. An example would be an individual member of the Dolce & Gabbana marketing group who verbally attacks a fellow group member because of his inadequate information about the negative dermatological effects of a floral scent. However, rather than framing the comment about the inadequacy of the individual's knowledge base, the aggressor comments about the inadequacy and incompetence of the individual who offered the comment.

In addition to the aggressor, the **blocker** is the individual who refuses to adopt the majority opinion, often out of spite and malicious tendencies. This individual impedes progress by being the sole dissenter. In a group that agrees that a decision will be made to the extent that a majority of its members are in favor, this sole blocker might not be such a large obstacle (DeStephen & Hirokawa, 1988). However, for the group that agrees a decision will be made only if all members are in favor, this blocker becomes problematic. An example would be an individual part of the Dolce & Gabbana marketing group who says she will not endorse the decision to market a new woody scent because purity and richness do not correspond with the mission statement of the company. This one group member stands in the way of the decision being

This QR code will direct you to a YouTube clip highlighting Solomon Asch's (1951) line experiment, which explains the role of social influence in decision making practices.

http://www.youtube.com/watch?v=Rrm6U1SgE74

brought to those in administrative positions. The **dominator,** another self-centered role that emerges in certain small groups, is the individual whose need for power and need for authority trump collective action. The dominator uses forceful and potentially demeaning dialogue to control intragroup discussion. This communicative action not only monopolizes viewpoints and decision perspectives, but also makes other group members hesitant to bring forth ideas that may seem, comparatively speaking, unmerited.

A final self-centered role, which clearly detracts from effective group communication, is the **clown**, whose interest in forming social relationships supersedes an interest in making a good, well-informed decision (Benne & Sheats, 1948). Although this person might think this form of humor is a helpful component of the decision-making process, it is more likely to distract than benefit collective action if not used properly (Romero & Pescosolido, 2008). Given the Dolce & Gabbana marketing group example, the clown might ask the group members to think whether a male mate is more likely to enjoy a floral, oceanic, or woody scent. After all, isn't the goal of a perfume's olfaction to attract the woman's relational partner? This example might provide some initial humor, poking fun at the role of gender in product decision making, but can also lead the group to stray from the task, rethink its initial decision, and/or treat this "clown" as a sexist.

Although Benne and Sheats' (1948) discussion about small group roles has informed and influenced the small-group process since its launch, it is important that students, scholars, and practitioners of organizational communication remember three things. First, these roles are not necessarily mutually exclusive, meaning that a single group member can adopt a task role and a maintenance role simultaneously. It is common, for example, that the elaborator also becomes the harmonizer during times of intragroup conflict. Second, based on the principle of holism, all three types of group roles must be successful if the small group is to be effective. For example, even if the group is able to forward many ideas and if conflict is resolved, the small group will ultimately fail if those adopting self-centered roles dominate the discussion. Finally, not all the aforementioned roles are adopted in all small groups. In the most effective small groups, for example, self-centered roles do not emerge, and maintenance roles are limited (Benne & Sheats, 1948). In the most ineffective small groups, task roles are weak, maintenance roles are insufficient, and self-centered roles dominate. In the end, however, knowing, understanding, and adopting these group roles is often the difference between successful and unsuccessful group communication.

Types of Small Group Networks

Understanding how social actors within groups are socially and structurally connected to each other is important for understanding group discussion, intragroup dynamics, and group success. Alexander Bavelas, a social

FIGURE 7.1
Chain Network

psychologist interested in the link between a group's network structure and the group's productivity, developed four types of social networks that emerge in, and come to differentially affect, small groups (Bavelas, 1948). The first group network, the **chain**, is the idea that in order to communicate within a small group, ideas must flow from individual to individual to individual in a linear format. For example, assume there are five people comprising an organizational group. Within a chain network, individual A communicates an idea to individual B, who communicates the idea to individual C, who communicates the idea to individual D, who finally communicates the idea to individual E (see Figure 1). This is analogous to a hierarchical chain of command, where individual E (the most powerful member of a given group) only hears of the idea once it has been filtered through three other people first. This clearly is problematic because as the communication spreads through this chain, there is the opportunity for **reframing** (distortion of) information. Assume, for example, that a group of five people must determine the negative consequences for a fellow employee who constantly ridicules others during monthly organizational meetings. Assume that, within the chain network, individual A tells individual B that she thinks this employee should merely meet with the chief executive officer to discuss the problems of the inappropriate behavior. However, what then stops individual B from altering this message before delivering it to individual C? Although this might be viewed as unethical, this type of message reframing is facilitated in the chain network due to the unchecked information transferred from person to person. Although communication does not become repetitive and reaches one individual at a time due to the structured nature of discussion, this network can have two unintended consequences. First, there might be a lack of collective deliberation from all group members (i.e., each communication episode can receive feedback from only one isolated individual). Second, there is an

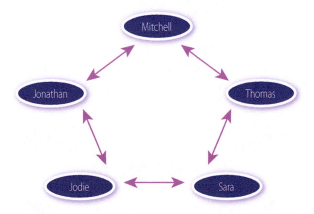

FIGURE 7.2
Circle Network

increased potential for communication censorship and reframing. Due to the nature of the network (linear in nature), this chain is not always conducive for maximum communication and optimal productivity.

The second type of group network, the **circle** network, posits that communication is most effective when all individuals have the opportunity to interact with two others. That is, if we situate individuals A, B, C, D, and E in a circular network configuration rather than a chain, person A can communicate with persons B and E; person B can communicate with persons A and C; person C can communicate with persons B and D; person D can communicate with persons C and E; and person E can communicate with persons D and A (see Figure 2). Behaviorally speaking, the circle network eliminates the strict chain of command offered in the previous network configuration and allows each person to receive feedback from two people, rather than only one. In the chain network, in order for person E to have access to this dialogue, the message must travel from person A to person B to person C to person D to person E. This is a total of three communicative steps. In the circle network, however, because individual A is structurally connected to individual E, that dialogue is immediately ready for transmission. In a circle group network, every individual can communicatively reach all others in two or fewer steps (Bavelas, 1948). Although this group formation is still problematic in terms of lack of access to others, it does expedite the social process by eliminating an extra degree of separation between and among members in the chain network.

The third type of group network, the **wheel** network, is the idea that one person has access to all others, but all others do not have access to each other. This individual is the hub for the group network and, thus, all information is mediated through him or her (see Figure 3). Although this saves the group time in that all members receive information in only two steps (i.e., from individual A to individual B and then from individual B to individuals C, D, and E), the same problem that exists in the chain network exists in the circle network, which is the lack of collective deliberation from all group members and the potential for communication censorship and reframing. Although person C can engage in dialogue with person B, person C does not have structural access to persons A, D, or E, thus inhibiting the communication process between and among group members.

The final type of group network, the **all-channel network**, is the idea that all individuals have communicative access to all others (see Figure 4).

FIGURE 7.3
Wheel Network

FIGURE 7.4
All-Channel Network

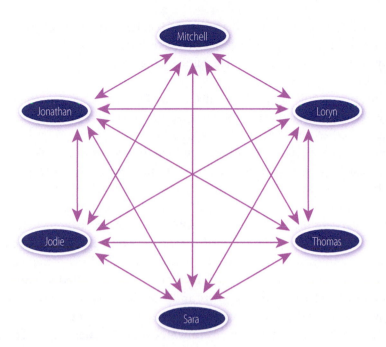

Remembering the original definition of a group offered at the start of this chapter (a collection of individuals, ranging in number from three to 11, who are brought together because of a common interest and must work collaboratively and interdependently to achieve a collectively accepted goal), this type of network configuration is most advantageous. The flow of ideas is not inhibited and the communication process has no structural barriers. Although the optimal type of group configuration depends on many variables (the organization's culture, the task at hand, the number of individual group members, and the roles adopted), Bavelas (1948) highlighted the importance of group configuration on communication, introducing a structural component to the decision-making process.

The Role of Technology in Small Groups

A discussion about group communication in the organizational context would be remiss without mentioning the role and importance of technology. One such technological innovation that began to appear in organizations during the mid-1980s is known as a Group Decision Support System (GDSS), which introduced electronic technology into the decision-making process. The GDSS attempted to alleviate many of the variables that routinely complicated the group communication process, such as apprehension, conformity, fear of advocating a novel idea, and fear of conflict (Sosik, Avolio, & Kahai, 1997). Gerardine Desanctis and Brent Gallupe, two management scientists interested in the small-group process within organizations, claimed that among the essential needs of decision-making groups are: (a) communicating ideas to all group members, (b) developing a group strategy,

(c) indicating individual preferences, and (d) participating equally (Desanctis & Gallupe, 1987). The use of electronic technologies in the 1980s, such as electronic messaging and teleconferencing, made possible technology-mediated communication.

Such electronic support systems allowed groups to engage in the four aforementioned group tasks by letting group members anonymously post ideas and other intellectual contributions, providing each group member a viewing screen to monitor group discussion, providing a summary of ideas circulated by all group members, and offering group members the opportunity to anonymously solicit the input and feedback of others (Dennis, George, Jessup, Nunamaker, & Vogel, 1988). Such technologies in the 1980s and 1990s were met with mixed results. Some groups benefited from the increased discussion and decreased communicative hesitation (more group members actively and willingly adopted task roles and maintenance roles), while other groups found that such mediated forums created too much of a no-holds-barred environment where individuals' social behaviors impeded group productivity (more group members became self-centered).

In today's organizational environment, Group Decision Support Systems and electronic technologies like them are more necessary than optional, as much group decision making occurs between and among individuals who are geographically dispersed. In short, an electronic support system helps overcome some of the obstacles associated with time and space. However, as with all forms of media, there are advantages and disadvantages associated with electronic communication. From a group perspective, such support systems stimulate increased participation, reduce the fear of nonconformity and social loafing, decrease interpersonal domination, and increase collaboration. Paradoxically, however, such support systems also provide an increased opportunity for information overload, a decrease in the speed at which a group moves through the stages of the decision-making process, a lack of nonverbal communication cues to gauge important social variables, and a potential increase in the amount of small-group conflict. It is important that organizations that use such technologies for group decision making enhance the positive effects and alleviate the negative effects associated with a GDSS and the communicative effects of it.

Summary

Groups are extremely important for organizations, though their creation, maintenance, and functioning are not without problems. If structured and managed properly, group work can lead to more effective and creative decision making, the presentation of a diversity of ideas, an increase in collective involvement, the distribution of tasks, and an accumulation of shared knowledge. If structured and managed poorly, however, group work can lead to communication breakdown, create too much social cohesion, take more time to make a decision, and result in social loafing. Although no two groups are the same in terms of social roles, social structure, and social norms, it is clear that harnessing the benefits associated with group work is important for organizations. The key is to determine how communication aids a group in its social practices and how group members can work collaboratively to achieve a common goal. Think about the organizational world around you. Even the seemingly most isolated jobs are filled by people working with others to provide a product and/or service. This highlights a claim made in the opening paragraph of this chapter, which stated that there is a semantic difference between the terms *organization* and *organize,* where people do the latter to create the former. People are doing work not individually, but collectively. They are, in other words, working in groups.

Questions for Discussion and Review

1. Explain why small groups in organizations likely have a ceiling effect and provide certain ways to overcome the potential negative effects of having too many people in one group.

2. Explain the differences between contrived and emergent groups and give an example of each.

3. One claim made early in this chapter is that there are several types of groups, although they are not necessarily mutually exclusive. Explain what this means and give an example of the overlapping nature of certain types of groups.

4. Explain what happens in each of the four group formation stages. Give an example of the communication issues that might arise as a group moves from orientation to reinforcement.

5. Explain why social influence has both positive and negative effects for small group communication within organizations.

6. Define Katz and Kahn's (1966) idea of holism and give a small-group example of how this informs the communication process.

7. One claim made early in this chapter is that risky shift mentality is an advantage of working in small groups. Create an argument that could reframe a risky shift as a small group's disadvantage and explain why this might become problematic.

8. Create a hypothetical small-group situation in which different people adopt task roles, maintenance roles, and self-centered roles. What do the different roles seem to provide group members? What would happen if one of the roles did not exist? How do these roles complement each other?

9. Differentiate among the chain network, the circle network, the wheel network, and the all-channel network. Explain the advantages and disadvantages of each. Is one type of network better suited for organizational work than another?

10. Explain how technology both eases and complicates the small-group decision-making process and give examples of times when using technology might be a strategic and successful decision.

References

Asch, S. E. (1951). Effects of group pressure upon the modification and distortion of judgments. In H. Guetzkow (Ed.), *Groups, leadership, and men* (pp. 177–190). Pittsburgh: Carnegie Press.

Alderton, S. M., & Frey, L. R. (1986). Argumentation in small group decision-making. In R. Y. Hirokawa & M. S. Poole (Eds.), *Communication and group decision-making* (pp. 157–173). Beverly Hills, CA: SAGE Publications.

Ancona, D. G. (1990). Outward bound: Strategies for team survival in the organization. *Academy of Management Journal, 33,* 334–365.

Bales, R. F., & Borgatta, E. F. (1966). Size of group as a factor in the interaction profile. In A. P. Hare, E. F. Borgatta, & R. F. Bales (Eds.), *Small groups: Studies in social interaction* (pp. 396–413). New York: Knopf.

Bavelas, A. (1948). A mathematical model for group structure. *Applied Anthropology, 7,* 16–30.

Beatty, M. J. (1989). Group members' decision rule orientations and consensus. *Human Communication Research, 16,* 279–296.

Benne, K. D., & Sheats, P. (1948). Functional roles of group members. *Journal of Social Issues, 4,* 41–49.

Bennis, W. G., & Shephard, H. R. (1956). A theory of group development. *Human Relations, 9,* 415–437.

Bonito, J. A., & Hollingshead, A. B. (1997). Participation in small groups. In B. R. Burleson (Ed.), *Communication Yearbook 20* (pp. 227–261). Newbury Park, CA: SAGE Publications.

Bray, S. R., & Brawley, L. R. (2002). Role efficacy, role clarity, and role performance effectiveness. *Small Group Research, 33,* 233–253.

Burke, K. (1950). *A rhetoric of motives.* Berkeley, CA: University of California Press.

Chang, A., Duck, J., & Bordia, P. (2006). Understanding the multidimensionality of group development. *Small Group Research, 37,* 327–350.

Cline, R. J., & Cline, T. R. (1980). A structural analysis of risky shift and cautious shift discussions: The diffusion of responsibility theory. *Communication Quarterly, 28,* 26–36.

Collins, B. E., & Guetzkow, H. (1964). *A social psychology of group processes for decision-making.* New York: Wiley.

Desanctis, G., & Gallupe, B. R. (1987). A foundation for the study of group decision support systems. *Management Science, 33,* 589–609.

Dennis, A. R., George, J. F., Jessup, L. M., Nunamaker, J. F., & Vogel, D. R. (1988). Information technology to support electronic meetings. *Management Information Systems Quarterly, 12,* 591–624.

DeStephen, R. L., & Hirokawa, R. Y. (1988). Small group consensus: Stability of group support for decision, task process, and group relationships. *Small Group Behavior, 19,* 227–239.

Farmer, S. M., & Roth, J. (1998). Conflict handling behavior in work groups: Effects of group structure, decision processes, and time. *Small Group Research, 29,* 669–713.

Fisher, B. A. (1970). Decision emergence: Phases in group decision making. *Speech Monographs, 37,* 53–66.

Gastil, J. (1993). *Democracy in small groups: Participation, decision-making, and communication.* Philadelphia: New Society Publishers.

Gersick, C. J. (1988). Time and transition in work teams: Toward a new model of group development. *The Academy of Management Journal, 31,* 9–41.

Gouran, D. S. (1969). Variables related to consensus in group discussions of questions of policy. *Speech Monographs, 36,* 387–391.

Gustafson, D. H., Shukla, R. K., Delbecq, A. L., & Walster, G. W. (1973). A comparative study of differences in subjective likelihood estimates made by individuals, interacting groups, Delphi groups, and nominal groups. *Organizational Behavior and Human Performance, 9,* 280–291.

Hansen, M., Mors, M. L., & Lovas, B. (2005). Knowledge sharing in organizations: Multiple networks, multiple phases. *Academy of Management Journal, 48,* 776–793.

Hirokawa, R. Y. (1988). Group communication and decision-making performance: A continued test of the functional perspective. *Human Communication Research, 14,* 487–515.

Hirokawa, R. Y. (1990). The role of communication in group decision-making efficacy: A task contingency perspective. *Small Group Research, 21,* 190–204.

Janis, I. (1972). *Victims of groupthink.* Boston: Houghton-Mifflin.

Karau, S. J., & Williams, K. D. (1993). Social loafing: A meta-analytic review and theoretical integration. *Journal of Personality and Social Psychology, 65,* 681–706.

Katz, D., & Kahn, R. L. (1966). *The social psychology of organizations.* New York: Wiley.

Hoegl, M., & Gemuenden, H. G. (2001). Teamwork quality and the success of innovative projects: A theoretical concept and empirical evidence. *Organization Science, 12,* 435–449.

Hoon, H., & Tan, M. L. (2008). Organizational citizenship behavior and social loafing: The role of personality, motives, and contextual factors. *Journal of Psychology, 142,* 89–108.

Ingham, A. G., Levinger, G., Graves, J., & Peckham, V. (1974). The ringelmann effect: Studies of group size and group performance. *Journal of Experimental Social Psychology, 10,* 371–384.

Mabry, E. A. (1999). The systems metaphor in group communication. In L. R. Frey, M. S. Poole, & D. S. Gouran (Eds.), *Handbook of group communication theory and research* (pp. 71–91). Thousand Oaks, CA: SAGE Publications.

Malone, D. (2002). Knowledge management: A model for organizational learning. *International Journal of Accounting Information Systems, 3,* 111–123.

Meyers, R. A., & Brashers, D. E. (1998). Argument in group decision making: Explicating a process model and investigating the argument-outcome link. *Communication Monographs, 65,* 261–281.

Monge, P. R., & Contractor, N. S. (2001). Emergence of communication networks. In F. M. Jablin & L. L. Putnam (Eds.), *New handbook of organizational communication* (pp. 440–502). Newbury Park, CA: SAGE Publications.

Monge, P. R., & Eisenberg, E. M. (1987). Emergent communication networks. In F. M. Jablin, L. L. Putnam, K. H. Roberts, & L. W. Porter (Eds.), *Handbook of organizational communication: An interdisciplinary perspective* (pp. 304–342). Newbury Park, CA: SAGE Publications.

Pelz, D. C. (1952). Influence: A key to effective leadership in the first line supervisor. *Personnel, 29,* 209–217.

Redding, C. W. (1966). The empirical study of human communication in business and industry. In P. E. Ried (Ed.), *Frontiers in experimental speech communication research* (pp. 47–81). Syracuse, NY: Syracuse University Press.

Rogers, E. M., & Kincaid, D. L. (1981). *Communication networks: Toward a new paradigm for research.* New York: Free Press.

Romero, E., & Pescosolido, A. (2008). Humor and group effectiveness. *Human Relations, 61,* 395–415.

Saunders, C. S., & Miranda, S. M. (1998). Information acquisition in group decision making. *Information and Management, 34,* 55–74.

Scheidel, T., & Crowell, L. (1964). Idea development in small discussion groups. *Quarterly Journal of Speech, 50,* 140–145.

Shaw, M. E. (1981). *Group dynamics: The psychology of small group behavior.* New York: McGraw Hill.

Sherif, M. (1935). *The psychology of social norms.* New York: Harper.

Sosik, J., Avolio, B., & Kahai, S. (1997). Effects of leadership style and anonymity on group potency and effectiveness in a GDSS environment. *The Journal of Applied Psychology, 82,* 89–103.

Stasser, G., & Titus, W. (1985). Pooling of unshared information in group decision making: Biased information sampling during discussion. *Journal of Personality and Social Psychology, 53,* 81–93.

Tuckman, B. W. (1965). Developmental sequence in small groups. *Psychological Bulletin, 63,* 384–399.

Vinokur, A., & Burnstein, E. (1974). The effects of partially shared persuasive arguments on group induced shifts: A group problem solving approach. *Journal of Personality and Social Psychology, 29,* 305–315.

Wallach, M. A., Kogan, N., & Bem, D. J. (1964). Diffusion of responsibility and level of risk taking in groups. *Journal of Abnormal and Social Psychology, 68,* 263–274.

Wheelan, S. A., & McKeage, R. (1993). Developmental patterns in small and large groups. *Small Group Research, 24,* 60–83.

Whitford, T., & Moss, S. A. (2009). Transformational leadership in distributed work groups: The moderating role of follower regulatory focus and goal orientation. *Communication Research, 36,* 810–837.

Xia, L., Yuan, Y. C., & Gay, G. (2009). Why don't we like to work with them: Personality, adversarial network and performance in project groups. *Management Communication Quarterly, 23,* 32–62.

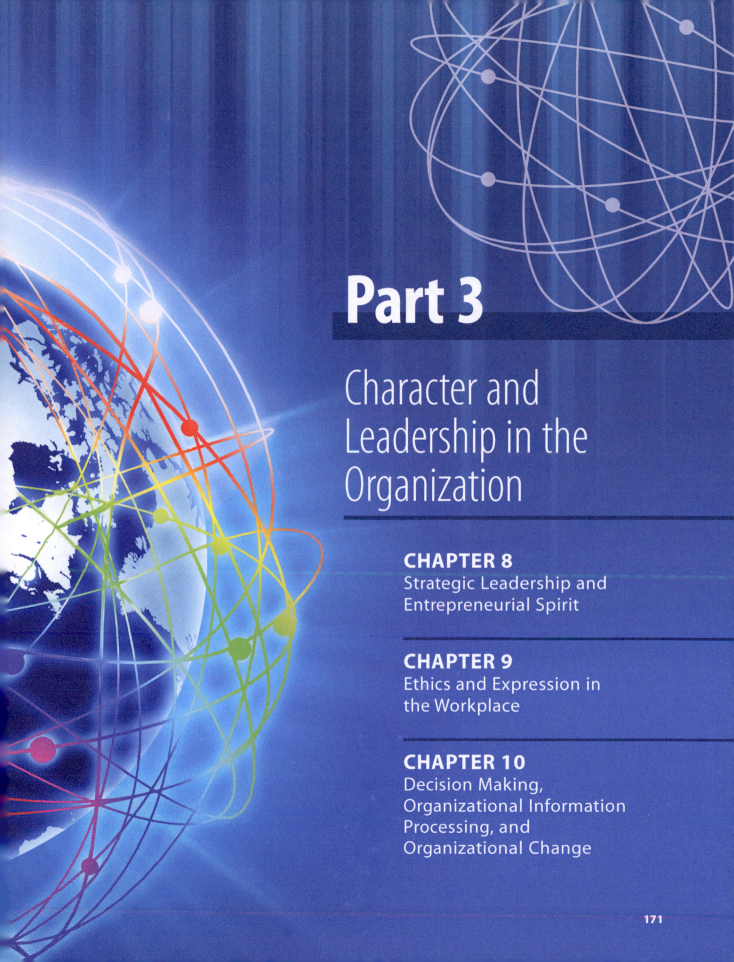

Part 3

Character and Leadership in the Organization

CHAPTER 8
Strategic Leadership and Entrepreneurial Spirit

CHAPTER 9
Ethics and Expression in the Workplace

CHAPTER 10
Decision Making, Organizational Information Processing, and Organizational Change

Chapter 8

Strategic Leadership and Entrepreneurial Spirit

Learning Objectives

Upon completion of the chapter, the student should be able to:

- Compare and contrast the trait leadership perspective and the situational leadership perspective.

- Compare and contrast the four leadership styles of Hersey and Blanchard.

- Compare and contrast hierarchy of needs theory, motivator hygiene theory, and acquired needs theory.

- Compare and contrast the three types of entrepreneurs.

Key Terms

Acquired needs theory

Contingency theory

Entrepreneurial spirit

Entrepreneurship

Exchange approaches to leadership

Great man theory of leadership

Hierarchy of needs

Leader-member exchange theory

Motivator hygiene theory

Situational leadership perspective

Situational leadership theory

Trait leadership perspective

One of the most important areas of research in organizational communication is the study of leadership. Throughout history people have hypothesized and theorized about what makes certain people exceed others' expectations and become legends. Our culture loves leaders and is constantly in search of the next "great person" to lead willing followers. This chapter presents assumptions about contemporary leadership perspectives as well as theories of human motivation, including what makes certain people strive continually to create new ideas, new products, and new ways of doing things. This chapter examines some of the most intriguing aspects of organizational life: leadership, motivation, and entrepreneurship.

Leadership

Before we present various perspectives on leadership, we must distinguish between management and leadership. Although most Americans confuse management with leadership, the differences between the two are immense. Perhaps the greatest differences lie in the perception of the status quo. The manager's role is to continue the status quo as efficiently as possible. This is not a negative thing if the status quo is efficient and profitable. On the other hand, leadership involves looking for the next development or opportunity for growth and change that may result in increased organizational growth, employee growth, profitability, and market share. Leaders look toward tomorrow to create the new status quo. That is, they engage in foresight more than present-sight. The manager's focus is on the here-and-now or what *is*, whereas the leader's focus is on tomorrow and what can be.

Managers generally do the "telling" ("This is the way we want you to do the job"), whereas leaders generally do the "selling" ("If we were to change this process, how would you do things differently?"). The manager's primary responsibility is to organize labor, whereas the leader's primary responsibility is to inspire labor. The reaction to information also highlights important differences between leaders and managers. Managers tend to be reactive to new information in an effort to maintain the status quo, whereas leaders tend to be proactive in that they use the untested and uncertain nature of new information as an opportunity for growth. The same is true with regard to vision. The manager sees the future through the prism of the past and present, whereas the leader sees the present through the future. A final important difference between managers and leaders is the power they use to get things done. Managers tend to use **legitimate power**, or power that is officially granted to them by the organization, as opposed to leaders, who use **referent power**, or the ability to get followers to act because the followers like the leader and believe in his or her vision (French & Raven, 1968). Given these vast differences between managers and leaders, we now focus on theories and perspectives of leadership.

Leadership Perspectives

It is a common assumption in our culture that people should "shoot for the stars." We are constantly bombarded with messages that tell us we should excel beyond our wildest dreams and reach some degree of superiority over others so that others may see us as successful. For example, consider the dramatic increase in viewership of professional sports—both the amount of different sports available as well as our interest in viewing and attending sporting events. The American culture thrives on competition and rising to the top. But for every victory there are countless failures. Is a person a good leader only if he or she succeeds? How do we measure success? Is success a tangible outcome, such as a higher score or victory in a game? Or is it a feeling or attitude? The answer is, it depends. To measure effective leadership, we must consider the goal of the leader and organization. Leaders of a for-profit company (e.g., Walmart) and a not-for-profit company (e.g., American Heart Association) are subject to different measures of success. Specifically, a for-profit company gauges success by quarterly revenue, whereas a not-for-profit organization measures success by the amount of donations (in dollars) received.

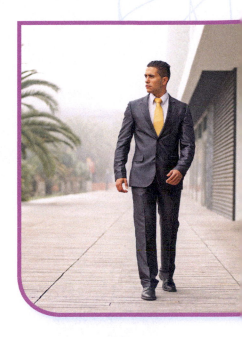

Trait Leadership Perspective

The **trait leadership perspective** holds that people either possess the attributes of a leader or they do not. For centuries, people have studied royalty and others in positions of power to determine what qualities they possess that make them effective leaders. This type of approach is known as the **great man theory of leadership**. In one of the first major contributions to the trait leadership perspective, Ralph Stodgill (1948, 1974) believed that leadership qualities are part of a person's personality and, therefore, research and theory on leadership must always account for personality traits.

There are several traits associated with leadership. First, leaders possess the trait of **narcissism**, which is the belief that they, as opposed to someone else, are qualified to lead. This trait assumes a higher level of self-confidence and self-efficacy in one's own ability to get things accomplished. Second, the trait of **charisma** reflects the leader's ability to display a high degree of communication competence, the ability to inspire confidence, the ability to inspire subordinates, as well as the ability to convince subordinates to buy into the leader's vision (Conger, Kanungo, & Associates, 1988). The term **communication competence** refers to the ability to be effective (i.e., achieve a desired goal) and appropriate (i.e., achieve goals in a way that respects other people and is deemed socially appropriate). The study of organizational leadership is prominent in the work of Max Weber (1947), who distinguished between charisma based on behavior (**pure charisma**) and charisma based on the position of power the person holds within the organization (**routinized charisma**). It is important to remember that leaders possess charisma regardless of whether their intent is for good or evil. Examples of people who

trait leadership perspective Perspective of leadership where leadership qualities are believed to be within an individual's personality.

great man theory of leadership Theory of leadership that assumes all great leaders have similar personality attributes.

are charismatic include John F. Kennedy, Oprah Winfrey, Charles Manson, Ronald Reagan, Barack Obama, Hillary Rodham Clinton, and David Koresh.

Interpretation of events distinguishes effective leaders from ineffective leaders. Locus of control is a trait that concerns how people attribute causes to outcomes in life (Rotter, 1966). Carl Anderson and Craig Schneier (1978) found that people who exhibit an internal locus of control (i.e., see outcomes as being a function of their own behavior) are more likely to be leaders than people who exhibit an external locus of control (i.e., see outcomes as a function of luck, chance, fate, other people, etc.). Internally oriented people reported having greater amounts of previous leadership experience (Hiers & Heckel, 1977) and emerge as group leaders more frequently than people who report being externally oriented (Lord, Phillips, & Rush, 1980).

There has been much debate about whether men or women are better leaders. Sex and gender are considered biological and psychological traits, respectively. That is, when we group people based on sex, we rely on biological indicators (male/female), whereas when we group people based on gender, we rely on psychological indicators (masculine/feminine). Because men and women do display differences in their leadership styles, both display effective and ineffective leadership behaviors. Rosabeth Kanter (1977) found that women in organizations tend to be more nurturing and socially sensitive, whereas men tend to be more assertive and use more overt power. More recently, researchers have found that the most effective leaders display a gender neutral style or display an **androgynous style**, which is a combination of both masculine and feminine behaviors (Hackman & Johnson, 2000). Although trait leadership studies have declined in recent years, a person's physical and psychological predispositions to lead remain viable in explaining effective versus ineffective leadership. The trait perspective assumes that because leadership is a consistent quality, the leader can lead regardless of the situation. However, another perspective holds that both situation and context determine which qualities and behaviors are considered leader-like. Therefore, leadership is believed to be situationally bound.

Situational Leadership Perspective

The **situational leadership perspective** assumes there is no such thing as a born leader; rather, people act as leaders depending on the situation. Consider the following list of people and whether they would be considered leaders without the particular situations in which they were involved Rosa Parks (without segregation), Abraham Lincoln (without the Civil War), Winston Churchill (without the Battle of Britain), Martin Luther King Jr. (without the Civil Rights struggles of the 1960s), Rudy Giuliani (without the terrorist attacks on the World Trade Center), and Mother Teresa (without Third World poverty and oppression). The **situational leadership theory** of Paul Hersey and Kenneth Blanchard (1977) assumes that any leadership style should be based on both the employee's **psychological maturity** (degree of self-efficacy and willingness to accept responsibility) and **job maturity**

This QR code will direct you to an article discussing both positive and negative organizational leadership strategies.

http://www.what-are-good-leadership-skills.com/effective-leadership-styles.html

situational leadership perspective Assumes there is no such thing as a born leader; rather, people act as leaders depending on the situation.

situational leadership theory Assumes that any leadership style should be based on both the employee's psychological maturity and job maturity.

(degree of skills and knowledge of the task). As employees' maturity increases, the most appropriate leadership style is more relationally focused than task focused. Specifically, there is a hierarchy of maturity levels, and each level requires a degree of both task and relational leadership styles.

At the most basic maturity level, a leader would use the **tell style**, which is high in task focus and low in relationship focus. The tell style is advocated for employees who have low self-efficacy and are unmotivated. Therefore, the leader must simply instruct or train employees in skills used in accomplishing the task. Second on the continuum is the **sell style**, which assumes that employees have some maturity and are resistant to being told what to do, yet are not fully motivated to show initiative. Therefore, the leader should be high in both task and employee focus. This type of leadership style includes explaining decisions and advising employees in an effort to motivate them toward task accomplishment. Third on the continuum is the **participative style**. This style assumes that employees have high levels of job maturity and low levels of psychological maturity. Therefore, a low task focus and high relational focus style are required because employees are capable of performing the task but are unwilling or resistant to perform the task. The final approach which is on the far end of the continuum is the **delegating style**, which reflects high levels of employee psychological and job maturity. With these employees, a low task focus and a low employee focus are required. In this case, employees are capable of performing the task and are motivated to do so. Therefore, the leader should allow employees to perform (Hersey, 1984).

Another situational leadership theory is Fielder's (1972) **contingency theory**, which holds that the degree of success of any leader is contingent on the situational demands (whether the leader should have a task focus or employee focus) and the amount of influence and control the leader has in the given situation. Basically, in situations that are in the extreme (very successful or very unsuccessful outcomes with no middle option), you would want a task-oriented leader. When the situation is moderate in gravity (moderately successful or moderately unsuccessful), an employee-focused leader is more effective.

Fielder (1972) believed that you cannot change the internal qualities of leaders and as such should find situations (task focused or employee focused) that match our specific qualities and offer a degree of control and influence over subordinates. For example, in professional sports you find coaches who have accomplished incredible things in terms of turning around a losing franchise or getting the most out of a difficult or underachieving player. However, when that same coach goes to a different team with a different culture and different players, he or she may only experience average success. The match of the person's strengths to the specific situation results in effective leadership but does not guarantee that the person will be successful in all situations because effective leadership is something that requires more than a leader's personality traits.

contingency theory Assumes that a leader's success is contingent on situational demands, such as whether the leader should have a task or employee focus and a leader's influence and control in a given situation.

The situational perspective gives hope to all of us who are afraid to speak in public, were not picked as captains of sport teams in grade school, or were not the most popular person on campus. What is important is that there is no "true" leadership style. Therefore, it is difficult to identify a leader before a situation occurs. There is little research to support a situational leadership perspective, yet it remains intuitively appealing in its assumptions, because it affords everyone the potential or chance of being a leader, given the right circumstances.

Exchange Approaches to Leadership

The perspectives of leadership discussed thus far have considered aspects of the individual, the situation, or a combination in determining what constitutes effective leadership. **Exchange approaches to leadership** looks at the quality of the relationship between organizational members to determine leadership effectiveness. In this section, we examine the two theories of leader-member exchange and transformational leadership.

Leader-member exchange theory (LMX) focuses on the **quality of relational linkages** between the superior (leader) and subordinates (members) as a major influence in determining effective leadership (Dansereau, Cashman, & Graen, 1973). More specifically, the way in which leaders and subordinates negotiate their specific roles influences how leaders and subordinates interpret work and the work experience. LMX theory assumes that leaders behave differently toward individual members of the organization based on the interpersonal nature of each relationship. That is, leaders develop either **high-quality links** or **low-quality links** with subordinates. A high-quality link is characterized by high trust, respect, and an overall positive tone, whereas a low-quality link is characterized by mistrust, lack of respect, and an overall negative tone. Subordinates with high-quality links to the leader are called **in-group members**, as opposed to subordinates with low-quality links to the leader, who are called **out-group members** (Dansereau, Graen, & Haga, 1975).

Research supporting the positive aspects of high-quality exchanges between leaders and members is bountiful. For example, in-group members are promoted more quickly and are more team oriented than out-group members (Erdogan, Liden, & Kraimer, 2006). According to LMX, the major influence on quality of leadership is the roles negotiated through interactions between the leader and individual members of the organization. The role development process consists of the **role-taking phase** (phase in which the supervisor seeks to discover the job-related talents and motivations of the member), the **role-making phase** (phase in which there is movement from the supervisor "telling" the subordinate his or her role to the subordinate seeking to alter the nature of the role as well as how the role is performed), and the **role-routinization phase** (phase in which the role of the subordinate is accepted by the supervisor and the subordinate's behavior becomes routine and expected).

exchange approaches to leadership Looks at the quality of the relationships between organizational members to determine leadership success.

leader-member exchange theory Describes how the relationship quality between superiors and subordinates is determined by the quality of their communication exchanges.

Another exchange-based leadership approach is **transformational leadership**. Our culture values equal rights and justice, but it also values competition and commitment. Transformational leadership focuses on empowering individual workers and helping the organization adapt to changes in both internal (e.g., implementing new technology) and external (e.g., changes in the market, community, or society at large) environments. This type of leadership is paradigmatic in that it represents a worldview rather than just another way to explain effective leadership behavior. The premises of transformational leadership are: (1) the leader is a change agent; (2) the leader emphasizes the self-actualization of subordinates; and (3) the leader pursues the goals of the organization as well as satisfies the higher-level needs of followers, including opportunities for growth and self-fulfillment. Tichy and Devanna (1986) highlighted seven characteristics that separate transformational leaders from other types of leaders. Table 8.1 lists these characteristics.

Transformational leadership involves constant change and adaptation. Given that society and organizational life are constantly changing, effective leaders must adapt appropriately to those changes. The only thing constant, according to the transformational approach, are the seven leadership characteristics described in Table 8.1.

Organizations as Leaders

When people generally think of leadership, they speak in terms of specific individuals. However, have you ever considered an organization as a whole

TABLE 8.1 Characteristics of Transformational Leaders	
Transformational Characteristics	**Thoughts, Feelings, and Behaviors**
Are identified as change agents	Understand that the only thing that remains stable in organizations is instability. Welcome the challenge of being innovating and changing as the environment demands.
Show courage	Will risk being ridiculed for the success of the organization and followers.
Have a clear vision	Are able to constantly envision the future and possibilities that accompany change and innovation.
Are driven by values	Demonstrate impeccable moral fiber and integrate this moral code into the day-to-day function of the organization and organizational members.
Never stop learning new information	Are life-long learners who are always interested in better ways of doing things. Rarely satisfied with the status quo and are always looking for the next innovation.
Welcome uncertainty and ambiguity	Thrive on chaos and welcome complex challenges. Uncertainty and ambiguity are motivating and represent an opportunity for growth.
Believe in workers	Have an undying commitment to bettering organizational members through opportunities for learning and growth.

when discussing leadership? The words *benchmarking* and *strategic planning* are terms that pertain to industry leaders. Generally speaking, when organizations set goals for the future, they base those goals on the organization that is the most effective at that time. Tom Peters and Robert Waterman (1982) authored a revolutionary book entitled *In Search of Excellence: Lessons from America's Best Run Companies* in which they tracked "excellent companies" to see what they were doing and how they were doing it. To be considered an excellent company, the following three criteria were developed. First, the company had to be on the *Fortune* 500 list (a list of the 500 U.S. companies that generate the greatest revenue). Second, the company had to experience above-average growth and financial return over a 20-year period. Finally, the company had to have a reputation of being an innovative organization within its field. Among the companies included in the analyses were Boeing, Hewlett-Packard, IBM, Johnson & Johnson, McDonald's, Proctor & Gamble, and 3M.

Peters and Waterman (1982), along with other colleagues, developed a set of seven interrelated concepts known as the **McKinsey 7-S Framework,** which is based on structure, strategy, systems, style, skills, staff, and shared values. Using this framework in their analysis, Peters and Waterman (1982) delineated eight attributes common to all 43 excellent companies studied.

1. **Bias for action:** These companies exhibit a "let's try it and see what happens" attitude. This shows a willingness to experiment with innovative ideas to see if there is any benefit to the company.

2. **Close to the customer:** These companies view customers as the sole reason they exist and constantly remind employees of this fact. Further, the customer is considered an invaluable resource for innovation and change.

3. **Autonomy and entrepreneurship:** Excellent companies support and encourage risk taking, internal competition, as well as a high number of innovations. They encourage innovations because the greater the number of total innovations (given that some will fail), the greater the number of successful innovations.

4. **Productivity through people:** Although these companies are totally performance centered, they see productivity not as a result of organizational control but as something born of the organization's great expectations for each employee. The culture that results filters out low-performing employees. Low-performing employees soon find that they do not fit in the organization and will self-select out. That is, they will actively seek other employment opportunities.

5. **Hands on, value driven:** People at all levels of the organization get involved in all of the tasks performed by the organization. For example, at Service Master Corporation, which is the largest facility maintenance organization in the world, all top management from the CEO down to front line supervisors will take one day out of the year,

put on work clothes and perform cleaning duties such as mopping floors, dusting, and vacuuming. This is done to remind all members of the organization that they are not too busy to serve other people as well to remind them of the business that they have chosen to be in. This commitment to the organizational-wide value system is the organization's cohesive glue. Excellent companies have a focused value system that permeates every aspect of the organization.

6. **Stick to the knitting:** Excellent companies focus only on doing what they do best. They do not seek to grow for the sake of growing (e.g., a high-tech company should not acquire an airline simply because it can afford to do so). Basically, this concept urges organizations to stick with the services, products, and/or sectors that brought success in the first place.

7. **Simple form, lean staff:** Companies that enjoy great success have highly streamlined organizational structures. Authority is well defined at all levels of the organization. For example, it was common practice in the Japanese automobile industry to cut resources down to where the organization was most efficient. Once achieved, management would attempt to cut another 10 percent of the resources and see how efficient and streamlined the organization could become. Once the cutting of resources resulted in decreased quality or performance, previous levels of funding were restored and the organization was deemed to be efficient and streamlined.

8. **Simultaneous loose-tight properties:** Excellent companies give departments and divisions a great degree of autonomy and latitude. At the same time, however, all departments and divisions are bound to the central value system and culture of the organization.

One of the key lessons from the Peters and Waterman (1982) book is that excellence is temporary. As society, technology, and consumer tastes change, excellent organizations must also adapt, change, and innovate to stay relevant (Peters, 1987). Simply put, *what is effective today will be ineffective tomorrow.*

Applied Leadership

It has become common practice in business to promote employees who are successful at what they do. For example, we seek out the most effective drill press operator and promote that person to manager of drill press operators. This is the best recipe for managerial disaster. What does the drill press operator know about managing people who operate a drill press? More often than not, this person may not be an effective leader. It is one thing to be a high-quality producer at a task and quite a different thing to manage people who produce. Simply put, doing something well does not necessarily give you the skill set to manage people who do the same thing. This notion is also known as the **Peter Principle**. That is, people rise to their level of incompetence. This is a **principle of hierarchiology** and holds that organizational members

This QR code will direct you to a YouTube clip highlighting different strategies of organizational leadership.

http://www.youtube.com/watch?v=Y47qRvPHoVU

are promoted to their highest level of competence. Any further promotion results in becoming incompetent (Peter & Hull, 1969). This is the same basic approach taken by Jack Welch (former CEO of General Electric and widely recognized as one of the most successful American organizational leaders).

Jack and his wife, Suzy, in their book entitled *Winning* (Welch & Welch, 2005), argue that when you become a leader, it is no longer about you; it is about your people. Success, therefore, is about growing other people through making your workers better, more intelligent, and more secure in their professional identities. This is accomplished through nurturing and support and is not as easy as it seems. For example, chances are you are reading this material because you hope to get one of the *best grades* in the course. When you complete your degree, you work hard to be promoted to a position of power. All of this focus is about you. This type of focus is vital to initial success (i.e., laying the foundation for your career). However, when you become a leader, you must turn off this tendency toward self-focus. That is, you must behave in ways that differ completely from the behaviors that brought you initial professional success. Further, the Welches advocate exhibiting positive energy and optimism and making every big event, whether positive or negative, an opportunity to teach a lesson to your team.

In a study cosponsored by *U.S. News & World Report* and the Center for Public Leadership at Harvard University's John F. Kennedy School of Government, a well-respected panel sought to determine the top 24 leaders of both public- and private-sector organizations. The committee comprised academic, government, business, and nonprofit leaders convened by the center. It defined an award-winning leader as a person who motivates people to collaborate with one another to accomplish amazing things. The committee used the following criteria in the selection process:

- *Sets direction.* This comprised 25 percent of the criteria. Sets direction consists of encouraging a shared sense of purpose, a movement toward positive social consequences, and strategic innovation.

- *Achieves results.* This comprised 50 percent of the criteria. Achieves results consists of results that are profound and have wide-ranging effects, have a positive social impact, are sustainable, and exceed expectations.

- *Cultivates a culture of growth.* This comprises the final 25 percent of the criteria. Cultivates a culture of growth consists of communicating and embodying the positive organizational core values and inspiring others to take initiative and be leaders.

Using these criteria, the committee chose the top 24 leaders and awarded them the honor of that designation (see Table 8.2).

Leaders have special qualities that transcend simple character traits, communication skills, or situational attributes. Effective leaders possess all three of these qualities, all of which contribute to effective leadership.

| **TABLE 8.2** | The Top 24 Leaders/Leadership Teams in Private and Public Sectors |

Name	**Position**
Lance Armstrong	Cyclist and Advocate
David Baltimore	Scientist
Regina Benjamin	Physician
Jeff Bezos	Corporate CEO
Robert Gates	22nd U.S. Secretary of Defense
Fiora Harrison & Maria Zuber	Scientists
Freeman Hrabowski	Education
Amory Lovins	Engineer
Anne Mulcahy	Corporate CEO
Terence Blanchard & Herbie Hancock	Musicians
Indra Nooyi	Corporate CEO
Benjamin Carson	Surgeon
Linda Rottenberg	Corporate CEO
Manny Diaz	Mayor
Jeffery Sachs	Economist
Marian Wright Edelman	Advocate
Steven Spielberg	Film Maker
Anthony Fauci	Physician
Michael Tilson Thomas	Symphony Director
Mike Feinberg & Dave Levin	Education
United States Junior Officers	Military

Source: http://www.usnews.com/news/special-reports/features/best-leaders

However, both leaders and followers must be motivated toward success if they are to be successful in the organization. The next section reviews some aspects of human motivation.

Motivation

The need to explain why people behave as they do has prompted researchers in all of the social sciences to provide dozens of explanations and theories for human behavior. Explaining why people work is no different. The reasons we go to work and pursue particular careers of interest are as unique and diverse as each one of us. Examples of why people work include money,

FIGURE 8.1
Maslow's Hierarchy of Needs.
Adapted from A. H. Maslow
(1943) a Theory of Human
Motivation, *Psychological Review,*
50, 370–396.

power, prestige, pride, and commitment. This next section reviews several ways of thinking about human motivation in general as well as motivation specific to the workplace.

Maslow's Hierarchy of Needs

hierarchy of needs Approach to motivation that holds that there are primary needs that must be satisfied before a person can pursue higher-level needs.

Abraham Maslow (1943) proposed a theory of motivation based on the pursuit to fulfill human needs. Maslow's **hierarchy of needs** approach to motivation holds that there are **primary needs** that must be satisfied before a person can pursue higher-level needs. These lower or more primitive needs sustain physiological survival (our need for air, water, food, etc.). Once these physiological needs are met, we are motivated to satisfy our **safety needs**, such as a life free of turmoil, relative stability, and a preference for predictability. Upon meeting the safety needs, we are motivated to satisfy our **love needs**, which include the need for affection and a sense of belonging to the larger human community. Once the love needs are met, we are motivated to satisfy our **esteem needs**, such as pursuing recognition, appreciation, and respect from other people. Once these needs are met, we are motivated to achieve our highest level need—**self-actualization**—in which we focus on reaching the pinnacle of our potential for achievement and meaning. Figure 8.1 depicts Maslow's hierarchy of needs. For example, when you feel that everything is going great in your world (family, work, personal, health, etc.), you are feeling self-actualized. However, it is important to understand that we are constantly trying to achieve self-actualization and are constantly fluctuating up and down this hierarchy of needs. Think about your future work life, which will likely last for at least 40 years. Throughout your work life you will encounter good health, sickness, death, success, and failure as well as a variety of other life circumstances that will bring about varying levels of motivation. No matter where you are in the hierarchy, such events will influence your motivation.

Motivator Hygiene Theory

This theory of motivation was developed by Fredrick Herzberg (1968) and is based on the degree of satisfaction and dissatisfaction workers experience in the workplace. **Motivator hygiene theory** is a departure from the more traditional theories of motivation, which are established on a single continuum ranging from satisfied to dissatisfied. Instead, Herzberg proposed a two-continua model in which the first continuum reflects a range from being satisfied to not being satisfied, and the second continuum reflects a range from being dissatisfied to not being dissatisfied. Figure 8.2 illustrates these continua. The rationale for creating two continua is based on the concept that the opposite of something is not something different. This concept is best illustrated by our legal system, in the handing down of verdicts. When a person is found not to have committed a crime of which he or she was accused, that person is found to be "not guilty" as opposed to "innocent." The absence of something (e.g., guilt) cannot be something else (e.g., innocent). Instead, it is not guilty. Simply put, the opposite of "apple" is "not apple".

Similar to Maslow's lower-level needs (physiological and safety needs), factors related to job dissatisfaction concern the person's need to avoid being deprived of physical and social rewards. Herzberg (1968) illustrates the pursuit of these needs using an analogy of the biblical characters Adam and Abraham. The **Adam personality** concept reflects behavior that occurred after Adam was sent out of the Garden of Eden. That is, he was faced with the need to satisfy the primal needs of food, security, safety, and so on. The motivation to satisfy these needs became Adam's sole focus. This is similar to the **hedonic philosophy of life**, which implies the pursuit of pleasure which is immediate gratification only to reemerge soon after fulfillment. Adam's banishment was a result of this hedonic (indulgent) behavior.

The factors associated with being satisfied in a job are similar to Maslow's concept of self-actualization and reflect the need to achieve the maximum of human potential and perfection (Pugh & Hickson, 1997). This type of motivation is reflected in the biblical character Abraham and is known as the **Abraham personality**. According to the Bible, God summoned Abraham because he believed that Abraham was capable of accomplishments that were far beyond primal needs. The pursuit of self-realization and great achievement for an entire people, rather than his own needs, was Abraham's primary focus. The Abraham personality is reflective of the **eudaimonic philosophy of life** in that people seek deeper meaning in life and move beyond the simple pursuit of pleasure and happiness.

Although both the Adam and Abraham personalities seek to be satisfied at work, they seek satisfaction in different places. The Adam personality seeks to avoid pain, which, in the workplace, means avoidance of dissatisfaction. This motivational force results in a search for ways to avoid pain in the immediate environment through things such as good pay, good coworker relationships, and a pleasant working environment. The Adam personality

motivator hygiene theory Theory of motivation that assumes people are motivated to action based on the degree of satisfaction or dissatisfaction they experience on the job.

This QR code will direct you to an article published by the *Chief Executive Group*, which discusses the 40 top-rated organizations in terms of leadership practices.

ttp://chiefexecutive.net/40-best-companies-for-leaders-2012-how-top-companies-excel-in-leadership-development

FIGURE 8.2
Herzberg's Motivator
Hygiene Continua

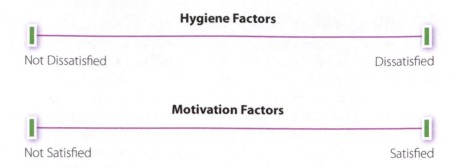

is motivated to avoid dissatisfaction and is not motivated toward achieving satisfaction. In contrast, the Abraham personality seeks achievement, recognition, and opportunity for growth.

Herzberg (1968) termed the things that make us dissatisfied **hygiene factors** (e.g., pay, working conditions, etc.). To use a biological analogy, poor hygiene can lead to disease, but good hygiene does not necessarily stop disease. In other words, just providing a worker with good pay and good working conditions does not mean that the worker will be motivated. On the other hand, the things that make us satisfied are known as **motivator factors** or **growth factors** and concern the need for great accomplishment, human growth, and self-realization. The lack of motivator factors will not cause a worker to be dissatisfied (assuming good hygiene is present) but will cause a worker to not be satisfied. This theory was tested and supported in research studies using engineers and accountants. The findings indicated that the factors that make workers satisfied are different from those that result in dissatisfaction. More specifically, the five factors that make people satisfied are *achievement, recognition, the attraction of the work itself, responsibility, and chance for advancement.* On the other hand, the factors associated with being dissatisfied were company policies/company administration, supervision, salary, interpersonal relations, and working conditions (Pugh & Hickson, 1997).

To test this theory, Herzberg (1982) assessed over 1,600 employees and found that 81 percent of motivator factors reflected human growth and development whereas 69 percent of hygiene factors contributed to dissatisfaction. The overall principle of motivator hygiene theory is that workers will be most likely to perform well if they are given all the appropriate tools. Although providing these tools will not motivate workers, it will keep them from becoming dissatisfied. Further, this theory encompasses the complexity of human nature and the innate need for human growth. Figure 8.2 illustrates this concept.

acquired needs theory
Assumes that people are motivated to behave in ways that help them acquire things that the culture at large deems important.

Acquired Needs Theory

The influence of culture on individuals is the underlying assumption of the **acquired needs theory** of motivation. This theory assumes that people are motivated to work to acquire the things that the culture at large deems important (McClelland, 1962). All the needs dictated by the culture can be broken down into three main or overarching needs that, according to Western culture, are pursued through work.

The first is the **need for achievement**. People who are high in this need are motivated to acquire positions of responsibility and strive to achieve moderate goals (they pursue moderate goals because goals that are seen as too easy will be reached by everyone and thus will not be viewed as a significant success; on the other hand, goals that are seen as too difficult will be reached by very few and thus may lead to failure). Research indicates that workers who are high in the need for achievement are also open, sensitive, and report higher levels of job satisfaction (Mitchell, 1984). The second need is the **need for power**. People who are high in this need are motivated to aspire to greatness and positions of respect (Kotter, 1988). This motivation also includes the pursuit for control, influence, and responsibility over other people.

Although it may seem that people who pursue the need for power have selfish intentions, people who are high in the motivation for power often use this power to help others around them (McClelland, 1975). The final need is the **need for affiliation**, which is the need to develop and enjoy quality relationships with others, avoid conflict, and be less dogmatic and less assertive in an effort to maintain these relationships. Overall, acquired needs theory highlights the different factors that motivate people and uses these factors to explain why people are motivated to perform certain jobs at certain productivity levels. For example, a productive social worker who makes an annual salary of $22,000 per year is motivated by different needs than a productive stockbroker who makes $220,000 per year.

Theories of worker motivation seek to predict, explain, and understand the things that motivate people to work as well as how to tap into these motivating factors to achieve maximum employee performance. Motivation will continue to be an intriguing aspect of productive organizational function. Beyond the theories reviewed here, there are many perspectives on how or why workers are motivated. However most differentiate the more primal needs (i.e., physiological needs) from higher-level needs (i.e., psychological needs). Regardless of how you view motivation, the fact remains that people are complex beings and have a wide range of needs that they strive to satisfy. The roles of communication and relationship building and maintaining are central in these theories of worker motivation. The ability to satisfy workers' physiological, psychological, and interpersonal needs results in motivated, committed, and long-term employees.

Entrepreneurial Spirit

Entrepreneurs can be considered innovators in terms of not only their vision of what is possible, but also in their acquisition and coordination of

TABLE 8.3	Some of the Greatest Entrepreneurs

Industry-Related	Entertainment
Ben Franklin (1706–1790)	P. T. Barnum (1810–1891)
Henry Ford (1863–1947)	Louis B. Mayer (1885–1957)
John D. Rockefeller (1839–1937)	Walt Disney (1901–1966)
Cyrus McCormick Sr. (1809–1994)	Berry Gordy Jr. (1929–)
Andrew Carnegie (1835–1919)	George Lucas (1944–)
Finance-Related	**Media Related**
Charles Schwab (1937–)	Martha Stewart (1941–)
Amadeo P. Giannini (1870–1949)	David Sarnoff (1891–1971)
J. P. Morgan (1837–1913)	Robert Johnson (1946–)
Charles Merrill (1885–1956)	Oprah Winfrey (1954–)
Transportation-Related	**Retail-Related**
Herb Kelleher (1931–)	Aaron Montgomery Ward (1843–1913)
Fred W. Smith (1944–)	Sam Walton (1918–1992)
William S. Harley (1880–1943)	Richard Sears (1863–1914)
Arthur Davidson (1881–1950)	Alvah Roebuck (1864–1948)
Franchising-Related	**Fashion-Related**
Roy Kroc (1902–1984)	Ralph Lauren (1939–)
Harland Sanders (1890–1980)	Levi Strauss (1829–1902)
Juan Trippe (1899–1981)	Phil Knight (1938–)
Technology-Related	**Consumer-Goods Related**
George Eastman (1854–1932)	Estee Lauder (1908–2004)
Steve Jobs (1955–2011)	Madam C. J. Walker (1867–1919)
Michael Dell (1965–)	Asa Chandler (1851–1929)
Bill Gates (1955–)	W. K. Kellogg (1860–1951)
Thomas Alva Edison (1847–1931)	Milton Hershey (1857–1945)
Ross Perot (1930–)	Eberhard Anheuser (1805–1880)
	Adolphus Busch (1839–1913)
Hospitality-Related	**Internet-Related**
William Becker (1921–2007)	Jeff Bezos (1964–)
Paul Greene (1914–1994)	Steve Case (1958–)
J. W. Marriott Jr. (1932–)	Pierre Omidyar (1967–)
Conrad Hilton Sr. (1887–1979)	Larry Page (1973–)
	Sergey Brin (1973–)

Source: Heisz, Ocker, & Skrhak (2011).

the resources necessary to make the venture successful. Many people have an entrepreneurial spirit, but many may use that spirit in ways unrelated to traditional business outcomes. For example, entrepreneurial spirit may take the form of developing a program to help the elderly or the homeless, to pursue a nonprofit venture, or to devise more efficient ways to organize household finances.

There are many definitions of **entrepreneurship**, including willingness to take the initiative, the ability to recognize and reorganize social and economic resources in practical ways, and acceptance of the inherent risk of failure in such practices (Cohen, 1990). We define entrepreneurship as the process of creating or synthesizing something new or unique and investing the necessary financial, social, psychological, and temporal capital to achieve independence related to personal, psychological, or professional ends. In the same vein, we define **entrepreneurial spirit** as the capacity to be predisposed to engage in the process of creating or synthesizing something new or unique and investing the necessary financial, social, psychological, and temporal capital to realize independence related to personal, psychological, or professional ends. Table 8.3 lists some of the greatest entrepreneurs of all time.

Although there is a general belief that people become entrepreneurs because they are entirely self-motivated, driven people, people choose to pursue entrepreneurship for a number of other reasons. Simply put, entrepreneurs can be divided into **push-factors** and **pull-factors**. Push-factors pertain to people who become entrepreneurs because environmental factors thrust them into that role. Examples of such environmental factors include events such as a lay-off, bankruptcy, or change in marital status. This sort of entrepreneurship reflects a need to cope with the present situation. Pull-factors reflect the pursuit of positive rewards rather than the need to survive and cope with a problematic situation. The need to be independent, wealthy, and respected represents pull-factors.

In addition to the various reasons for becoming an entrepreneur, entrepreneurs are categorized based on their specific motivations. There are three basic types of entrepreneurs based on the objectives of the specific person (Stanworth & Curran, 1976). The **artisan entrepreneur** seeks independence and autonomy as the primary goal; making money is not deemed as important as getting satisfaction from work. Organizations established based on these needs tend to start and remain small. The **traditional entrepreneur** seeks to maximize financial gain and is constantly pursuing growth for the company. Therefore, for the traditional entrepreneur, size matters and the larger the firm, the better. The psychological factors of independence and autonomy are secondary to monetary success for this type of entrepreneur. Finally, the **managerial entrepreneur** believes that making a good income and seeking higher social status are important, but so is the need to grow the organization. The managerial entrepreneur seeks both tangible and psychosocial rewards from the venture.

entrepreneurship The process of creating or synthesizing something new or unique and investing the necessary resources to realize independence related to personal, psychological, or professional ends.

entrepreneurial spirit The capacity to be predisposed to engage in the process of creating or synthesizing something new or unique and investing the necessary resources to realize independence related to personal, psychological, or professional ends.

Can a person obtain all or some of the goals of the entrepreneurial types yet remain employed within an organization? People who perform the actions of an entrepreneur (pursuit of autonomy, status, etc.) within an existing organization are known as **intrapreneurs** (Hisrich & Peters, 2002). An intrapreneur is generally given the autonomy and resources necessary to innovate and then have those innovations produced and marketed by the organization. Often teams of people are given autonomy to create and are expected to develop new and innovative projects in unorthodox ways. Such teams are referred to as **skunkworks**. This is a group of individuals brought together to achieve unusual results and given freedom to operate independent of existing organizational norms and rules. Skunkworks, then, are teams of intrapreneurs.

Background and Personality Factors

Many research studies demonstrate that entrepreneurs share particular personality and sociopsychological factors (Huuskonen, 1993). The typical entrepreneur is 25 to 40 years old, is the first born child, and (until recently

TABLE 8.4   Entrepreneurial Skill Sets.

Technical Skills	Business Management Skills
*Writing	Planning and goal setting
*Oral communication	*Decision making
Monitoring environment	*Human relations
Technical business management	*Marketing
Technology	Finance
*Interpersonal	Accounting
*Listening	*Management
*Ability to organize	Control
*Network building	*Negotiation
*Management style	Venture launch
*Coaching	Managing growth
*Team player	
Personal Entrepreneurial Skills	
Self-discipline	Persistent
Risk taker	Visionary leader
Innovator	Ability to manage change
Change oriented	

* = communication based or requires substantial communication skills

when women have made great strides in workplace representation) are typically male. Further, entrepreneurs have a great deal of self-confidence and relatively few family and economic ties. It is easier for a person without dependents, a spouse, or mortgage to take risks than it is for someone who has such ties.

In Chapter 6 we discussed the influence of personality on our work behavior. As discussed earlier in this chapter, effective leadership is a function of our personality. The same is true of the entrepreneur's personality characteristics. The entrepreneur generally has a strong feeling of being in control (i.e., an internal locus of control), has a high need to achieve (e.g., financially, status, independence, etc.), and a high need for autonomy and power (Brockhaus, 1987; Stanworth, Stanworth, Granger, & Blyth, 1989). Entrepreneurs often possess a difficult and rebellious personality, which may cause them to come across as rebellious and lacking in teambuilding skills. Nonetheless, entrepreneurs have the experience, requisite skill sets, and means of implementing financial, motivational, and predispositional characteristics that lend them to effective uncertainty management and strategic risk taking. Robert Hisrich (1992) outlines the skill sets necessary for effective entrepreneurship. He believes that entrepreneurial skillsets can be broken down into technical skills, business management skills, and personal entrepreneurial skills. In Table 8.4, we have placed an asterisk beside the skillsets that are either exclusively communication based or require substantial communication skill. As you will see, effective entrepreneurs must have effective communication skills if they are to achieve success.

Summary

Leadership, as presented in this chapter, continues to intrigue researchers and practitioners, alike. In any given year, dozens of books are written that attempt to explain the complex process of leading others effectively and appropriately. The research reviewed throughout this chapter provides evidence for the many ways people think about leadership (e.g., leaders are born, made, or a combination of both).

Leadership is not necessarily about individuals. As the review of excellent companies suggests, organizations that lead their industries are not necessarily successful because of a CEO or any one member of the organization. Instead, organizations are nothing more than a collection of people. When an organization has effective leaders and effective followers, that organization displays qualities of a leading organization.

Vision, risk, accountability, integrity, compassion, and vision are but a few of the characteristics that effective leaders share. For the most part, the literature suggests that we can learn most of these characteristics if we are willing to change and adapt to the environment around us. It is no coincidence that most of the people cited as effective leaders have years of experience with both success and failure. As was mentioned in earlier chapters, learning from failure can be far more meaningful and valuable than learning from success. Effective leaders do just that.

Motivation also continues to be an intriguing aspect of productive organizational function. There are many different perspectives concerning how and why people are motivated. Most, however, differentiate the more primal needs (i.e., physiological needs) from higher-level needs (i.e., psychological needs). Regardless of how you view motivation, the constant is that people are complex beings with a wide range of needs who strive to satisfy those needs. Satisfying workers' physiological and psychological needs, by most accounts, results in motivated, committed, and long-term employees.

Finally, we examined the concept of entrepreneurial spirit and the shared characteristics of entrepreneurs. Whether influenced by external circumstances beyond their control or an internal need for autonomy, control, and financial independence, entrepreneurs have a unique life perspective that is conducive to management of uncertainty, a predisposition toward risk taking, and the ability to communicate effectively.

Questions for Discussion and Review

1. Define trait leadership. Identify both the strengths and weaknesses of this perspective.

2. Define the basic idea behind situational leadership. Argue why the situational approach to leadership may be a better way to describe leadership than a trait approach.

3. Describe the basic premise underlying leader-member exchange theory. Explain what behaviors determine whether a worker becomes a member of the in-group or out-group.

4. Define transformational leadership. What is meant by the idea that this type of leadership is more paradigmatic or representative of a worldview than other approaches? Provide examples to support your answer.

5. Explain the McKinsey 7-S Framework. List the eight attributes of excellent companies.

6. Describe the Principle of Hierarchology. Provide an example.

7. Explain Maslow's hierarchy of needs. Provide an example.

8. Explain the basic idea behind Herzberg's motivator hygiene theory. Discuss how having satisfied and dissatisfied continua provide a unique perspective to motivation.

References

Anderson, C. R., & Schneier, C. E. (1978). Locus of control, leader behavior and leader performance among management students. *Academy of Management Journal, 21,* 690–698.

Brockhaus, R. H. (1987). Entrepreneurial folklore. *Journal of Small Business Management, 7,* 1–6.

Cohen, J. A. (1990). Footwear and the jet set. *Management Review, 1,* 42–45.

Conger, J. A., Kanungo, R. N., & Associates. (1988). *Charismatic leadership: The elusive factor in organizational effectiveness.* San Francisco: Jossey-Bass.

Dansereau, F., Cashman, J., & Graen, G. B. (1973). Instrumentality theory and equity theory as complementary approaches in predicting the relationship of leaders and turnover among managers. *Organizational Behavior & Human Performance, 10,* 184–200.

Dansereau, F., Graen, G. B., & Haga, W. J. (1975). A vertical dyad linkage approach to leadership within formal organizations: A longitudinal investigation of the role making process. *Organizational Behavior & Human Performance, 13,* 46–78.

Erdogan, B., Liden, R. C., & Kraimer, M. L. (2006). Justice and leader-member exchange: The moderating role of organizational culture. *Academy of Management Journal, 49,* 395–406.

Fielder, F. E. (1972). How do you make leaders more effective? *American Behavioral Scientist, 24,* 630–631.

French, J. R. P., & Raven, B. (1968). The bases for social power. In D. Cartwright (Ed.), *Studies in social power* (pp. 259–270). Ann Arbor, MI: University of Michigan Press.

Hackman, M. Z., & Johnson, C. E. (2000). *Leadership: A communication perspective.* Prospect Heights, IL: Waveland.

Heisz, D., Ocker, L., & Skrhak, K. S. (2011). *50 greatest entrepreneurs of all time.* Success Magazine. Retrieved from http://www.successmagazine.com/50-GreatestEntrepreneurs-of-All-Time/PARAMS/article/182/channel/15

Hersey, P. (1984). *The situational leader.* Escondido, CA: Center for Leadership Studies.

Hersey, P., & Blanchard, K. H. (1977). *Management of organizational behavior: Utilizing human resources* (3rd ed.). Englewood Cliffs, NJ: Prentice Hall.

Herzberg, F. (1968). 'One more time: How do you motivate employees?' *Harvard Business Review, 46,* 53–62.

Herzberg, F. (1982). *Managerial choice: To be efficient and to be human.* Provo, UT: Olympus.

Hiers, J. M., & Heckel, R. V. (1977). Seating choice, leadership, and locus of control. *Journal of Social Psychology, 103,* 313–314.

Hisrich, R. D. (1992, June). Toward an organizational model for entrepreneurial education. *Proceedings of the International Entrepreneurship Conference,* Dortmund, Germany.

Hisrich, R. D., & Peters, M. P. (2002). *Entrepreneurship* (5th ed.). Boston: McGraw-Hill.

Huuskonen, V. (1993). The process of becoming an entrepreneur: A theoretical framework of factors influencing entrepreneurs' start-up decisions. In H. Klandt (Ed.), *Entrepreneurship and business development* (pp. 43–54). Brookfield, VT: Ashgate Publishing.

Kanter, R. M. (1977). *Men and women of the corporation.* New York: Basic Books.

Kotter, J. P. (1988). *The leadership factor.* New York: Free Press.

Lord, R. G., Phillips, J. S., & Rush, M. C. (1980). Effects of sex and personality on perceptions of emergent leadership, influence, and social power. *Journal of Applied Psychology, 65,* 176–182.

Maslow, A. H. (1943). A theory of human motivation. *Psychological Review, 50,* 370–396.

McClelland, D. C. (1962). Business drive and national achievement. *Harvard Business Review, 40,* 99–112.

McClelland, D. C. (1975). *Power: The inner experience.* New York: Irvington.

Mitchell, T. R. (1984). *Motivation and performance.* Chicago: Science Research Associates.

Peter, L. J., & Hull, R. (1969). *The Peter Principle: Why things always go wrong.* New York: William Morrow & Co.

Peters, T. J. (1987). *Thriving on chaos: A handbook for management revolution.* New York: Macmillan.

Peters, T. J., & Waterman, R. H. (1982). *In search of excellence: Lessons from America's best run companies.* New York: Harper & Row.

Pugh, D. S., & Hickson, D. J. (1997). *Writers on organizations* (5th ed.). Thousand Oaks, CA: SAGE Publications.

Rotter, J. B. (1966). Generalized expectancies for internal versus external control of reinforcement. *Psychological Monographs, 80* (Whole No. 609).

Stanworth, M. J. K., & Curran, J. (1976). Growth and the small firm: An alternative view. *Journal of Management Studies, 13,* 95–196.

Stanworth, M. J. K., Stanworth, C., Granger, B., & Blyth, S. (1989). Who becomes an entrepreneur? *International Small Business Journal, 8,* 11–22.

Staw, B. M. (1977). *Intrinsic and extrinsic motivation.* Morristown, NJ: General Learning Press.

Stodgill, R. M. (1948). Personal factors associated with leadership: A survey of the literature. *Journal of Psychology, 25,* 35–71.

Stodgill, R. M. (1974). *Handbook of leadership: A survey of theory and research.* New York: Free Press.

Tichy, N., & Devanna, M. A. (1986). *The transformational leader.* New York: John Wiley & Sons.

U.S. News & World Report. (2012). America's best leaders. Retrieved from http://www.usnews.com/news/special-reports/features/best-leaders.

Weber, M. (1947). In A. M. Henderson & T. Parsons, (Trans.), *The theory of social and economic organization.* New York: Oxford.

Welch, J., & Welch, S. (2005). *Winning.* New York: HarperCollins.

Chapter 9

Ethics and Expression in the Workplace

Learning Objectives

Upon completion of the chapter, the student should be able to:

- Compare and contrast the six ethical perspectives.
- Compare and contrast the four dimensions of the ethical wheel.
- Explain how nonverbal behaviors can have ethical implications.
- Explain the six practices of ethical organizations.
- Compare and contrast the dimensions of organizational dissent.
- Compare and contrast the six organizational dissent strategies.

Key Terms

Deontological ethical perspective
Ethical wheel
Foundational ethical perspective
Indirect interpersonal aggression
Organizational dissent

Relationship-based
ethical perspective
Rights/justice-based
ethical perspective
Situational ethical perspective

Stakeholder theory
Three-filter test
Utilitarian ethical perspective
Whistleblowing

If you were to peruse the course offerings in any graduate program related to organizational life (e.g., MBA programs), you would find at least one course in ethics. However, just a decade ago this was not the case. The study of ethics throughout the social sciences (e.g., organizational communication, organizational psychology, organizational sociology, business management) is a relatively new study. Why is there a sudden need to study ethics in the workplace? Are we less noble than we used to be? Are people inherently self-interested without regard for their coworkers? Why are so many organizations being caught in fraudulent activity? These are tough questions with relatively easy answers. As a society, other disciplines (e.g., medicine and philosophy) have long struggled with ethical questions. In an ever-growing, diverse workplace, there is an equal amount of diversity regarding what constitutes proper or ethical behavior. Is it unethical to use the company copy machine for personal use? Is it ethical to use the Internet for personal gain (e.g., checking your bank account, writing blogs) at work? The answer is that it depends on whom you ask. People usually think of ethics as significant life-and-death decisions. However, imagine that every time you speak, you are making an ethical decision. Every day in our lives (even the most boring of days) we are making hundreds of ethical decisions. The workplace is no different.

Although it may seem that more white-collar crime is being committed, the truth is that contemporary organizations are no more greedy or fraudulent than at any other time in history. It is just that the authorities and government agencies have set up more effective controls that reveal more wrongdoing than in past generations. A large amount of unethical behavior in contemporary corporations involves accounting fraud. Table 9.1 highlights scandals over the last several years that have significantly impacted our perception of organizations' trustworthiness. You will notice that most of these corporations were involved in various financial frauds (e.g., under- or overreporting earnings, hiding debt/profit from shareholders) and represent financial, retail, telecommunications, and high-tech manufacturing sectors. This list is but a sample of the fraud cases that have emerged in recent years.

Ethical Perspectives

There are many perspectives on what constitutes ethical behavior in the workplace. Sometimes these perspectives are diametrically opposite of one another. However conceptualized, workplace ethics is a relatively new concept, and business schools throughout the United States have only recently developed courses in ethical decision making. The following perspectives have been developed by some of the most profound thinkers in philosophy and economics and can be readily applied to workplace behavior.

TABLE 9.1	A Sample of Corporations Caught in Corrupt Activity	
Adelphia Communications	Global Crossing
AOL-Time Warner	Halliburton
Arthur Andersen	Homestore.Com
Brystol-Myers Squibb	Kmart
ClearStream	Merke
CMS Energy	Mirant
Compass Group	Nicor
Duke Energy	Nortel
Dynasty	Phar-Mor
El Paso	Radio Shack
Enron	Tyco
Exxon	WorldCom
Fannie Mae	Xerox

Foundational Ethical Perspective

The **foundational ethical perspective** holds that ethical behavior is true in nature and universal. There is a core set of ethics that are to be followed. This perspective is representative of people who follow religious teachings, such as those taught in the Bible, Torah, and Koran (e.g., it is wrong to deceive customers or it is wrong to take advantage of a customer's ignorance about a product). This perspective assumes that people have a duty to obey moral guidelines and that adherence to duty is paramount. If an organization has an explicit professional code of ethics, the statements of that code generally reflect the foundational ethical perspective.

foundational ethical perspective Assumes that ethical behavior is true in nature and universal.

Situational Ethical Perspective

The **situational ethical perspective** assumes that ethical decisions are unique to any given situation and are not universal in nature. For example, Herb Kelleher, CEO of Southwest Airlines, rejects the long-held ethical assumption that "the customer is always right." This statement represents a foundational ethical perspective. Kelleher argues that belief in "the customer is always right" credo is a betrayal of your own people. In fact, he believes that many times the customer is not only wrong, but is often a drug addict or drunk. In these cases, employees are authorized to ban difficult customers from flying on Southwest Airlines. Particular situations call for an ethical standard that changes with the particular circumstances. Thus, the only rule in the situational ethical perspective is that there are no universal assumptions about what is and what is not considered ethical.

situational ethical perspective Assumes that ethical decisions are unique to any given situation and are not universal in nature.

Deontological Ethical Perspective

deontological ethical perspective Assumes that if a person's intentions are based on sound, ethical reasoning, then the action is ethical.

The **deontological ethical perspective** is also known as virtue ethics. Although mostly associated with the writings of Immanuel Kant, deontological ethics extend back to Aristotle and his writings on Nichomachean ethics. The ethical focus of this perspective is based on intentions. If a person's intentions are based on sound ethical reasoning, then the action is ethical. This focus on intention disregards the positive or negative consequences associated with the action. For example, a pharmaceutical corporation markets a drug that will increase the quality of life for millions of people, but the development and testing of the drug resulted in the deaths of dozens of animals and several human beings. In this case, with the intention to help millions of people, the loss of a few "test subjects" is not a compromise of ethical standards.

Utilitarian Ethical Perspective

utilitarian ethical perspective Assumes that ethical behavior is based on outcome as opposed to intention.

The **utilitarian ethical perspective** was derived in opposition to deontological ethics. That is, ethical behavior is based on outcomes, not intentions. Developed by a series of thinkers including Jeremy Bentham, John Stuart Mill, and Henry Sidgwick, this perspective distinguishes between one's personal moral commitments (e.g., a person's personal sense of duty) and how one actually behaves. Both moral commitments and behavior should be in a dialogue (i.e., acknowledge that both virtue and behavior exist in ethical decisions), but are not necessarily related to each other (i.e., the behavior may or may not be reflective of the person's moral commitments). The underlying assumption of utilitarianism is that actions should be aimed at increasing utility or happiness. Simply put, the best ethical decision is the one that guarantees the most happiness. If the overall result is good, then the action is ethical. This perspective is representative in the hedonic perspective discussed in Chapter 1.

Rights/Justice-Based Ethical Perspective

rights/justice-based ethical perspective Assumes that ethical behavior is based on a certain level of dignity, justice, and fairness for all.

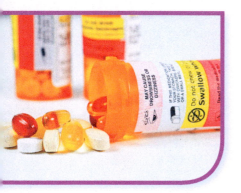

The **rights/justice-based ethical perspective** views ethical behavior as derived from natural law. An ethical person or organization is one in which a certain level of dignity and justice is maintained and in which there is fairness for all. An example of rights/justice-based ethics is Walmart's decision to provide a variety of generic prescription medications for $3 each. This decision resulted in making medications affordable to a wider segment of the population. There are two general types of rights/justice. **Distributive justice** reflects normative principles that concern what is just or right regarding the allocation of goods in an organization. **Procedural justice** reflects making and implementing decisions based on fair principles.

Relationship-Based Ethical Perspective

The **relationship-based ethical perspective** assumes that ethical behavior is created and maintained through communication. That is, all relationships within the organization as well as between the organization and its various external publics are based on quality and honest communication. Spontaneity devoid of ulterior motives also factors into honest communication. Another assumption of the relational ethical perspective is that dialogue (i.e., communication exchange between people) is the foundation on which all relationships are developed, maintained, and/or terminated. Therefore, a person engaged in communicating should remember the effect of dialogue on the other person and should be focused on the development of the other person. Johannesen (1996) argues that this perspective "allows free expression, seeks understanding, and avoids value judgments that stifle. One shows desire and capacity to listen without anticipating, interfering, competing, refuting, or warping meanings into preconceived interpretations" (p. 68).

> **relationship-based ethical perspective** Assumes that all relationships within and among the organization and its various external publics are based on quality and honest communication.

Stakeholder Theory

The term *stakeholder* defines parties whose interests are affected by business activity. The term emerged early in the development of business ethics as a reaction against the position advanced by Milton Friedman (1970) in his article entitled "The Social Responsibility of Business Is to Increase Its Profits." Friedman believed the social world is organized into separate zones of activity. That is, individual functions and roles should not overlap. For example, a businessperson is not trained in the same way as a lawyer, who is not trained in the same way as a Zen monk or a philosopher. This separation also holds true for political activity, economic activity, and social activity. That is, these are separate spheres of activity that should not be comingled.

Because these zones of activity are separate, Friedman (1970) believed the sole responsibility of a firm is to those people who own the instruments of production (i.e., the shareholders or stakeholders). The stakeholders, according to **stakeholder theory**, are internal or within the organization. Thus, an organization and its members are behaving ethically if they generate profits for the stakeholders. Ethical behavior within the economic realm is based on working solely to maximize investor profits within the limits of the law. When people talk about the obscene quarterly profits posted by "big oil" companies, they are making this statement based on more of a rights/justice-based perspective than stakeholder theory, which would argue that if profits were not as large as they can be, then the organization and organizational members are not behaving ethically.

> **stakeholder theory** Assumes that an organization's sole responsibility is to those people who own the instruments of production.

Given that stakeholder theory was advanced over 35 years ago, the question "What constitutes a stakeholder?" has been expanded to reflect the modern corporate environment. Internal stakeholders now include directors, managers, production workers as well as shareholders. Outside the organization, external stakeholders include customers, suppliers, competitors, local communities, government regulating bodies, and most recently with the development of eco-commerce, planet Earth. In the end, stakeholders fall into five categories: shareholders, customers, employees, suppliers, and the community.

Ethical Considerations in Communication

All the ethical perspectives discussed thus far either suggest the importance of communication (i.e., foundational, situational, deontological, utilitarian, rights/justice, and stakeholder ethical perspectives) or overtly highlight communication (i.e., relationship-based ethical perspective) as the central tenet. What should we consider when we communicate in the workplace? First, every communicative behavior has ethical implications (e.g., when to speak, what to say, when to say it, how to say it, when to be silent, when to listen, etc.). Second, similar to the relational ethical perspective, communication ethics should involve reflection on the motives of the sender and receiver as well as the impact of the messages being sent. Third, all communication occurs within a context that directly impacts the communicative exchange (e.g., who, what, where, when, how). Finally, there is a nonverbal component to ethical behavior. The next section discusses specific nonverbal aspects of behavior and possible ethical implications of each.

Nonverbal Behavior and Ethics

Discussions of ethical communication behavior often involves the spoken word. However, it is important to be aware of our nonverbal communication because it plays a major role in the impact of the spoken word. Birdwhistell (1970) believed that as much as 70 percent of the messages we send are sent by the body, 23 percent by the tone or inflection of our voice, and 7 percent by the actual words we use. Our nonverbal behavior serves as a **metamessage** (a message that sends information about a message). For example, if a supervisor says, "You are my best employee" while rolling her eyes, you will take that to mean that she is being sarcastic. In this example, the rolling of her eyes sends the metamessage of "Whatever I say, take it to mean the opposite." Given the mindless fashion in which people use nonverbal communication in the workplace, it is no mystery that nonverbal communication can have deleterious ethical effects on behavior and can contradict our spoken messages.

Some nonverbal behaviors have a greater influence than others (e.g., nonverbal behaviors such as haptics, occulesics, territoriality, clothing, and chronemics). **Haptics** concerns the use of touch when communicating. The use of touch can range from a supporting embrace to sexual harassment. Generally speaking, people should restrict touch to handshakes when in the workplace. Because there is so much room for misinterpretation of touch, restricting yourself to handshakes reduces ambiguity in terms of your intent. Given that the interpretation of what constitutes appropriate touch is in the mind of the receiver, you can never be entirely sure that your intended reason for touching someone will be relayed accurately. In addition, the person who has more power will initiate touch more often, control the length of touch, and violate the personal space of the person with lower status (Henley, 1977, 1995).

Occulesics concerns the use of the eyes when communicating. In all cultures, the eyes play a special role in relaying meaning. In Western cultures, many believe that the eyes are the window to the soul. In fact, direct eye contact is perceived as being a sign of credibility as well as honesty (i.e., leading to attributions of ethical behavior) (Burgoon & Saine, 1978). However, in other cultures, eye contact is seen as devious or aggressive. Given that research indicates that eyes can express aggressiveness, attractiveness, credibility, dominance, interest, intimacy, and persuasiveness (Burgoon & Dillman, 1995), it is important to understand that eye contact can influence others' attributions about how ethical your behavior is. This is further complicated by culture and gender influences.

The use of space, or **territoriality**, can influence the perception of ethical behavior. Although originally conceptualized as how people unconsciously organize their space (Hall, 1966), people often consciously manipulate their space to relay particular messages to others. For example, consider the Oval Office of the President of the United States. This room was designed to intimidate other world leaders (e.g., the large oversized desk, the smaller chairs for visitors, and the fact that the room has no corners). These signs of power were implemented as a psychological intimidating factor. Many people do not consider ethical implications when they set up their office space and assume that it really does not matter how your space is arranged. However, Avtgis (as cited in Wright, 2007) argues the following:

> Theoretically the things you display are at the core of your values, your moral center. … [T]he workplace does not guarantee free speech. You check that off at the door. Part of what you put on your desk is free speech, but depending on what it is, it could create a hostile work environment. (p. 6)

The invasion of space can also influence interpretations of ethical behavior. Generally speaking, the person who has more power in a relationship will violate the space of the less powerful person with greater frequency as well as violate the space for longer durations. The less powerful member generally has to ask permission to gain access to the more powerful person's space through things like making an appointment or checking to see if access will be appropriate (Anderson, 1999).

Clothing is also an extension of your ethical/value system. Clothing sends such an important message that some organizations require particular uniforms or dress codes to present a desired image to the public. In fact, it is common for organizations to provide a clothing allowance for employees in the sales department or for those who interact with external publics (e.g., the media, community) on a regular basis. Organizations also enact dress

TABLE 9.2	Thomsett's Eight Principles of Appropriate Dress Guidelines

1. Observe how other employees in the organization are dressed.

2. Strike a balance between being comfortable and career minded.

3. Your wardrobe should be varied enough to be appropriate for the region of the country in which you work as well as the varied seasons.

4. Your choice of clothing should be conservative in nature while avoiding any flashy or outrageous clothing.

5. Spend the extra money to purchase high-quality and practical clothing. In fact, treat the purchase of clothing as an investment in your professional future.

6. Although your organization may have an explicit dress code, become aware of the implicit or unspoken dress code.

7. Be conservative in your choice of accessories. This includes jewelry, fragrance, and other accessories.

8. Be mindful of and adhere to the basic rules of good grooming.

requirements to reflect a desired culture (Remland, 2003). For example, former President George W. Bush always wore a suit and tie (and also demanded formal dress of his staff) when in the Oval Office. This was in contrast to former President Bill Clinton, who used a more casual mode of dress when working in the Oval Office. How do we find out about what is appropriate dress for any particular organization? Thomsett (1991) believes that to figure out what is and is not appropriate, we should follow the eight principles detailed in Table 9.2.

The use of time or **chronemics** also involves ethical considerations. There are many aspects of time and its use that have ethical implications. Former President Clinton was notorious for being late to meetings. Being late to meetings implies, "I have the right to make you wait and, therefore, I am more powerful than you." Another example involves visiting a physician's office for treatment. The physician is almost always running late and behind schedule, and we have no choice but to wait (the physician has more power in this instance). However, if we were late to that appointment, the physician would simply move on to the next patient and we would have to reschedule our appointment. However, Thomsett (1991) dispels several myths of meeting times and being prompt, including the following: (1) The person who shows up last, and perhaps late for the meeting, is demonstrating power over the other person(s); (2) the person who is early to a meeting is put at a disadvantage; and (3) if you arrive promptly you are seen as anxious or neurotic. Thomsett argues that showing up early indicates courtesy to the other person and respect for the other person's time (i.e., professionalism). If you are late for a meeting or an appointment, an apology is in order. The use of time to demonstrate dominance and/or power is ethically questionable and should be avoided.

Practices of an Ethical Organization

According to May (2006), ethical organizations follow six practices. First is the ethical practice of **alignment**, which involves matching the organization's formal practices (e.g., performance appraisals, employee handbook) and informal practices (e.g., norms, rituals) to the needs of its members. This requires effort on the part of both the organization as well as organizational members. Second is the ethical practice of **dialogic communication**, which holds that open channels of communication constitute the cornerstone of teamwork. This open communication should be decentralized and lack a hierarchical structure. That is, all employees are encouraged to communicate with other members regardless of status or function. Third is the ethical practice of **participation**, in which feedback is valued and member contributions are recognized. Trust is a premium, and decision making involves members at all levels of the organization. Fourth is the practice of **transparent structure**, which holds that every practice the organization engages in should be up front and open (above board) to both internal publics (employees) and external publics (customers, community). Such transparent practices include employee appraisals, hiring policies, and organizational mission. Fifth is the practice of **accountability**, which involves going above and beyond the minimal standards set by the industry and government regulations. For example, organizations that offer free childcare for employees or an automobile manufacturer that constantly receives top reliability and safety ratings would be considered accountable. Sixth is the practice of **courage**, which means that the organization values employee dissent, listening to the dissent, as well as admitting when the organization has made a mistake. These six ethical practices are the hallmarks of ethical organizations. The focus on using corporate culture based on a sound ethical vision is growing in contemporary business. Explicit ethical codes guide the organization as well as all organizational members to a common interpretation of appropriate business practices.

This QR code will direct you to the homepage of Santa Clara University's *Markkula Center for Applied Ethics*, where you will be able to learn more about the role of organizational ethics in decision-making practices.

http://www.scu.edu/ethics/ publications/iie/v2n1/ homepage.html

ethical wheel A model of ethical decision making that reflects the impact that various dimensions of our lives exert on our ethical decision making and resulting behavior.

FIGURE 9.1
The Ethical Wheel.

The Ethical Wheel

It is easy to think of ethics as a singular concept. Yet ethics as a singular concept oversimplifies a fluid and dynamic idea. To match your definition of what is right or wrong behavior with that of your family, social group, organization, and profession is a difficult, if not an impossible thing to achieve. The **ethical wheel** (see Figure 9.1) illustrates the influences that various dimensions of our lives exert on our ethical or unethical decision making. Let's take a look at each of these dimensions of ethical influence and how they may influence behavior in the workplace.

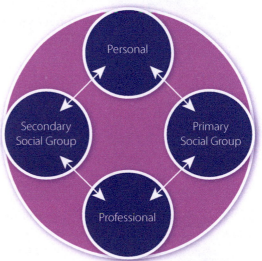

Personal Dimension of Ethics

We would be foolish to assume that we all focus on this dimension more than on the others. There is not a day that goes by in which we make decisions about our professional behavior that may compromise our personal ethics. The personal dimension of our ethical behavior consists of those standards of behavior that are an accumulation of our experiences. These experiences vary with each individual and are similar to DNA in that they are unique to each person. Given that our accumulated experiences are unique to each individual, when an organization puts forth ethical guidelines, it is difficult, if not impossible, to ensure that all organization members follow them in the same way.

Primary Social Group Dimension of Ethics

The primary social group's influence on ethical standards consists of the family or group that socialized the person to distinguish between right and wrong. We begin learning about work as soon as we are able to understand language. We see our parents come home from their jobs and we listen to the types of stories they tell about work and the work environment. Our family stories concerning careers and education are the foundation from which we calibrate what is and is not ethical behavior. The primary social group influence is as unique as are personal influences.

Secondary Social Group Dimension of Ethics

The secondary social group consists of groups that are not as influential as our primary group, but provide some psychological or social benefits to group members. Secondary groups can take the form of churches, civic clubs, fraternities, sororities, sports teams, and special interest groups. The secondary social group provides a guideline for ethical behavioral standards that may or may not be consistent with those derived from the personal and primary social group influences.

Professional Dimension of Ethics

The professional dimension consists of primarily professional standards of conduct mandated by professional organizations in our chosen career field. For example, if you are a lawyer, you are bound by standards of ethical behavior developed not only by your present employer but by the American Bar Association. An ASE-certified mechanic is bound by professional standards of the specific automotive repair shop but also by standards of the National Institute of Automotive Service Excellence.

One of the biggest concerns associated with all ethical influences in the ethical wheel is the inability to satisfy all four ethical dimensions simultaneously. Can you think of a time when you compromised your personal ethics for professional gain? Or compromised your professional ethics for personal gain? It is important to remember that the small ethical decisions far outnumber the larger ethical decisions. In ethics training, people generally focus on major ethical dilemmas (e.g., euthanasia, abortion). We should start to look at the small ethical decisions we make on a day-to-day basis. In time, the accumulation of these small decisions equate to the entire ethical profile of the person.

Organizational Dissent

Think of all the jobs you have held throughout your life. It would be safe to guess that there were many jobs you disliked and were not hesitant to let everyone around you know how you felt. Why were you complaining to these people? The answer to this question varies based on the specific job and the person answering it. Some of us express job dissatisfaction to others just to vent or get it off our chest. Sometimes we dissent to audiences (i.e., coworkers) or outside audiences (i.e., family and friends). Others voice their dissatisfaction in ways that anger the boss. All of these types of expression serve different functions. One way to define how employees express dissatisfaction is **organizational dissent** (Kassing, 1997, 1998).

organizational dissent
The way employees go about voicing disagreement or dissatisfaction about organizational issues.

Dimensions of Dissent

Organizational dissent is the way employees voice disagreement or dissatisfaction about organizational issues. The dissent concept consists of three basic types of expression. The first type of expression is called **articulated dissent** and occurs when we express dissatisfaction to people who can directly alleviate the problem. For example, consider a job in which you are having interpersonal problems with a coworker. This coworker has been spreading rumors about you and it is affecting your performance. In this situation you can go directly to the employee and ask that he or she refrain from spreading rumors, or you could go to your supervisor and request that the employee cease spreading rumors and be reprimanded for his or her behavior. In both of these cases, you are expressing your dissatisfaction directly to people who can improve the situation (i.e., the coworker and/or your supervisor). This type of dissent is considered prosocial and is most effective in bringing about change because it overtly confronts the behavior in an effort to make the behavior cease. Research shows that when people express articulated dissent, they experience positive outcomes in the workplace. For example, articulated dissenters report being higher in argumentativeness (i.e., tendency to enjoy arguing positions on controversial issues) and lower in verbal aggressiveness (i.e., tendency to attack a person's self-concept with the intent of inflicting psychological pain) than people who do not use articulated dissent (Kassing & Avtgis, 1999).

What if you were facing the situation just described and a coworker was spreading rumors about you? However, instead of confronting the coworker or going directly to the supervisor, you complained to family, friends, or other coworkers. In other words, you complained or expressed your dissatisfaction to people who really can't do anything about the situation. This is called **displaced dissent**. It occurs when we express dissatisfaction to people outside the organization who cannot alleviate the problem but will lend an ear as we vent our displeasure. This type of expression serves an important psychological support function. Consider a time when you called a friend or sibling and asked him or her not to offer advice, but just to listen as you tell them how difficult a coworker is being. Although the situation will remain the same the next morning at work, your ability to talk about it with other people "grounds you" and makes the situation a bit more tolerable. People who regularly use this type of dissent do so in a traitlike fashion. In other words, regardless of the issue, the importance of the topic, or the person involved, displaced dissenters use this form of dissent more because of their personality than for reasons concerning a specific situation or position (Kassing & Armstrong, 2002; Kassing & DiCioccio, 2004).

What lies between directly dissenting to a person who can change the situation from within the organization and expressing dissent to people external to the organization who cannot? The answer is **latent dissent**, which is defined as expressing dissatisfaction to people within the organization who cannot alleviate the issue. People who regularly use latent or antagonistic dissent report being more verbally aggressive (Kassing & Avtgis, 1999) and see outcomes in the workplace as being beyond their control (Avtgis & Kassing, 2001). We should all be aware of how we dissent in the workplace and understand the possible repercussions of each type of expression.

Issues of Dissent

The issues about which employees express dissent can be reduced to nine topics. This list was generated by Kassing and Armstrong (2002) by asking employees at all levels of organizations what topics they have complained about to their supervisors. The results of this study revealed that employees generally complain about the following issues: (1) decision-making practices, (2) treatment of employees, (3) employee and organizational-wide ethical practices, (4) inefficiencies/barriers to effective performance, (5) changes within the organization, (6) employee performance evaluations, (7) safety-related issues, (8) resources needed to perform tasks efficiently, and (9) lack of responsibility in and dissatisfaction with their current role in the organization.

We all have our own style of dissenting in the workplace. The key is to understand how you behave and make positive changes so that when you perceive an unjust situation in the workplace, you can use prosocial dissent tactics (i.e., articulated dissent) to alleviate the problem. However, it is important to understand that when you use articulated dissent, you must use it appropriately. In the example of the rumor-spreading employee, going directly to that person and saying, "If I hear another rumor about me, I am

This QR code will direct you to an assessment tool provided by Duke University's *Kenan Institute for Ethics*, which allows you to assess the role of ethics in one's organization.

http://kenan.ethics.duke.edu/
research/organizational-ethics/
measure-up/

going to stick my fist down your throat!" is certainly not advocated. This is an example of using articulated dissent inappropriately. A better approach is to use articulated dissent and appropriate language in a civil verbal and nonverbal tone.

Strategies of Dissent

Kassing (2002) argued that workers dissent upward (to people above them, such as a supervisor) in several ways that result in positive or negative consequences for the worker. The first three strategies result in positive consequences. The first strategy is **direct appeal**, which is based on fact followed by some sort of evidence (e.g., statistics, consensus opinion). The second type is **repetition**, which involves bringing up the issue consistently over time, such as at every meeting or whenever asked, "How are things going?" The third strategy is **solution presentation**, which is another upward strategy that centers on offering solutions while presenting the problem. For example, you may say, "I believe that some employees are taking advantage of long breaks and long lunch hours. I propose installing time clocks until people become more punctual and responsible."

The next two strategies hold the most potential for negative consequences. **Circumvention** occurs when an employee goes above his or her immediate supervisor to complain. Imagine how the supervisor would react upon learning that an employee went above their head to dissent. This would cause great relational strain between the subordinate and the immediate supervisor. The final upward dissent strategy is **threatening resignation**. Although this strategy is self-explanatory, one caveat is offered: Don't use this strategy unless you intend to quit your job. Imagine how embarrassing it would be for a person who has no intention of quitting her job to threaten resignation, only to be told by her supervisor that the complaint is not valid and nothing will be done about the issue.

Whistleblowing

In our culture we are bombarded with stories and fables of people who stand up in the face of adversity and end up triumphant. News stories have printed details of what happened when employees revealed organizational wrongdoings in corporations such as Enron, Phar-Mor, and Merrill Lynch. The concept of **whistleblowing** is firmly grounded in ethical decision making. Whistleblowing is different from dissent in that an employee reveals questionable organizational practices to an outside audience that can bring about justice or public awareness (e.g., people who live in an affected community, politicians, media). Whether it be a leak to the press from an unidentified insider or a high-profile executive who turns state's evidence, the goal of whistleblowing is to bring justice to those who have wronged or deceived others.

whistleblowing Revealing questionable organizational practices to an outside audience that can bring about justice or increase awareness in an affected public.

This QR code will direct to you a YouTube clip highlighting President Barack Obama's crackdown on organizational whistleblowers.

http://www.youtube.com/ watch?v=Z428H8EBRhk

On the face of it, the greater good is served when unethical practices and organizations are brought to justice. However, at what price to the whistle-blower? When the dust settles, the whistleblower is also a casualty of the justice process. It is not uncommon for whistleblowers to be "blackballed" in their respective industry and isolated from their professional contacts. Research shows that whistleblowing occurs more often when employees feel that the communication climate of the organization (the social tone of employees' relationships with coworkers and supervisors) is highly supportive and low in defensiveness. Other research indicates that the severity of the offense and relational closeness to the perpetrator are good indicators of whether someone will blow the whistle. Specifically, the closer we are to a coworker who does a wrongdoing, the less likely we are to blow the whistle. However, if the offense is severe enough in nature, relational closeness is less of a factor in whistleblowing (King, 1997). Another factor that influences whistleblowing behavior is the probability of retaliation to the whistleblower. Brown and Masser (1996) found that people will whistleblow when the offense is great, the threat of retaliation is low, and there is a perception that the whistleblowing will bring about change.

As increasing numbers of corporations are getting caught in ethically compromising positions, whistleblowing becomes an important tool in the process of justice and accountability. Congress and other legal bodies are constantly discussing the protection of whistleblowers to counter the silencing created by the fear of being blackballed. More often than not, whistleblowers have involvement in the wrongdoing. People frequently find themselves on the cusp of getting caught, so they either cut a deal with authorities or simply want out of the situation. In these cases, the whistleblower is equally dirty as the other perpetrators of the wrongdoing. Further, the whistleblower is engaging in whistleblowing merely to preserve self-interest rather than to promote ethical business practices. In this situation the whistleblower is of questionable moral character.

Indirect Interpersonal Aggression

indirect interpersonal aggression A "dark side" communication behavior in which people try to harm others' credibility or performance indirectly, thus avoiding a face-to-face encounter.

A fairly new body of research focuses specifically on antagonistic types of dissent behavior called **indirect interpersonal aggression**. This is a "dark side" behavior in which people try to harm the credibility or performance of others in indirect ways. For example, consider a person who spreads a rumor about a manager who physically assaulted his supervisor. Although the event never occurred, the rumor could have definite consequences for this manager's career aspirations. Indirect verbal aggression is defined as "a predisposition to harm other people without engaging in face-to-face interaction" (Beatty, Valencic, Rudd, & Dobos, 1999, p. 105).

Consider how conflict plays out in the workplace. How often have you witnessed a direct verbally aggressive exchange between two coworkers? The encounter may be loud and dramatic but usually blows over relatively quickly. In contrast, indirect interpersonal aggression does long-term damage to the victim, such as loss of potential professional opportunities and a damaged or destroyed reputation (Beatty et al., 1999).

Indirect interpersonal aggression in the workplace takes the form of spreading rumors, withholding information, failing to relay messages, destroying personal property, backstabbing, and generally undermining other people (Rancer & Avtgis, 2006). People who use this type of expression in the workplace are hostile and unpleasant to be around. These people savor any information that can be used to hurt others. Unfortunately, because people who practice indirect interpersonal aggression work behind the scenes and under the radar, you never can truly realize the damage that such behavior causes.

The flow of faulty information in an organization is not necessarily because of malicious intent. Instead, sometimes rumors become a function of uncertainty created by a lack of information. This lack of information does not have to be real as much as perceived. In general, subordinates think they do not receive enough information from superiors, and superiors believe they provide too much information to subordinates. Whether real or perceived, Lussier (1999) argues that rumors start because of a concerted effort by the organization to conceal information from employees.

Can rumors ever be productive? **Rumors** may be a useful tool through which management receives feedback from subordinates about changes the organization is considering. Rumors can be defined as unsubstantiated messages presented as verified fact. **Strategic ambiguity** is the concept of purposely giving less information than is needed for complete understanding. Management often uses this tactic to see how employees react or behave in the reduction of the uncertainty created by inadequate information. For example, when seeking out possible candidates for promotion, candidates are often given "tests" to see how they will react in uncertain situations. The successful television show *The Apprentice* uses strategic ambiguity to test the creativity and resolve of candidates. It is important to note that sometimes rumors and uncertainty can destroy an entire organization (Light & Landler, 1990).

Real-World Misbehaviors in the Workplace

We asked several hundred workers to list the worst things that were ever done to them or said to them. These workers ranged from nonmanagement to top management and were drawn from sectors that included education, government, service, manufacturing, and high tech. The results were surprising in that regardless of career level (e.g., management versus nonmanagement) or specific sector, the same interpersonal and ethical failures resonated throughout the respondents. Table 9.3 illustrates some examples of those responses.

Practical Advice on When to Speak

As you have probably concluded from this chapter and your own experiences with work, everything we say and do has ethical implications. So how do we behave in ways that are in our own best interest? Using rumors or spreading unverified information to hurt other people or help ourselves is something that human beings have struggled with for thousands of years, as evidenced by a parable involving the ancient Greek philosopher Socrates and one of

TABLE 9.3 Questionable Ethical Behavior in the Workplace

Current Position	Sector	Perpetrator	Incident
Teacher	Education	Supervisor	Asked a demeaning question in a meeting of colleagues.
Nonmanagement	Service	Supervisor	Forbid me to use the telephone while on the job but allowed my coworkers to continue using the telephone.
Nonmanagement	Service	Coworker	Backstabbed, lied to the boss about things I have done.
Top management	Education	Supervisor	Repeated to leadership something told in confidence.
Top management	Education	Coworker	Took credit for my work on a recent project. Stole from the company by padding timesheets.
Middle management	Government	Supervisor	Repeated to a job applicant something that I told him in confidence.
Middle management	Government	Coworker	Repeated something that I said in a joking way to another employee but in a hurtful way. Person in charge of doing timesheets told others about people's use of sick leave and time off.
Middle management	Civil service	Coworker	Lied about me to others about something I said.
Nonmanagement	High tech	Supervisor	Singled me out in front of other coworkers. Did not follow through on her promises. Played favorites with certain people.
Nonmanagement	High tech	Coworker	Played a practical joke on me my first day on the job.
Nonmanagement	Service	Supervisor	Spoke negatively about me to other employees at my level.
Nonmanagement	Service	Coworker	Brought me into a conflict I was not originally part of.
Lower management	Manufacturing	Coworker	Blamed me for something they did. Got mad at me for not covering for their illegal behavior. Told me something about the job that was not true.
Middle management	Civil service	Coworker	Claimed credit for my ideas. Lied about taking money.

his associates. This parable highlights the level of ethics and responsibility toward which all people in and out of the workplace should strive. The parable is called the **three-filter test**.

A colleague of Socrates approached him one day and said, "Socrates, do you want to hear of the information that I have just heard about one of your students?" Socrates said, "Before you do this, I would like you to pass my three-filter test." The colleague looked bewildered and asked, "Three-filter test?" The great philosopher said, "Yes! This is a way to distinguish between information that is noble and that which is not. The first filter is the **filter of truth**. Is what you are about to tell me about my student absolutely true?" The man stammered and replied, "No, in fact, I have no evidence of it being true." Socrates said, "So you are not entirely convinced that this is true information." The man looked a little embarrassed and said, "No." Socrates then said, "Let's move to the second filter, the **filter of goodness**. Is what you are about to tell me about my student something good?" The colleague replied, "Oh, on the contrary, it is very bad." Socrates said, "So you want to tell me something that you are not sure is true and is not good?" At this point the man was thoroughly embarrassed and hurt. Socrates said, "Do not worry; there is still one filter that may render the information worthy. The third filter is the **filter of usefulness**. Is what you are about to tell me about my student useful to me?" The man replied, "No." Socrates then concluded, "So what you are about to tell me about my student is not true, not good, and not useful. Then why tell me at all?"

three-filter test A test developed by Socrates to assess whether information or knowledge is valuable and worth sharing with others.

Summary

This chapter details the difficulties that every worker and organization faces regarding ethical behavior. Human expression, almost by definition, assumes ethical implications. When we communicate within the organization, whom we speak to, what we speak about, where we say it, and when we say it all have possible ethical issues attached. Throughout this chapter we have presented ways of thinking about ethical behavior within the organization (i.e., foundational, situational, deontological, utilitarian, rights/justice-based, relationship-based, and pertaining to the stakeholder theory). By understanding how we as well as others in the organization deem what is and is not ethical, we can better understand the perspective of others as well as how a behavior we deem unethical is viewed as perfectly ethical from another perspective.

Ethical organizations exhibit a variety of behaviors or practices (alignment, dialogic, participation, transparent structure, accountability, and courage) that sets them apart from other organizations. It is important to understand that just because an organization is seen as ethical does not necessarily mean it will be successful. Therefore, high ethical standards are no guarantee of great organizational success; they are only a good standard of behavior.

The ethical tensions introduced by the ethical wheel demonstrate the constant tension we experience daily in trying to balance all the ethical demands placed on us from a variety of sources (personal, primary social group, secondary social group, and professional). Most people would agree that given the diversity of sources influencing our ethical standards, simultaneously meeting all the ethical standards demanded by the four sources is difficult if not impossible to achieve.

The expression of employee voice was exemplified in the organizational dissent construct. As indicated, there are productive ways of speaking out on issues that concern us (articulated dissent) and less productive avenues for expression (displaced and latent dissent). Other voice expressions within the organization include whistleblowing, indirect interpersonal aggression, rumors, and strategic ambiguity.

Also presented were several ways that people use voice in the organization. Some techniques (articulated dissent) are seen as more ethical than others (indirect interpersonal aggression). Human beings, especially within organizations, are faced with thousands of ethical decisions. We argue that ethical perfection is a myth in any decision or choice we make. That is, when we make a choice, we simultaneously do not choose other options. How do we reconcile this discrepancy with ethical integrity? Such a pursuit is difficult and will continue to intrigue people as we move into the new global economy.

Questions for Discussion and Review

1. Define the following ethical perspectives: situational, deontological, utilitarian, rights/justice, and relationship. Give an example of each.

2. Explain the basic tenets of stakeholder theory. Do you agree with Milton Friedman in his focus on profits? Provide an argument that supports your answer.

3. Based on the chapter, define each of the components of the ethical wheel. Explain how each dimension contributes to the overall dynamic process of ethical behavior. How might these dimensions of ethics influence your behavior in the workplace?

4. Explain the basic idea behind organizational dissent. Describe the circumstances that influence the type of dissent that is enacted.

5. Argue why specific types of dissent are considered positive and others are considered negative. Provide examples to support your answer.

6. List and define the nine topics associated with employees expressing dissent.

7. Define whistleblowing and explain whether whistleblowing is considered positive or negative. Explain how you feel about whistleblowing.

8. Describe the three-filter test. Explain how this concept is relevant to organizational ethics.

9. Construct a code of ethics that could be applicable to any organization. Make sure the code of ethics is a minimum of one paragraph long. Which of the ethical perspectives best represents your code of ethics?

References

Anderson, P. A. (1999). *Nonverbal communication: Forms and functioning.* Mountain View, CA: Mayfield.

Avtgis, T. A., & Kassing, J. W. (2001). Dissention in the organization as it relates to control expectancies. *Communication Research Reports, 18,* 118–128.

Beatty, M. J., Valencic, K. M., Rudd, J. A., & Dobos, J. A. (1999). A "darkside" of communication avoidance: Indirect interpersonal aggressiveness. *Communication Research Reports, 16,* 103–109.

Birdwhistell, R. L. (1970). *Kinesics and context: Essays on body motion communication.* Philadelphia: University of Pennsylvania Press.

Brown, R., & Masser, B. (1996). 'When would you do it?' An investigation into the effects of retaliation, seriousness of malpractice and occupation on willingness to blow the whistle. *Journal of Community & Applied Social Psychology, 6,* 127–130.

Burgoon, J. K., & Dillman, L. (1995). Gender, immediacy, and nonverbal communication. In P. J. Kalbfleisch & M. J. Cody (Eds.), *Gender, power, and communication in human relationships* (pp. 63–82). Hillsdale, NJ: Earlbaum.

Burgoon, J. K., & Saine, T. (1978). *The unspoken dialogue.* Dallas: Houghton Mifflin.

Friedman, M. (1970, September 13). The social responsibility of business is to increase its profits. *The New York Times Magazine,* 122–126.

Hall, E. T. (1966). *The hidden dimension.* Garden City, NY: Doubleday.

Henley, N. M. (1977). *Body politics: Power, sex, and nonverbal communication.* Englewood Cliffs, NJ: Prentice Hall.

Henley, N. M. (1995). Body politics revisited: What do we know today? In P. J. Kalbfleisch & M. J. Cody (Eds.), *Gender, power, and communication in human relations* (pp. 27–31). Hillsdale, NJ: Earlbaum.

Johannesen, R. L. (1996). *Ethics in human communication* (4th ed.). Prospect Heights, IL: Waveland Press.

Kassing, J. W. (1997). Articulating, antagonizing, and displacing: A model of employee dissent. *Communication Studies, 48,* 311–330.

Kassing, J. W. (1998). Development and validation of the organizational dissent scale. *Management Communication Quarterly, 12,* 183–229.

Kassing, J. W. (2002). Speaking up. *Management Communication Quarterly, 16,* 187–209.

Kassing, J. W., & Armstrong, T. A. (2002). Someone's going to hear about this: Examining the association between dissent-triggering events and employees' dissent expression. *Management Communication Quarterly, 16,* 39–65.

Kassing, J. W., & Avtgis, T. A. (1999). Examining the relationship between organizational dissent and aggressive communication. *Management Communication Quarterly, 13,* 100–115.

Kassing, J. W., & DiCioccio, R. L. (2004). Testing a work place experience explanation of displaced dissent. *Communication Reports, 17,* 113–121.

King, G. (1997). The effects of interpersonal closeness and issues of seriousness on blowing the whistle. *Journal of Business Communication, 34,* 419–436.

Light, L., & Landler, M. (1990, December 24). Killing a rumor before it kills a company. *Business Week,* p. 23.

Lussier, R. N. (1999). *Human relations in organizations* (4th ed.). Boston: McGraw-Hill.

May. S. (2006). Ethical perspectives and practices. In S. May (Ed.), *Case studies in organizational communication: Ethical perspectives and practices* (pp. 19–48). Thousand Oaks, CA: SAGE Publications.

Rancer, A. S., & Avtgis, T. A. (2006). *Argumentative and aggressive communication: Theory, research, and application.* Thousand Oaks, CA: SAGE Publications.

Remland, M. S. (2003). *Nonverbal communication in everyday life* (2nd ed.). Boston, MA: Houghton Mifflin.

Thomsett, M. C. (1991). *The little black book of business etiquette.* New York: AMACOM.

Wright, C. (2007, October 7). Is your work space professional? *Clarksburg Gazette,* pp. C5–C6.

Chapter 10

Decision Making, Organizational Information Processing, and Organizational Change

Learning Objectives

Upon completion of the chapter, the student should be able to:

- ◆ Compare and contrast the functional approach to decision making and Thompson's decision types.

- ◆ Compare and contrast Vroom's decision-making styles and Simon's activity approach to decision making.

- ◆ Explain the difference between organizational change and organizational innovation.

- ◆ Compare and contrast proactive scanning strategies and reactive scanning strategies of environmental information gathering.

- ◆ Compare and contrast information systems theory and uncertainty management theory.

- ◆ Compare and contrast the idea-generation techniques of brainstorming and the inventional system.

Key Terms

Brainstorming

Decision making

Functional approach to
   decision making

Information

Information systems theory

Informational reception
   apprehension

Innovation

Inventional system

Simon's activity approach to
   decision making

Strategic change

Thompson's uncertainty model

Uncertainty management theory

Vroom's decision-making styles

Regardless of the type of work we find ourselves doing, much of our day is spent in information processing and decision making. Each day we are bombarded with data that we choose to either ignore or attend to (see Chapter 1). Each individual as well as each organization processes information differently; some people and organizations are more efficient and effective at processing information than others. The same is true for decision making. As discussed in this chapter, the ways people and organizations process information have profound effects on organizational success and failure. Decision making and information processing are also vital for successful organizational change. Successful organizational change depends on organizational members as well as the surrounding environment. This chapter examines some of the ways individuals and organizations make decisions and process information, ranging from the most mundane (e.g., what to have for lunch) to the more profound (e.g., whether to retool an entire assembly line). Further, this chapter investigates how organizations introduce change and the critical factors involved in bringing about successful organizational change.

Decision Making

decision making Process of choosing one alternative or course of action over another.

It is important to distinguish between **decision making** and **problem solving**. Many decisions are made during the problem-solving process. Simply put, all problem solving involves decision making, yet not all decision making involves problem solving. Decision making consists of choosing of one alternative or course of action over another. Problem solving, on the other hand, involves rectifying a situation, process, or procedure that has been deemed inappropriate, ineffective, or faulty.

Functional Approach

functional approach to decision making An approach to decision making that requires more than a structured and systematic five-step sequence.

One way people make decisions is through a structured pattern known as the **functional approach to decision making** (Gouran & Hirokawa, 1983, 1996). This approach to decision making can also be used effectively in problem solving and involves the following five steps: (1) having a full understanding of the issue; (2) determining the criteria for the development of effective solutions; (3) identifying all possible solutions; (4) reviewing the positive aspects and negative aspects of each solution; and (5) selecting the best option to solve the issue. The functional approach has been proven to be effective in determining and implementing quality solutions. The effectiveness of the functional approach lies in the fact that each decision is addressed without preconceived ideas or perceptions. All decisions move through the five steps, and high-quality decisions result from this process.

Thompson's Uncertainty Model

Using the concept of uncertainty as a primary influence on decision making, James Thompson (1967) developed a variety of strategies that can be used based on decision makers' relative certainty about the outcome as well as the link between the decision and the situation. "The making of decisions involves beliefs or assumptions as to what will happen if this, rather than that, is done and preferences as to what is most desirable. There is less certainty about some beliefs and preferences than there is about others" (Pugh & Hickson, 1997, p. 60).

The four quadrants of **Thompson's uncertainty model** reflect the degree to which people believe there is a direct cause-and-effect relationship between decision and outcome as well as the degree to which people are clear about the desired outcome (see Figure 10.1). A person may view an increase in sales as a direct link to an increase in production. This perceived link (increased sales = increased production) results in the increase in production being the most logical decision to address the issue of "what to do about increased sales." This example indicates a high degree of certainty in a cause-and-effect relationship (increased sales causes an increase in production) as well as high certainty in the desired outcome (increased sales volume). This type of decision making is known as the **computational strategy**. What if the cause-and-effect relationship is not so clear? In other words, what if the increase in production requires hiring new, unskilled workers and purchase of new machinery? In this case, we remain certain about our outcome but uncertain about whether the added labor and machinery will immediately satisfy the growing demand (e.g., it may take time to train new employees and install, calibrate, and inspect new machinery). This illustration exemplifies the **judgmental strategy**, which is linked to the added risk involved (i.e., when decision makers are certain as to the outcome they desire but uncertain as to whether the proposed solution will solve the problem).

Thompson's uncertainty model An approach to decision making based on the degree of cause-and-effect relationship between decision and outcome as well as the degree to which people are clear about the desired outcome.

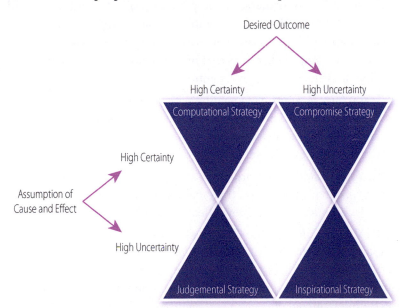

FIGURE 10.1
Thompson's Four Quadrants of Decision Making.

Source: Adapted from Thompson (1967). *Organization in Action.* Columbus, OH: McGraw-Hill.

The third quadrant reflects a situation in which decision makers are uncertain of what they want (e.g., such as a difference in perspective on whether to increase production or reduce future sales orders), yet see both ideas as effective in satisfying the issue of increased sales. This reflects the **compromising strategy**, which provides decision makers with some of what they wanted such that all parties are partially satisfied.

The final quadrant occurs when decision makers are uncertain about their desired outcomes and degree to which the proposed solutions will solve the issues. This strategy is considered a "shot in the dark" or "a wish and a prayer" and is called the **inspirational strategy**. Pugh and Hickson (1997) argue that "the aim of management and administration when designing organizations and making decisions must be the effective alignment of organizational structure, technology, and environment" (p. 61). This perspective reflects the idea that decision making is a holistic process influenced from all factors occurring within and beyond the organization.

Vroom's Decision-Making Styles

Victor Vroom (1974), along with his colleagues (Vroom & Jago, 1988; Vroom & Yetton, 1973), developed an approach to decision making that reflects the varying degree of input that management seeks from employees and the degree to which that information is acted upon. The **Vroom decision-making styles** include the **autocratic-oriented** (i.e., AI and AII), **consultative-oriented** (CI and CII), and **group-oriented** (GII) decision-making styles. **Vroom's decision-making styles** are outlined by Pugh and Hickson (1997):

AI: You solve the problem or make the decision on your own using information available to you at the time.

AII: You solicit information from your subordinates and then decide on the solution to the problem yourself. The subordinates may or may not be aware of the fact that you are problem solving when you ask for information. Their role is that of information giver as opposed to aiding or evaluating possible solutions.

CI: You engage in problem solving with several individual subordinates but do not bring them together as a group. You then make the decision on your own, and that decision may or may not reflect the input of the subordinates.

CII: You consult the subordinates as a group about the problem and solicit group feedback. You then make the decision on your own, and this decision may or may not reflect the group input.

GII: You consult the subordinates as a group. Working with the group, you generate solutions and evaluate those solutions in an effort to reach an agreement. Thus, the role of the manager is more of a chairperson who manages the process rather a manager who acts unilaterally.

Vroom's decision-making style A decision-making style that reflects the varying degree of input that management seeks from employees and the degree to which that information is acted upon.

In light of these different decision-making processes, Vroom and Yetton (1973) distinguished between what decision-making processes managers *should* utilize as opposed to what decision-making processes managers *do* utilize. Given that a key goal of their research was to develop a prescriptive or guideline for decision makers to follow when developing a solution (i.e., answering the issue of what decision-making processes managers should utilize), they identified three classes of consequences that influence the effectiveness of decision making. These consist of *the quality or rationality of the decision* (any detraction from a rational process is detrimental to a quality decision); *the acceptance or commitment on the part of the subordinates to execute the decision* (regardless of the quality of the decision, if the subordinates do not support it and believe in it, it will fail); *the amount of time required to make the decision* (with all else being equal; i.e., quality of the decision, etc.), decisions made in a short time are more effective than decisions made over an extended time.

All three decision processes (i.e., autocratic, consultative, and group) can be appropriate in any given situation. For example, if one solution is clearly better than the others, if there is sufficient information to make a quality decision, and if that decision need not be accepted and endorsed by subordinates, then an autocratic decision (AI) would be best. On the other hand, if there is clearly no one best solution, acceptance by subordinates is crucial to successful decision implementation, and if the manager made the decision

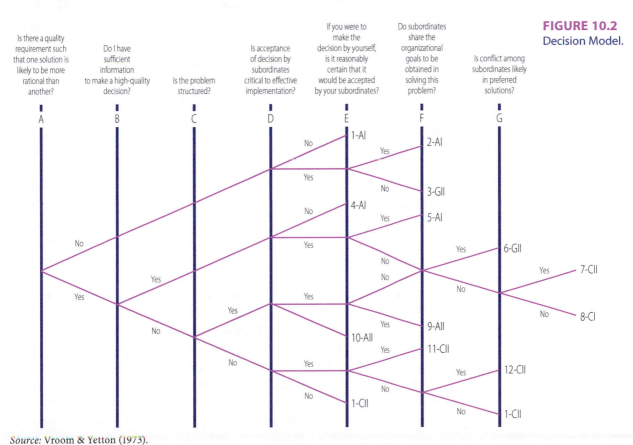

FIGURE 10.2
Decision Model.

Source: Vroom & Yetton (1973).

by him- or herself, then the group process (GII) would be most effective. This proscriptive approach to decision making offers managers a model by which the most effective decision-making strategy can be employed given the appropriate situation. Figure 10.2 shows the Vroom and Yetton (1973) decision-making matrix.

Simon's Activity Approach

Simon's activity approach to decision making
A three-stage process of decision making comprised of intelligence, design, and choice activity.

Another effective approach to decision making is Herbert Simon's (1960) idea that management and decision making can be considered synonymous. That is, management can be considered the process of making decisions. **Simon's activity approach to decision making** contains three stages: **intelligence activity, design activity,** and **choice activity**. Intelligence activity is the process of seeking out situations in need of decision making. Design activity reflects the invention, development, and analysis of possible courses of actions. The final stage is choice activity, which is the process of selecting one course of action from the available choices.

These three stages are considered linear in that we move sequentially through intelligence activity, design activity, and then choice activity. Simon (1977) differentiated among the different ways in which people make decisions. The first assumes that people make decisions in a rational way and is known as the **economic man model**. This model assumes the best course of action is that which is rational and results in maximum return. Given that most, if not all, people make decisions with little or no rational thinking, the economic man model tends to be an unrealistic explanation.

The second model is known as the **administrative man model** and seeks to "satisfice," or find a solution that is satisfactory or one that is both satisfactory and will suffice. This model highlights the importance of "muddling through" decisions. As Pugh and Hickson (1997) state, "Most decisions are concerned, not with searching for the sharpest needle in the haystack, but with searching for a needle sharp enough to sew with" (p. 118). As highlighted by this quote, this decision-making approach seeks solutions that are meant to be good enough and is less concerned with optimal solutions. As indicated in previous models, decisions that are made in a shorter time tend to be more effective or better than those that take longer. Given the nature of the administrative man model, seeking out good solutions, in general, takes a shorter time than looking for the optimal solution (as is the case with the economic man model).

The tension between the optimal decision and the satisfactory decision is further complicated by the concept of whether the decisions are routine or new to the organizations. **Programmed decisions** are "repetitive and routine or a definite procedure has been worked out to deal with them" (Pugh & Hickson, 1997, p. 119). For example, the decisions involved in processing a customer complaint are considered ordinary decisions that occur many times during the day and, thus, are given relatively little thought. **Unprogrammed decisions** are those that are "new and unstructured or where there is no cut-and-dried method for handling the problem" (Pugh & Hickson, 1997, p. 119). Examples of unprogrammed decisions include launching a new product line, merging with another company, and expanding operations to a new country.

Given that the difference between programmed and unprogrammed decisions is basically that of the novel from the mundane, unprogrammed decisions are less efficient and more costly. However, in today's organizations, decisions can be made with computer-simulated models as well as probability models. That is, each possible decision scenario can be simulated and the resulting consequences analyzed.

Decision Making as Art and Politics

The final approach is that of James March (1988), who views decision making as part art and part politics. According to Pugh and Hickson (1997), "Decision making can be understood in much the same nonrational way as a painting by Picasso or a poem by T. S. Eliot" (p. 121). During the decision-making process, the perceptions and views of the decision makers as well as the relationships among the decision makers are continually changing and must be considered.

In an unpredictable and capricious world, people often do not use much rationality when making decisions. In fact, people often make decisions without necessarily knowing what they are doing. Similar to Simon's activity approach, rationality is limited by our ability to think about a decision. Complicating this limited rationality further is that people are idiosyncratic and, as such, may communicate their preferences for a decision in strange ways. For example, consider a person who is engaged in generating possible solutions to a problem. When it comes time for this person to express her solution or decision, regardless of how rational her decision-making process, this person expresses the possible solution in an awkward way, resulting in the perception that she derived this solution through a strange or idiosyncratic process. According to March (1994), everyone in the organization has a different view about how things should be done. For example, people in the production department of the organization believe in certain ways of doing things that differ from those of management, the sales department, human resources, shareholders, and so on. Given this, there is no one best way or rationality but a negotiated or agreed-on rationality that is accepted by the various people and groups in the organization. This is known as **organized anarchy**.

Decision making is affected by four influences. First is the influence of **quasi resolution of conflict**, which is the most common influence on decision making. The term *quasi* is used here because there are so many political views and perspectives in the organization that no one ever really gets entirely what he or she wants. People may argue that "the boss always gets what he wants!" This is not true in that a boss may have made a decision that results in a desired outcome for him- or herself, but it may be at the expense of angry employees, suppliers, and so on. Given that everyone views a "good" decision differently, March (1994) terms this **local rationality**, in that we are able to hold the belief that we are being rational with regard to our immediate concerns. For example, the marketing department is concerned with how to brand a product, whereas the production department is focusing on meeting supply needs. The localization of each unit's needs ensures that everyone gets some (i.e., quasi resolution of conflict) of what he or she desires. This is in contrast to seeking only optimal solutions for any one specific party. The **acceptable level decision rule** does not concern the optimal possibilities but, instead, concerns the level at which all parties can perceive the decision as something they can live with. The final concept associated with the quasi resolution of conflict is **sequential attention to goals**, which is used in situations where many goals are not being satisfied simultaneously and the situation therefore becomes uncontrollable. When this occurs, isolating and analyzing each goal, solving the problems associated with the goal, and then moving on to the next goal is the advocated course of action. For example, in an organizational crisis where customers are quickly switching to other competitors, the many decisions and issues that need to be addressed can quickly become overwhelming. Thus, prioritizing and addressing the most significant issues first and then moving to the less significant issues result in making the crisis more manageable.

The second influence on decision making is **uncertainty avoidance**. Uncertainty avoidance is a state in which all organizations exist. Every element of the organization is uncertain. For example, uncertainty can come from external factors such as the economy and customer needs, or it can come from internal factors such as the solvency of the company, the worker talent base, and employee needs. Decision making is a process that occurs in the present, not the future. Any decision we make is based on information in the here and now. Decisions for the future are generally avoided due to the great level of uncertainty associated with events in the future. For example, to reduce uncertainty in the marketplace, an organization may engage in exclusive contracts with suppliers and retailers and conform to competitors in terms of price setting; the organization may establish these behaviors as standard practices of doing business because they afford the organization a degree of certainty and control. Such practices are regularly employed by Walmart and Apple.

The third influence on decision making is **problemistic search**. Given that uncertainty is an inevitable state and organizations seek to reduce it, problems require solutions. Whenever something is termed a problem, a search is conducted to find a solution. When people look to the future for "strategic planning," they are creating problems that require a problemistic search that will help them address any problematic issues. In other words, they are conjecturing about future problems and seeking solutions to those problems. This type of problem-search/solution cycle is considered

This QR code will direct you to a website that provides an interactive tool to practice and further develop your own decision-making skills and strategies.

http://www.decision-making-solutions.com/decision_making_activities.html

simple minded (March & Olsen, 1980) in that it introduces unneeded uncertainty into the organization. Pugh and Hickson (1997) present the following argument:

When a problem arises, search for a solution is concentrated near the old solution. Radical proposals are brushed aside, and a safer answer is found, not much different from what was there before. When a U.S. university sought a new dean to head a major faculty, prominent outsiders were passed over and an established insider chosen because of fears that outsiders might make too many changes (pp. 123–124).

The problemistic search phenomenon can also be seen in the National Football League, the National Basketball Association, and Major League Baseball, where coaches and managers move from one team to another regardless of their past performance. Due to the consistency of being known (regardless of records accumulated with previous teams) or being considered an insider, this gives the league owners and stakeholders more predictability of the incoming coach's behavior.

The final concept concerns how organizations learn throughout the decision-making process. Organizations do not have all knowledge before making a decision; knowledge and information are gained through the process of engaging in decision making. This process is known as **organizational learning**.

The uncertainty and seemingly nonrational approaches that people and organizations take when making decisions led to the **garbage can model of organizational choice** (Cohen, March, & Olsen, 1972). According to Pugh and Hickson (1997), "When people fight for the right to participate in decision making and then do not exercise it, when they request information and then do not use it, when they struggle over a decision and then take little interest in whether it is ever carried out, something curious must be going on" (p. 124). People tend to be more concerned with the right or opportunity to engage in decision making rather than interest in the actual decision. In other words, people are more concerned with having a voice and less concerned with what that voice is saying.

March (1994) believed that decisions emerge through **resolution, oversight,** or **flight**. Decision by resolution occurs when the choice or solution resolves the original problem. Decision by oversight occurs when the choice or solution is made quickly and capriciously from other choices available in an effort to solve the problem quickly. Finally, decision by flight refers to a situation in which the original problem has disappeared and so the choice or solution is made by default, without the problem-solving process.

This approach to decision making highlights the nonrational way in which people and organizations make decisions. If people tend to engage in decision making that is in the heat of the moment and based on emotion, then they should act before they think and not concern themselves with the future impacts of a decision because, after all, that decision is based on current information and the here-and-now (Pugh & Hickson, 1997).

As indicated in these models of decision making, the process of selecting the best alternative sometimes can be found, not in the search for the optimal solution, but in the search for the solution that provides each person involved with a sense of control over the decision and a decision that everyone finds acceptable or tolerable.

Idea Generation

Underlying all approaches to decision making is the fact that good decisions are a product of good information. Good information is brought about the ways of thinking about an issue from different perspectives. Therefore, it becomes crucial that quality ideas be developed on which to base the decision. There are two techniques for generating ideas that work particularly well in the decision-making process: **brainstorming** and the **inventional system**. Both systems were developed not only to generate as many ideas as possible, but to offer a systematic evaluation of each idea so that a "best" solution can be derived.

As discussed in Chapter 7, brainstorming is an idea-generation procedure focused on generating as many possible approaches or solutions to problems. One major assumption of brainstorming is that in the generation of many ideas, one of the ideas will be deemed most appropriate for the problem or decision. Brainstorming is generally used in a group setting but can also be effective when used individually. Brainstorming is a simple and popular idea-generation technique, and one that 70 percent of businesspeople report using in their organization (Kelley & Littman, 2001). The seven rules for effective brainstorming are as follows: (1) Have a clear statement of the problem, (2) express as many solutions as possible, (3) record these ideas on paper or electronically so the responses can be seen and/or heard, (4) avoid being evaluative when producing possible ideas, (5) generate as many ideas as quickly as possible with as little delay as possible so the flow of thoughts is not interrupted, (6) generate as many creative or "wild and crazy" ideas as possible, and (7) combine or "piggyback" ideas to create truly unique ideas. Following these seven steps provides the foundation from which to generate good possible solutions.

brainstorming A decision-making procedure focused on generating more ideas or solutions to problems than can be generated by individuals working alone.

inventional system An idea-generation technique designed to assist people in the development or generation of arguments or positions.

The Inventional System

Another system that is especially effective at generating ideas for solving problems is the inventional system. This system was developed by Dominic Infante (1988) and was designed to assist people in developing or generating arguments or positions. Although this system was originally developed to generate arguments in a debate or argumentative exchange, the system is extremely effective for decision-making idea generation.

Problem solving is about the analysis of a given problem and the development of an effective intervention or solution. Within the organization, these decisions can range from the more mundane (e.g., how to make sure the overnight cleaning crew vacuums all the carpets) to the more profound (e.g., how do we make our product safer in an effort to reduce risks to children?). Issues involved in decision making and problem solving generally take three forms: (1) **issues of policy** (e.g., our current policy of maternity leave should be expanded to include male employees); (2) **issues of fact** (e.g., implementing pay raises for all employees will reduce the amount of funds available for our annual donation to local nonprofit organizations); and (3) **issues of value** (e.g., is it right to offer benefits to spouses of employees without offering the same benefits to people with domestic partners?). The inventional system is effective in all aspects of the problem-solving process regardless of the issue at hand.

The inventional system consists of four main components, each containing sub-issues (Infante, 1988). The main categories of the system consist of **problem, blame, solution,** and **consequence**. The problem (i.e., What is the problem?) and blame (i.e., Who is to blame for the problem?) components concern the need for a change, whereas the solution (i.e., How do we fix the problem?) and consequence (i.e., What are the results of implementing our solution?) components reflect concern about how implementing the solution will satisfy the problem (Rancer & Avtgis, 2006).

The problem component contains three subissues: the *signs of the problem,* the *specific harm of the problem,* and *the widespread effects of the problem.* For example, if we are examining poor coworker relationships, we may see signs of the problem as rumor spreading, overtly aggressive communication exchanges, and avoidance behavior. The harm would be lack of productivity, increase in turnover, and potential for harassment lawsuits.

The blame component contains three subissues: the *causes of the problem,* determining whether the *current system is at fault,* and determining whether the *present system should be changed.* In our example, this would concern issues such as finding out who or what is responsible for the deteriorating coworker relationships. This could include exploring whether the ways we socialize, hire, or train employees in the workplace are responsible for this condition as well as whether changing some or all of these procedures will alleviate the problem.

The solution component contains two subissues: *identifying the possible solutions* and *identifying the best of these solutions.* For example, how can we change the way employees are treated (e.g., communication training, conflict mediation, employee retreat)? Once these solutions are identified, we decide which solution(s) is(are) best for alleviating the problem (e.g., poor coworker relationships).

The final component of the inventional system is consequence, which contains two subissues: *identifying the positive outcomes resulting from the solution* and *identifying the negative outcomes resulting from the solution.* For example, sending employees on a retreat may aid in resolving the conflict but will require a large financial expense. Developing and implementing a communication training program in effective conflict behavior may not necessarily address the specific issues related to the original employee conflict but may result in avoiding future conflict.

The inventional system allows people to think in a methodological and structured way when engaging in problem solving. Once a person commits this system to memory and employs it correctly, it becomes a habitual tool through which all problems can be analyzed. Furthermore, it also serves as a filter for determining whether a person has enough information to engage in the problem solving process. In other words, the system will reveal whether further information or research is needed before a problem can be solved. Rancer and Avtgis (2006) argue that "given the series of questions posed by the inventional system, a person may quickly realize he or she does not have enough information" (p. 203).

The process of decision making is as complex and varied as the decisions themselves. Each of the approaches presented represents some of the most popular, well-developed approaches to decision making. Successful decision makers often rely on one or all of these strategies to arrive at optimal solutions. Underlying the making of effective decisions is the ability to generate appropriate alternatives and ideas. These alternatives represent the basis from which the decision will be rendered.

Information Processing

Information Bits of data that are created when people assign them significance.

Information can be defined as bits of data that are created when people assign them significance. For example, when economists hypothesize about the state of the economy, they use particular pieces of information, which may include the number of new home startups, existing home sales, gross national product, gross domestic product, valuation of the dollar, current exchange rates, long-term and short-term interest rates, and the unemployment rate. Which of these data are more indicative of the state of the economy? The answer is that it depends on the particular person making the evaluation. Any piece of information is both replete with and devoid of information depending on the degree of meaning people assign to it. Is an organization considered healthy only if its stock price remains stable or begins to climb? Or is the health of an organization dependent on the health of the market it serves as well as internal factors such as quality employee relationships and quality working conditions? The study of information and information processing is a diverse area because it encompasses how the individual as well as the organization engage in sense-making behavior and the meaning and value assigned to particular bits of data.

The way in which people identify and attribute significance to bits of information in the environment is called **information scanning**. People's scanning behavior tends to be either proactive or reactive in nature. **Proactive scanning** reflects the tendency to identify and assign significance to data that may/will be used in future decision making or problem solving.

Reactive scanning refers to the tendency to identify and assign significance to data only after a problem or a situation requiring a decision presents itself.

The following practices are believed to aid in developing proactive scanning within the organization: (1) Keep in contact with all organizational members and publics, including employees at all levels of the organization, other organizations, consumers, and others in the community; further, encourage all members of the organization to do the same; (2) develop information profiles or information databases on competitors, consumers, and industry trends and make this information easily accessible to all organizational members; (3) openly discuss the internal and external influences on the organization and organizational goals and work collaboratively to interpret these data from these influences; and (4) develop practices that improve the proactive scanning of organizational members by manipulating the environment (e.g., changing the position of a piece of office furniture or adding a new analysis to a report that distinguishes between who will recognize the new data and who will overlook it) (Choo, 2006). Other practices that encourage proactive information scanning behavior, especially in groups, include keeping decision-making and problem-solving groups together for longer periods and ensuring that group members represent diversity of expertise and culture (Sutcliffe, 2001).

Information Systems Theory

Karl Weick (1979) proposed a theory of how people make sense of information in an environment. The main goal of **information systems theory** is to explain how information and sense making are perceptual processes that vary from person to person. That is, what constitutes information and information quality is unique to each individual. Each person brings his or her own sense-making tools and processes to every event.

According to Pugh and Hickson (1997), sense making consists of at least seven distinguishing characteristics:

information systems theory Seeks to explain how information and sense making are perceptual processes that vary from person to person. It also seeks to identify how ambiguity and equivocal information lead people to different realities.

1. Organizational sense making is grounded in the construction of identity, which is the way in which people are constantly defining and redefining themselves.

2. Organizational sense making is retrospective in that people are constantly reconstructing experience and do not make sense of something until the event has already been experienced. For example, reflect on a bad work experience you have had in the past. Chances are you engaged in a good deal of reflection to make sense of the event and, after reflection, concluded that the event was a bad experience.

3. Organizational sense making becomes part of sensible environments. In other words, because we engage in sense making, we become part of the environment we are making sense of. For example, for a long time the U.S. Postal Service believed that it had a monopoly on package shipping services and disregarded competition from

small-sized shipping companies such as FedEx and DHL resulting in the delivery of poor-quality customer service. However, this complacency led to a drastic decline in business as the "small" competitors grew into major competitors through quality customer service.

4. Organizational sense making is a social process, meaning that people make sense of events in relation to other people both inside and outside the organization.

5. Organizational sense making is an ongoing process in that people are always making sense of events around them. Therefore, sense making is believed to have no beginning and no end.

6. Organizational sense making is focused on cues. These cues indicate that sense making occurs from common or familiar points of reference. For example, if a supervisor informs her subordinates that someone from "headquarters" is coming for a visit, this may serve as a cue for subordinates to be on their best behavior. Given that the information of a visit from headquarters prompts subordinates to behave in more productive ways, the supervisor can use this cue to control the sense making behavior of subordinates.

7. Organizational sense making can be driven by the plausible, not the probable. In other words, when people make sense of events, their sense making may or may not be based on what was probable, but on what was plausible. An example is someone who regularly concludes that many events in his life occur because there is a "conspiracy" involved. Another example would be an employee who receives a negative evaluation because his quality of work was lacking. However, the employee blames the negative evaluation on other factors (e.g., the employee's coworkers did not care for him and, as a result, actively worked to sabotage his productivity). Although the employee's interpretation is not the most probable, it is plausible, and the employee is convinced of its veracity.

Information systems theory seeks to identify how ambiguity and equivocal information lead people to different realities. Thus, organizations should seek to ensure that there is a "most single" reality that is shared by all members of the organization. Simply put, organizations should seek to reduce uncertainty or equivocation (i.e., **requisite variety**) with regard to information.

Weick (1995) argues that organizations operate or exist within an environment that is both physical and informational. People within the organization are in a constant state of **organizing**. Weick believes that we should use verbs such as *managing* and *organizing* as opposed to nouns such as *management* and *organization*. The use of verbs reflects the fluidity of the sense-making process, whereas the use of nouns reflects a stationary or fixed process. People create their environment through **enactment**, which is the action of making sense. Any one person will attribute different realities to information. Given that people have different **perceptual schemas** and **selective perception**, people create different information environments. In a low equivocal environment, people use **assembly rules**, which are standard processes that help people establish standard routines for making sense of information. **Sense making** involves not only interpreting information but also generating what was interpreted. As Weick argues, "People know what they think when they see what they say" (Weick, 1979, p. 175). For example, your college or university has a student handbook that explicitly provides standardized procedures for everything from academic standards of conduct to the steps necessary to apply for graduation. These standards help increase the probability that each student will enact these processes in a similar way. On the other hand, when there is high equivocation, people engage in **communication cycles**, which are sense-making actions through which people create and react to ideas. For example, a professor gives an assignment with only the following instructions: "I want you to develop a term paper on the Civil War. The length of the paper should be as long as it needs to be to cover the topic satisfactorily." The information provided by the professor is full of uncertainty and equivocal information. In this case, students will probably engage in communication cycles to make sense of the equivocal directions. Weick (1979) believes that both assembly rules and communication cycles are used most during the **selection stage of organizing**. "The selection process selects meanings and interpretation directly and it selects individuals, departments, groups, or goals indirectly (Weick, 1979, p. 175). On the other hand, when sense making is effective and people are sharing the same information environment, people are utilizing the **retention stage of organizing.** Organizations should document both assembly rules and communication cycles as a rubric for future sense-making processes. The retention stage of organizing involves deciding whether assembly rules and communication cycles should be retained or discarded in future sense making. It is argued that the more information that is retained from past information processing, the more difficult it will be to process more complex information in the future. However, some retention of past sense making is valuable. Simply put, Weick believes we should "treat memory as a pest." The rules that an organization has developed and engages in are known as **organizational intelligence** (Kreps, 1979) (see Figure 10.3). Information systems theory serves as a rubric from which shared sense making can be accomplished in the process of organizing. Figure 10.3 illustrates how this process is enacted.

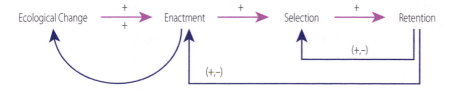

FIGURE 10.3
Structure of the organizing process.
Adapted from Weick (1973), *The Social Psychology of Organizing.* Reading, MA: Addison-Wesley.

Informational Reception Apprehension

informational reception apprehension A habit of information processing characterized by anxiety and antipathy regarding information reception, perception, processing, or adjustment.

Informational reception apprehension (IRA) is a habit of information processing that reflects "a pattern of anxiety and antipathy that filters informational reception, perception, and processing, and/or adjustment (psychologically, verbally, physically) associated with complexity, abstractness, and flexibility" (Wheeless, Preiss, & Gayle, 1997, p. 166).

Some people experience anxiety about incoming information or stimuli that have specific characteristics. For example, some people experience anxiety when faced with complex information whereas others may experience anxiety when the information contains a lot of names and numbers. Stimuli can vary in complexity, abstractness, and flexibility. **Complexity** reflects both the amount and details of the message as well as the cognitive capacity of the person receiving the information. **Abstractness** reflects the concreteness of the information as well as the capacity of the person receiving the message to think abstractly. **Flexibility** is "the demands of the external environment for openness, adaptability, change, etc., as well as the ability of a person to select, receive, and deal with such information" (Wheeless, Eddleman-Spears, Magness, & Preiss, 2005, p. 146).

Every person has a threshold for information processing that, when crossed, impairs that person's ability to process information properly. For example, consider the following two situations. In the first situation your supervisor enters your office and says, "Tomorrow we will have a mock sales meeting at which you will pitch your new idea to your coworkers, and at the conclusion of your presentation we will all talk about the positives and negatives of the presentation." In the second situation your supervisor walks into your office and says, "Tomorrow you will pitch your new idea to our biggest client and then, following the presentation, we will all talk about your future with the company." The changing environmental demands (i.e., mock sales presentation versus being terminated or promoted based on one sales pitch) may cause you to experience severe informational reception apprehension when developing or reviewing the sales presentation simply because of the gravity associated with the potential outcomes of the sales presentation.

Informational reception apprehension is believed to contain three dimensions: **listening apprehension**, **reading anxiety**, and **intellectual inflexibility.** Listening apprehension is the fear associated with either anticipated or real listening situations. Reading anxiety refers to the degree of anxiety a person experiences when reading information. Intellectual inflexibility reflects the degree to which people are unwilling to consider different points of view. In a study looking at IRA and argumentative and aggressive communication, Paul Schrodt and Lawrence Wheeless (2001) found that listening apprehension and intellectual inflexibility were predictors of both argumentativeness and verbal aggressiveness. That is, people reporting high levels of IRA also reported higher levels of verbal aggressiveness and lower argumentativeness. The way we cognitively and emotionally respond to information directly determines the type of information we seek, the amount of information we seek, and how accurately we recall that information. For example, it is not uncommon for people to suffer listening apprehension when meeting people for the first time. Have you ever forgotten someone's name when you first meet him? Is this a pattern for you? If so, you might suffer from information apprehension when meeting people for the first time. Forgetting people's names, especially when first meeting them, is common because people are nervous and generally concerned with making a good first impression. The focus on impression formation takes our focus away from effectively processing the incoming information.

Uncertainty Management Theory

We have all heard the mantra that "change is good." But to some, change means new information, adjustment, and an overall sense of being overwhelmed. Some people and organizations are in industries where change is part of everyday life (e.g., high technology, personal electronics), whereas others are in stable environments where there is little new information that leads to change (e.g., natural resources, energy). One can consider the processing of new information as the introduction of uncertainty into an environment. The introduction of new information to a person or organization creates a state of uncertainty that must be managed effectively to facilitate sense making.

One such theory designed to explain the uncertainty management process is **uncertainty management theory** (UMT). UMT was developed by Dale Brashers (2001a) as a reaction to the simplistic way that the term *uncertainty* has been conceptualized in communication theory. He believes that uncertainty is a multifaceted concept that can be more valuable and serve more functions when not treated as an aversive state to be avoided or reduced. UMT was originally conceptualized to explain how people react to health-related uncertainty (Brashers, 2001b; Brashers, Goldsmith, & Hsieh, 2002) but UMT can explain uncertainty in the organization just as effectively.

According to Afifi and Matsunaga (2008), UMT consists of three features: (1) the meaning and the experience of uncertainty, (2) the role of an individual's response to uncertainty, and (3) the psychological and communicative strategies used to manage uncertainty. Unlike other theories that conceptualize uncertainty as something that should be reduced or avoided, a key term with UMT is *management of uncertainty* as opposed to *reduction of uncertainty*. In fact, Brashers (2001a) argues that the equation of "more information = less uncertainty" is false. He argues that information and uncertainty are not unidimensional constructs but that they are separate constructs. The key question is, How much information is enough? The concept of "enough" varies from person to person. Therefore, Brashers believes that when people feel insecure about the amount of knowledge they possess or the amount of knowledge available, uncertainty is present. Simply put, "Abandon the assumption that uncertainty will produce anxiety" (Brashers, 2001a, p. 477).

uncertainty management theory A theory that explains how people react to uncertainty. Uncertainty is believed to be a multifaceted concept that can be more valuable if not treated as if it needs to be reduced or avoided.

A plethora of other emotions accompany experiences of uncertainty. For example, consider a poorly performing subordinate who has been asked to report to the supervisor's office at the end of the day. Given that it is a Friday afternoon, the subordinate decides to go directly home instead of reporting to the supervisor. The subordinate's lack of effort in reporting to the supervisor's office (and resulting lack of information about his or her job status) can make the subordinate feel comfortable—the uncertainty may give the subordinate hope of keeping his or her position. Another example is a person who sends out a résumé for a position but fails to make a follow-up phone call to the employer to determine if he or she is being considered for the position. This lack of definitively knowing if he or she is being considered for the position provides the candidate with a degree of hope.

Another key component of UMT concerns our reaction to uncertainty and how it directly impacts the influence of uncertainty on our psychological well-being. For instance, if a person interprets uncertainty in a negative fashion (i.e., negative emotional response), uncertainty is considered a dangerous state that should be avoided whenever possible. On the other hand, if a person perceives uncertainty as a positive experience (i.e., positive emotional response), uncertainty becomes beneficial to his psychological well-being. For example, a person who has a negative emotional response to uncertainty would be ideal for an assembly line position that contains very little uncertainty in things such as work hours, break times, and required tasks. However, a person who has a positive emotional response to uncertainty will be ideal for a position such as a stockbroker or salesperson, because pay in those jobs is based on performance, some work shifts may be longer than others based on customer interest, and volatility is a regular occurrence. Figure 10.4 illustrates the uncertainty management process.

Research on information seeking has provided scholars with an abundance of findings whose primary focus is based on the premise that the more information we seek, the more control information provides to us. This process has been described from a skills development perspective as a way to gain control over a particular situation (Cegala & Lenzmeir Broz, 2003) as well as a personality characteristic that predisposes people to seek out information (Lefcourt, 1981). However, UMT holds that our perceptions of uncertainty (positive versus negative) directly impact the strategies and

FIGURE 10.4
Model of uncertainty management.

types of communication we engage in and expose ourselves to when trying to manage the uncertainty. The following experiment illustrates this point: Ask 10 people you know the following question: If you had a choice, would you want to know the types of diseases you will develop in the future? Chances are that some people will respond "yes." In this case, uncertainty is a negative state that must be reduced if it is to be maintained effectively. By *maintained* we mean that every person has a level of uncertainty he or she feels comfortable living with. Some people can only effectively manage uncertainty if it is greatly reduced or eliminated, whereas others can effectively manage some degree of uncertainty. Others feel comfortable in managing high levels of uncertainty. People who respond "no" to the question posed above perceive the function of uncertainty differently. For these people, uncertainty is a positive state that must be maintained because knowing what diseases they will develop in the future causes them more anxiety than not knowing.

Applying Brashers' (2001a) uncertainty management concepts to the organization, there are three additional ways in which people can interpret information. First, some people who live with chronic states of uncertainty adapt to the state of chronic uncertainty (e.g., It's something that I have to deal with, so I might as well get used to it). Second, social networks such as family and friends as well as social role models (e.g., people in the organization who have been there a long time and have been successful in their position) aid in managing high uncertainty. For example, an employee facing downsizing can rely on family and friends but may also rely on people who have been laid off from similar jobs. Third, we engage in uncertainty management at a metalevel. That is, we manage our uncertainty management. We can metamanage uncertainty in two ways: First, we can manage our uncertainty by distributing our need for certainty in one area of our lives and uncertainty in other areas of our lives. This is not to suggest that there is a finite amount of uncertainty management. Rather, our psychological makeup, in a protective way, naturally determines where our uncertainty management efforts are needed (i.e., where uncertainty management is vital for effective management) and where they are discretionary (i.e., desired but not vital). For example, if we are experiencing a great deal of uncertainty about our job security, we may simply come to terms with the lack of employment security and seek certainty in other areas of our lives, such as playing on a sports team or engaging in a hobby, which afford us certainty in terms of a set schedule and control over the amount of time we want to spend engaged in the tasks. Second, through time and experience, people develop the flexibility to discern what information is trustworthy and relevant from that which is not. An example of this would be the difference between the way a new employee and a long-term employee react to rumors of organizational downsizing. Chances are, the newcomer will become extremely anxious and uncertain because she has never been exposed to such information with this particular organization and thus will have trouble managing the uncertainty. On the other hand, the long-term employee will probably be unfazed by rumors because he has experienced (and learned to manage effectively) such information (i.e., lay-off rumors) in the past and concludes that lay-off rumors are not worth the worry.

The ability to identify important information in the environment as well as process that information properly is a key factor for organizational success. With new information comes a degree of uncertainty that may cause some people to experience high levels of anxiety, whereas other people may be comfortable processing the information. As identified in this section, how we manage uncertainty and scan information environments tends to be traitlike in that we develop ways of accruing environmental information and habitual ways of reacting to such information. In the next section we discuss organizational change, which inherently contains uncertainty for organizational members and the organization as a whole.

Organizational Change

In reading the previous chapters of this text, it should be clear that change, whether in terms of communicating with coworkers and customers or adjusting to the workplace, is the only thing that is consistent. Organizations experience change in both minor and dramatic ways, just as people do. The word *change* can mean different things to different people and affects how management strategies evolves (see Chapter 2) as well as whether organizations survive or fail based on how they handle change (see Chapter 1). This section introduces two important concepts: how strategic change is implemented and how organizational innovation or change is communicated throughout the organization.

Strategic Change

strategic change A complex, situation-dependent, and continuous process that is purposefully implemented and monitored

Andrew Pettigrew is a distinguished professor of organizational behavior who argued that **strategic change** should be thought of as a complex, situation-dependent, and continuous process. Strategic change should also be purposefully implemented and monitored. According to this approach, change can only be fully understood when **context** (both the environment within the organization and society as a whole), **content** (the objectives that are to be achieved by the change), and **process** (the way in which the organization goes about implementing the change) are accounted for. Given that there are so many factors involved in the process of organizational change; change can be considered a political process.

The change process, according to Pettigrew (1973), moves through a sequential four-step process. First, the **development of concern** is the process of sensing that a problem exists, which leads to legitimizing the idea of change to the point that change is put on the organization's agenda. Second, **acknowledgment of understanding the problem** builds a culture that advocates change. This process may take time; when implementing any significant change, there is an effect on "power structures, career paths, and reward systems and [the change] is therefore unlikely to be straightforward in its application" (Pugh & Hickson, 1997, p. 172). **Planning and acting** is the third stage and reflects selling the vision of what the future will be like when the change is successfully implemented. This process is necessary so that successful planning and commitment to the organization can be established and change can be generated. The final stage is the **stabilizing of change**, which is the ability of management to make sure that the entire organizational process supports the change. This involves ensuring that the reward system, flow of information, power, and authority support the new "organizational reality."

In a study of how organizations manage change, Pettigrew and Whipp (1991) identified five interdependent problems of managing strategic change that can adversely affect companies:

1. *Assessing the environment,* which entails making sure that all top management is aware of the constant learning required to keep the activities and practices of the organization moving toward the desired end state.

2. *Leading change,* which is the need to build a climate that encourages innovation and change as well as building the necessary resources to bring about the change.

3. *Linking strategic and operational change,* which assumes that whenever a strategic plan is implemented over time, not only do the expected changes take place, but also unexpected change. This outcome of both expected and unexpected change is known as **operational changes**. Therefore, it is important to ensure that the actual result remains closely related to the original strategic plan.

4. *Treating human resources as assets and liabilities,* meaning that members of the organization must be willing to acquire and be capable of acquiring new knowledge and skill as well as able to unlearn patterns that would be detrimental to the desired change.

5. *Developing a coherent approach,* which assumes it is imperative to keep the organization together while attempting to change or reinvent it. Pettigrew's (1973) approach to organizational change is predicated on the fact that change is a multidimensional and fluid concept in which factors within, throughout, and beyond the organization influence the success or failure of any change.

Organizational Innovation

Everett Rogers (1995) defined **innovation** as "an idea, practice, or object that is perceived as new by an individual or other unit of adoption" (p. 11). It is important to emphasize that there is little difference between *change* and *innovation.* Trying to articulate the difference between change and innovation is unnecessary because "the communication patterns for change and

innovation The idea, practice, or object that is perceived as new by people or units of adoption.

innovation in organizations are rather similar" (Rogers & Agarwala-Rogers, 1976, p. 153). Innovation, then, is something that "is change" as well as something that "requires change."

The **innovation process** consists of two phases: the **initiation phase** and the **implementation phase**. The initiation phase consists of gathering relevant information and making the necessary plans to accompany the upcoming change. When we refer to accompanying the change, we mean making sure there is a clear need for the change and the change will result in added value for the organization as well as making sure the organization's strategic plan is consistent with the proposed change or innovation (Rogers, 1983). For example, the Turner Broadcasting Station (TBS) was a "general entertainment" cable network and offered programming that included comedy and professional wrestling. In an effort to invigorate the network, energize the staff, and boost ratings, Steve Koonin (formerly of Coca-Cola) was hired as chief operating officer (COO). The decision was made to switch the network's programming to include only drama. The TBS staff met this drastic change in programming format with trepidation. However, top management's decision to cancel the station's highest rated program (*World Championship Wrestling*) because it did not fit into the network's strategic plan symbolized upper management's commitment to becoming a leader in dramatic programming. The result was a complete transformation both in ratings and programming, and TBS is now an industry leader in the drama genre.

The second phase of the innovation process is the implementation phase. This phase reflects all of the communication, decisions, and actions necessary to ensure the change is successfully integrated into the organization. This implementation phase may require adapting the innovation or altering the organization in an effort to achieve a "best fit" scenario between the

FIGURE 10.5
The Innovation/Change
Model of Innovation
Adoption.

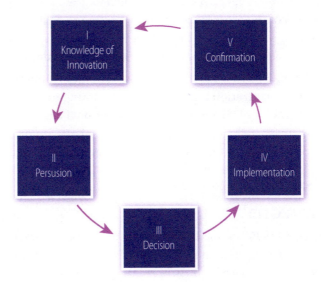

change and the organization. Eventually, a successful implementation would be merging the identity of the change and the organization such that the change becomes part of the organization and vice versa.

The innovation/change process, as presented here, is linear in nature. It is important to note that the success of any innovation is contingent on its malleability, or ability to be altered. For example, if a new technology or business model does not allow for the idiosyncratic practices of the particular organization (i.e., the organization's "own way" of doing things), the innovation may be deemed unfit or inefficient and thus discarded simply because it was not crafted or customized to the specific organization. The process of adopting any idea or innovation can be considered a "life cycle" in that innovations are created, mature, and then give way to new ways of doing things. Rogers (1986) proposed a five-stage model of innovation decision making that consists of "the mental process through which an individual or other decision-making unit passes from first knowledge of an innovation, to forming an attitude toward the innovation, to a decision to adopt or reject, to implementation of the new idea, and to confirmation of this decision" (p. 119). Figure 10.5 illustrates the five-stage model of innovation/change adoption.

First is the **knowledge stage**, which consists of the organization or personnel within the organization becoming aware that the innovation or idea exists and may be beneficial to the organization. The second stage is the **persuasion stage**, which reflects the appeal of the actual characteristics of the innovation or proposed change. More specifically, these innovation attributes are **relative advantage** (will adoption of this innovation allow the organization to operate more efficiently or more consistently with the strategic plan than it currently does?); **compatibility** (to what degree does the innovation agree with the organization's current values/mission and/or future mission?), **complexity** (is the innovation something that is easily understood and/or used by all members of the organization?); **trialability** (to what degree can the innovation be implemented on a trial basis? Can we commit some units of the organization to the change on a trial basis?); and **observability** (to what degree are the results of the innovation visible to members of the organization or those who are making the final decisions?). All these elements factor into the persuasion stage of innovation adoption. Third is the **decision stage**, in which those who hold decision-making power determine if the innovation or change is worth making or adopting. This type of decision, given the scope of the innovation, is generally made at the upper levels of the organization. The fourth stage, the **implementation stage**, involves putting the innovation into practice throughout the organization. This can be a monumental task depending on the type of change. As mentioned earlier, TBS decided to transform its entire station brand from general entertainment to dramatic programming. This level of profound change required all members of the organization to alter or completely change their current ways of doing things. Unlike the previous three stages, which are considered more mental in nature because they do not require any actual physical change to the organization, during the implementation stage the organization changes physically (e.g., the new computer system is installed or the new production line is turned on). The **confirmation stage** is the fifth and final stage and consists of determining if adoption of the innovation has resulted in the promised results or has failed to deliver the promised benefits articulated in the persuasion stage.

These stages of innovation adoption are considered universal in that all organizations and all innovation/change will, to one extent or another, go through these stages when considering whether to invest (financially, emotionally, and organizationally) in an innovation.

Summary

This chapter provided an overview of the ways in which organizations and organizational members make decisions, the processes associated with information, and the reasons that quality information processing is crucial to successful change and innovation adoption.

Decision making and decision-making processes are rational processes but are also unique to each individual decision maker. The knowledge bases from which people draw when making decisions can be based on both fact and intuition. The models presented in this chapter account for all styles of decision making and provide a foundation for gauging and assessing your own decision-making tendencies.

The processing of information and the ways people use information in the organization, as discussed in this chapter, provide many interesting insights into why, when it comes to significant change, people and organizations tend to be "ahead of the curve" and others tend to be "behind the curve." Information can come in many forms and is only considered valuable if the person or organization deems it valuable. What one person views as valuable information, another person may consider useless. This is further complicated by our psychological capacity to process information. Some people are predisposed to process more complex information better than others and to be more comfortable with high degrees of uncertainty than others. This individual difference can differentiate effective from less effective decision making.

Finally, organizational change and the organizational change process are dynamic and sequential. If any change is to be successful, it must be embraced by organization members at all levels. Further, the organization's culture must be willing to accept change and innovation as well as adapt successfully to the change. The concept of change is inherent in today's workplace, and successful employees will effectively process and adapt to change.

Questions for Discussion and Review

1. Compare and contrast decision making and problem solving. Provide an example to support your answer.

2. List and define the five steps of the functional approach to decision making. Why would an organization or group move through all five steps?

3. List and define the four strategies associated with Thompson's uncertainty model. Describe when an organization would likely engage in each strategy. Provide examples to support your answer.

4. According to Vroom and Yetton, there are decision-making processes managers *should* utilize versus those that they *do* utilize. Explain the difference between the two and provide an example for each.

5. List and define the three stages of Simon's activity approach. Explain why these stages are considered linear.

6. Explain the difference between a good solution versus an optimal solution. Provide examples to support your answer.

7. According to March, decision making is affected by four influences. List and explain each of these influences and explain how each affects the quality of decisions.

8. Define organizational innovation and describe what occurs at each stage of the innovation process.

References

Afifi, W. A., & Matsunaga, M. (2008). Uncertainty management theories: Three approaches to a multifarious process. In L. A. Baxter & D. O. Braithwaite (Eds.), *Engaging theories in interpersonal communication: Multiple perspectives* (pp. 117–132). Thousand Oaks, CA: SAGE Publications.

Brashers, D. E. (2001a). Communication and uncertainty management. *Journal of Communication, 51,* 477–497.

Brashers, D. E. (2001b). HIV and uncertainty: Managing treatment decision making. *Focus: A guide to AIDS research, 16*(9), 5–6.

Brashers, D. E., Goldsmith, D. J., & Hsieh, E. (2002). Information seeking and avoiding in health contexts. *Human Communication Research, 28,* 258–271.

Cegala, D. J., & Lenzmeier Broz, S. (2003). Provider and patient communication skills training. In T. L. Thompson, A. M. Dorsey, K. I. Miller, & R. Parrot (Eds.), *Handbook of health communication* (pp. 95–120). Mahwah, NJ: Erlbaum.

Choo, C. W. (2006). *The knowing organizations: How organizations use information to construct meaning, create knowledge, and make decisions* (2nd ed.). New York: Oxford University Press.

Cohen, M. D., March, J. G., & Olsen, J. P. (1972). A garbage can model of organizational choice. *Administrative Science Quarterly, 17,* 1–25.

Gouran, D. S., Hirokawa, R. Y. (1983). The role of communication in decision-making groups: A functional perspective. In M. S. Mander (Ed.), *Communication in transition: Issues and debate in current research* (pp. 168–185). New York: Praeger.

Gouran, D. S., & Hirokawa, R. Y. (1996). Functional theory and communication in decision-making and problem-solving groups: An expanded view. In R. Y. Hirokawa & M. S. Poole (Eds.), *Communication and group decision making* (2nd ed., pp. 55–80). Thousand Oaks, CA: SAGE Publications.

Infante, D. A. (1988). *Arguing constructively.* Prospect Heights, IL: Waveland Press.

Kelley, T., & Littman, J. (2001). *The art of innovation: Lessons in creativity from IDEO, America's leading design firm.* New York: Currency.

Kreps, G. (1979). Human communication and Weick's model of organizing: A field experimental test and revaluation. *Dissertation Abstracts International, 40, 07A.*

Lefcourt, H. M. (1981). *Research with the locus of control construct: Vol. 1. Assessment methods.* New York: Academic.

March, J. G. (1988). *Decisions and organizations.* Hoboken, NJ: Blackwell.

March, J. G. (1994). *A primer on decision making.* New York: Free Press.

March, J. G., & Olsen, J. P. (1980). *Ambiguity and choice in organizations* (2nd ed.). New York: Oxford University Press.

Pettigrew, A. (1973). *The politics of organizational decision making.* Hampshire, UK: Tavistock.

Pettigrew, A., & Whipp, R. (1991). *Managing change for competitive success.* Hoboken, NJ: Blackwell.

Pugh, D. S., & Hickson, D. J. (1997). *Writers on organizations.* Thousand Oaks, CA: SAGE Publications.

Rancer, A. S., & Avtgis, T. A. (2006). *Argumentative and aggressive communication: Theory, research, and application.* Thousand Oaks, CA: SAGE Publications.

Rogers, E. M. (1983). *Diffusion of motivation.* New York: The Free Press.

Rogers, E. M. (1986). *Communication technology: The new media society.* New York: The Free Press.

Rogers, E. M. (1995). *Diffusion of innovations* (4th ed.). New York: The Free Press.

Rogers, E. M., & Agarwala-Rogers, R. (1976). *Communication in organizations.* New York: The Free Press

Schrodt, P., & Wheeless, L. R. (2001). Aggressive communication and informational reception apprehension: The influence of listening anxiety and intellectual inflexibility on trait argumentativeness and trait verbal aggressiveness. *Communication Quarterly, 49,* 53–69.

Simon, H. A. (1960). *Administrative behavior* (2nd ed.). New York: Macmillan.

Simon, H. A. (1977). *The new science of management decision.* Englewood Cliffs, NJ: Prentice Hall.

Sutcliffe, K. M., (2001). Organizational environments and organizational processing. In F. M. Jablin & L. L. Putnam (Eds.), *The new handbook of organizational communication: Advances in theory, research, and methods* (pp. 197–230). Thousand Oaks, CA: SAGE Publications.

Thompson, J. D. (1967). *Organization in action.* Columbus, OH: McGraw-Hill.

Vroom, V. H. (1974). A new look at managerial decision-making. *Organizational Dynamics, 5,* 66–80.

Vroom, V. H., & Jago, A. G. (1988). *The new leadership: Managing participation in organizations.* Englewood Cliffs, NJ: Prentice Hall.

Vroom, V. H., & Yetton, P. W. (1973). *Leadership and decision-making.* Pittsburgh: University of Pittsburgh Press.

Wheeless, L. R., Eddleman-Spears, L., Magness, L. D., & Preiss, R. W. (2005). Informational reception apprehension and information from technology aversion: Development and test of a new construct. *Communication Quarterly, 53,* 143–158.

Wheeless, L. R., Preiss, R. W., & Gayle, B. (1997). Receiver apprehension, information receptivity, and cognitive processing. In J. A. Daly, J. C. McCroskey, J. Ayers, T. Hopf, & D. M. Ayres (Eds.), *Avoiding communication: Shyness, reticence, and communication apprehension* (pp. 151–187). Cresskil, NJ: Hampton Press.

Weick, K. E. (1979). *The social psychology of organizing* (2nd ed.). Reading, MA: Addison-Wesley.

Weick, K. E. (1995). *Sense-making in organizations.* Thousand Oaks, CA: SAGE Publications.

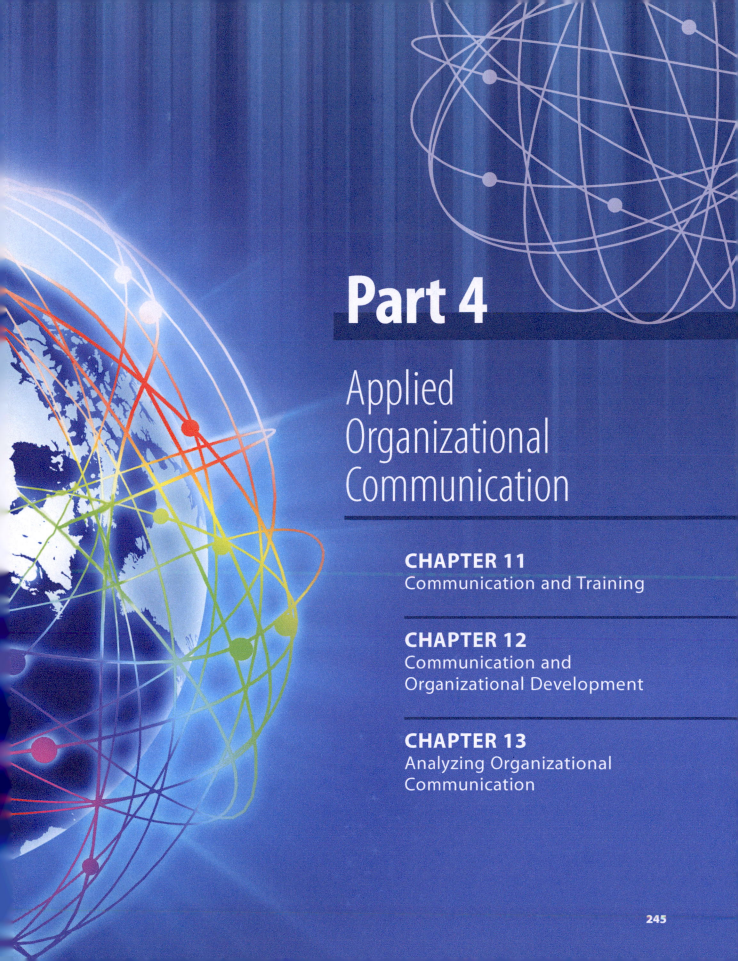

Part 4

Applied Organizational Communication

CHAPTER 11
Communication and Training

CHAPTER 12
Communication and
Organizational Development

CHAPTER 13
Analyzing Organizational
Communication

Chapter 11

Communication and Training

Learning Objectives

Upon completion of the chapter, the student should be able to:

- Compare and contrast knowledge acquisition and skills acquisition.

- Compare and contrast the various training and development functions within the structure of the organization.

- Explain the nine critical skills and abilities that are essential for a career in training.

- Compare and contrast the four levels of competency.

- Compare and contrast behavioral objectives and instructional objectives.

- Compare and contrast role-play, case studies, games, and instruments as devices for the organizational trainer.

Key Terms

Andragogy
Behavioral objectives
Case study
Communication training
Course delivery
Data-analysis skills
Employee relations function
Employment/staffing function
Evaluation
Facilitation skills
Instructional design
Instructional objectives
Instructor's manual

K.A.S.H. formula
Learning
Lecturette
Lesson content
Needs analysis
Needs assessment
Notes to instructor
Objectives
Organizational development function
Organizational training
Participants' manual
Presentational skills

Role-play
Rule of 16
Skills acquisition
Subject-matter expert
Training function
Training need
Unconscious competence
Unconscious incompetence
Understanding the adult learner
Vocalic competence
Written communication skills

Training is one of the most important functions in the contemporary organization. The American Society for Training and Development, the leading association for trainers and organizational development specialists, estimates that U.S. organizations spent almost $130 billion on employee training and development in 2006 (www.astd.org). In this chapter, we (1) define organizational training, (2) identify where hard skills training (learning software or new accounting procedures) as well as soft skills training (learning communication conflict management or persuasion techniques) are located in the structure of most organizations, (3) discuss when and why training is needed, (4) present the major application categories of training, (5) describe the essentials of adult learning theory, (6) outline skills and abilities critical for a career in communication training, (7) describe two major job functions of communication training, (8) present several methods of delivering training, (9) describe the process of developing communication-based training programs, and (10) describe how we can evaluate whether training has been successful.

Defining Organizational Training

organizational training
Process of acquiring knowledge and skills necessary for individuals to perform effectively on the job.

skills acquisition Training employees to perform a particular behavior.

Organizational training involves the acquisition of knowledge and skills necessary for individuals to perform effectively on the job. There are two critical components of training: **knowledge acquisition** and **skills acquisition**. Knowledge acquisition is a component of organizational training that is designed to enhance what people know about an organizational process or issue. For example, new employees are often trained in the process or steps for reporting safety issues through the necessary channels. Skills acquisition refers to training employees to perform a particular behavior. For example, an employee, after being shown a demonstration of the process for inputting account information, is asked to perform the data input procedure just demonstrated. Thus, training involves presenting information designed to enhance what people *know,* and what they will be able to *do* on the job. Generally speaking, skill acquisition is of particular importance to organizations because it tends to have more impact on bottom-line productivity.

communication training
Training that encompasses the presentation of knowledge and skills designed to enhance individuals' competence in presenting information to others and helping people work more effectively with each other.

Although there are many types of training conducted in organizations, in the context of this textbook, we focus on aspects of **communication training**. Communication training usually encompasses the presentation of knowledge and skills designed to enhance individuals' competence in presenting information to others (presentation skills training) and to help individuals work more effectively with each other (interpersonal and group communication training). Communication training has been defined as the process of developing communication skills to perform a specific job more effectively (Beebe, Mottet, & Roach, 2004). Table 11.1 presents several topics often covered in communication training.

TABLE 11.1	Common Topics in Communication Training
Presentational skills	Managing the media
Listening skills	Team building
Managing organizational change	Cultural diversity
Written communication—writing skills	Conducting effective meetings
Delegation	Dealing with difficult people
Group decision making	Effective telephone skills
E-mail etiquette	Sexual harassment

Organizational Training in the Structure of the Organization

Many companies have human resources departments, which were formerly referred to as personnel departments. Human resources departments usually have four major functions: compensation and benefits, employment/staffing, employee relations, and training and organizational development. The **compensation and benefits function** encompasses job evaluations, structure and merit plans, and executive compensation plans. The **employment/staffing function** includes internal and external staffing and hiring, managing college and other recruitment and internship programs, administering EEO/AAP (Equal Employment Opportunity and Affirmative Action Programs), and career counseling. The **employee relations function** concerns evaluating performance, handling management issues, managing safety and health services, dealing with disciplinary and attendance issues, and fostering positive employee relations. The **training function** imparts knowledge and skills that enable employees to be more effective in their positions. This function is our primary focus in this chapter. The **organizational development function** concerns organizational design and structure, intervention design and implementation, and quality of work-life processes. When the term *organizational development* is used, the goals are usually larger and are frequently designed to effect widespread organizational change and transformation (Beebe, Mottet, & Roach, 2004, p. 9). We discuss the organizational development function in chapter 12.

When Training Is Needed, and When It Is Not

While it may be easy to conclude that organizational training can be used to "cure" any and all problems an organization encounters, there are times when training is not only inappropriate, but can actually make the organizational issue that the training was supposed to fix even worse. For example, if a manager is displeased with the conduct of her or his subordinates, you

compensation and benefits function Responsible for job evaluations, structure and merit plans, and executive compensation plans.

employment/staffing function Responsible for handling internal and external staffing and hiring, managing college and other recruitment, handling internship programs, administering EOE/AAP, and engaging in career counseling.

employee relations function Responsible for evaluating performance, handling management issues, managing safety and health services, handling disciplinary and attendance issues, and fostering positive employee relations.

training function Responsible for imparting necessary knowledge and skill so employees become more effective in their positions.

organizational development function Responsible for organizational design and structure, intervention design and implementation, and quality of work-life processes.

might hear a call for a training program on Enhancing Employee Motivation or Improving Listening Skills, designed to "fix" the problem. Clearly, a well-crafted and delivered training program designed to provide knowledge and skills on how to motivate subordinates may ameliorate the perceived problem of lackluster employee performance. Similarly, a well-designed program to enhance employees' ability to listen with greater comprehension or provide them with the skills necessary to paraphrase superiors messages may reduce the dysfunctional "conduct issues" perceived by a supervisor.

Martin (2007) identified five organizational situations in which training may not be the first, the best, or even the most appropriate response to perceived or real organizational deficiencies. Training may not be appropriate when it is used in the following situations: (1) *When lack of skill is not the problem.* As mentioned, training is designed to enhance understanding of a concept and most importantly to develop a set of skills in a particular domain of performance (e.g., listening, delivering a presentation, conflict management, persuading customers, etc.). If members already possess the skills needed to do their jobs effectively, then training designed to develop those skills is not necessary and may be seen by management as counterproductive and a waste of time and money. Martin (2007) suggests that if a problem does exist, it might emanate from "a poorly designed work process" that thwarts employees from accomplishing their tasks easily and with competence. Whatever the task may be, if the existing process is deficient it is the process, not the employee, that can be implicated in the failure to get the job done competently and expeditiously. (2) *When training is a substitute for corrective action.* That is, organizations often use training as a corrective action when disciplining an employee or employees would be more effective and appropriate. Martin (2007) illuminates this misapplication of training. A manager, frustrated with a few employees returning late from lunch, orders the entire work group to attend a training program on "time management." Thus, instead of using corrective action directed at the few tardy employees, training becomes the misapplied substitute for the corrective action. Such a substitute is an unwarranted waste of organizational time and resources. (3) *When training is used to satisfy a "requirement" for professional development.* Martin (2007) argues that training should only be conducted when it is needed to develop or enhance the skills and understanding of a group. The operative terms here are *develop* and *enhance.* Training should not be solely focused on compliance. For example, offering a workshop on sexual harassment just to document trainee attendance in order to reduce the organization's liability should that trainee be faced with a charge of sexual harassment is a misapplication of training. Compare this to a training program designed to prepare employees to effectively identify and report situations before they lead to sexual harassment charges. This latter application of the training would be deemed appropriate. Some training programs are offered just because a training department has to offer courses throughout the year. While this may appear to be desirable problem, it creates a culture where training can be seen as a nonessential or trivial component of employee's professional development instead of a critical component in the development of specific skills and knowledge that a group needs to be more competent on the job. (4) *When performance expectations have not been properly communicated.* For employees to perform up to a certain expectation, they must know exactly what is expected of them to accomplish their jobs. If those expectations are either not known, or if the training does not address the specific skills and knowledge needed for proper job performance, it is not likely the employees will actually use that knowledge base or those skills to perform their tasks. Martin (2007) states, "Before you get someone in to do a training session, first make sure that you've set the right expectations for performance that will encourage workers to use what they're being taught" (p. 2). (5) *When management lacks understanding and commitment to training.* Training requires the commitment of upper level management. If the managers do not know about the training content or skills that are being taught, it is unlikely that employees will actually use it, since that knowledge and skill set will not be reinforced by their managers. If this occurs, training becomes a "nice to know" rather than a "need to know" (Martin, 2007, p. 2).

The Role of the Communication Trainer

Communication trainers perform a number of functions in the organization, including corporate trainer, instructor/course delivery specialist, competency expert, curriculum development specialist, instructional designer, performance improvement technologist, technical trainer, and e-trainer. Many trainers with several years of experience are commonly promoted to positions as training coordinator and then training manager. The training manager is responsible for planning, organizing, and staffing the organization's training department. As they ascend the corporate structure, trainers often learn more about the other dimensions of human resources we described above (e.g., compensation, benefits, employee relations, staffing) and can move on to positions such as vice president of training and development and ultimately vice president of human resources.

Communication training is primarily divided into two areas: **instructional design** (the development of training modules and training programs) and **course delivery** (the presentation or delivery of training programs). We describe these two major roles within the training department. Instructional design involves research, planning, writing, and producing the actual training modules and training programs. Instructional designers are responsible for writing and producing the training program that they may or may not deliver. Instructional designers develop the content of training programs, including writing the course learning objectives. They are also responsible for producing the content of manuals for the program (usually the instructor's or trainer's manual and the participants' manual) and are responsible for developing the experiential activities that the trainees will engage in

instructional design
The development of training modules and training programs.

course delivery
The presentation or delivery of training programs.

during the program to ensure the course or program objectives are met. Depending on the size of the organization, the instructional designer may also be responsible for producing the manuals for the training program (collating, photocopying, binding).

The second major job function of a communication trainer is delivering the program. When performing this task, the trainer can be referred to as the instructor, trainer, or facilitator. Usually, the trainer is not the same individual who designs the program (the instructional designer), although again, depending on the size of the organization, the course delivery specialist may have a role in designing and writing the training program. The trainer delivers the content of the program to participants and administers the training to the participants.

Although instructor-led training is still the most common delivery method for training (www.trainingmag.com, November/December 2007, p. 16), organizations are more frequently incorporating technology within the training function. Consequently, some organizations are making greater use of online training methods in which the trainee is taught via computer. This method has been labeled e-learning. E-learning or e-instruction seems to be more acceptable for "hard" skills training (e.g., sales procedures and completing complaint forms) and is employed less frequently in "soft" skills training (e.g., training in presentational communication skills, interpersonal skills, customer service, executive development, and sales training), where instructor-led and face-to-face training still dominates. Online methods are often used to supplement face-to-face instruction in what has recently been termed **blended learning**. With the increase in e-learning, more organizations are hiring content development specialists (a type of e-instructional designer and e-technology specialist) to produce their training programs. In addition, organizations are often outsourcing their training and hiring contract trainers or training consultants to do both the instructional design and course delivery. The reasons an organization would outsource instructional design and course delivery can range from the specialization of the training topic (e.g., how to diffuse an aggressive customer using diffusing communication strategies) to the fiscal health of the organization. If an organization cannot afford to employ an in-house trainer, it will hire outsiders for its training needs. If a training program is delivered in too many locations simultaneously, an individual who is well versed in distance learning is often consulted, resulting in a new position title such as distance learning coordinator or distance learning director.

In the training function, trainers often conduct **needs analyses** to identify problems or other organizational issues and to determine if training is the most appropriate response. In addition, the training function is concerned with assessing the outcomes of training, also referred to as **evaluation**. Trainers are often responsible for obtaining trainees' reactions to the program at the conclusion of the program. Since so much time and money are spent on training, management must know whether the training outcomes

evaluation Process of determining if the objectives created for the particular training program were accomplished and how to improve future versions of a particular program.

have been met. Thus, comprehensive, systematic, and empirical training evaluations are often conducted to determine if indeed there was an increase in the participants' knowledge and skills.

Skills and Abilities Critical for a Career in Training

Individuals who are thinking about a career in training must possess several key skillsets. If you are considering a career as an organizational trainer, one of the first questions you should ask yourself is, "Do I enjoy getting up in front of groups and presenting information, facilitating discussions, and helping individuals learn in a fun and engaging fashion?" If the answer is "no," then a career in communication training is probably not for you. However, if you answered "yes" to this question, then you may have the personality traits that will help you become an effective trainer.

There is more to becoming a successful communication trainer than simply enjoying delivering information to groups. Certain skills, abilities, and competencies are essential if you are to emerge as a successful communication trainer. In the following list, these skills and abilities are not rank ordered (most important followed by less important) because they all need to be developed and refined if one is to become a successful trainer.

1. **Presentational Skills**—Trainers must be in front of different-sized groups for hours, if not days, at a time. Trainees have come to expect that the person delivering the program will at minimum keep them awake and interested, and maximally, stimulated and energized throughout the entire program. Effective trainer presentation skills are a prerequisite to being a successful trainer. This means you must deliver the content of the module or program with energy and vitality. You must use proper vocal articulation and pronunciation, and you must be perceived as an active and dynamic communicator. Successful trainers channel energy through their body by using appropriate gestures, facial expressions, and vocal variety (varied pitch, tone, rate, and inflection) and avoid being monotone. Trainers must engage in eye contact with the trainees; that is, they should try to increase the perception of nonverbal immediacy (closeness) by looking at all of the trainees several times throughout the program.

   presentation skills The ability to deliver the content of the program with energy, to use proper vocal articulation and pronunciation, and to be perceived as a dynamic communicator.

2. **Written Communication Skills**—Successful trainers must possess effective written communication skills, especially if they are to succeed in the instructional design dimension of training. They must be adept at putting ideas together and arranging the content of training programs in a way that maximizes engagement and results in effective and successful learning. Successful trainers must be skilled in developing course learning objectives (we cover this skill in detail later in this chapter).

   written communication skills The ability to write effectively and persuasively; arranging the content of training programs in a way that maximizes engagement and results in effective and successful learning.

andragogy The art and science of teaching or training adults.

3. **Active Listening Skills**—Trainers interact with many types of people, and because **andragogy** (the art and science of teaching or training adults) requires that the participants be recognized as an integral part of the training program, successful trainers must be active listeners. That is, they must be able to listen with comprehension and to paraphrase (restate in their own terms) trainees' comments and suggestions so these comments and suggestions can be incorporated into the program or module.

facilitation skills The ability to lead and guide individual and group discussions during training programs.

4. **Facilitation Skills**—The ability to lead and guide individuals and groups is a necessary skill in delivering training. A good facilitator can transform a training session from dull and uninteresting into one that trainees perceive as lively, dynamic, and productive. Facilitation skills come into play throughout all aspects of the delivery of training. As we discuss later in this chapter, getting the trainees actively involved in the module or program is essential, because training encompasses more dimensions than the mere delivery of content. Trainees must be actively involved in the program, and one way this is accomplished is through design and delivery of experiential activities that make the material come alive. A successful trainer who is skilled at facilitation can change trainees' perception of an activity from boring and a waste of time to important, engaging, and even fun. A skilled facilitator knows how to solicit responses from the entire group, even those who may initially seem reluctant or apprehensive. A successful facilitator knows how to elicit information and ideas from reluctant trainees as well as knowing how to manage the "talkaholic" trainee who dominates the group. A skilled facilitator is able to ask the right questions, either prepared in advance or on the fly, so that participant responses can be shared with the group and incorporated into the lesson content.

5. **Interpersonal Communication Skills**—Trainers must be sensitive and competent in interpersonal communication interactions. One of the most critical interpersonal communication skills is empathy. **Empathy** is the ability to understand the attitudes, beliefs, and values of another person, to be able to put yourself into their shoes. When conducting training programs on topics such as Cultural Diversity, Assertiveness, or Employment Interviewing, it is especially important for the trainer to exhibit empathy because trainees will likely offer numerous and divergent responses. A successful trainer must be able to understand why a particular response was given as well as make the trainee's contributions understood and not dismissed by the trainer or the group. Openness, self-disclosure, the ability to manage others, and the ability to provide appropriate feedback are other interpersonal communication skills important to all successful trainers.

6. **Data-Gathering Skills**—Earlier in this chapter we identified one of the functions of a training and development specialist as being a needs analyst. We suggested that in performing this function, the trainer or organizational development specialist identifies the discrepancy between what the trainees already know or can do, and what they should or must know or be able to do. The difference between the actual and desired knowledge level and skill level is defined as the **training need**. Although not every training effort begins with a formal needs analysis, conducting a **needs analysis** or assessment significantly enhances the likelihood that a training program will be successful. It may also help identify whether training will be the solution to the problem or whether some other type of intervention strategy (e.g., team building or a change in job description) should be implemented. To conduct a successful needs analysis, a trainer must be able to design or select appropriate data-gathering tools and measures (more on this is presented in chapter 13), know several methods of data gathering (e.g., surveys, interviews, focus groups, observation), and be able to assemble the data for analysis.

    training need The difference between the actual and desired knowledge level and skill level.

    needs analysis An analysis of the discrepancy between what trainees already know or can do and what they should or need to know or be able to do.

7. **Data-Analysis Skills**—Trainers must be able to evaluate and interpret the information gathered so they can correctly identify training gaps or other organizational problems that may or may not require a training solution. Being skilled in both quantitative and qualitative research methods/data analysis techniques, statistical analyses, and the use of business software tools, including programs such as Excel and SPSS (the Statistical Package for the Social Sciences), is critical to effective assessment efforts.

    data analysis skills The ability to evaluate and interpret gathered information and correctly identify training gaps or other problems that may or may not require a training solution.

8. **Political Skills**—You may wonder why we have included political skills in the list of skills required of successful trainers. Political skills are important in today's organizational and economic climate. Today, training (and development) must be considered as part of the bottom line for any organization. That is, training must be directly tied to the organization's business goals, profit structure, competitive structure, and economic health. It is not enough that successful training be perceived as fun or something that is good for the employees' sake. Organizations' CEOs must see training as a necessity that contributes to the success and economic health of the organization. Corporate executives must be able to see clearly that training and development enhance the organization through investing in the quality of the workforce. Successful trainers, training managers, and vice presidents of human resources must be able to negotiate delicate organizational relationships. They must be able to convince upper management that training and organizational development do indeed contribute to the profitability of the organization. Today, the training and development departments of organizations must demonstrate that training and

development programs as well as interventions deliver a return on investment. Thus, trainers must possess the political savvy that will allow them to make this case persuasively.

understanding the adult learner The ability to understand the concept of andragogy and the assumption that skills training should be problem centered and immediately applicable.

9. **Understanding the Adult Learner**—One of the most fundamental sets of concepts a trainer or instructional designer must be aware of is andragogy, or the art and science of helping adults learn. *Andragogy* is a term developed by Malcolm Knowles, considered the father of adult education (*andra* from the Greek *aner,* meaning adult, and *gogy* from the Greek *ago,* meaning leading). Andragogy is differentiated from pedagogy, or the art and science of teaching children. Training adults is different from teaching students in traditional school or college settings. Andragogy assumes several things about adults and learning. First, adults are task- and problem centered in their orientation to learning. That is, the adult learners' focus tends to be on the development of immediate skills necessary to accomplish task- and work-related activities (i.e., give me useful information that I can employ today, not obscure knowledge that I cannot use in my job). Second, adults learn best when they take an active role in the learning process. Adults need to be active learners, intensely involved in the learning process. As active learners, they need to be involved both cognitively (thought provoking) and behaviorally (task performing), and the techniques used to train the adult learner must incorporate activities and exercises in addition to content presentation. We discuss how to do this later in this chapter when we discuss the use of experiential training vehicles.

The Need for Training

Employees seek training for numerous reasons. First, an individual's job may change within the organization. An employee may be asked to take on additional responsibilities in his or her job category, and these new responsibilities may require extra skills and knowledge. For example, a successful employee may suddenly find herself promoted to a managerial position in which she must supervise a group of employees. Although she might have been successful in doing her job, she is now responsible for managing a group and will need leadership skills, coaching skills, and specialized communication training (conflict management, listening, presentation communication skills, interviewing skills). Second, changes in the organizational culture or structure mandate new knowledge and skills. For example, if an employee who has been accustomed to working alone is suddenly required to perform his job function in a team setting, he may require additional training in collaboration, idea generation, and problem solving. Third, technological innovations may require acquisition of new knowledge and skills. For example, a new computer hardware system is introduced into the organization, and the employee must learn how to operate it effectively and efficiently. Or a new software program is unveiled that is different from the software the employee had been working with. Although the employee might have tried to learn the software on her own through trial and error or "playing around with it," she lacks the proper knowledge and ability to fully implement the software's features.

Thus, individuals come (or are sent by their employer or manager) to training for several reasons that can be summarized in two broad categories: (1) The individual or employee does not know something he or she needs to know (what, why, or how) to accomplish organizational tasks; or (2) the individual or employee cannot do something he or she must be able to do to accomplish organizational tasks (an employee lacks the skills necessary to do his job effectively). Occasionally, an individual or employee will not do what is required to accomplish organizational tasks (the employee has the necessary knowledge and skillset but does not have the motivation to perform). Although the first category can be overcome through training, the second category likely requires some other type of intervention, such as organizational development efforts, disciplinary efforts, and, in extreme cases, termination.

Levels of Competency

There are four steps involved in skill acquisition. The first step is **unconscious incompetence**, which occurs when we cannot perform a behavior or skill and we do not know that we cannot perform it. If you have ever observed an individual performing a task or behavior and thought, "That looks easy. I'm certain I could do it," such thinking exemplifies unconscious incompetence. Whether it is operating a piece of equipment or a software program, unconscious incompetence occurs before we actually try to perform the skill or behavior. In other words, performing a task competently involves more than observing the task and concluding that we know how to do it simply because we have seen it done. The second step is **conscious incompetence,** which occurs when we try to perform the skill or behavior and we realize that we cannot either do it at all or we do it unsatisfactorily. Probably one of the most frequently cited examples of conscious incompetence is learning to drive a car with a stick shift. Most people in their first attempt to drive such a vehicle have experienced the car stalling or the clutch slipping, with the result that the car does not move. Our need for skill development is obvious to us in this situation. The third step is **conscious competence**, in which we can perform the skill, but we still must exert mental effort to accomplish the task or perform the behavior.

The fourth and final step in skill development is **unconscious competence**, which usually occurs after training has been completed and we have had some time to practice the new skill or behavior. Unconscious competence occurs when we can perform the skill or behavior without putting

unconscious incompetence
Level of competence in which we cannot perform a behavior or skill and we do not know that we cannot perform it.

unconscious competence
Level of competence in which we can perform the skill or behavior without putting much thought into it.

much thought into it. Revisiting the example of learning to drive a car with a stick shift, unconscious competence occurs when you are able to operate the stick shift without having to think about the process of shifting gears or working the clutch. Another example of unconscious competence is when you have driven a particular route to a destination so often that it seems as if the vehicle almost drives you there automatically; you have driven so frequently from point A to point B that you drive almost on autopilot without actually having to think about your route (of course, however, you pay attention to safe driving practices).

Thus, training as a function in the organization is needed primarily because a gap exists between what individuals need to know and be able to do, and their current level of knowledge and skill. Training can decrease the skill deficiency gap, especially when we follow what has been referred to as the **K.A.S.H. formula** for training (**K**nowledge, **A**ttitude, **S**kills, **H**abits). Training can fill the gap and increase our content knowledge, improve our attitude toward work, develop or enhance skills and behaviors needed to accomplish tasks more effectively, and build work habits that will likely enhance our on-the-job performance.

K.A.S.H. formula An effective formula for reducing the skill deficiency gap. The formula consists of trainee knowledge, attitude, skills, and habits.

Creating an Interactive Training Program

Conducting a Needs Assessment

Before a training program is designed, a needs assessment should be conducted. A needs assessment is a systematic examination of the cause and extent of the problem that has prompted the request for training. A thorough, objective, and systematic assessment of the problem will help determine the extent of the skills or performance gap. Suppose the training department of an organization has been called in and asked to deliver a program on conflict management. This program has been requested because the manager of a given team believes there is lack of cooperation and congeniality among members of this work unit. To determine if training is the answer to this perceived problem or to determine the content of such a program, a **needs assessment** is conducted.

needs assessment A systematic examination of the cause and extent of the problem that prompted the request for training.

Several reasons have been identified for conducting a needs assessment:

1. It allows us to identify the current level of skills and performance. If there is a skill or performance gap, the needs assessment can often identify the causes of the gap.

2. It helps us determine if training is the correct answer to the problem. Using the example mentioned above, the needs assessment may reveal that the perceived lack of cooperation and congeniality among members of the work team may not exist, except in the mind of the manager. Rather this excessive conflict may be due to the manager's lack of effective communication, lack of feedback, and poor coaching

skills, not due to any interpersonal difficulties among the team members. If this is the case, then no amount of training will resolve the problem because the problem is not the employees' behavior but the manager's behavior. If the problem can be ameliorated by training, then a needs assessment can determine exactly what knowledge, skills, attitudes, and behaviors must be taught to the trainees to correct the situation. The needs assessment will also discern how long it will take until the desired results are obtained.

Needs assessments depend on gathering data to assess training needs, and there are several data collection methods available. Although a complete treatment of data-gathering techniques is beyond the scope of this chapter (data gathering is covered in chapter 13 in the discussion on conducting communication audits), a few of the more common techniques are mentioned here.

Interviews with individuals are an effective tool. Interviews, especially face-to-face, allow for greater in-depth information to be gathered and frequently employ open-ended questions (questions that allow employees to elaborate on their answer if they choose). **Questionnaires**, containing both open- and closed-ended questions, are especially useful when attempting to gather data from a large group. Questionnaires can take the form of surveys, scales, and self-report instruments, which are tools developed by individuals external to the organization. These instruments have been evaluated for their reliability (consistency, stability, and accuracy) and validity (measurement efficacy, which ensures the scales measure what they say they do) to ensure they are assessing what the trainer intends to measure. Several books are available that contain many instruments used in communication and human relations training (see, for example, Pfeiffer, Heslin, & Jones, 1976; Rubin, Palmgreen, & Sypher, 2004). Another frequently employed method of conducting a needs assessment is **observation**. In this method, a trainer observes others on the job. To go back to our example of the team in need of conflict management training, before the training is designed and conducted, a trained individual visits with the team at its worksite, observes and records his or her perceptions of team members' communication behaviors, and analyzes the information from this observation session. Although this method may be more effective for hard skills training, it is possible for the observation method to be used effectively for more soft skills training, such as communication. The observer would note, for example, how team members interacted with each other, when and if verbally aggressive communication was used, and the use of any nonverbal aggressive behaviors. The observer may even attend meetings to see how team members interact with each other.

After the data are gathered from any or all of these techniques, the data are analyzed, and a clearer picture of the problem should emerge. It is only then that a decision can be made as to whether training is the cure for the problem or whether another form of organizational intervention would be more appropriate (see chapter 12, which discusses organizational development).

This QR code will direct you to the homepage of *Dale Carnegie Training*, where you will be able to learn more about the role and process of organizational assessments.

http://www.dalecarnegie.com/
organizational-development-
human-resources-training/

Selecting and Narrowing the Topic

After conducting the needs assessment, you will likely know the general topic for the training program or module. Almost every topic for communication training has a plethora of subtopics that could be covered in a program. Although you would like to cover every subtopic imaginable, it is impractical to think your program can go for more than a few hours or a few days at most. Unlike taking a 15-week semester-long course in college, most trainees cannot leave their jobs for more than a half-day (four hours), full day (eight hours), or two to three days at most. Thus, you must decide on exactly what will be covered during the program to enhance the trainees' knowledge and develop their skills on a particular topic. It is also possible, and often highly likely, that your client will dictate to you exactly how long your training program can be.

The objectives of your program determine exactly what the trainees need to know and be able to do upon completion of the program. Thus, your objectives help you determine what subtopics should and should not be included in the training program. We discuss designing and developing course objectives later in this chapter. Your learning objectives will help you with the tests of "excess and defect." That is, after you write and design your learning objectives, you know what subtopics are extraneous to your program (these would be considered excess and should be eliminated from the module) and what topics that are considered essential to successfully completing your objectives but are not yet listed in the program design (these would be considered the "defect," or what is missing from the program). It is also important to determine what content the trainees absolutely must know to accomplish the objectives as opposed to what would be "nice" for them to know (Lawson, 1998).

Suppose we are asked to design a training program on the general topic of The Employment Interview. Further, we propose to write the program from the vantage point of the interviewee; that is, the person who is going through the employment interview process. The first topic of this training would be subsumed under the topic The Interview, followed by the more narrow topic The Employment Interview. However, even this is a broad topic with many subtopics, including What to Expect in the Employment Interview, How to Tell the Interviewer About Yourself, Your Nonverbal Presence, Taking Personality Tests, Asking Questions, and How to Answer Questions in the Employment Interview. We could not possibly cover all the subtopics of the employment interview in a half- or even full-day training program. Thus, we need to examine our course learning objectives to determine exactly what subtopics must be covered during the program to meet those objectives.

Conducting Research and Developing Content

After you have selected the topic for the training program or module, you need to gather information to develop the program content. One avenue for gathering information is to consult with a **subject-matter expert**. A subject-matter expert, often referred to as a SME, or "smee", is an expert in a particular subject or content area. SMEs are often used in the design of a successful training program. Individuals responsible for the training program design (instructional designers) consult with SMEs during the course development to determine what content belongs in a training program. The SME works with the instructional designer to develop the instructional and behavioral objectives for the program and then helps develop and organize the program or module content. After the program is written, the instructional designer turns over the program to the trainer, who delivers the program.

How do you find material for your training module? There are both internal and external sources for finding material (Beebe, Mottet, & Roach, 2004). If you are an expert on the topic of the program you are designing, then it is relatively easy to find material. If you have developed an expertise in a subject area of communication, then you can draw on that knowledge base to help you write the program. However, if you are not a subject-matter expert in a particular content area, you probably need to conduct research to develop the program. When developing program content, it is helpful if you consult with a SME. What if you do not know someone who is considered an expert on a topic? You then need to consult with other external sources to develop the program content.

We are fortunate to live in the Information Age. We can access external sources of information easily. Begin by searching websites that contain not only scholarly books, but books that are more applied and professional in nature. For example, search sources such as Amazon.com, which lists millions of titles. A search of your local library's resources might also be helpful because you may find books on the topic of your program. Returning to our example of preparing the training program on employment interviewing, if you type the terms *employment interview* in the search box on Amazon.com, you will encounter a plethora of titles that focus on appropriate behavior for the interviewer, the interviewee, or both during an employment interview. Of course, you will also encounter textbooks written by communication scholars that will be helpful in developing your program content. Once you select titles that seem appropriate for your content, go to your local library's home page and see which, if any, titles can be found there and which are available through interlibrary loan. Your library should also have databases you can search for articles to help you develop program content. Some helpful databases for communication-related articles include ERIC, Academic Search Complete, Business Source Complete, and Communications and Mass Media Complete. Depending on the type of libraries you consult (e.g., university libraries versus public libraries), you may have some if not all of these databases available.

There are also many books and materials available from commercial publishing companies directly related to the training industry. The appendix of this chapter lists some of them. These sources of information can help

subject-matter expert (SME)
A person who is an expert in a particular subject or content area.

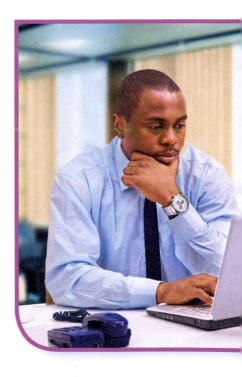

you develop the content of your training program. It is imperative that you provide proper citations and give credit to all external sources of information you use in developing your program. In addition to proper citation protocols, including a page of references in the participants' manual is helpful to your trainees. The references tell the trainees where the information originated in case they want to reference the original material.

Writing Instructional and Behavioral Objectives

An adage suggests that "If you don't know where you are going, how do you know when you've arrived?" This section discusses how to write training goals and objectives. Simply put, "Training goals and objectives serve as the road map when creating a training program" (Ittner & Douds, 1988, p. 9).

Robert Mager has been called the "father of learning objectives." His book, *Preparing Objectives for Programmed Instruction* (1961), influenced pedagogical efforts for the last several decades and continues to influence many corporate training programs developed today. Mager argued for the use of specific, measurable objectives that guide designers during course development and aid trainees in the learning process. Mager (1984) recommends that

> before you prepare instruction, before you select instructional procedures or subject matter or material, it is important to be able to state clearly just what you intend the results of that instruction to be. A clear statement of learning objectives will provide a sound basis for choosing methods and materials and for selecting the means for assessing whether the instruction has been successful. (p. v)

It is important to distinguish between goals and objectives in training. McCroskey (2002) suggests that "the long-term goals are the forest whereas our daily instructional objectives are the trees" (p. 6). Another way to conceptualize these constructs is that **goals** are the broad statements that indicate what the trainee will learn, whereas **objectives** are easily measurable and often include specific, demonstrable skills. Goals serve as the "target" for achievement of a given module or program and often serve as the basis for writing objectives.

Objectives provide the basis for all the content and activities that follow in the instructional design process. One of the most important tasks in creating a training program is development of the instructional and behavioral objectives that spell out exactly what the participants should know and be able to do at the end of the program. In creating objectives, it is helpful to ask, "What are the knowledge, skills, and behaviors the trainee needs to know and be able to do at the end of a training program?"

objectives Goals that are easily measurable and often include specific, demonstrable skills.

Reasons for Objectives

Objectives are useful for trainees, trainers, and instructional designers. Objectives are used to (1) select and design instructional content, materials, and methods; (2) ultimately improve performance; and (3) determine whether the training has been successful. By clearly stating what we want the trainees to accomplish, we can identify whether the trainees have acquired the knowledge and skills that we said they would.

It is helpful to differentiate between instructional and behavioral objectives. **Instructional objectives** are what you as the trainer want the trainees to *know* at the end of the program, whereas **behavioral objectives** are what you want the trainees to be able to *do* at the end of the program. Today, training is highly outcome based. That is, we must be able to demonstrate the training has had a favorable impact on the bottom line of the organization and the training has a positive impact on the performance of the employees as well as the organization as a whole. Therefore, we must write instructional and behavioral objectives that specify that some change (i.e., increased knowledge and skill) will occur. Human resources executives demand of the training department that the program participants are really getting what the program said they were going to get and that the training department can demonstrate the success of instruction in terms of whether the trainees have accomplished the program's instructional and behavioral objectives.

Let's return to an example of a training program discussed earlier in this chapter. Suppose we are designing a training program on the topic *How to Achieve Success in an Employment Interview*. The program content includes a module on presenting the trainees with correct and appropriate responses to questions they are likely to be asked in an employment interview. In planning the content of this module, titled *How to Respond to the Most Difficult Questions During an Employment Interview*, you need to develop a set of instructional and behavioral objectives. Here is a sample:

> *Instructional Objectives (IO)*
>
> Upon completion of this module, participants will:
>
> *IO#1:* Understand four components of answering employment interview questions successfully.
>
> *IO#2:* Understand how to respond to the 10 most difficult personal questions asked during employment interviews.
>
> *Behavioral Objectives (BO)*
>
> Upon completion of this module, participants will
>
> *BO#1:* Use four components to answer questions in a mock employment interview.
>
> *BO#2:* Respond verbally and appropriately to at least seven difficult personal questions asked during employment interviews.

There are set criteria for developing well-crafted learning behavioral objectives. They should be *observable;* that is, they should include some type of

instructional objectives
That the trainer wants the trainees to know at the end of the program.

behavioral objectives
What the trainer want trainees to know at the end of the program.

behavior that you can literally observe in the trainee in some way. One of the behavioral objectives listed in the sample objectives above specifies a particular behavior the trainee must display "verbally and appropriately" when asked a personal question by an employment interviewer. In addition, behavioral objectives should be *measurable;* you should be able to assess how accurately or effectively a given behavior was performed. If potential answers to these personal employment interview questions are provided during the module, the trainees are expected to learn these responses and use them when asked a personal question during an interview. Finally, behavioral objectives must be *realistic*. Note that in the behavioral objective specified above, we require that the trainee respond appropriately to at least seven personal questions that might be asked during an employment interview (e.g., Why do you want to work here?). Asking trainees to be able to respond appropriately to all 10 of the difficult questions may be unrealistic and unattainable.

Writing the Instructor's and Participants' Manuals

Once the research is done, the instructional designer must write and assemble both the **instructor's manual** (trainer's manual) and the **participants' manual**. What should be included in each of these important documents? First we discuss the essential material to include in the instructor's manual.

The Instructor's Manual

The instructor's manual, also called the trainer's manual or the leader's/facilitator's guide, is *the* most important guidebook for the trainer. The instructor's manual provides detailed content and instructions for delivering the training program. It contains what the trainer is going to say to trainees, guidelines on how the program should proceed, debriefing questions to present to trainees, and instructions to the trainer on when to show certain slides, how to conduct the activities and experiential vehicles that will be delivered to trainees, time frames for these activities, and other information that assists the trainer in delivering the training program smoothly and efficiently.

In some cases and for some organizations, the instructor's manual provides the *exact* content (a verbatim script) regarding what is to be said to the trainees. Some organizations, and especially many training companies, demand complete consistency in the manner in which the content is presented to the trainees; no deviation is permitted. Other organizations allow some leeway for the trainer to deviate from "the script" and present details and sections of the content in his or her own words.

instructor's manual
The most important guidebook for the trainer; provides detailed content and instructions for delivery of the training program.

participants' manual
Manual given to participants so trainees can adequately review the course material during and after they leave the training program.

The instructor's manual, at minimum, should include the following:

◆ A cover with the title of the program or training module

◆ A table of contents for the instructor's manual (i.e., on what page of the instructor's manual each topic is presented)

◆ The content of the training program or training module

◆ Master copies of all handouts to be distributed to trainees

◆ Copies of all experiential vehicles to be used during the delivery of the program or module (ice-breakers, activities, exercises, role-plays, games, simulations, case studies)

◆ Instructions on how to conduct these experiential activities

◆ Instructions on how to debrief these experiential activities

◆ A program icon key (a sheet listing all the icons used in the instructor's manual and the meaning of each)

◆ A copy of the participants' manual

◆ The references used to write the program

Although there are numerous designs and layouts for effective instructor's manuals, we recommend that new trainers use a two-column format for the layout of the instructor's manual. The two columns consist of **Lesson Content** and **Notes to Instructor**. A sample page of a two-column instructor's manual is presented in Table 11.2.

Icon Key for Instructor's Manual

The following key will help guide you through the instructor's manual:

 Turn to PowerPoint slide

 Refer to participants' manual

 Hand out candy

 Ask question

 Point to information on slide

 Important information

 Timed exercise

The Lesson Content portion of each page provides exactly what the trainer is going to say to trainees during the session (some statements are more detailed than others). The Notes to Instructor column provides guidelines for the trainer (directions or actions) that help the trainer deliver this content (e.g., Watch your time, Turn to Slide PP-24, Ask trainees to turn to page 18 in their manual.). The instructor's manual is usually built module by module, taking into account the instructional and behavioral objectives you want the

lesson content Contains exactly what the trainer is going to say to trainees during the session.

notes to instructor Contains guidelines (directions or actions) for the trainer that help the trainer deliver the content.

TABLE 11.2   Sample Page of Instructor's Manual

Lesson Content	Notes to Instructor
	The following supplies are needed to conduct a successful training session:
	1. Instructor's manual
	2. Participants' manual (one per trainee, plus one for trainer's reference)
	3. PowerPoint capabilities
	4. Stopwatch
	5. Activity handouts (to include with the participants' manuals)
	6. Name tags (one per trainee)
	7. Pens and markers (one per trainee)
	8. Giveaways (candy, pens, etc.)
	9. Certificates of completion
Hello! My name is _____. I would like to welcome all of you to our training session on The Employment Interview.	Show Slide # PP-1.
Does everyone have a participant manual and a participant name tag?	
Review table of contents	
I would like to go over the objectives of today's program:	Tell trainees to turn to page 1 in their manual.
Instructional Objective #1	
Upon completion of this program, participants will understand the 10 key components of effectively presenting oneself in an employment interview.	Show Slide # PP-2.
Behavioral Objective #1	
Upon completion of this program, participants will demonstrate how to respond to 10 of the most difficult questions asked in an employment interview.	Slide # PP-3.
Let's get started. I'm going to distribute these index cards. Please do not put your name on the card. I would, however, like you to write a response on the card to this question: What was the worst experience you have ever had during a job or employment interview?	Distribute index cards to trainees.

trainees to accomplish during the program. Each module is then added to the next one, until the entire instructor's manual is complete and ready for use by the trainer who will deliver the program.

The Participants' Manual

Almost all training programs include distribution of a participants' manual. This manual is usually distributed to trainees either before the program begins or at some point during the early part of the training. The participants' manual should contain, but is not limited to, the following:

- A cover page with the title of the program and the name of the organization presenting the program
- The instructional and behavioral objectives to be covered during the training
- Copies of all handouts to be used during the program or module (activities, exercises, role-plays, games, simulations, case studies)
- A summary of the key information presented during the program. Some participants' manuals contain copies of all of the slides shown during the program, and an area in which trainees can take notes. (There is a feature in PowerPoint that allows the user to print the slides out as handouts that include room for such note taking.)
- References trainees can refer to for additional information about the program content

There are no universal guidelines regarding what should go into a participants' manual. However, it might be useful to follow this general rule: *There should be enough content in the participants' manual that trainees can adequately review the course material after they leave the program.*

Delivering the Program

There is a maxim that goes something like this: "If you tell people something, they might remember about one quarter of it. If you tell people something and then show them how to do it, they might remember about half of it. However, if you tell them something, show them how to do it, and then have them actually do it, they will remember about 70 percent of it." This maxim is critical in the context of training. When trying to impart new skills to an individual or group, it is important to have that person or group actively involved in the learning process, especially by having the individual or group display the skills or behaviors you have just presented.

Delivering a Lecture

In our discussion of the differences between pedagogy and andragogy presented earlier in this chapter, we highlighted the difference between training and teaching. Traditional pedagogy is a relatively passive learning process; andragogy is more active and attempts to involve the participants in the learning process. In this section, we describe several ways to involve trainees when delivering training content. Beebe, Mottet, and Roach (2004, p. 111) identify a number of advantages of the **lecture method**, including presenting a lot of content in a short time; giving the trainer greater control over what occurs in the training session; and being able to accommodate any size group, from five to 500. Occasionally, the goal of training is primarily to present information or expose trainees to the new information so they are aware that such new information exists. If this is the case, the nature of that learning goal may require the trainer to present information and content matter in a lecture format. Indeed, if your course or program objectives only involve cognitive learning (what we have described earlier as instructional objectives), then lecturing may be an appropriate presentation method.

One method used often in presenting information to participants is the **lecturette**, a brief lecture or short talk typically ranging from five to 15 minutes. In a lecturette, the trainer explains a process or principle relevant to the immediate needs of the learners. Lecturettes are often used as an introduction to a group activity or event, such as before another planned activity. In this case, the lecturette serves as a setup to the more experiential activity the participants will engage in. To illustrate using a rock concert analogy, the lecturette is the opening act whose job is to work up the energy level of the audience for the arrival of the headline act.

Although the lecture and lecturette have their purposes in training, they also have disadvantages. Training is considered a highly interactive enterprise, and lectures are considered a one-way transmission of information (information flows from the lecturer to the lectured). Consequently, lectures are viewed as a *trainer-centered* versus *trainee-centered* delivery format. When lecturing, the trainer is in charge. Thiagarajan (2005) has coined the term *interactive lecture* to discuss how lectures can be made more interactive and foster two-way communication between the trainer and the trainees. Rather than abandoning the lecture format entirely, Thiagarajan (a.k.a. Thiagi) recommends that trainers incorporate a number of techniques to increase interaction. Among the suggestions he offers are requiring trainees to review and summarize lecture content during a program, interspersing reviews of key points throughout a training program rather than presenting them at the conclusion, conducting quiz activities throughout a lecture, and having the trainees teach program content to each other (team teaching).

Trainers have at their disposal several devices and activities to enliven training and make it more interactive. We describe these tools in the following section.

lecturette A short lecture in which the trainer explains a process or principle relevant to the immediate needs of the learners. Also used as an introduction to a training activity.

Designing and Including Experiential Activities in Training

Experiential vehicles, or activities, can be used in conjunction with lectures or lecturettes or, in some cases, they can replace the lecture format. The most frequently used experiential vehicles are role-plays, case studies, games, and instruments.

The Role-Play

The **role-play** allows trainees to put into practice the knowledge, skills, and behaviors they have just learned. When engaged in a role-play, participants apply the knowledge and skills they acquired from the training program in a real-world situation. Role-playing forces participants to practice and experiment with the new skills and behaviors and to receive feedback on their behavior from the trainer and the other participants. The simplest role-play involves two participants (role-players) who are asked to act out a scenario that requires the display of newly acquired skills and knowledge. It is critical when using a role-play that it is clearly written and realistic, and that it fits the program's objectives.

Here is an example of how a role-play might be used in a training program. Suppose you have just delivered a training program that covered the topic *How to Achieve Success in an Employment Interview*. Part of the program content included presenting the trainees with correct and appropriate behaviors to engage in during an employment interview. You have reached the end of this training segment, in which you have presented content to the trainees. It is now time to have them display the knowledge they acquired and practice the skills and behaviors they have just learned. A role-play would be an effective experiential activity to accomplish this objective. Trainees would be split into dyads (groups of two), with one trainee acting as the interviewer and one as the interviewee. A mock employment interview would proceed in which the "interviewer" would ask a series of questions to the "interviewee." Included among those questions would be several more difficult questions interviewees must respond to during an employment interview ("Tell me about yourself," "What is your greatest weakness?" and "Why do you want to work here?").

After the mock interviews, the trainer debriefs this role-playing activity by asking the trainees who acted as the interviewer in each dyad to share how their interviewee responded to those questions and whether the interviewee used the recommended responses taught during the content portion of the program.

Case Studies

Case studies are a popular experiential vehicle in training. Case studies allow trainees to use the knowledge gained through training to enhance

role-play Activity that allows participants to apply the knowledge and skills they acquire from their training in a real-world situation.

case studies A training vehicle that allows trainees to use the knowledge gained through the training as a way to enhance problem solving; involves presenting trainees with a scenario in which the trainee analyzes an organizational problem and offers possible solutions.

problem solving. The typical case study method involves presenting the trainees with a scenario (a case or critical incident) in which the trainee analyzes an organizational problem and offers alternatives and solutions to the problem based on the content presented in the training.

Usually cases are presented in written form in the participants' manuals. An example of a case study is found on the textbook's website. The following guidelines are important when using a case study as an experiential training vehicle: (1) The entire case study, including the instructions for debriefing, must be included in the instructor's manual; (2) in addition to the actual details of the case, an overview of the case should be included that describes the key characters involved in the case and explains the nature of the relationship among the characters or between the organization and the characters; (3) learning objectives should be tied to the case study so trainees can identify what communication issue(s) or problem(s) exist and understand how effective communication can impact positively on those issues; and (4) most important, a series of discussion questions regarding the case must be included so trainees can analyze how communication plays a significant role in the case.

Games

Games are among the most popular experiential vehicles used in training because they are considered low risk, adapt to most forms of content, and foster participation. Most important, games are fun and stimulate competition and team development. Games are often used successfully when testing the trainees' content knowledge in a dynamic and interactive fashion. Indeed, there is empirical evidence that games increase student learning and motivation. Using an experimental method, Garard, Hunt, Lippert, and Paynton (1998) randomly assigned students to one of two learning conditions (traditional lecture versus instruction via a game). The same course material was covered in both groups. After the instruction, the researchers administered scales to measure affective and cognitive learning, as well as a scale to measure motivation to learn. Although no significant differences were observed between the two groups on affective learning (the degree to which they liked the content), the results indicated that students in the game group reported significantly higher levels of cognitive learning and more interest and motivation than the group that received the traditional lecture format.

The game show format provides a robust method for helping trainees prepare for testing and functions as an interactive, light-hearted way to review content (Yaman & Covington, 2006). Rather than giving the trainees a quiz over the material covered during a program, having the trainees play a game show can achieve the same goal, but in a more interactive and entertaining way. As a consequence, information comprehension and retention are enhanced. Several TV game shows have been successfully adapted to the learning environment, including *Jeopardy!, Family Feud, Wheel of Fortune,* and *Who Wants to Be a Millionaire?* There are some modifications that must be made when converting a TV game show into an experiential training vehicle. Yaman and Covington (2006) argue that "a classroom game show allows you to review, elaborate, correct, and apply your content, as well as place it in a real-world scenario" (p. 10). They offer numerous recommendations for converting games shows successfully from the television format to a training format, such as always using teams, emphasizing what was learned as opposed to who won, changing the rules (e.g., no need to ring in to answer a question, but instead letting teams take turns answering questions), and de-emphasizing the glitz while emphasizing content. Of course, the game show format is only one way in which games can be integrated into the training process, and numerous sources are available to help trainers select the most appropriate game format to maximize interaction and learning.

Instruments

The use of instruments (surveys, diagnostic tools, self-report measures, inventories) can add life, interest, and stimulation to the training process. Through the use of an instrument, trainees can find out more about themselves (their attitudes, their predispositions, their behaviors) as well as make certain points of a theory come alive. In Chapter 6 we discussed several personality and communication traits that are relevant to organizational communication (argumentativeness, verbal aggressiveness, communication apprehension, Machiavellianism, and locus of control). Self-report instruments enable a trainee to evaluate the degree to which you possess these traits.

An instrument is used in training for several purposes:

1. As a result of completing and scoring the instrument, the trainer can supply personal feedback to trainees about their scores (Are you high, moderate, or low in argumentativeness? Verbal aggressiveness?).

2. When a group of trainees completes an instrument, each individual's score can be compared with the group's scores. For example, suppose a group of new managers is going through communication training to enhance their knowledge and communication skills. An instrument with great importance in organizational communication is the Communicator Style Measure (CSM) (Norton, 1983). This instrument consists of 51 items covering the dimensions of communicator style (e.g., open, dramatic, dominant, contentious, relaxed, friendly, attentive, animated, impression leaving). Several dimensions of communicator style (relaxed, friendly, and attentive), along with the aggressive communication traits of argumentativeness and verbal aggressiveness, form the basis of the theory of independent mindedness, which was presented in chapter 2. A trainer can administer the CSM, along with the Argumentativeness (Infante & Rancer, 1982) and Verbal Aggressiveness (Infante & Wigley, 1986) scales, to the group of new managers during a training program. After completing the instruments, each manager can determine by his

or her scores on the three instruments which of the communication trait profiles he or she falls under (see the discussion of TIM Profiles in Chapter 2). The trainer can then tell the group which of these profiles engenders the greatest employee commitment, satisfaction, and productivity.

3. The use of instruments in training also facilitates longitudinal assessment of change. Suppose you are presenting a training program on the topic *Arguing Constructively*. The trainer administers the Argumentativeness Scale in the beginning of the program as a diagnostic tool to determine how motivated the trainees are to engage in argumentative communication (which is considered a constructive trait and carries an important set of behaviors, especially in the organizational context). The trainees are then presented with content knowledge on the importance of being argumentative, along with training on how to use the **Inventional System** (Infante, 1988). The Inventional System is a way to help individuals generate arguments regardless of the topic or the participants in the argument. At the end of the program, the Argumentativeness Scale is re-administered. This allows the trainer and trainee to determine if there has been a change in the argumentativeness predisposition from pre- to posttraining.

As stated earlier, many instruments can be used to teach communication theory and other concepts important in effective communication. As Pfeiffer, Heslin, and Jones (1976) state, "When participants have invested time and energy in an activity such as completing an inventory related to the model being explored, they have also invested in learning the theory, and the entire process becomes more meaningful and easily relatable in terms of the group experience" (pp. 8–9).

Using Instructional Aids

In today's training environment, it is customary to include **instructional aids** (presentation aids) in the delivery of a training program. Instructional aids serve a number of purposes in delivering training, including getting the attention of the trainees, reinforcing key points of the presentation, adding emphasis to what the trainer is saying, and aiding in information retention (Lawson, 1998).

There are several types of instructional aids available (overhead projectors, videotapes, electronic whiteboards, etc.), but we recommend two of the most frequently used aids: **presentation software** and **flip charts**. The most frequently used visual aid today is presentation software such as PowerPoint. PowerPoint enhances the delivery of training by adding visuals (such as pictures), sound, animation, and even video to slides that contain information content. Although a complete treatment of creating PowerPoint slides is beyond the scope of this chapter (see Earnest, 2008, for a complete treatment on designing effective PowerPoint slides), we provide a few suggestions here. First, do not crowd the slide with too many words. There are a number of suggestions for the maximum amount of words to be placed on each slide; however, we recommend using the **Rule of 16**. That is, do not include more than 16 words on each PowerPoint slide you create. It is better to have a larger number of slides than to crowd too many words on each slide. Second, although we certainly endorse the use of sound, animation, and transitions in slides, try to limit the amount you use. Too many sounds, transitions, and animations can distract trainees and prevent them from receiving and remembering the information. Finally, although the use of color is clearly recommended, carefully select the background color of each slide. Some background colors tend to obscure the text, making it difficult for trainees to read the slide.

Rule of 16 A rule of thumb for using PowerPoint slides that recommends including no more than 16 words on any slide so as not to overwhelm trainees

One of the training industry staples is the flip chart. Long before computers and presentational software were invented, the flip chart was trainers' major instructional aid. Even today, flip charts have their place in the training industry. The flip chart has essentially two uses: (1) If presentational software is unavailable, training content can be put on flip chart pages instead of, or in addition to, PowerPoint slides; and (2) flip charts can be used to record information elicited from the trainees during training. As the program progresses, many trainers ask trainees for their responses to questions, and these responses can be neatly printed on flip chart paper. In addition, many trainers use blank flip chart pages to write down questions that trainees ask during a program and to which the trainer can respond at the end of the session. In both cases, the trainer will want to tear off these flip chart pages and post them on a wall of the training room. Today, flip chart pads are available with sticky top sections (like a giant Post-It® note) so tape is no longer needed to secure the page to the wall. The flip chart is the instructional aid of choice when engaging in problem solving such as the nominal group technique (see chapter 7).

Essential Presentation Skills

Try to recall your best and worst learning experiences from anytime in your life (high school, college, or a training program you have taken). Think about what made them the best and the worst experiences. When we ask students and trainees about the single most important factor in the success or failure of that learning experience, most respond that it was the instructor. Therefore, it is essential to have effective presentational skills when delivering a training program.

There are numerous presentation skills that engender a successful and competent training presentational style, but we focus on three of the most important ones: eye contact (**occulesics**), body motion and movement (**kinesics**), and vocalics (**paralanguage**).

Eye contact with trainees is essential in keeping them focused on you and the training. Eye contact is one of the behaviors associated with **nonverbal immediacy** (Mehrabian, 1971). **Immediacy** refers to the degree of closeness people feel. People feel psychologically closer to each other when they use certain nonverbal cues, such as greater proximity and more direct eye contact. Immediacy behaviors develop a positive relationship between the trainer and trainees. Regardless of whether you have 20 or 200 trainees in the room, it is essential that you create a sense of nonverbal immediacy by using eye contact.

We recommend that rather than trying to "scan" the group by giving each trainee just a second or two of eye contact, a trainer should lock eyes on one trainee for several seconds before moving on to the eyes of another participant. It is critical to use this behavior in a smooth rather than a "robotic" fashion.

Another presentation skill essential to the success of a trainer is **kinesics**, or body motion and movement. Whether you are presenting a half-day, full-day, or two-day training program, you are likely to quickly lose your group if you do not incorporate gestures into your repertoire of trainer presentational skills. However, when using your body to deliver the program, do not use movements that are distracting to the trainees. For example, do not pace excessively around the training room, do not rock side to side when speaking, and do not use so many gestures that you appear to be manic.

vocalic competence The use of voice that is appropriate in volume and displays variety.

The final essential presentation skill is **vocalic competence**. Vocalic competence is achieved by using several voice techniques. The first vocalic behavior is appropriate volume. A trainer who cannot be heard from the middle to the back of the training room soon engenders looks of boredom and disdain from the trainees. Second, vocal variety is necessary. Vocal variety means using inflection and pitch with your voice. You have probably heard presenters who lacked vocal variety. You likely became bored with their monotone, one-pitch delivery and tuned out. Thus, it is essential to be vocally dynamic when delivering training.

Evaluating Training

Have you ever taken a college course or attended a training program in which you had a lot of fun but did not learn much? On the surface this experience might have seemed enjoyable; however, on reflection you probably felt dissatisfied because critical information you needed to know was missing or key skills you needed to acquire were not taught. This issue speaks to the importance of evaluation in training.

There are several reasons why training evaluation is important. The most fundamental reason for evaluating training is to determine if the objectives you offered for the program were accomplished. That is, did the trainees acquire both the content knowledge and the skills and/or behaviors you promised them in the beginning of the program? Second, evaluation helps determine whether the program needs to be modified. For example, after evaluation you may discover that certain portions of the training were under-developed, whereas others may have been presented too comprehensively. Thus, evaluation helps determine how to improve future training. Finally, and perhaps most important in times of economic contraction, evaluation helps the training department make a strong case for how it contributes to the organization's bottom line. Evaluation can help trainers "justify their existence" (Kirkpatrick & Kirkpatrick, 2006, p. 17).

Kirkpatrick (1994) proposed the most systematic model for evaluating training. The model consists of four levels, with each level having an impact on the next one. Level 1 is referred to as **reaction**. This is the most basic level of evaluation, and it measures trainees' satisfaction with the program. Just as you may be asked to complete an evaluation of a college course at the end of a semester, trainees almost always are asked to provide an evaluation of the training they just completed. In the training industry, level 1 evaluations are often referred to as "smile sheets," because they measure how much the trainee "liked" the program. Kirkpatrick and Kirkpatrick (2006) suggest that obtaining a positive reaction to the training program is important because what trainees say to management about a program might determine if a particular training company will be hired again. In addition, obtaining a favorable reaction to training is important because "if participants do not react favorably, they probably will not be motivated to learn" (Kirkpatrick & Kirkpatrick, 2006, p. 22). Level 1 (reaction) evaluations are usually conducted at the end of the training.

Level 2 evaluation focuses on **learning**. Level 2 evaluation assesses the degree to which trainees learned from the program. That is, did the train-ees obtain content knowledge, change their attitudes, acquire new skills, or increase their skill level as a result of taking the program? According to Kirkpatrick and Kirkpatrick (2006), "Learning has taken place when one or more of the following occurs: Attitudes are changed. Knowledge is increased. Skill is improved. One or more of these changes must take place if a change in behavior is to occur" (p. 22). In training, learning is most often assessed through tests, observation of behavior, and interviews.

Level 3 evaluation focuses on **behavior**; that is, did the trainees' behavior change when returning to the organization as a result of their participation in the training? As you might imagine, level 3 evaluation is more difficult to obtain or assess than levels 1 or 2 evaluations. Level 3 evaluation requires a commitment from the organization in that the evaluator is allowed to go into the organization and collect data through surveys, observation of behavior, and interviews. Kirkpatrick and Kirkpatrick (2006) state, "It is important to evaluate both reaction and learning in case no change in behavior occurs. Then it can be determined whether the fact that there was no change was the result of an ineffective training program or of the wrong job climate and lack of rewards" (p. 24).

learning Level 2 of the Kirkpatrick model that involves assessing the degree to which trainees obtain content knowledge, change their attitudes, acquire new skills, or increase their skill level as a result of the training.

Level 4 evaluation focuses on **results**. That is, it seeks to determine how the training has impacted the organization's goals, objectives, and bottom line. Is there increased productivity among employees as a result of the training? Is there greater quality in their output? Are there fewer employee mistakes? Greater sales? More customer satisfaction? Higher organizational profits? It is probably obvious that level 4 evaluation is the most demanding of all four evaluation levels. In addition, not all training programs are amenable to level 4 evaluation. However, as mentioned earlier, in times of organizational retrenchment, training programs and departments are among the first to be eliminated. Thus, level 4 evaluation, especially if it supports the value of training to the organization's bottom line, may be the most valuable form of evaluation.

The Efficacy of Communication Training

After reading this chapter, two fundamental questions surface: How effective is communication training? Does communication training really make a difference on a trainee's performance? Two studies from the communication discipline have addressed these questions.

The first study (Papa & Graham, 1991) asked this question: Do managers whose performance is assessed and who receive assessment-based communication skills training receive different performance ratings than managers who do not receive such training? (p. 370). Two groups of mid-level managers participated in the study. One group received diagnostic assessment without subsequent training on communication skills, and one group received both the diagnostic assessment *and* the communication skills training. Participants were assessed along 12 behavioral dimensions: integrity, logical reasoning, assertiveness and decisiveness, organization, innovativeness, tenacity, organizational awareness and vision, persuasiveness, time sensitivity, social intelligence, written communication, and nonverbal communication.

Participants in the training group received follow-up communication skills training based on their needs identified in the assessment. The training included five three-hour modules on the topics of interpersonal communication, listening, performance counseling, nonverbal communication, selection interviewing, assertiveness, leadership, participative decision making, and written communication. The results indicated that those managers who received the communication skills training were rated significantly higher on performance evaluation ratings of written communication, oral communication skills, and interaction abilities (e.g., assertiveness, behavioral flexibility, and persuasiveness) than managers who did not receive such training (Papa & Graham, 1991, p. 381).

The researchers offered several reasons for these results. First, assessing each manager's communication skills prior to placement in a training program allowed the trainers to construct a program better suited to the trainee's needs. Second, the individual meetings held between trainers and trainees after the training module allowed trainees to discuss how they planned to transfer the skills they learned into a real organizational setting. Finally, the focus on communication skills training is clearly the activity or set of behaviors that is "most critical to managerial performance" (Papa & Graham, 1991, p. 381).

A second study supports the importance of communication and presentational skills training. Seibold, Kudsi, and Rude (1993) asked an important question: Does communication (i.e., presentation skills) training make a difference? Using three of the four levels of Kirkpatrick's training evaluation model discussed earlier, Seibold et al. (1993) offered the following research questions: (1) Does presentation skills training produce positive reactions among participants (reaction level)?; (2) does presentation skills training promote learning related to program objectives (learning level)?; (3) does training produce short-term improvement in participants' presentation skills (behavior level)?; and (4) does training produce long-term improvement in participants' presentation skills (behavior level)?

The researchers tested employees from a variety of organizations. In addition to this experimental group, a control group that did not receive the training was used for comparison purposes. The two-day training program focused on presentational skills (e.g., speech organization, making effective introductions and conclusions, using visual aids) and enhancing delivery skills (e.g., using gestures, rate of speech, volume, eye contact, vocal variety).

To measure the efficacy of the training, participants were provided with scales (measures) and assessed how satisfied they were with the training (reaction) and how much they learned from the training (learning). To evaluate skill enhancement (behavior), rating scales were given to coworkers (and supervisors) as well as the training instructor, who then rated each participant on the 16 skills he or she was supposed to learn during the training.

The results supported the efficacy of the communication skills training program. First, communication skills training produced positive reactions (reaction level) regarding enjoyment of and satisfaction with the program. Next, the training promoted learning of the instructional and behavioral objectives (the content) of the training. Finally, the training produced both short-term and long-term improvement in the participants' presentational skill abilities (behavior level). The results of these two studies indicate strong support that communication training in general, and communication skills training in particular, improve an individual's communication performance.

Summary

Training is one of the most important functions in an organization. In this chapter we first defined training, provided an overview of the training industry, placed training within the structure of the contemporary organization, described several job functions of trainers, and described several skills and abilities needed for a career in training. Next we provided details on how to develop, design, and conduct communication-based training programs. Specifically, we discussed how to conduct a needs assessment, how to select and narrow the topic for training, and how to conduct research for the content portion of the training program. Finally we discussed how to write instructional and behavioral objectives and how to design and produce manuals for the trainer and the program participants, and we provided guidelines on several factors associated with the delivery of training programs, discussed the inclusion of experiential activities in training, and concluded with a discussion of how to evaluate training results.

It should be clear that people who enjoy researching, writing, presenting information, and facilitating communication would enjoy a career in communication training. We anticipate that training will continue to be a job with abundant opportunities in contemporary organizations. The need for training has never been greater as job requirements constantly change, technology continually advances, and communication-based knowledge and skills are at the forefront of the global organization.

Questions for Discussion and Review

1. Recall from the chapter the definition of organizational training. List and explain the two critical components of training and provide examples of both. Also explain why communication training is important to personal and organizational success.

2. Based on the information in the chapter, list and describe the functions of a human resources department. Explain and provide examples of the ways in which communication plays an important role in the daily interactions within this department.

3. Based on what you read about the role of communication training, describe and explain the two major areas of concentration within the training department and the ways in which both hard and soft skills apply. Provide examples to support your answer.

4. List and explain the nine skills person must develop and refine to become a competent communication trainer. Of these skills, in your opinion, which one is the most important? Support your answer.

5. Recall from the chapter the section on the need for training. List and explain in your own words several of the reasons a person would seek training. Choose from any chapter in the book and explain how training would benefit the employee's understanding of the concepts highlighted in that chapter. Provide examples to support your answer.

6. Recall the four steps that describe a person's state of skill acquisition. Explain how each of the four steps builds on the preceding step in the progression toward competence in the selected area of training. How would this process relate to communication competence training?

7. Based on what you read in the chapter, list and explain the components found in the K.A.S.H. formula. Explain how this formula facilitates narrowing the gap between what an individual currently knows and what he or she needs to know.

8. Recall from the chapter the importance of a needs assessment. Explain what a needs assessment is and provide several reasons for conducting such an assessment. Lastly, explain how a needs assessment can reveal communication deficiencies within a department.

9. What types of tools do trainers use to conduct a needs assessment? List the benefits and liabilities of each of these tools, in your opinion. Which do you think is the best and why?

10. List the steps a trainer must go through in conducting a training session, from selecting a topic for the training module to delivering the actual training. Then explain how each of these steps is important to the overall success of the program.

11. List and explain several activities that can be used in conjunction with lectures during a training session. Which of these do you think is most effective? Provide support for your answer.

References

Beebe, S. A., Mottet, T. P., & Roach, K. D. (2004). *Training and development*. Boston: Pearson.

Earnest, W. (2008). *Save our slides*. Dubuque, IA: Kendall Hunt Publishing Company.

Garard, D. L., Hunt, S. K., Lippert, L., & Paynton, S. T. (1998). Alternatives to traditional instruction: Using games and simulations to increase student learning and motivation. *Communication Research Reports, 15*, 36–44.

Infante, D. A. (1988). *Arguing constructively*. Prospect Heights, IL: Waveland Press.

Infante, D. A., & Rancer, A. S. (1982). A conceptualization and measure of argumentativeness. *Journal of Personality Assessment, 46*, 72–80.

Infante, D. A., & Wigley, C. J. (1986). Verbal aggressiveness: An interpersonal model and measure. *Communication Monographs, 53*, 61–69.

Ittner, P. L. & Douds, A. F. (1988). *Train the trainer: Practical skills that work*. Amherst, MA: HRD Press.

Kirkpatrick, D. L. (1994). *Evaluating training programs: The four levels*. San Francisco: Berrett-Koehler Publishers.

Kirkpatrick, D. L., & Kirkpatrick, J. D. (2006). *Evaluating training programs: The four levels* (3rd ed.). San Francisco: Berrett-Koehler Publishers.

Lawson, K. (1998). *The trainer's handbook*. San Francisco: Jossey-Bass/Pfeiffer.

Mager, R. (1961). *Preparing objectives for programmed instruction*. San Francisco: Fearon Publishers.

Mager, R. (1984). *Preparing instructional objectives* (2nd ed.). Belmont, CA: Pitman Learning, Inc.

Martin, M. (2007). *5 reasons you don't need training*. From http://michelemartin.typepad.com/thebambooprojectblog/2007/02/5_reasons_you_d.html

McCroskey, J. C. (2002). Learning goals and objectives. In J. L. Chesebro & J. C. McCroskey, *Communication for teachers* (pp. 3–7). Boston: Allyn & Bacon.

Mehrabian, A. (1971). *Silent messages*. Belmont, CA: Wadsworth.

Norton, R. (1983). *Communicator style: Theory, applications, and measures*. Beverly Hills, CA: SAGE Publications.

Papa, M. J., & Graham, E. E. (1991). The impact of diagnosing skill deficiencies and assessment-based communication training on managerial performance. *Communication Education, 40,* 368–384.

Pfeiffer, J. W., Heslin, R., & Jones, J. E. (1976). *Instrumentation in human relations training* (2nd ed.). La Jolla, CA: University Associates, Inc.

Rubin, R. B., Palmgreen, P., & Sypher, H. E. (2004). *Communication research measures: A sourcebook*. Mahwah, NJ: Erlbaum.

Seibold, D. R., Kudsi, S., & Rude, M. (1993). Does communication training make a difference? Evidence for the effectiveness of a presentation skills program. *Journal of Applied Communication, 21,* 111–131.

Thiagarajan, S. (2005). *Thiagi's interactive lectures*. Alexandria, VA: ASTD Press

Yaman, D., & Covington, M. (2006). *I'll take learning for 500: Using game shows to engage, motivate, and train*. San Francisco: Pfeiffer/John Wiley & Sons.

Appendix to Chapter 11

Resources Helpful in Developing Training Content

Braithwaite, D. O., & Wood, J. T. (2000). *Case studies in interpersonal communication.* Belmont, CA: Wadsworth/Thompson Learning.

The Crisp Series on Communication. Axzo Press (www.axzopress.com).

Keyton, J., & Shockley-Zalabak, P. (2006). *Case studies for organizational communication.* Los Angeles: Roxbury Publishing Company.

May, S. (Ed.). (2006). *Case studies in organizational communication.* Thousand Oaks, CA: SAGE Publications.

Newstrom, J. W., & Scannell, E. E. (1980). *Games trainers play.* New York: McGraw-Hill.

Nilson, C. (1995). *Games that drive change.* New York: McGraw-Hill.

Petit, A. (1994). *Secrets to enliven learning.* San Diego: Pfeiffer & Company.

Pfeiffer, J. W., & Jones, J. E. (1974). *A handbook of structured experiences, Vols. I–X.* San Francisco: Jossey-Bass/Pfeiffer.

Sashkin, M. (1989). *Structured activities for management training in communication.* King of Prussia, PA: Organization Design and Development, Inc.

Scannell, E. E., & Newstrom, J. W. (1983). *More games trainers play.* New York: McGraw-Hill.

Scannell, E. E., & Newstrom, J. W. (1991). *Still more games trainers play.* New York: McGraw-Hill.

Silberman, M. (1995). *101 ways to make training active.* San Francisco: Jossey-Bass/Pfeiffer.

Tamblyn, D., & Weiss, S. (2000). *The big book of humorous training games.* New York: McGraw-Hill.

Chapter 12

Communication and Organizational Development

Learning Objectives

Upon completion of the chapter, the student should be able to:

- Compare and contrast action research and appreciative inquiry.
- Explain Lewin's three-step model of organizational change.
- Compare and contrast Lewin's three-step model of organizational change and Klein's model of communication strategies for organizational change.
- Compare and contrast appreciative inquiry and appreciative action research models.
- Explain the appreciative inquiry approach to team building.

Key Terms

Action research (AR)

Appreciative action research model (AARM)

Appreciative inquiry (AI)

Communication during the moving stage

Communication during the refreezing stage

Communication during the unfreezing stage

Communication medium dimension

Communicative role of change agents

Organizational development function

Process conflict

Process orientation

Relationship conflict

T-groups/training groups

Task conflict

Team building

Three-step model of organizational change

As we maintain throughout this text, without communication it would be impossible for organizations to exist. Communication allows individuals to work together and function as teams, to exchange information, and to establish and maintain relationships. As systems, organizations are subject to internal changes and external pressures from the environment. Like other systems, organizations are subject to entropy (chaos and disorder). The ability to adapt and change separates successful organizations from those that are less successful. Communication is the main element in successful organizational functioning and change, and without communication, progressive entropy would surely spell the demise of any organization.

In this chapter, we define and describe the practice known as **organizational development** (OD). We trace the historical development of OD and describe the characteristics of organizational development efforts. In doing so, we describe the relationship between OD and communication, paying special attention to the role of communication in the facilitation and management of organizational change. Finally, we describe two types of OD interventions: team building and appreciative inquiry.

organizational development function Responsible for organizational design and structure, intervention design and implementation, and quality of work-life processes.

What Is Organizational Development?

Organizational development is an area of organizational studies that has a clear, applied focus centering on or about organizational change. As we have mentioned throughout this text, if organizations are to survive and thrive, they must be able to implement change strategies successfully. This notion is especially true today, when the modern organization is buffeted by rapid information exchange, technological advancement, instantaneous communication, and global competition.

There are numerous definitions and conceptualizations of organizational development (alternatively referred to as *organization development*). One of the first organizational scholars to provide a working definition of OD was Richard Beckhard. Beckhard offered what has come to be called a "classic" definition of organization development. He defines OD as "an effort (1) *planned,* (2) *organization-wide,* and (3) *managed* from the top, to (4) increase *organizational effectiveness* and *health* through (5) *planned interventions* in the organization's 'processes,' using (6) *behavioral science knowledge*" (Beckhard, 1969, p. 9).

In this definition, several key elements of OD efforts are highlighted. Organizational development involves the systematic diagnosis of an organization followed by a new "strategic plan" for improving the organization. OD efforts attempt to implement change in the entire organization, as in the case of changing the entire organization's culture or managerial strategy. The organization's top management actively supports and is committed to the organizational change process. OD efforts are initiated to enhance an

organization's effectiveness, including the organization's ability to communicate information (internally and externally; horizontally and vertically) in the most unbiased and undistorted way possible.

In today's global economy, change is a constant and something that organizations need to be cognizant of and proactive with. OD is a collection of theories, principles, and strategies for managing change at the individual, group, intergroup, organizational, and interorganizational levels (Rothwell & Sullivan, 2005). Another pioneer in organizational development, Gordon L. Lippitt defined OD as a "process of initiating, creating, and confronting those changes needed—so as to make it possible for organizations to become or remain viable, to adapt to new conditions, to solve problems, to learn from experiences, and to move toward greater individual, group and organization maturity" (Lippitt, 1982, p. 15).

Kreps (1990a) notes that organizational communication researchers are particularly suited to help organizations increase their effectiveness because much of what is accomplished in organizations is done through communication and information exchange. Kreps suggests,

> By using organizational communication research to evaluate the effectiveness of internal and external communication activities, communication researchers can identify communication difficulties, develop intervention strategies to reduce these problems, and help direct organizational development to promote organizational effectiveness. (1990a, p. 104)

Organizational development is an applied discipline in which data can be gathered and analyzed to develop strategies and recommendations to assist organizations in promoting more effective communication and to make changes that can lead to greater organizational effectiveness. Organizational problems and constraints identified during the diagnostic phase of an OD effort can be managed more productively by applied communication researchers, who can suggest strategies to overcome problems and to manage change more effectively.

The Roots of Organizational Development

From where did the field of organizational development evolve? Organizational scholars, such as W. Warner Burke (2006), suggest that there were essentially three roots of the OD development tree: sensitivity training (also referred to as T-groups), sociotechnical systems change (developed at the Tavistock Institute in London), and survey feedback (the use of surveys and questionnaires for data collection, organizational diagnosis and assessment, and ultimately for organizational change and improvement; see chapter 13).

Some people argue that findings from the Hawthorne studies (see chapter 2) contributed to the development of OD efforts. For example, Burke

(2006) suggests that several theories and theorists could also be mentioned for their contributions to the development of OD. For example, under the heading of individual perspective on change, Abraham Maslow and Frederick Herzberg are recognized for their needs theories of motivation (see chapter 8); Edward E. Lawler III and Victor Vroom are noted for their expectancy theories; and J. Richard Hackman and Greg R. Oldham are noted for models of job satisfaction. Under the heading of group perspective on change, Kurt Lewin is considered the preeminent theorist; he conceptualized organizations as social systems and held that groups form the basis of an organization's subsystems. Also mentioned as contributing to our understanding of behavior changes within the group is theorist Chris Argyris. Finally, under the heading of the total system perspective on organizational change, Rensis Likert is recognized for his four major models (autocratic, benevolent autocratic, consultative, and participative) of organizational structure and design (see chapter 2).

Action Research: The Foundational Method for Organizational Change

OD efforts use action research based on gathering both "objective" quantitative and qualitative data and analyzing those data to uncover problems and implement solutions to those problems (Beckhard, 2006; Waclawski & Church, 2002). **Action research** is a fundamental method used in contemporary organizational development efforts designed to produce change in organizations and other social systems (Fitzgerald, Murrell, & Newman, 2002). OD is based on open-systems theory, and it uses the action research method to examine existing organizational processes (e.g., how things are done in the organization) to decide what changes are needed and how to implement those changes. Social scientist Kurt Lewin is considered one of the first advocates, if not the developer, of the action research process. You may already be familiar with Lewin from his statement, "There is nothing so practical as a good theory" (Lewin, 1951, p. 169), often mentioned in communication theory courses and textbooks (see, for example, Infante, Rancer, & Avtgis, 2010).

The goal of action research is to foster change in groups and organizations by focusing on "research and data-driven decision-making" (Dickens & Watkins, 2006, p. 185). Cunningham (1993) defines action research as "a spectrum of activities that focus on research, planning, theorizing, learning, and development. It describes a continuous process of research and learning in the researcher's long-term relationship with a problem" (p. 4). In essence, Lewin's conceptualization of action research is the application of traditional social science methods of research applied to social and organizational problems. Unlike traditional experimental research, however, action research takes place in naturally occurring (i.e., field) settings, such as organizations.

action research (AR)
A fundamental method used in contemporary organizational development efforts designed to produce change in organizations and other social systems.

Most important, "action researchers attempt to make scientific discoveries while also solving practical problems" (Dickens & Watkins, 2006, p. 190).

One of the goals of action research is to have participants engage in self-reflection while attempting to solve or correct a problem. The action research process begins with the identification of a problem. In the spirit of the content of this book, let's assume that it is an organizational problem. Data are collected via interviews, surveys, or other methods (see chapter 13). These data are analyzed, and problems (if any) are identified. Solutions to the problem(s) are generated. Next, action researchers implement the changes identified as potential "corrections" to the problems identified. They then test the effects that these changes have made on the organization by engaging in more data gathering, evaluation, and assessment. Action researchers repeat this process "until they have exhausted the problem that they identified initially" (Dickens & Watkins, 2006, p. 193). This "cycle" of problem identification and solving is repeated until the organization's problems are identified and adequately solved.

Resistance to Change

As we have argued elsewhere in this text (in chapter 10 and earlier in this chapter), change occurs in all organizations and to all members within an organization. Change may occur as the result of a major structural realignment of an organization (e.g., two units are being combined into one, or one large division is split into two), the introduction of new technology (e.g., replacing traditional PCs with tablet computers), a new top-level management change or new ownership of an organization, or a merger of two organizations, to name just a few.

Regardless of what precipitates change, organizational change is difficult for many individuals to cope with. Among the negative feelings associated with change include employees feeling a sense of loss, such as a loss of security ("Where do I now stand in this organization?"), feeling a lack of competence ("I don't know how to use this new device"), feelings of failure ("I don't know how to do this new job"), or even negative or anxious emotional expressions resulting from a loss of interpersonal relationships due directly to the change ("I don't know anyone in this new work unit") (Scott & Jaffe, 1995).

Resistance to change is exhibited in a number of ways. Employees often display a multitude of emotional and behavioral resistance strategies that include increases in anger, apathy, complaining, stubbornness, job-related errors, or even complete emotional and psychological withdrawal (Scott & Jaffe, 1995, p. 57). Some human resource scholars even argue that people resist change due to physiological reasons (brain activity). They suggest that a part of the brain, the amygdala, may interpret the change as a threat to the body, resulting in release of stress hormones. The amygdala thus works to protect the body from change (Emerson & Stewart, 2011). As such, employees interpret any change as a threat, thus, there is an innate physiological and emotional reaction to organizational change and a person's resistance to it.

Managing Organizational Change

In chapter 10 we introduced the concept of organizational change by presenting Pettigrew's (1973) concept of the multidimensionality of the change process. In this chapter we elaborate on the process of change by presenting how organizational development theorists and practitioners have conceptualized and studied the implementation of organizational change.

As we have mentioned, Kurt Lewin was instrumental in the creation of organizational development and of three social scientific techniques used in OD: T-groups, survey research, and action research (Carlock, 1994). As a psychologist, Lewin used what was then a new collaborative approach to research by incorporating the active participation of his research subjects in problem solving. Lewin's background and experiences growing up in Europe led him to conclude that the best way to help solve social and organizational problems is to involve everyone in the process. Indeed, "Lewin's philosophy of the role of collaboration in problem solving became a core value of contemporary OD" (Carlock, 1994, p. 52).

Lewin's Three-Step Model of Organizational Change

OD scholars pay homage to Kurt Lewin for his many contributions to OD, including his application of theories of personality, his focus on the impact of psychological influences on behavior, his identification of forces that can either promote or discourage change, and his development of the "action research" paradigm (Mirvis, 2006). However, it was his development of the **three-step model of organizational change** that represents Lewin's greatest achievement toward the development of the OD discipline.

three-step model of organizational change
A three-step process of organizational change developed by Kurt Lewin consisting of unfreezing, moving, and refreezing.

Change, according to Lewin (1951), comes about as a result of a three-step process. Step 1 is labeled **unfreezing**, which assumes that motivation for change must exist before a change occurs. In this unfreezing step, an individual's equilibrium needs to be destabilized or "unfrozen" before an individual's old behavior can be abandoned and a new behavior adopted. This has been interpreted by OD scholar Bernard Burnes to mean that individuals who encounter change "have to feel safe from loss and humiliation before they can accept the new information and reject old behaviors" (2006, p. 142). Unfreezing is geared toward readying the organization and its employees for change as well as challenging the status quo (Klein, 1996).

Step 2 in the change process is labeled **moving**. Lewin recognized that unfreezing by itself is not enough for planned change to occur. Rather, Lewin suggested that individuals facing change must assess all the options available during the change process. Only by doing this type of assessment can people "move from a less acceptable to a more acceptable set of behaviors" (Burnes, 2006, p. 142). The moving step is geared toward beginning the process of change, developing momentum for change, and evaluating pilot efforts involved in the change (Klein, 1996).

Step 3, labeled **refreezing**, represents the last step, and reflects an attempt to ensure the new ideas or behaviors are relatively stable and that they do not regress to the old ideas and behaviors. In terms of organizational behavior, refreezing mandates changes to the organization's culture, policies, and practices (Burnes, 2006, p. 143). Step 3 in the three-step model of organizational change is geared toward reinforcing the change, making final corrections to problems found as a result of the change, and institutionalizing the change (Klein, 1996).

Although Lewin's three-step model of organizational change has been met with some criticism throughout the last six decades, Elrod and Tippett (2002) compared models of organizational change and found that more contemporary models of organizational change bore "striking" similarities to Lewin's three-step model. Thus, it may be safe to say that Lewin's model has withstood the test of time (Burnes, 2006).

The Role of Communication in Managing Organizational Change

As we argue throughout this text, communication scholars, researchers, and practitioners are especially well suited to enhance the functioning of organizations. Communication theories, concepts, and principles can be applied to organizational issues to assist in the examination and amelioration of organizational communication. This can be done by identifying key issues that affect the efficacy of organizational communication and organizational behavior, and by helping organizations adapt to change.

Effective communication is clearly a component in successful change efforts (Lewis, 2000). Indeed, Lewis has suggested that communication factors and the process of organizational change are "inextricably linked" (1999, p. 44). Effective communication can help employees understand the need for change or, at minimum, can help employees accept the implementation of an already-decided-on change process. Effective communication can also help prepare organizational members for the change at a personal level as well as provide social support. An effective communication strategy during a change process can also "be used to reduce resistance, minimize uncertainty, and gain involvement and commitment as the change progresses which may, in turn, improve morale and retention rates" (Goodman & Truss, 2004, pp. 217–218). Additionally, lack of communication or ineffective communication has been suggested as a factor contributing to the failure of organizational change programs (Goodman & Truss, 2004).

Using Lewin's three-step model of organizational change, Klein (1996) developed a set of communication strategies to help organizations implement change more effectively. Three assumptions guide the choice of these strategies: (1) Change should be viewed positively and created for the improvement of the organization; (2) change will proceed conditionally and will be closely monitored and subject to modification; and (3) change is likely to be comprehensive and will result in a radical overhaul of the organization or unit. Klein suggests that the implementation of a total quality management system throughout an organization or the development of self-managed work teams throughout an organization would qualify as examples of radical organizational change efforts. The difficulties associated with the implementation of organizational change can be significantly reduced or dealt with more effectively if there is a communication strategy in place to deal with the problems of organizational change. "It seems to us that a well-planned communications process can be most helpful in easing the way to a more effective process" (Klein, 1996, p. 44).

Klein's (1996) model focuses on both the content of communication and the medium by which communication is disseminated throughout the organization. The **communication content dimension** focuses on what messages and information are conveyed to organizational members before, during, and after the change efforts. And, much like one section of the International Communication Association Audit (an instrument used for diagnosing several dimensions of organizational communication, see chapter 13), it also highlights what type of information or feedback should be sought from employees before, during, and after a change initiative (Goodman & Truss, 2004). Communication content assists in reducing uncertainty, helps overcome resistance to change, gains commitment from employees for the change effort, and helps secure input from organizational members during the change process. The **communication medium dimension** used to share information "should fit the significance and complexity of the message as well as the stage in the change process" (Goodman & Truss, 2004, p. 218). The communication medium employed during a change process can include general bulletins (e.g., circular, announcements on mediated notice boards, blogs), personal "memoing" (e.g., tailored memos and letters, targeted e-mails), interactive media (e.g., videoconferencing), and face-to-face interactions (e.g., one-to-one meetings, group meetings).

communication medium dimension Reflects how information is shared and the degree to which the medium fits the significance and complexity of the messages and the stage in the change process.

A Blueprint for Communication During the Implementation of Organizational Change

Step 1—Communication During the Unfreezing Stage

The first step of **communication during the unfreezing stage** is the most difficult step in the implementation of organizational change because it is the stage where resistance to change is usually the strongest. Traditional methods of behavior, communication, structure, and "doing business" usually are being challenged during change, and it is likely that organizational members may attempt to mount resistance to the change efforts. Klein (1996) suggests that a carefully planned communication strategy should be in place to meet

communication during the unfreezing stage Used during the most difficult step in organizational change, where resistance is usually strongest, as there needs to be a carefully planned communication strategy in place to meet any resistance to change.

this resistance movement. This step requires the organization or its change agents to clearly communicate the objectives of the change, what is going to happen to the organization and its members as a result of the change, and why the change is needed.

If the change is systemwide (i.e., the entire organization), Klein recommends the CEO should be the main communicator of the change. If change is unit-wide, the unit or department manager should be the major spokesperson. It is critical, however, that the need for the change be communicated explicitly to the employees who will be affected by it. Messages as to the ineffectiveness of the status quo must be delivered, and a well-reasoned rationale for the change must be provided. Klein suggests that the message of change needs to be communicated to organizational members repeatedly, and he advocates the use of several media to communicate that message (e.g., e-mail, written memos and letters, intranet). However, face-to-face sessions should also be used for maximum effectiveness. "Give-and-take" group forums at each successively lower organizational level are especially helpful in addressing organizational members' concerns. Senior management should be present and take an active role in these question-and-answer sessions. Opinion leaders should be kept informed of all relevant information about the change process and its consequences. Finally, all messages should be consistent and reinforcing.

Step 2—Communication During the Moving (Changing) Stage

During the **communication during the moving stage**, as the change is being implemented, rumors and uncertainty abound throughout the organization and its members. Klein (1996) suggests that the communication strategy at the moving stage should have three primary objectives: (1) Provide detailed information about the status of the change effort to those not initially involved with, or impacted by, the change; (2) inform those not yet affected how they will be impacted and how the change will directly affect them; and (3) challenge any misinformation about the change process.

This step in the change process should be marked by detailed information dissemination designed to reduce uncertainty in organizational members. Klein (1996) recommends that senior management provide constant communication that highlights the change implementation progress. This information should again be disseminated via group Q&A sessions and via written communication (e.g., memos, letters, e-mail). More specific details regarding employees' new jobs and role expectations should also be shared.

Step 3—Communication During the Refreezing Stage

At the critical **communication during the refreezing stage**, the primary goal of management and the change agents should be "building structures and processes that support the new ways" and addressing the question "Is the organization more effective than before?" (Klein, 1996, p. 42). At this stage,

communication during the moving stage Attempts to provide detailed information about the status of the change effort to nonstakeholders, provide information about how the change will impact those not yet affected, and challenge misinformation relating to the change process.

communication during the refreezing stage Attempts to disseminate information in a specific, continuous, and multidirectional manner so employees fully understand how the changes affect the organization, their jobs, and their lives as organization members.

all organizational members are likely to have been impacted by the elements put in place during the change process. Klein (1996) recommends that information dissemination during this stage be multidirectional, specific, and continuous so employees will have a "full understanding" of how the changes affect the organization, their jobs, and their lives as organization members.

Case Studies in Managing Organizational Change

Case studies involving organizations undergoing change initiatives investigated how communication strategies were used in the stages of change, as well as the efficacy of those strategies. Two organizations were studied by Goodman and Truss (2004). In one of the organizations, labeled PubCo by the authors, introduction of new working hours constituted the change. In the other organization, labeled OilCo by the authors, a physical relocation of the company's offices constituted the change. In PubCo, there was no clearly defined communication strategy for the change implementation, whereas the other organization, OilCo, had a clear system of communication in place and informed employees two years in advance of the change. PubCo adopted a reactive and ad hoc approach to implementing the change and used a variety of media to disseminate messages about the change, with some change managers using e-mail, others using written memos, and still other managers using group meetings and notice boards. OilCo used a uniform set of media to communicate the change efforts, including face-to-face meetings, e-mail, and surveys, "all of which were interactive and designed to gain employees' input" (Goodman & Truss, 2004, p. 222).

The researchers observed some interesting yet surprising findings regarding employees' perceptions of the adequacy of the change efforts and their satisfaction with those efforts. First, employees in both organizations felt the amount and type of communication delivered during the change process was inadequate. This perception surfaced even in the organization where a clear communication strategy was in place and employees were notified about the changes two years in advance. This finding underscores how unsettling major changes are to employees and highlights the importance of providing an employee-feedback mechanism so that the communication strategies "are continually updated and refined to ensure maximum employee awareness and commitment" (Goodman & Truss, 2004, p. 225). Despite this finding, employees in the organization with the clear communication strategy in place had more positive responses to the change regarding the personal effects of change, level of consultation, updating of the change effort, and clarity of the organization's messages than employees in the organization without a communication strategy in place. The researchers concluded that change managers must continually adjust the communication strategies used and view the communication process during change in a holistic fashion. Simply put, any communication strategy is more effective than no communication strategy.

This QR code will direct you to a YouTube clip highlighting the role of change in organizations, as well as how to manage such change.

http://www.youtube.
com/watch?v=__
IlYNMdV9E&feature=related

A **taxonomy of communication** during the change process was developed by Goodman and Truss (2004) and includes decisions on four components: (1) *messages* (what employees must know, should know, could know); (2) *media* (the specific combination of media that should be employed during the change process, i.e., verbal, written, electronic); (3) *channels* (the specific channels to be employed during the change process to disseminate information, i.e., senior management, managers, team leaders, groups, informal groups), and (4) *approaches* (which approach would best facilitate organizational change, i.e., directive/coercive, participative, consultative). The results of their research also revealed that employees favored face-to-face verbal communication for the main set of change messages. This finding supports Klein's (1996) change model discussed earlier, which suggests that group meetings attended by senior management in which questions and answers are exchanged can facilitate the dissemination of information most effectively and with the greatest employee satisfaction. The findings also suggest, however, that multiple media should be used, and the four elements of messages, media, channels, and approach must be considered holistically to facilitate change. One of the reasons that the change efforts at OilCo met with only partial success was that, even though a clear strategy for change was in place, a mismatch among the medium, channels, and approach of communication existed. That is, although the media used (verbal communication) and the channels used (managers, team leaders, groups) were appropriate, the approach used (directive) was inappropriate because employees had little choice but to accept the change (the relocation of the offices), and the messages did not supply employees with information that they "must know" (Goodman & Truss, 2004).

Many of the recommendations offered by both Klein (1996) and Goodman and Truss (2004) for communication during organizational change efforts were also suggested in practitioner-oriented texts on change initiatives. In a unique research effort, Lewis, Schmisseur, Stephens, and Weir (2006) investigated what themes about communication emerged in best-selling "popular" or "practitioner-oriented" books on organizational change. Lewis and her colleagues suggest that these books often have great impact on actual organizational practices because managers and organizational change agents who read these books often implement the recommendations and suggestions contained in them.

A **thematic analysis** (the systematic identification of dominant themes or recurring trends in advice) of these books was conducted. Three general categories emerged from their analyses. Under the first category, labeled **communicative role of change agents**, three themes emerged regarding the function of change agents in the organization. This theme suggested functions of the change agent in promoting communication and participation in the change process, such as facilitating change by guiding others and the role of the change agent in establishing or maintaining the organization's vision for the change (Lewis et al., 2006, pp. 118–119).

communicative role of change agent Defines the functions of the change agent in promoting communication and participation in the change process, facilitating change by guiding others, and establishing or maintaining the organization's vision for the change.

The second major category resulting from their analysis was labeled **general strategies for communication and introduction of change**. This category contained several recommendations for organizational leaders regarding communicating and introducing the change initiatives in the organization. Four themes emerged in this category: (1) the need for change agents to encourage organizational members to participate fully in the change process; (2) the need to create an organizational culture that facilitates change; (3) the need to garner support for the change from the organization's members by establishing a clear purpose and vision for the change; and (4) the development of a communication-focused strategy about the change. This included the need for change messages to be clear, consistent, and frequent (Lewis et al., 2006, pp. 120–122).

The third major category that emerged from their analysis was labeled **specific communicative tactics for change**. This category presented specific advice on how to implement the change process. Seven themes emerged in this category: (1) asking for input and developing tactics to increase participation in the change process; (2) using informal organizational communication networks to spread the change messages; (3) giving advice on the dissemination of information, such as providing all "stakeholders" with information about change early in the change process, using multiple channels to disseminate information, and using repetition of change messages; (4) providing suggestions on how to present the content of change messages to establish credibility; (5) using motivational communication strategies during change (e.g., providing compliments to employees); (6) formulating specific communication plans, including when to use specific media to communicate the change information and using multiple channels to communicate the messages about change; and (7) creating and communicating a clear and relevant vision for change to all employees (Lewis et al., 2006, pp. 123–128).

Several conclusions were reached by Lewis and colleagues (2006) based on this study. First, encouraging participation from all organizational members in the change process was stressed in these popular books. Lewis and coworkers (2006) noted that "participation was a strong current of the scholarly literature as well" (p. 129). Second, advice from these books underscores the importance of keeping a constant flow of information throughout the organization and its members. Again, Lewis and colleagues (2006) noted that "at the level of general principle, there is clear agreement between these practitioner-oriented sources and the scholarly literature that information dissemination be honest and open" (pp. 130–131). Finally, the importance of communicating a clear purpose for the change initiative to organizational members along with the creation of a clear vision understood by organizational members engenders a more favorable reaction to the change. As with the other two recommendations, the researchers noted that "scholarly literature has examined the role of vision in change communication and found similar results for providing general information" (Lewis et al., 2006,

p. 131). Thus, Lewis and her colleagues concluded that there exists a "surprising alignment" between the findings from the scholarly literature and what is contained in these practitioner-oriented change management texts. Therefore, the knowledge presented in this text contains, to a large degree, similar content to leading manuals advocating organizational change.

Two Approaches to Communication and Organizational Development

Appreciative Inquiry

Earlier in this chapter we introduced a foundational method for conducting organizational change efforts: action research. Recall that action research refers to a systematic process of gathering objective data in order to uncover problems in organizations with the ultimate goal of finding and implementing solutions to those problems. Many conceptualizations of action research include the term *problem* in the definition. For example, Dickens and Watkins (2006) state, "Kurt Lewin developed the action research model in the mid-1940s to respond to problems he perceived in social action" (p. 186), and Cunningham (1993) defined action research as "a continuous process of research and learning in the researcher's long-term relationship with a problem" (p. 4).

In the last 20 years, a paradigm shift has taken place in the discipline of organizational development with the introduction of a new way of looking at and approaching the improvement of organizations and organizational change. Called **appreciative inquiry**, it has spread quickly among organizational development theorists and practitioners and has made its way into the communication discipline as well. Developed by Cooperrider and Srivastva (1987), appreciative inquiry can be seen as a reaction against the traditional "action research" model of organizational development, which emphasizes that organizations have "problems" that need to be solved.

appreciative inquiry (AI)
An organizational development perspective that rejects the problem-solving or "deficit-based" approach of action research, and focuses on "doing things right" and using those things to build the future of the organization.

Although it has by no means replaced action research (AR) as the dominant model in organizational development efforts, appreciative inquiry (AI) has been gaining support from academics in both the communication and organizational development disciplines. This approach has also been adopted by a number of communication and OD practitioners in their consulting and training efforts. Indeed, AI appeals to many scholars and practitioners, especially on the qualitative side of the communication discipline, because of its focus on language, discourse, and stories within the organization (Lewis, Passmore, & Cantore, 2008). Organizational communication scholars have long used the concept of stories and storytelling as a method of preserving and sharing important information about organizational life. Kreps (1990b) noted, "The information value of stories as repositories for and disseminators of organizational intelligence implies that organizations can utilize stories to promote organizational development" (p. 201).

Assumptions of Appreciative Inquiry

One of the major differences between the AI and AR models of organizational development is that AI rejects the emphasis on identifying organizational problems as the key step in the OD process. Rather than focusing on *what is wrong* in the organization, AI theorists and practitioners try to focus on *what is right*. AI rejects the problem-solving or deficit-based approach to organizational change; AI advocates believe the problem-solving approach leads to feelings of demoralization and hopelessness. That is, if organizational members focus exclusively on identifying problems and their causes, a repetitive cycle of deficit thinking is established (Sharma, 2008, p. 25). Rather, AI suggests that productive and well-functioning organizations are guided by what gives hope and joy to the organization and its members. AI offers the principle that all social systems, including organizations, tend toward the most positive images held by their members. Thus, "instead of viewing an organization as having problems, AI views an organization as doing things right, and using those right things to build the organization's future" (Egan & Lancaster, 2005, p. 33). This approach to organizational development mirrors the positive psychology movement, which seeks to build on a person's strengths as opposed to using the more traditional problem-solving approach.

Five Steps in the Appreciative Inquiry Process

The organizational development process under the AI model involves a five-step process: (1) define; (2) discover; (3) dream; (4) design; and (5) determine destiny. In this section we define and describe each of the steps in the model.

Step 1—Define

Before organizational change can be implemented, an organization must define the focus of the inquiry or what type of change is required. The **define step** is also referred to as topic selection or the affirmative topic choice. In this step, positive phrasing is stressed. That is, the outcome must be capable of being positive for those involved in the change. In coming up with the type of change or the topic identification, Lewis and colleagues (2008) recommend that the OD consultant resist the tendency to frame the issues as a problem. Rather, under the rubric of AI, it is critical that the topic be reframed as a set of questions to be addressed. For example, Lewis and colleagues (2008) suggest that rather than focusing on "reducing work absence" in the organization, the organization should reframe this issue under the AI model as "creating a work environment where what we do every day matters to our clients" (p. 49). Other examples of this reframing would be instead of the desired change being defined as "increasing profits," it would be reframed as "retaining existing customers and finding new customers." Instead of asking "What can we do to decrease customer complaints?" ask, "When customers have been especially pleased with our service, how can we apply these successful moments to all of our customer service interactions?" (Lewis et al., 2008, p. 51).

Step 2—Discover

The **discover step** in the AI process involves conducting interviews to secure information that reveals the organization's strengths, and uncovering or discovering the unique and positive qualities of the organization. The goal is to identify common themes and stories from organizational members and then communicate these themes and stories to everyone in the organization. During this stage "the members of the organization have the opportunity to come to know the history of their organization as history of positive possibilities rather than problematic past events, crises, and forgotten or irrelevant events" (Lewis et al., 2008, p. 49). Again, the focus of this step of discovery is on interviews with all members of the organization involved in the change so they can share their experiences and stories about the organization at its best. The concept behind this experience sharing is that the elicitation of positive stories about the organization generates excitement about the organization's positive aspects and what the organization can accomplish in the future.

Step 3—Dream

The **dream step** in the AI intervention process takes the ideas, stories, and themes uncovered during the discover phase and expands them to develop "a statement summarizing the organization's vision, purpose, and strategic intent" (Egan & Lancaster, 2005, p. 34). Information gathered from employees during the discovery step is examined and analyzed for recurring themes, which are then labeled as a "dream" of and for the organization's future. The dream step allows organizational members to uncover what the organization looked like at its best, and then determine how those moments of success can be applied to the organization's future.

This QR code will direct you to a website dedicated to organizational development and will provide both input and strategies on coping with development and change in organizations.

http://www.organizational
development.com/

AI practitioners accomplish the dream step by engaging in many activities, including rewriting the organization's mission to better represent its dream, engaging in "dream sharing" in which organizational members share their personal dreams with others, and even creating a "dream map." A *dream map* is a visual representation of the organization's dream that uses pictures and words cut from magazines and displayed for all members to see and discuss (Lewis et al., 2008).

Step 4—Design

The **design step** is where the dreamed themes and ideas are transformed into more concrete, tangible, and agreed-on actions and principles that are implemented in the final step of the AI process. The AI intervention team plans the structure, strategies, communication systems, and policies for achieving the organization's desired future. In essence, "The design phase is concerned with making decisions about the high level actions which need to be taken to support the delivery of the dream" (Lewis et al., 2008, p. 58). During this step, small-group discussions are organized around answering the question, "What does this organization need to do in terms of its structure, style, and communication to deliver this dream?" Small groups of employees answer this question and responses are shared among groups.

Step 5—Destiny

Perhaps the most concrete step in the AI process, step 5 was originally labeled the "delivery" step. Relabeled the **destiny step**, it is where the organizational members actually write action plans and implementation strategies that will bring the organization to the future it dreams of. In this step, organizational members develop the specific actions or changes to the organizational processes that lead to dream fulfillment or to the future the dream created. In practical terms, this could involve the development of new customer service programs in which employees are trained to communicate in a way that respects and appreciates all customers, development of new methods of organizational decision making, development of a mentoring program for new employees, or development of an employee recognition program (Krattenmaker, 2001).

An Assessment of the AR and AI Models of Organizational Development and Change

Both the dominant, "traditional" model of organizational development and change (AR) and the newer model (AI) have their strengths and weaknesses. As mentioned earlier in this chapter, advocates of the AI approach suggest that the AR model is limiting because it tends to focus almost exclusively on the negative aspects with its emphasis on uncovering organizational problems rather than looking for the positive aspects or uncovering what works well in an organization (which is the stated mission of AI). On the other hand, the AI method of OD has been criticized as having generated little research to support it (McLean, 1996) as well as for being biased in favor of those holding positions of power in the organization in that employees only think of the positive accomplishments of the organization and its leadership (Golembiewski, 1999).

To better understand the contributions of both models, Egan and Lancaster (2005) conducted an assessment of both AR and AI aimed at uncovering the strengths and challenges of both models of OD. Organizational development professionals and consultants representing a variety of large and small public and private sector organizations and from a variety of industries (e.g., financial, retail merchandising, food, energy, health care, schools) were interviewed and asked to provide their perceived strengths and weaknesses of both models. Every study participant was an experienced AI facilitator. The OD practitioners generated a number of strengths and limitations of each model. We report a few of them here (Egan & Lancaster, 2005, pp. 41–43):

Strengths of AI Model of OD

1. Invites imagination and positive imagery into the organization.
2. Captures positive organizational stories.

3. Connects organizational members to a collective positive past.

4. Helps groups realize what is working well.

5. Clarifies a new future picture for the organization.

Weaknesses of AI Model of OD

1. Difficult interpersonal situations may be overlooked.

2. Feelings of anger or frustration not voiced.

3. Dissatisfied organizational members retreat and withdraw.

4. Managers may avoid challenges by focusing exclusively on "the positive."

5. External constituents expect problem-solving process.

Strengths of the AR Model of OD

1. Uses assessment and evaluation from broad data collection.

2. Describes and defines key organizational processes.

3. Provides measurability that can mark progress over time.

4. Aligns well with organizations oriented toward empiricism.

5. Leads to improved performance.

Weaknesses of the AR Model of OD

1. Lacks vision for what the organization could become.

2. Opportunities overshadowed by negative perceptions or feelings.

3. Negative organizational histories given too much attention.

4. Managers may use the process to blame employees for problems.

5. Overly focusing on measurement may feel dehumanizing.

An interesting additional finding emerged from the Egan and Lancaster (2005) study. Practitioners who reported using an organizational development approach that combined both AI and AR models suggested that a combination might be most beneficial in helping organizations manage change and grow. Egan (2004) created a new model called the **appreciative action research model**, which combines the strengths of AI while minimizing the limitations of the AR model. This new AARM model supports the discovery, dream, and design steps in AI with the more objective assessment, feedback, and evaluation steps in AR. The new AARM model can be seen at the website of this textbook.

Incorporating elements of the discovery and dream steps of the AI model while retaining the advantages of the problem-oriented focus of the traditional AR model makes this combined model potentially more efficacious in OD efforts. Although this assertion awaits empirical confirmation, there is clearly something appealing regarding the integration of two disparate OD perspectives. Indeed, Cady and Caster (2000) suggest that combining the more humanistic side of OD with the empirical data–driven diagnostic side

appreciative action research model (AARM)
An organizational development perspective that combines the strengths of appreciative inquiry while minimizing the limitations of the action research model.

"allows for seemingly polar opposite theories, such as the problem approach and the appreciative approach, to exist in a synchronous relationship" (p. 90).

Team Building

One of the most frequent organizational development interventions involves the creation of more effective teams and groups. Woodman and Passmore (2002) state that over one-third of an organizational development consultant's time is spent on team building and group process consulting. Indeed, it has been suggested that the field of OD developed from scholars and practitioners interested in team functioning and team dynamics (Dyer, 2005). Early OD efforts focused on the use of **T-groups** or **training groups** sponsored by the National Training Laboratories, which traces its roots to the sociopsychological theory of Kurt Lewin. T-groups involved eight to 12 individuals getting together with a professional trainer to discuss their behavior. The trainer then used his or her authority to get group members to express positive and negative feelings about themselves and the other members of the group (Gorden, 1979). The impact of T-groups appeared to have resulted in enhancing interpersonal competencies of individuals rather than having a significant and positive impact on team or organizational performance. As a consequence, a new model of team development began, called **team building** (Dyer, 2005, p. 404).

In subsequent years, interest in team building among communication and OD scholars has escalated. This was largely due to the conclusion reached by scholars and practitioners that motivated and cohesive teams outperform unmotivated and fragmented teams.

Although a comprehensive examination of group- and team-based development and communication is beyond the scope and purpose of this chapter, scholars and researchers have identified several key factors that influence the effective functioning of teams: **commitment, trust, involvement, team goals, process orientation** (defined as having problem-solving techniques), and **communication** (Hartley, 1997). Clearly, effective communication is one of the most important dimensions of teamwork.

Dyer (2005) recommends that during a team-building intervention, the OD consultant or practitioner should ask the following questions specifically about communication within and among the team: "(1) Who communicates? How often? For how long?, (2) Who communicates to whom?, and (3) Who talks to whom?, Who interrupts whom?" (p. 408). By obtaining answers to these questions, the OD consultant can determine who has the power and influence on the team, if there are any coalitions among team members, and whether the patterns of communication facilitate or thwart the team in reaching its goals.

Another set of questions related to communication within the team to be addressed deals with how the team makes decisions. Does the team make decisions by majority rule? By consensus? By formal authority? How

T-groups/training groups Involves a group of eight to 12 individuals with a professional trainer to discuss their behavior; including expressing positive and negative feelings about themselves as well as others.

team building A technique used to create and enhance commitment, trust, involvement, team goals, a process orientation, and communication.

process orientation A key factor of team building contributing to effective team functioning.

is conflict managed in the team? Team conflicts usually center around three types: relationship, task, and process. **Relationship conflicts** are based on style, personality, and social issues, which usually lie outside of work-related issues and almost always create negativity within the team. **Task conflict** involves differences in how tasks are to be performed. **Process conflict** involves differences in the methods and strategies used to accomplish tasks. Task and process conflict are not nearly as destructive as relationship conflict. In fact, according to Dyer, both task and process conflict "can actually enhance team performance, for such conflicts can motivate the team to search for better solutions to its problems" (2005, p. 409).

Dyer (2005) created a team-building checklist to determine if team building might be an effective OD intervention strategy. Figure 12.1 presents this checklist.

If the checklist results indicate that a team-building intervention is needed, the next question to ask is whether the team manager feels competent in handling the team-building program or whether an external OD, communication consultant, or practitioner should be brought in to do the intervention. If it is determined that an external consultant is needed for the intervention, then decisions must be made to determine what type of team-building activities would be appropriate for this particular team.

To accomplish this, a data-gathering effort must be conducted through interviews and questions regarding several factors. The first factor deals with the **organizational context** (What tasks is this team required to perform? Does this team have the authority and autonomy to determine its own goals and methods or does a manager or leader oversee this?). The second factor relates to the **composition of the team** (What is the size of this team? What knowledge, skills, and abilities do the team members possess?). The third factor deals with the **processes the team currently employs to get tasks accomplished** (Who communicates with whom? Which members have the most power and influence in the group? Are there any cliques and coalitions within the team? What communication patterns exist to accomplish team goals? How are decisions made in this team or group?) (Dyer, 2005).

Once this and other data have been gathered, Dyer (2005) recommends that a team brainstorming session be conducted to solve the team's problems: "The consultant should encourage the team to reach consensus regarding those activities and actions that are most likely to improve team performance" (p. 413). Note that this type of team intervention likely falls under the AR model, in which organizational interventions and programs are designed to solve problems. However, the AI model of organizational development has also tackled the team-building process.

An Appreciative Inquiry Approach to Team Building

Recall our discussion earlier in this chapter about the major tenets of the AI model of organizational development. The major question to address in an organizational development effort is, What things are this organization

relationship conflicts One of the three most common types of conflict found in teams; based on style, personality, and social issues, and almost always creates negativity within the team.

task conflict One of the three most common types of conflict; involves differences in how tasks are to be performed.

process conflict One of the three most common types of conflict; involves differences in the methods and strategies used to accomplish tasks.

and its employees doing right that will help build this organization's future? Conversely, proponents of AI suggest that team-building efforts from the traditional AR-oriented model begin by asking the question, What problems exist in this team? (see Table 12.1 for a checklist of potential team problems). Once this has been accomplished, organizational development specialists

| **TABLE 12.1**   Team Building Checklist 1 |

Problem Identification: To what extent is there evidence of the following problems in your work unit?	Low Evidence		Some Evidence		High Evidence
1. Loss of production or of work-unit output	1	2	3	4	5
2. Grievances or complaints within the work unit	1	2	3	4	5
3. Conflicts or hostility among unit members	1	2	3	4	5
4. Confusion about assignments or unclear relationships between people	1	2	3	4	5
5. Lack of clear goals or low commitment to goals	1	2	3	4	5
6. Apathy or general lack of interest or involvement of unit members	1	2	3	4	5
7. Lack of innovation, risk taking, imagination, or taking initiative	1	2	3	4	5
8. Ineffective staff meetings	1	2	3	4	5
9. Problems in working with the boss	1	2	3	4	5
10. Poor communication: people afraid to speak up, not listening to one another, or not talking together	1	2	3	4	5
11. Lack of trust between leader and members or among members	1	2	3	4	5
12. People do not understand or agree with decisions	1	2	3	4	5
13. People feel that good work is unrecognized or unrewarded	1	2	3	4	5
14. People are discouraged from working together in better team effort	1	2	3	4	5

Scoring: Add up the score for the 14 items. If your score is between 14 and 28, there is little evidence that your unit needs team building. If your score is between 29 and 42, there is some evidence, but no immediate pressure, unless two or three items are very high. If your score is between 43 and 56, you should seriously think about planning a team-building program. If your score is over 56, team building should be a top priority for your work unit.

Source: From *Team Building: Proven Strategies for Improving Team Performance,* 4th ed. by William G. Dyer, Jeffrey Dyer, and Edgar Schein. Copyright © 2007. Reprinted by permission of John Wiley & Sons, Inc.

begin the process of uncovering or developing solutions to the problems identified. As you can see, these are very different processes or models as applied to team building.

The AI model has been applied in major organizational development efforts in a variety of businesses and nonprofit organizations nationally and internationally. AI as a method of engaging people in productive conversations, dialogue, and storytelling has also been applied more specifically to build teams and enhance team performance. The AI approach begins by formulating a series of positive questions to discover the causes of the team's successful functioning.

Whitney, Trosten-Bloom, Cherney, and Fry (2004) suggest that the existing deficit-based team-building models developed from the AR paradigm usually require team members to work through problem solving, conflict, and hidden agendas in order to progress toward team development, unity, and effectiveness. They suggest that applying the tenets of AI, specifically to team building, can lead to more satisfied, cohesive, effective, and productive teams. By asking positive questions, "[team] members are more likely to eagerly anticipate coming together and to interact with words and stories that create positive images about past and future teamwork" (Whitney et al., 2004, p. 3).

Applying the AI model involves using positive questions throughout the entire team-building process, which includes selecting team members, establishing team norms, aligning the strengths of team members, and creating a vision and goal for the team (Whitney et al., 2004). For example, to stimulate open and honest communication among team members, a positive question should be posed to all members of the team, such as "what three small changes could you and your teammates agree to that together would enhance the level of open and honest communication within the team? (Whitney et al., 2004, p. 64), or "think of a time when this team functioned very effectively as a cohesive and productive unit. How did the team members communicate with each other that increased efficiency, increased group consensus, and increased team effectiveness?

At the conclusion of the sharing process, the team should be able to apply the design phase (Step 4) of the generalized AI model to develop concrete and tangible norms, principles, and procedures for team building that can be implemented in the destiny phase (Step 4) and will lead to an improved, satisfied, and productive team. Thus, according to AI advocates, rather than dwelling on team conflict moments, the AI model makes the team focus on cooperative moments; and instead of focusing on moments of low team morale, the focus is shifted to moments of excitement and future building (Cherney, 2003).

Using the AI model, Bushe and Coetzer (1995) asked new team members to recall stories of "exceptional team experiences," and then asked them to share those experiences with the other team members. From these stories, "best team practices" themes emerged that were incorporated into plans for the emerging team. Bushe and Coetzer suggest that using this AI process leads the group to higher team effectiveness and greater team cohesion.

Summary

Like other systems, organizations are subject to constant change. The ability to adapt to and affect change separates successful from less successful organizations. Organizational development is the area of organizational studies that focuses on the implementation and management of organizational change.

In this chapter, we first defined organizational development, traced its roots, and provided a brief history of the OD movement. Next, we presented the foundational method for conducting organizational change efforts, the action research model. In particular, we presented Kurt Lewin's three-step model of organizational change. This model has helped guide organizational change efforts for the past five decades. We then presented several communication strategies for the implementation of organizational change that emerged from Lewin's model.

We concluded the chapter by introducing two major approaches to communication and organizational development: appreciative inquiry and team building. Appreciative inquiry represents a relatively new way to approach the organizational improvement and organizational change. Rather than focusing on identifying problems in an organization and then developing solutions to those problems, appreciative inquiry asks organizational members to examine what works well. By sharing these stories and moments of success, the AI model seeks to develop action plans to implement these successful strategies.

We also introduced one of the most frequent types of OD interventions, team building. We first presented a more traditional action research approach to team building in which team problems are revealed and then solutions to those problems are developed. Finally, we presented an AI approach to team building in which the team's best practices are elicited through the use of positive questions.

After reading this chapter, you should understand more about how communication and organizational development specialists assist organizations and manage the change process to improve the quality of organizational life for all members.

Questions for Discussion and Review

1. Discuss the significant advances in the evolution of organizational development as a distinct subdiscipline of communication studies.

2. Explain the underlying assumptions of action research. How would a consultant approach organizational development from this perspective?

3. Describe the elements of Lewin's three-step model of organizational change. How can these factors within the organization foster or inhibit change?

4. Identify the types of communication associated with each step of the three-step model of organizational change.

5. Discuss the three categories of organizational change as identified by Lewis, Schmisseur, Stephens, and Weir (2006) and how each of these steps is necessary for a complete organizational development effort.

6. Explain the underlying assumptions of appreciative inquiry and describe the five steps of this approach.

7. List and describe three of the five strengths and weaknesses for the action research and appreciative inquiry approaches to organizational development.

8. Explain the underlying assumptions of the appreciative action research model of organizational development. Do you agree that this perspective is superior to either action research or appreciative inquiry approaches? Explain your answer.

9. List and define the key factors for effective team functioning. Describe a team to which you belonged that possessed all or none of these factors.

References

Beckhard, R. (1969). *Organization development: Strategies and models.* Reading, MA: Addison-Wesley.

Beckhard, R. (2006). What is organization development? In J. V. Gallos (Ed.), *Organization development* (pp. 13–38). San Francisco: Jossey-Bass.

Burke, W. W. (2006). Where did OD come from? In J. V. Gallos (Ed.), *Organization development* (pp. 3–12). San Francisco: Jossey-Bass.

Burnes, B. (2006). Kurt Lewin and the planned approach to change. In J. V. Gallos (Ed.), *Organization development* (pp. 133–157). San Francisco: Jossey-Bass.

Bushe, G. R., & Coetzer, G. (1995). Appreciative inquiry as a team development intervention. *Journal of Applied Behavioral Science, 31,* 13–30.

Cady, S. H., & Caster, M. A. (2000). A DIET for action research: An integrated problem and appreciative focused approach to organization development. *Organization Development Journal, 18,* 79–93.

Carlock, R. S. (1994). *The need for organization development in successful entrepreneurial firms.* New York: Garland Publishing, Inc.

Cherney, J. K. (2003, April 2). *Appreciative teambuilding: Creating a climate for great collaboration.* Retrieved from http://www.teambuildinginc.com/article_ai.htm

Cooperrider, D. L., & Srivastva, S. (1987). Appreciative inquiry in organizational life. In R. W. Woodman & W. A. Passmore (Eds.), *Research in organizational change and development, Vol. 1* (pp. 129–169). Greenwich, CT: JAI Press.

Cunningham, J. B. (1993). *Action research and organizational development.* Westport, CT: Praeger.

Dickens, L., & Watkins, K. (2006). Action research: Rethinking Lewin. In J. V. Gallos (Ed.), *Organization development* (pp. 185–201). San Francisco: Jossey-Bass.

Dyer, W. Gibb, Jr. (2005). Team building: Past, present, and future. In W.J. Rothwell & R.L. Sullivan (Eds.). *Practicing organizational development* (2nd ed., pp. 403-419). San Francisco, CA: Pfeiffer.

Dyer, W., Dyer, W. G., & Dyer, J. H. (2007). *Team building: Proven strategies for improving team performance* (4th ed., pp. 79–80). New York: John Wiley and Sons, Inc.

Egan, T. M. (2004). *An affirmative action research model.* Unpublished manuscript.

Egan, T. M., & Lancaster, C. M. (2005). Comparing appreciative inquiry to action research: OD practitioner perspectives. *Organization Development Journal, 23,* 29–49.

Elrod, P. D. II, & Tippett, O. D. (2002). The 'Death Valley' of change. *Journal of Organizational Change Management, 15,* 273–291.

Emerson, T., & Stewart, M. (2011). *The change book.* Alexandria, VA: ASTD Press.

Fitzgerald S. P., Murrell, K. L., & Newman, H. L. (2002). Appreciative inquiry: The new frontier. In J. Waclawski & A. H. Church (Eds.), *Organization development: A data-driven approach to organizational change* (pp. 203–221). San Francisco: Jossey-Bass.

Golembiewski, R. (1999). Fine-tuning appreciative inquiry: Two ways of circumscribing the concept's value-added. *Organization Development Journal, 17,* 21–27.

Goodman, J., & Truss, C. (2004). The medium and the message: Communicating effectively during a major change initiative. *Journal of Change Management, 4,* 217–228.

Gorden, W. I. (1979). Experiential training: A comparison of T-groups, Tavistock, and EST. *Communication Education, 28,* 39–48.

Hartley, P. (1997). *Group communication.* New York: Routledge.

Infante, D. A., Rancer, A. S., & Avtgis, T. A. (2010). *Contemporary communication theory.* Dubuque, IA: Kendall Hunt.

Klein, S. M. (1996). A management communication strategy for change. *Journal of Organizational Change Management, 9,* 32–46.

Krattenmaker, T. (2001, October). Change through appreciative inquiry. *Harvard Management Communication Letter, 4,* 5–6.

Kreps, G. L. (1990a). Organizational communication research and organizational development. In D. O'Hair & G. L. Kreps (Eds.), *Applied communication theory and research* (pp. 103–121). Hillsdale, NJ: Erlbaum.

Kreps, G. L. (1990b). Stories as repositories of organizational intelligence: Implications for organizational development. In J. A. Anderson (Ed.), *Communication yearbook 13* (pp. 191–202). Newbury Park, CA: SAGE Publications.

Lewin, K. (1951). Frontiers in group dynamics. In D. Cartwright (Ed.), *Field theory in social science* (pp. 188–237). New York: Harper & Row.

Lewis, L. K. (2000). 'Blindsided by that one' and 'I saw that one coming': The relative anticipation and occurrence of communication problems and other problems in implementers' hindsight. *Journal of Applied Communication Research, 28,* 44–67.

Lewis, S., Passmore, J., & Cantore, S. (2008). *Appreciative inquiry for change management: Using AI to facilitate organizational development.* London: Kogan Page Limited.

Lewis, L. K., Schmisseur, A. M., Stephens, K. K., & Weir, K. E. (2006). Advice on communicating during organizational change. *Journal of Business Communication, 43,* 113–137.

Lippitt, G. (1982). *Organizational renewal* (2nd ed.). Englewood Cliffs, NJ: Prentice Hall.

McLean, G. N. (1996). AR in OD: RIP? *Human Resource Development Quarterly, 7,* 1–3.

Mirvis, P. H. (2006). Revolutions in OD. In J. V. Gallos (Ed.), *Organization development* (pp. 39–88). San Francisco: Jossey-Bass.

Pettigrew, A. (1973). *The politics of organizational decision making.* Hampshire, UK: Tavistock.

Rothwell, W. J., & Sullivan, R. (2005). *Practicing organization development: A guide for consultants* (2nd ed.). San Francisco: Pfeiffer.

Scott, C. D., & Jaffe, D. T. (1995). *Managing change at work* (Rev. ed.). Menlo Park, CA: Crisp Publications.

Sharma, R. (2008). Celebrating change: The new paradigm of organizational development. *The ICFAI University Journal of Soft Skills, 2,* 23–28.

Waclawski, J., & Church, A. (2002). Introduction and overview of organization development as a data-driven approach for organizational change. In J. Waclawski & A. H. Church (Eds.), *Organization development* (pp. 3–26). San Francisco: Jossey-Bass.

Whitney, D., Trosten-Bloom, A., Cherney, J., & Fry, R. (2004). *Appreciative team building.* Lincoln, NE: iUniverse, Inc.

Woodman, R. W., & Passmore, W. A. (2002). The heart of it all: Groups and team-based interventions in organization development. In J. Waclawski & A. H. Church (Eds.), *Organization development* (pp. 164–176). San Francisco: Jossey-Bass.

Chapter 13

Analyzing Organizational Communication

In this chapter, we examine the importance of formally assessing an organization's communication. Communication has been said to be the "lifeblood" of an organization (Downs & Adrian, 2004), so it is critical that these assessments take place from time to time to determine how well communication and information are being disseminated among employees and between work teams and other organizational units. In addition, formal organizational communication assessments are essential to obtain a sense of employees' attitudes toward the organization's internal and external communication efforts and to determine if any communication problems exist that must be addressed.

First, we discuss the nature of survey research in the organization. We discuss what constitutes organizational survey research, how survey research is conducted in the organization, issues of reliability and validity in organizational communication survey research, how surveys are constructed, and the process of gathering data using surveys. We then focus on how to conduct formal communication audits in the organization. We describe the most frequently used instruments, audit tools, and techniques in organizational diagnostic efforts, including interviews, formal communication auditing tools such as the International Communication Association's Communication Audit, the Downs-Hazen Communication Satisfaction Questionnaire, and the Organizational Identification and Organizational Commitment Instrument. We conclude by describing how to conduct an organizational network analysis.

The Importance of Assessing Organizational Communication

Think about your best and your worst work-related experiences. Surely the amount of financial compensation you received for your work is probably an important factor in ranking your job as good or bad as well as ranking your experiences with the organization as satisfying or unsatisfying. However, if you are like many people, the amount of money you received may be secondary to other factors regarding assessing your satisfaction with that job. As we have stressed throughout this text, perceptions of the communications you receive from your superiors and colleagues are often ranked as more important considerations in assessing your job satisfaction. Reviewing some of the research discussed throughout this text has led researchers to conclude that effective communication is significantly correlated with job satisfaction and organizational commitment (Hargie & Tourish, 2000). Indeed, it is suggested that effective internal organizational communication could positively affect employees' behavior by increasing productivity, increasing the quality of output (both service and products), increasing innovativeness, reducing employee absenteeism, reducing employee turnover, and thus, reducing overall organizational costs (Clampitt & Downs, 1993; Downs & Adrian, 2004; Hargie,

Tourish, & Wilson, 2002; Ray, 1993). The quality of communication between a subordinate and her or his superior is so critical that Goldhaber (1986) stated that it was the *most important* contributor to job satisfaction (p. 236).

Success and communication are also important with regard to an organization's external communication with clients and customers. Hargie and Tourish (2000) suggest that a positive corporate image helps increase sales and contract acquisition. They report a "direct correlation between the willingness of organizations to address their external customer relations on the one hand, and their management of internal communication issues on the other" (pp. 14–15). As examples, Hargie and Tourish cite companies such as IBM, Ben & Jerry's, Apple, and 3M, which have clearly defined their organizational culture, communicated this culture both externally to customers and internally to their employees, and have successful external and internal communication programs. Communication assessments often include audits of an organization's climate. Communication climate includes factors such as participative decision making, supportiveness between superiors and subordinates, trust, the openness in organizational communication, and how performance goals are communicated within the organization.

What Is a Communication Assessment?

How does an organization know if its communication is successful? Recently, we have witnessed organizations that thought they were successful, only to discover, often too late, that this perception was inaccurate (e.g., Enron, Circuit City, Lehman Brothers). The only effective way for an organization to objectively and systematically assess the state of its internal (and often external) communication is to conduct an audit or assessment. Downs and Adrian (2004) define **communication assessment** as a "diagnostic process that collects important data to be used in constructing a realistic description of the actual organization" (p. 7). They suggest six characteristics for a communication assessment:

communication assessment
A diagnostic process that collects important data to be used in constructing a description of an organization.

1. **Independence**—A communication assessment should be conducted by trained individuals external to the organization. In conducting an audit or assessment, confidentiality must be assured, and the best way to achieve this is by using individuals external to the organization. Often, individuals will refuse to respond to assessment instruments or will provide false responses or data if they feel their answers to items will be transparent, and hence, the organization could use their answers against them.

2. **Professionalism**—Organizational communication assessment must be conducted by professionals who have expertise in communication analysis and communication consultation.

3. **Diagnostic thoroughness**—A diagnosis must be systematic and must be made about all areas of communication considered important in that organization.

4. **Skilled evaluation**—The data gathered must be held to some criteria in judging the adequacy of the current state of the organization's communication; that is, "Observations must always be put into some context historically, organizationally, industrially, or economically" (p. 8). One of the communication auditing techniques we describe later in this chapter is called the **International Communication Association (ICA) Communication Audit**. One of the benefits of this auditing tool is that data have been gathered on many different organizations and norms have been developed with which an auditor can interpret any new data gathered. This type of skilled evaluation, as Downs and Adrian describe it, allows the auditor to respond effectively to questions, such as "What are the criteria for judging whether this organization's communication is effective?" Indeed, conducting multiple communication audits of the same organization are beneficial because they allow us to compare the results of the data obtained at Time 1 and Time 2 from the same organization. In this way, we can both evaluate change and have some objective criteria with which to evaluate the organization against its "developmental past" (Downs & Adrian, 2004, p. 9).

5. **Tailored design**—Communication assessments should be tailored to the specific organization. That is, some data-gathering techniques work well with some organizations but not with others. Attempting to use an organizational survey designed for a large organization in an organization with few employees may not be prudent. For this type of organization, other techniques such as confidential interviews and focus group interviews may be more effective.

6. **Current time frame**—Remember that organizations are dynamic and communication patterns change constantly. Even though we gather data about an organization at one point in time, generalizations about the communication in that organization are often limited to that particular time. If one high-ranking member suddenly leaves the organization, the conclusions drawn about the communication in that organization obtained from a prior audit may no longer be relevant. To draw conclusions about current communication activity, another assessment must be conducted.

International Communication Association (ICA) Communication Audit Assessment that measures information received, information sent, follow-up, sources of information, timeliness, organizational communication relationships, outcomes, and channels of communication.

Benefits of Conducting a Formal Organizational Communication Assessment or Audit

To employ a medical analogy, when you go to a doctor because of some illness or other problem, the physician will likely gather data on your health by conducting a series of diagnostic tests (e.g., an MRI; an EKG; blood profile, including HBA1C and cholesterol level; colonoscopy). The doctor does this to verify your health or to determine what might be ailing you. Further, the doctor uses these tests to increase the chances of obtaining an accurate diagnosis rather than having to take a guess by simply observing your symptoms or making a diagnosis by inference. Although a competent doctor may be able to diagnose a medical condition accurately through a simple medical interview, the data from these tests provide the doctor with a more valid and reliable diagnosis. The same is true for the communication specialist who requests a systematic communication assessment or audit of the organization's communication. Rather than merely guessing, a communication audit can reveal more valid and reliable information about the organization's communication systems.

Survey Research in the Organization

Organizational surveys are a popular and ubiquitous method of assessing a number of issues associated with organizational life, including employee attitudes, perceptions, and behaviors. Indeed, several large organizations employ individuals, often from the company's human resource department, who are responsible for designing, conducting, interpreting, and presenting employee attitude surveys.

organizational survey
Popular method of assessing a number of issues associated with organizational life, including employee attitudes, perceptions, and behaviors.

Surveys can be defined as "a systematic process of data collection designed to quantitatively measure specific aspects of organizational members' experience as they relate to work" (Church & Waclawski, 2001, p. 5). The information generated by surveys can be attitudinal (e.g., what employees think and feel), informational (e.g., what employees know), or both. Organizational surveys most often use a standardized questionnaire or instrument that contains a series of items with some type of **response format** (a formal method by which individuals respond to the items on the questionnaire or scale). The definition we presented by Church and Waclawski contains a few assumptions about the nature of survey research that must be stressed. The first is that survey research is a *systematic process*. The importance of organizational research mandates that it bes done with care and planning. Each step of the survey process (which we identify in the next section) must be planned and prepared.

Second, although survey research can contain both quantitative and qualitative elements, this text focuses largely on the *quantitative examination* of organizational communication. Hence, in this chapter we focus primarily on the quantitative dimensions of survey research. Later in the chapter we offer several organizational communication assessment tools, most of which focus on gathering quantitative data. Gathering this type of data requires several considerations regarding the type of questions asked and the type of measurement desired.

The third element in the definition offered above, *specific aspects of organizational members' experience,* refers to the many dimensions or issues that are investigated in organizational survey research. Most of the instruments we focus on pertain primarily to organizational *communication.* However, there are other organizational issues that can have a direct or indirect effect on communication practiced within the organization. Among them are issues related to employee satisfaction, organizational change, perceptions of employee empowerment, employee compensation and benefits, organizational leadership, relationships within the organization, and commitment to the vision or mission of the organization (Church & Waclawski, 2001, p. 7). These are but a few of the many additional topics that organizational surveys can investigate.

Advantages of Organizational Survey Research

This QR code will direct you to a website containing the Baldrige Program, which highlights both the role and practice of organizational assessments.

http://www.nist.gov/baldrige/

If you have ever worked in an organization, it is likely that you have been a participant in organizational survey research. Survey research is a popular technique for assessing a host of organizational issues, and it is estimated that over 70 percent of U.S. organizations use this method of information gathering (Church & Waclawski, 2001). Why is survey research so popular as an information-gathering technique? According to organizational scholars (e.g., Church & Waclawski, 2001; Downs & Adrian, 2004), there are several answers to this question. First, surveys are relatively easy to conduct. Surveys can be distributed easily to employees who are already on the job and can be completed during work hours. Today, with the Internet, private organizational intranets, personal digital assistants (PDAs), cell phones, and e-mail, administering surveys has become even easier and less costly. Even large-scale communication audit instruments (e.g., the ICA Audit) can be administered online (Goldhaber, 2002).

Second, surveys and organizational questionnaires allow for a degree of anonymity, which allow respondents to provide information that they might not share in other types of data-gathering efforts, such as in a personal interview or a focus group interview. The issue of anonymity is a critical one, and confidentiality must be ensured if you expect employees to respond to the survey or questionnaire honestly and accurately, or expect them to respond at all. Several years ago, one of the authors of this text attempted to conduct a communication audit of health care workers in a large metropolitan hospital. One of the groups targeted for data gathering was nurses, all three shifts of the nursing schedule. Part of the communication audit included a section on the communication between the nurses and their supervisors.

After gathering the data, the research team noticed that for one of the nursing shifts, most of the nurses left blank the items measuring interpersonal relational satisfaction with their supervisors. It quickly became apparent to the researchers that there were some difficult and strained interpersonal relationships between the nurses and their supervisors, as evidenced by the nurses' unwillingness to complete that section of the survey. When we queried some of the employees about this missing data, they indicated they were afraid they might be identifiable from their responses to the demographic section of the survey and their responses could be used against them. Although assurances of confidentiality were underscored, it was clear that mistrust and poor interpersonal relations existed between the supervisors and subordinates at that facility.

Surveys allow for the examination of many topics within a single data-gathering effort. For example, the ICA Communication Audit questionnaire contains 122 questions covering eight content areas (receiving information from others, sending information to others, follow-up on information sent, sources of information, timeliness of information received from key sources, organizational communication relationships, organizational outcomes, and channels of communication). This instrument will be presented later in this chapter. Gathering data of this scope on organizational communication using personal interviewing techniques would involve much more time on the part of both the researcher and the respondent. Finally, surveys and questionnaires usually yield quantitative data that are relatively easy to assemble, organize, and analyze.

FIGURE 13.1
Systematic Procedures for Effective Organizational Survey Research.

Source: Church & Waclawski, 2001. Used with permission from Jossey-Bass Publishers.

The Seven Steps of Effective Organizational Survey Research

Church and Waclawski (2001) offer a systematic seven-step process for conducting organizational survey research. Figure 13.1 outlines the seven steps.

Step 1: Gaining Support for the Survey

The first step in the organizational survey process is securing the organization's commitment to the survey research process by gaining the support of key organizational members. Obtaining support from upper (senior) management is critical because it enhances the credibility of the survey effort. If the survey will be used to aid in some organizational change efforts, then support from upper management is essential. Employees from all organizational levels must also be part of the survey effort right from the beginning. If management and employee support is not secured, then they will be unlikely to participate in the survey process.

You may find that organizational members are often jaded about organizational survey research efforts. This can happen because results of prior survey research efforts have been ignored by the organization, the results were never shared with organizational members, or the change promised as a consequence of the research was never realized. Thus, employee commitment and participation in future survey research efforts are diminished, and survey efforts are met with cynicism and resistance (Church & Waclawski, 2001, p. 42). These reactions must be overcome if the survey process is to succeed. Before the survey is designed, it is critical that you set clear objectives regarding the survey's purpose and obtain upper management commitment for the survey process. Further, you must attempt to overcome any suspicion, resentment, or negativity from employees, ensure anonymity and confidentiality in the data-gathering process, inform employees how the survey will be used, and decide what content areas will be examined and what demographic information will be gathered.

For an organizational survey to be successful, a set of clear, observable, and measurable objectives must be identified. These requirements appear similar to the requirement in the development of training objectives we discussed in Chapter 11. These goals and objectives must be presented to and agreed on by key organizational members (Church & Waclawski, 2001, p. 32). For example, your survey's objectives might be to assess (1) the overall employee satisfaction with communication in this organization, (2) the effectiveness of upward and downward communication as a consequence of the organization's recent structural change, (3) the effectiveness of communication channels used in the organization (email, intranet, newsletters), (4) the quality of interpersonal relationships within the work unit, and (5) the conflict management style of members of a work team (Hargie & Tourish, 2004).

Church and Waclawski (2001) suggest that three questions must be addressed at this step in the survey process: (1) What is the purpose of the survey? (Are we measuring attitudes? Are we measuring employee morale?);

(2) What are the expected outcomes of the survey? For example, will the survey be used to make some structural or procedural changes in the organization?; and (3) Who will be involved in the survey? (Will there be representatives of a cross-section from organizational units? Different levels? Different functions?) (p. 34).

Step 2: Developing the Survey

Step 2 in Church and Waclawski's (2001) process of conducting organizational survey research concerns developing the survey content. Designing the survey items and the survey questions is critical to the success of the survey process. The results and implications of many an organizational survey have been limited by poorly chosen and poorly written items. One of the first decisions researchers must make is whether to use an existing survey or questionnaire previously used with other organizations or to develop a custom-designed survey for the current organization or client.

We discuss and present two preexisting reliable and valid organizational communication auditing instruments later in this chapter (e.g., the ICA Communication Audit Questionnaire and the Downs-Hazen Communication Satisfaction Questionnaire). However, we begin our discussion by presenting several important issues in developing a custom-designed survey. Whether you are working alone or with a **survey design team** (i.e., key members of the organization, often from the corporate communication and human resources departments, who are charged with developing the questionnaire), there are several considerations that must be carefully planned regarding item and question development. Several issues will arise regarding the actual survey instrument that will have to be decided before the items or questions are written. These considerations include, but are not limited to (1) what dimensions or content areas of organizational communication you want to include in the survey (general attitudes toward the organization, perceptions of the adequacy of upward and downward communication, satisfaction with communication from superiors, satisfaction with intergroup communication); (2) the type of questions asked (open-ended versus closed-ended); (3) the type of response format that will be presented to the respondents (agree–disagree, almost always true–almost never true, yes–no, frequent–infrequent, very satisfied–very dissatisfied); (4) the level of measurement of the items on the survey (nominal, ordinal, interval, ratio); and, (5) the overall length of the survey.

Open-Ended Versus Closed-Ended Items

One of the most important decisions in organizational survey design and construction is the composition of items. There are two types of items used in surveys, questionnaires, and other instruments: open-ended and closed-ended. **Open-ended items** do not restrict participants' answers, but rather allow them to respond with their own words and provide as much or as little detail and content as they want. An example of an open-ended survey item is, "What changes would you like to see implemented in the way information is shared among teams in this organization?" Several advantages of open-ended items have been suggested and include providing more detailed and potentially more robust information, allowing for more respondent individuality, and allowing for subjects to let off steam (Church & Waclawski, 2001; Downs & Adrian, 2004). On the other hand, there are disadvantages in using open-ended responses in organizational surveys. First, respondents' answers often contain irrelevant information; further, because respondents must elaborate on their attitudes and perceptions, they often leave such questions blank. Critical or negative open-ended responses are not easily analyzed and converted to quantitative form (partly due to verbally aggressive written rants about coworkers or the organization in general). Often, responses to open-ended items require the researcher to use **content analysis** to determine patterns of responses and to convert the data into a form that can be summarized easily.

content analysis

A data analysis procedure that seeks to determine patterns of responses and to convert the data into a form that can be easily summarized.

Closed-ended items are more restrictive and present the survey participant with a predetermined response format to use in replying to the item. Multiple-choice questions, checklists, rating scales, and true-false questions are examples of closed-ended items. An example of a closed-ended item that might be used in an organizational communication survey is as follows: "How satisfied are you with the amount of feedback you receive from your immediate supervisor?" satisfied ____:____:____:____:____ dissatisfied

This is an example of a semantic–differential scale with a five-space response format. In this case, the respondent would be asked to put a check mark in one of the spaces of that scale. A check in the first space from either side would mean *extremely satisfied* or *extremely dissatisfied,* a check in the second space would mean *satisfied* or *dissatisfied,* and a check in the middle space would indicate being *neither satisfied nor dissatisfied.*

Closed-ended questions have a number of benefits and limitations. In terms of benefits, they are easier for the participant to respond to, they provide a uniformed response format for all participants, and most important, they are easier for the survey analyst to analyze and quantify. On the other hand, closed-ended questions do not allow respondents to elaborate on their answers, may not provide a response that is fully within the range of respondents' feelings and/or attitudes, and provide less information than would be obtained if using an open-ended item. However, it is recommended that organizational researchers use both open- and closed-ended items in their surveys and questionnaires (Downs & Adrian, 2004).

The most common types of formats used with closed-ended questions in organizational communication survey research are **Likert-type scale items, semantic-differential-type scale items**, and items that require some type of rank ordering of information. The first two formats (Likert and semantic-differential) yield interval-level data, whereas the third format (rank ordering) yields ordinal level data (see Infante, Rancer, & Avtgis, 2010). Examples of items with these formats are presented later in this chapter when we provide some survey items from preexisting organizational communication assessment instruments.

It is customary on organizational surveys to provide respondents with either a five- or seven-space response format with which participants can indicate their perceptions, attitudes, or some other type of response. For example, if you want to assess respondents' levels of satisfaction with the amount of feedback they receive from their supervisor, you could ask, How satisfied are you with the feedback you receive from your supervisor?

Very satisfied	Satisfied	Neutral	Dissatisfied	Very dissatisfied
5	4	3	2	1

Another type of item that gets at the same issue and employs a Likert-type scale with a different response format is to provide the following statement: I am satisfied with the amount of feedback I receive from my supervisor.

Strongly agree	Agree	Neutral	Disagree	Strongly disagree
5	4	3	2	1

Another question designed to assess a different dimension of this issue is to ask a respondent the following question: How frequently do you receive feedback from your supervisor?

Always	Very often	Sometimes	Almost never	Never
5	4	3	2	1

Other Issues in Developing Survey Items

It is important to include enough survey items to address adequately all the issues and concepts related to the organizational concerns under study. It is also important that you do not overwhelm respondents with so many items that **participant fatigue** ensues. Participant fatigue causes people to respond to long surveys by filling in answers without reading the question or simply leaving them blank. It is also important to be careful in the wording used to construct scale items. It is especially critical to avoid writing **double-barreled items**, or single items that attempt to measure more than one idea (e.g., How satisfied are you with the amount and type of feedback you receive from your supervisor?). Avoid crafting items that may be biased in some way. An example of a biased survey item is, "Which of the following problems do you believe should be addressed first in organizational development efforts?" This question is considered biased because the item wording suggests to respondents that there are indeed problems in the organization (respondents may feel there are no problems) or that there are more problems than those the listed in the answer choices.

When asking respondents for demographic data, do not ask for demographics that you do not intend to investigate in your analyses. Recall that by asking for too much personal demographic information (e.g., age, department, length of service in the company, gender), respondents might believe their anonymity will be compromised and will avoid responding truthfully to sensitive items. Further, it is recommended you put the demographic questions at the end of the survey (Downs & Adrian, 2004).

Other Considerations in Survey Development

Before large-scale administration of an organizational survey, it is prudent to conduct a **pilot test**, or pretest, of the survey. This is done by asking a sample of respondents from the organization, who are similar to those who will ultimately receive the final instrument, to provide feedback on the instrument and identify any issues or concerns (bad questions, confusing items) before the instrument is disseminated to its intended recipients. By conducting this pilot test, analysts or auditors can determine whether the respondents are interpreting the items as the developers intended (Downs & Adrian, 2004). This extra assessment step helps ensure that threats to the instrument are identified and corrected before it is administered to all employees and, thus, potentially save valuable organizational resources (time, money).

Church and Waclawski (2001) suggest that three criteria be used to assess the efficacy of a questionnaire in a pilot test:

1. *Clarity:* Are the items clear to the respondents?

2. *Relevance:* Are the items relevant to the respondent's experiences in the organization?

3. *Specificity:* Do the items measure participants' perceptions and attitudes sufficiently or are the items too vague? For example, assume that one of the main objectives of the survey or communication audit is to obtain an understanding of superior–subordinate communication. Suppose also that one of the items asks participants to respond to the following statement: I receive adequate feedback about my job performance from my immediate supervisor, with a 1–5 response format ranging from 5–*Strongly Agree* to 1–*Strongly Disagree.* If the greatest frequency of responses to this item is 2–*Disagree,* that information is meaningful in that we know that most of the respondents feel they are not receiving adequate feedback from their supervisors. However, it might be useful to use a follow-up item that asks for greater detail about the *type* of feedback employees want to receive.

Step 3: Communicating the Survey's Purpose and Objectives

To secure the success of an organizational communication assessment survey, it is critical to communicate the survey's purpose and objectives well before employees receive it. Employees need to be informed about why the survey is being undertaken and why their participation is integral to the process. This preparation work can be accomplished via multiple communication channels and media. Among your options for disseminating this information are "corporate videos, newsletters, glossy pamphlets, booklets, electronic documents posted on intranets and Websites, e-mails, letters and memos, town meetings, formal announcements at other gatherings such as 'all hands on' management meetings, and postings on bulletin boards" (Church & Waclawski, 2001, pp. 97–98). Although all these information channels are viable, it is most effective to use the channel(s) most widely used by employees (e.g., email). It is also highly recommended that high-ranking organizational officials (CEOs, vice presidents of human resources) send a formal letter, addressed to each employee individually, stating the objectives and what is required for participation in the assessment.

When employees receive the survey, it should be accompanied by a cover letter and instructions for completing the instrument. The primary purpose of these components is to motivate respondents to complete the survey and lend credibility to the survey project and assessment process (Downs & Adrian, 2004). Remember that several employees may have already been through the survey process without seeing any discernible organizational change or follow-up despite their participation. Hence, the motivation and credibility boost (via cover letter and instructions) are essential to garner respondent cooperation and support. Finally, the cover letter can underscore the confidentiality and anonymity of respondent answers.

Step 4: Administering the Survey

Once the organizational assessment survey is written, it is time to get the survey into the respondents' hands. There are several considerations you must be aware of during the process of survey administration. Because organizational members are busy doing their jobs, it is important to provide a time window during which respondents can complete and return the survey. At one end of the time frame continuum, Church and Waclawski (2001) recommend that you give employees one month to complete and return the survey. This time frame can vary depending on the method of survey delivery (e.g., in person, U.S. mail, email, or website). At the other end of the time continuum, Downs and Adrian (2004) suggest that three days are sufficient for surveys to be returned and that, in all cases, the time frame for returning surveys should not exceed one week. As indicated, although researchers disagree about the optimal time frame for survey completion, a time frame that ranges from three days to one month usually works well.

Depending on the size of the organization, you might decide to survey all employees (conduct a **census**), or select only a sample of employees to receive the questionnaire. With smaller organizations, it is recommended that you survey *all* employees. With larger organizations (e.g., 10,000+ employees), you can also choose to administer the survey to all employees, although, depending on the exact size of the organization, it could be time consuming and costly to do so. If proper sampling techniques are used, the data collected from a sample will be both reliable (consistent, stable, accurate) and valid (the survey measures what it is intended to measure). However, it is suggested that "where the survey effort is fully supported by senior management and part of

census An assessment that includes every employee of the organization.

the fabric of a much larger organization development and change initiative, a full-scale, all-employee census is probably preferred (Church & Waclawski, 2001, p. 121).

The task of distributing the survey to employees can take several forms, with each form having its respective strengths and weaknesses. First, you can have members of the organization distribute surveys to all employees. One of the most common methods of distribution involves giving the survey instrument to the managers of each division, who then distribute them individually to their subordinates or **direct reports**. Second, employees can gather in an **orchestrated group session** (Church & Waclawski, 2001) to complete the survey. An orchestrated group session involves gathering employees in a specific place to complete the necessary assessment instruments and then return to their jobs. Third, surveys can be distributed via mail and sent to employees' home addresses or be put in their office or workplace mailboxes. Finally, the survey can be posted online, using the organization's intranet or other data-gathering website (e.g., surveymonkey.com).

Response return rates tend to be enhanced via personal paper-and-pencil or optical scan administration, although electronic distribution via email, intranet, or Web page appeals greatly to a younger or more technologically savvy demographic that has grown up with and is more comfortable using these technologies. Recognize, however, that email responses can sometimes compromise anonymity and confidentiality because email programs leave a **trace point** from the respondent's computer (Church & Waclawski, 2001; Downs & Adrian, 2004). A trace point is a "fingerprint" that identifies the email sender. Although e-distribution methods for surveys are increasing in popularity, "the paper-and-pencil and optical scan methods of distribution are still used most frequently" (Church & Waclawski, 2001, p. 143).

Although organizational communication research analysts would like a 100 percent employee participation and response return rate, this percentage is almost impossible to achieve. Whereas a 50 percent response return rate is considered acceptable for data analysis, a 65–70 percent response return rate is considered "adequate" (Fink, 2009).

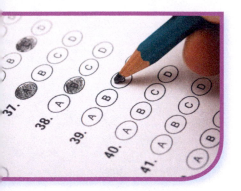

Step 5: Analyzing Survey Data

Depending on the type of data and the level of measurement you obtain, there are a number of analyses you can conduct to make sense of and interpret the data you have gathered. It is critical, however, that you do not lose sight of the ultimate purpose of the survey—to help the client understand employees' perceptions of the organization's communication effectiveness as well as what employees think of other aspects of the organization at that specific time and place.

Although a lesson on statistics is clearly beyond the scope of this chapter, we refer to a few statistical techniques you may already be familiar with from your coursework in statistics or communication research methods. If you need more background or a refresher in statistics, you can consult sources that will provide a foundation for such information (see Salkind, 2008). Data analysis involves taking all the raw data and summarizing and synthesizing it to provide a "picture" of the perceptions, attitudes, opinions, experiences, and suggestions of the respondents. Although the survey may yield some "statistically significant" findings, it is important to recognize that if the survey was well designed, even nonsignificant findings may be important to the organization. This is especially true as it relates to organizational change and development.

The organizational assessment survey team should provide some results to senior management about two to three weeks from the close of the data-gathering effort (Church & Waclawski, 2001). There is usually some lag time between providing results to senior management/organizational leadership and then to all the employees who provided the data (who tend to be at the nonexecutive levels of the organization). Keeping this reporting time lag as short as possible will go a long way toward affirming employees' favorable perceptions of your survey efforts as well as their belief that the findings will yield some concrete and positive impact on the important issues identified in the assessment. Such positive perceptions will aid in organizational efforts to change procedures and policies identified in the survey as well as employee participation in future surveys.

Data analysis is facilitated when the survey team uses optical scan forms for respondents' answers. Web-based response systems, in which respondent answers are automatically entered into a data file for analysis, are also efficient mechanisms for data analysis. Before submitting the data file for analysis, it is a good idea to go through a **data cleaning** process. The process of data cleaning consists of checking for and correcting problems such as missing data, duplicate responses from the same person, a **response set** (in which a respondent, for example, will provide a response of 3 for all items on the survey regardless of what the questions are asking), and incorrect use of scales (e.g., a person checking the divider of a scale, not the space, or providing a response of 8 on a scale that has a 1–5 response format) (Church & Waclawski, 2001).

Once data cleaning has been accomplished, you are ready to conduct data analyses. At a minimum, it is suggested that you conduct descriptive statistics on all the items on the survey. This involves obtaining a frequency distribution for all items (e.g., for Item 1, My supervisor treats me with respect, the number of people who responded with 5, 4, 3, 2, and 1), calculating percentages of those responses for each item, calculating measures of central tendency (mean, median, and mode) for items that have interval and/ or ratio level measurement, rank ordering the means by agreement for all items, and calculating measures of dispersion (range, standard deviation, and variance) for each item.

Where appropriate, you may want to conduct additional correlational analysis between key survey items to determine how two items relate to one another. For example, you might want to conduct a correlation on the data from the item "My supervisor provides me with sufficient information to allow me to do my job effectively," and the item "I am satisfied with my job." Although correlation does not prove causality, correlations provide additional insight on how certain organizational issues or perceptions relate to one another. In other words, the correlation between these two items in our example indicates that as perceptions of supervisor information-giving increases (as reported by subordinates), the more satisfied are the subordinates. This is not to say that giving subordinates the perception that they are receiving sufficient information causes them to be satisfied, just that the two (perceptions of receiving adequate information and satisfaction) are positively related.

You may want to conduct some type of statistical comparisons among groups. These analyses allow you to see if significant differences exist in survey ratings "by various groups, functions, areas, experiences, demographic information, or other categorizing variables that differentiate among types of people" (Church & Waclawski, 2001, pp. 186–187). Downs and Adrian (2004) suggest that some types of comparisons could involve different work units, gender, managers versus nonmanagers, length of time on the job, work status (e.g., full time versus part time), and job mobility (number of previous job titles held within the organization).

Finally, if you provided room for open-ended responses that allow respondents to provide their own comments (e.g., the ICA Communication Audit Questionnaire allows for this type of data collection), you need to content analyze these open-ended responses and identify any themes that emerge. For example, you may collect open-ended data in which many of the respondents indicate that more information needs to be provided by top management. Therefore, you may conclude that there is a "lack of information" theme emerging from the data.

Step 6: Presenting Survey Results and Findings

Thus far we have focused on several important steps involved in the organizational survey assessment process. We have discussed securing involvement in the survey process from key organizational members, discussed the development of appropriate reliable and valid survey items and questions, described communicating the purpose of the survey to employees, discussed how you can administer the survey to employees, and described how to analyze the data you have obtained. Step 6 in this process represents the culmination of those efforts—presenting the results and findings of the survey to organizational members. Indeed, this is the step that all organizational members should eagerly anticipate. Rather than being the end of the process, it is really the beginning, because the findings and results should help drive organizational enhancement and change efforts. Any intervention that is implemented is directly due to the results of your analysis.

Often called the **roll-out process** (Church & Waclawski, 2001), there are multiple audiences with whom you need to share the results and findings.

These include, but are not limited to, upper management, divisional or departmental middle-level management, and ultimately, all members of the organization.

When preparing the survey report, a hard copy of the entire document should be presented to senior and upper-level management. Of course, this hard copy can be supplemented with PowerPoint presentations, and if given permission by senior management, be posted on an intranet or other organizational Web pages.

Typically the report contains (1) a cover page; (2) an executive summary (a summary of the major findings identified in the data analysis); (3) a discussion of the methodology employed in conducting the survey (instrument development, survey administration procedures, sample selection process, if used); (4) comprehensive reporting on the results (means, frequencies, percentages, standard deviations for all closed-ended items, analysis of statistical comparisons between groups, functions, demographic information); (5) conclusions and recommendations; (6) an appendix that includes a copy of the actual survey instrument administered and a content analysis of the actual open-ended responses identifying the major themes or issues that emerged. When reporting the results of the survey, it is recommended that, in addition to statistics, a graphical representation of the data also be included, such as pie charts and bar charts.

Step 7: Using Survey Results to Guide Change and Improvement

As we discussed earlier in this chapter, one of the goals of organizational communication survey assessment efforts is to help an organization implement change and improve its communication effectiveness. As Church and Waclawski (2001) state, "Even if the survey construction, administration, communication, analysis, and delivery are conducted with the utmost competence, if the survey results are not absorbed and ultimately used by the organization members to make key decisions, the survey cannot be considered to have been maximally effective" (p. 231). This can mean several things, including presenting information to employees that suggests that, although they are generally satisfied with the communication procedures and practices, some change in the status quo is needed to increase overall levels of satisfaction.

In the preceding chapter we presented several options to help implement organizational development and change. We do not report those here. Rather, we recommend some strategies that can help move organizational leaders toward implementing change that emerged as a result of the communication assessment. You must recognize that the client or senior management who requested the organizational assessment may be apprehensive or skeptical about the findings. This can be especially true if some of the communication or morale problems were created by the client or senior management that arranged for the assessment in the first place. At the extreme, senior management might even challenge the findings of the survey or challenge your procedures or your sample. First, it is critical that you underscore to management that organizational change was a goal of the survey process right from the beginning of the assessment, if indeed it was. Second, to help with implementation of change, you should recommend the creation of organization-wide **ad hoc committees** (committees assembled to complete a specific task). These ad hoc committees should be charged with the task of developing or recommending specific organizational development programs (e.g., conflict resolution, decision making) for their own work teams and units based on the survey results that were specific to that work group, division, department, or unit.

The Issues of Reliability and Validity in Organizational Survey Research

Regardless of whether you use an existing survey or communication audit instrument in your organizational communication assessment (see the section in this chapter where we present examples) or develop your own survey instrument or measure, the issues of reliability and validity are sure to surface. It is critical that any survey instrument you distribute to employees be both reliable and valid. The information you gather from these surveys and instruments must be reliable and valid if you are to use the data to make meaningful changes to the organization, develop training programs, or alter the organizational structure. That is, using reliable and valid instruments or measures allows you to have confidence in the conclusions you derive from the findings (Davis, Gallardo, & Lachlan, 2010). Making organizational changes, developing training programs, or deciding to adopt a particular public relations campaign from data obtained from unreliable or invalid instruments is risky at best, and could be financially catastrophic at worst. In this section we answer the questions, What are *reliability* and *validity?* and "Why are they important in organizational survey research?

Reliability

Reliability refers to the stability, consistency, and accuracy of a measurement scale, test, or instrument (Infante, Rancer, & Avtgis, 2010). Reliability, in the case of surveys, assesses how well your scale, test, or measure produces the same results on repeated trials. You might identify with the concept of reliability a bit more if we provide a few examples outside of traditional organizational communication research.

The consistency, stability, and accuracy (i.e., reliability) of personal possessions and other nonpaper-and-pencil instruments are also critical. For example, would you consider your current automobile to be "reliable" or "unreliable?" Does your car start every time? Does it always transport you from one place to another? If so, you might consider your car to be reliable. If you get in your car and do not feel confident that it will start or will get you to where you want to go, then you would probably consider your car to be unreliable and in need of replacement. Over the last several years, reliability has been an important attribute for automobiles, especially when American-made cars are compared to cars from Japan and Europe. After decades of questionable reliability, and for first time in 24 years, American automobiles are frequently rated as equal to and even better in reliability than European automobiles (*USA Today,* 2004).

Reliability is also a major issue in health management. Individuals who have diabetes use a device called a *glucometer* as a measurement tool in the management of this disease. Most glucometers must be calibrated whenever a new set of test strips are introduced in order to obtain a stable and accurate reading of one's blood sugar levels. Obtaining a reliable measurement of one's blood sugar is of utmost importance for healthy functioning. That is, if the glucometer produces a reading that is unreliable, then a diabetic is at risk for either hypo- (too low) or hyperglycemia (too high). The ramifications of inaccurate and unreliable glucometer readings can produce disastrous consequences for a diabetic.

Have you ever received a speeding ticket? Quite a few of our students admit to this indiscretion. If you were ever pulled over for speeding, it is likely the police officer used a radar gun to clock your vehicle's speed. In most states, a police officer on "speed control" must calibrate the radar gun at several intervals during the day to demonstrate that the radar gun has produced reliable readings of automobile speed. Some students report that their speeding tickets have been nullified because they were able to prove in court that the reporting officer did not calibrate their radar instrument, thus challenging the reliability of the speed measurement, not the integrity of the officer. In this example, the successful challenge was to the measurement, not the person doing the measuring.

A final example illustrates the perils of not using reliable instruments in organizational communication research. Suppose your organization's public relations department wants to create greater awareness of the local United Way chapter. One outcome of this increased awareness might be greater donations. Your company has decided to hire an organizational research consultant to test the efficacy of a new PR campaign your organization is thinking about using to replace the existing campaign.

The creative team designs the new campaign, and a pilot study is conducted. The researcher administers an online questionnaire to determine the effectiveness in increasing both awareness and intentions to donate time and money to the local United Way chapter. After the data are collected, the consultant presents the findings. He suggests the findings reveal that the new PR campaign will be more effective than the one your organization currently uses. Based on these findings, an executive decision is made to adopt the new campaign. In adopting the new campaign, there are large initial costs in terms of printing and advertising, media, etc.

This QR code will direct you to the *Minnesota Council for Quality,* where you will learn more about organizational assessments as well as the benefits and processes associated with them.

http://www.councilforquality.org/assess.cfm

Several weeks later it is discovered that the questionnaire used had weak reliability, and that there really is no difference between PR Campaign A (the old one) and PR Campaign B (the new one) in influencing public opinion toward the United Way. You have just spent a great deal of time and money on a new campaign that was no better than the existing one. The lesson here is that using instruments, questionnaires, surveys, and tests without first assessing and ensuring their reliability (and validity) can yield data that lack confidence. Thus, recommendations and actions taken on the basis of that data may not be justified or helpful.

Thus, before you employ a scale, test, questionnaire, or some other measure to obtain data about the communication behavior of employees, it is critical that you establish the measure's reliability. Of course, if you use an existing instrument, the reliability of that scale, test, or measure most likely has already been established and you can likely use that scale with confidence. While a thorough discussion of reliability is beyond the scope of this introduction, this serves as an overview of an important concept that organizational communication professionals must be aware of.

Validity

Measurement validity with specific reference to surveys and tests asks the question as to whether the measurement instrument actually measures what it says it is measuring (Infante, Rancer, & Avtgis, 2010). As with reliability, a test, scale, or some other measure must possess **validity**. If the instrument you are using is designed to measure employee satisfaction with the amount of communication they receive within their organization, it must measure that concept and not something else, such as the quality of that communication. In this example, quantity and quality are two distinct properties of communication; the amount of versus the quality of.

In your preparation to attend college or graduate school, did you take one of the popular standardized tests such as the ACT, SAT, or GRE? Although these measures, according to the Educational Testing Service (ETS), serve as predictors of success at the next level of education (e.g., ACT and SAT for undergraduate studies and the GRE for success in graduate education), there is debate as to the validity of these tests. That is, exactly what are these standardized tests measuring? Some believe these tests measure intelligence, while others believe they measure how much you learned in your coursework in high school or college. Such questions and concerns reflect issues related to the validity of these measures.

Nicholas Lemann (1999), who studied the history of the SAT, argues that those students who think these standardized tests (ACT/SAT/GRE) measure intelligence may not be far off (http://www.pbs.org/wgbh/pages/frontline/shows/sats/interviews/lemann.html). Others feel the SAT/ACT may be a valid measure of vocabulary fluency (for the verbal component) and college algebra and geometry (for the quantitative portion) and not a valid measure of potential for success in college or graduate school, as it does not seem to measure things such as motivation, passion, and desire. Regardless of your opinions on this issue or even your own scores on such tests, obtaining a particular score on these standardized tests can impact opportunities that influence the rest of a person's life. So the validity of these standardized tests is an important issue for many students as many people claim their score on such tests greatly influenced their college decision-making process. Similar to what was expressed about reliability, this discussion of validity is meant as an introduction to tests, scales, and instruments used by the organizational communication professional.

This section is a brief introduction to the concepts of reliability and validity in terms of survey research use regarding traditional or well-established scales, tests, and instruments. Over years of use, many communication scales, tests, and measures are subject to reliability and validity challenges. This is done to ensure both the accuracy of measurement (reliability), and to ensure that the instrument is measuring what it was intended to measure (validity). Indeed, even a well-established instrument such as the International Communication Association (ICA) Communication Audit presented in this chapter has been examined and changes have been recommended to enhance reliability and validity (DeWine & James, 1988). Such challenges may be due in large part to societal changes and the way meanings of concepts evolve over time. Therefore, what was once defined as X is now defined as Y. For example, 30 years ago you may have found a work satisfaction scale that refers to "secretaries." In today's world, such a word and concept has evolved to include an abundance of related professions, which include "administrative assistant" or "administrative support personnel" among others.

Benefits of Conducting a Communication Audit

The term **communication audit** was first used by Odiorne (1954). The concept of a communication audit or organizational assessment is often likened to a visit to a doctor or an accountant. When you visit a doctor, the doctor often uses a number of instruments to get an assessment of your health. The physician using these tools is able to offer a diagnosis of the health of various systems of your body, such as your respiratory, digestive, endocrine, and reproductive systems. The concept of the audit has also been linked with the practice of diagnosing an organization's financial health. That is, an accountant or financial analyst often examines the organization's financial books to obtain a picture of the organization's financial condition. In both cases, however, these assessments have been said to have both diagnostic and prescriptive phases (Hargie & Tourish, 2000). In other words, here is the problem (diagnostic) and here is what must be done to fix it (prescription). A weather forecasting analogy has also been applied to communication audits because these audits "help managers recognize whether storms, earthquakes, or sunshine lies ahead" (Hargie & Tourish, 2000, p. 27).

communication audit
An assessment tool used to measure a variety of communication factors in the organization.

Goldhaber (1986) identified a number of benefits to conducting a formal communication audit: (1) comparing pre- and posttest data to assess a restructuring of the organization or the introduction of new hardware or software; (2) assessing the efficacy of new organizational development programs (see chapter 12 for a discussion of organizational development); (3) determining whether the structure of the organization needs reexamination; (4) developing communication training programs that may be developed to deal with problems identified in the audit; (5) determining how much structural or procedural change to implement in the organization; and (6) identifying formal and informal channels of communication used in the organization (pp. 400–401). In the following sections, we examine in detail several specific questions formal communication audits can answer.

Established Communication Assessment and Audit Tools

The International Communication Association (ICA) Communication Audit

When we discussed conducting an organizational communication assessment survey, we noted that the survey team has two choices in creating an instrument: You can create a new instrument or survey for the client organization, or you can use an existing reliable and valid instrument that has been developed and used by other organizations. One such instrument, which has been one of the most frequently used in the communication discipline since the late 1970s (DeWine, 1994), is the ICA Communication Audit Survey (Goldhaber & Rogers, 1979).

The ICA Communication Audit Survey contains 122 questions divided into eight components (DeWine, 1994; Downs & Adrian, 2004; Goldhaber & Rogers, 1979). The first component assesses the amount of **information received** (and that needs to be received) about key work-related topics. It includes items designed to assess information about individual performance, information needed to do one's job effectively, and information needed to keep informed about organizational matters. The second component assesses the amount of **information actually sent** (and that needs to be sent) about key work-related topics. It includes items that assess upward communication, including reports, complaints, and requests for additional information. The third component of the audit assesses the amount of **action or follow-up taken** (and that needs to be taken) on information sent to organizational members. This section measures how well subordinates, coworkers, supervisors, and management respond to messages. The fourth component measures the amount of information received (and desired) from **sources of information**. This section of the audit allows employees to indicate how much information they are receiving and would like to receive from specific sources, such as subordinates, coworkers, supervisors, and management, as well as from meetings, presentations, and the "grapevine." Downs and Adrian (2004) suggest that the data gathered from this section of the audit should be interpreted with some care. The data from this section provide "only general reactions to the sources. They do not, for example, tell the auditor specifically what information is needed but is not being passed on" (p. 130). In addition, they suggest the data gathered from this section must be compared by units or departments to make it meaningful. For example, if 50 out of 250 employees evaluate their immediate supervisor as low in communicating information, are those 50 employees spread out across several departments or are they clustered in only one or two departments? This knowledge is crucial in interpreting the data.

The fifth component of the audit assesses the **timeliness of information received** from key organizational sources. That is, the extent to which the information received from others (e.g., supervisors, coworkers, etc.) is received when they need it. Downs and Adrian (2004) suggest that if information is obtained too early, then information overload can result. If information is obtained too late, subordinates may not be able to perform their job as effectively as they would if the information were obtained earlier. The sixth component is one of the most important dimensions because it assesses perceptions of the **quality of organizational communication relationships** employees have with supervisors, management, coworkers, and the organization in general. Think about the jobs you have had in the past. What was the quality of the communication you had with your immediate supervisor? If it was satisfying, then you might have a favorable perception of the organization and your job. If it was not, then your satisfaction with the organization and your job may have been low. Downs and Adrian (2004) suggest that the employee-supervisor relationship is one of the most important determinants of an employee's commitment to the organization. Component seven assesses **satisfaction with organizational outcomes**. DeWine (1994) suggests that the 13 items in this part of the audit measure both the individual's personal efforts and achievement as well as organizational outcomes, whereas Downs and Adrian (2004) suggest that this section of the audit actually measures what has been called "communication climate." For example, if employees express significant dissatisfaction with their pay, upward mobility, and organizational recognition (these are all items assessed in this section), then their dissatisfaction may cause them to leave the organization.

Finally, the eighth component of the audit assesses the amount of information received (and that needs to be received) from **channels of communication**. These channels include internal media (video, film, slides), external media (TV, radio, newspapers), face-to-face communication, bulletin boards, telephone, and internal publications (newsletters, corporate magazines). Since the development of this section of the ICA audit, new technologies have evolved (intranet, organizational websites), and it is highly recommended that these new media be incorporated into this section of the audit instrument through the addition of items worded to reflect the new technologies. In addition, it is highly recommended that this list of channels be adapted to fit each organization assessed. That is, some organizations may rely heavily on websites, whereas others may rely more on email exchanges. Because of its historical importance, comprehensiveness, and extensive use, we have chosen to present the entire ICA survey in Table 13.1.

The ICA Communication Audit Survey established itself as a productive tool for assessing organizational communication, and it remains so today. It has been used in a plethora of organizations, such as banks, colleges, hospitals, manufacturing plants, airlines, retail organizations, governmental organizations, and the military. As with any measurement tool, in the years since its development, organizational communication researchers have suggested modifications and changes to the instrument (DeWine & James, 1988; Downs, Clampitt, & Laird, 1981; Greenbaum, DeWine, & Downs, 1987). However, it "still remains as one of the best sources of information about organizational relationships and the kind of information that moves throughout an organization" (DeWine, 1994, p. 197) and is used by organizational communication researchers and practitioners alike.

The ICA Communication Audit employs five data-gathering tools. In addition to the ICA Communication Audit Survey we have just presented, **interviews, network analysis, critical incident analysis,** and the **communication diary** are also valuable tools for auditing communication (Goldhaber & Rogers, 1979). The interview portion of the audit is conducted one-on-one with selected organizational members. It is used primarily so employees can substantiate and/or expand on the information gleaned from the audit instrument. Network analyses are used so employees can report on the frequency with which they communicate with members of their work unit, department, and other departments in the organization. The results of a network analysis allow us to place organizational members into the roles of isolate, liaison, or group member. We further describe the network analysis later in this chapter.

network analysis
A component of the ICA Communication Audit that has employees report on the frequency with which they communicate with members of their work unit, department, and other departments.

critical incident analysis
A component of the ICA Communication Audit that concerns asking employees to describe "critical" communication episodes that they feel are representative of successful and unsuccessful communication experiences they have had with members of the organization.

communication diary
A component of the ICA Communication Audit that concerns asking people to record certain communication activities for a one-week period.

TABLE 13.1	ICA Communication Audit Questionnaire

QUESTIONNAIRE SURVEY
by
The International Communication Association

Instructions

Please mark all your responses on the enclosed answer sheet. Please use the pencil supplied, as ink or hard lead pencils will not be recorded. Also, please carefully erase any stray pencil marks. Please answer all questions since each is important for possibly improving the operation of your organization. If there are any questions which do not apply to you, leave them blank. If there are questions which you do not understand, please ask us about them. We appreciate your patience for this important survey.

PLEASE MARK ONLY ONE RESPONSE TO EACH QUESTION

You may find the following definitions useful as you answer the questions on this survey:

[A client-specific glossary of key terms goes here if necessary.]

Receiving Information from Others

Instructions for Questions 1 through 26

You can receive information about various topics in your organization. For each topic listed on the following pages, mark your response on the answer sheet that best indicates: (1) the amount of information you *are* receiving on that topic and (2) the amount of information you *need* to receive on that topic, that is, the amount you *have to have* in order to do your job.

Topic Area		This is the amount of information I receive now						This is the amount of information I need to receive				
		Very Little	Little	Some	Great	Very Great		Very Little	Little	Some	Great	Very Great
How well I am doing in my job.	1.	1	2	3	4	5	2.	1	2	3	4	5
My job duties.	3.	1	2	3	4	5	4.	1	2	3	4	5
Organizational policies.	5.	1	2	3	4	5	6.	1	2	3	4	5
Pay and benefits.	7.	1	2	3	4	5	8.	1	2	3	4	5
How technological changes affect my job.	9.	1	2	3	4	5	10.	1	2	3	4	5
Mistakes and failures of my organization.	11.	1	2	3	4	5	12.	1	2	3	4	5
How I am being judged.	13.	1	2	3	4	5	14.	1	2	3	4	5
How my job-related problems are being handled.	15.	1	2	3	4	5	16.	1	2	3	4	5
How organization decisions are made that affect my job.	17.	1	2	3	4	5	18.	1	2	3	4	5
Promotion and advancement opportunities in my organization.	19.	1	2	3	4	5	20.	1	2	3	4	5
Important new product, service or program developments in my organization.	21.	1	2	3	4	5	22.	1	2	3	4	5
How my job relates to the total operation of my organization.	23.	1	2	3	4	5	24.	1	2	3	4	5
Specific problems faced by management.	25.	1	2	3	4	5	26.	1	2	3	4	5

Sending Information to Others

Instructions for Questions 27 through 40

In addition to receiving information, there are many topics on which you can send information to others. For each topic listed on the following pages, mark your response on the answer sheet that best indicates: (1) the amount of information you *are* sending on that topic and (2) the amount of information you *need* to send on that topic in order to do your job

		This is the amount of information I send now						*This is the amount of information I need to send now*				
Topic Area		Very Little	Little	Some	Great	Very Great		Very Little	Little	Some	Great	Very Great
Reporting what I am doing in my job	27.	1	2	3	4	5	28.	1	2	3	4	5
Reporting what I think my job requires me to do	29.	1	2	3	4	5	30.	1	2	3	4	5
Reporting job-related problems	31.	1	2	3	4	5	32.	1	2	3	4	5
Complaining about my job and/or working conditions	33.	1	2	3	4	5	34.	1	2	3	4	5
Requesting information necessary to do my job	35.	1	2	3	4	5	36.	1	2	3	4	5
Evaluating the performance of my immediate supervisor	37.	1	2	3	4	5	38.	1	2	3	4	5
Asking for clearer work instructions	39.	1	2	3	4	5	40.	1	2	3	4	5

Follow-up on Information Sent

Instructions for Questions 41 through 50

Indicate the amount of *action* or *follow-up* that *is* and *needs* to be taken on information you send to the following:

		This is the amount of follow-up now						*This is the amount of follow-up needed*				
Topic Area		Very Little	Little	Some	Great	Very Great		Very Little	Little	Some	Great	Very Great
Subordinates	41.	1	2	3	4	5	42.	1	2	3	4	5
Co-workers	43.	1	2	3	4	5	44.	1	2	3	4	5
Immediate supervisor	45.	1	2	3	4	5	46.	1	2	3	4	5
Middle Management	47.	1	2	3	4	5	48.	1	2	3	4	5
Top Management	49.	1	2	3	4	5	50.	1	2	3	4	5

Sources of Information

Instructions for Questions 51 through 68

You *not only* receive various kinds of information, but can receive such information from *various sources* within the organization. For each source listed below, mark your response on the answer sheet that best indicates: (1) the amount of information you *are* receiving from that source and (2) the amount of information you *need* to receive from that source in order to do your job.

Sources of Information		This is the amount of information I receive now						This is the amount of information I need to receive				
		Very Little	Little	Some	Great	Very Great		Very Little	Little	Some	Great	Very Great
Subordinates (if applicable)	51.	1	2	3	4	5	52.	1	2	3	4	5
Co-workers in my own unit or department	53.	1	2	3	4	5	54.	1	2	3	4	5
Individuals in *other* units, department in my organization	55.	1	2	3	4	5	56.	1	2	3	4	5
Immediate supervisor	57.	1	2	3	4	5	58.	1	2	3	4	5
Department meetings	59.	1	2	3	4	5	60.	1	2	3	4	5
Middle Management	61.	1	2	3	4	5	62.	1	2	3	4	5
Formal management presentations	63.	1	2	3	4	5	64.	1	2	3	4	5
Top management	65.	1	2	3	4	5	66.	1	2	3	4	5
The "grapevine"	67.	1	2	3	4	5	68.	1	2	3	4	5

Timeliness of Information Received from Key Sources

Instructions for Questions 69 to 74

indicate the extent to which information from the following sources is usually *timely* (you get information when you need it—not too early, not too late).

		Very Little	Little	Some	Great	Very Great
Subordinates (if applicable)	69.	1	2	3	4	5
Co-workers	70.	1	2	3	4	5
Immediate supervisor	71.	1	2	3	4	5
Middle Management	72.	1	2	3	4	5
Top Management	73.	1	2	3	4	5
"Grapevine"	74.	1	2	3	4	5

Organizational Communication Relationships

Instructions for Questions 75 through 93

A variety of communicative relationships exist in organizations like your own. Employees exchange messages regularly with supervisors, subordinates, co-workers, etc. Considering your relationships with others in your organization, please mark your response on the answer sheet which best describes the relationship in question.

Relationship		Very Little	Little	Some	Great	Very Great
I trust my co-workers	75.	1	2	3	4	5
My co-workers get along with each other	76.	1	2	3	4	5
My relationship with my co-workers is satisfying	77.	1	2	3	4	5
I trust my immediate supervisor	78.	1	2	3	4	5
My immediate supervisor is honest with me	79.	1	2	3	4	5
My immediate supervisor listens to me	80.	1	2	3	4	5
I am free to disagree with my immediate supervisor	81.	1	2	3	4	5
I can tell my immediate supervisor when things are going wrong	82.	1	2	3	4	5
My immediate supervisor praises me for a good job	83.	1	2	3	4	5
My immediate supervisor is friendly with his/her subordinates	84.	1	2	3	4	5
My immediate supervisor understands my job needs	85.	1	2	3	4	5
My relationship with my immediate supervisor is satisfying	86.	1	2	3	4	5
I trust top management	87.	1	2	3	4	5
Top management is sincere in their efforts to communicate with employees	88.	1	2	3	4	5
My relationship with top management is satisfying	89.	1	2	3	4	5
My organization encourages differences of opinion	90.	1	2	3	4	5
I have a say in decisions that affect my job	91.	1	2	3	4	5
I influence operations in my unit or department	92.	1	2	3	4	5
I have a part in accomplishing my organization's goals	93.	1	2	3	4	5

Organizational Outcomes

Instructions for Questions 94 through 106

One of the most important "outcomes" of working in an organization is the *satisfaction* one receives or fails to receive through working there. Such "satisfaction" can relate to the job, one's co-workers, supervisor, or the organization as a whole. Please mark your response on the answer sheet which best indicates the extent to which you are *satisfied* with:

Outcome		Very Little	Little	Some	Great	Very Great
My job	94.	1	2	3	4	5
My pay	95.	1	2	3	4	5
My progress in my organization up to this point in time	96.	1	2	3	4	5
My chances for getting ahead in my organization	97.	1	2	3	4	5
My opportunity to "make a difference"—to contribute to the overall success of my organization	98.	1	2	3	4	5
My organization's system for recognizing and rewarding outstanding performance	99.	1	2	3	4	5
My organization's concern for its members' welfare	100.	1	2	3	4	5
My organization's overall communicative efforts	101.	1	2	3	4	5
Working in my organization	102.	1	2	3	4	5
My organization, as compared to other such organizations	103.	1	2	3	4	5
My organization's overall efficiency of operation	104.	1	2	3	4	5
The overall quality of my organization's product or service	105.	1	2	3	4	5
My organization's achievement of its goals and objectives	106.	1	2	3	4	5

Channels of Communication

Instructions for Questions 107 through 122

The following questions list a variety of channels through which information is transmitted to employees. Please mark your response on the answer sheet which best indicates: (1) the amount of information you *are* receiving through that channel and (2) the amount of information you *need* to receive through that channel.

Channel		This is the amount of information I receive now						This is the amount of information I need to receive				
		Very Little	Little	Some	Great	Very Great		Very Little	Little	Some	Great	Very Great
Face-to-face contact between two people	107.	1	2	3	4	5	108.	1	2	3	4	5
Face-to-face contact among more than two people	109.	1	2	3	4	5	110.	1	2	3	4	5
Telephone	111.	1	2	3	4	5	112.	1	2	3	4	5
Written (memos, letters)	113.	1	2	3	4	5	114.	1	2	3	4	5
Bulletin Boards	115.	1	2	3	4	5	116.	1	2	3	4	5
Internal Publications (newsletter, magazine)	117.	1	2	3	4	5	118.	1	2	3	4	5
Internal Audio-Visual Media (Videotape, Films, Slides)	119.	1	2	3	4	5	120.	1	2	3	4	5
External Media (TV, Radio, Newspapers)	121.	1	2	3	4	5	122.	1	2	3	4	5

Background Information

This section is for statistical purposes only and will be used to study how different groups of people view your organization. We do not want your name, but would appreciate the following information.

123. How do you receive most of your income from this organization?

   1. Salaried
   2. Hourly
   3. Piece work
   4. Commission
   5. Other

124. What is your sex?

   1. Male
   2. Female

125. Do you work:

   1. Fulltime
   2. Parttime
   3. Temporary Fulltime
   4. Temporary Parttime

126. How long have you worked in this organization?

    1. Less than 1 year

    2. 1 to 5 years

    3. 6 to 10 years

    4. 11 to 15 years

    5. More than 15 years

127. How long have you held your present position?

    1. Less than 1 year

    2. 1 to 5 years

    3. 6 to 10 years

    4. 11 to 15 years

    5. More than 15 years

128. What is your position in this organization?

    1. I don't supervise anybody

    2. First-line supervisor

    3. Middle management

    4. Top management

    5. Other (Please specify:_____)

129. What was the *last* level you completed in school?

    1. Less than high school graduate

    2. High school graduate

    3. Some college or technical school

    4. Completed college or technical school

    5. Graduate work

130. What is your age?

    1. Under 20 years of age

    2. 21 to 30 years of age

    3. 31 to 40 years of age

    4. 41 to 50 years of age

    5. Over 50 years of age

131. How much training to improve your communicative skills have you had?

    1. No training at all

    2. Little training (attended *1* seminar, workshop, training activity or course)

    3. Some training (attended a few seminars, workshops, training activities, or courses)

    4. Extensive training (attended a great number of seminars, workshops, training activities, or courses)

132. How much money did you receive from this organization last year?

    1. Less than $9,000

    2. $9,000 to $11,999

    3. $12,000 to $17,999

    4. $18,000 to $25,000

    5. Over $25,000

133. During the past ten years, in how many other organizations have you been employed?

    1. No other organizations

    2. One other organization

    3. Two other organizations

    4. Three other organizations

    5. More than three others

134. Are you presently looking for a job in a different organization?

    _____ Yes

    _____ No

(from: Goldhaber, G.M., & Rogers, D.P. (1979). *Auditing Organizational Communication Systems: The ICA Communication Audit* (pp. 35–53). Dubuque, IA: Kendall Hunt Publishing Company. Used with permission).

The critical incident component asks employees to describe "critical" communication episodes that they feel are representative of successful or unsuccessful communication experiences they have had with members of the organization. In this technique, employees are asked to report on their concrete behavior that culminated in a successful or unsuccessful communication experience. In the communication diary, participants are asked to keep a diary of certain communication activities (e.g., conversations with organizational members, phone calls, emails, meetings) for a one-week period. The data from these diaries are then analyzed, and these data provide "indications of actual communication behavior among individuals, groups and the entire organization" (Goldhaber & Rogers, 1979, p. 10).

The Downs-Hazen Communication Satisfaction Questionnaire

Research suggests a strong positive relationship between communication satisfaction and job satisfaction (Pettit, Goris, & Vaught, 1997). Communication satisfaction, as experienced in the organizational context, comprises a number of factors, including the amount of information employees receive, the overall climate of the organization, the receptivity of upward communication, and how frequently employees interact with each other (Zwijze-Koning & deJong, 2007).

The **Communication Satisfaction Questionnaire** (CSQ) (Downs & Hazen, 1977) was developed as another communication audit tool that can be used instead of or in addition to the ICA Communication Audit Survey. (Cal W. Downs was a member of the development team of the ICA Communication Audit Survey.) The CSQ consists of a 40-item instrument that measures eight dimensions of satisfaction with communication, information, relationships, channels of communication, and organizational climate. It is a Likert-type scale that employs a 1–7 response format, ranging from 1–Very Dissatisfied to 7–Very Satisfied.

The first dimension, **satisfaction with communication climate**, assesses whether the organization motivates employees to meet organizational goals, whether the organization encourages employees to identify with the organization, the degree of employee perception of communication competence, and the degree to which information flow helps employees perform their jobs. The second dimension assesses **satisfaction with communication with supervisors**. Items assess upward and downward communication with superiors, and subordinates' perceptions of how open their supervisors are to their ideas. **Satisfaction with organizational integration** is the third dimension and assesses the degree to which employees receive information about their work environment and information about organizational policies and benefits. Dimension 4, **satisfaction with media quality** assesses employees' perceptions of organizational communication channels (e.g., meetings, written directives) and their reactions to them. **Satisfaction with horizontal and informal communication** (dimension 5) assesses perceptions of organizational information networks and includes perceptions of the "grapevine." It gauges the accuracy of the information on these networks. **Satisfaction with organizational perspective** (dimension 6) assesses how well informed employees feel about organizational change and information about the organization's mission and financial standing. Dimension 7 assesses **satisfaction with communication with subordinates**. This set of items is only completed by those in supervisory or management roles. It measures how receptive subordinates are to downward communication and how willing they are to provide upward communication. The final dimension is **satisfaction with personal feedback**, which is also completed only by managers and assesses the extent to which supervisors feel their subordinates are receptive to evaluation, suggestions, and criticism. Three additional items are included on the CSQ, one that measures employees' overall level of job satisfaction, one that asks whether employees' satisfaction has changed within the last six months, and open-ended items that ask employees to indicate what things they believe need to be changed about the communication in their organization and, if changed, would improve their satisfaction (Downs, 1994).

The CSQ has been subjected to much empirical scrutiny over the years, and this scrutiny has resulted in support for both the reliability and validity of the measure (Gray & Laidlaw, 2004; Zwijze-Koning & deJong, 2007). It is an effective tool to use in assessing communication satisfaction and the "role

Communication Satisfaction Questionnaire Assesses dimensions of satisfaction. These include communication, information, relationships, channels of communication, and organizational climate.

of communication and its relationship to key dependent variables such as job satisfaction, productivity, organizational commitment, trust, and overall organizational performance" (Gray & Laidlaw, 2004, p. 444).

Organizational Identification and Organizational Commitment

Two concepts that have engendered a great deal of interest and scholarship in organizational communication over the past several decades are organizational identification and organizational commitment. These concepts have been found to be of great importance regarding how employees feel about their organization. In this section we define the two concepts and present the most frequently used measurement scales designed to measure these most important organizational factors.

Organizational Identification

Organizational identification A feeling of attachment, belonging, and pride in being an organizational member; a perception that the employee and organization are similar in values and goals.

The concept of organizational identification was introduced several decades ago from the disciplines of Management, Organizational Behavior, and Industrial and Organizational Psychology. However, organizational identification received traction and widespread interest in the communication discipline when it was reconceptualized, and a systematic program of research was developed by Cheney (1982, 1983) and Tompkins and Cheney (1983). **Organizational identification** is conceptualized as a feeling of attachment, belonging, and pride in being an organizational member, loyalty to the organization, and a perception that the employee and the organization are similar in terms of shared values and goals (Gautam, Dick, & Wagner, 2004). That is, when employees possess "organizational identification" they identify with their organization and behave and communicate in a manner consistent with the organization's perspective. It can also be thought of as "a process of internal and external persuasion by which the interests of an individual merge with the interests of an organization, resulting in the creation of identifications based on those interests" (Johnson, Johnson, & Heimberg, 1999, p. 160). Because organizational identification is seen as a social, rhetorical, and discursive process (see Cheney & Tompkins, 1987), communication scholars view identification as a process whereby employees actively create, recreate, and ultimately adopt an organizational identity congruous with their personal identity (Liberman, 2011). It occurs when one's individual identity and the organizational identity mutually and positively coincide or overlap (Liberman, 2011).

From Cheney's communicative perspective, organizational identification can be seen as both a *process* (organizational members actively and socially identify through interaction and communication) and a *product* (identification is the result of a need for affiliation, sense-making, and organizational membership). An employee who identifies with an organization is more

TABLE 13.2   The Organizational Identification Questionnaire

Response format: 7 = Very strong agreement; 6 = Strong agreement; 5 = Agreement; 4 = Neither agreement nor disagreement; 3 = Disagreement; 2 = Strong disagreement; 1 = Very strong disagreement.

1. I would probably continue working for this organization even if I did not need the money.
2. In general, the people employed by this organization are working toward the same goals.
3. I am proud to be an employee of this organization.
4. This organization's image in the community represents me well.
5. I often describe myself to others by saying "I work for this organization" or "I am from this organization."
6. I try to make on-the-job decisions by considering the consequences of my actions for this organization.
7. We at this organization are different from others in our field.
8. I am glad I chose to work for this organization rather than another company.
9. I talk up this organization to my friends as a great company to work for.
10. In general, I view this organization's problems as my problems.
11. I am willing to put in a great deal of effort beyond that normally expected to help this organization to be successful.
12. I become irritated when I hear others outside of this organization criticize the company.
13. I have warm feelings toward this organization as a place to work.
14. I would be willing to spend the rest of my career with this organization.
15. I feel that this organization cares about me.
16. The record of this organization is an example of what dedicated people can achieve.
17. I have a lot in common with others employed by this organization.
18. I find it difficult to agree with this organization's policies on important matters relating to me. (*Recode*)*
19. My association with this organization is only a small part of who I am. (*Recode*)*
20. I tell others about projects that this organization is working on.
21. I find that my values and the values of this organization are very similar.
22. I feel very little loyalty to this organization. (*Recode*)*
23. I would describe this organization as a large "family" in which most members feel a sense of belonging.
24. I find it easy to identify myself with this organization.
25. I really care about the fate of this organization.

Note: The higher the score, the greater the organizational identification.

*Items 18, 19, and 22 need to be recoded before you can compute your score on this questionnaire. That is, if you responded to these items with a "7", you must now give yourself a score of "1". If you responded to these items with a score of "6", you must now give yourself a score of "2". If you responded to these items with a score of "5", you must now give yourself a score of "3". If you responded to these items with a score of "4", leave the score as a "4". If you responded to these items with a score of "3", you must now give yourself a score of "5". If you responded to these items with a score of "2", you must now give yourself a score of "6". And finally, if you responded to these items with a score of "1", you must now give yourself a score of "7".

Source: From *Communication Monographs*, Vol. 50, No. 4, December 1983 by George Cheney. Reprinted by permission of Taylor & Francis, via Copyright Clearance Center.

likely to be receptive to influence attempts by members of that organization. Cheney (1983) adds that organizational identification also affects employee attitudes toward the organization. Certain processes assist an employee in the organizational identification process, including being socialized and assimilated into the organization, participating in, and active involvement with organizational decision-making processes.

Why is Organizational Identification important? Research has revealed a number of positive outcomes associated with organizational identification, including greater organizational effectiveness, higher employee motivation, more employee satisfaction, and greater organizational commitment (see the next section for a treatment of organizational commitment).

In developing a scale to measure the concept of organizational identification, Cheney developed items from other instruments used to assess both organizational identification and commitment. Because of this, the OIQ (Organizational Identification Questionnaire) has some overlap with scales that measure organizational commitment (e.g., the Organizational Commitment Questionnaire, Allen & Meyer, 1990), although the concepts of identification and commitment are suggested to be both theoretically and empirically distinct (Gautam et al., 2004).

The OIQ was developed to measure this concept of organizational identification (Cheney, 1982, 1983). It consists of 25 items measuring three "components" of organizational identification: *membership* (feelings of attachment to an organization), *loyalty* (being loyal to the organization), and *similarity* (similarity between employee and the organization in terms of shared characteristics, values, and goals). However, Cheney (1982, 1983) conceptualized Organizational Identification to consist of one dimension (so that respondents receive only one score on the scale), and this assumption has been supported by more recent research (Miller, Allen, Casey, & Johnson, 2000). Table 13.2 presents the OIQ.

Organizational Commitment

organizational commitment
An overall physical, emotional, and/or psychological attachment to an organization.

A concept closely related to, but clearly different from, organizational identification is **organizational commitment**. As with identification, organizational commitment emerged from the disciplines of Organizational Behavior and Industrial/Organizational Psychology and has been defined and interpreted in several ways over the past several decades. It was initially defined as "[a] strong belief in and acceptance of the organization's goals and values, a willingness to exert considerable effort on behalf of the organization, and a strong desire to maintain membership in the organization (Mowday, Porter, & Steers, 1982, p. 27). More recently, commitment has been conceptualized as "one's physical, psychological, and/or emotional attachment to an organization" (Liberman, 2008, p. 3). The more an employee is committed to his or her organization, the more he or she feels either a real, perceived, or assumed level of attachment to the organization.

Why is organizational commitment important? Multidisciplinary research has suggested that the greater the organizational commitment an employee feels toward his or her organization, the less likely an employee will arrive to work late, have lower rates of absenteeism, be less likely leave or quit the organization, report greater job satisfaction, receive more favorable job performance evaluations, and most important from a communication perspective, report better quality and greater amount of communication between and among other employees (Liberman, 2008, p. 7).

Two industrial and organizational psychologists, John Meyer and Natalie Allen, are recognized as leading scholars and researchers in this area of commitment. Their scale, the Organizational Commitment Questionnaire (OCQ), is considered the most frequently used instrument to measure this concept of organizational commitment. As a multidimensional concept, the questionnaire allows researchers to determine whether, and to what extent, an individual is committed to the organization. It measures three types of organizational commitment: affective, continuance, and normative.

Affective commitment is seen as an employee's emotional attachment, identification, and involvement in the organization. Affective commitment represents an employee's emotional commitment to the organization ("I want to be a committed employee because it will make me more content"). Employees with affective commitment stay with the organization "because they want to do so" (Meyer & Allen, 1991, p. 67). **Continuance commitment** represents an employee's awareness of the costs associated with leaving the organization (I want to be a committed employee because I fear what will happen if I am not). Employees with continuance commitment stay with the organization "because they need to do so" (Meyer & Allen, 1991, p. 67). **Normative commitment** is based on a feeling of obligation to continue working for the organization due, in large part, to perceived pressure from others in their social and personal environment (I want to be a committed employee because social others tell me that I must and I don't want to let them down). Employees with normative commitment stay with the organization because they feel "that they ought to" (Meyer & Allen, 1991, p. 67). Table 13.3 presents the Organizational Commitment Questionnaire.

It can be argued that the foundation of both organizational identification and organizational commitment is communication. As Cheney and Tompkins (1987) state, "The approach is language-centered in its terminological focus and its reliance on Burkean theory (Burke, *A Rhetoric of Motives*) to help explain identification and commitment" (p. 1). Kenneth Burke was a philosopher and rhetorical theorist. In his influential work, *A Rhetoric of Motives* (1969), he argued that for persuasion to occur, an individual must "identify" with the target of the persuasive effort. The Burkean concept of identification was broadened to include the notion of "belonging" to a group, such as a family, profession, or organization (Cheney, 1983, p. 347). The work of Burke, especially his concept of identification, has received much attention in the communication discipline. This concept has been modified and

TABLE 13.3	The Organizational Commitment Questionnaire (OCQ)

Response format: 7 = Strongly agree; 6 = Agree; 5 = Slightly agree; 4 = Neither agree nor disagree; 3 = Slightly disagree; 2 = Disagree; 1 = Strongly disagree

1. It would be very hard for me to leave my organization right now, even if I wanted to.

2. I do not feel any obligation to remain with my current employer. (*Recode*)*

3. I would be very happy to spend the rest of my career with this organization.

4. One of the few negative consequences of leaving this department would be the scarcity of available alternatives.

5. Even if it were to my advantage, I do not feel it would be right to leave my organization now.

6. I really feel as if this organization's problems are my own.

7. Right now, staying with my organization is a matter of necessity as much as desire.

8. I do not feel a strong sense of "belonging" to my organization. (*Recode*)*

9. I believe that I have too few options to consider leaving this organization.

10. I do not feel "emotionally attached" to this organization. (*Recode*)*

11. I would feel guilty if I left my organization now.

12. I do not feel like "part of the family" at my organization. (*Recode*)*

13. This organization deserves my loyalty.

14. If I had not already put of much of myself into this organization, I might consider working elsewhere.

15. I would not leave my organization right now because I have a sense of obligation to the people in it.

16. This organization has a great deal of personal meaning for me.

17. Too much of my life would be disrupted if I decided I wanted to leave my organization now.

18. I owe a great deal to my organization.

Legend:

AC = Affective Commitment Scale Items (6 items – 3, 6, 8, 10, 12, 16)

NCR = Normative Commitment Scale Items (Revised) (6 items – 2, 5, 11, 13, 15, 18)

CC = Continuance Commitment Scale Items (6 items – 1, 4, 7, 9, 14, 17)

Note: The higher the score, the greater the organizational commitment

*Items 2, 8, 10, and 12 need to be recoded before you can compute your score on this questionnaire. That is, if you responded to these items with a "7", you must now give yourself a score of "1". If you responded to these items with a score of "6", you must now give yourself a score of "2". If you responded to these items with a score of "5", you must now give yourself a score of "3". If you responded to these items with a score of "4", leave the score as a "4". If you responded to these items with a score of "3", you must now give yourself a score of "5". If you responded to these items with a score of "2", you must now give yourself a score of "6". And finally, if you responded to these items with a score of "1", you must now give yourself a score of "7".

Source: From *Journal of Occupational and Organizational Psychology,* March 1990 by Natalie Allen & John Meyer. Reprinted by permission of John Wiley & Sons, via Copyright Clearance Center.

FIGURE 13.2

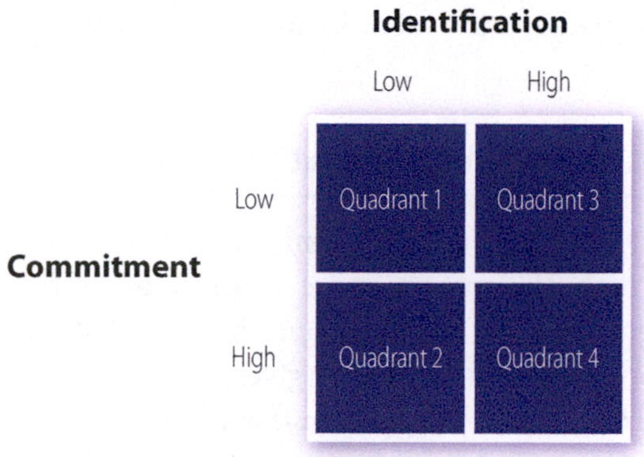

Identification

	Low	High
Low	Quadrant 1	Quadrant 3
High	Quadrant 2	Quadrant 4

Commitment

Adapted from: Cheney & Tompkins (1987).

applied to the study of organizations by Cheney and Tompkins who state that both the process and product of organizational identification are expressed through language.

Cheney and Tompkins offer a matrix containing four quadrants combining both of these organizational concepts:

Quadrant 1 represents those organizational members who have low identification and low commitment; *Quadrant 2* represents those members who have low identification and high commitment; *Quadrant 3* represents those members who have high identification and low commitment; and *Quadrant 4* represents those organizational members who have high identification and high commitment.

Think about the jobs you have had and the organizations you have worked with in the past. Perhaps you can place yourself into one of these quadrants for each of those jobs and organizations. One could argue that the most productive, satisfying, and least dissonance-producing combination of identification and commitment resides in Quadrant 4, in an employment situation where you had high organizational identification and high organizational commitment. Research has revealed the benefits of organizational identification and commitment, including greater well-being, job satisfaction, and productivity. Gautam et al. (2004) suggest that managers can engender organizational identification by "implementing programs that strengthen feelings of corporate identity and that create a positive image of the organization as a whole" (p. 312).

Organizational commitment can be enhanced by organizations taking certain measures. For example, positive relationships have been found between perceived fairness of organizational policies (e.g., drug testing) and affective commitment. The manner in which an organization communicates its policies and procedures can promote greater affective commitment. Organizational commitment has been associated with the degree of autonomy an employee has on their job, how challenging their job is perceived, how much their manager allows them to participate in decision making, how fairly they are treated, and how much support they receive from their supervisor

(Meyer & Allen, 1997). These antecedents to organizational commitment suggest the importance of developing training programs (see Chapter 11) that are designed to enhance superior-subordinate communication.

Communication Network Analysis

communication networks
Reflects the roles individuals occupy in a communication network. These roles are communication patterns that connect each member of the organization to the flow of communication in the network.

Messages are exchanged by organizational members through **communication networks**. These networks may comprise a minimum of two people or can involve every member of the organization. The roles that individuals occupy in a communication network have been given labels. These labels, or roles, are defined by the communication pattern that connects each member of the organization to the flow of communication in the network (Goldhaber, 1986). A **group** is defined as three or more individuals who exchange communication messages primarily with each other. **Bridges** are defined as group members who interact with members of other groups. **Liaisons** interact mainly with members of two or more groups but themselves are not members of any one group. **Stars** are individuals who occupy a central role in the organization's communication network. Finally, individuals who have no, or relatively few, links to others in the organization are called **isolates**.

What exactly is a communication network? Rogers (1995) defined a communication network as "interconnected individuals who are linked by patterned flows of information" (p. 308). What makes a network analysis so interesting and important to the organization is that it shows who is really communicating with whom, and who gets information from whom, despite or in addition to what might be specified on the formal "organizational chart." As Goldhaber and Rogers (1979) state, "One thing is to describe a person's attitude toward receiving information. But an infinitely more complete picture appears when we know who the information came from and how each person passes it to others" (p. 164).

TABLE 13.4	ICA Network Analysis

Network Analysis

As part of our study we would like you to complete this communication flow form. Although people's names are included here, *your individual responses will not be made available to anyone in the organization.* The purpose of this part of the audit is to quickly and efficiently assess the abilily of the communication network to provide people with the information they need to do their job effectively and happily.

As you complete this form we want you to think about the people you usually communicate with in a typical work day. This includes face-to-face interaction, telephone calls, and written memos.

You will notice that we have asked about two different channels of communication. In the first, we want you to think of the times you communicate (sending and receiving) about work related matters through the *formal organizational structure* (e.g., committee or staff meetings, memos, official notices oral or written, business communications).

In the second question, we want you to think of the times you communicate through the *informal (grapevine) structure* (e.g., chance conservations, spontaneous meetings, personal notes and phone calls).

To fill in the form, you should:

1. Find your name in the list and circle it.

2. Write the I.D. number found to the right of your name below:

   _____

3. Scan down the list of names until you locate a person with whom you usually communicate in a typical work day.

4. Decide whether each communication is part of either the formal or informal structure.

5. Write the number of communications that typically take place, in the space beside the appropriate heading (formal and / or informal).

6. For the person with whom you typically communicate, decide how important these communications *usually* are to you. Next to the number of communications, for either or both of the channels you have chosen, circle:

   "1" If the communications are usually *not at all important*

   "2" If they are *somewhat important*

   "3" If they are *fairly important*

   "4" If they are *very important*

   "5" If they are *extremely important*

7. Continue this process for each person on the questionnaire for which you feel that you communicate each day.

Example

During the typical work day I usually communicate about work related matters with the following people through the:

	I.D.	Formal Organizational Structure	Informal Organizational Structure
Jones, Charles, clerk	2056	—2— 1 2 3 4 ⑤	——1 2 3 4 5
Smith, Harry, manager	2057	—5—1 2 ③ 4 5	—2—1 ② 3 4 5

In this example, the person filling out the form indicated that he or she communicated two times a day with Charles Jones in business meetings or through official memos and these are extremely important to him or her. In another example, the respondent indicated that he or she typically communicated with Harry Smith about 5 times a day using formal channels and about twice a day using informal channels. In the first case interactions were usually fairly important and in the second case only somewhat important.

Notice the last page of this form contains some blank spaces for other personnel whose names were not included in this form. If you communicate with others whose names are not on this list, please print their names, work location, and the number of formal and informal communications you usually have with them in a typical work day. Also, circle the importance of each of these interactions just as before.

Thank you for your cooperation.

(from: Goldhaber, G.M., & Rogers, D. P. (1979). *Auditing Organizational Communication Systems: The ICA Communication Audit* (pp. 166-167). (Dubuque, IA: Kendall Hunt Publishing Company. Used with permission).

Everyone in an organization has a personal network (a flow of information and communication from one person to another). Hence, everyone's personal network is connected to others' personal networks, which creates the "actual" flow of communication and information among members of the organization. This is precisely why communication auditors conduct network analyses—to uncover the "real" or "actual" flow of communication and information among and between organizational members.

A few components of the ICA Communication Audit Survey discussed earlier can identify some of the communication flow among organizational members. However, only a dedicated communication network analysis can "(1) identify where information flow is blocked or overloading a communication network; (2) identify who is blocking or overloading the flow of information; (3) construct new structures to reduce information blocks or overloads" (Downs & Adrian, 2004, p. 193).

The ICA Communication Audit Survey instrument contains a dedicated network analysis component (see Table 13.4). The primary goals of this component are to identify the flow of information in a given organization, compare the "actual" communication networks with the formal networks identified by the organizational chart, and compare the roles of organizational liaisons, groups, and isolates identified by the analysis with the roles these individuals are expected to occupy based on their job descriptions or their place on the organizational chart. This is done to help the organization manage information flow more effectively (Goldhaber, 1986; Goldhaber & Rogers, 1979).

Although conducting a network analysis in a small organization can be accomplished by simple data analysis (by making charts of who communicates with whom), conducting a network analysis in a larger organization is virtually impossible without the use of sophisticated data-analysis computer software packages such as NEGOPY (Lesniak, Yates, Goldhaber, & Richards, 1977; Richards, 1975) and UCINET (Borgatti, Everett, & Freeman, 1995; see www.analytictech.com). Fortunately, the ICA Communication Audit Survey contains an instrument designed to help gather data for a network analysis.

Once you gather the data, arrange them according to the requirements of the particular software program you are using and submit the data for analysis. Then you are ready to interpret the output. A comprehensive discussion of interpreting network analysis output is beyond the scope of this chapter, because it depends on the software program you are using and the type of output provided. However, regardless of the program used, the analyses should provide you with a comparison of the *actual* networks identified versus the networks you expected to find, given the organizational chart, identification of organizational members and the groups they belong to, identification of any liaisons and isolates within the organization, and comparison of the actual versus expected network roles. This information, combined with the data gathered from the use of the other ICA Communication Audit Survey components, should provide you with a comprehensive picture of the communication in that organization.

Summary

Research has demonstrated that effective communication positively affects a wide range of employee perceptions and behaviors, including job satisfaction and productivity. How does an organization know if its communication processes and procedures are successful? The only effective way to objectively and systematically assess the state of an organization's internal and external communications is to conduct a formal communication assessment or communication audit.

In this chapter we discussed the importance of conducting organizational communication assessments and audits. We presented a seven-step process for conducting organizational communication research and described each of the steps in detail. We included information on how to design survey items and how to present survey results and findings to the organization. Next, we discussed two well-established communication audit and assessment tools. First, we presented the International Communication Association (ICA) Communication Audit Survey, which assesses eight dimensions of organizational communication, including perceptions of the amount of information received, quality of organizational communication relationships, and satisfaction with organizational outcomes. In addition to describing what this survey does, we described how to use this instrument and included the actual ICA Survey Questionnaire. Next, we presented the Downs-Hazen Communication Satisfaction Questionnaire, which measures satisfaction with eight dimensions, including satisfaction with communication, information, relationships, communication channels, and organizational climate. We then introduced you to two organizational communication concepts (organizational identification and organizational commitment) which assess how employees feel about their organization. Finally, we described the process of conducting a communication network analysis. After reading this chapter, you should be equipped with enough information to analyze organizational communication by either developing your own survey or by using one of the established measures described in this chapter.

Questions for Discussion and Review

1. Recall from the chapter the importance of assessing organizational communication. List and explain several of the organizational and personal benefits associated with assessing communication interactions in the workplace.

2. Based on the information in the chapter, define and describe the six characteristics of a communication assessment. In your opinion, which of these is the most valuable? Provide examples to support your answer.

3. Based on what you read about the benefits of conducting a formal communication assessment, describe and explain the analogy between a visit to a doctor and a communication assessment.

4. List and explain the advantages and disadvantages of survey research. Based on what you read in the chapter, do you think the benefits outweigh the drawbacks? Support your answer.

5. Recall Figure 13.1. Explain each of the seven steps associated with effective organizational survey research. Provide examples of each step.

6. Recall the seven steps associated with effective organizational survey research. Define a pilot test, and explain why a researcher would want to conduct one. Explain the benefits and drawbacks associated with a pilot test.

7. Based on what you read in the chapter, describe the benefits associated with conducting a communication audit. How does the health care metaphor illustrate the process of conducting a communication audit? Provide examples to support your answer.

8. Recall from the chapter the ICA Communication Audit Survey. Explain each of the eight components and provide sample questions for each. Based on what you read in the chapter, which four of the eight components do you feel are most important? Provide a rationale to support your answers.

References

Allen, N. J., & Meyer, J. P. (1990). The measurement and antecedents of affective, continuance and normative commitment to the organization. *Journal of Occupational Psychology, 63,* 1–18.

Borgatti, S., Everett, M., & Freeman, L. (1995). *UCINET V.* Columbia, SC: Analytic Technologies.

Burke, K. (1969). *A rhetoric of motives.* Berkeley, CA: University of California Press.

Cheney, G. (1982). *Organizational identification as a process and product: A field study.* Unpublished master's thesis, Purdue University.

Cheney, G. (1983). On the various and changing meanings of organizational membership. A field study of organizational identification. *Communication Monographs, 50,* 342–362.

Cheney, G., & Tompkins, P. K. (1987). Coming to terms with organizational identification and commitment. *Central States Speech Journal, 38,* 1–15.

Church, A. H., & Waclawski, J. (2001). *Designing and using organizational surveys.* San Francisco: Jossey-Bass.

Clampitt, P., & Downs, C. (1993). Employee perceptions of the relationship between communication and productivity: A field study. *Journal of Business Communication, 30,* 5–28.

Davis, C. S., Gallardo, H. P., & Lachlan, K. A. (2010). *Straight talk about communication research methods.* Dubuque, IA: Kendall Hunt Publishing Co.

DeWine, S. (1994). International communication association audit. In R. B. Rubin, P. Palmgreen, & H. E. Sypher (Eds.), *Communication research measures: A sourcebook* (pp. 193–205). New York: Guilford Press.

DeWine, S., & James, A. C. (1988). Examining the communication audit: Assessment and modification. *Management Communication Quarterly, 2,* 144–168.

Downs, C., & Hazen, M. (1977). A factor analytic study of communication satisfaction. *Journal of Business Communication, 14,* 63–73.

Downs, C. W. (1994). Communication satisfaction questionnaire. In R. B. Rubin, P. Palmgreen, & H. E. Sypher (Eds.), *Communication research measures: A sourcebook* (pp. 114–119). New York: Guilford Press.

Downs, C. W., & Adrian, A. D. (2004). *Assessing organizational communication.* New York: Guilford Press.

Downs, C., Clampitt, P., & Laird, A. (1981, May). Critique of the ICA communication audit. Paper presented at the annual meeting of the *International Communication Association,* Minneapolis.

Fink, A. (2009). *How to conduct surveys* (4th ed.). Los Angeles: SAGE Publications.

Gautam, T., Dick, R. V., & Wagner, U. (2004). Organizational identification and commitment: Distinct aspects of two related concepts. *Asian Journal of Social Psychology, 7,* 301–315.

Goldhaber, G. M. (1986). *Organizational communication* (4th ed.). Dubuque, IA: Wm. C. Brown.

Goldhaber, G. M. (2002). Communication audits in the age of the Internet. *Management Communication Quarterly, 15,* 451–457.

Goldhaber, G. M., & Rogers, D. P. (1979). *Auditing organizational communication systems: The ICA communication audit.* Dubuque, IA: Kendall Hunt.

Gray, J., & Laidlaw, H. (2004). Improving the measurement of communication satisfaction. *Management Communication Quarterly, 17,* 425–448.

Greenbaum, H. H., DeWine, S., & Downs, C. W. (1987). Management and organizational communication measurement: A call for review and evaluation. *Management Communication Quarterly, 1,* 129–144.

Hargie, O., & Tourish, D. (2000). *Handbook of communication audits for organizations.* New York: Routledge.

Hargie, O., Tourish, D., & Wilson, N. (2002). Communication audits and the effects of increased information: A follow-up study. *Journal of Business Communication, 39,* 414–436.

Hargie, O., & Tourish, D. (2004). How are we doing? Measuring and monitoring organizational communication. In D. Tourish & O. Hargie (Eds.), *Key issues in organizational communication* (pp. 234–251). New York: Routledge.

Infante, D. A., Rancer, A. S., & Avtgis, T. A. (2010). *Contemporary communication theory.* Dubuque, IA: Kendall Hunt.

Johnson, W. L., Johnson, A. M., & Heimberg, F. (1999). A primary- and second-order component analysis of the Organizational Identification Questionnaire. *Educational and Psychological Measurement, 59,* 159–170.

Lemann, N. (1999). *The big test: The secret history of the American meritocracy.* New York: Farrar, Straus and Giroux.

Lesniak, R., Yates, M., Goldhaber, G., & Richards, W. (1977, May). NETPLOT: An original computer program for interpreting NEGOPY. Paper presented at the annual meeting of the *International Communication Association,* Berlin.

Liberman, C. J. (2008, October). *Birds of a feather flock together, or do they? Understanding the homophily/heterophily debate within the organizational communication context.* Paper presented at the annual meeting of the New York State Communication Association, Kerhonkson, NY.

Liberman, C. J. (2011). Why organizational identification matters as a communication variable: Past, present, and future trends. *Proceedings of the New York State Communication Association,* 132–151.

Meyer, J. P., & Allen, N. J. (1991). A three-component conceptualization of organizational commitment. *Human Resource Management Review, 1,* 61–89.

Meyer, J. P., & Allen, N. J. (1997). *Commitment in the workplace.* Thousand Oaks, CA: SAGE Publications.

Miller, V. D., Allen, M., Casey, M. K., & Johnson, J. R. (2000). Reconsidering the Organizational Identification Questionnaire. *Management Communication Quarterly, 13,* 626–658.

Mowday, R. T., Porter, L. W., & Steers, R. M. (1982). *Organizational linkages: The psychology of commitment, absenteeism, and turnover.* San Diego: Academic Press.

Odiorne, G. (1954). An application of the communication audit. *Personnel Psychology, 7,* 235–243.

Pettit, J. D., Goris, J. R., & Vaught, B. (1997). An examination of organizational communication as a moderator of the relationship between job performance and job satisfaction. *The Journal of Business Communication, 34,* 1–98.

Ray, R. L. (1993). The business of running a business. In R. L. Ray (Ed.), *Bridging both worlds: The communication consultant in corporate America* (pp. 13–35). Lanham, MD: University Press of America.

Richards, W. (1975). *A manual for network analysis: Using NEGOPY network analysis program.* Stanford, CA: Institute for Communication Research, Stanford University.

Rogers, E. (1995). *Diffusion of innovations* (4th ed.). New York: Free Press.

Salkind, N. J. (2008). *Statistics for people who think they hate statistics* (3rd ed.). Los Angeles: SAGE Publications.

Tompkins, P. K., & Cheney, G. (1983). Account analysis of organizations: Decision making and identification. In L. L. Putnam & M. E. Pacanowsky (Eds.), *Communication and organizations: An interpretive approach* (pp. 123–146). Beverly Hills, CA: SAGE Publications.

Zwijze-Koning, K., & deJong, M. (2007). Evaluating the Communication Satisfaction Questionnaire as a communication audit tool. *Management Communication Quarterly, 20,* 261–282.

Conclusion

When the field of organizational communication began in the 1960s, it was for a particular reason. In short, it was because W. Charles Redding, the father of organizational communication, claimed that although organizational behaviorists, administrative scientists, and industrial/organizational psychologists were studying the right things, they were, unfortunately, neglecting one important independent factor: communication. Our goal in this textbook was to illustrate the central role that communication plays in organizations of all types, with a particular emphasis on those areas that are most informing of organizational success.

In so doing, we highlighted how communication is inextricably linked to (a) the process of organizing (Chapter 2); (b) the role of an organization's culture in the creation of a unified identity (Chapter 3); (c) the manifestation of language within the organizational confines (Chapter 4); (d) the creation and effects of relationships and their role in many organizational practices and processes (Chapter 5); (e) personality and the character traits that emerge and inform many interpersonal and small-group behaviors (Chapter 6); (f) interactions that take place between and among individuals as they work in small groups to complete certain tasks (Chapter 7); (g) effective leadership practices (Chapter 8); (h) the use of ethics when employees engage in or disengage from organizational behaviors (Chapter 9); (i) the process of decision making that transpires when employees congregate (Chapter 10); (j) the process of training through which employees oftentimes must navigate; and (k) the role of change and development necessary for continued organizational success.

Given that our title includes the phrase *Strategies for Success,* we believe not only that there are recipes for organizational effectiveness and failure, but also that such recipes can be taught and learned. In Chapter 4, for example, you learned that mindfulness, or the process of communicative awareness, is a necessary prerequisite for the use of language within the organizational environment. All too often, however, such mindfulness is either nonexistent or masked, which can provide an uncomfortable, unwanted, and unwelcoming organizational environment. Simply by being mindful, employees can make the work environment more creatively fertile and dynamic, which are the very features necessary for organizations to survive and perhaps prosper. In Chapter 7, you learned that understanding the small-group process and appreciating the incorporation of divergent perspectives, novel ideas, and even different personalities can aid organizations in the decision-making process. At the same time, you also learned that the small-group process can be constraining if, for example, there is an assumed pressure for conformity and/or self-centered roles begin to negatively affect decision making. In Chapter 11, you learned the importance of training and development as they relate to organizational success and how communication competencies are necessary. At the same time, you learned that it is crucial to conduct a needs assessment prior to such training and development programs if they are to be successful. In the end, we framed all the topics, concepts, theories, and perspectives in our units and the chapters within them as teachable, learnable, and most importantly, communication centered.

As we swiftly find ourselves embedded in this 21st century, the areas of study within the world of organizational communication have not changed much. In fact, the same issues (leadership, decision making, conflict management, training, relationships, organizational change, organizational development, organizational assessment) still routinely surface as main chapters in contemporary textbooks, articles published in scholarly academic journals, and case studies. The main difference, however, is that nearly 50 years of organizational communication research has enlightened practitioners about best practices associated with many organizational processes. As we highlighted throughout this text, it is important for these practitioners to find ways to harness the advantages and rid organizations of potential problems, both of which are realized through proper use of communication and sound application of organizational communication theory. In the end, if employees and managers can effectively do this, and we believe they can, then the organization, regardless of its form or function, will be a place where people can realize some of the most fundamental human aspirations and needs.

Glossary

A

Abraham personality
A motivational tendency to focus on the need to achieve the maximum of human potential and perfection.

Abstractness The degree to which information is concrete as well as the capacity of the person receiving the message to think abstractly.

Acceptable level decision rule
The degree to which the consistency between one decision and another is minimal enough to be tolerated.

Accountability An ethical practice of going above and beyond the minimal standards set by the industry and government regulation.

Acknowledgment of understanding the problem The building of a culture that advocates change that affects power structures, career paths, and reward systems.

Acquired needs theory Theory of motivation that assumes people are motivated to behave in ways that help them acquire things that the culture at large deems important.

Acquisition The process by which one organization takes control of another.

Action is locally organized A component of conversational analysis referring to (a) what is relevant to the interactants within a specific or particular context, and (b) adjacency or sequence of actions as a process for communicators to work together in predictable ways to construct a recognizable course of action.

Action is structured A component of communication analysis that assumes not only that talk is an action, but that action is guided by a structure that allows the communicators to coordinate the interaction in a way that allows for things such as turn taking and establishes patterns of interactions.

Action or follow-up taken
A component of the ICA communication audit that assesses how well subordinates, coworkers, supervisors, and management respond to messages.

Action research A fundamental method used in contemporary organizational development efforts designed to produce change in organizations and other social systems.

Action-oriented listening style
This type of listener is characterized by an interest in straight, concise, error-free, and well-organized presentations.

Active listening skills The ability to listen with comprehension and to paraphrase trainee comments and suggestions so that they may be incorporated into the program or module.

Actor-observer bias A perceptual bias in which our actions are never interpreted as being as negative as the actions of others.

Ad hoc group A small group that organizes members for a particular reason and, either on completion of the group's task or failure of the group to overcome internal conflict, these members part ways.

Ad-hoc committee
A committee that is formed to complete a specific task.

Adam personality A motivational tendency to focus on immediate satisfaction and pleasure.

Adaptation The degree to which we alter our behavior in response to the behavior of another person.

Additional resources Combination of brain power, creativity, and experiences each member brings to the group.

Administrative man model
A decision-making type in which people seek to "satisfice" or find a solution that is satisfactory or one that is both satisfactory and will suffice.

Affective commitment
An employee's emotional attachment to and identification and involvement with an organization.

Affirming communicator style
A communicator style that reflects the validation of another person's selfconcept.

Agenda An organizational tool, a road map for the group discussion that helps group members remain focused on their task.

Aggressor A small-group role whose major responsibility is to make personal attacks in the hope that such degradation will impede the small-group process and lower one's assumed status.

Alignment An ethical practice that matches the organization's formal practices and informal practices to the needs of its members.

All-channel network A type of small-group network wherein all individuals have communicative access to all others.

Andragogy The art and science of teaching or training adults.

Androgynous style Style of leadership that contains both masculine and feminine communication behaviors.

Animated style A dimension of communicator style that reflects the frequent use of nonverbal behaviors when communicating.

Anticipatory socialization All socialization efforts prior to the newcomer entering the organization (e.g., talking with parents, watching work life on television, etc.).

Anticipatory stage The first stage of the socialization process within which employees begin to anticipate life within the organization.

Antinepotism Policies that prohibit the hiring of family members and that restrict working relationships between family members.

Appreciative action research model (AARM) An organizational development perspective that combines the strengths of appreciative inquiry while minimizing the limitations of the action research model.

Appreciative inquiry (AI) An organizational development perspective that rejects the problem-solving or "deficit-based" approach of action research, and focuses on "doing things right" and using those right things to build the future of the organization.

Appropriate disclosure A dimension of communicative adaptability that reflects the degree to which a person reveals personal information in the appropriate amount as dictated by any given situation.

Appropriateness A dimension of communication competence that reflects the ability to be socially appropriate when pursuing goals.

Argument approach A motivation toward arguing that reflects the degree to which a person likes to approach argumentative situations.

Argument avoid A motivation toward arguing that reflects the degree to which a person likes to avoid argumentative situations.

Argumentativeness A communication trait in which a person has a predisposition to advocate positions on controversial issues while simultaneously refuting the positions that others take.

Articulated dissent Expressing dissatisfaction to people who can directly alleviate the problem.

Articulation A dimension of communicative adaptability that reflects the degree to which a person is skilled in the expression of ideas.

Artifact A symbolic element that comes to shape and create employee knowledge and understanding.

Artisan entrepreneur Seeks independence and autonomy as the primary goal; the making of money is not deemed as important as getting satisfaction from the work.

Assembly rules Standard processes that aid people in establishing standard routines for making sense of information.

Assertiveness The tendency to assert one's rights when a perceived wrong or injustice has occurred.

Asynchronous communication Communication that is not time bound, meaning that a message can be sent at any time or location and the receiver can access the message at his or her convenience (e.g., e-mail).

Attending Dimension of the Myers-Briggs Type Indicator that reflects how people interpret information.

Attentive style A dimension of communicator style that reflects communicating in a way that suggests interest and involvement in a conversation.

Attribution The process by which we give meaning to behavior.

Audio & video conferencing A set of interactive telecommunication technologies that allow two or more locations to interact via two-way video and audio transmissions simultaneously.

Authoritarianism A predisposition to rely on structure and rules for determining what is right or wrong. An authoritarian person has great respect for power and status.

Authority The ability to get people to obey orders voluntarily.

Authority rule Authority figure inside or outside the organization makes the decision. This entity may be either a member of the group or an influential non-group member.

Autocratic-oriented style A decision-making style in which managers solve the decision with the information available to them at the time or when managers solicit information from subordinates but still make the decision by themselves.

Autonomy and entrepreneurship Attribute of a company that supports and encourages risk taking, internal competition, as well as a high number of innovations.

B

Basic attribution error Overestimating internal attributions (dispositional factors) to the behavior of others while underestimating external attributions (situational factors).

Behavior Level 3 of the Kirkpatrick model that involves assessing the degree to which trainees' on-the-job behavior actually changed as a result of their participation in the training.

Behavioral objectives Objectives that you as a trainer want trainees to know at the end of the program.

Benevolent-authoritative type Also known as System 2. Type of management that uses rewards for employee motivation. Employee input is sought only to the extent that management deems appropriate.

Betweenness centrality One's level of importance based on his or her ability to socially connect previously disconnected people.

Bias for action Attribute of a company that shows a willingness to experiment with innovative ideas to see if there is any benefit to the company.

Blame A component of the inventional system that concerns who or what is responsible for the issue or problem.

Blended learning A training method that uses both face-to-face instruction and online methods.

Blocker A small-group role whose major responsibility is to refuse to adopt the majority opinion, oftentimes out of spite and malicious tendencies.

Blood type A Most artistic of blood types and indicates people who have deep-rooted strength, are steadfast in times of crisis, are shy, and avoid conflict.

Blood type AB Most undesirable of blood types and indicates people who are outgoing yet shy and have a predisposition to be interpersonally difficult people.

Blood type B Most practical of blood types and indicates people who are goal directed, are nonconformists, and rely on logic in decision making.

Blood type O Most desirable of blood types and indicates people who are socially outgoing and energetic; yet easily defeated and undependable.

Blood typing An assessment method that assigns particular personality characteristics based on the type of blood a person possesses.

Brainstorming A decision-making procedure focused on generating more ideas or solutions to problems than can be generated by individuals working alone.

Bridges A role in which people interact with members of other groups.

Bureaucratic management A management perspective that advocates a tight structure with many levels in the hierarchy as well as control over employees.

C

Case studies A training vehicle that allows trainees to use the knowledge gained through the training as a method to enhance problem solving. This involves presenting trainees with a scenario in which the trainee analyzes an organizational problem and offers possible solutions.

Ceiling effect The process by which too many parts of the same group begin to counteract the benefits of being in such a group.

Census An assessment that includes every employee of the organization.

Centrality The level of importance based on one's position within a given social network.

Chain network A type of small-group network that requires that ideas flow from individual to individual to individual in a linear format.

Channels of communication A component of the ICA audit that assesses the amount of information received (and needed) from channels of communication.

Character attacks A type of verbal aggression that involves a person's lack of character or moral fiber.

Charisma A personality trait that reflects displaying a greater than average communication competence and the ability to inspire subordinates as well as have subordinates inspired by the leader's vision.

Chinese zodiac A chronologically based personality assessment grounded in ancient folklore that ascribes personality characteristics based on year of birth.

Choice activity The process of selecting one course of action from available choices.

Chronemics The use of time when communicating. Can also have organizational ethical implications. For example, is it ethical to purposely show up late for a meeting in order to show that you are in control of time and thus, in a more powerful position.

Circle network A type of small-group network wherein communication is most effective when all individuals have the opportunity to interact with two others.

Circumvention A negative strategy of organizational dissent in which an employee goes above his or her immediate supervisor to complain about an issue.

Close to the customer Attribute of a company where customers are viewed as the sole reason the organization exists and where the customer is considered an invaluable resource for innovation and change.

Closed system A system that does not exchange information with the immediate environment.

Closed-ended items Assessment items that are more restrictive and present the survey respondent with a predetermined response format to use when responding to the item.

Closeness centrality The number of steps necessary to reach all other parts of a given social network.

Clothing An important aspect of nonverbal behavior that can have organizational ethical implications.

Clown A small-group role whose major responsibility is to form social relationships that supersede an interest in making a good, well-informed decision.

Club culture Based on the work of Handy, this organizational culture is structured after the Greek god Zeus and is highlighted by a focus on strong leadership.

Cognitive flexibility The degree to which a communicator considers options for behaving in different situations, as well as, enacts the correct behavioral option in accordance within the situation at hand.

Cohesiveness The degree to which group members cooperate and are committed to group goals. This includes ideas such as the degree of members' attraction toward one another, their sense of groupness, and their perceptions of loyalty to one another, the group, and the organization.

Collaboration Involves group members seeking to exchange information, examine differences, understand the problem, and show openness toward each other.

Collective versus individualistic tactics Involves grouping newcomers together and putting then through a common set of experiences rather than exposing each newcomer to unique experiences.

Collectivistic culture A culture that tends to focus on collective goals, needs, and views of the group rather than those of any one person.

Commitment A key factor of team building that contributes to the effective functioning of teams.

Common goal The purpose or objective toward which the group is directed. It is the notion of a common goal that allows for the interdependence of groups to be successful.

Communication (group) Allows the group experience to occur. The verbal and nonverbal messages that generate shared meaning among group members account for the attainment of the group's goals.

Communication (OD) A key factor of team building that contributes to the effective functioning of teams.

Communication accommodation theory (CAT) A language theory that was developed to examine the underlying motivations and con sequences of shifts in language patterns.

Communication assessment A diagnostic process that collects important data to be used in constructing a description of an organization.

Communication audit An assessment tool used to measure a variety of communication factors in the organization.

Communication competence The ability to communicate in appropriate and effective ways.

Communication content dimension A communication strategy that focuses on what messages and information are conveyed to organizational members before, during, and after the change efforts.

Communication cycles Sense-making actions whereby people create and react to ideas.

Communication diary A component of the ICA audit that concerns asking people to record certain communication activities (e.g., conversations with organizational members, phone calls, e-mails, meetings) for a one-week period.

Communication during the moving stage A strategy of change implementation that attempts to provide detailed information about the status of the change effort to nonstakeholders, provide information to those not yet affected about how the change will impact them, and challenge any misinformation relating to the change process.

Communication during the refreezing stage A strategy of change implementation that attempts to disseminate information in a specific, continuous, and multidirectional manner in order for employees to fully understand how the changes have affected the organization, their jobs, and their lives as members of the organization.

Communication during the unfreezing stage Communication during the most difficult step in organizational change, where resistance is usually strongest, as there needs to be a carefully planned communication strategy in place to meet any resistance to change.

Communication flexibility A communication trait reflecting the degree to which communicators are able to adapt communication behavior to specific situations and develop behavioral options to use as situations demand.

Communication medium dimension A communication strategy that reflects how information is shared and the degree to which the medium fits the significance and complexity of the messages and the stage in the change process.

Communication network An analysis technique that reflects the roles that individuals occupy in a communication network. These roles are patterns of communication that connect each member of the organization to the flow of communication in the network.

Communication satisfaction survey A communication audit tool that assesses dimensions of satisfaction. These include communication, information, relationships, channels of communication, and organizational climate.

Communication training Training that encompasses the presentation of knowledge and skills designed to enhance individuals' competence in presenting information to others and helping people work more effectively with each other.

Communicative adaptability The ability to perceive sociointerpersonal relationships and adapt interaction goals and interpersonal behaviors.

Communicative role of change agent A category of change that defines the functions of the change agent in promoting communication and participation in the change process, facilitating change by guiding others, and establishing or maintaining the organization's vision for the change.

Communicator image A combination of substyles that when combined determine the degree to which a person is seen as a competent and effective communicator.

Communicator style A communication trait reflecting how a person verbally and para-verbally interacts with others to signal how literal meaning should be taken, interpreted, filtered, or understood.

Compatibility Attribute of an innovation that concerns whether or not the innovation agrees with the organization's current values/mission and/or future mission.

Compensating patterns Part of Interaction Adaptation Theory that involves the balancing out of the other's behavior and seeks to represent the whole spectrum of the interaction.

Compensation and benefits function Responsible for job evaluations, structure and merit plans, and executive compensation plans.

Competence attack A type of verbal aggression that denigrates someone's ability to do something.

Complexity The amount and details of the message as well as the cognitive capacity of the person receiving the message. Also an attribute of an innovation that concerns the degree to which the innovation is easily understood and/or used by all members of the organization.

Composition of the team A factor in organizational development data gathering concerning specific characteristics of the team and team members (e.g., size of team, skill set of team).

Compound request A long request that asks listeners to (a) make a decision whether or not they mind completing the request and (b) make a decision whether or not to comply with what is being asked of them.

Compromise A form of decision making characterized as an agreement based on mutual concession.

Compromise A small, loud minority of group members persuades the group to adopt its decision or idea.

Compromising strategy A decision-making type that reflects a high degree of certainty in cause-and-effect relationships and low degree of certainty in desired outcomes.

Computational strategy A decision-making type that reflects a high degree of certainty in cause-and-effect relationship and high certainty in desired outcomes.

Computer A machine that manipulates data according to a list of instructions.

Computer networks A group of interconnected computers.

Computer-mediated communication (CMC) Originated in the organizational context and involves the use of computer technology to facilitate interpersonal communication.

Concertive control There is consensus among employees that helps shape their behaviors in accordance with the core set of values and vision of the organization.

Confirmation stage Stage of innovation adoption that determines whether or not adoption of the innovation has resulted in the promised results or failed to deliver the promised benefits articulated in the persuasion stage.

Conflict A disagreement that accrues within a relationship based on divergent viewpoints and perspectives.

Connotative meaning Subjective association people attach to verbal messages.

Conscious competence Level of competence in which we can perform the skill, but we still must exert a great deal to accomplish it.

Conscious incompetence Level of competence in which we try to perform the skill or behavior and realize we cannot do it at all, or we do it unsatisfactorily.

Consensus A form of decision making that requires all group members to be in agreement.

Consensus attribution Attributing meaning to behavior based on whether or not the person is behaving in a way similar to others.

Consequence A component of the Inventional System that concerns the positive and negative effects of implementing a solution.

Consistency attribution Attributing meaning to behavior based on whether or not the person behaves consistently over time.

Constructive conflict Conflict negotiated through a set of communicative exchanges that focus on saving, protecting, giving, or maintaining face and self-worth.

Consultative type Also known as System 3. Type of management that uses reward and punishment to motivate employees. Smaller decisions are left to the employees whereas bigger decisions are made by upper management.

Consultative-oriented style A decision-making style in which the manager engages in problem solving with particular individual subordinates or consults the particular individual subordinates as a group and then makes the decision by him/ herself.

Contagion The process through which attitudes and/or behaviors are either adopted or barred by people, based on the quantity of others who have created similar attitudes or engaged in similar behaviors, as they make both collective and individual decisions.

Content The specific objectives that are to be achieved by strategic change.

Content analysis A data analysis procedure that seeks to determine patterns of responses and to convert the data into a form that can be easily summarized.

Content-oriented listening style Reflects an interest in intellectual challenge and in complex information.

Contentious style A dimension of communicator style that reflects communicating in a way that is combative or antagonistic.

Context Factor of strategic change characterized by knowledge of the environment within the organization and society as a whole.

Contingency theory A theory of leadership that assumes that a leader's success is contingent on situational demands, such as whether the leader should have a task or employee focus and a leader's influence and control in a given situation.

Continuance commitment An employee's awareness of the costs associated with leaving an organization.

Contractual tactics Focus on the subordinate's willingness to conform to or exceed organizational and supervisor expectations and conventions. For example, the subordinate volunteers to stay late to finish a project for an important client or offers to pick needed materials from local vendors.

Contributor A small-group role, whose primary responsibility is to provide responses to the information seeker's query. Also known as *initiator*.

Contrived group A small group that is deliberately and artificially constructed.

Contrived relationship A forced relationship that an employee has no jurisdiction over.

Control The ability to overtly or covertly manipulate the thoughts, feelings, and behaviors of others.

Convergence How people use language to adapt to one another by slowing down or speeding up speech rates, lengthening or shortening utterances, and using pauses and specific forms of language, including tag questions, verbal intensifiers, various forms of politeness, tone quality, vocal energy, phrasing, enunciation, and pronunciation.

Conversational analysis A theory of language that views communication as actions constructed by communicators out of talk and body behavior.

Conversational desires A person's optimal expectations that are highly personalized and reflect things such as one's personality and other individual differences.

Conversational expectations Formed by societal norms of appropriateness as well as the degree of knowledge developed from past interactions with a specific person.

Conversational repair A technique used not only to clarify problems of communication or meaning but also to achieve other communication goals.

Conversational requirements A person's basic psychological/physiological needs related to approach-avoidance behavior and believed to be unconscious.

Corporate we A unified sense of identity among employees.

Country club manager A management style that indicates a high concern for workers and a low concern for the task.

Courage An ethical practice in which the organization values employee dissent, listens to employee dissent, and admits when the organization has made a mistake.

Course delivery The presentation or delivery of training programs.

Critic A small-group role, whose major responsibility is to play the devil's advocate. Also known as *evaluator*.

Critical advisor This role involves probing ideas without threatening or alienating members or challenging leadership. The critical advisor also seeks idea clarification and evaluates most procedural functions for greater understanding.

Critical incident analysis A component of the ICA audit that concerns asking employees to describe "critical" communication episodes that they feel are representative of successful and unsuccessful communication experiences they have had with members of the organization.

Critical perspective A perspective that seeks to uncover imbalances of power and control as well as make those who suffer from such oppression aware that this imbalance exists.

Cultural networks The communication systems through which the values of the organization are communicated.

Current time frame A characteristic of communication assessment that states that organizations are dynamic and communication patterns are constantly changing. As such, generalizations about communication are limited to one point in time.

Cyberethics The ways in which ethical traditions and norms are negotiated and broken in the realm of computer technology.

Cybernetic learning A type of learning that reflects adjusting thoughts and behaviors based on feedback from the environment (e.g., management).

Cybernetic system A system that is self-regulating based on feedback from the environment.

D

Dangling carrot approach An approach to performance that assumes people only work for tangible rewards.

Data cleaning Ensuring that the collected data is free from systematic or random error that can adversely affect the data.

Data-analysis skills The ability to evaluate and interpret gathered information and correctly identify training gaps or other organizational problems that may or may not require training as the solution.

Data-gathering skills The ability to design or select appropriate data-gathering tools and measures, know several methods of gathering data (e.g., surveys, interviews, focus groups, observation), and be able to assemble the data for analysis.

Deciding Dimension of the Myers-Briggs Type Indicator that refers to how people make decisions.

Decision making Happens many times in the process of problem solving and involves a judgment such as a choice between alternatives.

Decision stage Stage of innovation adoption in which those who hold decision-making power determine if the innovation or change is worth making or adopting.

Defensive organizational climates Climates high in emotional exhaustion, role overload, and depersonalization.

Defensive routines When workers develop preventative or reactive routines instead of being proactive in the workplace.

Define step Part of appreciative inquiry process in which positive phrasing is stressed, where the outcome must be capable of being positive for the stakeholders involved in the change.

Degree centrality A quantitative measure of the number of relationships that a single employee has compared to all others.

Delegate A situational leadership style in which the leader is neither task nor employee focused because the subordinate is capable of completing the work.

Delegating style A situational leadership style which reflects high levels of employee psychological and job maturity.

Denotative meaning The literal or dictionary meaning of a word.

Deontological ethical perspective Assumes that if a person's intentions are based on sound, ethical reasoning, then the action is ethical.

Depersonalization The process of focusing all interaction in the workplace on task completion and discouraging interactions that are relational in nature.

Design activity The invention, development, and analysis of possible courses of action.

Design step Part of appreciative inquiry process where several small groups are organized in an attempt to transform the dreamed themes and ideas into more concrete, tangible, and agreed-upon actions and principles.

Destiny step Part of appreciative inquiry in which organizational members actually write action plans and implementation strategies that will bring the organization to the future it dreamed of.

Destructive conflict A level of disagreement coupled by hostility that subsumes the group to the extent that it changes the group dynamics in such a way the group ceases to function.

Development of concern Process of sensing that a problem exists, which then leads to legitimizing the idea of change to a point that change is put on the organization's agenda.

Diagnostic thoroughness A characteristic of communication assessment that states that diagnosis must be systematic and must be made about all areas of communication that are considered important to the organization.

Dialogic communication An ethical practice that emphasizes open channels of communication that constitutes the cornerstone of teamwork.

Differentiation perspective Reveals inconsistencies in interpreting the organizational culture. There may be several different subcultures within the organization that do not adhere to the same set of values and beliefs.

Dimensions of dissent The way employees go about voicing disagreement about organizational issues. Consists of articulated, displaced, and latent/antagonistic dissent.

Direct appeal A positive strategy of organizational dissent that is based on fact followed by some sort of evidence, such as notes, figures, and consensus and opinion.

Direct personalization A dimension of taking conflict personally that refers to the bad feelings that people experience in a conflict episode.

Direct report One of the most common methods of report distribution that involves giving the survey instrument to the managers of each division, who then distribute them individually to their subordinates.

Direct tactics Include overtly defining relational expectations, and allowing subordinates to protest relational injustices and express opinions.

Disagreement Part of the tolerance for disagreement communication trait and reflects a difference of opinion on an issue.

Disbanding group A small group that organizes members for a particular reason and, either upon completion of the group's task or failure of the group to overcome internal conflict, these members part ways. Also known as *ad hoc group*.

Discover step Part of appreciative inquiry that involves conducting interviews to secure information that reveals the organization's strengths, and uncovering or discovering the unique and positive qualities of the organization.

Disdain A cause of verbal aggression that assumes a deep-seated dislike for another person.

Disengagement and exit Involves the employee either being physically transferred out of the department or leaving the organization through resignation.

Displaced dissent Expressing dissatisfaction to people who cannot alleviate the problem but will lend an ear as we vent our displeasure.

Distinctiveness attributions Attributing meaning to behavior based on whether or not the person acts differently to various people.

Distributive justice Normative principles that concern what is just or right regarding the allocation of goods in the organization.

Diversity of ideas The range of alternatives available to group members as they make a decision.

Diversity The variety of resources people bring with them to workgroups, including prior experiences, culture, race, gender, and attitudes.

Dogmatism A predisposition to be rigid in belief systems about what is right and wrong and unwilling to consider alternative points of view.

Domestic organizations Organizations that identify with one country and its culture.

Dominant style A dimension of communicator style that reflects communicating in a way that takes charge of a situation.

Dominator A small-group role whose major responsibility is to use both forceful and potentially demeaning dialogue in order to control intragroup discussion.

Double-barreled items Single items that attempt to measure more than one idea (e.g., "How satisfied are you with the amount and type of feedback you received from your supervisor?").

Double-loop learning Also known as generative learning. Type of learning that entails learning the process and understanding the rationale for the process and how this process contributes to the function of the entire organization.

Downward communication Messages that flow from the supervisor down to the worker.

Downward distortion One's decision to emphasize the positive elements embedded in a message when communicating with superiors and subordinates.

Dramatic style A dimension of communicator style that reflects communicating in a way that either understates or overstates information.

Dream step Part of appreciative inquiry that takes the ideas, stories, and themes uncovered during the discovery phase and expands them to develop statements of the organization's vision, purpose, and strategic intent.

E

Ecological perspective A view of organizations that assumes that organizations are bound to other organizations of their kind and that some of these organizations will survive and some will become extinct. Only in stability can organizations survive.

Economic man model A decision-making type where people make decisions in a completely rational way.

Effectiveness A dimension of communication competence that reflects the ability to achieve a desired goal.

Eigenvector centrality One's level of importance based on whether he or she is connected to people with degree, betweenness, and/or closeness centrality.

Elaborator A small-group role whose primary responsibility is explaining the ideas (not the merits of the ideas) to other group members to reduce any ambiguities that might exist.

Electronic mail Often abbreviated as e-mail; is a store-and-forward method of writing, sending, receiving, and saving messages over electronic communication systems.

Emancipation A term describing workers who take control of the means of production and gain freedom and independence from oppression.

Emergence The third stage of the group development process wherein the development of a decision through communication by group members transpires.

Emergent group A small group that comes into being based on volunteerism, self-interest, and expertise.

Emergent relationship A relationship based on self-determination and choice.

Empathy The ability to understand the attitudes, beliefs, and values of another person, to be able to "put yourself in their shoes." Employee relations function Responsible for evaluating performance, handling management issues, managing safety and health services, handling disciplinary and attendance issues, and fostering positive employee relations.

Employee identification The extent to which an employee sees him- or herself as part of the larger collective and engages in behaviors and actions representative of his or her attachment to the organization.

Employee relations function Responsible for evaluating performance, handling management issues, managing safety and health services, handling disciplinary and attendance issues, and fostering positive employee relations.

Employment/staffing function Responsible for handling both internal and external staffing and hiring, managing college and other recruitment, handling internship programs, administering EOE/AAP (Equal Opportunity Employment and Affirmative Action Programs), and engaging in career counseling.

Enactment The action of making sense of information.

Encounter stage The second stage of the socialization process within which employees begin to learn the ropes and experience the realities of the organization.

Encourager A small-group role whose major responsibility is to provide praise and admiration for the ideas brought forth by group members.

Enculturation A process of socialization that allows personal cultures to be passed from one generation to another.

Energizing Part of the Myers-Briggs Type Indicator that refers to specific factors that motivate people.

Enterprise resource planning Computer programs designed to manage entire workplaces, including organizations in multiple locations; can include accounting, inventory, and purchasing functions.

Entrepreneurial spirit The capacity to be predisposed to engage in the process of creating or synthesizing something new or unique and investing the necessary financial, social, psychological, and temporal capital to realize independence related to personal, psychological, or professional ends.

Entrepreneurship The process of creating or synthesizing something new or unique and investing the necessary financial, social, psychological, and temporal capital to realize independence related to personal, psychological, or professional ends.

Entropy A system that exchanges information with the immediate environment.

Epistemics of social relations Assumes that our various role identities (e.g., friend, brother, sister, parent) are enacted through communication within relevant situations.

Equifinality There are multiple ways to reach or achieve the same goal.

Espoused theory What the manager tells employees about the manager's ethics, management style, and management philosophy.

Esteem needs One of Maslow's hierarchy of needs reflecting the need for recognition, appreciation, and respect from other people.

Ethical wheel A model of ethical decision making that reflects the impact that various dimensions of our lives exert on our ethical decision making and resulting behavior.

Ethnocentrism The belief that one's own culture is superior to other cultures.

Eudaimonic view A perspective that the chief goal in life is the pursuit of our inner potential.

Evaluation Process of determining if the objectives you created for the particular training program were accomplished and how to improve future versions of a particular program.

Evaluation perspective Part of the training function that concerns the effectiveness of training outcomes.

Evaluator A small-group role whose major responsibility is to play the devil's advocate.

Evolutionary perspective See *ecological perspective*.

Existential culture Based on the work of Handy, this organizational culture is highlighted by Dionysus, the god of wine and song. This culture places the aims and needs of its members before those of the organization as a whole.

Expert power An employee's ability to have certain control over others based on the knowledge that he or she has about a particular topic.

Exploitative-authoritative type Also known as System 1. Type of management that uses fear and threats to motivate employees. Decisions are made at top levels of the organization and handed down to workers. Employee input is devalued.

External attribution Attributing behavior to external or situational factors such as the situation, the environment, or the influence of other people.

External locus of control A predisposition to view outcomes in life as being due to chance, fate, luck, or powerful others who are responsible for outcomes.

External work locus of control Predisposition to interpret outcomes at work as being the result of outside forces such as luck, chance, and fate and not due to our own purposeful action.

Extroverted Dimension of the Myers-Briggs Type Indicator that refers to people being motivated by outside factors such as people, places, and things.

F

Face Refers to a claimed sense of desired social self-image in a relational or group setting.

Face-loss Occurs when we are being treated in such a way that our identity claims are being either directly or indirectly challenged or ignored.

Face-negotiation strategies Ways of creating and maintaining a desired special self-image.

Face-negotiation theory Indicates that people in all cultures try to maintain and negotiate face in all communication situations.

Face-saving strategies Behaviors employed to regain face once one's face has been threatened or lost.

Face-threats Behaviors that appear to be threatening to one's self-concept.

Facilitation skills The ability to lead and guide individual and group discussions during training programs.

Facilitator The group member who prepares the agenda for the meeting, distributes the agenda for approval, makes sure the agenda is followed, upholds the rules, and adjourns the meeting.

Facsimile (FAX) Refers to a machine that facilitates the transmission of documents from one location to another via telephone connections.

Fayol's bridge Also known as the gangplank; the lateral exchange of information between members at the same level in the organization.

Feedback Information obtained by the system that comes from the environment.

Feeling Dimension of the Myers-Briggs Type Indicator that refers to the degree to which people use feelings and value-based judgment when making a decision.

Filter of goodness Part of the three-filter test that assesses the absolute positiveness of information or knowledge.

Filter of truth Part of the three-filter test that assesses the absolute verifiability of information or knowledge.

Filter of usefulness Part of the three-filter test that assesses the absolute utility of the information or knowledge.

Fixed versus variable tactics Provides a set timetable for the assumption of a new organizational role as opposed to no set timetable for role adoption.

Flexibility The demands of the external environment for openness, adaptability, and change as well as a person's ability to select, receive, and respond to such information.

Flight A decision in which the original problem has disappeared, resulting in the choice or solution being made but solving nothing.

Flip chart An instructional aid that allows us to record information elicited from trainees. Charts are easily mounted on the training room walls for easy reference.

Formal versus informal tactics Involves segregating newcomers from experienced employees during a socialization period as opposed to immediately integrating newcomers and experienced employees.

Foundational ethical perspective Assumes that ethical behavior is true in nature and universal.

Four-factor model Assumes that sexual harassment consists of two internal factors (motives for harassment and overcoming internal inhibitors) and two external factors (overcoming external inhibitors and overcoming victim resistance).

Fragmentation perspective Assumes that ambiguity and uncertainty are inevitable and are present at all levels of the organization regardless of a person's role.

Friendly style A dimension of communicator style that reflects communicating in a more intimate way.

Functional approach to decision making An approach to decision making that requires more than a structured and systematic five-step sequence.

G

Games A popular experiential training activity that are adaptable to almost all forms of content and foster a great deal of participation.

Gangplank Also known as Fayol's bridge; is the lateral exchange of information between members at the same level in the organization.

Garbage can model of organizational choice A model of decision making in which people are more concerned with the right or opportunity to engage in decision making than with the actual decision.

General strategies for communication and introduction of change A category of change that includes encouraging organizational members to participate fully in the change process, creating an organizational culture that will facilitate change, establishing clear purpose and vision, and developing a communicationfocused change strategy.

General systems theory Theory that applies the properties of living systems to a variety of phenomena.

General tendency to argue The tendency toward argument based on the degree to which we approach argumentative situations and the degree to which we avoid argumentative situations.

Generative learning See *double-loop learning*.

Global organizations Companies that identify with a global system of doing business rather than that of any single nation.

Globalization Technological developments including major advances in communication and transportation capacities that facilitate international production and exchange of goods and services across international borders.

Goal Broad statements indicating what the trainee will learn.

Goodness-of-fit principle Role acquisition is based on a group member's traits and skills that parallel the requirements of a given role.

Great man theory of leadership Theory of leadership that assumes great leaders all have similar personality attributes.

Greater creativity The ability of the group to generate more innovate ideas and creative solutions than individuals could generate working alone.

Group A collection of individuals, ranging in number from three to 11, who are brought together because of a common interest and who must work collaboratively and interdependently to achieve a collectively accepted goal.

Group Three or more individuals who exchange the majority of communication messages with each other.

Group cohesion The idea that those part of a small group will table their own attitudes, ideas, and opinions if they go against the majority.

Group decision support system A form of electronic technology that helps small-group members as they engage in the process of decision making.

Group decision support systems Computer technologies designed to provide decision-making structures for use by groups and/or individuals.

Group roles Based on a number of characteristics and behaviors members perform in order to help the group achieve its goals. Group roles are either emergent (elected) or assigned.

Group size The ideal workgroup size is 5 to 7 members, yet can range from a minimum of 3 to a maximum of 15.

Group-oriented style A decision-making style in which the manager consults subordinates as a group and then, working with the group, evaluates those solutions to reach an agreement.

Groupthink Faulty decision making that results from in-group pressures and often results from an excessive amount of cohesion in the group.

Groupthink The process by which those who are part of a collective social unit are fearful of not supporting a behavior or decision because of the inherent social dangers of nonconformity.

Growth factors Factors of motivation that reflect the need for growth, accomplishment, and self-realization.

H

Hands on, value driven Attribute of a company in which people at all organizational levels get involved in all of the organization's tasks.

Haptics The use of touch when communicating.

Harmonizer A small-group role whose major responsibility is to quickly and effectively diffuse the unwanted consequences of group conflict.

Hawthorne effect A threat to the internal validity of an experiment in which a change in experimental conditions brings about change in the behavior of the participants.

Hawthorne studies A series of studies between 1927 and 1932 that gave rise to the human relations approach to management.

He A component of business success that involves the smooth functioning of groups or society.

Hearing A physiological process that occurs when sound waves enter the ear canal and vibrations are converted to electrical signals sent to the brain.

Hedonic view A perspective that assumes the chief goal in life is the pursuit of happiness or pleasure.

Hegemonic view When the oppressed accept the ideology of the organization that reinforces the oppressed position.

Hegemony Occurs when subordinates in an organization accept their role as the oppressed.

Hierarchy of needs Approach to motivation that holds that there are primary needs that must be satisfied before a person can pursue higher level needs.

High-quality linkages Part of LMX theory characterized by high trust, respect, and an overall positive tone.

Holism The idea that individuals who are part of a group are only as strong as their weakest link.

Homeostasis The dynamic balance of a system. The balance of inputs, throughputs, and outputs within a system.

Homogeneity Individuals in a group share many similar characteristics to the extent that they all appear to be the same individual.

Hostile work environment A form of sexual harassment that reflects a sexually charged work atmosphere.

Human relations approach A management approach that advocates that management should satisfy the interpersonal and emotional needs of workers.

Human resource approach A management approach that holds that employees are a valuable asset that should be developed for the benefit of both the organization and the worker.

Hurtful teasing An aggressive and hurtful communicative event encountered by a target in which the perpetrator's efforts to mitigate the negative effects of the tease are unsuccessful and the target experiences hurt or humiliation.

Hygiene factors Factor of motivation based on being dissatisfied with working conditions and interpersonal relationships.

I

Ideology A set of ideas that inform employees about their organization's goals, practices, aspirations, needs, and expectations.

Illusion of agreement A perception that the group as a whole has reached an agreement but individual group members are not actually in favor of the decision.

Illusion of unanimity Belief that everyone agrees. Even silence is seen as agreement.

Imagination The reinterpretation of ourselves as well as the work we perform.

Immediacy The degree of psychological closeness created by the use of verbal and nonverbal behavior.

Implementation phase Phase of innovation consisting of all the communication, decisions, and actions ensuring that the change is successfully integrated into the organization.

Implementation stage Stage of innovation adoption where the innovation is put into practice throughout the organization.

Impoverished manager A management style that indicates a low concern for workers and a low concern for task.

Impression-leaving style A dimension of communicator style that reflects communicating in a way that is memorable.

In-group members Organizational members who have a high-quality link to their supervisor.

In-group relationships Employees with high-quality communication exchanges with their supervisors and who are given preferential treatment by their supervisors in the form of social support, trust, decision making, and influence.

Independence A characteristic of communication assessment that states that assessment should be conducted by trained individuals external to the organization.

Indirect interpersonal aggression A "dark side" communication behavior in which people try to harm others' credibility or performance in an indirect way, thus avoiding a face-to-face encounter.

Individualism A characteristic of culture proposed by Hofstede that reflects the degree to which a culture encourages individual success as opposed to group success.

Individualistic culture Cultures such as the U.S. in which the concerns and wants of the individual supersede the wants and needs of the group.

Information Bits of data that are created when people assign them significance.

Information actually sent A component of the ICA communication audit that assesses upward communication, including reports, complaints, and requests for additional information.

Information provider One of the most shared roles; responsible for providing accurate and concise data instantly on any given topic. Requirements of this role include good research skills and the ability to contribute new ideas and critically evaluate others' ideas.

Information received A component of the ICA communication audit that assesses information about individual performance, information needed to do one's job effectively, and information needed to keep informed about organizational matters.

Information scanning The way in which people identify and attribute significance to bits of information in the environment.

Information seeker A small-group role, whose primary responsibility is to use communication to gauge member insight.

Information systems theory A theory that seeks to explain how information and sense-making is a perceptual process that varies from person to person. It also seeks to identify how ambiguity and equivocal information lead people to different realities.

Information-seeking tactics Tactics used by newcomers to reduce uncertainty and take control of the socialization process.

Informational reception apprehension A habit of information processing characterized by anxiety and antipathy regarding information reception, perception, processing, or adjustment.

Initiation phase Phase of innovation consisting of gathering relevant information and making the necessary plans to accompany the upcoming change.

Initiator A small-group role, whose primary responsibility is to provide responses to the information seeker's query.

Innovation The idea, practice, or object that is perceived as new by people or units of adoption.

Innovation process The process of adopting new ideas, technologies, or practices; is comprised of both initiation and implementation phases.

Inputs Elements or data flowing into a system.

Inquiry Entails directly and overtly asking another person for information.

Inspirational strategy A decision type that reflects a low certainty in cause-and-effect relationship and low certainty in desired outcomes.

Instant messaging Abbreviated as IM; refers to technologies that create the possibility of real-time, text-based communication between two or more participants over the Internet.

Instructional aids Training devices that are designed to get the attention of the trainee, reinforce key points of the presentation, and aid in the retention of information presented in the training.

Instructional design The development of training modules and training programs.

Instructional objectives Things that the trainer wants the trainees to know at the end of the program.

Instructor's manual The most important guidebook for the trainer; provides detailed content and instructions for delivery of the training program.

Instrument A training device that allows trainees to find out more about themselves through self-perception scales and other-perception (e.g., coworkers) scales.

Integration perspective Depicts culture as consistent, clear, and understood by all members.

Intellectual inflexibility The degree to which people are unwilling to consider different points of view.

Intelligence activity The process of seeking out situations that are in need of decision making.

Interaction The shared mutual respect, and the acknowledgment of each member for his or her unique and individual contributions. These interactions are accomplished through communication.

Interaction adaptation theory A theory developed to explain conscious communicative behavior or behavior that is mindful, intentional, and symbolic.

Interaction attributes Part of the perceptual organizational process that is based on a person's interaction style.

Interaction involvement Communication competence-based construct that reflects the degree to which people are cognitively and behaviorally engaged in interpersonal interactions.

Interaction position Individualized communication information that is comprised of our desires, expectations, and requirements.

Interactionist perspective of personality A belief that personality is developed by both biological and environmental factors.

Intercultural communication competence The ability to (help) shape the process of intercultural interaction in a way that avoids or contextualizes misunderstanding while creating opportunities for cooperative problem solving in a way that is acceptable and productive for all involved.

Intercultural competence The understanding of the cultural rituals, rites, roles of other cultures.

Interdependence The extent to which group members are affected and influenced by the attitudes and behaviors of other members.

Internal attribution Attributing behavior to internal or dispositional factors within a person, such as a personality trait, values, and attitudes.

Internal locus of control A predisposition to view outcomes in life as being due to purposeful action and not chance, luck, or fate.

Internal work locus of control Predisposition to interpret outcomes at work as being under our control and not the control of some external source (e.g., fate or the boss).

Internal-stable factors Attributing outcomes to personal traits that are difficult to change.

Internal-unstable factors Attributing outcomes to personal traits that are easy to change.

International Communication Association (ICA) Audit The most widely used organizational communication assessment that measures information received from others, information sent to others, follow-up on information sent, sources of information, timeliness of information received from key sources, organizational communication relationships, organizational outcomes, and channels of communication.

International organizations Companies that identify with two or more countries as well as unique and distinct cultures within those countries.

Internet A global data communication system comprised of the hardware and software infrastructure that provides connectivity among computers.

Interpersonal communication skills The ability to be sensitive and competent in interpersonal interactions.

Interpretation Part of the perception process that involves how we make sense of organized data by giving meaning to these data.

Interview Data-gathering technique that allows in-depth information to be gathered and frequently uses open-ended questions. Also a component of the ICA audit that allows one-on-one interviews in which employees can substantiate and/or expand on information gleaned from the audit instrument.

Intrapreneur A person who is given the autonomy and resources necessary to innovate and whose innovations are produced and marketed by the organization.

Introverted Dimension of the Myers-Briggs Type Indicator that refers to people being motivated by emotions and internal perceptions.

Intuition Dimension of the Myers-Briggs Type Indicator that refers to the degree to which people tend to envision that which is not yet created.

Inventional system A system for generating arguments regardless of the argument topic or the person with whom we are arguing.

Investiture versus divestiture tactics Affirm the newcomer's identity and personal attributes rather than denying them or stripping them away.

Involvement A key factor of team building contributing to the effective functioning of teams.

Invulnerability A symptom of groupthink occurs when an organization is overly confident and willing to take big risks because it believes it is invincible.

Isolates A role in which people have no, or relatively few, links to others in the organization.

Issues of dissent Types of organizational issues in which employees express dissent. There are nine central issues.

Issues of fact Issues that concern whether or not something "is or is not" and are based on objective evidence.

Issues of policy Issues that concern whether or not something should or should not be done.

Issues of value Issues that concern whether something is or is not right, moral, or ethical.

J

Job maturity Degree of skills and knowledge acquired in performing a task.

Judgment Dimension of the Myers-Briggs Type Indicator that refers to the degree to which people prefer an organized and structured life.

Judgmental strategy A decision type that reflects a low degree of certainty in cause-and-effect relationship and high certainty in desired outcomes.

K

K.A.S.H. formula An effective formula for reducing the skill deficiency gap. The formula consists of trainee knowledge, attitude, skills, and habits.

Kinesics The study of body movement and motion. Proper use of body movements is critical to being a successful trainer.

Knowledge acquisition A component of organizational training that is designed to enhance what people know about an organizational process or issue.

Knowledge stage Stage of innovation adoption in which the organization or personnel within the organization become aware that the innovation exists and may be beneficial to the organization.

L

Language A collection of signs, symbols, codes, and rules used to construct and convey messages.

Language expectancy theory (LET) A theory that seeks to explain why some linguistic forms of persuasive messages are more effective than others.

Latent dissent Expressing dissatisfaction to people within the organization but who cannot alleviate the issue..

Leader-member exchange theory Originally called the vertical dyadic linkage theory; describes how the relationship quality between superiors and subordinates is determined by the quality of their communication exchanges.

Lean media channels Channels that fulfill very few if any of the information carrying capacity.

Learned helplessness Repeated negative consequences result in the worker showing little initiative, if any.

Learning Level 2 of the Kirkpatrick model that involves assessing the degree to which trainees obtain content knowledge, change their attitudes, acquire new skills, or increase their level of skill as a result of the training.

Lecture method A method of delivery that allows for a great deal of content to be delivered in a short amount of time and affords the trainer a great amount of control over what occurs in the training session.

Lecturette A short lecture (between 5 and 15 minutes) in which the trainer explains a process or principle that is relevant to the immediate needs of the learners. Also used as an introduction to a training activity.

Legitimate power An employee's ability to have certain control over others based on his or her official position within an organization.

Legitimate power Power that is officially granted by the organization.

Length of request Linguistic factor that indicates the longer the request, the more powerless the speaker; the shorter the request, the more powerful the speech.

Lesson content Contains exactly what the trainer is going to say to trainees during the session.

Liaisons A role in which people interact mainly with members of two or more groups but they themselves are not members of any group.

Like/dislike valence A dimension of taking conflict personally; refers to the degree to which people enjoy engaging in conflict.

Likert-type scale items An answer format that accesses the degree to which people agree or disagree with a statement and results in interval data (generally uses a 1–5 or 1–7 scale).

Limited resource A certain advantage that exists within an organization, but one that not all employees have equal access to.

Listening The process of receiving, constructing meaning from, and responding to spoken and/or nonverbal messages.

Listening apprehension Fear associated with either anticipated or real listening situations.

Listening styles The way in which a person usually listens to others; defined as a set of attitudes, beliefs, and predispositions about the how, where, when, who, and what of information reception and encoding.

Local rationality A view of decision making reflecting the belief that we are being rational with regard to our immediate concerns and that everyone involved gets some of what he or she desires.

Locus of control A predisposition that refers to the way in which people view outcomes in their lives as being due to forces beyond their control or to their own behavior.

Love needs One of Maslow's hierarchy of needs reflecting the need for affection and belonging.

Low-quality links Part of LMX theory characterized by mistrust, lack of respect, and overall negative tone.

M

Machiavellianism A predisposition to do whatever is necessary to achieve a desired goal. This may include lying and cheating in an effort to achieve a desired goal.

Maintenance role A small group role, the focus of which is on interpersonal relationships and intragroup harmony.

Majority rule A decision-making practice in which the majority (greater than 50%) vote determines the group's course of action. This is the most commonly used decision-making method in U.S. culture.

Majority vote A form of decision making wherein at least one more individual is in favor of a decision than against it.

Maledictions A type of verbal aggression that involves using phrases or sayings that wish someone harm.

Managerial entrepreneur Type of entrepreneur who believes that making a good income and seeking higher social status are important but so is the need to grow the firm.

Manufactured consent Employees willingly adapt and reinforce the power of the organization and their subsequent oppression.

Masculinity A characteristic of culture proposed by Hofstede that reflects the degree to which a culture values optimum performance and the pursuit of material success.

Maslow's hierarchy of needs Theory of motivation that holds people are motivated to satisfy essential human needs starting at the physiological and moving to higher psychological needs.

McKinsey 7-S framework A set of interrelated concepts to measure the success of an organization (structure, strategy, systems, style, skills, staff, and shared values).

Media richness theory A theory that involves the process by which managers select one form of communication channel over another. The channel choice is based on the complexity and ambiguity of the message.

Meeting A scheduled gathering of group members for a relatively structured discussion guided by an agenda and a facilitator.

Mentoring A concept related to trust; from a communication perspective, defined as discourse intended to provide support and guidance to a subordinate for the purpose of enhancing the progress of his or her career while furthering the goals of the organization.

Merger The process by which two organizations combine to create a new entity.

Meta-message A message that sends information about a message.

Metamorphosis stage The third and final stage of the socialization process within which employees begin to accept and manifest organizational norms and become organizational insiders.

Metaphor A term that comes to symbolically and comparatively represent, by association, something else.

Mindfulness Being aware of your behavior and basing your behavior on a specific situation as opposed to simply enacting a generic script that is used for a variety of situations.

Mindguarding Protects members from adverse information or opposition that may go against what the group already thinks.

Mindlessness Interacting in ways that are generic, without thought, and without regard to the specific context.

Minority influence A decision supported by few, but that can be adopted if the "right" people use the "right" persuasive strategies.

Mission statement A set of organizational goals that provides employees and consumers with information about what the organization in question deems most important.

Model I approach Management approach that assumes unilateral goals, self-reliance, failure to disclose negative opinions, and reliance on objectivity and logic.

Model II approach Management approach that assumes proaction, consultative decision making, solution implementation, and the ability to adapt if the solution needs adjustment.

Moderate manager A management style that indicates a moderate concern for workers and a moderate concern for task.

Monitoring Involves attending to a situation, attending to the behavior of others, or doing both in an attempt to obtain informational cues.

Morality Ignoring ethical and moral consequences because the group believes its position is morally right.

Motivator factors Factors of motivation that reflect the need for growth, accomplishment, and self-realization.

Motivator hygiene theory Theory of motivation that assumes people are motivated to action based on the degree of satisfaction or dissatisfaction they experience on the job.

Motives for harassment A component of the four-factor model of sexual harassment; reflects a range of motives, such as the need for power and the need for control.

Moving A step in the three-step model of organizational change that is geared toward beginning the process of change, developing momentum for change, and evaluating pilot efforts involved in the change.

Multicultural organizations Organizations that identify with one country but realize the need to be culturally diverse.

Multinational organizations Organizations that identify with one nationality while doing business with many nations.

Myers-Briggs type indicator A test that assesses important personality characteristics pertinent to a person's preference for certain career paths.

N

Name generator technique A methodology for obtaining social network data whereby organizational participants are asked to name the five people with whom they communicate most often.

Narcissism A personality trait that reflects the degree to which people have self-confidence, self-efficacy, and a belief that it is them, not others, who can best lead the group or organization.

Need for achievement Factor of acquired needs theory; reflects striving to acquire positions of responsibility and to achieve moderate goals.

Need for affiliation Factor of acquired needs theory; reflects the need for relationships, conflict avoidance, and nonassertiveness.

Need for power Factor of acquired needs theory; reflects the need to aspire to greatness and seek control over other people.

Needs analysis An analysis of the discrepancy between what trainees already know or can do and what they should or need to know or be able to do.

Needs assessment A systematic examination of the cause and extent of the problem that prompted the request for training.

Negative language Language use that creates an impression of someone who is pessimistic, insecure, and threatened by situations, people, and places.

Negative organizational culture Culture that places the interests of employees, customers, and shareholders second to other corporate interests, including personal profit and power.

Negative relational effects A dimension of taking conflict personally; refers to the belief that conflict is negative and only leads to damaged relationships.

Negativity effect The psychological impact of negative events tends to be longer lasting and have a greater influence on a person's state of mind than the impact of positive events.

Nepotism Reflects any favor or favoritism shown to another person based on familial relation.

Network analysis A component of the ICA audit that has employees report on the frequency with which they communicate with members of their work, unit, department, and other departments in the organization.

Nominal group technique An ideageneration technique that maximizes participation of group members while minimizing some of the interpersonal problems associated with group interaction.

Nonaffirming communication style A communicator style that reflects communicating in a way that negates or threatens another person's self-concept.

Nonsummativity The whole system is more than the sum of the system's parts.

Nonverbal immediacy The use of nonverbal behaviors, such as direct eye contact, open-body position, and physical closeness, that results in increasing the psychological closeness between the speaker and the audience.

Nonverbal verbal aggression A type of verbal aggression that involves using nonverbal gestures to intimidate or humiliate another person.

Normative commitment A feeling of obligation to continue working for the organization due, in large part, to perceived pressure from others.

Normative information Any behavior or attitude that the organization deems valuable or expects from employees.

Notes to instructor Contains guidelines (i.e., directions or actions) for the trainer that help the trainer deliver the content.

O

Objectives Goals that are easily measurable and often include specific skills that are demonstrable.

Observability Attribute of innovation that concerns the degree to which the results of the innovation are visible to members of the organization or those who are making the final decision.

Observation A data-gathering technique in which the researcher observes other people's behavior in a natural setting.

Occulesics The use of eye behavior when communicating. Proper use of the eyes (e.g., eye contact that is appropriate and immediate) is critical to being a successful trainer.

Open style A dimension of communicator style that reflects communicating in an extroverted and spontaneous way.

Open system A system that exchanges information with the immediate environment.

Open-ended items Assessment that does not restrict participants' answers but allows them to respond in their own words and to provide as much or as little detail and content as they want.

Operational changes Part of strategic change reflecting the results or outcomes of both expected and unexpected change.

Opinion seeker A small-group role whose primary responsibility is to engage the members in discussion about the merits and drawbacks of all ideas presented.

Oppressor A term describing management's use of power and control to alienate and subjugate workers.

Orchestrated group session Involves employees being gathered in a specific place to complete the necessary assessment instrument and then return to their jobs.

Organization Part of the perception process that involves the ordering of incoming stimuli in an attempt to make sense of the world.

Organizational assimilation The process of teaching those ongoing behaviors and cognitive processes by which individuals join, become a member of, and exit the organization.

Organizational climate The overall feeling of an organization. Climates are the aggregate perceptions of the employees. These include formal and informal policies, practices, and procedures of the organization.

Organizational commitment An overall physical, emotional, and/or psychological attachment to an organization.

Organizational communication The process through which people, connected by and through a common mission, sets of goals, and culture, create, share, and distribute information to both internal and external constituents in an effort to achieve objectives and generate collective meaning.

Organizational context A factor in organizational development data gathering concerning how the team performs.

Organizational culture A shared set of assumptions and values that guide the everyday behaviors of organization members. These assumptions are agreed-upon, correct ways to perceive, think, and feel.

Organizational development An applied discipline in which data are gathered and analyzed to develop strategies and recommendations that can assist organizations in promoting more effective communication and in making changes that can lead to greater organizational effectiveness.

Organizational development function Responsible for organizational design and structure, intervention design and implementation, and quality of work-life processes.

Organizational disengagement/exit A process (as opposed to an event) highlighted by the employee withdrawing from personal relationships with coworkers and supervisors as well as a general withdrawal from work and the organization.

Organizational dissent The way employees go about voicing disagreement or dissatisfaction about organizational issues.

Organizational entry stage Begins as newcomers enter the organization (i.e., their first day on the job) and continues until newcomers have made the transition from outsiders to integrated members of the organization.

Organizational heroes People who personify the corporate values of the organization and epitomize the strength of the organization through their actions and behaviors.

Organizational identification A feeling of attachment, belonging, and pride in being an organizational member; a perception that the employee and organization are similar in values and goals.

Organizational intelligence The variety of rules an organization has developed and in which it engages.

Organizational learning An influence on decision making in which organizations do not have all knowledge before making a decision; knowledge and information are gained through the process of engaging in decision making.

Organizational norms Sets of established behavioral patterns within any given organization.

Organizational peer relationships Relationships comprised of employees at the same hierarchical level who have no authority over each other.

Organizational romance A relationship between two members of the same organization that a third party perceives to be characterized by sexual attraction.

Organizational rules Formalized proscribed behaviors that are mandated by the organization (e.g., in the employee handbook).

Organizational social network A representation of how employees are structurally and socially connected to each other.

Organizational socialization The process by which newcomers learn the ropes of their organization's culture.

Organizational survey Popular and ubiquitous method of assessing a number of issues associated with organizational life, including employee attitudes, perceptions, and behaviors.

Organizational symbol The socially constructed representation of an organization's image.

Organizational tie Any type of relationship that one employee shares with another.

Organizational training Process of acquiring knowledge and skills necessary for individuals to perform effectively on the job.

Organizational values The clear and explicit philosophy about how the company conducts business.

Organizations as brains A metaphor that assumes that intelligence is found at all levels of the organization and the organization is constantly learning and adapting.

Organizations as cultures A metaphor that assumes that organizations have an overall corporate culture that is comprised of many subcultures.

Organizations as living organisms A metaphor based on biology; concerns the organization's ability to adapt to the environment.

Organizations as machines A metaphor that assumes that organizations are logically arranged and have clear authority and power structures.

Organizations as places of domination A metaphor that assumes that the organization, as a result of the organization's quest for power, becomes a source of stress, sickness, pollution, and human exploitation.

Organizations as political systems A metaphor that assumes that organizations are places in which politics are at work and that these politics range from autocratic to democratic.

Organizations as psychic prisons A metaphor that assumes that employees give the organization power over their thoughts and behavior.

Organizations as roles A metaphor that assumes that the organization provides us with purpose and structure. Our role in the organization becomes our reality.

Organizations as systems in flux A metaphor that assumes that the organization is in a constant state of creating and re-creating itself.

Organized anarchy A type of decision making in which there is no one best way or rationality but a negotiated or agreed upon rationality that is accepted by the various people and groups in the organization.

Organizing Part of information systems theory that reflects the fluidity of the sense-making process.

Orientation The first stage of the group development process wherein individuals begin to engage in informal dialogue in an effort to get to know one another and reduce the initial uncertainty that accompanies any novel social situation.

Out-group members Organizational members who have a low-quality link to their supervisor.

Out-group relationships Employees who develop low-quality communication exchanges with their supervisors, are not afforded preferential treatment, and are met with little support from their supervisors.

Outputs Elements or data flowing out of a system.

Overcoming external inhibitors A component of the four-factor model of sexual harassment; reflects overcoming organizational reaction to the behavior as well as avoiding any legal ramifications.

Overcoming internal inhibitors A component of the four-factor model of sexual harassment; reflects overcoming fears of retaliation from the victim and the perpetrator's personal sexual inhibitors.

Overcoming victim resistance A component of the four-factor model of sexual harassment; reflects the ability to use things such as job status, which dictates that the more powerful person is the initiator of most communication with subordinates, to overcome the victim's refutations.

Overconvergence Occurs when a person adapts to the language patterns of another person to the point that the language use is perceived as condescending and ridiculing.

Oversight A decision in which the solution is chosen quickly and capriciously from among other available choices in an effort to solve the problem quickly.

P

Panoptic A form of surveillance designed to enhance the organization's level of control over its employees.

Paralanguage Use of all elements associated with the voice other than the actual words we use. The elements include vocal rate, inflection, accent, and pitch.

Participant fatigue Occurs when people respond to long surveys by simply filling in answers without reading the question or simply leaving the questions blank.

Participant's manual Manual given to participants that at the least should contain enough information that trainees can adequately review the course material after they leave the training program.

Participate A situational leadership style in which the leader is employee focused in an effect to offer social support to subordinates.

Participation An ethical practice of valuing feedback and recognizing contributions of organizational members.

Participative style A situational leadership style where employees have high levels of job maturity and low levels of psychological maturity.

Participative type Also known as System 4. Type of management that emphasizes quality interpersonal relationships to maximize individual potential and organizational productivity.

People-oriented listening style Involves listening centered on the concern for other people; their emotions and interests are emphasized.

Perception A process that involves the selection, organization, and interpretation of stimuli in the environment. Is also a part of the Myers-Briggs Type Indicator that refers to the degree to which people prefer to live their life in a spontaneous and flexible way.

Perceptual schema A process of organizing and interpreting information or stimuli that is unique to each person.

Permanent group A small group that is ever-present and rarely changes its members.

Permeable boundaries The limits of a system in which elements are exchanged between the system and the larger environment.

Persecution feelings A dimension of taking conflict personally; refers to the tendency to avoid conflict episodes.

Personal culture Comprised of a person's experiences, beliefs, values, attitudes, meanings, social hierarchies, religion, notions of time, roles, norms, values, beliefs, rules, and behaviors.

Personal dimension of ethics A dimension of the ethical wheel that consists of standards of behavior that are an accumulation of our experiences.

Personal tactics Involve behaviors such as frequent small talk, informal discussion of nonwork concerns, joke sharing, and compliment giving (examples of small talk include the well-being of the supervisor's family and the performance of local sports teams).

Personality attacks A type of verbal aggression that involves attacking characteristics of a person's social and psychological characteristics.

Personality traits Idiosyncratic and individual factors that set one person apart from another person.

Personality/task congruity The degree to which a person's personality matches his or her assigned tasks in the workplace.

Persuasion stage Stage of innovation adoption concerning the level of appeal of the innovation's characteristics.

Peter principle Principle that assumes people rise to their level of incompetence.

Physical attributes Part of the perceptual organizational process that is based on a person's physical characteristics.

Physiological needs One of Maslow's hierarchy of needs reflecting the need for air, food, water, and other essentials.

Pilot test A process of asking a sample of respondents from the organization (who are similar to those who will ultimately receive the final instrument) to provide feedback on the instrument and identify any issues or concerns before the instrument is disseminated to everyone.

Planning and acting Part of strategic change; reflects selling the vision of what the future will be like when the change is successfully implemented.

Political correctness Language that is strategically used to replace other language so as to not be viewed as discriminatory, harassing, or offensive to others.

Political skills The ability to negotiate delicate organizational relationships and convince upper management that training and organizational development efforts do indeed contribute to the profitability of the organization.

Populations Organizations of a similar type.

Positive language Language use that projects a confident, well-meaning, and team-oriented person.

Positive organizational culture A culture that provides employees with a sense of security and stability as a result of a deep-rooted, well-defined past and a sense of predictability that forecasts the future.

Positive relational effects A dimension of taking conflict personally; refers to the belief that conflict is positive and results in better quality relationships.

Positive-face A sense of positive self-concept that can take place either at the individual level, group level, or both.

Power The ability to force people to do what you want regardless of their willingness or unwillingness to do so.

Power differential approach Assumes that the larger the power difference between people, the more probable that there will be sexual harassment.

Power-distance A characteristic of culture proposed by Hofstede that reflects the degree to which a culture values power and status.

Precise style A dimension of communicator style that reflects communicating in a way that is exact and detailed.

Predicted outcome value A theory that assumes people formulate judgments about the likelihood of engaging in future interactions.

Presentation skills The ability to deliver the content of the module or program with energy and vitality, to use proper vocal articulation and pronunciation, and to be perceived as an active and dynamic communicator.

Presentation software An instructional aid that includes adding visuals, such as pictures, sounds, animation, and video, to slides.

Pressure on dissent Pressures members to agree by treating like outsiders those who disagree.

Primary needs Primitive needs that sustain physiological survival (e.g., air, water, food, etc.).

Primary social group dimension of ethics A dimension of the ethical wheel that concerns the influence of family or the group; this influence socializes a person to distinguish between right and wrong.

Principle of hierarchiology Principle that assumes organizational members are promoted to their highest level of competence.

Proactive scanning Tendency to identify and assign significance to data that may or will be used in future decision making or problem solving.

Problem A component of the Inventional System that concerns the clear definition of the issue or problem at hand.

Problem solving group Process of rectifying a situation, process, or procedure that has been deemed inappropriate, ineffective, or faulty.

Problemistic search A factor influencing decision making; whenever something is termed a problem, a search is conducted to find a solution.

Procedural justice Reflects making decisions and implementing those decisions based on fair and sound principles.

Process Factor of strategic change reflecting the way in which the organization goes about implementing change.

Process conflict One of the three most common types of conflict; involves differences in the methods and strategies used to accomplish tasks.

Process orientation A key factor of team building contributing to the effective functioning of teams.

Processes the team currently uses to get tasks accomplished A factor in organizational development data gathering concerning the various communication and power dynamics of the team.

Productivity through people Attribute of a company that is performance centered and views productivity not so much as a result of organizational control but more as a result of great expectations that exist for each employee.

Profanity A type of verbal aggression that involves the use of obscene words and vulgar language.

Professional dimension of ethics A dimension of the ethical wheel consisting of professional standards of conduct mandated by professional organizations in a given career field.

Professionalism A characteristic of communication assessment that states that assessment should be conducted by professionals who have expertise in the analysis of communication and communication consultation.

Programmed decisions Decisions that are repetitive and routine or a definite procedure worked out to address specific issues.

Project group A small group whose ultimate objectives are more specific and more micro-driven than a work group.

Psychological attributes Part of the perceptual organizational process that is based on a person's psychological state of mind.

Psychological climate Involves employee perceptions of how the work environment impacts psychological well-being.

Psychological maturity
A person's degree of self-efficacy and willingness to accept responsibility.

Psychopathology Explanation for verbal aggression that assumes people carry around repressed hostility from past traumatic experiences and, when faced with similar situations, act out in an aggressive way.

Public relations The communicative construction of an organization's public image, and the goodwill that results, for such external bodies as government officials, social activists, consumers or potential consumers, investors or potential investors, and media outlets.

Pull-factors Reflect the pursuit of positive rewards rather than the need to survive and cope with a problematic situation.

Punctuated equilibria Long periods of stability marked by short periods of sudden change.

Punishment power An employee's ability to have certain control over others based on his or her ability to deny incentives or rewards.

Pure charisma Charisma based on the behaviors that a leader exhibits.

Push-factors Environmental factors that thrust people into the role of an entrepreneur, such as a lay-off or bankruptcy.

Q

Qingmian A component of business success that involves respecting the feelings of others.

Quality improvement group
A collection of individuals whose main responsibility is to determine strategies for increasing an organization's effectiveness, efficiency, and productivity.

Quality of relational linkage
A major component of LMX Theory that reflects how the leader and subordinate negotiate their specific roles and how this directly impacts how both leaders and subordinates interpret work and the work experience.

Quality or organizational communication relationships
A component of the ICA communication audit that assesses the quality of our relationships with supervisors, management, coworkers, and the organization in general.

Quanix A component of business success that involves valuing friendship.

Quasi-resolution of conflict
Occurs when there are so many political views and perspectives in the organization that no one ever really gets what he or she wants.

Questionnaires Data-gathering technique that is useful when attempting to gather data from large groups of people. May take the form of surveys, scales, or self-report instruments.

Quid pro quo A form of sexual harassment that is defined as sexual behavior in exchange for something.

R

Rational-legal authority system
A system of bureaucratic management that advocates that organizations should be designed to achieve certain goals through the use of rules and regulations developed by the organization.

Rationalization Making excuses; discounting warnings no matter how strong the warnings are.

Reaction Level 1 of the Kirkpatrick model that involves assessing trainees' levels of satisfaction with the program.

Reactive scanning Tendency to identify and assign significance to data only after a problem or a situation requiring a decision presents itself.

Reading anxiety The degree of anxiety a person experiences when reading information.

Reality shock Occurs when expectations about a new job are different from what is actually experienced.

Reciprocating patterns Part of interaction adaptation theory that involves matching the behavior or reciprocating the behavior of another person.

Recorder A designated role in which the person is not necessarily an active participant in the group discussion but whose function is to take the minutes of the meeting.

Recorder A small-group role whose major responsibility is to keep track of everything communicated during the small-group deliberation.

Referent The thing that a sign is representing.

Referent power A base of power reflecting the ability to get followers to act because the followers like you and believe in your vision.

Referent power An employee's ability to have certain control over others based on his or her perceived worth and respect.

Reframing The distortion of information that occurs during the process of message transmission.

Refreezing A step in the three-step model of organizational change that ensures that the new ideas or behaviors are relatively stable and that employees do not regress to the old ideas and behaviors.

Reinforcement The fourth and final stage of the group development process wherein group members continue to rationalize their decision and reinforce its validity.

Relational communication Verbal and nonverbal messages that create the social fabric of a group by promoting relationships between and among its members.

Relational dialectic An inherent inconsistency between two salient variables, which results when competing interpersonal needs surface at the same time.

Relational dissolution The process by which relationships come to an end, either through a gradual process (passing away) or an isolated incident or event (sudden death).

Relational maintenance strategy Actions individuals engage in with the intent of maintaining a relationship.

Relational-based ethical perspective Assumes that all relationships within the organization as well as among the organization and its various external publics are based on quality and honest communication.

Relationship A symbiotic social connection between two people in which certain limited resources are shared, resulting in more effective and efficient productivity for both parties.

Relationship conflicts One of the three most common types of conflict found in teams; is based on style, personality, and social issues that usually lie outside of work-related issues and almost always create negativity within the team.

Relative advantage Determining whether an innovation's adoption will allow the organization to operate more efficiently or more consistently than it currently does.

Relaxed style A dimension of communicator style that reflects communicating in a way that lacks anxiety or tension.

Reliability The stability, consistency, and accuracy of a measurement scale, test, or instrument.

Repetition A positive strategy of organizational dissent that involves bringing up an issue consistently over a period of time.

Replacement Occurs when new organizations emerge in direct relation to a changing environment. New organizations developed specifically for the new environment are more effective than existing organizations that try to adapt to the new environment.

Requisite variety Occurs when an organization seeks to ensure that there is a "most single" reality that is shared by all members of the organization (e.g., reduce uncertainty and equivocation).

Resolution A decision in which the choice or solution resolves the original problem.

Response format A formal method in which individuals respond to the items on a questionnaire or scale.

Response set A threat to data in which a respondent places the same value (e.g., 3) for every question regardless of what is asked.

Results Level 4 of the Kirkpatrick model that involves the degree to which the training has impacted the organization's goals, objectives, and bottom line.

Retention stage of organizing Process of organizing that decides whether or not assembly rules and communication cycles should be retained or discarded in future sense-making.

Reward power An employee's ability to have certain control over others based on his or her ability to provide incentives.

Rich media channels Channels that fulfill all or most of the carrying capacity criteria (e.g., FTF interactions).

Rights/justice-based ethical perspective Assumes that ethical behavior is based on a certain level of dignity and justice and a level of fairness for all.

Risky shift The idea that social beings are more likely to make a riskier, rather than safer, decision when working in a group with others as opposed to when working alone.

Rites and rituals Ceremonies or events that recognize and celebrate the values of an organization.

Ritual A type of sign that is neither totally arbitrary (like a symbol) nor symptomatic (like a signal).

Robber barons People who control an entire industry, crush competition, and amass an incredible amount of personal wealth.

Role attributes Part of the perceptual organizational process that is based on a person's role in society.

Role culture Based on the work of Handy, this organizational culture is modeled after the Greek god Apollo and is epitomized by attention to order and rules.

Role-making phase A phase marked by the movement away from the process in which the supervisor tells newcomers their role as a process in which newcomers seek to alter the nature of their given role as well as the manner in which the role is performed.

Role-play Training activity that allows training participants to apply the knowledge and skills they acquire from the training program in a "real world situation."

Role-routinization phase A phase that reflects the point at which the role of the newcomer and expected behaviors of the supervisor are accepted and understood.

Role-taking phase The sampling phase in which the superior attempts to discover members' relevant talents and motivations through iterative test sequences.

Roll-out process The process of sharing the results of the organizational assessment; includes upper management, divisional or departmental middle-level management, and, ultimately, all members of the organization.

Routinized charisma Charisma based on the position of power a person holds in the organization.

Rule of 16 A rule for using Power-Point slides that suggests people should not include more than 16 words on any given slide because doing so can overwhelm trainees.

Rumors Unsubstantiated messages presented as verified fact.

S

Safety needs One of Maslow's hierarchy of needs reflecting the need for a life free of turmoil and characterized by relative stability and a preference for predictability.

Sapir-Whorf hypothesis Also known as the theory of linguistic relativity. Assumes that all higher levels of thought depend on language and that the structure of language we use influences the way we perceive the environment.

Satisfaction A component of the ICA audit that assesses both an individual's personal efforts and achievements as well as organizational outcomes.

Satisfaction with communication climate Part of the ICA Audit that assesses whether the organization motivates employees, level of identification, communication competence, and information flow.

Satisfaction with communication with subordinates Part of the ICA Audit that assesses how receptive subordinates are to downward communication and how willing they are to provide upward communication.

Satisfaction with communication with supervisors Part of the ICA Audit that assesses upward and downward communication.

Satisfaction with horizontal and informal communication Part of the ICA Audit that assesses perceptions of organizational networks.

Satisfaction with media quality Part of the ICA Audit that assesses employee's perceptions of organizational communication channels and their reaction to them.

Satisfaction with organizational integration Part of the ICA Audit that assesses the degree to which employees receive information about their work environment including policies and benefits.

Satisfaction with organizational perspective Part of the ICA Audit that assesses how well informed employees feel about organizational change, information about the organization's mission and financial standing.

Satisfaction with personal feedback Part of the ICA Audit that assesses the extent to which supervisors feel their subordinates are receptive to evaluation, suggestions, and criticism.

Scalar chain Type of information transfer that reflects a clear hierarchical exchange of information.

Scientific management A management perspective that assumes any worker can be productive if given a scientifically efficient task. This perspective does not concern the well-being of the worker and is focused on efficient task completion.

Scientifically efficient A term used to reflect a task that has been analyzed for efficiency so that any worker can optimally perform that task.

Scripts Recipes that are borrowed, followed, and modified by individuals to get things done.

Secondary social group dimension of ethics A dimension of the ethical wheel that consists of groups that are not as influential as the primary group, but provide some psychological or social benefits to group members.

Selection Part of the perception process that involves determining what stimuli get our attention.

Selection stage of organization Process that selects meanings and interpretation directly and selects individuals, departments, groups, or goals indirectly.

Selective perception The tendency to pay attention to particular elements or information in the environment while ignoring other elements or information.

Self-actualization The process of allowing our value systems, personal needs, interpersonal needs, professional needs, and talents to drive our behavior in and out of the workplace.

Self-censorship Doubting our own opinions; being unwilling to disagree or dissent in order to maintain group harmony.

Self-centered role A small-group role, the focus of which is on disturbing intragroup harmony and detracting the group from its productivity.

Self-disconfirming prophecy Occurs when our original beliefs, perceptions, and expectations influence our behavior in a way that prevents the original beliefs, perceptions, and expectations from being supported.

Self-fulfilling prophecy Occurs when we have false expectations about a situation; it results in behavior that makes the false expectation come true.

Self-handicapping The adoption or advocacy of impediments to success in a situation where the person anticipates failure.

Self-realization See *self-actualization.*

Sell A situational leadership style in which the leader is task and employee focused and thereby hopes to motivate subordinates.

Semantic differential-type scale items An answer format that uses bipolar adjectives to assess how people feel about particular issues (e.g., not credible_ _ _ _ _credible) and results in interval level data.

Sense-making The interpretation of a perceptual process that varies from person to person. What constitutes information and information quality is unique to each individual.

Sensing Dimension of the Myers-Briggs Type Indicator that refers to the degree to which people tend to see things at face value.

Sequential attention to goals Decision-making approach used in situations where many goals are not being satisfied simultaneously. Isolates and analyzes each goal, solves it, and then moves on to the next goal.

Sequential versus random tactics Involve a set sequence of steps (rather than an unsystematic sequence of steps) that end in the assumption of a new role.

Serial versus disjunctive tactics Involve newcomer socialization by experienced workers as opposed to unaided learning of a job and role.

Sex-roll spill-over approach Assumes that when the sex ratio is disproportionate, there is a higher probability for sexual harassment.

Sexual harassment Involves unwelcomed sexual advances, requests for sexual favors, and other verbal or physical conduct of a sexual nature when this conduct explicitly or implicitly affects an individual's employment, unreasonably interferes with an individual's work performance, or creates an intimidating, hostile, or offensive work environment.

Shared knowledge The pooled information to which people have access that enables employees to engage in work practices.

Signals Signs that have a direct, one-to-one relationship with the things they represent.

Signs Things that stand for or represent something else.

Simon's activity approach A three stage process of decision making comprised of intelligence, design, and choice activity.

Simple form, lean staff Attribute of a company that has a streamlined organizational structure and well define authority.

Simultaneous loose-tight properties Attribute of a company that gives a great degree of autonomy and latitude to departments and divisions yet at the same time all departments and divisions of the organization are bound to the central value system and culture of the organization.

Single-loop learning Learning how a process is executed, not why it is executed. This type of learning is believed to be self-oppressive.

Situational ethical perspective Assumes that ethical decisions are unique to any given situation and are not universal in nature.

Situational leadership perspective A leadership perspective that assumes there are no true-born leaders; rather, people act as leaders in different situations. Anyone can effectively adapt the appropriate leadership style to a given situation and follower(s).

Situational leadership theory Assumes that any leadership style should be based on both the employee's psychological maturity and job maturity.

Skilled evaluation A characteristic of communication assessment that states that data gathered must be held to some criteria in judging the adequacy of the current state of the organization's communication.

Skills acquisition A component of organizational training that refers to training employees to perform a particular behavior.

Skills deficiency Assumes that a lack of arguing skills leads a person to resort to verbal aggression.

Skunkworks A term used to refer to people who are given autonomy to create and are expected to develop new and innovative projects in unorthodox ways.

Small bandwidth Occurs when a person is given a small degree of linguistic freedom.

Social composure A dimension of communicative adaptability that reflects the degree to which a person is calm, cool, and collected in social situations.

Social confirmation A dimension of communicative adaptability that reflects the degree to which a person can affirm or maintain the other person's face or self-image while interacting.

Social experience A dimension of communicative adaptability that reflects the degree to which a person actually experiences, or is willing to experience, novel situations.

Social identity theory The idea that individuals construct a certain sense of self based on the groups in which they find themselves embedded.

Social influence The influence of coworkers and superiors on the way in which members perceive reality.

Social information processing theory Assumes that communicators form impressions about others based on the relatively limited nonverbal and physical cues available through mediated communication.

Social learning Assumes the tendency to be verbally aggressive is developed through modeling significant others in our environment based on reward or punishment resulting from behavior.

Social loafer The member of a group who exerts less energy and effort toward the group's task because he or she expects others will pick up the slack.

Social loafing Group members who do not contribute to the group at a level equal to their abilities.

Social solidarity A network's or small group's willingness to agree that certain behaviors are deemed appropriate and others inappropriate.

Social support The support system created by in-group or network members.

Social-emotional leader The group member who focuses on people and is experienced with handling interpersonal problems.

Sociopsychological approach Assumes that there are particular combinations of an individual's personality and a specific situation that, when aligned, bring about sexual harassment.

Soldiering The assumption that workers purposely work below their capacity.

Solution A component of the Inventional System that concerns the possible ways of fixing or correcting an issue or problem.

Solution presentation An upward strategy of organizational dissent that centers around offering solutions along with the presentation of the problem.

Source credibility The degree to which people are perceived as being trustworthy and having expertise.

Sources of information A component of the ICA communication audit that assesses how much information people are receiving, and would like to receive, from specific sources, such as subordinates, coworkers, supervisors, and management, as well as from meetings, presentations, and the grapevine.

Specific communicative tactics for change A category of change reflecting specific advice on how to implement the change process. This includes asking for input to increase participation, using informal networks to spread the message, using multiple channels to disseminate information, suggesting how to present the content of change, using motivational strategies, formulating specific communication plans, and creating and communicating a clear and relevant vision of change for all employees.

Spontaneous cooperation The fostering of relationships and teamwork among workgroup members.

Stabilizing of change Part of strategic change reflecting the ability of management to ensure that the entire organizational process is in support of change.

Stakeholder theory Assumes that the sole responsibility of an organization is to those people who own the instruments of production.

Standing group A small group that is ever-present and rarely changes its members. Also known as *permanent group*.

Stars People who occupy a central role in the organization's communication network.

Stereotyping Generalizations or assumptions that people make about the characteristics of all members of a group, based on an image (often wrong) about what people in that group are like.

Stereotyping outsiders Occurs when an organization considers opposition too weak and stupid to make real trouble for the organization.

Stick to the knitting Attribute of a company that only focuses on doing what it does best or sticks to the services, products, and/or sectors that have brought success in the first place.

Strategic ambiguity Purposely giving less information than is needed for complete understanding.

Strategies of dissent The specific messages that employees use to express dissent to management; can have both positive and negative consequences.

Stress reaction A dimension of taking conflict personally refers to the psychological and physical discomfort a person experiences in a conflict episode.

Strong cultures A culture with a system of formal and informal rules that indicate how employees and the organization as a whole are to behave. Thus, a strong corporate culture enables workers to feel as if they are making a positive contribution to the organization, which results in more productive workers.

Structuration theory A theory that assumes that structure and action are a duality in that structures are recursive in that they are produced and reproduced through behavior.

Structure The process of assigning a recorder to take the minutes of the meeting and making sure the agenda is circulated.

Style of living Dimension of the Myers-Briggs Type Indicator that reflects a person's preferred lifestyle.

Subject-matter expert (SME) A person who is an expert in a particular subject or content area.

Subjugated A term that describes workers who are oppressed and exploited by management.

Subsystem A system that operates within a larger system.

Supportive organizational climate A supportive communication climate that invites openness among employees, encourages the use of empathetic listening, promotes constructive conflict management procedures, and encourages behaviors that build morale and creativity.

Suprasystem A larger system within which smaller systems operate.

Surveillance The use of technology in the workplace as a form of power and control that subjugates workers through continual monitoring.

Survey design team Key members of the organization often coming from the corporate communication and human resource departments and charged with developing the assessment questionnaire.

Symbol A type of sign that is human made or an artificial phenomenon.

Symptom A type of sign that bears a natural relationship to that for which it stands.

Synchronous communication Messages that are time bound in that the receiver must be present to receive the message and can respond to the message immediately or in real time (e.g., face-to-face communication).

System adaptation A self-regulating system utilizing feedback to adapt or change.

System maintenance A self-regulating system utilizing feedback to maintain itself.

Systems 4 management approach A human resource approach to management that ranges from depersonalization of employees to the full integration of employee input and potential.

Systems perspective A perspective rooted in biology that explains organizational processes by viewing the organization as an organism.

T

T-groups/training groups Early organizational development technique involving 8 to 12 individuals getting together with a professional trainer to discuss their behavior; including expressing positive and negative feelings about themselves, as well as others.

Tag questions A form of powerless language use that when tagged to the end of the statement greatly detracts from the power and status of the speaker.

Tailored design The belief that communication assessments should be tailored to the specific organization, not to organizations in general.

Taking conflict personally A communication trait that refers to the degree to which people view conflict as a punishing situation and something that should be avoided.

Talk is action A component of conversational analysis that assumes that to understand interpersonal interaction, we must understand that talk is something people do.

Task conflict One of the three most common types of conflict; involves differences in how tasks are to be performed.

Task coordination difficulties Problems associated with arranging the various factors needed for efficient team function.

Task culture According to Handy, this organizational culture is based on Athena, the goddess of knowledge, and focuses on the problem-solving ability of the organization.

Task leader Usually talks more than others in the group, is very mature, is well educated, is knowledgeable about the group task, and has good problem-solving skills along with a command of communication rules and strategies.

Task manager A management style that indicates a low concern for workers and a high concern for task.

Task role A small group role, the focus of which is on productivity and making certain the group achieves its defined goals.

Task socialization Involves acquiring information about the job and understanding the tasks for which one has been hired.

Taxonomy of communication A four component class of decisions employed during the change process, consisting of messages, media, channels, and approaches.

Team building A technique used to create and enhance commitment, trust, involvement, team goals, a process orientation, and communication.

Team goals A key factor of team building contributing to the effective functioning of teams.

Team manager A management style that indicates a high concern for workers and a high concern for task.

Teasing and ridicule A type of verbal aggression that involves making light of someone's shortcomings in an antagonistic fashion.

Tell A situational leadership style in which the leader focuses on tasks in training employees.

Temperament A part of personality predispositions that is believed to be based in biology and is comprised of different areas of the brain and their subsequent interaction.

Tension releaser Someone who can be funny while being aware of the sensibilities of the group. This role involves using tension-releasing humor to resolve interpersonal conflict and lessen the intensity of awkward moments.

Territoriality How people consciously and unconsciously organize their space.

Text messaging A common term for the sending of short text messages from mobile phones.

Thematic analysis An analysis technique involving the systematic identification of dominant themes or recurring trends in data.

Theory in use The actual behaviors that a manager engages in with employees that expose the manager's ethics, management style, and management philosophy.

Theory of independent mindedness A communication-based organizational theory that advocates cultural congruity between the organization and the larger culture within which it operates. Based on the three communication traits of argumentativeness, verbal aggressiveness, and communicator style.

Theory of linguistic relativity Also known as the Sapir-Whorf hypothesis. Assumes that all higher levels of thought depend on language and that the structure of language we use influences the way we perceive the environment.

Theory X approach A management approach that assumes workers are lazy, have little ambition, and are motivated by coercion and threats.

Theory Y approach A management approach that assumes workers are motivated by an internal need to excel and actively pursue responsibility.

Theory Z approach Approach to management that advocates matching the organization's culture to that of the larger society and assumes that involved workers are the key to increased productivity.

Thinking Dimension of the Myers-Briggs Type indicator that refers to the degree to which people use logic and structured information in decision making.

Thompson's uncertainty model An approach to decision making based on the degree of cause and effect relationship between decision and outcome as well as the degree to which people are clear about the desired outcome.

Threatening resignation A negative strategy of organizational dissent in which a person threatens to quit his or her job unless the problem is resolved.

Threats A type of verbal aggression that involves insinuating physical or psychological harm to another person.

Three-filter test A test developed by Socrates to assess whether information or knowledge is valuable and worth sharing with others.

Three-step model of organizational change A three-step process of organizational change developed by Kurt Lewin, consisting of unfreezing, moving, and refreezing.

Throughputs Elements flowing through the system.

Time-oriented listening style Listening style characterized by a focus on time-efficient communication.

Timeliness of information received A component of the ICA communication audit that concerns the degree to which information is received in a timely manner.

Tolerance for disagreement A communication trait that reflects the amount of disagreement a person can tolerate before he or she perceives the existence of a conflict in a relationship.

Trace point A "fingerprint" that identifies the sender of an e-mail and that can compromise anonymity and confidentiality of employee responses.

Traditional entrepreneur Type of entrepreneur who seeks to maximize financial gain and is constantly pursuing growth for the company.

Training function Responsible for imparting necessary knowledge and skill so employees become more effective in their positions.

Training need The difference between the actual and desired knowledge level and skill level.

Trait argumentativeness The tendency to present and defend positions on controversial issues while simultaneously attacking the positions that others take on those issues.

Trait leadership perspective Perspective of leadership where leadership qualities are believed to be within the personality of an individual.

Trait perspective of leadership A perspective of leadership that assumes people either possess the attributes of a leader or they do not.

Trait verbal aggressiveness A predisposition to attack the self-concept of another person with the intent to inflict psychological harm or pain.

Transformational leadership A leadership perspective that is focused on the empowering individual workers and helping the organization adapt to changes in both internal and external environments.

Transparent structure An ethical perspective that assumes every practice the organization engages in should be up front and open.

Trialability Attribute of an innovation that concerns the degree to which the innovation can be implemented on a trial basis.

Trust The degree to which relational partners have confidence in their counterpart's predictability of actions or words as well as their good intentions for a counterpart's wellbeing. Also a key factor of team-building contributing to the effective functioning of teams.

Type A organization An organization that uses typical American management style of individuality, short-term employment, and rapid advancement.

Type J organization An organization that uses typical Japanese management style of collectivism, long-time employment, and nonspecialized career paths.

U

Ultimate attribution error
An extreme case of basic attribution error in which we see the failures in other people as due to internal factors and our own failures as due to external factors.

Uncertainty avoidance
A characteristic of culture proposed by Hofstede that reflects the degree to which a culture copes with novelty.

Uncertainty management theory
A theory that explains how people react to uncertainty. Uncertainty is believed to be a multi-faceted concept that can be more valuable and serve many more functions if not treated as an aversive state that needs to be reduced or avoided.

Unconscious competence Level of competence in which we can perform the skill or behavior without putting much thought into it.

Unconscious incompetence Level of competence in which we cannot perform a behavior or skill and we do not know that we cannot perform it.

Understand the adult learner The ability to understand the concept of andragogy and the assumption that skills training should be problem centered and immediately applicable.

Unfreezing A step in the three-step model of organizational change that assumes that motivation for change must exist before any change occurs.

Unprogrammed decisions
Decisions that are new and unstructured or for which there is no cut-and-dried method for handling the problem.

Upward communication Messages that flow from the worker up to the supervisor.

Upward distortion One's decision to emphasize the positive elements embedded in a message when communicating with superiors and subordinates.

Utilitarian ethical perspective
Assumes that ethical behavior is based on outcome as opposed to intention.

V

Validity
Addresses the question of whether the measurement instrument actually measures what it says it is measuring.

Verbal aggressiveness
A predisposition to attack the self-concept of another person with the intent to inflict psychological harm or pain.

Verbal intensifiers Words that increase the intensity of the emotion the speaker is experiencing as opposed to the literal information contained in the message.

Verbal qualifiers Words that reduce the strength and impact of an utterance.

Verbal self-handicaps
A handicapping strategy that reveals to the evaluator that the condition exists.

Vocalic competence The use of voice that is appropriate in volume and with great variety.

Vroom's decision making style
A decision-making style that reflects the varying degree of input that management seeks from employees and the degree to which that information is acted upon.

W

Web site A collection of web pages, images, videos, or other digital media hosted by one or more web servers, usually accessible via the Internet.

Wheel network A type of small-group network wherein one person has access to all others, but all others do not have access to each other.

Whistleblowing Revealing questionable organizational practices to an outside audience that can bring about justice or increase awareness in an affected public.

Wide bandwidth Occurs when a person is given a large degree of linguistic freedom.

Wit A dimension of communicative adaptability that reflects the degree to which a person uses humor in appropriate situations to diffuse escalating aggressive communication exchanges.

Work alienation A feeling of being psychologically disconnected from the organization.

Work group A collection of individuals whose main purpose is to achieve an overarching task that ultimately benefits the organization and those who are part of it.

Work-life boundaries
The distinction between home and work that have become blurred because technology such as computers, blackberries, and cell phones has enabled a 24-hour workday in which employees are always connected to their jobs.

Work-specific locus of control
A predisposition to view outcomes within the organization as being due to forces beyond our control or our own behavior.

Workgroup communication
The interaction of 3 to 15 people who are communicating and working interdependently to achieve a common goal.

Workgroup socialization Involves newcomers learning particulars about their workgroup and the behaviors associated with the group's rules, goals, and values.

Working poor A situation derived from progressive capitalism in which workers are unable to afford the products they produce.

Workplace bullying The repeated mistreatment of one employee targeted by one or more employees with a malicious mix of humiliation, intimidation, verbal abuse, and work interference.

Workplace friendships Typically emerge among peers who are working in close proximity to one another on joint tasks, and who socialize together.

Workplace relationship Any relationship a person has with a coworker, such as a supervisor-subordinate, peer, or mentoring relationship.

World marketplace Concept referring to the degree to which the U.S. economy is connected to the economies of other countries around the world.

World Wide Web One of the services communicated via the Internet. It is a collection of interconnected documents and resources, linked by hyperlinks and URLs.

Written communication skills The ability to write effectively and persuasively when putting ideas together.

Subject Index

A

Abraham personality, 185
abstractness, 232
acceptable level decision rule, 224
accountability, practice of, 205
acknowledgment of understanding the problem, 236
acquired needs theory, 186–87
acquisition, 63
action or follow-up taken, 330
action research (AR)
    defined, 295
    in organizational change, 286–87
active listening skills, 254
actor-observer bias, 14
Adam personality, 185
adaptation, 81–82
ad hoc committees, 326
ad hoc group. *See* disbanding group
administrative man model, 222
adult learner, understanding, 256
affective commitment, 345
Affirmative Action Programs (AAP), 249
affirming communication style of communication, 43
aggressor, role of, 159
alignment, 205
all-channel network, of small group, 162–63
American business, 6
American culture, 15
    to consumerism and individual advancement, 26
American organizations (Type A organizations), 35–36
American Red Cross, 147
American Society for Training and Development, 248
Amish people, 5
andragogy, 254, 256

androgynous style, of leadership, 176
animated style, 43
anticipation, 60
anticipatory stage, of socialization process, 58
applied leadership, 181–83
appreciative action research model (AARM), 299
appreciative inquiry (AI), 295–98
    assumptions of, 296
    defined, 295
    steps in process of, 296–98
    in team building, 301–3
Apprentice, The (NBC), 153
appropriate disclosure, 136
appropriateness, 4
argument approach, 129
argumentativeness, 42, 43
Argumentativeness Scale, 272
articulated dissent, 207
articulation, 136
artifacts, 52
artisan entrepreneurs, 189
assembly rules, 231
assertiveness, 129
attentive style of communication, 43
attributions for behavior, 12
    biases in, 14–15
    external, 12
    internal, 12
    rules for, 13
authoritarianism, 123
authority, defined, 28
autocratic-oriented decision-making style, 220–21

B

bandwidth, 85–86
basic attribution error, 14

behavior (level 3 of the Kirkpatrick model), 275
behavioral contagion, 51
behavioral objectives, 263
benchmarking, 180
benevolent-authoritative type of management, 33
betweenness centrality, 107
Big Bang Theory, The, 102
Blake and Mouton's managerial grid, 39–41
blame in inventional system, 227
blended learning, 252
blocker, role of, 159
blood type A, 121
blood type AB, 121
blood type B, 121
blood type O, 121
blood typing, 121
blueprint, 60
brain-derived neurotrophic factor (BDNF), 120
brainstorming
    in decision-making process, 226
    in workgroups, 226
breaking-in period of socialization process, 58
bridges, defined, 348
bureaucratic management, 28
business ethics, development of, 201

C

case studies, 269–70
ceiling effect, 146
census, 321
centrality, 106
chain, 161
change agents, communicative role of, 293
channels of communication, 205, 331

character attacks, 128

charisma trait, 175

childhood labor, 25

Chinese Zodiac, 121–22

choice activity stage, in decision-making, 222

chronemics, 204

circle network, of small group, 161–62

circumvention, 209

closed-ended items, 318–19

closed system, 8

closeness centrality, 107

clothing, 203–4

clown, 160

cognitive flexibility, 134–35

cognitive learning, 270

Cold Stone Creamery, 61, 62

collective commitment, 151

collective involvement, 151

commitment, in team building, 300

communication, 33

   channels of, 331

   competence, 175

   content dimension, 290

   ethical considerations in, 202–4

   during implementation of organizational change, 290–92

   Klein's model of, 290

   medium dimension, 290

   nonverbal, 202

   in organization, 4

   role in managing organizational change, 289–90

   taxonomy of, 293

   in team building, 300

   training (See communication training)

   trait profiles, 44

communication accommodation theory (CAT), 79–81

communication assessment. See also organizational communication, assessment of

   benefits of conducting, 313

   current time frame in, 312

   defined, 311–12

   diagnostic thoroughness in, 312

Downs-Hazen communication satisfaction questionnaire, 340–42

ICA Communication Audit Survey, 312, 330–40

independence in, 311

professionalism in, 311

skilled evaluation in, 312

tailored design in, 312

tools for, 330–42

communication audit

   benefits of, 313, 329–30

   Downs-Hazen communication satisfaction questionnaire, 340–42

   ICA Communication Audit Survey, 312, 330–40

   questionnaire, 332–40

   tools for, 330–42

communication conflict-related traits, 126–33

   argument approach, 129

   argumentativeness, 129–30

   assertiveness, 129

   character attacks, 128

   competence attacks, 128

   general tendency to argue (ARGgt), 129

   interactionist perspective of personality, 129

   maledictions, 128

   nonverbal verbal aggression, 128

   personality attacks, 128

   taking conflict personally (TCP), 130–31

   teasing and ridicule, 128

   threats, 128

   tolerance for disagreement (TFD), 131–33

   verbal aggressiveness, 127–28

communication cycles, 231

communication diary, 332

communication, in organizational change

   general strategies for, 294

   during moving stage, 291

   during refreezing stage, 291–92

   role of, 289–90

   during unfreezing stage, 290–91

communication network analysis, 348–51

communication trainer

   instructor's manual, 251, 264–67

   lectures, delivering, 268

   notes to instructor, 265

   role of, 251–53

   skills and abilities critical for, 253–56

communication training

   common topics in, 249

   communication trainer (See communication trainer)

   competency levels in, 257–58

   defined, 248

   efficacy for, 276–77

   evaluating, 274–76

   experiential activities in, 269–72

   instructional aids, 272–73

   interactive training program (See interactive training program)

   Kirkpatrick's model for evaluating, 275

   manuals, writing, 264–67

   need for, 256–57

   online methods of, 252

   organizational training and, 248

   presentation skills, 253, 273–74

communicative adaptability, 135–37

communicative role, of change agents, 293

communicator image, 133

communicator style (CS), 42, 133–34

   dimensions, 43

Communicator Style Measure (CSM), 271

compatibility, 239

compensating patterns, 82

compensation and benefits function, 249

competence attacks, 128

competence-related traits, 133–37

   animated style of interaction, 133

   attentive style of interaction, 133

   cognitive flexibility, 134–35

   communicative adaptability, 135–37

   communicator image style of interaction, 133

communicator style construct (CS), 133–34

contentious style of interaction, 133

dominant style of interaction, 133

dramatic style of interaction, 133

friendly style of interaction, 133

impression leaving style of interaction, 133

open style of interaction, 133

precise style of interaction, 133

relaxed style of interaction, 133

substyles of interaction, 133

competency levels, 257–58

competent communication, 4

complexity, 232, 239

composition of the team, 301

compound requests, 78

compromising strategy, 220

computational strategy, 219

concertive control, 10

confirmation stage of innovation adoption, 240

conflict, 104, 150

quasi resolution of, 223

connotative meaning, 73–74

conscious competence, 257

conscious incompetence, 257

consequence in inventional system, 227

consultative-oriented decision-making style, 220

consultative type of management, 33

contagion, 51

content analysis, 318

content in strategic change, 236

contentious style, 43

context in strategic change, 236

continuance commitment, 345

contributors, role of, 157

contrived group, 147

contrived relationships, 98

convergence, 80

converging speech patterns, 80, 82

conversational desires, 83

conversational expectations, 83

conversational requirements, 83

"corporate we," notion of, 50

corporations caught in corrupt activity, 199

corporatist theory, 42

country club manager, 40

courage, practice of, 205

course delivery, 251

critical incident analysis, 332

critical perspective of organizations, 9–10

cultural artifacts, 52–53

current time frame, in communication assessment, 312

cybernetic learning, 39

cybernetic system, 8

D

dangling carrot approach to management, 27

data-analysis skills, 255

data cleaning, 323

data-gathering skills, 255

deciding in Myers-Briggs Type Indicator, 120

decision-making, 146, 150, 155, 158

as art and politics, 223–26

clown, role in, 160

ethical, 209

five-stage model of innovation, 239

functional approach to, 218

Group Decision Support System (GDSS), 163–64

idea generation and, 226

inventional system and, 226–28

Simon's activity approach and, 222–23

Thompson's uncertainty model and, 219–20

Vroom's decision-making styles and, 220–22

decision stage, of innovation adoption, 239

defensive routines, 37

define step of appreciative inquiry, 296

degree centrality, 106

delegating style, of leadership, 177

denotative meaning, 73

deontological ethical perspective, 200

depersonalization, 28

design activity stage, in decision-making, 222

design step, of appreciative inquiry, 297

destiny step, of appreciative inquiry, 298

development of concern stage, in decision-making, 236

diagnostic thoroughness, in communication assessment, 312

dialogic communication, 205

direct appeal, 209

direct personalization, 131

direct reports, 322

disbanding group, 149

discover step, of appreciative inquiry, 297

disdain, 127

displaced dissent, 208

dispositional factors, 12

dissent. *See* organizational dissent

distributive justice, 200

divergence, 80–81

diversity of ideas, 151

dogmatism, 123–24

dominant style, 43

dominator, role of, 160

double-barreled items, 319

double-loop learning, 39

Downs-Hazen communication satisfaction questionnaire, 340–42

downward

communication, 34

distortion, 103

dramatic style, 43

dream step, of appreciative inquiry, 297

dress guidelines, Thomsett's eight principles of, 204

E

economic man model, 222

Educational Testing Service (ETS), 328

effectiveness, 4

eigenvector centrality, 108

e-instruction. *See* e-learning

elaborators, role of, 157

e-learning, 252

electronics industry, technological advancements in, 6

electronic support systems, 164

emancipation, 9

emergent group, 147

emergent relationships, 98

empathy, 254

employee
    view of an organization, 15–16
    willingness to adopt, 10

employee-centered system, 34

employee relations function, 249

employee's subjugated position, 10

employment interviews. *See* interviews, in needs assessment

employment/staffing function, 249

enactment, in decision-making, 230

encounter stage, of socialization process, 58, 60

encouragers, role of, 158

energizing in Myers-Briggs Type Indicator, 120

English language, 72

Enhancing Employee Motivation training program, 250

entrepreneurial spirit, 187–91
    background and personality factors, 190–91
    defined, 189
    entrepreneurial skill sets and, 190
    greatest entrepreneurs and, 188

entrepreneurship
    categories of, 189
    defined, 189

entropy, 8

Equal Employment Opportunity (EEO), 249

equifinality, 7

espoused theory, 38

esteem needs, in hierarchy of needs, 184

ethical perspectives, in the workplace, 198–202
    corporations caught in corrupt activity, 199

deontological ethical perspective, 200
    foundational ethical perspective, 199
    relationship-based ethical perspective, 201
    rights/justice-based ethical perspective, 200
    situational ethical perspective, 199
    stakeholder theory, 201–2
    utilitarian ethical perspective, 200

ethical reasoning, 200

ethical wheel, 205–7

ethics. *See also* ethical perspectives, in the workplace; organizational dissent
    considerations in communication, 202–4
    indirect interpersonal aggression and, 210–11
    misbehaviors in the workplace and, 211
    nonverbal behavior and, 202–4
    personal dimension of, 206
    practical advice on when to speak, 212–13
    practices of ethical organizations, 205
    primary social group dimension of, 206
    professional dimension of, 206–7
    secondary social group dimension of, 206
    three-filter test and, 213
    virtue (*See* deontological ethical perspective)
    whistleblowing and, 209–10

eudaimonic philosophy of life, 185

eudaimonic view, of organizational life, 16

evaluation, 252

evaluator/critic, role of, 158

evolutionary/ecological perspective of organizations, 6–7

experiential training activities, 269–72
    case studies, 269–70
    games, 270–71
    instruments used in, 271–72
    role-play, 269

exploitive-authoritative type of management, 33

external attributions, 12

external locus of control, 125

external work locus of control, 126

extroverted, in Myers-Briggs Type Indicator, 120

F

facilitation skills, 254

Fayol's bridge, 29

Fayol's lateral communication, 29

feedback, 8

FEMA (U.S. Federal Emergency Management Agency), 147

filter of goodness, 213

filter of truth, 213

filter of usefulness, 213

flexibility, 232

flight in decision-making, 225

flip charts, 272, 273

Fortune 500, 180

foundational ethical perspective, 199

four-factor model, of sexually harassing behavior, 88

French fries, process of making, 38

friendly style of communication, 43

functional approach, to decision making, 218

Functional Magnetic Resonance Image (MRI), 120

G

games, 270–71

gangplank, 29

garbage can model of organizational choice, 225

general personality traits, 122–26
    authoritarianism, 123
    dogmatism, 123–24
    locus of control, 125–26
    Machiavellianism, 124–25

general systems theory, 7

generative learning, 39

Great Depression, 32

Group Decision Support System (GDSS), 163–64

group, defined, 146, 348

group handicapping behavior, 152

group orientation, 150

group-oriented decision-making style, 220

groupthink phenomenon, 155

growth factors of motivation, 186

H

Habitat For Humanity, 147

haptics, 202

harmonizers, role of, 158–59

Hawthorne effect, 32

Hawthorne Studies, 31–32

hedonic philosophy of life, 185

hedonic view of organizational life, 15

hegemonic view, 10

Herzberg's motivator hygiene continua, 186

hierarchiology, principle of, 181–82

higher education, 7

high-quality links, 178

holism, concept of, 151, 156, 158, 160

homeostasis (the dynamic balance of the system), 7

hostile work environment, 87

How to Lose a Guy in Ten Days (movie), 103

human productivity, 24

human relations, approach to management, 31–32

human resource, approach to management

    Argyris' Model I and Model II approach, 37–39

    Blake and Mouton's managerial grid, 39–41

    Likert system 4 management approach, 33–34

    McGregor's Theory X and Theory Y approach, 34–35

    Ouchi's Theory Z approach, 35–37

    theory of independent mindedness (TIM), 41–44

hygiene factors, of motivation, 186

I

ICA Communication Audit Questionnaire, 324

idea generation in decision-making, 226

ideology, 52

imaginization, concept of, 18

immediacy, 274

implementation phase, of innovation adoption, 238

implementation stage, of innovation adoption, 239

impoverished manager, 40

impression-leaving style, 43

Improving Listening Skills training program, 250

independence, in communication assessment, 311

indirect interpersonal aggression, 210–11

industrialization, 5

information actually sent, 330

informational reception apprehension (IRA), 232–33

information processing, 228–36

    informational reception apprehension and, 232–33

    information systems theory and, 229–31

    uncertainty management theory and, 233–36

information received, 330

information scanning, 228

information seekers, role of, 157

information-sharing, 96

information systems theory, 229–31

in-group members, 178

in-group membership, 51

initiation phase, of innovation, 238

initiators, role of, 157

innovation

    defined, 237

    five-stage model of decision-making in, 239

innovation/change model, of innovation adoption, 238–39

innovation process, phases of, 238

inputs (elements flowing into the system), 7

In Search of Excellence: Lessons from America's Best Run Companies (Peters and Waterman), 180

inspirational strategy, 220

instructional aids, 272–73

instructional and behavioral objectives, writing, 262

instructional design, 251

instructional manuals

    instructor's, 264–67

    participant's, 267

instructional objectives, 263

instructor. *See* communication trainer

instructor's manual, 251, 264–67

    icon key for, 265–67

    sample page of, 266

instruments, used in training, 271–72

intellectual inflexibility, 232

intelligence activity stage, in decision-making, 222

interaction adaptation theory (IAT), 81–83

interactionist perspective of personality, 129

interaction position, 83

interactive lecture, 268

interactive training program

    instructional and behavioral objectives, writing, 262

    needs assessment, conducting, 252, 258–59

    reasons for objectives, 263–64

    research and development, 260–62

    selecting and narrowing the topic, 260

interchangeable gun part, 5

interdependent systems, 8

internal attributions, 12

internal locus of control, 125

internal-stable factors, 126

internal-unstable factors, 126

internal work locus of control, 126

International Communication Association (ICA) Communication Audit, 290, 312, 329, 330–40, 350
interpersonal communication skills, 254
interpretation of information, 12
interviews, in needs assessment, 259, 261
intrapreneurs, 190
introverted, in Myers-Briggs Type Indicator, 120
intuition in Myers-Briggs Type Indicator, 120
inventional system, 226–28, 272
isolates, 348
issues of fact, in decision-making, 227
issues of policy, in decision-making, 227
issues of value, in decision-making, 227

J

Japanese blood typing, assessment method, 121
Japanese culture values, 121
Japanese organizations (Type J organizations), 35–36
job maturity, 176–77
job satisfaction, 111, 125–26, 187, 286, 310, 340
Johnson and Johnson, 53
judgmental strategy, 219
judgment in Myers-Briggs Type Indicator, 120
justice
    distributive, 200
    procedural, 200

K

K.A.S.H. formula, 258
kinesics, 273–74
Kirkpatrick's model, for evaluating training, 275
K-Mart, 7
knowledge acquisition, 248
knowledge stage, of innovation, 239
knowledge transfer, 153

L

Lambda Pi Eta, 7
language
    connotative meaning, 73–74
    defined, 72
    denotative meaning, 73
    English, 72
    gender influence on, 75
    interaction and, 79–84
    main function of, 72
    perception, 76–77
    power and, 77–79
    sexual harassment and, 86–89
    styles, 74–76
    technological, 72
    within the workplace, 74
language expectancy theory (LET), 84–86
latent dissent, 208
laziness, 12
leader-member exchange theory (LMX), 178
leadership
    applied, 181–83
    communication competence, 175
    contingency theory of, 177
    criteria in the selection process, 182
    difference with management, 174
    great man theory of, 175
    high-quality and low-quality links with subordinates, 178
    legitimate and referent power, 174
    organizations as industry leaders, 179–81
    and quality of relationship with organizational members, 178
    role development process, 178
    styles of, 176–77
    top 24 leaders/leadership teams in private and public sectors, 183
    transformational, 179
leadership perspectives
    exchange approaches to leadership and, 178–79

situational leadership perspectives, 176–78
    trait leadership perspectives, 175–76
learned helplessness, 37
learning (level 2 of the Kirkpatrick model), 275
lecture method, 268
lecturette, 268
legitimate power, 174
length of the requests, 78
lesson content, 265
Lewin's three-step model, of organizational change, 288–89
liaisons, 348
life expectancy, technological advancements and, 24
like/dislike valence, 131
Likert-type scale items, 318
limited resources, 96
linguistic expectations, 85
linguistic freedom, 85
linguistic relativity, theory of, 76
listening apprehension, 232
local rationality, 224
locus of control, 125–26
love needs, in hierarchy of needs, 184
low-quality links, 178

M

Machiavellianism, 124–25
maintenance roles, in organizational group, 157
maledictions, 128
management training, effectiveness of, 39
managerial behavior, 38
managerial entrepreneurs, 189
managerial grid, 39–41
manager's espoused theory, 38
managing organizational change, 288–95
    case studies in, 292–95
    communication, role of, 289–90
    Lewin's three-step model of, 288–89

manufactured consent, 10
Maslow's hierarchy of needs, 184
mass production of goods, 5
McKinsey 7-S framework, 180
merger and organizational culture, 63
metamessage, 202
metamorphosis stage, 60
metaphors of organizations, 55
    as brains, 17
    as cultures, 17
    as living organisms, 17
    as machines, 16–17
    as place of domination, 18
    as political systems, 17
    as psychic prisons, 18
    as roles, 17–18
    as systems in flux, 18
mindfulness, 74
mindlessness, 74
minority influence, 102
misbehaviors, in the workplace, 211
Model I and Model II approach to
    management, 37–39
moderate managers, 40
moral commitments, 200
Morgan's multiple perceptions, 16–18
motivation, 183–87
    acquired needs theory and, 186–87
    Maslow's hierarchy of needs
        and, 184
    motivator hygiene theory
        and, 185–86
motivator factors, of motivation, 186
motivator hygiene theory, 185–86
motives for harassment, 88
moving stage
    of communication, 291
    Lewin's three-step model of
        organizational change, 288–89
Myers-Briggs employee assessment,
    120
Myers-Briggs Type Indicator, 119

N

name generator technique, 111
narcissism trait, 175

National Communication Association,
    147
National Institute of Automotive
    Service Excellence, 206
National Training Laboratories, 300
need for achievement, 187
need for affiliation, 187
need for power, 187
needs analysis, 252
needs assessment, conducting, 252,
    258–59
negative language, 74–76
negative relational effects, 131
NEGOPY software package, 350
network analysis, 332, 348–49
nonaffirming communication style of
    communication, 43
nonsummativity, 8–9
nonverbal behavior and ethics, 202–4
nonverbal communication, 202
nonverbal immediacy, 274
nonverbal verbal aggression, 128
normative commitment, 345

O

objectives, in communication
    training, 262
observability, 239
observation, in communication
    training, 259
occulesics, 203, 273
online training, 252
open-ended items, 317–18
open style of communication, 43
open system, 8
operational changes, 237
opinion seekers, role of, 158
oppressors (management), 9
orchestrated group session, 322
organizational change, 6–7
    action research and, 286–87
    assessment of AR and AI models
        of, 298–300
    communication during
        implementation of, 290–92
    managing (See managing
        organizational change)

organizational innovation
    and, 237–40
    resistance to, 287–88
    strategic change and, 236–37
organizational choice, garbage can
    model of, 225
organizational commitment, 344–48
Organizational Commitment
    Questionnaire (OCQ), 344, 345, 346
organizational communication,
    assessment of, 4–5, 310–11
    audits, benefits of, 313
    communication network analysis,
        348–51
    ICA Communication Audit Survey
        used in, 312
    organizational surveys used
        in, 313–30
    quantitative examination
        for, 313–14
    role in professional development, 4
    as scholarly discipline, 4
organizational context, 301
organizational culture, 50
    constraining factors, 62
    cultural artifacts, 52–53
    as enabling and constraining,
        60–64
    factors associated with an, 52–56
    formal, 53
    merger and, 63
    role in developing sense of
        collective identity, 61
organizational development (OD)
    appreciative inquiry used
        in, 295–98
    assessment of AR and AI models
        of, 298–300
    defined, 284–85
    function, 249
    roots of, 285–86
    team building in, 300–303
organizational dissent
    dimensions of, 207–8
    issues of, 208–9
    strategies of, 209
organizational identification, concept
    of, 342–44

Organizational Identification Questionnaire (OIQ), 343, 344
organizational innovation, 237–40
organizational intelligence, 231
organizational learning, 225
organizational perception process, 11–12
organizational relationship, 97–98
  advantages, 100–102
  complications associated with, 103–5
  disadvantages, 105
  information flow and dissemination, 102
  methods of studying, 110–11
  superior/subordinate, 99–100
organizational relationships, 4
organizational socialization, 56–60
organizational social network, 105–9
organizational surveys, 313–30
  advantages of, 314–15
  considerations in survey development, other, 320
  defined, 313
  effective, seven steps in
    administering the survey, 321–22
    analyzing survey data, 322–24
    communicating survey's purpose and objectives, 320–21
    developing the survey, 317–20
    gaining support for, 316–17
    presenting results and findings, 324–25
    using results for change and improvement, 325–26
  issues in survey development, other, 319–20
  open-ended vs. closed-ended items, 317–19
  reliability, issues of, 326–28
  response format of, 313
  survey design teams, 317
  systematic procedures for, 315
  validity, issues of, 328–29
organizational ties, 109–10

organizational training. See also communication training
  defining, 248
  in the structure of the organization, 249
organizations
  as brains metaphor, 17
  as cultures metaphor, 17
  eudaimonic view of, 16
  evolutionary/ecological perspective of, 6–7
  hedonic view of, 15
  as living organisms metaphor, 17
  as machines metaphor, 16–17
  as a place of domination metaphor, 18
  as political systems metaphor, 17
  population ecology of, 6
  as psychic prisons metaphor, 18
  as roles metaphor, 17–18
  as systems in flux metaphor, 18
  systems perspective of, 7–9
organized anarchy, 223
organizing
  in information systems theory, 230
  retention stage of, 231
  selection stage of, 231
out-group members, 178
outputs (elements flowing out of the system), 7
overcoming external inhibitors, 88
overcoming internal inhibitors, 88
overcoming victim resistance, 88
overconvergence, 80
oversight in decision making, 225
Oxford Pocket Dictionary and Thesaurus, 73

P

paralanguage, 77, 273
participant fatigue, 319
participant's manual, 264, 267
participation, ethical practice of, 205
participative style, of leadership, 177
participative type of management, 34
Pelz effect, 154

perception in Myers-Briggs Type Indicator, 120
perception process, 11–12
perceptual schemas, 11, 231
permanent group, 148
permeable boundaries, 7
persecution feelings, 131
personal dimension of ethics, 206
personality attacks, 128
personality/task congruity, 138
personality traits, 119–26
  accounting for individual differences, 118
  assessment methods
    Chinese Zodiac placemat, 121–22
    Japanese blood typing, 121
  authoritarianism, 123
  communication conflict-related traits, 126–33
  competence-related traits, 133–37
  deciding, 120
  dogmatics, 123–24
  energizing, 120
  feeling, 120
  general, 122–26
  introvert, 120
  intuition, 120
  judgment, 120
  locus of control, 125–26
  Machiavellianism, 124–25
  perception, 120
  sensing, 120
  thinking, 120
person's interaction position, 83
persuasion stage of innovation, 239
Peter Principle, 181
physical attributes, 11
pilot test, 320
planning and acting stage of strategic change, 237
political correctness (PC), 87
political skills, 255–56
population ecology of organizations, 6
positive language, 74–76
positive relational effects, 131

power
    differential approach, 87
    types of, 97
precise style of communication, 43
Preparing Objectives for Programmed Instruction (Mager), 262
presentation skills, 253, 273–74
presentation software, 272
primary needs in hierarchy of needs, 184
primary social group dimension of ethics, 206
proactive scanning, 228
problem in inventional system, 227
problemistic search, 224
problem solving, 150, 218, 270. *See also* decision-making
procedural justice, 200
process conflicts, in team building, 301
process in strategic change, 236
process orientation, in team building, 300
profanity, 128
professional dimension of ethics, 206–7
professionalism, in communication assessment, 311
programmed decisions, 222
project group, 147
psychological attributes, 11
psychological maturity, of employee, 176–77
psychopathology, 127
public relations and organizational relationship, 110
pull-factors, 189
punctuated equilibria, 6
pure charisma, 175
push-factors, 189

Q

quality improvement group, 148
quality of organizational communication relationships, 331
quality of relational linkages, 178
quasi resolution of conflict, 223
questionable ethical behavior, 212

questionnaires, 259
quid pro quo, 87

R

rational-legal authority system, 28
reaction (level 1 of the Kirkpatrick model), 275
reactive scanning, 229
reading anxiety, 232
reciprocating patterns of interaction, 82
recorder in workgroups, 158
RED, IAT hierarchy of, 83–84
referent, defined, 72
referent power, 174
reframing, of information, 161
refreezing stage
    communication during, 291–92
    Lewin's three-step model of organizational change, 289
relational dialectic, 103
relational dissolution, 104
relationship
    complications associated with, 103–5
    defined, 96
    organizational, 97–98, 100–105, 110–11
    public relations and, 110
    superior-subordinate, 99–100
relationship-based ethical perspective, 201
relationship conflicts, in team building, 301
relative advantage, 239
relaxed style, 43
reliability, of organizational surveys, 326–28
repetition, 209
replacement, 6
requisite variety, 230
resistance, to organizational change, 287–88
resolution, 225
response format, of organizational surveys, 313
response set, 323

results (level 4 of the Kirkpatrick model), 276
retention stage, of organizing, 231
Rhetoric of Motives, A (Burke), 345
rights/justice-based ethical perspective, 200
risky shift, 152
ritual, 73
robber barons, of the 19th century, 24
    well-known and the industries they dominated, 25
role attributes, 11
role-development process
    role-making phase of, 178
    role-routinization phase of, 178
    role-taking phase of, 178
role-making phase of role development, 178
role-play, 269
role-routinization phase of role development, 178
role-taking phase of role development, 178
roll-out process, 324
routinized charisma, 175
rule of 16, 273
rumors, 211

S

safety needs in hierarchy of needs, 184
Sapir-Whorf hypothesis, 76
satisfaction with communication climate, 341
satisfaction with communication with subordinates, 341
satisfaction with communication with supervisors, 341
satisfaction with horizontal and informal communication, 341
satisfaction with media quality, 341
satisfaction with organizational integration, 341
satisfaction with organizational outcomes, 331
satisfaction with organizational perspective, 341

satisfaction with personal feedback, 341

scalar chain, 29

scientifically efficient, 27

scientific management, 26

   approach, assumptions of, 27

   communication in, 27

   Fayol's lateral communication and, 29

   perspective, 28

   principles of, 28

secondary social group dimension of ethics, 206

selection, 11

selection stage, of organizing, 231

selective perception, 231

self-actualization needs in hierarchy of needs, 184

self-centered roles, in organizational group, 157

self-disconfirming prophecy, 14

self-fulfilling prophecy, 14

self-handicapping, 78–79

sell style, of leadership, 177

semantic-differential-type scale items, 318

sense making, 231

sensing in Myers-Briggs Type Indicator, 120

sequential attention to goals, 224

Service Master Corporation, 180

sex-role spillover approach, 87

sexual harassment at workplace, 86–89

sexually harassing behavior, 88

shared knowledge, defined, 153

signals, 72

signs, 72

Simon's activity approach to decision making, 222–23

single-loop learning, 38

situational ethical perspective, 199

situational factors, 12

situational leadership perspective, 176–78

skilled evaluation, in communication assessment, 312

skills acquisition, 248

skills deficiency, 127

skunkworks, 190

small bandwidth, 85

small groups

   advantages of, 151–54

   definition of, 146

   different types of, 147–49

   disadvantages of, 154–56

   networks, types of, 160–63

   roles in, 157–60

   stages for formation of, 149–51

   technology, role of, 163–64

social composure, 136

social confirmation, 136

social experience, 136

social identity theory, 51

socialization process, 9

social learning, 127

social loafer, 156, 164

social solidarity, 101

social support, 101

sociopsychological approach, 88

soldiering, 26

solution in inventional system, 227

solution presentation, 209

source credibility, 86

sources of information in ICA audit, 330

specific communicative tactics for change, 294

"sponsor" of harassment, 89

spontaneous cooperation, 32

stabilizing of change stage, 237

stakeholder theory, 201–2

standing group, 148

Starbucks, 54

stars, 348

strategic ambiguity, 211

strategic change, managing, 236–37

strategic planning, 180

stress reaction, 131

subject-matter expert (SME), 261

subjugated (exploited) workers, 9

subsystem, 7

superior-subordinate communication, 99–100

superior/subordinate organizational relationship, 99–100

suprasystem, 7

survey design teams, 317

symbols, 54, 72

symptom, 72

system 4 management approach, 33

system adaptation, 8

system maintenance, 8

systems perspective, of organizations, 7–9

T

tag questions, 78

tailored design, in communication assessment, 312

taking conflict personally (TCP), 130–31

task and role distribution, 152

task conflicts, in team building, 301

task manager, 40

task roles, in organizational group, 157

taxonomy of communication, 293

team building

   appreciative inquiry approach to, 301–3

   checklist, 302

   commitment in, 300

   communication in, 300

   composition of the team, 301

   defined, 300

   goals in, 300

   involvement in, 300

   process conflicts in, 301

   process orientation in, 300

   process the team currently employs to get the task accomplished, 301

   relationship conflicts in, 301

   task conflicts in, 301

   trust in, 300

team manager, 41

teasing and ridicule, 128

tell style, of leadership, 177

temperament of the person, 127

territoriality, 203

TFI Fridays, 61–62

T-groups/training groups, 300

thematic analysis, 293

theory in use, 38

theory of independent mindedness (TIM), 41–44

theory of linguistic relativity, 76

Theory of the Leisure Class: An Economic Study of Institutions, The, 24

Theory X and Theory Y, McGregor's, 34–35

Theory Z, Ouchi's, 35–37, 42

thinking in Myers-Briggs Type Indicator, 120

Third World countries, 25

Thompson's uncertainty model, 219–20

threatening resignation, 209

threats, 128

three-filter test, 213

three-step model, of organizational change, 288–89

throughputs, 7

timeliness of information received in ICA audit, 331

time-motion efficiency, Taylor's, 26–28

tolerance for disagreement (TFD), 131–33

trace point, 322

traditional entrepreneurs, 189

training, components of, 248

training function, 249

training need, 255

trait argumentativeness, 129

trait leadership perspective, 175–76

transformational leadership, 179
    characteristics of, 179

transparent structure, practice of, 205

trialability, 239

Triangle Shirtwaist Company disaster, 31

trickle-down economics, 9

trust, in team building, 300

Turner Broadcasting Station (TBS), 238

Type A (American) organizations, 35

Type J (Japanese) organizations, 35

U

UCINET software package, 350

ultimate attribution error, 14

uncertainty avoidance, 224

uncertainty management theory (UMT), 233–36

unconscious competence, 257

understanding the adult learner, 256

unfreezing stage
    communication during, 290–91
    Lewin's three-step model of organizational change, 288

United States
    agricultural America, 26
    child labor in, 25
    consumerism and individual advancement, 26
    home ownership, 52
    industrialization in, 25–26
    sexual harassment charges filed in, 87
    technological advancements, 26
    watershed period of American labor history, 31

unprogrammed decisions, 222

upward communication, 33

upward distortion, 103

U.S. Equal Employment Opportunity Commission (EEOC), 86

U.S. News & World Report, 182

utilitarian ethical perspective, 200

V

validity, of organizational surveys, 328–29

verbal aggressiveness, 127–28

verbal intensifiers, 77

verbal qualifiers, 77

verbal self-handicaps, 79

virtue ethics. *See* deontological ethical perspective

vocalic competence, 274

Vroom's decision-making styles, 220–22

W

Walmart, Little Rock, 7

Weber's bureaucracy, 28–29

Western Electric Company, 31

wheel network, of small group, 162

whistleblowing, 209–10

wide bandwidth, 85

Winning (Welch and Welch), 182

wit, 136

worker productivity, understanding
    Fayol's lateral communication, 29–30
    Taylor's time-motion efficiency, 26–28
    Weber's bureaucratic management, 28–29

workers' psychological well-being, 32

work groups, 147

workgroups
    recorder in, 158

working poor, 9

workplace
    practical advice on when to speak, 212–13
    questionable ethical behavior in, 212

work-specific locus of control, 126

written communication skills, 253

Y

yin and yang, 82

Author Index

A

Adams, G. A., 110–11
Adelman, M. B., 101
Adorno, T., 123
Adrian, A. D., 310–12, 314, 318, 320, 322, 324, 330, 331, 341, 350
Afifi, W. A., 233
Agarwala-Rogers, R., 238
Albrecht, T. L., 101
Alderton, S. M., 150
Allen, M., 344
Allen, N. J., 344–45, 348
Amato, P. P., 79
Ancona, D. G., 149
Anderson, C. A., 135
Anderson, C. R., 176
Anderson, C. M., 43
Anderson, J., 78
Anderson, P. A., 203
Anheuser, E., 188
Argyris, C, 37–39, 286
Arkin, R. M., 79
Armstrong, T. A., 208
Asch, S. E., 155
Ashforth, B. E., 51, 62
Athanassiades, J. C., 104
Avolio, B., 163
Avtgis, T. A., 42, 43, 72, 79, 80, 126, 128, 130, 134–36, 203, 207–8, 211, 227–28, 286, 318, 326, 328

B

Bales, R. F., 155
Bandura, A., 125
Barch, S. L., 131
Barker, J., 10
Barnum, P. T., 188
Barry, B., 96
Bate, B., 75

Baumgardner, A. H., 79
Baumgardner, S. R., 16
Bavelas, A., 160–63
Baxter, L. A., 100, 103
Beatty, M. J., 137, 150, 211
Beavin-Bavelas, J., 37, 111
Becker, J. H., 125
Becker, W., 188
Beckhard, R., 284, 286
Beebe, S. A., 248–49, 261, 268
Bem, D. J., 152
Benne, K. D., 157–60
Bennis, W. G., 146
Bentham, J., 200
Berman, E. M., 103
Bezos, J., 188
Birdwhistell, R. L., 202
Bjorn, L., 88
Blackstone, T., 101
Blake, R., 39–41, 100
Blanchard, K., 176
Blyth, S., 191
Bonacich, P., 108
Bonito, J. A., 146
Bordia, P., 149
Borgatta, E. F., 155
Borgatti, S., 350
Bowker, J., 75
Boyd, B., 96
Bradac, J. J., 75, 80
Brannigan, A., 32
Brashers, D. E., 151, 233, 235
Brass, D. J., 107
Brawley, L. R., 153
Bray, S. R., 153
Bridge, K., 100, 103
Brin, S., 188
Brockhaus, R. H., 191
Brooks, R. D., 84
Brown, R., 210

Burgoon, J. K., 203
Burgoon, M., 81, 83–86
Burke, K., 50, 152, 345
Burke, W. W., 285
Burnes, B., 288–89
Burnstein, E., 151
Burt, R. S., 111
Busceme, S., 101
Busch, A., 188
Bushe, G. R., 303
Bush, G. W., 204

C

Cady, S. H., 299
Cahill, D. J., 105
Canary, D. J., 126
Cantore, S., 295–97
Carlock, R. S., 288
Carnegie, A., 24, 25, 188
Carroll, G. R., 6
Cartwright, S., 63
Case, S., 188
Casey, M. K., 344
Cashman, J., 178
Caster, M. A., 299
Cegala, D. J., 234
Chandler, A., 188
Chang, A., 149
Cheney, G., 342, 344–45, 347
Cherney, J., 303
Cherney, J. K., 303
Chesbro, J. L., 135
Choo, C. W., 229
Church, A. H., 286, 313–14, 316–18, 320–25
Churchill, W., 176
Clampitt, P., 310, 332
Cline, R. J., 152
Cline, T. R., 152
Clinton, B., 204

Clinton, H. R., 176
Cody, M. J., 126
Coetzer, G., 303
Cohen, J. A., 189
Cohen, M. D., 225
Collins, B. E., 152
Conger, J. A., 175
Contractor, N. S., 96–98, 105, 108, 147
Cooke, J., 25
Cooper, C. L., 63
Cooperrider, D. L., 295
Courtney-Staley, C., 78
Covington, M., 270–71
Crant, M., 96
Crocker, C., 25
Cronkhite, G., 72
Crothers, M. K., 16
Crowell, L., 151
Cunningham, E. M., 126
Cunningham, J. B., 286, 295
Curran, J., 189

D

Dallinger, J. M., 130–31
Daly, J. A., 126
Dangello, F., 125
Dansereau, F., 178
Davenport, T. H., 96
Davidson, A., 188
Davidson, C., 54
Davis, C. S., 326
Deal, T. E., 53
Deci, E. L., 15
deJong, M., 340–41
Delbecq, A. L., 151
Dell, M., 188
Denison, D. R., 50
Denning, V. P., 84
Dennis, A. R., 164
Desanctis, G., 163–64
DeStephen, R. L., 159
Devanna, M. A., 179
Devine, I., 101
DeWine, S., 329–32
DiCioccio, R. L., 208
Dickens, L., 286, 287, 295

Dick, R. V., 342
Dickson, W. J., 31, 32
Diener, E., 15
Dillman, L., 203
Dina, R., 63
Disney, W., 188
Dobos, J. A., 210–11
Dose, J. J., 55
Downs, C., 310, 332, 341
Downs, C. W., 310–12, 314, 318, 320, 321, 322, 324, 330, 331, 332, 341, 350
Drew, D., 25
Duck, J., 149
Duran, R., 135–37
Dyer, J. H., 302
Dyer, W., 302
Dyer, W. G., 302
Dyer, W. G., Jr., 300–301

E

Earnest, W., 273
Eastman, G., 188
Eddleman-Spears, L., 232
Edison, T. A., 188
Egan, T. M., 296–99
Eisenberg, E. M., 147
Eliot, T. S., 223
Elrod, P. D. II, 289
Emerson, T., 287
Equal Employment Opportunity Commission (EEOC), 86
Erdogan, B., 178
Everett, M., 350
Ewing, D., 42

F

Fairhurst, G. T., 53
Falcione, R. L., 58, 59
Farace, R. V., 8
Farmer, S. M., 146
Fayol, H., 29
Feldman, S. P., 54
Fiechtner, S. B., 124
Fielder, F. E., 177
Fink, A., 322

Fisher, B. A., 149–50
Fisk, J., 25
Fitzgerald, L. F., 87
Fitzgerald, S. P., 286
Flagler, H., 25
Ford, H., 188
Foster, B., 53
Fox, M. J., 53
Franke, R. H., 32
Franklin, B., 188
Freeman, J., 6
Freeman, L. C., 106–7
Freeman, L., 106, 350
French, J. R. P., 96–97, 174
Frenkel-Brunswik, E., 123
Frey, L. R., 150
Frick, H. C., 25
Friedman, M., 201
Fry, R., 303

G

Gable, M., 125
Gallardo, H. P., 326
Gallupe, B. R., 163–64
Garard, D. L., 270
Gastil, J., 154
Gates, B., 188
Gates, J. W., 25
Gautam, T., 342, 344, 347
Gay, G., 147
Gayle, B., 232
Gemuenden, H. G., 148
George, J. F., 164
Gersick, C. J., 148
Giannini, A. P., 188
Gibbons, P., 75
Giedd, J. L., 88
Giffords, E., 63
Giles, H., 77, 79, 80, 81
Giuliani, R., 176
Glauser, M. J., 102
Goldhaber, G. M., 98, 311, 314, 330, 332, 340, 348, 350
Goldsmith, D. J., 233
Golembiewski, R., 298
Goodman, J., 289–90, 292–93

Gorden, W. I., 42–44, 130, 300
Gordy, B., Jr., 188
Goris, J. R., 340
Gould, J., 25
Gouran, D. S., 150, 218
Graen, G. B., 178
Grafton-Small, R., 54
Graham, E. E., 130, 276–77
Granger, B., 191
Granovetter, M., 109
Graves, J., 156
Gray, J., 341–42
Greenbaum, H. H., 332
Greene, P., 188
Gruber, J. E., 88
Guetzkow, H., 152
Gunn, E. P., 120
Gustafson, D. H., 151
Gutek, B. A., 87, 89

H

Habermas, J., 10
Hackman, J. R., 286
Hackman, M. Z., 176
Haga, W. J., 178
Hall, E. T., 203
Hamilton, M. A., 86
Hample, D., 130–31
Hannan, M. T., 6
Hansen, M., 154
Hargie, O., 310–11, 316, 329
Harley, W. S., 188
Harriman, E. H., 25
Harris, R. N., 78
Hartley, P., 300
Hazen, M., 341
Heckel, R. V., 176
Heider, F., 12, 107
Heimberg, F., 342
Henkel, J., 124
Henley, N. M., 203
Hersey, P., 176–77
Hershey, M., 188
Herzberg, F., 185–86, 286
Heskett, J. L., 99
Heslin, R., 259, 272

Hickson, D. J., 16, 34, 185–86, 219, 220, 222, 223, 225, 229, 237
Hiers, J. M., 176
Higgins, R. L., 78
Hill, J. J., 25
Hilton, C., Sr., 188
Hirokawa, R. Y., 101, 146, 151, 159, 218
Hisrich, R., 190–91
Hoegl, M., 148
Hofsteade, G., 60
Hollingshead, A. B., 146
Hollon, C., 125
Hoon, H., 156
Hopkins, M., 25
Hsieh, E., 233
Hull, R., 182
Hunter, J. E., 86
Huntington, C. P., 25
Hunt, S. K., 270
Hurt, H., 131
Huuskonen, V., 190

I

Infante, D. A., 41–44, 72, 80, 127–30, 226–27, 271–72, 286, 318, 326, 328
Ingham, A. G., 156

J

Jablin, F. M., 29, 57–59, 98, 99, 100, 101, 104, 105
Jackson, D. D., 37, 111
Jaffe, D. T., 287
Jago, A. G., 220
James, A. C., 329, 332
Janis, I., 155
Jessup, L. M., 164
Jex, S. M., 110–11
Jobs, S., 188
Johannesen, R. L., 201
Johnson, A. M., 342
Johnson, C. E., 176
Johnson, J. R., 344
Johnson, P., 80
Johnson, R., 188
Johnson, W. L., 342
Jones, J. E., 259, 272

Jones, S. B., 85
Jordan, J. M., 53

K

Kahai, S., 163
Kahneman, D., 15
Kahn, R. L., 151–52
Kanter, R., 176
Kanungo, R. N., 175
Kant, I., 200
Karau, S. J., 156
Kassing, J. W., 43, 128, 130, 207–9
Kato, T., 36
Katz, D., 151–52
Kaul, J. D., 32
Kausilas, D., 101
Kazlow, C., 124
Kelleher, H., 188, 199
Kelley, T., 226
Kellogg, W. K., 188
Kelly, L., 136
Kendall, J., 55
Kendall, K., 55
Kennedy, A. A., 53
Kennedy, J. F., 176
Keyton, J., 89
Kincaid, D. L., 147
King, G., 210
King, M. L., Jr., 176
Kirkpatrick, D. L., 275
Kirkpatrick, J. D., 275
Kirmeyer, S. L., 101
Klein, S. M., 288–93
Knight, P., 188
Knowles, M., 256
Knutson, P. K., 131–32
Knutson, T., 131
Kogan, N., 152
Koonin, S., 238
Koresh, D., 176
Koss, M. P., 89
Kotter, J. P., 99, 187
Krackhardt, D., 109
Kraimer, M. L., 178
Krattenmaker, T., 298
Krayer, K. J., 124

Kreps, G. L., 231, 285, 295
Kroc, R., 188
Krone, K. J., 98–100
Kudsi, S., 277

L

Lachlan, K. A., 326
Laidlaw, H., 341–42
Laird, A., 332
Lake, E. A., 79
Lakoff, R., 78
Lancaster, C. M., 296–99
Landler, M., 211
Langer, E., 74
LaPoire, B. A., 81
Lauder, E., 188
Lauren, R., 157, 188
Lawler III, E. E., 286
Lawson, K., 260, 272
Leary, M. R., 79
Lefcourt, H. M., 125–26, 234
Lemann, N., 328
Lenzmeir Broz, S., 234
Lesniak, R., 350
Levinger, G., 156
Levin, J., 124
Levinson, D., 123
Lewin, K., 286, 288, 295, 300, 304
Lewis, L. K., 289, 293–94
Lewis, S., 295–97
Liberman, C. J., 342, 344–45
Liden, R. C., 178
Light, L., 211
Likert, R., 33, 286
Lilly, J. D., 126
Lincoln, A., 176
Linstead, S. A., 54
Lin, T., 101
Lippert, L., 270
Lippitt, G. L., 285
Littman, J., 226
Lord, R. G., 176
Lovas, B., 154
Lucas, G., 188
Luck, G., 126

Lundgren, S., 101
Lussier, R. N., 211

M

Mabry, E. A., 146
McClelland, D. C., 187
McCormick, Cyrus, Sr., 188
McCroskey, J. C., 125–26, 131–33, 262
McCroskey, L. L., 131
McGregor, Douglas, 34–35, 36
Machiavelli, N., 124
McKeage, R., 146
McLean, G. N., 298
McPhee, R. D., 98
Mael, F., 51, 62
Mager, R., 262
Magness, L. D., 232
Malone, D., 153
Manson, C., 176
March, J., 223–25
Markiewicz, D., 101
Marriott, J. W., Jr., 188
Marshall, L., 137
Martin, J., 51
Martin, M., 250–51
Martin, M. M., 43, 133–35
Marx, K., 9
Maslow, A., 100, 184–85, 286
Masser, B., 210
Matsunaga, M., 233
Mayer, L. B., 188
Mayo, E., 31, 32, 97–98
May, S., 205
Mehrabian, A., 274
Mellon, A., 25
Merrill, C., 188
Meyer, J. P., 344–45, 348
Meyers, R. A., 151
Miller, V. D., 344
Mill, J. S., 200
Miranda, S. M., 154
Mirvis, P. H., 288
Mishra, A. K., 50
Mitchell, T. R., 187
Monarsh, B., 87

Monge, P. R., 8, 96–98, 105, 108, 147
Morgan, G., 16, 18, 55, 56
Morgan, J. P., 24, 25, 188
Morrison, R., 98, 101, 111
Mors, M. L., 154
Moss, S. A., 147
Mottet, T. P., 248–49, 268
Mouton, J. S., 39–41, 100
Mowday, R. T., 344
Mulac, A., 75, 80
Mumby, D., 10
Mumby, D. K., 52
Murrell, K. L., 286
Myers, S., 136

N

Neuwirth, K., 53
Newman, H. L., 286
Nielsen, I. K., 110–11
Norton, R., 42, 133, 271
Nunamaker, J. F., 164

O

Obama, B., 176
Odiorne, G., 329
O'Donohue, W., 88
O'Hair, D. H., 125
O'Hare, E., 88
Oldham, G. R., 286
Olsen, J. P., 225
Omidyar, P., 188
Ouchi, W., 35–37
Ouellette, J. A., 101

P

Page, L., 188
Palmgreen, P., 259
Papa, M. J., 276–77
Parks, M. R., 134, 135
Parks, R., 176
Passmore, J., 295–97
Passmore, W. A., 300
Patterson, B. B., 128

Paynton, S. T., 270
Pearce, J. A., 54
Peckham, V., 156
Pelz, D. C., 154
Perot, R., 188
Perry, T., 105
Pescosolido, A., 160
Peter, L. J., 182
Peters, M. P., 190
Peters, T. J., 180–81
Pettigrew, A., 54, 236–37, 288
Pettit, J. D., 340
Pfeiffer, J. W., 259, 272
Phillips, J. S., 176
Poole, M. S., 101, 104
Porter, L. W., 344
Pratt, M., 53
Preiss, R. W., 232
Prusak, L., 96
Pryor, J. B., 88
Pugh, D. S., 16, 34, 185–86, 219–23, 225, 229, 237
Pullman, G. M., 25
Putnam, L. L., 29, 55, 104

R

Rafaeli, A., 53
Rancer, A. S., 42–43, 72, 79–80, 126, 128–30, 134–35, 211, 227–28, 271, 286, 318, 326, 328
Ravasi, D., 61
Raven, B., 96–97, 174
Ray, R. L., 310–11
Reagan, R., 176
Redding, C. W., 146
Redding, W. C., 357
Reichel, P., 124
Remland, M. S., 204
Richards, W., 350
Richmond, V. P., 125, 131–33
Richter, M. N., 103
Roach, K. D., 248–49, 268
Roberts, L., 84
Rockefeller, J. D., 24, 25, 188
Roebuck, A., 188
Roethlisberger, F. J., 31, 32
Rogers, D. P., 330, 332, 340, 348, 350

Rogers, E., 147, 237–39
Rokeach, M., 123
Romero, E., 160
Rosenthal, R., 81
Ross, L., 14
Roth, J., 146
Rothwell, W. J., 285
Rotter, J. B., 125, 176
Rubin, R. B., 259
Rubin, R., 134
Rudd, J. A., 210–11
Rudd, J., 137
Rude, M., 277
Rush, M. C., 176
Russell, H. M., 8
Ryan, R. M., 15

S

Saine, T., 203
Salkind, N. J., 323
Sanders, H., 188
Sanford, R., 123
Sarnoff, D., 188
Saunders, C. S., 154
Scheidel, T., 151
Schein, E. H., 50, 52, 53, 56, 58, 60, 63
Schmisseur, A. M., 293–94
Schneider, M., 89
Schneier, C., 176
Schon, D., 37, 38
Schrag, J. L., 78
Schrodt, P., 232
Schultz, B., 78
Schultz, M., 61
Schwab, C., 188
Schwarz, N., 15
Scott, C. D., 287
Sears, R., 188
Seibold, D. R., 277
Seligman, M. E. P., 15, 37
Sharma, R., 296
Shaw, M. E., 153
Sheats, P., 157–60
Sheehan, E. P., 124
Shephard, H. R., 146
Shepperd, J. A., 79

Sherif, M., 155
Shintaku, M., 121
Shukla, R. K., 151
Shullery, M. M., 130
Shullman, S. L., 87
Sias, P. M., 98, 105
Sidgwick, H., 200
Siehl, C., 51
Simon, H., 222
Sirimangkala, P., 43
Smith, F. W., 188
Snyder, C. R., 78
Sorensen, G., 126
Sosik, J., 163
Spates, J. L., 124
Spector, P. E., 126
Srivastva, S., 295
Stanko, B. B., 89
Stanworth, C., 191
Stanworth, M. J. K., 189, 191
Stasser, G., 152
Steers, R. M., 344
Steinfatt, T. M., 72
Stephens, K. K., 293–94
Stewart, D., 85
Stewart, M., 188, 287
Stodgill, R., 175
Strauss, L., 188
Street, R. L., 81
Strine, M., 9
Sullivan, R., 285
Sutcliffe, K. M., 229
Sypher, H. E., 259

T

Tajfel, H., 51, 61–62
Tan, M. L., 156
Taylor, E., 128
Taylor, F., 26–28, 99
Teven, J. J., 125, 133
Thiagarajan, S., 268
Thomas-Maddox, C., 128
Thompson, J., 219
Thomsett, M. C., 74, 204
Thweatt, K. S., 133–35
Tichy, N., 179

Tippett, O. D., 289
Titus, W., 152
Tjosvold, D., 41
Tompkins, P., 10
Tompkins, P. K., 342, 345, 347
Tourish, D., 310–11, 316, 329
Trippe, J., 188
Trosten-Bloom, A., 303
Truss, C., 289–90, 292–93
Tuckman, B. W., 154
Turner, J. C., 51, 61–62

V

Valencic, K. M., 210–11
Vanderbilt, C., 25
Van Maanen, J., 58
Vaught, B., 340
Vinokur, A., 151
Virick, M., 126
Vogel, D. R., 164
Von Bertalanffy, L., 7
Vroom, V., 220–22, 286

W

Waclawski, J., 286, 313–14, 316–18, 320–25
Wagner, U., 342
Walker, M. C. J., 188
Wallach, M. A., 152
Walster, G. W., 151
Walton, S., 188
Ward, A. M., 188
Waterman, A. S., 15
Waterman, R. H., 180–81
Watkins, K., 286, 295
Watzlawick, P., 37, 111
Weber, M., 28, 103, 175
Weick, K. E., 64, 229–31
Weir, K. E., 293–94
Welch, J., 182
Welch, S., 182
West, J. P., 103
Wheelan, S. A., 146
Wheeless, L., 131, 232
Whipp, R., 237

White, C. H., 81
Whitford, T., 147
Whitney, D., 303
Wiemann, J. M., 77, 79
Wiener, N., 8
Wigley, C. J., 42–43, 127, 132, 271
Wilkins, A., 56
Williams, K. B., 88
Williams, K. D., 156
Wilson, C. E., 58
Wilson, N., 310–11
Winfrey, O., 176, 188
Woodman, R. W., 300
Wood, W., 101
Wright, C., 203

X

Xia, L., 147

Y

Yaman, D., 270–71
Yates, M., 350
Yetton, P. W., 220–22
Yuan, Y. C., 147

Z

Zakahi, W. R., 136–37
Zwerman, W., 32
Zwijze-Koning, K., 340–41